ZOLAR'S
ENCYCLOPEDIA
& DICTIONARY
OF DREAMS

ZOLAR'S

ENCYCLOPEDIA & DICTIONARY OF DREAMS

PRENTICE
HALL
PRESS

New York   London   Toronto   Sydney   Tokyo   Singapore

PRENTICE HALL PRESS
15 Columbus Circle
New York, New York 10023

PRENTICE HALL PRESS and colophon are registered trademarks
of Simon & Schuster, Inc.

Library of Congress Cataloging-in-Publication Data
Zolar.
  [Encyclopedia and dictionary of dreams]
  Zolar's encyclopedia and dictionary of dreams / by Zolar.
    p.   cm.
  Reprint. Originally published: Garden City, N.Y. : Doubleday, 1963
  ISBN 0-13-984014-1
  1. Dreams.   1. Title.
  BF1091.Z65   1989   89-4008
  135'.3'03—dc20   CIP

Manufactured in the United States of America

10 9 8 7 6 5 4 3

Preface

There have been professional dream interpreters for many thousands of years. Among the ancient peoples of Babylon, Chaldea, and Judea, dream interpretation was recognized as an accomplished art. The earliest record we have of a published work on the interpretation of dreams was compiled by Artemedorus Dalidarius in the second century A.D. This work was translated into English and published in London sometime during the seventeenth century. It has since been reprinted and translated into every language. Many of the interpretations used in this *Dictionary of Dreams* have been taken from this ancient document. Since Dalidarius' time the interest in the study of dreams has never diminished. Some of the best-known psychologists, such as Freud, Jung, Rhine, McDougall, and Zener, have devoted their lifetime to the subject.

The average reader does not have the time or the will to delve deeply into this intriguing subject. Therefore I suggest that the information contained in this book be used broadly, as a form of entertainment.

On January 10, 1937, the New York Sunday *Mirror* published an article in its magazine section entitled "Dreamed This Tragedy and It Was True." It told of a man who, while on board ship in mid-ocean, dreamed his son had been killed in an automobile accident. He actually saw the accident in his dream. The next morning, he received a cablegram telling of his son's death in almost the exact circumstances as were revealed in his dream the night before.

"THE AWFUL DREAM" CAME TRUE

The following article appeared in the
NEW YORK WORLD-TELEGRAM & SUN on
MONDAY, March 3, 1958.

MIAMI BEACH, MARCH 3: Handicappers are going to have to start including dreams in their figures. Remember how Willie Shoemaker blew the Derby last May, how he suddenly stopped riding and stood up in the irons, thinking he had passed the finish line a winner? All this, Gallant Man's owner, Ralph Lowe, had seen in a dream several nights before. From the same mysterious unconsciousness, Elizabeth Arden Graham learned she was to win the Flamingo, only to have Jewel's Reward's victory erased on a foul by the stewards. "Of course, dreams are silly, meaningless things," the first lady of cosmetics told us yesterday. "Still that was all I could think of as I stood there in the winner's circle waiting for the stewards to reach a decision.

"The awful dream was coming true right in front of my eyes. The close finish. The announcement that a foul had been claimed. The long tense wait. Try as I might to ignore the whole thing I knew there now could be but one result. Our number was coming down. A very upsetting even clammy experience it was."

It must have been an embarrassing experience, too. This had been an incredibly rough race. Over the last eighth of a mile the two leaders, Jewel's Reward and Tim Tam had engaged in a boisterous equine version of rock and roll. Six different times they collided.

To everyone who had a clear view of the stretch run it should have been obvious that the stewards would examine the film of the race before allowing the result to stand, yet some unthinking official immediately rushed Mrs. Graham to the winner's circle. No time was to be lost. It seems the TV cameras were waiting.

The humiliation to which the great lady was subjected was senseless. To her credit she stood up under it in the magnificent manner of the thoroughbreds she breeds and races. Though visibly shaken, and perhaps dazed by the portentous dream, she uttered no complaint. "Like the official, I thought we had won too," she said.

THE STRANGE DREAM OF PRESIDENT ABRAHAM LINCOLN

There is a strange account of a dream, told by Abraham Lincoln on the day that he was assassinated. Mr. and Mrs. Lincoln were entertaining a few friends in the White House. The President told how he had been troubled by a strange dream. He said, "It seems strange how much there is about dreams in the Bible. There are sixteen chapters in the Old Testament and four or five in the New in which dreams are mentioned, and there are many other passages throughout the Bible, which refer to visions. If we believe the Bible, we must accept the fact that many things are made known in our dreams. I had one the other night that has haunted me ever since. I heard sobs as if a number of people were quietly weeping, but the mourners were invisible.

"I went from one room to another but no living person was in sight; however, the same mournful sounds of distress followed me as I went along. Every object was familiar to me, but nowhere could I see people who were grieving as though their hearts would break. I was puzzled and alarmed. When I entered the East Room, I met with a sickening surprise. Before me was a dais, on which rested a corpse in funeral vestments. Around it were stationed soldiers who were acting as guards, and there was a throng of people gazing mournfully at the corpse, whose face was covered. 'Who is dead in the White House?' I demanded of one of the soldiers. 'The President,' was his answer. 'He was killed by an assassin.' Then came a loud burst of grief from the crowd which awoke me from my dream. It is only a dream," said the President, "but it has strangely annoyed me; however, let us say no more about it."

A little after ten o'clock that night, Good Friday, April 14, 1865, despite all the precautions taken to guard the President, Abraham Lincoln was fatally shot. The rest is history, but the dream remains an enigma for the world to ponder.

On March 17, 1937, most of the New York papers carried the following headline: DREAM BOOK DID IT, SAYS MRS. G.P. WHEN INFORMED THAT SHE HAD WON $31,116.00 IN THE IRISH SWEEPSTAKES. Once before in 1930 she had won $2,300.00. Mrs. G.P. stated that the lucky numbers pertaining to her dream revealed the lucky sweepstake numbers that she played.

It has often been said that "coming events cast their shadows before them." Many years of study and research in this interesting science enables me to offer you my interpretations of your most important dreams.

Sigmund Freud, the father of modern dream interpretation said, "A reminiscence of the concept of the dream that was held in primitive times seems to underlie the evaluation of the dream which was current among people of antiquity. They took it for granted that dreams were related to the world of the supernatural beings in whom they believed, and that they brought inspirations from the Gods and the Demons. Moreover, it appeared to them that dreams must serve a special purpose in respect to the dreamer—that, as a rule, they predicted the future. The pre-scientific conception of the dream which obtained among the ancients was, of course, in perfect keeping with their general conception of the universe."

Many persons have written me about various sums of money they have won from time to time with the aid of their dream numbers. Personally, I believe that in most cases coincidence played the major part in their good fortune. It has been my experience that Lady Luck is very unpredictable and that in the long run, except in very rare cases, persons lose much more than they win in any form of speculation. Because there are always exceptions to the rules, and due to popular demand, I will explain how to convert dream interpretations into number vibrations.

FRANKLIN'S ASTRAL RULE

Benjamin Franklin, who was deeply versed in mystic mathematics, left the following rule by which a number may be found that will show the month and day of birth and the age of any person.

Set down the number of the month of birth; annex it to the day of birth; multiply the number so found by two; add five; multiply by fifty; add age; subtract 365; and add 115. The quotient will show the month and day of birth and age, when pointed off in the digits.

Number is the language of the Infinite. Throughout the cosmos the science of numbers must eternally be the same. All that exists, every atom, dimension, motion, form, or manifestation, is capable of being represented by, and has perfect correspondence with, numbers. The individual number of any specified Ego will disclose every change of such Ego's existence by the numerical action of such number.

Take any set of three numbers or more, reverse them to obtain a second set of numbers, subtract one from the other, and the digits of the remainder will always, by addition, reduce into nine, and the remainder itself will always be nine or a multiple of nine. This operation is a spiral movement of the numbers employed, and the nine, therefore, represents a circle. An eternal spiral motion may be properly represented by an endless row of nines, each nine symbolizing one complete revolution of the spiral movement. The relation between this endless spiral motion and all other motions must be determined by such a scale number as will forever measure the cycles or complete revolutions of all other motions, itself included. Such a scale is found in the relations of the sum of the primary numbers to the number representing a complete circle-nine. The scale number so found will measure the complete revolution of every cosmic factor, and as every revolution has correspondence with nine, so the measure must have correspondence also; so that when the digits of the scale number shall have given nine for depth, nine for width, and nine for length, then such a cycle will be complete and a new cycle begun. The infinite evolution is measured off by such numbers into well-defined periods or eras.

Table of the Alphabets

The science of numerology is basically founded on the digits of single numbers from 1 to 9. Each letter in the alphabet vibrates to one of these numbers:

1	2	3	4	5	6	7	8	9
A	B	C	D	E	F	G	H	I
J	K	L	M	N	O	P	Q	R
S	T	U	V	W	X	Y	Z	

If you will study the above table, you will notice that the letters *A, J,* and *S* vibrate to the number 1; *B, K,* and *T* vibrate to the number 2; and so on.

By using the above table you can find the favorable number (vibrations) for any dream or word. Should you have a dream that is not interpreted in this book and want to know the lucky number, simply reduce the letters to numbers. For example, the word *cat.* By referring to the table of the alphabet above, you will readily see that *C* vibrates to the number 3, *A* to the number 1, and *T* to the number 2. *Cat,* therefore, vibrates to 3 plus 1 plus 2; add them up and you get 6, which is the primary number for *cat.* Should you want two numbers that vibrate to *cat,* use any two numbers that add to 6, for example, 1 and 5, 4 and 2, 3 and 3, and so on.

Should you want three numbers that add up to 6, use 1–2–3, or 2–1–3. or 4–0–2, and so on.

In the event that your word should result in a total of two numbers. follow this method. Take, for example, the word *winter.* Checking with the table of the alphabet, we note that *W*—5, *I*—9, *N*—5, *T*—2, *E*—5, *R*—9. When we add 5 plus 9 plus 5 plus 2 plus 5 plus 9 we get a total of 35: we then add 3 plus 5, or 8, which is the primary number for *winter.*

This system can be applied to the dreams appearing in any dream book or for any word, name, or sentence.

Time Number Vibrations

The months of the year vibrate to the following digits:

TABLE OF MONTHS

JANUARY	1	JULY	7
FEBRUARY	2	AUGUST	8
MARCH	3	SEPTEMBER	9
APRIL	4	OCTOBER	1
MAY	5	NOVEMBER	2
JUNE	6	DECEMBER	3

The days of the week vibrate to the following digits:

TABLE OF DAYS

MONDAY	1
TUESDAY	2
WEDNESDAY	3
THURSDAY	4
FRIDAY	5
SATURDAY	6
SUNDAY	7

The hours of the day vibrate to the following digits:

TABLE OF HOURS

1:00 A.M. vibrates to 1	1:00 P.M. vibrates to 4
2:00 A.M. vibrates to 2	2:00 P.M. vibrates to 5
3:00 A.M. vibrates to 3	3:00 P.M. vibrates to 6
4:00 A.M. vibrates to 4	4:00 P.M. vibrates to 7
5:00 A.M. vibrates to 5	5:00 P.M. vibrates to 8
6:00 A.M. vibrates to 6	6:00 P.M. vibrates to 9
7:00 A.M. vibrates to 7	7:00 P.M. vibrates to 1
8:00 A.M. vibrates to 8	8:00 P.M. vibrates to 2
9:00 A.M. vibrates to 9	9:00 P.M. vibrates to 3
10:00 A.M. vibrates to 1	10:00 P.M. vibrates to 4
11:00 A.M. vibrates to 2	11:00 P.M. vibrates to 5
12:00 A.M. vibrates to 3	12:00 P.M. vibrates to 6

Ptolemy, the greatest mathematician of ancient times, said, "Judgment must be regulated by thyself, as well as by the sciences—it is advantageous to make choice of days and hours at a time constituted by your number vibration."

There are many systems and methods of making predictions, but none more interesting than numerology, since anyone may by a little concentration and study work it out.

The ancient Egyptians, Greeks, Romans, and Arabians had various systems which were remarkably accurate. These teachings have come down to us from the remotest antiquity. Since all letters have their numerical equations, then, all combinations of letters respond to a certain numerical value. The universe operates with exact mathematical precision, calculated to a fraction of a second. Every action or expression responds to a numerical measure of time. When you listen to music or a speech, you are unconsciously vibrating to certain number influences in the words and music. Every day of life brings good or bad reaction to the magnetic influence of the numerical equations that surround you. They are in everything you see, feel, or hear. It is impossible to escape them.

It is false to believe that the occult science of numerology sets the final hand of fate upon events and people or that such a thing as bad luck or good luck is ordained. This is not true; this science does not compel, nor does it indicate that when the vibrations or conditions are not favorable it is impossible to have some measure of good fortune. Rather it tells us when our chances are more or less aided by natural causes. Remember that the rays or vibrations help cause us to be hasty or slow, bright or dull, calm or explosive, according to the conditions under which they vibrate at a given time. These forces help to shape our thoughts and actions.

The 12 Signs of the Zodiac

Astrology is a scientific study of the sun, moon, planets, and stars. It indicates mathematical calculations required to determine the exact position of the planets on the date of birth.

The zodiac is that portion of the sky through which the sun, moon, and planets move from east to west. The zodiac is divided into twelve portions, called the "House of Heaven." Each is named for a constellation of the zodiac.

AQUARIUS	THE WATER BEARER	January 20 to February 18
PISCES	THE FISHES	February 19 to March 20
ARIES	THE RAM	March 21 to April 20
TAURUS	THE BULL	April 21 to May 21
GEMINI	THE TWINS	May 22 to June 21
CANCER	THE CRAB	June 22 to July 22
LEO	THE LION	July 23 to August 22
VIRGO	THE VIRGIN	August 23 to September 21
LIBRA	THE BALANCE	September 22 to October 22
SCORPIO	THE SCORPION	October 23 to November 21
SAGITTARIUS	THE CENTAUR	November 22 to December 21
CAPRICORN	THE GOAT	December 22 to January 19

GOOD AND BAD DAYS OF THE MOON
FOR DREAMS OCCURRING FROM THE 1ST TO THE 31ST OF EACH MONTH

1. Will be good
2. Will not come true
3. Will have no effect
4. Will be very good
5. Will not enjoy good things
6. Don't reveal dream to others
7. Everything will come as you wish
8. Beware of enemies
9. Will have what is desired this day
10. Will come through with happiness
11. Will see the effect in four days
12. Will have adversity
13. Your dream will come true
14. Long time before happiness comes
15. Dream will come true in thirty days
16. Your wish will bring good results
17. Keep the dream secret for thirty days
18. Don't trust your friends
19. Will be very happy in your affairs
20. Dream will come true after four days
21. Don't have confidence in anyone
22. Your desire will be accomplished
23. Dream will be explained in three days
24. Will have much happiness
25. Dream will come true after nine days
26. Will receive much unexpected help
27. Will receive good news
28. Your wish will come true
29. Will receive plenty of money
30. Will receive good news in the morning
31. Will receive sad news

DATES OF FAVORABLE AND UNFAVORABLE DREAMS OCCURRING EACH MONTH

FAVORABLE		UNFAVORABLE	
January	3—20—27—31	January	13—23
February	7—8—18	February	2—10—17—22
March	3—14—22—26	March	1—7—9—17
April	5—27	April	4—30
May	1—2—4—6—9—24	May	3—12—19
June	3—17—19	June	14—29
July	5—7—14—19—26	July	1—7—20—21

August	2—5—10—11—14—22	August	7—27
September	19—22—26—28	September	2—14—16—29—30
October	15—22—31	October	19—27
November	6—11—22	November	8—16—26
December	14—15—18—25—31	December	13

TABLE OF DREAMS ON PREGNANCY

For a pregnant woman to find whether she will give birth to a girl or a boy use the following process:

Use only the letters of the first name of the mother and father: check each letter of both names by taking the equivalent number from the following table:

```
A—B— C—D— E—F— G—H— I—J— K— L—M
10—2—20— 4—14— 6—16— 7—81—7—11—11—12

N— O—P— Q—R— S— T—U—V—W—X—Y— Z
4—14—0—16— 8—18—10—0— 2— 2— 2— 4—14
```

Then add all numbers of both names found under each letter of the table. After that add to the total numbers of the two names the number for the day of the week that the dream occurred, as follows:

MONDAY	add:	51	THURSDAY	add:	31
TUESDAY	"	52	FRIDAY	"	68
WEDNESDAY	"	103	SATURDAY	"	41
	SUNDAY	add: 106			

Add the total of all numbers; then divide the total by 7. If the number resulting from the division ends with an *even* number she will give birth to a *girl;* if it ends with an *odd* number she will give birth to a *boy.*

A

A:
The letter *A* printed or written: Good business.

Printing or writing the letter *A:* Happiness in life.

Others printing the letter *A:* Will have a long life.

ABANDON:
Of abandoning: Will live a long life.

Abandoning your wife: Will be in trouble.

Abandoning your husband: Loss of friends.

Abandoning your father: Recovery of lost valuables.

Abandoning your mother: Illness.

Abandoning your children: Loss of money.

Abandoning your relatives: Good times are coming.

Abandoning your sweetheart: Will be plunged into debts.

Abandoning your lover: Will be guilty of foolish actions.

Abandoning your friends: Expect failure in your affairs.

Abandoning your home: Happiness.

Abandoning your religion: Poverty.

Abandoning your business: Quarrels.

Abandoning your position: Change for the better.

Abandoning influential people: Will have enjoyment in life.

Abandoning ship: Failure in business.

Abandoning ship and reaching land: Good financial earnings.

ABBESS:
Of a convent superior nun: Big joy.

Meeting an abbess after an illness: Comfort.

Being an abbess: Will have high ambitions with an interesting future.

Being an abbess of a bad monastery: Will have a pleasant future.

ABBEY:
Of entering an abbey: Will receive many honors.

Being in an abbey: Will be free from anxiety.

Praying to God in an abbey: Will have joy and happiness.

Being seated in an abbey: Changes in present affairs.

An abbey fully decorated: Will have a trial over inheritance.

Building an abbey: Must endure many afflictions.

Conversing with others in an abbey: Will soon commit a sin.

ABBOT:
Of an abbot: Should calm your passions.

Wanting to be an abbot: Will lose the trust of friends.

Being an abbot: Will have many disappointments.

Meeting an abbot: Recovery from an illness.

Several abbots: Must endure pain and grief.

An abbot having bad behavior: Will be pitied by your friends.

ABDICATE:
A king or president abdicating: Disorder in business.

Abdicating from a prominent position: Recovery of money.

Relatives abdicating from their position: Joy.

Friends abdicating from their position: Postponement of success.

ABDOMEN:
Of the abdomen: Great expectations.

Having pains in the abdomen: Favorable affairs.

Feeling the naked abdomen: Recovery of money.

A married person dreaming of the abdomen: Unfaithfulness of one mate.

A lover's abdomen: Treachery on the part of one of the lovers.

A man seeing his abdomen growing: Will have high honors.

A woman seeing her abdomen growing: She will become pregnant.

ABDUCT:

Being abducted: Plans will be carried out well.

Being carried away by force: Good future ahead.

A woman being abducted: Very important and beneficial event to come.

A child being abducted: A mystery will be solved.

ABHOR:

Of abhorring something: Difficulties in your path.

Abhorring someone: Inheritance.

Abhorring an article and getting rid of it: Worries are over.

Being abhorred by others: Are prone to being selfish.

ABJECT:

Being abject: Hard times ahead for a little while.

Relatives being abject: Shame and sorrow.

Others being abject: Avoid your rivals.

Being in lowest abject condition: Unexpected good news.

ABODE:

Of own abode: False statements are being made against you.

Going into a strange abode: Will venture new undertakings.

Being in a strange abode: Affairs are in disorder.

Being refused admission to an abode: Be cautious in your plans.

Being locked out of an abode: Be meticulous in avoiding needless risk.

ABORTION:

Of an abortion: End of your love affairs.

Having an abortion: Happiness in the family.

Performing an abortion: Troubles ahead.

A successful abortion: Will live a long life.

Others having an abortion: Loneliness and trouble.

ABOVE:

Something hanging above you: Will receive good news.

Something falling near you from above: Will escape money losses.

Being hit by something falling from above: Sudden death.

Something from above falling on others: Beware of jealous friends.

ABROAD:

Going abroad: A change of work will take place.

Being abroad: Unsettled mind and way of thinking.

Returning from abroad: Changes in present conditions.

Others going abroad: Triumph over enemies.

Others being abroad: Will be deceived.

ABSCESS:

Of an abscess: Must get rid of bad friends.

Having an abscess: Will have an immediate recovery.

An abscess being operated on: A mystery will be solved.

Others having an abscess: Emotional sorrows.

Having an abscess on the neck: Sickness.

ABSCOND:

Someone absconding with your money: Treachery among those nearby.

Absconding with money: Will recover losses.

Relatives absconding: Beware of enemies.

Friends absconding: Be circumspect in all your dealings.

ABSENT:
A loved one being absent: Danger in love matters.
Other people being absent: Will have mastery over many matters.
Rejoicing over the absence of a relative: Frivolity.
Rejoicing over the absence of a friend: Loss of an enemy.
The death of an absent friend: A wedding is being planned.

ABSINTHE:
Drinking this green liquor: Family quarrels.
Others drinking absinthe: Doomed for disappointment.
Friends drinking absinthe: Recovery of money.
Enemies drinking absinthe: Advancement in your position.
Having absinthe in the house: Must endure painful things.
Getting drunk on absinthe: Small unhappiness will end with joy.

ABSTAIN:
Refusing a drink: Avoid your rivals.
Abstaining completely from drinking: Important events, very beneficial.
Relatives abstaining from drinking: Will live a long life.
Friends abstaining from drinking: Beware of jealous friends.

ABUNDANCE:
Having overabundance: Must calm your bad temper.
Having abundance: Big success in your plans.
Having abundance of money: A mystery will be solved.
Relatives having abundance of everything: Approaching money.
Others having abundance: Good results in love matters.

ABUSE:
Being abused: Business affairs will go badly.
Abusing another person: Others will take advantage of you.
Abusing your children: Success in love affairs.

Being abused by friends: Warning of troubles.

ABYSS:
Of an abyss: Difficulties ahead of you.
Falling into an abyss: Be careful in all business transactions.
Escaping from an abyss: Will overcome difficulties.
Falling into an abyss but not hurt: Don't lend money, it will not be returned.
Others falling into an abyss: Be circumspect in all your dealings.

ACACIA:
Of this flower when in season: Great disappointments ahead.
This flower when out of season: Realization of your wishes.
Receiving a gift of acacia flowers: You have a loyal friend.
Giving a gift of acacias: Must control your passions.
Smelling the perfume of acacia: Good times are coming.

ACADEMY:
Being single at an academy: Intended marriage will be marked by adversity.
Being married at an academy: Will overcome enemies with perseverance.
Being an academy professor: Will have unhappiness.
An academy officer: Discouragement in your affairs.
Being an academy cadet: Must endure humiliation.

ACCENT:
Having an accent: Will take a long trip.
Speaking with a foreign accent: Take care of your health.
Hearing others speaking with foreign accent: Will receive good news.
Putting an accent between words: Change of surroundings.

ACCEPT:
Being accepted: Will have mastery over many matters.

A lover being accepted: Affairs will not prosper.
Refusing to be accepted: Family quarrels.
Accepting an invitation: Expect an inheritance.

ACCIDENT:

Of an accident: A warning to avoid unnecessary travel.
Being in an accident: Your life is threatened.
An accident on land: Good personal and business ventures.
An accident at sea: Disappointment in love affairs.
An accident in the air: Will have a vigorous mind.
An accident in an automobile: Approaching money.

ACCLAIM:

Acclaiming others: Sorrowful consequences.
Receiving acclaim: Deprived of original simplicity.
Others showing acclaim: Will be double-crossed by friends.
Acclaiming a prominent person: Troubles ahead.

ACCOMPANY:

Accompanying someone: Failure of enemies.
Being accompanied: Very important and beneficial events to come.
Being accompanied by friends: Change of surroundings.
Having musical accompaniment: A mystery will be solved.
Accompanying a funeral procession: Poverty.
Accompanying a close friend to a cemetery: Riches and fortune.
Accompanying unknown person to a cemetery: Will be in need of money.

ACCOST:

Being accosted by a man: Will be scorned by others.
Being accosted by a woman: Honor.
Being accosted by a business person: Profit.

Being accosted by a poor person: Will receive money.
Being accosted by a friend: Will receive a legacy.

ACCOUNTS:

Adding up accounts: Loss of money by giving credit.
Working on accounts and bills: Hard work awaits.
Figuring others' accounts: Dignity and distinction.
Figuring employer's accounts: Beware of enemies.

ACCUSE:

Being accused: Beware of scandal.
Accusing others: Danger and misfortune.
Proving innocence when accused: Will overcome difficulties.
A righteous accusation: Serious troubles ahead.
Being accused by others of committing a crime: Will be beset by doubts.
Accusing yourself of wrongdoing: Will have plenty of money.
Being accused by a secret service official: Will be in trouble.
Being accused by a woman: Approaching business disaster.
Being accused by a man: Big success.

ACE:

The ace of diamonds: Quarrels.
The ace of Clubs: Money.
The ace of Hearts: Bad luck.
The ace of Spades: Good news.
Of an ace pilot: Another person is enjoying what you hoped to win.
Being an ace pilot: Will be deceived in love matters.

ACHE:

A woman having a severe ache: Very important and beneficial events to come.
A man having an ache: Good and prosperous business.
A farmer having an ache: Will have a good harvest.
A sailor having an ache: Will have a successful trip.

A lover having aches: Suitable time to pursue suit.

ACID:
Of acids: Will fulfill your promises.
Handling acids: Danger ahead through a promise.
Using acids: Will come out well from a present peril.
Others handling acids: Death of an enemy.

ACORN:
Collecting acorns: Will receive a legacy.
Holding acorns in the hands: Good fortune.
A lover holding acorns: Happiness.
An ill person holding acorns: Will have an immediate recovery.
Gathering acorns: Luck and prosperity.
Being under a tree: Will enjoy a wonderful life.

ACQUAINTANCE:
Of an acquaintance: Good luck.
Visiting an acquaintance: Will have enjoyment in life.
Making new acquaintances: A change in life will soon come.
Quarreling with an acquaintance: Your health will not be good.
Others being with your acquaintances: Will have a vigorous mind.

ACQUIT:
Being acquitted by a court: Failure of enemies.
Not being acquitted: Big prosperity.
Guilty people being acquitted: Will experience ups and downs.
Others being acquitted: Will have prosperous business.
Others not being acquitted: Misfortune.

ACROBAT:
An acrobat having an accident: Will escape all dangers.
Watching acrobats performing: Do not take a trip for nine days.
Being an acrobat: Will overcome enemies.

A relative being an acrobat: Will be deceived.

ACROSTIC:
This composition in verse: Don't make hasty decisions.
Completing an acrostic: Realization of speculations.
Not completing an acrostic: Are in trouble with business matters.
Others completing an acrostic: Will be jilted by a lover.

ACTING:
Of acting: Plans will not succeed.
Others acting: Will take a short trip.
Watching actors acting: Friends will cheat you.
Watching an actress acting: Will receive a letter with good news.
Watching children acting: Will have pleasant work and good news.

ACTOR OR ACTRESS:
Being introduced to an actress: Will have troubles at home.
Being introduced to an actor: Beware of much gossip.
Seeing many actors and actresses: Big satisfaction in life.
A comedian actor or actress: Good success in present business.
A tragic actor or actress: Unhappiness.
Being an actor: Loss of friends.
Being an actress: Will have much uneasiness.

ADAM AND EVE:
Of Adam and Eve: Prosperity.
Speaking to Adam: Wishes will come true.
Speaking to Eve: Misfortune in love.
A woman dreaming of Adam: Will give birth to a child.
A man dreaming of Eve: Will give a big family dinner.
A young girl dreaming of Adam: Will be happy in love.
A young man dreaming of Eve: Will find new employment.

ADDER:
Of this snake: Will have disputes with your mate.

6

Many adders: Beware of false friends.
Seeing an adder in a cage: A false friend is nearby.
Killing an adder: Will have victory over enemies.

ADDRESS:
Writing an address: Be careful of entering risky speculations.
Others writing an address: Misfortune in business.
Writing a business address: Luck and prosperity.
Writing address on love letters: Will receive good news.

ADIEU:
Bidding adieu to people: Will have bad health.
Others bidding adieu to you: Will take a tedious journey.
Bidding adieu to mate: Good times are coming.
Bidding adieu to children: Approaching money.

ADJUTANT:
Of an adjutant: Death of an enemy.
Being an adjutant: Troubles ahead.
Being in company of an army adjutant: Will make new friends.
Being in company of a high-ranking adjutant: Friends will be advantageous.

ADMINISTRATE:
Of an administrator: Disappointment in affairs.
Being summoned by an administrator: Improvement in business.
Administrating own business: Will receive an inheritance.
Administrating others' affairs: Good business activities.

ADMIRAL:
Of an admiral commanding his fleet: Good future.
Being in the company of an admiral: Big events to come.
Being an admiral: Danger in love matters.
Being the wife of an admiral: Insurmountable obstacles confront you.

ADMIRE:
Being admired: A change in life will come soon.
Admiring other people: Unhappiness.
Being admired by someone you like: Friendship.
Being admired by children: Will live a long life.

ADOPT:
Adopting someone: Relatives will ask for help.
Being adopted: Beware of enemies.
Having adopted children: Difficulties in love.
Being an adopted person: Financial gains.

ADORE:
Adoring children: Big success in all affairs.
Adoring your husband: Happiness and long life.
Adoring your wife: Wealth.
Adoring your sweetheart: Misfortune in business.
Adoring or worshiping an idol: Failure of affairs.
Adoring God and praying to him: Contentment and joy.

ADORN:
Being adorned: Difficulties and troubles ahead.
Adorning your children's room: Good times are coming.
Adorning your home: Changes in circumstances soon to come.
Others being adorned: Death of a relative.

ADRIFT:
Being adrift in a boat: Difficulties ahead.
Others being adrift: Changes in present environment.
Being adrift and reaching land safely: Happiness and riches.
Being adrift and boat overturning: Expect serious trouble.

ADULTERY:
Committing adultery: Your morals are excellent.

Other people committing adultery:
Loss of money.

Wife committing adultery: Quarrels
with neighbors.

Husband committing adultery: Will receive an inheritance.

ADVANCE:

Advancing in love affairs: Success in
business plans.

Advancing to become own boss: Success is certain.

Advancing in present position: Beware
of jealous friends.

Advancing in a law suit: Will lose the
case.

ADVANTAGE:

Taking advantage: Improvement in affairs in the future.

Others taking advantage of you: Will
have small disputes.

Taking advantage of others: Consolidation of business affairs soon.

Taking advantage of poor people: Will
receive good news.

Friends taking advantage of you: Will
lead a life of ease.

People taking advantage to get money:
Family prosperity in the future.

ADVENTURE:

Being an adventurer: Will be tormented a great deal.

Dreaming of exciting adventures: Big
change in your future.

Going on an adventure with a man:
New interest and surroundings.

Going on an adventure with a woman:
Someone is watching you.

Participating in adventures: Will be
bothered by women screaming.

ADVERSARY:

Of an adversary: Will win against rivals.

Fighting with an adversary: Doomed
for disappointment.

Having an adversary partner in business: Financial losses.

Having an adversary attorney: Worries will be smoothed away.

Being an adversary attorney: A false
friend is near.

ADVERSITY:

Having adversity: Prosperity.

Being persecuted by adversity: Discovery of money.

Having adversity in business: Will
realize high ambitions.

Having adversity in love: Be on guard
against spiteful gossip.

ADVERTISE:

Placing an advertisement: Difficulties
and disappointment ahead.

Reading an advertisement: Realization
of plans.

Advertising a sale: Loss of money.

Receiving a favorable advertisement:
Social activities of a happy nature.

ADVICE:

Receiving advice: Beware of false
friends.

Receiving advice from a priest: Loneliness and troubles.

Receiving advice from an attorney:
Will be humiliated.

Giving advice to others: Friendship of
many people.

Giving advice to children: Hard work
ahead.

Giving professional advice: See that
affairs are carried out well.

Giving financial advice: Will receive
a large payment.

ADVOCATE:

Being a counselor: Are considered
well to do by others.

Becoming an advocate: Will have
safety and money.

Children being an advocate: Happiness
is assured.

Hiring an advocate to defend you:
Will not have good results.

Being introduced to an advocate: Bad
news to come.

AFFECTION:

Of affection: Troubles for those near
you.

Having affection: Dignity and distinction.

Not having affection: Will have a long
life.

Affection between two loved ones: Inheritance.

Having the affection of children: Will receive unexpected money.

AFFILIATION:
Affiliating the soul to God: Big joy.

Being affiliated with a party: Beware of enemies.

Affiliating someone as a member: Will receive many honors.

Affiliating with another person: A change for the better to come.

AFFLICT:
Being afflicted: Success is certain.

Husband or wife being afflicted: Rapid success in business.

Being in a state of affliction: Happy destiny in view.

Being afflicted by others: A change for the better is coming soon.

AFFLUENCE:
Of affluence: Big success in plans.

Having affluence of wealth: Loss of business and money.

Having affluence of property: Loss of an estate.

Others having affluence of property and everything: Avoid rivals.

AFFRONT:
Receiving an affront: Loss of an inheritance.

Being affronted by relatives: Death in the family.

Being affronted by friends: Troubles ahead before having joy.

Affronting others: Must control passions.

AFLOAT:
Seeing something afloat: Will have troubles caused by others.

A small boat afloat: Good business ahead.

A big ship afloat: Abundant means.

A fish afloat: Will have good earnings.

A dead person afloat in the sea or river: Happy destiny ahead.

AFRICA:
Of Africa: Financial gains.

Seeing Africa on a map: Advancement of fortune will take place.

Taking a trip to Africa alone: Will make new friends.

Taking a trip to Africa with others: Will be guilty of foolish actions.

Going to Africa: Big joy.

Returning from Africa: Big disappointment ahead.

Being deported to Africa: Will have prosperity and good fortune.

AFTERNOON:
A beautiful afternoon: Good times are coming.

A cloudy afternoon: Very small profits ahead.

A foggy afternoon: Have faith in yourself.

A rainy afternoon: Will have good profits in business.

AGE:
To worry of your own age: Approaching illness.

Other people's age: Will have many very close friends.

Partner's age: Are being deceived.

Relative's age: Death in the family.

Friend's age: Will have a vigorous mind.

AGED PEOPLE:
Of an aged person: Joy without profit.

Member of family being aged: Approaching money.

Several aged people: Good luck and health.

Poor aged people: Difficulties ahead.

AGENT:
An agent soliciting: Will have good earnings.

Being an agent: Will influence people to do good.

Having dealings with an agent: Change of surroundings to come.

Others who are agents: Be circumspect in all your dealings.

AGONY:
Being in agony: Good sign for business affairs.

Husband and wife being in agony: Will have plenty of money.

Relatives being in agony: Will have a long life.

Children being in agony: Financial gains.

Others being in agony: Recovery from an illness.

AGREEMENT:

Of an agreement: Dignity and distinction.

Reading an agreement without signing it: Friends will cheat you.

Signing an agreement: Success of plans.

Canceling an agreement: Will have uncertain profits.

Not going through with an agreement: Hard work awaits.

Making an agreement with the devil: Big success for fishermen.

AGRICULTURE:

Of agriculture: Abundance.

Being an agriculturist: Prosperity.

Making money in agriculture: Success will come through hard work.

Having difficulties in agriculture: Arguments caused by vanity.

Losing money in agriculture: Will receive news of a marriage.

An agriculturist measuring land: Must be very diligent.

Being new in the agriculture business: Will have security.

AIR:

Clear air and blue sky: Success.

Cold air: Unhappiness in family relations.

Hot air: Are doing wrong by causing oppression.

Misty air: Are being deceived.

Foggy air: Reconsider present plans for action.

Damp air: Misfortune will end optimistic hopes.

Calm air: Happiness.

Stormy air: Will soon have an illness and be in danger.

AIR GUN:

Of an air gun: Should postpone decisions for a little while.

Having an air gun: A change in life will soon come.

Buying an air gun: Are being deceived.

Receiving an air gun: Will be double-crossed in love.

Others using an air gun: Enemies are endeavoring to destroy you.

AIRPLANE:

An airplane taking off: Success in your affairs.

An airplane landing: Beware of jealous friends.

Taking a trip in an airplane: Will soon experience many ups and downs.

Being in an airplane with a friend: A change in life will soon come.

Being in an airplane with a loved one: Will be guilty of foolish actions.

Being in an airplane with family: Study plans well and will earn money.

Being in an airplane disaster but not killed: Financial gains.

Being killed in an airplane accident: Must control passions.

Others being killed in an airplane accident: Will have a vigorous mind.

AISLE:

The aisle of a church: Will be beset by difficulties and misfortune.

Aisle in other buildings: Will take a long trip.

Aisle of a theater: Death of a friend.

Walking down the aisle of a theater: Will be guilty of bad actions.

ALARM:

Giving an alarm: Speed your plans to completion.

Hearing a fire alarm while asleep: Unexpected bad news ahead.

Hearing an alarm when awake: A change in life will soon come.

Being frightened by an alarm when sleeping: Troubles ahead.

ALBATROSS:

Of an albatross: Will receive good news from a stranger.

Several albatross on the sea: Relatives will ask for help.

An albatross on top of a ship mast: Don't lend money.

Shooting an albatross: Will escape a present peril.

ALDERMAN:

Being an alderman: Insurmountable obstacles confronting you.

Having dealings with an alderman: Will improve present estate.

Being in the company of an alderman: Do not speculate.

Others with an alderman: Beware of jealous friends.

ALEHOUSE:

Being inside an alehouse: Will be put in prison.

Going to an alehouse: Troubles and illness ahead.

Having a drink at an alehouse: Hard work awaits.

Meeting friends at an alehouse: Will find new interests and surroundings.

ALIEN:

Being an alien: Big love and friendship.

Being an undesirable alien: Shame and sorrow.

Being introduced to an alien: Will collect money.

An alien changing citizenship: Very important and beneficial events to come.

ALIMONY:

Paying alimony: Will get into serious trouble.

Receiving alimony: Will have a good future.

Refusing to pay alimony: Are highly considered by others.

Collecting alimony: Will live a long life.

ALIVE:

Being alive: Will be blamed for wrongdoings.

Being burned alive: Will do bad financial business.

Being drowned alive in water: Will

have many worries.

Being buried alive: Unhappiness.

Being alive at the expense of others: Will be short of money.

Children being alive: Happy days ahead.

ALLERGY:

Having an allergy: Will receive good news.

Being allergic to fruits: Will be persecuted.

Children being allergic to flowers: Will acquire new good friends.

Others having allergies: Fortune in present enterprises.

ALLEY:

Of an alley: Will have good neighbors.

A dead-end alley: Think well before acting.

An alley lined with trees: Honor and dignity.

A dark alley: Gossip of neighbors.

ALLIGATOR:

Of an alligator: Are surrounded by enemies.

Several alligators: Be careful in making new speculations.

Having alligator shoes: A change for the better will come soon.

Having alligator handbag: Will have good earnings.

ALMANAC:

Of an almanac: Changes will take place affecting future destiny.

Owning an almanac: Big scandal will be caused by present actions.

Buying an almanac: Will quarrel with someone very dear to you.

Consulting an almanac: Will be in debt and sued for payment.

ALMONDS:

Of almonds: Sorrow for a short time.

Buying almonds: Triumph over enemies.

Eating almonds: Will live a long life.

Almonds having a bitter taste: Present ventures will fail.

ALMOND TREE:

Of an almond tree: Riches.

An almond tree in blossom: Will have joy and satisfaction.
An almond tree with unripened fruit: Troubles ahead.
An almond tree with ripe fruit: Happiness in the home.

ALMS:
Of alms: Sorrow caused by affection for another.
Receiving alms: Loss of your home.
Giving alms freely: Great happiness.
Someone begging alms from you: Misfortune if you refuse to give.

ALOE:
Of aloe trees: Will have a serious illness.
Picking aloe leaves: Big joy.
Boiling aloe leaves: A change for the better will come.
Taking aloe juice as a medicine: Good health.

ALPACA:
Of an alpaca: Will receive a valuable present.
Having alpaca material: Will be lucky in receiving money.
Having alpaca suits: Will be advanced in present position.
Others with alpaca suits: Insurmountable obstacles confront you.

ALPHABET:
Of the alphabet: An absent friend will return.
Writing the entire alphabet: Unexpected good news to come.
Printing the entire alphabet: Worry will be smoothed away.
Counting the foreign alphabet: A mystery will be solved.

ALPINE CLIMBER:
Of an alpine climber: Be on guard against spiteful gossip.
A climber ascending a mountain: Will have good health and long life.
A climber descending a mountain: Will have success in affairs.
Seeing a mountain from a distance: Will receive good news.

ALTAR:
Of an altar: Discovery of lost money.
Kneeling at an altar: A secret desire will be fulfilled.
Being married and dreaming of an altar: Will have many small vexations.
Being outside the altar building: Big fortune.
A decorated altar: Will undertake a long trip.
An altar in confusion: Will be annoyed by enemies.
An altar being destroyed: Death of one of the children.
An altar being constructed: Will enjoy wealth.

ALTERATION:
Alterations being made: Will have good earnings.
Making various alterations: Prompt engagement.
Making alterations to children's clothes: Happiness in the family.
Others making alterations for you: Temptations will come to you.

ALTERCATION:
Having a heated dispute: Avoid rivals.
Having altercation with relatives: Watch neighbors carefully.
Having an altercation with a loved one: Happiness in love.
Having an altercation with a friend: Pride will be injured.
Others having an altercation: Failure of enemies.

ALUM:
Of alum: Luck and prosperity.
Having alum at home: Success in money matters.
Using alum: Someone beneath you is bitter against you.
Others using alum: Will be cheated by a friend.

AMBASSADOR:
Of an ambassador: Faithful friends are nearby.
Being an ambassador: Will lose present position.
Recalling an ambassador from his

post: Social activities of a happy nature.

Being in conference with an ambassador: Will realize high ambitions.

AMBER:

The color of amber: Warning against pride.

Having something of amber: Obstacles between you and loved one.

Receiving something made of amber as a gift: Approaching money.

Giving something made of amber as a gift: Abundant means.

AMBULANCE:

A full ambulance: Realization of all desires.

An empty ambulance: Loss of a friend.

Calling an ambulance for a relative: Will have financial troubles.

Calling an ambulance for yourself: Will soon recover from an illness.

AMERICA:

Of America: Many people are envious of you.

Being an American: Will have happiness in old age.

Seeing America on a map: Big joy.

Being in America: Happiness derived through own efforts.

Taking a trip to America alone: Will be married soon.

Taking a trip to America with others: Will have an unsettled future.

Going to America from abroad: Wealth and prosperity.

Going abroad from America: Ventures are faraway.

Being deported to America from abroad: Will be falsely accused.

Being deported from America: Will be guilty of foolish actions.

(See also **NORTH, CENTRAL,** and **SOUTH AMERICA.**)

AMETHYST:

Of an amethyst: Contentment in life.

Having an amethyst: Unexpected good news.

Buying an amethyst: Will be jilted.

Losing an amethyst: An enemy is seeking your ruin.

AMMONIA:

Of ammonia: Misfortune in love affairs.

Having ammonia: Danger through an accident.

Buying ammonia: Will have vexations.

Using ammonia: Quarrels with a friend.

AMOROUS:

Being an amorous person: Will be a victim of scandal.

Others being amorous toward you: Be careful in love affairs.

A man being amorous: Be careful of relationships with others.

A woman being amorous: Are demanding too much.

Young girls being amorous: Will make a wrong marriage.

AMPUTATE:

Seeing an amputation: Will have a healthy life.

A leg being amputated: Loss of a friend.

An arm being amputated: Loss of a relative.

A hand being amputated: Death of an enemy.

A foot being amputated: Death of a friend.

AMULET:

Of an amulet: Beware of jealous friends.

Wearing an amulet: Important decision must be made soon.

Buying an amulet for protection against evil: Will marry soon.

Selling an amulet: Unhappiness.

Receiving a gift of an amulet: Will experience the loss of a lover.

AMUSEMENT:

Of a place of amusement: Use your time more wisely.

Amusing yourself: Unhappiness.

Amusing yourself and family: Will have arguments.

Amusing yourself with friends: Loss of money.

Amusing yourself with a sweetheart: Will have very high hopes.

Others amusing themselves: Will marry a dancer.

ANARCHIST:

Of an anarchist: New interests and surroundings.

Several anarchists: Use caution in financial affairs.

An anarchist being killed: Will live a long, honest life.

Being an anarchist: Loss of freedom.

ANCESTORS:

Of ancestors: Don't trust people who say they are in love.

Ancestors who are dead: Happiness.

Great grandparents: Small illness to come.

Grandparents: Speedy recovery from an illness.

Other people's ancestors: Fortune is ahead.

ANCHOR:

An anchor on the bow of a ship: Good fortune.

An anchor hanging on the side of a ship: Luck and prosperity.

An anchor being down in the water: Will have disappointments.

Raising an anchor from the water: Will have good earnings.

Losing an anchor: Financial gains.

ANCHOVIES:

Of anchovies: Will have a good deal of suffering.

Buying anchovies: Good fortune.

Eating anchovies: Will have memories of first lover.

Using anchovies in a salad: Will receive a legacy.

ANECDOTE:

Hearing an anecdote: Big social event to come.

Telling an anecdote: Important and very beneficial event to come.

Hearing an anecdote from someone on stage: Doomed for disappointment.

Hearing an anecdote from a friend: A mystery will be solved.

ANGEL:

Of an angel: Success in love.

Several angels: Will receive an inheritance.

A nonsinful person dreaming of an angel: Will receive honors.

A sinful person dreaming of an angel: Will have to repent.

A healthy person dreaming of an angel: Happiness.

An ill person dreaming of an angel: Death.

An angel coming into your home: Prosperity.

An angel being close to you: Will enjoy peace and well-being.

ANGER:

Being angry: Avoid rivals.

Becoming very angry: Will be so upset that you cannot catch your breath.

Becoming angry with a loved one: Important events.

Becoming angry with a relative: Will benefit through that person.

Becoming angry with strangers: Will receive unexpected good news.

Becoming angry and fighting: Will enjoy good friendships.

Becoming angry with children: Will get invitation from a prominent person.

ANGLING:

Of angling: You are wasting your talents.

Angling and catching fish: Good news will follow.

Angling but not catching fish: Evil will come to you.

Angling in the deep sea: Will be alone and annoyed.

Angling in a river: Loss of a friend.

Angling with nets: Will do business with a smart woman.

Telling others of going angling: They will gossip about you.

Others going angling: Worry will be smoothed away.

ANIMALS:

Caressing animals: A big fortune is ahead.

Feeding animals: Wealth.

Beating animals: Expect joy.

Beating animals to death: Good results in business.

Pushing animals away: Will soon be divorced.

Animals resting in a stable: Unfortunate in love.

Animals resting in a field: Financial gains.

Animals on a mountain: Loss of money in business.

A dangerous wild animal: Will have adversity.

Being pursued by wild animals: Will be offended by a friend.

A bull or cow: Will make good investments.

A dog: Prosperity.

A horse: Important and very beneficial event to come.

A monkey: Social activities of a happy nature.

A crocodile: Poverty.

A fat animal: Abundance during the year.

A skinny animal: Must endure starvation.

A tame animal: Are surrounded by enemies.

Talking to animals: Will benefit by associating with people of society.

Talking to a dog: Pleasant work and good news.

Talking to a parrot: You expect too many favors of other people.

A parrot talking to you: The parrot's words will come true.

Buying animals: Trouble is ahead.

Selling animals: Success will be postponed.

Other people's animals: A mystery will be solved.

ANKLE:

Of own ankles: A friend is trying to help you secretly.

Ankles being injured: Difficulties followed by success later.

Breaking an ankle: Death of someone in a foreign country.

Other people's ankles: A mystery will be solved.

A woman showing her ankles: Realization of her desires.

A man dreaming of beautiful ankles: Health and joy.

Having big ankles: Fortune and honor.

Having very small ankles: Separation from mate in near future.

Having extraordinarily large ankles: Happiness secured from people abroad.

Having beautiful ankles: Will have plenty of money in old age.

Having long ankles: Loss of a son.

A man's broken ankle bleeding: Will die faraway from loved ones.

A woman dreaming of a man's ankles: Will lose husband and children.

Poor people having nice ankles: Big fortune.

ANNOUNCE:

Making a public announcement: Luck and prosperity.

Announcing own marriage: Failure of enemies.

Announcing a relative's marriage: Immediate recovery.

Others announcing their marriage: Discovery of lost valuables.

Announcing family affairs: Divorce is in sight.

Announcing a death: Danger through a secret.

Announcing a birth: Are being deceived.

Announcing the arrival of friends: Troubles ahead.

Others announcing news to you: A change in life will soon come.

A happy announcement: Illness and death.

ANNOY:

Being annoyed: Good fortune ahead for all plans.

Annoying others: Will have good earnings.

Annoying a married person: Avoid rivals.

Annoying children: Danger through a secret.

ANT:

Ants at work: Good business activity.

Having ants in the house: Illness within the family.

Ants climbing a tree: Vexations to come.

Ants on food: Happiness is assured.

ANTEATER:

Of an anteater: Will go bankrupt.

An anteater eating ants with wings: Loss of real estate.

An anteater eating worms: Loss of friends.

ANTELOPE:

Of an antelope: Someone dear has placed confidence in you.

Having antelope leather: Prosperity in money matters.

Having antelope shoes: Will be very healthy.

Having an antelope handbag: Will have sufficient money all your life.

Others with an antelope bag: Will be deceived.

ANTHEM:

Singing a national anthem: Temptation will come to you.

Hearing a national anthem: Happiness.

Hearing an anthem at an official ceremony: Will receive good news.

Hearing an anthem in church: Illness in the family.

ANTIQUES:

Of antiques: Will live a long life.

Buying antiques: Inheritance is forseen.

Selling antiques: Big loss of money.

Taking advantage of an antiquary in a deal: Increased prosperity.

ANVIL:

Of an anvil: Good results through work.

Buying an anvil: Happiness is assured.

Hitting metals on an anvil: Will have a change in present affairs.

Other people using an anvil: Good times are ahead.

ANXIETY:

Having anxiety: Will overcome enemies.

Having painful anxiety of the mind: Happy days are ahead.

Having anxiety over children: Will have good health.

Having anxiety over mate: Troubles are ahead.

APARTMENT:

Being in an apartment: Avoid rivals.

Owning an apartment: Family quarrels.

Being in an apartment alone: Loneliness and disappointment.

Being in an apartment with someone else: Good luck in love.

Hiding in an apartment: Will receive costly gifts.

The apartment of another person: Troubles ahead.

APE:

Poor people dreaming of apes: Good earnings.

Rich people dreaming of apes: Troubles and illness.

Apes dancing: Good business in real estate.

Apes in a cage: Opposition in love.

A baby ape: Will have good hopes in love.

APOLOGY:

Receiving an apology: Happiness in love.

Receiving an apology from children: Will overcome enemies.

Apologizing to friends: Return of a former friend.

Receiving an apology from a friend: Change of companionship.

APPAREL:

Of new apparel: Will encounter domestic troubles.

Wearing ragged apparel: Inheritance.

Being without any apparel: Unexpected money will reach you.

Others without any apparel: Favorable time for love.

Wearing apparel from a show window: Unexpected death of a relative.

APPARITION:
Of an apparition: Will receive very good news.

The apparition of a robber: A loyal friend is nearby.

Being frightened by an apparition: Will have ill health.

The apparition of a dead relative: luck and prosperity.

APPETITE:
Having a big appetite: Loss of relatives.

Having a small appetite: Ill health ahead.

Having an appetite for a big feast: Loss of money.

Losing the appetite: Danger through a secret.

APPLAUSE:
Receiving applause: Are prone to vanity.

Giving applause: Are unselfish and not envious of others.

Applauding a prominent person: Troubles ahead.

Others applauding: Treachery by friends.

APPLES:
Having apples: Big earnings and a good life.

Eating sweet apples: Good means and a favorable event.

Eating sour apples: Will cause trouble for yourself.

Eating applesauce: Change for the better to come.

APPOINTMENT:
Making an appointment: Will do business with untrustworthy person.

Missing an appointment: Are prone to insincerity.

Changing time of an appointment: Enemies are within the home.

Others missing an appointment: False friends are nearby.

APPREHENSION:
Having apprehension: Do things your own way as in the past.

Having apprehension over children: Will escape a present peril.

Having apprehension over finances: Family quarrels.

Having apprehension over friends: You expect too many favors.

APPROACH:
Being approached by a woman of quality: Will be humiliated.

Being approached by a business man: Good results in projects.

Being approached by an important person: Honor and profit.

Being approached by relatives: Family arguments.

Being approached by friends: Dishonor.

Being approached by strangers: Adversity.

APRICOT:
Eating apricots: Calamity is near from a hypocritical person.

Eating apricots during season: Good health and happiness.

Eating apricots out of season: Loss of hope.

Apricots growing on the tree: Pleasure and contentment in the future.

Picking apricots: Coming prosperity in business and love.

Having spoiled apricots in the hands: Trouble and loss of a relative.

Canned or preserved apricots: Will be cheated by friends.

Dried apricots: Big annoyance to come.

APRIL:
April 1st, foreign nations' Labor Day: Will make a trip abroad.

April Fools' joke played on you: Will have power over someone.

Fooling others on April Fools' Day: Loss of a friend.

Fooling relatives on April Fools' Day: Good times are ahead.

Fooling children on April Fools' Day: Happiness in the family.

Fooling a loved person on April Fools' Day: Difficulties in love.

The month of April during this month: Postponement of success.

The month of April during other months: Must mend ways in life.

Being born in April: Will be happy in love affairs.

Children being born in April: Will have important position in life.

APRON:

Of an apron: Happiness.

Wearing an apron: Lasting love.

A married woman wearing an apron: Will have ups and downs.

An unmarried woman wearing an apron: Will soon be engaged.

A man wearing an apron: Change for the better.

A widow wearing an apron: Will have several good friends.

Tearing an apron: Small benefit.

Losing an apron: Danger in love affairs.

Having lost an apron: Will lose your sweetheart.

Tying an apron: Will receive big honors.

Untying an apron: Will lose a loved one.

A blue apron: Gossip by other women.

AQUAMARINE:

Having an aquamarine stone: Affection of a youthful friend.

Buying an aquamarine stone: Happiness is assured.

Selling an aquamarine stone: Disappointment in love.

Losing an aquamarine stone: Danger in love matters.

AQUEDUCT:

Of an aqueduct: Will receive fortune from parents.

An aqueduct being built: Postponement of success.

An aqueduct being repaired: Will realize high ambitions.

Much water flowing through an aqueduct: Wealth.

ARAB:

Of an Arab: Will be molested during a trip.

Being an Arab: A change of fortune for the better to come.

Many Arabs: Will have a love affair.

Going with an Arab: Will have an important and good transaction.

ARBITRATION:

Of an arbitration: Loss of money through injustice.

Winning an arbitration: Projects will not succeed.

Losing an arbitration: Will have future financial benefits.

Being an arbitrator: Important and beneficial events to come.

ARBOR:

Of an arbor: Will hear secrets of other people.

Being in an arbor: Personal secrets will be revealed.

Walking in an arbor: Will receive good news.

An arbor being on fire: Affliction in love affairs.

ARCH:

Of an arch: Wealth and advancement.

A damaged arch: Must mend ways in life.

Passing under an arch: Many will seek favors from you.

The arch of a violin: Others will interfere in love affairs.

ARCHER:

Of an archer: Unhappiness in love matters.

Being an archer: Unfitted to fill your position.

Being a married archer: Danger is nearby.

An unmarried archer: Engagement is near.

ARCHITECT:

Of an architect: Will have much pleasure in life.

Being an architect: Suitable time to pursue suit of lover.

Being with an architect: Luck and prosperity.

Talking with an architect about a construction: Family quarrels.

ARENA:

Of an arena: Use caution in business ventures.

Being in an arena: A false friend is nearby.

Fighting in an arena: Will realize high ambitions.

Spectators being in an arena: Misery.

ARGUE:

Having an argument: Good and long life.

Arguing with family: Troubles caused by prying into affairs of others.

Arguing with relatives: Will have a strenuous time.

Arguing with an attorney: Troubles ahead.

Arguing with other people: An enemy is seeking your ruin.

ARISE:

Arising very early in the morning: Will make plenty of money.

Arising with the sun: Big happiness.

Arising from bed: Sickness.

Arising from the floor: Troubles and affliction.

Arising from a chair: Good news.

Arising from a couch: Will receive an unexpected letter.

Arising with a loved one: Will have disputes.

ARK:

Of an ark: Important and very beneficial events to come.

Having an ark: Safety and protection.

An ark in a sacred place: Long comfortable life.

The ark of the Ten Commandments: Abundant means.

ARM:

Of own arms: Victory over enemies.

Having a nice arm: Will have good friendships.

Having arms covered with hairs: Will be very rich.

Having big arms: Big joy ahead.

Having small arms: Will have plenty of money.

Very thin arms: Will soon be rich.

Having unusually big arms: Joy and contentment.

Having an arm cut off: Loss of a relative.

Having pain in the arms: Unlucky results in business.

Dirty arms: Big misery ahead.

A man having a broken arm: Family quarrels.

A woman having a broken arm: Loss of her husband.

Having both arms broken: Illness.

Having an accident with the arms: Ill health within family.

Right arm being amputated: Death of a male in the family.

Left arm being amputated: Death of a female in the family.

Breaking an arm: Big peril ahead.

Having skin disease on the arms: Will work hard without profit.

Having freckles on the arms: Must mend ways in life.

ARMCHAIR:

Of an armchair: Will receive urgent good news.

Many armchairs: Honor and dignity.

Sitting in an armchair: High consideration by others.

Others sitting in armchairs: Unwelcome guest will come to visit.

ARMENIANS:

Of an Armenian: Doomed for disappointment.

Being in Armenia: Important and very beneficial event to come.

Being with an Armenian: Return of a former friend.

Many Armenians: Will receive a long-awaited letter.

ARMISTICE:

Of Armistice Day: Promotion of affairs.

An armistice ending hostilities: Loss of a friend.
Making an armistice: Happiness.
An armistice ending in your favor: Will receive high honors.

ARMS:
Of firearms: Rapid success for own hopes.
Having a revolver: Discovery of lost valuables.
Having a rifle: Another person is enjoying what you hoped to win.
Being armed with guns: A good opportunity will come.
Having several guns: Postponement of success.
Others being armed with guns: Worry will be smoothed away.

ARMY:
Of an army: War within the family.
Several armies of different countries: Fortune and joy.
The army of own country: Will have small business success.
An army fighting: Treason and persecution.

AROUND:
Going around: Will receive good news.
Going around with people of poor morals: Will have an operation.
Going around with a loved one: Will receive good news.
Going around with children: Gossip by neighbors.

ARRANGE:
Arranging things in the house: Desires will not be realized.
Arranging family affairs: Hard work will bring fortune.
Arranging business: Misfortune.
Arranging clothes: Will receive an unexpected visit.
Arranging for a trip: Beware of gossip by friends.
Others arranging things: Profit.

ARREST:
Being arrested: Will have misery followed by joy.
Being arrested: Misfortune is near.

Being released from arrest: Unexpected and sudden success.
Others being arrested: Will receive an unexpected gift.

ARRIVAL:
Business people arriving: Good earnings.
The arrival of a relative: Loss of money.
The arrival of many relatives: Loss in business.
The arrival of a friend: Will receive a pleasant surprise.
The arrival of a mate: Family reunion.
The arrival of children: Happiness.

ARROW:
Being hit by an arrow: Misfortune caused by unsuspected person.
Throwing an arrow: Unhappiness.
Many arrows: Friends are working against you.
Having many arrows: Are surrounded by enemies.
A broken arrow: Failure in business.
Breaking an arrow: Failure in love.

ARSON:
Arson on land: Change for the better.
Arson at sea: Successful ventures.
Arson committed to others' homes: Dignity.
Arson committed in home causing fire with clear flames: Good employment.
Arson committed in home causing fire with dark flames: Financial ruin.
Arson committed in home causing fire with small flames: Will be fortunate.

ART:
Of works of art: Honor.
Buying works of art: Will have to work hard.
Selling works of art: Loss of money.
Being an art dealer: Diligence will be compensated.

ARTERY:
Having strong arteries: Will receive a message with good news.

Having weak arteries: Slow recovery from an illness.

Own arteries being cut: Will live a long life.

An artery of a river: Worries will be smoothed away.

ARTICHOKES:

Of artichokes: Will be able to surmount present troubles.

Having artichokes: Will have happiness and contentment.

Eating artichokes: Dissension within the family.

Growing artichokes: Luck and prosperity.

ARTIST:

Of an artist: Success will be yours.

Being an artist: Will receive many honors.

Having an artist paint your portrait: Treachery of a friend.

Posing for a sculptor: You expect too many favors from others.

An artist painting portrait of another: Will risk failure to plans.

ASHAMED:

Being ashamed: Fortune in business.

Being ashamed of chastity: Will meet a rich person.

Being ashamed of actions: Are stricken with a guilty conscience.

Being ashamed of children: Listen to advice of friends.

A mate being ashamed of the other: Separation will soon take place.

ASHES:

Of ashes: Loss of something through carelessness.

Having ashes in own fireplace: Loss of money.

Cremated ashes of a relative: Will live a long life.

Cremated ashes of a relative being put in an urn: Approaching money.

ASIA:

Of Asia: Will soon collect money.

Seeing Asia on a map: Advancement within present position.

Taking a trip to Asia alone: Will meet a new friend.

Taking a trip to Asia with others: Will have emotional sorrow.

Returning from Asia: Will have a love affair.

Being deported to Asia: Unhappiness in love affairs.

Being deported from Asia: Business will halt.

ASPARAGUS:

Having asparagus: Will have big success.

Raw asparagus: Success in own enterprises.

Handling asparagus: Will have a very healthy life.

Cooking asparagus: Own plans will be successful.

ASS:

Of an ass: Will not benefit from quarrels.

Riding on a donkey: Will fall into disgrace.

Having a donkey: Will have a dispute with best friend.

Being pulled by a donkey: Good luck in love affairs.

An ass running: Will receive bad news.

An ass moving very slowly: Plenty of security is forthcoming.

Purchasing an ass: Joy within the family.

Selling an ass: Big loss in business.

Loading an ass: Good business ahead.

A loaded ass: Will make money.

Sitting on a donkey: Will have plenty of work and fortune.

Children sitting on a donkey: Happiness.

Taking a donkey out of the stable: Business will be dissolved.

Hitting a donkey: Will receive unpleasant news.

Being kicked by a donkey: Misfortune in love.

Putting shoes on a donkey: Will do hard work in the future.

Seeing a donkey dead: Will live a long life.

Killing a donkey: Will lose all your fortune.

The ears of a donkey: Will be confronted with a big scandal.

Hearing a donkey bray: Disgrace within the family.

A wild donkey: Are not operating business well.

Many donkeys: Will be jilted by lover.

Donkeys belonging to others: Will have many loyal friends.

ASSAULT:

Being assaulted: Good information will be given to you.

Assaulting others: Monetary gain.

Children being assaulted: Family quarrels.

Others being assaulted: Unhappiness in love affairs.

ASTER:

Of asters: Pleasant happiness.

Picking asters: Will receive a letter with good news.

Gathering asters: A mystery will be solved.

Receiving a gift of a bouquet of asters: Abundance.

ASTHMA:

Of asthma: Plans will not work out well.

Having asthma: Will recover soon by changing residence to another state.

Contracting asthma: Financial gains.

Others having asthma: Doomed for disappointment.

ASTONISH:

Being astonished: Are in line to receive a cabinet post.

Astonishing other people: Big joy ahead.

Being astonished by actions of others: Riches.

A member of the family acting astonishingly: Will receive good news.

ASTROLOGY:

Of astrology: Happiness.

A rich person studying astrology: Loss of money.

A poor person studying astrology: Death.

Studying astrology at night: Important and very beneficial event to come.

ASTRONOMER:

Of an astronomer: Will realize high ambitions.

Being an astronomer: Sickness within the family.

Being in the company of an astronomer: Failure of enemies.

Others being with an astronomer: Will have good earnings.

ASYLUM:

Of an asylum: Will live a long healthy life.

Being in an asylum: Serious troubles ahead.

Avoiding being put in an asylum: Take care of own health.

A young girl dreaming of being in an asylum: Will marry soon.

ATHLETE:

Of an athlete: Family quarrels.

Being an athlete: Financial problems.

Becoming an athlete: Beware of overdoing.

Being in the company of an athlete: Avoid rivals.

ATLAS:

Of an atlas: Change of residence.

Having an atlas: Social activities of a happy nature.

Consulting an atlas: Will have plenty of money.

Buying an atlas: Will take a long trip abroad.

ATMOSPHERE:

Of atmosphere: Prosperity in money matters.

A clear atmosphere: Happiness within the family.

Cloudy atmosphere: Are without faithful friends.

Rainy atmosphere: Abundant means.

Very stormy atmosphere: Will have financial troubles.

ATTACHMENT:
Having an attachment for unpaid taxes: Will have financial embarrassments.
Having an attachment for money due: Dissolution of hopes for future.
Putting an attachment upon others: Will have ridiculous disputes.
Attaching bank accounts: Be careful in business affairs.

ATTACK:
Of an attack: A mystery will be solved.
Being attacked and injured: Will suffer an insult.
Being attacked but not harmed: Will soon have good fortune.
Attacking others: Danger is nearby.

ATTEND:
Attending a wedding: Immediate recovery.
Attending a funeral: Will have changes for the better.
Attending a party: Good times are coming.
Attending a dinner party: Accord among friends.
Others attending a party: Beware of rivals.
Attending to other people's affairs: Temptation will come.
Others attending to your affairs: Loss of a friend.

ATTENDANT:
Of an attendant: Dignity and distinction.
Having an attendant: Advancement within present position.
Dismissing an attendant: Love affairs will be disturbed.
Others having attendants: Will be cheated by friends.

ATTIC:
Of an attic: Will come out well from a present peril.
A married person dreaming of an attic: Should avoid flirtations.
A single person dreaming of an attic: Prompt engagement.
The attic of others' homes: Are confronted by insurmountable obstacles.

ATTORNEY:
Of an attorney: Will become very weary.
Hiring an attorney: Acquaintances will take advantage of you.
Consulting an attorney: Will be confronted with worries.
Being an attorney: Unexpected good news.
Being in court with an attorney: Avoid speculation in stocks.
Dealing with an opposing attorney: Big catastrophe ahead.
Having conferences with several attorneys: Troubles ahead.

AUDIENCE:
Of an audience: Will receive high distinction.
Having an audience with a prominent person: Will have good earnings.
Having an audience with a political person: Good times are coming.
Having an audience with a priest: Will soon be in trouble.
Having an audience with social people: Will have pleasure and distinction.

AUGUST:
Of August during this month: Will receive fortune from parents.
Of August during other months: Big success in life.
Being born in August: All will go well in life.
Children being born in August: Big fortune.
Of August during the spring: Will receive bad news.
Of August during the summer: Unexpected good news.
Of August during the fall: Warning of troubles.
Of August during the winter: Will take a long trip.

AUNT:
Of an aunt: Success in money matters.
Being an aunt: A successful matrimony is being planned.

Husband's aunt: Good times are coming.

Wife's aunt: Beware of jealous friends.

Visiting with an aunt: Will receive a legacy.

Other people's aunts: Shame and sorrow.

AUSTRALIA:

Being in Australia: Are being cheated by friends.

Traveling to Australia: Social events to come.

Traveling abroad from Australia: Will have sorrow.

Being deported to Australia: Misfortune in love affairs.

Being deported from Australia: Must bring affairs into order.

AUTHOR:

Of an author: Happiness.

Dealing with an author: Good times are coming.

Married people dreaming of an author: Fortune within the family.

Single people dreaming of an author: Unexpected good news to come.

A promoter dreaming of an author: Should handle his business better.

AUTHORITIES:

Of authorities: Troubles ahead.

Being called before government authorities: Will receive insults.

Seeking help from government authorities: Will incur debts.

Being persecuted by government authorities: Advancement within position.

Others being before government authorities: Danger through a secret.

AUTOMATIC:

Automatic machines: Will have a change for the better.

Acting automatically: Own weaknesses will be discovered.

Having automatic power: Good events will come as a surprise.

Handling automatic machines: Approaching money.

AUTOMOBILE:

Of an automobile: Hasty news will be sent to you.

Owning an automobile: Will receive an important gift.

Riding alone in an automobile: New surroundings are anticipated.

Riding with family in an automobile: Will be confronted by gossip.

Riding with lover in an automobile: Must control passions.

Riding with sweetheart in an automobile: Own weaknesses will be known.

Riding with others in an automobile: Be on guard against false news.

Having an automobile accident: Approaching money.

Escaping from the path of an overturning automobile: Avoid rivals.

Riding with friends in an automobile: Will soon discover a secret.

Riding with a woman: Scandal will be brought upon your name.

AUTUMN:

Of autumn: Will have a change of surroundings.

Autumn in the spring: Unfriendly influences are nearby.

Autumn in the summer: Will experience many ups and downs.

Autumn in the winter: Good times are coming.

AVALANCHE:

Of an avalanche: Are confronted by insurmountable obstacles.

Seeing an avalanche: Will soon have good fortune.

Being buried under an avalanche of snow: Good profits.

Others being buried under an avalanche: Change of surroundings.

AVOCADO:

Having avocados: Will receive a marriage proposal.

Buying avocados: Will be loved by many people.

Eating avocados: Will be visited by a loved one.

Making a salad with avocados: Good times are coming.

AWAKEN:
Being awakened: Be on guard against coming troubles.
Awakening yourself: Will have very good business success.
Awakening the family: Failure of enemies.
Awakening other people: Favorable events to come.

AX:
Owning an ax: A danger can be averted by own bravery.
Swinging an ax: Will receive a business promotion.
A rusty or broken ax: Loss of fortune.
A man dreaming of an ax: Will have love troubles.
A woman dreaming of an ax: Will have a loved person worthy of her.
A young woman dreaming of an ax: Will have a wealthy lover.

AXLE:
Of an axle: Recovery from an illness.

The axle of a wheel on a car: Will be guided by others.
The axle of a wheel on a truck: Will have ill health.
The axle on a machine: Abundant means.
A broken axle: Beware of enemies.

AZALEA:
Of beautiful azaleas: Will receive an unexpected gift.
Receiving a bouquet of azaleas: Approaching money.
Buying azaleas: Will receive a long-awaited letter.
Wearing clothes the color of azaleas: Financial gains.

AZURE BLUE:
Of the azure blue color: Promotion in own employment.
Azure blue sky: Contentment in love affairs.
Materials of any kind that are azure blue in color: Happiness.
Wearing dresses azure blue in color: Will have a change for the better.

B

BABY:
A beautiful baby: Will have happiness.
A woman dreaming of a baby: Pregnancy.
A married, pregnant woman dreaming of a baby: Big success in love.
A married woman dreaming of having a baby when not pregnant: Happiness.
A single woman dreaming of having a baby: Sorrow.
A widow dreaming of having a baby: Avoid rivals.
A widow dreaming of expecting a baby: Success in everything.
A baby sucking milk from mother's breast: Pleasure in life.
A baby sucking milk from a wet nurse: Painful illness.

A very smart baby: Will be surrounded by good friends.
An ugly baby: Misfortune ahead.
Holding a baby on your breast: Will soon have another baby.
A baby in swaddling clothes: Good hope in love.
A baby taking the first steps: Difficulties in business.
A woman nursing a baby: Will be deceived by a trusted person.
A baby being sick: Serious illness within the family.
Hearing a baby crying: Disputes in the family.
A helpless baby: Disappointments in love.
A baby in a bed: Are being watched by one with evil intentions.

Other people's babies: Failure of enemies.

Many babies: Abundance in your life.

BACCHUS:
A man dreaming of this Greek god: Abundance in money matters.

A woman dreaming of Bacchus: Hard work ahead.

A farmer dreaming of Bacchus: Will have a good crop.

A sailor dreaming of Bacchus: Will realize a higher position.

An unmarried woman dreaming of Bacchus: Will receive marriage proposition.

BACHELOR:
Of a bachelor: Beware of deceitful people.

Being a bachelor: A change in life will soon come.

A young bachelor: Will find a rich widow to marry.

An old bachelor: Misfortune in love affairs.

Becoming a bachelor after an annulled marriage: Financial gains.

A middle-aged man being a bachelor: Big joy in life.

An old man being a bachelor: Loss of a friend.

A young man being a bachelor: Will marry soon.

A bachelor getting married: Will find a rich woman to marry.

BACK:
Of own back: Misfortune in life and will die in misery.

Back being broken: Will have ulcers.

Back being full of sores: You have many enemies.

A woman turning her back on you: Opposition in love.

A man turning his back on you: Serious difficulties.

A person walking away from you: Jealous people are against you.

A person turning around and facing you: Will be spared from illness.

A young girl turning her back on you: Wealth.

A young man turning his back on a young girl: Loss of money.

BACK DOOR:
Using the back door: Will have good changes in life soon.

Letting a lover go out the back door: Will be married soon.

Relatives entering the back door: Family arguments.

Friends entering the back door: Caution must be used in business ventures.

Robbers breaking down the back door: Approaching money.

BACKGAMMON:
Playing backgammon: Financial gains.

Winning a game of backgammon: Expect an inheritance.

Losing a game of backgammon: Expect a business loss.

Others playing backgammon: Triumph over enemies.

BACON:
Purchasing bacon: Ill health.

Frying bacon: Will receive an unexpected gift.

Eating bacon alone: Money will come easily throughout life.

Eating bacon in company of others: Wealth.

Receiving bacon as a gift: Will be highly compensated.

BADGE:
Of a badge: Are under observation for a promotion.

A badge being pinned on you: Big security.

Pinning a badge on others: Warning of troubles.

Pinning a badge on a policeman: Family reunion.

Enemies wearing a badge: Treason and unfaithfulness.

BADGER:
Of a badger: Big work ahead.

Killing a badger: Will fall in love.

Catching a badger: Good luck attends you.

Others catching a badger: Beware of enemies.

BAG:
Of traveling bags: Abundance.
Carrying only one bag: Will incur plenty of debts.
Carrying several bags: Treachery from a friend.
Bags being on a wagon: Business will push forward.
Bags being in a car: Unexpected money will arrive.
Other people's bags: Misfortune in love affairs.

BAGGAGE:
Baggage being inside the house: Cancellation of a trip.
Baggage being on the street: Belongings will be stolen.
Losing your baggage: An inheritance will soon come.
Being unable to find baggage: Will be provoked by others.
Other people's baggage: Changes in love matters will occur.

BAGPIPE:
Of a bagpipe: Loss of money.
Owning a bagpipe: Pleasure is ahead.
Playing a bagpipe: Are greatly loved.
Others playing a bagpipe: Will have a marriage proposition.
Others having a bagpipe: Matrimonial worries.

BAIL:
Requesting bail: Present condition in life will improve.
Furnishing bail: Trouble will arise with an old friend.
Not granting bail: Will soon have a change in affairs.
Forfeiting bail: Good times are coming.

BAILIFF:
Being a bailiff: Will receive good news soon.
Being in custody of a bailiff: Advancement within position.
Talking with a bailiff: Unexpected money will come soon.

Having trouble with a bailiff: Will have a misfortune.

BAIT:
Putting bait on a fishhook: Will have a big joy.
Putting out bait for rats: Future depends on own intelligence.
Others putting out bait: Disappointments.
Others attempting to please by baiting you: Don't trust them blindly.

BAIZE:
Of this type of material: Exciting times are ahead.
Owning baize: Will be in need of money.
Dying baize: Troubles are in store for you.
Selling baize: Will have big earnings.
Spreading out baize: Will have very little money.

BAKERY:
Of a bakery: Will be rich.
Owning a bakery: Prosperity and success.
Being at a bakery: Will have a prosperous year.
A baker at work in a bakery: Will receive good news.
Being a baker at a bakery: Profits in business ventures.

BAKING:
A married woman dreaming of baking: Unlucky events to come.
A single woman dreaming of baking: Loss of friends through bad temper.
A widow dreaming of baking: Expect too many favors from others.
A man dreaming of baking: Will have plenty of money.

BALCONY:
Standing on a balcony: Will lose present position.
Sitting on a balcony: Will be unable to keep what you now have.
Being on a balcony alone: Financial gains.
Being on a balcony with a person of opposite sex: Big love.

Lovers saying farewell on a balcony: A long separation will follow.

Leaving a balcony with a loved one: Big disappointments.

BALD:

Going bald: Serious illness is in sight.

Being bald all over the head: Will be loved very much.

Being bald in the front of the head: Will be in big trouble.

Being bald in the back of the head: Will live in poverty.

Being bald on the right side of the head: Death of a friend.

Being bald on the left side of the head: Death of a relative.

A woman going bald: Will have difficulties in love affairs.

A baby being bald: Will enjoy love.

BALE:

Bales of cotton: Good fortune.

Owning bales of wool: Will have many troubles.

Buying bales of cotton: Will overcome enemies.

Selling bales of cotton: Approaching money.

BALL:

Of a gala ball: Will inherit plenty of money.

Young girls being at a ball: Will lose plenty of money.

Dancing with a young girl at a ball: Will have many good friends.

Dancing with a young man at a ball: Discovery of a secret.

A woman dancing with her husband at a ball: Will have success.

A married woman dancing with another man: Gossip by friends.

Unmarried woman dancing with a married man: Friends will cheat you.

Unmarried woman dancing with an unmarried man: Avoid rivals.

A woman dancing with her boyfriend at a ball: Illness.

A widow dancing with a married man at a ball: Will soon divorce his wife.

Young girls dancing at a ball: Will have plenty of money.

A professional dancer at a ball: Will meet a very pleasant person.

A professional man dancing at a ball: Will encounter obstacles.

Attending a masquerade ball: Beware of a trap.

Attending a wedding ball: Misfortune in own affairs.

Attending a small ball: Happiness.

Being among the dancers at a ball: Will receive good news.

Attending a ball with well-dressed women: Good luck.

A ball but you are not present at the ball: Will soon be engaged.

Watching a ball without dancing: Will soon receive a legacy.

Playing ball games: Will have many good friends.

Different balls for games: Will not have any friends.

Playing with a billiard ball: Good news.

Cannon balls: Great sorrow.

Baseball or cricket: Will receive good news.

Football: Uneasiness.

Tennis or rubber balls: Certain birth of a child.

BALLAD:

Playing a ballad: Good times are coming.

Singing a ballad: Someone for whom you care thinks unkindly of you.

Hearing a ballad: Beware of false judgments.

Composing a ballad: Will have dignity and distinction.

BALLAST:

A broken ballast: Friends are not trustworthy.

A ship in full ballast: Partner cannot be trusted.

A ship and ballast sinking: Abundant means.

Taking a ballast from a ship: Approaching money.

BALLET:
A woman dreaming of a ballet: Warning of troubles.
A young woman dreaming of a ballet: Infidelity with her lover.
A man dreaming of a ballet: Failure in business.
A widow dreaming of a ballet: Will soon marry a rich banker.
A stage ballet with professional dancers: Will have poor health.

BALLOON:
Of a balloon: Inventive mind will cause disappointment.
Being in a balloon: Happiness is assured.
Ascending in a balloon: Will have misfortune during a journey.
Descending in a balloon: Will make unfavorable money ventures.

BALLOT:
A ballot box: Present surroundings are not good.
Casting a ballot: Will have a change of companionship.
Others casting their ballot: Defeat in present affairs.
Opening a ballot box: A change for the better to come.

BALM:
Of balm: Are hated by others.
Buying balm: Will have a change in environment.
Using a soothing balm: True friendship is nearby.
Others using balm: Will experience emotional sorrow.

BALUSTRADE:
Of a balustrade: Will be in an accident.
A broken balustrade: Are confronted with insurmountable obstacles.
Placing hands on a balustrade: Will have much success in love.
Others with hands on a balustrade: Death of an enemy.

BANANA:
Buying bananas: Prosperity.
Eating bananas: Will be imposed upon to fulfill some duty.

Selling bananas: Unprofitable business ahead.
Decaying bananas: Will undertake a distasteful affair.
Growing bananas: Will have a small business venture.

BANDAGE:
Wearing bandages: Expect good news.
Children having bandages on: Good times are coming.
Putting bandages on others: Abundant means.
Others wearing bandages: Will receive bad news.

BANDIT:
Of a bandit: Prosperity in own affairs.
Several bandits: Are in big danger.
Being attacked by a bandit: Beware of accidents.
Attacking a bandit: Rely upon own vigor and good judgment.

BANISHMENT:
Being forced to accept banishment: Will be fortunate in love.
Being banished: Conditions will change for the best.
Being in exile: Troubles will last for only a short time.
Other people being banished: Will soon receive plenty of money.
Being banished forever: Prosperity.
Being banished from own home: Financial condition will be very bad.

BANJO:
Owning a banjo: Must endure sorrow.
Playing a banjo: Poverty.
Playing a banjo on the stage: Will receive big consolation.
Others playing a banjo: Joy.

BANK:
Being in a bank: Will receive false promises.
Dealing with a bank: Sudden loss of money.
Owning a bank: Friends are making fun of you.
Borrowing money from a bank: Financial losses ahead.

Receiving money from a bank: Bankruptcy is near.

Being in a money changer's bank: Will receive unpleasant news.

BANKRUPT:
Being bankrupt: Business will prosper well.

Going into bankruptcy: Will receive esteem of friends.

Having to declare bankruptcy: Avoid speculation.

Others being bankrupt: Business needs immediate watching.

BANNER:
Of a banner: Own personal position is not good.

A red banner: Will receive help from friends abroad.

The banner on a ship: Will take an ocean voyage.

A banner on a house: Failure of enemies.

Receiving a banner: A promised gift will not be given.

BANQUET:
Being in attendance at a banquet: Pleasures will be costly.

Young people dreaming of a banquet: Love and happiness.

Old people dreaming of being at a banquet: Will have abundant means.

Being in attendance at a wedding banquet: Are surrounded by good friends.

Attending a Christmas banquet: Happiness within the family.

Attending a political banquet: Disappointments.

BAPTIZE:
Having been baptized: Will have a prosperous life.

Relatives being baptized: Will be disappointed by best friend.

Children being baptized: Big joy.

Children of others being baptized: Accord among friends.

BAR:
Of a bar: Will be guilty of foolish actions.

Having a drink alone in a bar: A false friend is nearby.

Drinking with company in a bar: Must control passions.

Others drinking in a bar: Are more highly esteemed by friends than realized.

Single women drinking in a bar: Financial gains.

BARBARIC:
Being with barbaric people: Will make a love conquest.

A man being barbaric: Worries ahead.

A woman being barbaric: Avoid rivals.

Barbaric people fighting: Failure of enemies.

Barbaric people being killed: Danger through a secret.

BARBER:
Being in a barber shop: Difficulties in business.

Going to the barber: Success as a result of applied hard work.

Being a barber: Will have big success.

Calling a barber to the home: Will have an illness.

Having hair cut by a barber: Big profit in business.

Having a shave at the barber's: Loss of money.

Having haircut and shave by a female barber: Will have good clothes.

BAREFOOT:
A man going barefooted: Postponement of success.

A woman going barefooted: All her life, will never have a lasting love.

Children going barefooted: Shame and sorrow.

Only the feet being bare: Expect trouble and difficulty.

Feet and legs to knees being bare: Dishonor in social life.

Feet and legs to hips being bare: Will serve a small prison term.

BARGAIN:
Of bargaining: Should trust only your own opinions.

Being cheated out of a bargain: Own home will be robbed.

Having made a good bargain: Advancement within position.
Others making a good bargain: Have loyal friends.

BARGE:
Of a barge: Will travel quite a distance soon.
Being aboard a barge: Will soon get married.
A loaded barge: Triumph over enemies.
An empty barge: Troubles will arise from prying into affairs of others.

BARKING:
Hearing a dog barking: Take the advice of friends.
Seeing a dog barking: It is not opportune time to do business.
A dog barking at friends: A mystery will be solved.
Hearing several dogs barking: Important and beneficial event to come.

BARLEY:
Having a lot of barley: Abundance and plenty of money.
Eating barley: Will have rugged health.
Buying barley: Unhappiness within the family.
Selling barley: An enemy is very near.
Handling barley with hands: Joy and profit.
Eating bread made of barley: Big satisfaction and good health.

BARMAID:
Of a barmaid: Danger in love affairs.
Being a barmaid: Own affairs will improve slowly.
Having a barmaid: Difficulties due to own carelessness.
Dating a barmaid: Beware of jealous friends.
Being married to a barmaid: Will soon experience troubles.

BARN:
Being in a barn: Will win a law suit.
Being in a barn with other people: Inheritance.
An empty barn with doors open: Misfortune.

A full barn: Will marry a wealthy person.
Handling grain in a barn: Will live a happy life.

BAROMETER:
Having a barometer: Sickness.
A barometer registering good weather: Happiness.
A barometer registering bad weather: Unhappiness.
A barometer registering fair weather: Pleasure.
A barometer registering rainy weather: Disappointments.

BARON:
Of a baron: Will be deceived.
Being a baron: Are prone to being a proud person.
Being in the company of a baron: Dignity and distinction.
Married people dreaming of a baron: Big happiness.
Unmarried people dreaming of a baron: Will soon be married.

BARRACKS:
Of barracks: Hard work is ahead.
Being a soldier living in barracks: Difficulties will soon end.
Not living in barracks: Will get into trouble.
Many soldiers living in barracks: Warning of troubles ahead.

BARREL:
An empty barrel: Will be in poverty.
A full barrel: Will be wealthy.
An upright and full barrel: Prosperity.
A rolling empty barrel: Hard times to come.
Owning a barrel: Will receive an unexpected gift.
Having a large number of barrels: Abundance of money.
Having a full barrel of wine: Better times are ahead.
Having a full barrel of alcohol: Good success in business.

BASEBALL:
Playing a game of baseball: Future prosperity.

Others playing a game of baseball: Will have domestic contentment.

Not scoring in a game of baseball: Disappointment in love.

Making a good score in a game of baseball: Divorce is ahead.

Pitching the ball to the batter: Will have family troubles.

BASHFUL:

Being bashful: Will have a pleasant time at a large party.

Having bashful children: Joy.

Having bashful friends: Warning of troubles ahead.

BASIN:

Of a basin full of water: Joy within the family.

Using a full basin of water: Will have plenty of money.

An empty basin: Will incur many debts.

Drinking from a basin: Difficulties ahead in love affairs.

Eating from a basin: Will not marry the person you love.

BASKET:

Of a full basket: Good business ventures.

Having a full basket: Will make plenty of money.

Having an empty basket: Will lose money.

Other people's baskets: Family will increase in number.

BASTARD:

Of a bastard: Discovery of a secret.

Having a bastard: Will have dissatisfaction and regret.

Being a bastard: Will overcome difficulties.

BATH:

Of a bathtub: Will become very angry.

Being in a bathtub: Anxiety.

Taking a bath in ice water: Disgrace.

Taking a bath in cold water: Big sorrow.

Taking a bath in warm water: Will be separated from a loved one.

Taking a bath in lukewarm water: Wealth.

Taking a bath early in the morning: Will soon get married.

Taking a bath at noon: Pleasures and good health.

Taking a bath in the evening: A false friend is nearby.

Taking a bath at bedtime: Will surrender to sweetheart.

Preparing a bath: Will have a fight with some person.

Preparing a bath for yourself: Serious illness.

Preparing a bath for mate: Will realize high ambitions.

Preparing a bath for loved one: Will have a luxurious life.

Preparing a bath for children: Happiness.

Preparing a bath for sweetheart: This love affair will break up.

Getting in a bathtub clothed: Will quarrel with your lover.

Being in a bathtub with the one you love: Will receive an inheritance.

Undressing but not getting in the tub: Will have love troubles.

An empty bathtub: Will have business worries.

BATHING:

Bathing in the open: Success and good health.

Bathing in clear water: Success in business.

Bathing in dirty water: Expect difficulties.

Bathing in muddy water: Death of a relative.

Bathing in the open sea: Will receive a big fortune.

Bathing in water choked with weeds: Death of an animal.

Bathing in a river: Unusually good business ahead.

Bathing in a canal: Will be very rich.

Bathing in a lake: Will be unhappy.

Bathing in a swimming pool: Illness.

Bathing in a marsh: Will be very unlucky.

Bathing at a bathhouse: Will have ulcers.

Bathing in a cascade of water: Present projects will be a failure.

Bathing in a house: Anxiety.

Going bathing at sea with your mate: Will realize own hopes.

Going bathing at sea with children: Happiness within the family.

Going bathing at sea with a loved one: Will have luxurious life.

Going bathing at sea with a sweetheart: End of this love affair.

Going bathing in the nude: Will receive an inheritance.

Going bathing with clothes on: Will have an argument.

BATS:

A gray bat: Will have an easy life.

A black bat: Will quarrel and disaster awaits.

A white bat: Recovery of a sick person.

Many bats: Death within the family.

BATTLE:

Of a battle: Will enter into risky ventures.

Watching a battle: Will be persecuted.

A naval battle: Will be triumphant.

A battle on land: Will live a long life.

A battle with fists: Double cross in love affairs.

Being defeated in battle: Unwise business dealings of others will hurt you.

Fighting a battle alone: Things will turn out right for you.

Winning a battle: Will have a good future.

BAYONET:

Of a bayonet: Will have quarrels with friends.

Having a bayonet: Postponement of success.

Carrying a bayonet in the hands: Success in own enterprises.

Others holding a bayonet: Will be under the power of enemies.

A soldier having a bayonet: Worries will be smoothed away.

BAZAAR:

Of a bazaar: Luck and prosperity.

Being at a bazaar: Happiness in love.

Buying things at a charity bazaar: Will realize high ambitions.

People selling things at a charity bazaar: Will receive a proposal.

BEACON:

Of a beacon: Accord among friends.

Watching a beacon: Avoid quarrels, attempt a reconciliation.

Operating a beacon station: Will have vexations.

Others operating a beacon station: Disappointments.

BEADS:

Stringing beads: Will receive favors from a wealthy person.

Buying beads: Will have false friends.

Scattering beads: Loss of reputation.

Losing beads: Will be molested.

Counting beads: Will have much joy and deep content.

Finding beads: Misery and tears.

Selling beads: Beware of untrue friends.

Fishing beads: Scarcity.

BEAM:

A beam of wood: Will have a change of environment.

A very heavy beam of wood: Will have a burden to bear.

A light beam of wood: Will receive a well-merited reward.

A beam of steel: Will soon collect money.

BEANS:

Having beans: Difficulties ahead.

Beans growing: Worries ahead.

Buying beans: Will be criticized and slandered.

Eating beans: Will contract a contagious illness.

Cooking beans: Good business enterprises.

BEAR:

Of a bear: Will receive sad news.

A bear dancing: Will be tempted into speculations.

A bear in a cage: Success in the future.

Several bears: People are gossiping about you.

Being attacked by a bear: Will be persecuted.

Driving off a bear that is attacking: Will have big success.

A dead bear: You have many rich friends.

Killing a bear: Will have victory over enemies.

Drinking bear milk: Other people are envious of you.

Eating bear meat: Will have a long sickness.

Being transformed into a bear: Will receive sad news.

BEARD:
Having a beard: Financial distress.

A very short beard: Riches.

A man having a full beard: Unexpected success to come.

A very long beard: Will receive plenty of money.

A married woman dreaming of a man with a beard: Will soon leave husband.

A pregnant woman dreaming of a man with a beard: Will give birth to a son.

A girl dreaming of a man with a beard: Will soon marry the one she loves.

Pulling off own beard: Ruin and poverty.

Others pulling off a beard: Will have to pay creditors.

Cutting and shaving the beard: Loss of money.

Cutting the beard of someone you know: Security.

Someone else washing your beard: Grief.

Washing own beard: Anxiety.

Having a handsome beard: Complete success in own enterprises.

Having a curly beard: Will make the impression you desired.

Not having a beard: Big gain in business.

Making a beard smaller: Danger of losing wealth.

Losing hairs from the beard: Loss of a relative.

A black beard: Promising success in business.

A reddish beard: Provocation.

A white beard: Very big prosperity.

A brown beard: Misery.

A gray beard: Loss of money.

The beard turning gray: Will suffer from gossip and slander.

A very thin beard: Death of a member of the family.

A married woman dreaming of having a small beard: Divorce.

Unmarried woman dreaming of having a small beard: Gambling losses.

A pregnant woman dreaming of having a small beard: Abortion.

A widow woman dreaming of having a small beard: Loss of an estate.

A young girl dreaming of having a small beard: Matrimony.

BEAST:
Talking to animals: Hardship and misfortune.

Beasts making babbling noises: Will suffer grief.

Beasts fighting: Sickness.

Beasts scuffling: Cruel suffering.

Being pursued by beasts: Vexation caused by enemies.

Beasts starting a fight: Will be molested by friends.

Beasts running: Serious illness.

BEATEN:
Being beaten: Unhappiness in home relations.

Others being beaten: Loss of money.

A dog being beaten: Fidelity.

A cat being beaten: Treachery.

A horse being beaten: Happiness.

A snake being beaten: Triumph.

BEATING:
Beating a husband or a wife: Both will be very happy.

Married people dreaming of beating someone: Will live a peaceful life.

Bachelors dreaming of beating someone: Good fortune in love affairs.

Unmarried girls dreaming of beating men: Success in love.

A lover beating his mistress: The affair will be ended.

A woman beating her suitor: Big triumph in love.

A husband beating his wife: Happiness and a comfortable home.

A wife beating her husband: Long-lasting marriage.

A man beating a woman who is not his wife: Favorable business.

Parents beating their children: Unexpected good affairs.

Beating the children of strangers: Long illness.

A man beating a sweetheart: Future engagement.

A woman beating her sweetheart: Happiness in love.

Beating a friend: Contentment.

Being beaten by a friend: Unhappiness in love.

A bachelor slapping someone on the face: Will soon fall in love.

A married man slapping someone on the face: Marriage will last forever.

A married woman slapping a man on the face: She is faithful to husband.

Beating a pig or other animals: Damages in own affairs.

BEAUTIFUL:

Being beautiful: Illness.

Other people who are beautiful: They will be an invalid.

A man dreaming of a beautiful woman: Treason.

Of a beautiful girl: Joy and happiness.

A woman dreaming of a handsome man: Love will not last long.

A man being with his beautiful wife: Pleasing time in love.

A man being with a beautiful woman: Will have agreeable pastimes.

BED:

Resting comfortably in own bed: Will have security and love.

A bed made neatly: Will have a contented heart.

Having clean white sheets on a bed: Will have cause to worry.

Having clean colored sheets on a bed: Arrival of unexpected guests.

Making a bed: Change of residence to come.

An empty bed: Death of a friend.

Sitting on own bed: Will have an early marriage.

Being in a strange bed: Good turn of events in own affairs.

Remaining in bed for a long time: Misfortune is nearby.

Being in bed but unable to sleep: Will soon become ill.

A bed being in disorder: Secrets will be discovered.

Being sick in bed: Complications will develop or death.

A stranger being in your bed: Matrimonial unfaithfulness.

Being in bed in a hotel room: Friends will visit you unexpectedly.

A bed for camping: Will purchase real estate.

Burning a bed: Secrets will be divulged.

Old people going to bed: Death is near at hand.

Children going to bed: Will be unfortunate.

BEDBUGS:

Of bedbugs: Will be annoyed in relationship.

Many bedbugs: Death of a relative.

Being bitten by bedbugs: Will have wealth and abundance of property.

Crushing bedbugs and blood appearing: Serious illness.

Crushing bedbugs and water appearing: Will have an accident, not fatal.

Many bedbugs on a mattress: Will be provoked by a friend.

BED CLOTHES:

Many bed clothes: Will receive a big inheritance.

Purchasing bed clothes: Peril is ahead.

Wealthy people having many bed clothes: Loss of money.

Wealthy people dreaming of bed clothes: Improvement in life.

Poor people dreaming of bed clothes: Financial condition will be good.

BEDROOM:
Of own bedroom: Changes in own affairs.
Someone's luxurious bedroom: Delays in present affairs.
A bedroom in an apartment: Concealment of family secrets.
Sleeping in a hotel bedroom: Stupid gossip will be passed around.
Sleeping in the bedroom of a friend: Will become drunk.

BEEF:
Eating beef: Will be comfortably well off.
Eating roast beef: Will have a pleasant life.
Dropping beef in boiling water: Will derive pleasure out of life.
Eating boiled beef: Will be in deep melancholy.
Having more beef than able to eat: Will never be rich.
Purchasing beef to cook: Winnings at gambling.
Eating raw beef: Death is near at hand.
Eating beef stew: Long-lasting happiness.
Throwing away beef: Imminent danger.
A beef being killed in a fire: Infirmity.
Displaying a beef at a show: Actions will be rewarded.
Beef fighting: Happiness within the family.
Beef running: A secret will be divulged.
A herd of beef drinking water: Loss of something.
One beef drinking: Good fortune.

BEEHIVE:
Of a beehive: A great honor will come to you.
A beehive being full of bees: Abundance and wealth.
A beehive being empty: Poverty.
A beehive overturned: Will have plenty of money.

BEER:
Drinking beer: Monetary loss in speculations.
Being at an establishment selling beer: Loss of a loved one.
Being at a beer-drinking party: Be careful of betting.
Others drinking beer but not yourself: Will have a little money.
People making beer: Will have a life free of troubles.
Bottles of beer: Small business loss.
Friends becoming drunk from beer: Will receive a letter with bad news.

BEES:
Many bees: Happiness in life.
Being stung by bees: Beware of being double-crossed by friends.
Not being stung by bees: Success in love.
Rich people dreaming of bees: Will have upsets in business.
Poor people dreaming of bees: Will have good earnings.
Moving bees in swarms: Will have a fire in own house.
Moving bees in the morning: Good success in affairs.
Moving bees at noon: Good earnings.
Moving bees in the evening: Will make a well-known profit.
Moving bees with the honey: Will have plenty of money.
Bees making honey in own house or shed: Will overcome enemies.
Bees making honey on top of own house: Will be unlucky.
Bees coming into your house: Will be damaged by enemies.
Bees making honey in a tree: Big financial gains.
Bees flying around their beehive: Will have productive business.
Killing bees: Will have a big loss and ruin.
Making honey on own property: Complete success in business.

BEETLES:
Of beetles: Will make money.
Many beetles: Will have quarrels with friends.

Killing beetles: Will set matters right quickly.

BEETS:
Beets growing in a field: Prosperity in own affairs.
Many beets piled up: Good dealing in big business.
Eating beets: Love affairs will go well.
Buying beets: Will receive an expensive gift.

BEGGAR:
Of one beggar: Will receive unexpected help.
Many beggars: Will have fortune and happiness.
An aged beggar: Exercise economy.
A crippled beggar: Disputes within the family.
Giving money to a beggar: Love will be reciprocated.
A beggar coming into the house: Troubles and worry will come.

BEGGING:
Of begging: Misfortune within the family.
Others begging from you: Will be very fortunate.
Enemies begging: Will escape a present danger.
Friends begging: Will receive a legacy.

BEHEAD:
Being beheaded: Complete accomplishment of business dealings.
Being beheaded at a guillotine: Will have a very easygoing life.
Being beheaded by murderers: Loss of real estate.
Businessmen dreaming of being beheaded: Happiness.
Murderers being beheaded: Will be wounded and die.
Enemies being beheaded: Will realize present desires.

BELFRY:
A very high belfry: Will live a very long life.
The belfry of a church: Unexpected disgrace will come to you.

The belfry of a fortress: Will resist efforts of enemies.
The belfry of a building: Will be free from embarrassment.
The belfry of a cathedral: Big fortune.
Bells ringing from a belfry: Will receive financial credit.
A belfry partially demolished: Loss of employment.

BELL:
Hearing one bell ringing: Dissension within the family.
Hearing many bells ringing: Will receive good news.
Hearing church bells ringing: Be on guard against enemies.
A church bell without the knocker: You are impotent.
Hearing a doorbell ringing: Quarrels and seduction.

BELLE OF THE BALL:
Of the belle of the ball: Troubles in love affairs.
Being the belle of the ball: Will encounter much opposition.
Dancing with the belle of the ball: Avoid rivals.
Neglecting the belle of the ball: Happiness.

BELLOWS:
Of one bellow: Absent friends are desirous of seeing you.
Many bellows: Will receive a false report.
Using bellows on a fire: Will be confronted with difficulties.
Lending bellows: Good results in love.

BELLY:
Of own belly: Health and joy.
Having pains in the belly: Will have business disturbances.
A swollen belly: Serious illness.
A very large belly: Enlargement of own fortune.
A big belly and not being pregnant: Beware of untrue friends.
A small belly: Free yourself of bad affairs.
Unmarried woman dreaming of a big belly: Will soon be married.

Something moving in a belly: Hard labor ahead of you.

BELLY BUTTON:
Of own belly button: Will receive bad news from parents.
Belly button hurting: Birth of a child.
Children playing with belly button: Big wealth ahead.
The belly button of relatives: Will be assisted by influential person.

BELT:
Of many belts: Will soon have a love affair.
Putting on a belt: Happy future.
Others putting on a belt: Will go to court.
A broken belt: Will receive some damage.
An old belt: Will have to work harder.
A new belt: Honor.
A blue belt: Happiness.
A black belt: Death.
A brown belt: Illness.
A green belt: Good wishes.
A gold belt: Big earnings.
A silver belt: Profit.
A yellow belt: Treason.

BENCH:
Of a bench: Attend to work carefully or may lose your job.
Sitting on a bench: Will have a comfortable life.
Children sitting on a park bench: Good times are coming.
Others sitting on a bench: Death of an enemy.

BENEFITS:
Conferring benefits on others: Happiness.
Receiving benefits from others: Will have a trust estate.
Receiving benefits from family: Big joy.
Friends being beneficial: A mystery will be solved.

BEQUEST:
Bequeathing money to someone: Will be unhappy for only a day.
A bequest being made in own favor:

Will inherit money very soon.
Canceling a bequest: Fights within the family.
Writing a bequest for another person: Profit and joy.
Bequeathing all fortune to strangers: Will live a short life.
Bequeathing nothing to relatives: Imminent death.

BEREAVEMENT:
Being bereaved: News of marriage of friend soon to take place.
Suffering bereavement: Someone else will benefit by your actions.
Others suffering bereavement: A loyal friend is nearby.

BERET:
Owning a beret: Someone will pull a dirty deal that will not go through.
Having a cotton beret: Friendship is being abused by a friend.
Having a silk beret: Good results in life.
Having a traveling beret: Will be cheated by friends.
Children's berets: Riches.
Wearing a nightcap: Abundance in business.

BERRIES:
Of berries: Will enjoy social activities of a happy nature.
Picking berries: Financial gains.
Eating berries: Abundant means.
Buying berries: Important and very beneficial events to come.

BEST MAN:
Of a best man: Big joy.
Being a best man: Plans will fail because of a false friend.
A woman dreaming of a best man: Confidence and security.
Other people having a best man: Will be deceived.

BET:
Of making bets: Do not trust own opinions too much.
Others making bets: Don't allow opinions of others to interfere with you.

Winning a bet: Will have a change for the better.

Losing a bet: An enemy is seeking your ruin.

BETROTHED:

Being betrothed but not engaged: Will have troubles with lover.

Becoming engaged: Expect troubles within the family.

Relatives becoming betrothed: Family arguments.

Friends becoming betrothed: Will realize high ambitions.

BIBLE:

Reading the Bible: Family troubles to come soon.

Taking a Bible to church: Happiness.

Believing in the Bible: With perseverance will overcome enemies.

Children reading the Bible: Joy without profit.

BICYCLE:

Owning a bicycle: Happiness.

Riding a bicycle: Will have to make an important decision.

Selling a bicycle: Good wishes.

Buying a bicycle for children: Advancement in own affairs.

BIER:

Of a coffin and its litter: Death of a friend is near.

Lying in a bier: Triumphant end to hopes.

Relatives lying in a bier: Will receive a legacy.

A friend lying in a bier: Advancement in own position.

BIG:

Being a very big person: Riches and honors.

Being extra big and tall: Will be loved by the opposite sex.

Having a high rank in society: Persecution.

Being a big talker around women: Honor and dignity.

Being visited by big people: Abundance.

BIGAMY:

Committing bigamy: Assurance of a happy life.

Being a bigamist: Prosperous married life.

A bigamist being punished: Will have a vigorous mind.

Not being a bigamist: Approaching money.

Not believing in bigamy: Will enjoy much happiness with mate.

BILLIARDS:

Playing billiards: Dissipation of money.

Playing billiards regularly every day: Big difficulty ahead.

Engaged people playing billiards: Will have opposition from in-laws to-be.

Married people playing billiards: Love of mate is sincere.

Single people playing billiards: Will soon be married.

BILLS:

Paying bills: Immediate financial gains.

Not paying bills: Danger in business.

Having overdue bills: Others are speaking evil of you.

Being solicited to pay bills: Are disliked by your boss.

BINDING:

Binding books: Will find something that was hidden away.

Binding heavy things together: Will have trouble with justice department.

Binding wood together: Will receive sad news.

Portion of body being bound with tape: Unhappiness.

BINOCULARS:

Owning binoculars: Will have happiness in the future.

Men looking through binoculars: Happiness.

Women looking through binoculars: Will be greatly compensated in life.

Military people using binoculars: Will be damaged in personal affairs.

Viewing a loved one through binoculars: Loss of a distant relative.

Being watched through binoculars: Think carefully before acting.

Buying binoculars: A woman of poor morals is nearby.

BIRDS:

Of birds: Avoid rivals.

Birds sleeping: Will receive false news.

Birds in their nest: Family happiness.

Birds flying: Prosperity.

Birds fighting: Will make a change in employment.

Many birds: Big family reunion and gain of a suit.

Night birds: Lasting joy.

Wild birds: Will be oppressed by people.

Sea birds: Disappointment in business.

Birds that can be eaten: Will form a corporation.

Putting birds in a cage: Poor harvest.

Hearing birds singing: Great joy is in store for you.

Seeing birds singing: Will receive a valuable gift.

Catching birds: Immediate marriage for unmarried people.

A woman seeing birds with brilliant plumage: Will have an honest husband.

Unmarried woman dreaming of birds: Will marry a wealthy man.

A single girl dreaming of beautiful birds: Will soon be engaged.

Wealthy people dreaming of birds: Reverse of luck in business.

Poor people dreaming of birds: Improvement of own circumstances.

BIRD'S EGGS:

Bird's eggs in a nest: Will receive money.

Baby birds coming out of the eggs: Will receive good news.

People destroying bird's eggs: Business loss.

Animals eating bird's eggs: Will soon have a change in surroundings.

BIRD'S NEST:

Of only one bird in a nest: Will receive a package with a gift.

Several birds' nests: Happiness within the family.

Finding several birds in a nest: Big profit.

An empty bird's nest: Termination of affairs.

Destroying birds' nests: Poverty is near.

BIRTH:

A married woman giving birth to a child: Joy will be hers.

Single woman giving birth to a child: Will be abandoned by her lover.

Divorced woman giving birth to a child: Will inherit a large legacy.

Widow giving birth to a child: Will be guilty of foolish actions.

Assisting with the birth of a child: Joy and prosperity.

Assisting with the birth of twins or triplets: Very large success.

Assisting with the birth of a dead child: Failure of present projects.

Assisting with a Caesarean birth: Will have a dangerous illness.

Birth endangering life of pregnant woman: Will hear news of a marriage soon.

Pregnant woman dreaming of having a boy: Complete success in enterprises.

Pregnant woman dreaming of having a girl: Social pleasures followed by pain.

Man dreaming of wife having twins: Wealth and riches to come soon.

A father receiving news of a birth while away: Good wishes.

The birth of an eagle: Will have a very prosperous future.

The birth of a cat or other animals: Death of an enemy.

Of a birth occurring: Prosperity and abundance.

Giving birth to a child: Good fortune.

Only one baby being born: Will be treated with force.

Twins being born: Will have good luck in affairs.

The birth of close relatives: Abundant means.

Birth of fish: Will soon rain.

BIRTHDAY:

Of own birthday: Good results in financial matters.

Relative's birthday: Good business affairs.

Friend's birthday: Will benefit shortly.

Sweetheart's birthday: Abundance of money soon coming.

Wife's birthday: Good times are coming.

Husband's birthday: Abundant means.

Children's birthday: Approaching money.

BISCUITS:

Making biscuits: Will have a prosperous journey.

Buying biscuits: Will always have a good appetite.

Giving biscuits away: Are prone to enjoying pleasures too much.

Eating sea biscuits: Good health.

Giving sea biscuits to sailors: Prosperous married life.

BISHOP:

Of a bishop: Will have troubles with Justice officials.

Talking to a bishop: Business will be satisfactory.

Several clergymen being with a bishop: Ill health to come.

The dressing of a bishop: A false friend is nearby.

BITE:

Of a bite: Are about to sustain a loss.

Biting someone else: Will be embarrassed.

Biting the tongue: Loss of consideration from other people.

Being bitten by a woman: A jealous person is nearby.

Being bitten by a man: Beware of quarrels.

Being bitten by an animal: Will have troubles over love affairs.

Being bitten several times: Are being slandered by other people.

BITTER:

Tasting something bitter: Will have a rash all over the body.

Taking bitter medicine: Will quarrel with help.

Children eating bitter things: Family quarrels.

Feeling bitter: Will be attacked by thieves.

Other people feeling bitter toward you: Will quarrel with other people.

BLACK:

The color black: Will have a very unfortunate time.

A black dress: Sadness.

Black colors at a funeral: Good news will arrive soon.

Purchasing black clothes: Are being deceived.

BLACKBERRIES:

Of blackberries: Will have many trials to endure.

Gathering blackberries: Will be unlucky.

Eating blackberries: Will suffer losses.

Buying blackberries: Will be wounded in an accident.

Blackberries hanging on bushes: Big abundance.

A married woman picking blackberries: Will soon be pregnant.

Making blackberry jelly: Avoid rivals.

Receiving a gift of blackberry jelly: Are being cheated by friends.

Giving a gift of blackberry jelly: Family quarrels.

BLACKBIRD:

Of a blackbird: Will be unfortunate.

A woman dreaming of hearing blackbirds singing: Will have two husbands.

A man dreaming of hearing blackbirds singing: Will have two wives.

Unmarried person hearing blackbirds singing: Will soon be engaged.

BLACKSMITH:
Of a blacksmith: Agony and misfortune.
Being a blacksmith: Will soon lose faith in yourself.
Talking to a blacksmith: People do not have faith in you.
A blacksmith shoeing a horse: Will have obstacles ahead.
A blacksmith's fire: Riches.

BLADDER:
Of a bladder: Joy is forthcoming soon.
Having a bladder disease: Will receive a small inheritance.
Having a bladder operation: Will fall into disgrace in the near future.
Others having a bladder operation: Will have a secret sorrow.
Mate having a bladder removed: Will contract pneumonia.

BLAME:
Being blamed for something: Be humble toward superiors.
Blaming others: Joy.
Being blamed by other people: Sickness.
Blaming husband or wife for something: Joy following an argument.
Blaming children for something: Will receive gift from a foreign country.
Blaming friends for something: Will be cruelly deceived.

BLANKET:
Wealthy person dreaming of buying new blankets: Expect loss of money.
Average income people buying new blankets: Improvement of conditions.
Poor people dreaming of buying new blankets: Success.
Having old blankets: Good news is on the way.

BLASPHEMY:
Using the name of God to curse: Will have bad luck.
Being cursed by others using the name of God: Ambitions will be realized.
Other people taking the name of God in vain: Difficulties are surmounted.

Friends using blasphemy toward you: Failure of enemies.

BLEAT:
Hearing the bleating of one lamb: Prosperity in business.
Hearing several lambs bleating: Happiness within the home.
Seeing lambs bleating: Abundant means.
Hearing a large number of lambs bleating: Prompt engagement.

BLEEDING:
Own nose bleeding: Will he beld in contempt by others.
Others' nose bleeding: Will encounter opposition.
Bleeding a little from own body: Achievement of own desires.
Bleeding heavily from own body: Will fall into a trap.
Blood flowing onto the floor: Good success.

BLESSING:
Receiving a blessing: Will be forced into a marriage.
Children receiving a blessing: Happiness.
Family receiving blessings: Joy without profit.
Receiving a blessing from a priest: Will be very fortunate.
Several others receiving blessings: Will have a happy family.

BLIND:
Being blind: Will be double-crossed by someone nearby.
Becoming blind: Poverty.
Someone being born blind: Will commit a serious error.
A young person going blind: False friends are nearby.
A baby being born blind: Jealousy and sorrow.
Leading a blind person: Strange adventures to come.
A woman becoming blind: Some person will appeal to you for help.
A man becoming blind: Be cautious in business ventures.

Many people losing their sight: Triumph over enemies.

Friends losing their sight: Trouble and desolation.

Relatives losing their sight: Family quarrels.

Losing own eyesight: Unfortunate love affairs.

BLINDFOLDED:

A woman being blindfolded: Will bring disappointment to others.

A man being blindfolded: Will be a widower.

Being among blindfolded people: Persecution by a friend.

Other people being blindfolded: Will have a troubled conscience.

BLOAT:

Being bloated: Will receive bad news.

Relatives being bloated: Richness.

Friends being bloated: Honor.

Others who are bloated: Death of an enemy.

BLOOD:

Having blood on yourself: Unfortunate love affairs.

Having blood on hands: Will have very bad luck.

Blood flowing from a wound: Sickness and worry are hovering nearby.

Blood on cotton pads: Be careful in the choice of friends.

Garments stained with blood: Successful career is hampered by enemies.

Blood on other people: Severe disappointment.

(See also **TRANSFUSION.**)

BLOSSOM:

All sorts of trees blossoming: Joy and comfort.

Own flowers blossoming: Danger through a secret.

Neighbor's flowers blossoming: Triumph over enemies.

Blossoming trees and flowers growing: Will enjoy much recreation.

BLOT:

Making a blot on clean white paper: Will sleep in a strange bed.

Making a blot on colored paper: Will travel in near future.

Blotting an important document: Change for the better.

Blotting the writing on a check: Happiness is assured.

BLOW:

Wind blowing: Will have a litigation.

Blowing out a fire: Gossip is being spread about you.

Blowing in someone's face: Will be tricked by a woman who is cheating.

Blowing on hands to warm them: Will receive several gifts.

Blowing dust or other things: Will receive a letter with good news.

BLOWS:

Receiving blows: Reconciliation following a quarrel.

Giving blows to others: Good fortune coming from a friend.

Friends giving blows to each other: Warning of troubles.

Enemies receiving blows: Change of surroundings.

Children giving blows to each other: Advancement in own position.

BLUE:

Buying clothes of blue color: Will have a vigorous mind.

The color of the blue sky: Big love for children.

Navy blue color: Prosperity through other people.

Azure blue color: Promotion in own employment.

Any other shade of blue: Comfortable happy married life.

BLUNDER:

Of a blunder: Will do unexpectedly well in new undertaking.

Blundering about clumsily: Success in all affairs.

Other people blundering: Accord among friends.

Relatives blundering: Good times are coming.

BLUSH:
Blushing with shame: Will be obligated to offer explanations.
Blushing with pleasure: Will have to take a laxative.
Blushing when caught in wrongdoing: Will be loved by an old woman.
Children blushing: Will breakup with best friends.
Sweethearts blushing: They will get married before date set.

BOAR:
Chasing a wild boar: Unsuccessful efforts.
Being chased by a boar: Separation from lover.
Killing a boar: Advancement in position.
A boar being in a zoo: A secret will soon be discovered.

BOARDER:
Being a boarder: Death of an enemy.
Having a boarder: Betrayal.
Others who are boarders: Approaching troubles.
Being a boarder at a friend's home: Misfortune in love affairs.

BOARDS:
Sawing boards: Death in the family.
Planing boards: Will have to put a stubborn person in their place.
Buying boards: Good news.
Selling boards: Will make errors.
Assembling several boards: Good friendships.

BOAT:
Being aboard a boat: Will attain aim in life.
Sailing a boat in smooth water: Fortune in business.
Sailing a boat in rough water: Will have to face many difficulties.
Falling from a boat: Troubles will prove to be too much to handle.
A boat sinking: Termination of present love affairs.
A boat in a clear stream: Happiness.
A boat in a muddy stream: Disgrace.
A boat on a river: Security in own affairs.
A boat moving very slowly: Must have patience in life.

BODY:
Of own body: Happiness.
The body of a woman: People are flirting with this woman.
The body of a man: Good business ventures.
The body of children: Will undertake a journey.
The body of a deformed person: Will have good fortune ahead.

BOGEY:
Of a frightening apparition: Exceedingly happy marriage.
Making a good golf score: Look for important news.
Others making better scores than you: Misfortune in love affairs.

BOIL:
Boiling water: Must moderate passions.
Boiling food: Will have much happiness.
Boiling coffee: Will have emotional sorrow.
Boiling soups: Financial gains.

BOILER:
Of a boiler: Own hopes are useless.
A steam boiler: Be careful in business ventures.
Owning a boiler: Will make new acquaintances.
Being a boilermaker: Unhappiness at home.
Operating a boiler: Don't listen to flattery.

BOLTS:
Fastening bolts on own door: Will be offended.
A fastened bolt being broken: Are prone to greed and selfishness.
Being bolted in room by others: Troubles ahead.
Attempting to open the bolt: Will make a new start elsewhere.

BOMB:
Of a bomb: Will receive dreadful news.
Hearing the sound of a bomb: Happiness within the family.
Having been injured by a bomb: Serious disaster ahead.

BOMBARDMENT:
Of a bombardment: Will have misfortune.
Having been bombarded: Will have an unhappy marriage.
Others being bombarded: Deception in love matters.

BONES:
Bones taken from meat: Poverty.
Skeleton bones of a man: Property coming to you from a will.
Skeleton bones of a woman: Death of children.
Bones of wild animals: Will have bad business transactions.
A few bones of dead people: Will have many troubles.
Bones of fish: Illness is near at hand.
The bones of a whale: Are prone to being conceited.
Animals gnawing on bones: Will fall into complete ruin.

BONNET:
A black bonnet: You have false friends of the opposite sex.
A young woman dreaming of a new bonnet: She is prone to flirting.
A man dreaming of a woman trying on a new bonnet: Good luck.
Losing a new bonnet: Loss of freedom.

BOOK:
Books in a library: Will have an unexpected experience.
Books at home: Happiness.
Reading a book: Will lose good friends.
Reading mystery books: Will receive consolation from friends.
Reading science books: Big joy.
Reading stories and detective books: Will lead a quiet life.
Reading religious books: Contentment.
Reading schoolbooks: Prosperity.

Binding books: Will find something that was hidden away.
Writing books: Will waste time and money.

BOOKCASE:
An empty bookcase: Expect good fortune through own endeavors.
A full bookcase: Will suffer because of negligent and careless work.
A half-empty bookcase: You have a bad personality.
Buying a bookcase: Loss of employment.
Selling a bookcase: Financial troubles in business.

BOOKKEEPER:
A bookkeeper working on other people's books: Wealth.
A bookkeeper working on own books: Expect good fortune.
Being a bookkeeper: Will lead an easy life.
Hiring a bookkeeper: Good times are coming.

BOOTS:
Wearing boots: Will have small amount of good business.
Buying new boots: Business will be very good.
Having new boots: Can rely on the faithfulness of servants.
Old boots: Will meet with difficulties.
Having brown boots: Will have good luck.
Old boots hurting the feet: Loss of money due to own carelessness.
Other people with new boots: Danger in love matters.

BORROW:
Borrowing money: Domestic sorrow.
Repaying borrowed money: Will sail in smooth waters.
Others repaying borrowed money: Good business in the near future.
Others borrowing money from you: Death of a friend.

BOSOM:
Bosom being enlarged: Illness to come.
Bosom being inflamed: Will have a tooth pulled.

Bosom being painful: You are pregnant.

Bosom is becoming larger: Will be happy in old age.

Having a beautiful and healthy bosom: Big joy ahead.

A woman having hair on her bosom: Her husband will pass away.

BOTTLE:

A full bottle: Prosperity.

An empty bottle: Misfortune.

Spilling the contents of a bottle: Expect domestic worries.

A bottle of wine: Will be in a bad humor.

An empty flask: Will be disappointed in love.

A bottle full of liquor: Will be divorced.

An empty bottle of liquor: Own affairs will be good.

A full bottle of perfume: Will enjoy much happiness.

An empty bottle of perfume: Love affairs are on the rocks.

BOUDOIR:

Being in a boudoir: Hard work ahead.

Being in the boudoir of a beautiful lady: Separation from mate.

Being in the boudoir of an ugly woman: Will have disputes.

Making love in a boudoir: Will soon be arrested.

Preparing a boudoir: Good results in love affairs.

A boudoir being filled with rare items: Unhappiness.

BOUND:

Being bound with ropes: Will be confronted with obstacles.

Others being bound with ropes: Troubles will overtake you.

Being bound with ropes by other people: Will fall into a trap.

Binding other people with ropes: Embarrassment and loss of money.

BOUQUET:

A beautiful bouquet: A legacy is ahead in the future.

A withered bouquet: Illness and ensuing death.

Receiving a bouquet: Much pleasure in life.

Giving a bouquet: Lover is constant.

Keeping a bouquet of flowers: Will receive a marriage proposal.

Throwing away a bouquet: Separation from a friend.

Preparing a bouquet of flowers: Will be married soon.

Receiving several bouquets: Will have a faithful love.

Receiving a small bouquet: Joy that will not last a long time.

BOW AND ARROWS:

Hitting the target with an arrow: Can rely upon good fortune.

Missing the target with an arrow: Expect difficulties.

Hitting a bull's eye with an arrow: Inheritance.

Losing the arrow: Difficulties because of carelessness.

Being hit by an arrow: Beware of enemies.

Having many arrows: Money losses.

BOWER:

Of a bower: Will have many children.

Being under a bower alone: Will receive a marriage proposal.

Being under a bower with others: Will be visited by lover.

Picking grapes from a bower: Will have a happily married life.

BOWLING:

Bowling and knocking down all the pins: Will realize high ambitions.

Bowling and knocking down most of pins: Fortune in everything.

Bowling and not hitting any pins: Defeat in business dealings.

Other people bowling: Unhappiness.

Other people winning a bowling game: Will be robbed.

BOX:

Having a box: Will go out of business.

Tying a box: Financial losses.

Opening a box: Will take a long journey.

Opening a full box: Will receive a marriage proposal.

Opening an empty box: Plans will be upset.

A church charity box: Will have misery.

A strongbox: Will be cheated.

Robbing a strongbox: Will lose entire fortune.

BOXING MATCH:

Watching a boxing match: Will receive an astonishing announcement.

Taking part in a boxing match: Loss of friends.

Winning a bet on a boxing match: Accord among friends.

Losing a bet on a boxing match: You have one loyal friend.

BOY:

Of boys: Increase in the family.

Boys fighting: Will make a good resolution.

Boys jumping: Will collect money.

Boys boxing: Something bad will occur very soon.

Having a boy: A woman will soon become pregnant.

A boy being sick: Obstacles are ahead.

Rescuing a boy from danger: Will rise to eminence.

A boy being killed: Misery caused by parents.

A crippled boy: Troubles are ahead.

Adopting a boy: Other children will dislike the adopted son.

A young boy: Will soon be married.

Several young boys: Will receive good news.

A young boy dating a young girl: Must keep house in better order.

A young boy working in a store: Will enjoy good business.

A young boy securing work at a store: Unhappiness.

BRACELET:

Of a gold bracelet: Will have joy.

Receiving a bracelet as a gift from a friend: Early and happy marriage.

A young woman dreaming of losing a bracelet: Worry and vexation.

Finding a bracelet: Acquisition of property.

Wearing a gold bracelet: Will be lucky in unexpected financial affairs.

Dropping a bracelet: Broken love affair.

BRAIN:

Of brains: Will have an accident.

Having a sane brain: Great knowledge will bring good results in affairs.

Having a sick brain: Loss of money.

Having a brain tumor: You do not have a good reputation.

Relatives having a poor brain: Dangers ahead in the future.

Other people having a sane brain: Will be a very intelligent person.

Having a brain operation: Are a very passionate person.

Young people dreaming of eating brains: Will fall in love.

Elderly people dreaming of eating brains: Good health.

Performing a brain operation: Everything will go well in the future.

Friends having a brain operation: Will find a valuable hidden object.

Enemies having a brain operation: Will enjoy good earnings.

BRAMBLES:

Of brambles: Poverty and privation.

Pushing through brambles without being scratched by thorns: Happiness.

Others pushing through brambles: Disappointment in love.

Cutting down brambles: Shame and sorrow.

BRANCHES:

Cutting branches from trees: Will have a small disagreement.

Being hurt by a branch: Will have an accident.

Gathering branches together: Will have an operation.

Burning branches: Will receive a legacy.

Cutting branches from palm trees: Big honors.

Cutting branches from an olive tree: Peace and serenity.

A tree with many fertile branches: Will receive an unexpected legacy.

A tree with broken branches: Misfortune.

A tree with dead branches: A friend is trying to help you secretly.

A tree with withered branches: Recovery from an illness.

BRANDY:

Drinking brandy: Pleasant love affairs.

Owning a bottle of brandy: Beware of untrue friends.

Buying a bottle of brandy: Will receive unexpected good news.

Offering a drink of brandy to others: Must control passions.

BRASS:

Of brass: Watch associates very carefully.

Having something made of brass: A friend will cause unhappiness.

Buying brass: Advancement in position.

Selling brass: Are being deceived.

Being a brass worker: Will have many troubles.

BRASSIERE:

Of own brassiere: Another person is enjoying what you desired.

The brassiere of your wife: Avoid rivals.

The brassiere of a sweetheart: Temptation will come.

The brassiere of others: Will be jilted by lover.

Buying a brassiere: Will have a vigorous mind.

Losing a brassiere: Will find someone new for whom you will care.

BRAVERY:

Acting with bravery: Will have a nervous illness.

Being without bravery: Are apt to underestimate yourself.

Showing courage and bravery: A friend holds a secret enmity against you.

Others acting with bravery: Troubles ahead.

BRAY:

Hearing a donkey bray: Expect to hear of the loss of a friend.

Hearing many donkeys braying: Will be visited by several friends.

Hearing horses braying: Will entertain an unwelcome guest.

Hearing many horses braying: A mystery will be solved.

BREAD:

Of bread crumbs: Will receive a gift.

Baking bread: Will meet with success.

Eating bread: Will be helped by friends.

A hot loaf of bread: Wealth and honor will be yours.

Stale bread: Domestic trouble.

A very hard loaf of bread: Physical well-being and comfort.

Having several loaves of bread: Honor.

Buying bread: Big success.

Eating white bread: Will make a big profit.

Eating dark bread: Contentment.

Eating black bread: Business losses.

Carrying several loaves of bread: Will have some financial damages.

BREAK:

Breaking the glass of a window: Will receive sad news.

Breaking furniture: Quarrels within the home.

Breaking a drinking glass: Will have a broken leg.

Breaking eyeglasses: Unexpected fortune.

Breaking dishes: Failure in own affairs.

Breaking bottles: Will have bad health.

Breaking wooden objects: Will receive news of death of a relative.

Breaking a bone in the body: Will receive a legacy.

Breaking bones of meat: Will have all kinds of losses.

Breaking wooden poles: Will have big work ahead.

BREAKFAST:
Preparing breakfast: Misery and illness.
Eating breakfast alone: Will commit some folly.
Eating breakfast with others: Will soon receive money.
Having breakfast in a coffee shop: Will have a new sweetheart.
Having breakfast in the home of others: Will take a trip before long.

BREAST:
Having a beautiful breast: Big joy ahead.
Resting on someone's breast: True and loyal friendship.
The breast of a woman: Wishes will be gratified.
The breast of a man: Will soon be married.
A breast covered with hair: Success in love.
A woman having hair on her breast: Her husband will soon pass away.
A baby sucking at the breast: Will enjoy lasting happiness.
Young people having breast wounded: Will have splendid future.
Old people having breast wounded: Will have misfortune.
Breast being wounded with a sword during a duel: Bad news.
Breast being wounded with a knife in a fight: Good friendship.
Breast being wounded by a gun: Will make plenty of money.

BREATH:
Of breath: A beloved friend wishes to see you.
Being out of breath: Troubles to come.
Having bad breath: Will be abandoned.
Other people having bad breath: Avoid rivals.
Children having bad breath: Death of a friend.

BREEZE:
Being out in a strong breeze: Successful speculation.
Enjoying a light breeze: Everlasting happiness.
Enjoying a pleasant breeze at night: Will receive a gift from a stranger.

BRIBE:
Of bribing: Will be guilty of foolish actions.
Accepting a bribe of money: Upright and honorable conduct.
Refusing a bribe of money: Will be repaid money unexpectedly.
Bribing an official person: Big sorrow.

BRIDE:
A young woman being a bride: Will soon have a large legacy.
Kissing a bride: Will have many friends and much joy.
Being kissed by a bride: Will have good health.
A bride being pleased with her gown: Will have many children.
A bride being displeased with her gown: Disappointment in love.

BRIDEGROOM:
A bridegroom having a rich bride: Loss of the father.
A bridegroom having a beautiful bride: Loss of the mother.
A bridegroom having a young bride: Sickness within the family.
A bridegroom having an elderly bride: Abundant means.

BRIDESMAID:
Being a bridesmaid: Great disappointment.
Several bridesmaids: Happiness and long life.
Not being a bridesmaid: Danger through a secret.
Girl friends being bridesmaids: Unhappiness in love affairs.

BRIDGE:
Crossing a bridge: Will have a change of business occupation.
A man crossing a bridge: Will have a change of home.

A woman crossing a bridge: Will have social activities of a happy nature.

A single person crossing a bridge: Will soon be married.

A bridge that opens in the center: Will pardon enemies.

A red bridge: Danger ahead.

A bridge burning: Will lose some friends.

A bridge falling while walking on it: Financial losses.

Falling from a bridge: Affairs will be bad.

A bridge being built: Will make good business.

Crossing a bridge under repairs: Will have many troubles.

Crossing a damaged bridge: Be careful in making new plans.

Driving over a bridge: Abandon present plans.

Others crossing a bridge: Will have delays in own business.

BRIDLE:

Of a bridle: Will handle affairs well.

Putting a bridle on a horse: Will soon have some money.

Holding reins of a bridle in the hands: Happiness.

A bridle on another person's horse: Advancement in own position.

BRIEFCASE:

Having a briefcase: Will have riches for a short time.

A briefcase full of papers: Will neglect some of own business.

A briefcase without any papers: Good results in enterprises.

Losing a briefcase: Will make good business.

Finding a briefcase: Failure in all affairs.

BRIERS:

Being pricked by briers: Will be injured by secret enemies.

A brier prick drawing blood: Expect heavy losses.

Passing through briers without harm: Triumph over enemies.

Children being pricked by briers: Will live a long life.

BRISTLES:

Of bristles: Social success.

Having bristles: Security in own business.

Others having bristles: Are confronted by insurmountable obstacles.

BROKER:

Of a broker: Will meet untruthful people in the near future.

Being a broker: Earnings will remain the same for a short while.

Dealing with brokers on a purchase: Pleasures ahead.

Dealing with brokers for sale of property: Loss of money.

Having dealings with several brokers: Be cautious in business affairs.

BRONCHITIS:

Having bronchitis: An enemy is seeking your ruin.

Recovering from bronchitis: Great prosperity in the future.

Others having bronchitis: Will have obstacles in business.

Relatives having bronchitis: Will live a long life.

BROOCH:

Of a brooch: Financial gains.

Wearing a brooch in own house: Inheritance.

Wearing a brooch in others' houses: Expect troubles.

Buying a brooch: Will be deceived.

Selling a brooch: Loss of a great deal of money.

BROOK:

Of a clear brook: Will have faithful friends.

A muddy brook: Loss of friends.

A brook being near own home: Will receive an honorable appointment.

A brook being nearly dry: Discovery of lost valuables.

BROOM:

Having a new broom: Will make plenty of money.

Having an old broom: Beware of false friends.

Throwing away an old broom: Good luck to one for whom you care.

Hitting something with a broom: Will have a change for the better.

BROTH:

Drinking broth: Affairs will prosper.

Boiling broth: Will be married soon.

Spilling broth on garments: Will receive a high honor.

Giving broth to a sick person: Abundance of money.

BROTHER:

A man dreaming of his brother: Expect quarrels.

A woman dreaming of her brother: Much domestic happiness.

Quarreling with a brother: Big fortune.

A brother dying: Destruction of enemies.

A brother getting married: Family quarrels.

BROTHER-IN-LAW:

Of a brother-in-law: Are being taken advantage of by relatives.

Marrying a brother-in-law: Will recover from an illness.

Flirting with a brother-in-law: Failure of enemies.

Having several brothers-in-law: Financial gains.

BROWN:

Of the color brown: Big friendship.

Brown material: Will be double-crossed by employees.

Brown hair: A change in life will soon come.

Buying brown clothes: Joy without profit.

BRUISES:

Being bruised: Will have emotional sorrow.

Other people having bruises on the body: Beware of enemies.

Other people having bruises on their face: Loss of money.

Relatives having bruises: Troubles ahead.

BRUSH:

Of a brush: Approaching trouble.

Using a brush: Fondest wish will be granted.

Having an old brush: Disappointments.

Buying a new brush: Good times are coming.

A shop selling brushes: Sickness.

A brushmaker: Will get drunk.

BUBBLES:

Of bubbles: Will escape a present peril.

Creating bubbles: Avoid wastefulness or may lose sweetheart.

Bubbles in a bathtub: Will find a protector.

Bubbles from boiling water: Dignity and distinction.

BUCKLE:

A woman having a buckle unfastened: Troubles and difficulties ahead.

A man unfastening a woman's buckle: Marriage will take place soon.

Having a fancy buckle: Will have a change for the better.

Buying a buckle: Avoid rivals.

A broken buckle: An enemy is seeking your destruction.

BUGLE:

Hearing a bugle call: Will have success in all efforts.

Playing a bugle: Will be unfortunate in love affairs.

Hearing children playing a bugle: Joy without profit.

Soldiers playing a bugle: Danger in love matters.

BUGS:

Of bugs: Success in business or worldly affairs.

Many bugs: Will have gold and silver given to you.

Killing bugs: Will have money.

Others killing bugs: Will go to prison.

Having bugs in the house: Will have a great deal of money.

Having bugs outside the house: Do not place blame on friends.

Having bugs in the bedding: Prosperity beyond fondest hopes.

BUILDING:
Big buildings: Will have changes in present life.
Small buildings: Present affairs will not prove successful.
Very tall buildings: Will have much success.
Several buildings: Will become very annoyed.

BULL:
Being chased by a bull: Will receive a present.
Not running away from a bull: Will have good luck.
A furious bull: Will have much success in love affairs.
Many bulls: Will receive high honors.
Finding a bull's liver: Will suffer a big business loss.

BULLDOG:
Owning a bulldog: Advancement in own position.
A bulldog being in the street: Will find a big protector.
Having a bulldog in the house: Good news from an absent friend.
Buying a bulldog: Happiness is assured.
Selling the puppies of a bulldog: An enemy is seeking your ruin.

BULL'S-EYE:
Hitting the bull's-eye: Watch for important news.
Missing the bull's-eye: Will have enemies or rivals in love affairs.
Others hitting the bull's-eye: Be careful in giving out confidences.
Friends hitting the bull's-eye: Will have a change of surroundings.

BUMP:
Of bumping: Will be tormented by jealousy.
Bumping into various things: Will be accused by untrustworthy friends.
Bumping into people: A well-matched matrimony will take place.

Bumping into a vehicle: Will make profits dishonestly.
Bumping into a door: Will loan money to someone.

BUNDLE:
Of a bundle: Will receive an invitation.
A bundle of hay: Will have hardships.
A bundle of tobacco leaves: Will receive false news.
A bundle of clothes: Will receive good news.
People carrying bundles: Will achieve desires with diligence.
Many people with bundles: Will receive a gift from a friend.

BUNION:
Suffering from a bunion: Return of a traveler.
Inflamation leaving a bunion: Will have a new admirer.
Relatives suffering from a bunion: Troubles ahead.
Friends suffering from a bunion: Are confronted with insurmountable obstacles.

BURDEN:
Carrying a burden: Will be dependent upon other people.
Other people carrying a burden: Expect a large inheritance.
Children carrying a burden: Advancement in own position.
Friends carrying a burden: Financial gains.

BURGLAR:
A burglar being in own house: Beware of treachery.
A burglar coming into the house at night: Approaching troubles.
Catching a burglar red-handed: Will gain good fortune.
Burglars having stolen valuable things: Good investments.

BURIAL:
Attending the burial of a friend: Are expecting an inheritance.
Attending the burial of a relative: Will be married soon.

52

Attending the burial of a relative when married: Divorce.

Attending the burial of mother or father: Good financial speculations.

BURIED ALIVE:
Being buried alive: Riches and power will come soon.

Others being buried alive: Will have wealth and influence.

Enemies being buried alive: Will triumph over enemies.

A traitor being buried alive: Will be cheated by friends.

BURN:
Having burns on own body: Will have valuable friendships during life.

Others who have burns on body: Prosperity in own affairs.

Being burned because of others: Approaching troubles.

Being burned while cooking: Will be jilted by a lover.

BURNING:
A house burning: Fortune will improve.

A building burning: Losses and worry.

Own house burning: Will be happy in love.

Own building burning: Happiness.

Friend's house burning: Triumph over enemies.

A burning house making a big fire: Inheritance.

A burning house making a small fire: Quarrels among relatives.

A big store burning: Loss of money.

Being burned inside a burning house: Ambitions are too high.

A bed burning: Prosperity.

Own bed burning but not being injured: Death of wife or husband.

BURST:
Of bursting: Will have amusement and joy.

Having burst something: Will receive an inheritance.

Friends bursting something: Good results in business.

Enemies bursting something: Give credit where credit is due.

BURYING:
Of burying: Will have good real estate holdings.

Burying a steel pan: Unhappiness.

Burying a pot of gold: Will have an accident.

Burying stolen property in a box: Will have a happy life.

Burying money: Dissolution of hopes.

BUSHES:
Pushing through bushes: Will have a change for the better.

Hiding behind bushes: Imminent danger.

Others hiding behind bushes: Opposition in love.

Cutting down bushes: Danger through a secret.

BUSINESS:
Doing business: Untruthful gossip.

Beginning a good business: Must fight for good results.

Making money in business: Will receive money from a friend.

Losing money in business: Will lose your temper.

BUSINESS DOCUMENTS:
A man handling business documents: Be careful of speculations.

A woman handling business documents: Will have a change for the better.

A notary handling business documents: Financial gains.

Handling partnership documents: A big profit will soon come.

Handling personal documents: Will receive a legacy.

Handling family documents: Discovery of lost valuables.

BUTCHER:
Of a butcher: Will see someone dear to you.

A butcher killing any animal: Death of a close friend.

A butcher serving you with cut meat: Will live a long life.

Being friendly with a butcher: False friends are nearby.

Arguing with a butcher: Are surrounded by unfortunate influences.

BUTTER:
Eating butter: Happiness.
Having plenty of butter: Good luck of some kind to come.
Purchasing butter: Will have a change for the better.
Cooking with butter: Will be fortunate in business.
Selling butter: Avoid financial speculations.
Making butter in own house: Will receive a present.
Frying with butter: Will have a new admirer.

BUTTERFLY:
A butterfly flitting from flower to flower: Great prosperity.
A beautifully colored butterfly in the sunshine: Happiness in love.
A butterfly being in the house: Will have some slight trouble.
A young woman dreaming of a butterfly: Will have a happy marriage.
Catching a butterfly: Infidelity.
Killing a butterfly: Will receive a gift.
Chasing a butterfly: Are surrounded by unfortunate influences.

BUTTERMILK:
Making buttermilk: Big joy.
Spilling buttermilk: Will suffer because of own foolishness.
Buying buttermilk: Will escape an imminent danger.
Children drinking buttermilk: Prosperity.
Single people dreaming of drinking buttermilk: Disappointment in love.

Married people dreaming of drinking buttermilk: Trouble, sorrow, and losses.

BUTTOCKS:
Of own buttocks: Fortune is ahead.
The buttocks of a man: Good business will soon come.
The buttocks of a woman: Happiness and love.
The buttocks of a baby: Family reunion.
The buttocks of animals: Will soon have money.
The buttocks of a dog: Will soon be visited by thieves.

BUTTONS:
A single man dreaming of sewing on buttons: Delay in love affairs.
A woman dreaming of sewing on buttons: Will receive unexpected money.
Losing buttons: Secret enmity of some person.
Buying buttons: Will have a vigorous mind.

BUY:
Buying different articles: Troubles ahead in financial matters.
Buying food: Will have an average success.
Buying vegetables: Family quarrels.
Buying fruits: Misfortune in love affairs.
Buying clothes: Big success ahead.
Buying face powder: Will be extravagant in spending money.
Buying things for children: Will have much good luck.

C

CAB:
Riding in a cab alone: Are engaged in a suitable hobby.
Riding in a cab with friends: Discovery of a secret.

A man riding in a cab with a woman: Name will be connected with scandal.
A woman riding in a cab alone: Will enjoy average success.

Riding in a cab at night: Are keeping secrets from friends.

Riding in a cab in the rain: Correspondence with friends living abroad.

Riding in a cab to meet sweetheart: Weaknesses will be known.

Riding in a cab with wife: Will have a long life.

Riding in a cab with children: Happiness within the family.

Riding in a cab with relatives: Will encounter gossip in the future.

CABBAGE:

Eating cabbage: Uncertain livelihood.

Buying cabbage: Good health and long life.

Boiling cabbage: Suitable work and good news.

Growing cabbage: Be cautious in business affairs.

Making a cabbage salad: Abundant means.

CABIN:

Being in the cabin of a ship: Domestic troubles.

Being in a cabin at the beach: Love affairs.

Being in a country cabin: Slow recovery from an illness.

Being in a cabin with the family: Good days ahead.

Being in a cabin with a lover: Death of an enemy.

Being in a cabin with friends: Danger in love matters.

CABINET:

Of a cabinet: Treachery from trusted people.

Buying a cabinet: Great financial gain.

Selling a cabinet: Dissension within the family.

Opening a cabinet: Will receive a long-awaited letter.

Closing a cabinet: Loss of a letter in the mail.

CACKLE:

Hearing a hen cackle at dawn: Warning that care is needed.

Hearing a hen cackle at noon: Fights between relatives.

Hearing a hen cackle in the evening: Big peril.

CADDY:

Of a caddy: Will receive a present.

Using services of a caddy: Misfortune is near.

Friends using services of a caddy: Good luck to one for whom you care.

CADET:

Of a cadet: Hard work ahead.

Cadets at an academy: Will be threatened by someone.

Cadets drilling: Will be deceived.

Cadets going home: Will be persecuted.

Cadets graduating: Will be cheated by a woman.

A relative being a cadet: Will receive news of the birth of a child.

CAGE:

An empty cage: A member of the family will elope.

A cage full of birds: Untold wealth.

Only one bird in a cage: Will have many lovely children.

Two birds in a cage: Successful love affairs.

Three birds in a cage: Engagement will be broken.

Wild animals in a cage: Danger of going to prison.

CAIN:

A man dreaming of Cain: Retrace footsteps and tread a different path.

A woman dreaming of Cain: Will be highly considered by others.

Unmarried people dreaming of Cain: Will soon be married.

CAKE:

Baking a cake: Will have a lucky turn of events.

Eating a piece of cake: Will lose sweetheart.

Buying a cake: Will enjoy the affection of a friend.

A woman dreaming of eating her wedding cake: Big peril.
Serving cake to friends: Are confronted with insurmountable obstacles.

CALCULATE:
Of calculating: Unhappiness.
Calculating expenditures: Expect bad news concerning business.
Calculating other affairs: Will make new acquaintances.
Others calculating for you: Will incur new enemies.
Having calculated wrongly: Damages in affairs.

CALENDAR:
Of a calendar: Are prone to being too impatient.
Buying a calendar: Will receive good news.
Tearing off calendar sheets: Will receive an unexpected gift.
Worrying about a calendar date: Will be fortunate in marriage.

CALF:
Owning a calf: Will have a very good future.
Buying a calf: Will be madly in love.
Selling a calf: Will soon be married.
A calf belonging to others: Fortune received from parents.
Married people dreaming of a calf: Marriage will last forever.

CALICO:
Of calico: Will have love affairs.
Buying calico: Unhappy events within twelve months.
Selling calico: Will soon have happiness.
Owning calico: Gossiping of other women.

CALL:
A single person dreaming of hearing name called: Will soon fall in love.
A married person dreaming of hearing name called: Will soon divorce.
Calling someone else: Look for important news.

Being called by several people: Will be insulted by a relative.

CALM:
Calming yourself: Will have many adventures.
Calming angry people: Illness of children.
Calming a relative: Loss of consideration from friends.
Calming the screaming of one suffering: You have a violent temper.
Calming husband or wife: Will have a violent family quarrel.
Calming sweetheart: Sickness.
Calming friends: Loss of money.
Calming other people: Misfortune in love affairs.
Ordering others to be calm: Will be loved and ridiculed.

CAMEL:
Of one camel: Will have hardship and obstacles to overcome.
Many camels: Great financial gain.
A camel carrying a load: Inheritance.
Riding on a camel: Will be wealthy.

CAMEO:
Of a cameo: Will receive high consideration of others.
Having a cameo: Promotion in own affairs.
Receiving a cameo as a gift: Recovery from an illness.
Buying a cameo: Happiness.
Losing a cameo: Death.

CAMERA:
Owning a camera: Will receive disagreeable news.
Looking into a camera: Will be deceived.
Buying a camera: Joy without profit.
Receiving a camera as a gift: Will have love troubles.

CAMP:
Of a camp: Will have peace in domestic affairs.
Of camping: Will have good days ahead.
Being in a camp: Good fortune in love affairs.

Going camping: Good change in business affairs.

Soldiers in a camp: Great financial gains.

Friends in a camp: Successful result of ventures.

CAMPHOR:

Of camphor: Are surrounded with evil.

Having camphor in the house: Will risk failure of plans.

Buying camphor: Will be cheated by friends.

Using camphor: Change of surroundings.

CAN:

Many cans: Will receive good news.

Drinking from a can: Great joy.

Opening a can: A rival will win affection of your sweetheart.

Buying several cans of juices: Avoid enemies.

Throwing away an empty can: Serious disaster ahead.

CANADA:

Of Canada: Will have good business.

Seeing Canada on the map: Will have a vigorous mind.

Going to Canada from abroad: You have many loyal friends.

Going abroad from Canada: Happiness is assured.

Taking a trip to Canada alone: Must endure a painful experience.

Taking a trip to Canada with others: You enjoy amusements too much.

Returning from a trip to Canada: Loss of business.

Being deported from Canada: Will find a new lover.

Being deported to Canada: There will be much discussion about you.

Having business dealings with Canada: Will be implicated in secret deal.

Being a citizen of Canada: Will make financial gains.

Living in Canada: An enemy is seeking your ruin.

CANAL:

A canal full of water: Security is forthcoming.

A canal with clean, clear water: Fortune is near at hand.

A canal with muddy water: Should save money for old age.

A canal covered with weeds: Coming trouble.

CANARY:

Having a canary in the home: Will have a happy and comfortable life.

Owning a canary: Will be deceived by a friend.

Buying a canary: Will soon make a trip.

A dead canary: Death of a very good friend.

CANCER:

Of cancer: Are short of money at present but will have plenty later.

Having cancer in the neck: Will have a long life.

Having cancer inside the body: Are very fond of too many amusements.

Others having cancer: Attempt to avoid talking too much.

Relatives having cancer: Will receive a legacy.

CANDLE:

Candles burning brightly: Expect an invitation to a feast.

Candles flickering: Expect to attend a funeral.

Lighting candles: Will meet with friends.

Putting out candles: Will quarrel with a friend.

Having colored candles: Will become a widow or a widower.

Buying candles: Are inclined to believe enemies.

Being burned by a candle: Will have a serious accident.

Making candles: Joy and satisfaction.

Carrying lighted candles: Death of a friend.

A sick person dreaming of candles: Will soon recover.

Unmarried people dreaming of candles: Will soon be married.

Business people dreaming of candles: Prosperous and good business.

CANDY:
Making candy: Will reap profit in business.
Eating candy: Pleasure in society.
Receiving a box of candy as a gift: Are very highly admired.
Giving a box of candy as a gift: Peace and happiness in the home.
Enjoying the taste of candy: Security is forthcoming.

CANE:
Owning a cane: Unhappiness.
Resting on a cane: Illness in the near future.
Hitting someone with a cane: Will have domination over enemies.
Killing someone with a cane: Will make good profits.
Carrying a cane on the arm: Good health.
Breaking a cane: Dissension within the family.
Having a cane to punish people with: Financial troubles.
A cane used by pilgrims: Will take a long trip.
A woman using a cane: Will have love affairs.
Sugar cane: Arguments between friends.
Bamboo cane: Will raise several children.
Cane of nutmeg: Big quarrels between business associates.
Wicker cane: Are prone always to doubt other people.
A small blowing cane: Several dogs will be killed.
A cane that holds a small bladed sword: High hopes.

CANISTER:
Having a canister: Doomed for disappointment.
Opening a canister: Will discover the secret of a friend.
Closing a canister: Are attempting to conceal secrets.
Having food in a canister: Will have a secret to keep.

CANNIBALS:
Of cannibals: A period of sorrow is about to come.
Animals being cannibals: Will receive disturbing news.
Humans being cannibals: Misfortune in love.

CANNON:
Of a cannon: Danger in love affairs.
A military man firing a cannon: Marriage to a beautiful girl.
A man dreaming of hearing a cannon fired: Danger in business.
A woman dreaming of hearing a cannon fired: Will marry a military man.

CANOE:
Owning a canoe: Lack of friends.
Being in a canoe alone: Danger of fire.
Being in a canoe with a loved one: Avoid rivals.
A canoe overturning: An enemy is seeking your ruin.

CANTALOUPE:
Having cantaloupe: Good success.
Eating cantaloupe: Good hopes.
Buying cantaloupe: Good luck in love affairs.
Cultivating cantaloupes: Will make money.
A sick person dreaming of eating cantaloupe: Will soon recover.

CAP:
Putting on a cap: Difficulties in love affairs.
Buying a cap: Will receive an inheritance.
Selling a cap: Are not operating own business well.
Having a cap given to you: Will have a happy marriage.
An old and dirty cap: Damages in business.

CAPTAIN:
Of a captain: Advancement and prosperity.
Being a captain: Fulfillment of hopes.

Marrying a captain: Will be confronted with a big scandal.

Being a captain's wife: Joy in the family.

Being a captain's sweetheart: Security is forthcoming.

Being a captain's servant: Will have misfortune.

CAPTIVITY:

Being in captivity: Will have an unhappy marriage.

Other people in captivity: Beware of overstrain.

Enemies in captivity: Beware of business losses.

Animals in captivity: Dignity and distinction.

CARCASS:

Of a carcass: Happiness and long life.

The carcass of an animal: Long life and good perspectives.

The carcass of wild animals: Abundant means.

CARDINALS:

Of a cardinal: Advancement in profession.

A priest being made a cardinal: Happiness.

A cardinal dying: Misfortune in own affairs.

Many cardinals: Sorrow caused by a secret.

Conclave of cardinals: Progress in business affairs.

A cardinal being appointed Pope: Misfortune in enterprises.

CARDS:

Playing cards: Will take a trip abroad.

Other people playing cards: Will have quarrels soon.

Playing cards and winning: Troubles ahead.

Playing cards and losing: Good business ventures are faraway.

Being a card dealer: Bad news.

CARESS:

A mother caressing her children: Anxious days because of illness.

A wife caressing her husband: Happy events.

A husband caressing his wife: Will have good earnings.

Sweethearts caressing each other: Will receive dreadful news.

CARETAKER:

Of a caretaker: Damages will be caused by an evil person.

Being a caretaker: Relief of pains.

The caretaker of a garden: Death.

Being caretaker of a bankruptcy case: A faithful friend is nearby.

CARNATIONS:

Of carnations: Vanity will be satisfied.

White carnations: Success in undertakings.

Red carnations: Quarrels with friends.

Pink carnations: Glorious success.

Flesh-colored carnations: Big friendship.

Bluish-red carnations: Prosperity through other people.

CAROLS:

Singing carols: Will have a happy marriage.

Hearing carols sung: Will have nothing to fear.

Children singing carols: Joy and happiness.

Singing carols in church: A loyal friend is nearby.

CARPENTER:

Being a carpenter at work: Success in financial matters.

Hiring a carpenter: Unexpected good news.

A carpenter working busily: Will overcome difficulties.

A carpenter fixing the house: Financial security.

CARPET:

Several carpets: Danger for the one who owns the carpet.

Making carpets: Big happiness.

Buying a carpet: A mystery will be solved.

A carpet burning: Be on guard against spiteful gossip.

Being in a carpeted room: Expect good news.

Exchanging a carpet for a new one: Dissatisfaction in love.

Laying a carpet: Big catastrophe ahead.

CARRIAGE:

Of a carriage: Wealth that will last for a short time only.

Riding in a carriage: Are subject to a short illness.

Getting out of a carriage: Loss of an estate.

Driving a carriage: Sickness.

Making a long trip in a carriage: Will be slow to achieve fortune.

Being the coachman of a carriage: Will have a faithful servant.

A broken carriage: A business partnership will be dissolved.

An overturned carriage: Misery.

CARROTS:

Of carrots: Profit through inheritance.

Having carrots in the home: Will have plenty of money.

Growing carrots: Accord among friends.

Eating carrots: Joy without profit.

Cooking carrots: Abundance.

CARRY:

Of being carried by anyone: Will have an uncertain future.

Being carried by a man: Will have anxious days because of illness.

Carrying a woman: Difficulties will soon be overcome.

Being carried by a woman: Will have new love affairs.

Being carried by a poor person: Happiness.

CARVING:

Doing own carving: Will have prosperity.

Carving for others: Others will benefit by own actions.

Other people carving for you: Will fall in love.

A cook carving meat: Are in the grip of deceitful people.

CART:

Of a cart: Honor.

Being carried in own cart: Will have might and authority.

Getting in a cart: Loss of employment.

Getting out of a cart: Loss of dignity.

A covered cart: Will not complete a planned trip.

Being tied to a cart to pull it: Will be in pain and bondage.

A cart loaded with hay: Wishes will be accomplished.

CASCADE:

Of a cascade: Abundant means.

Watching a cascade alone: Abundance of money.

Watching a cascade with a loved one: Big happiness.

Being near a cascade: Big success in everything.

CASHIER:

Of a cashier: Big joy without profit.

Being a cashier: Expect financial worry.

Watching a cashier: Freedom from want.

Several cashiers at a bank: Are being deceived.

CASTLE:

Of a castle: Expect the visit of good friends.

Entering a castle: You are madly in love.

Residing in a castle: Will receive a marriage proposal.

An ancient castle: Are surrounded by false friends.

The fortress of a castle: Good business ventures.

A small castle: Unhappiness.

A castle being on fire: Quarrels because of bad temper.

CASTOR:

Of the fur of a beaver: Will be very diligent.

Owning a beaver fur coat: Will receive a small inheritance.

Buying a beaver fur coat: You have a faithful lover.

Selling a beaver fur coat: Be cautious in business ventures.

Relatives having a beaver fur coat: Beware of spiteful gossip.

Friends having a beaver fur coat: A false friend is nearby.

CASTOR OIL:

Of a bottle of castor oil: Recovery from an illness.

Being ordered to take castor oil by a doctor: Short illness.

Giving castor oil to children: Will soon take a trip.

Relatives taking castor oil: Family quarrels.

CASTRATE:

Being castrated: Triumph over enemies.

Castrating a man: Society will get along much better.

Castrating a horse: Will be falsely accused.

Castrating a dog: Will have a very faithful companion.

Castrating a pig: Unhappiness.

Castrating a lamb: Will give a large dinner party.

Castrating a mule: Will be punished by a high official.

Castrating a donkey: A big affliction is to come.

Being hurt by a castrated animal: Will be found guilty of wrongdoing.

CAT:

Of brown, white, or gray cats: Are being deceived by a trusted person.

A black cat: Illness is near.

Defending yourself from a cat: Will be robbed.

Cats playing: Will be visited at home by enemies.

A furious cat: Will have arguments with lover.

A cat with her kittens: Unhappiness in marriage.

Being scratched by a cat: Someone is seeking your downfall.

A pregnant cat: Will be robbed.

A cat eating rats: Will receive payment of money loaned.

A cat sleeping: Small success.

A cat eating her food: Divorce.

A cat fighting with a dog: Will have quarrels with neighbors.

Hitting a cat: Will fall into bad company.

Many cats and dogs: Loss of profits in a business deal.

A cat being on the roof: Will be unsuccessful in affairs.

A cat delivering kittens: Divorce is near at hand.

CATALOGUE:

Of a catalogue: Good business ahead.

Receiving a catalogue: Will lose money.

Making a selection from a catalogue: Attempt to be diligent in future.

Cataloguing store merchandise: Will enjoy large gambling winnings.

Cataloguing machinery: Loss in personal affairs.

Cataloguing documents: Small unhappiness.

Cataloguing clothes and shoes: Friends will place blame upon you.

CATARACT:

A cataract with clear water running easily: Expect domestic happiness.

A cataract with murky water not running easily: Loss of money.

A cataract with muddy water: Financial gains.

CATECHISM:

Receiving oral instruction from a catechism: Happiness.

Reading a catechism manual: Good business activities.

Preaching from a catechism: Dignity and distinction.

CATERPILLAR:

Of this piece of machinery: May suffer from malicious tongues.

Owning a caterpillar: Watch own actions.

Working with a caterpillar: Good business ahead.

CATHEDRAL:
The interior of a cathedral: Take care of own business.
The outside of a cathedral: Good fortune.
Being in a cathedral: Will receive honors.

CATTLE:
Many cattle: Prosperity according to the number of cattle.
Black cattle: Troubles ahead in business.
Cattle of other colors: Prosperity in business.
Driving cattle: Must work hard.
Fat cattle: Will have a fruitful year.
Lean cattle: Will be in want of provisions.
Being followed by cattle: Loss in business.
Being rich and owning cattle: Disgrace and loss in business.
Being poor and owning cattle: Good profits.

CAULIFLOWER:
Of cauliflower: Good health and comfortable home life.
Eating cauliflower: Joy and honor.
Growing cauliflower: Treason by a friend.
Buying cauliflower: Will have good health.

CAUSEWAY:
Of a causeway: Troubles will increase.
Crossing over a causeway: Work will be of an artistic nature.
A causeway not yet paved: Will receive a letter with money.

CAVALRY:
Of a cavalry: Good love affairs.
Belonging to a cavalry: Will marry a beautiful woman.
A married woman dreaming of a cavalry man: Will divorce her husband.
A single woman dreaming of a cavalry man: Will marry a rich banker.

CAVE:
Being in a cave: Change and probable separation from loved ones.

Escaping from a cave: All will go well in business.
Falling into a cave: Expect business worries.
Being with others in a cave: Abundant means.

CAVERN:
Of a cavern: Fortune will change for the better.
A very deep cavern: Death of a friend.
Being in a cavern: Will always remain poor and unknown.

CEILING:
The ceiling of own room being damaged: Happiness.
A cracked ceiling: Will have troubles caused by a friend.
Repairing a ceiling: Good times are coming.

CELERY:
Of celery: Good health.
Eating celery: Will have domestic comfort.
Buying celery: Will escape from troubles.

CELL:
Of a prison cell: Prefer to be left alone.
Being in a prison cell: Joy and honor to come.
Others being in a prison cell: Good earnings in the future.
Several people in one cell: Have an appreciation for good music.
An empty cell: Love disputes.
Breaking out of a cell: Will live a long life.

CELLAR:
An empty cellar: Will have prosperity.
Sleeping in a cellar: Poverty.
Going into the cellar: Will be very fortunate.
Coal in a cellar: Will receive good news from far away.
Many things stored in a cellar: Good business.
A woman dreaming of a cellar with wines: A gambler will propose marriage.

CEMENT:
Of cement: Will receive a present.
Buying cement: Will have important events.
Working with cement: Will receive unexpected money.

CEMETERY:
Of a cemetery: Will conquer all things.
Being in a cemetery: Will soon have prosperity.
A bride passing a cemetery on way to marriage: She will lose husband.
Children gathering flowers in a cemetery: Coming prosperity.
Elderly people putting flowers in a cemetery: Will have no grief.

CENTRAL AMERICA:
Being in Central America: Security in business.
Going to Central America from abroad: New interests and surroundings.
Going abroad from Central America: Expect difficulties in home life.
Being deported to Central America: Misfortune in business.
Being deported from Central America: Avoid enemies.

CERTIFICATE:
Receiving a certificate: Do not see things from others' point of view.
Giving a certificate: People will recognize your innocence.
Receiving a stock certificate: Financial losses.

CHAFF:
The chaff of grain: Plans will not succeed.
Separating chaff from the seed: Will be very fortunate.
Storing the chaff of grain: Will have a vigorous mind.

CHAGRIN:
Being chagrined: Joy.
Children being chagrined: Will acquire new friendships.
Members of family being chagrined: Disputes with mother-in-law.

Friends being chagrined: Rely on own good judgment.

CHAINS:
Of iron chains: Will escape from some difficulty.
Cutting a chain: Will have worries for a short time.
Wearing a chain: Expect bad days in the near future.
A gold chain around a woman's neck: Good fortune with friend or lover.
A person wearing chains in jail: Business will be bad.
Succeeding in breaking the chains: Will be free of social engagements.
Others in chains: Ill fortune for them.
Being bound in chains: Will soon be relieved of burdens.

CHAIR:
Of an empty chair: Will receive news from an absent friend.
Sitting in a comfortable arm chair: Will have prosperity.
Sitting in a chair and being moved by others: Will receive high honors.

CHALK:
Of chalk: Disappointment in some cherished hope.
Buying chalk: Will have a long life.
Handling chalk: Will soon be married.

CHALLENGE:
Being challenged: Will reconcile with enemies.
Challenging someone to a duel: Immediate death of a relative.
Challenging someone to boxing match: Will be a public shame to community.
Others challenging: Be prudent in the future.

CHAMPAGNE:
Drinking champagne: Will be unfortunate in love affairs.
Buying champagne: Big happiness.
Being at a champagne party: Will be happy with lover.

CHAMPIONS:
Of champions: Pull yourself together and be more careful.

Being a champion: Financial gains.
Own team being champions in a game: Very small success in business.

CHANDELIER:
Church chandeliers: Will go to prison.
Chandeliers with candles hanging from the ceiling: Prosperity.
Chandeliers with globes hanging from the ceiling: Wealth.
A table chandelier with candles: Misfortune in love affairs.

CHANGE:
Of conditions in life changing: Damages to present condition.
A woman changing her sex: A son will be born to bring honor to family.
A man changing his sex: Great family dishonor.
Other people changing their sex: Infirmity.
Changing course while driving: Many troubles ahead.
Changing clothes: Will receive a large damage.

CHAPEL:
Of a chapel: Will have unmeasured joy and true friends.
Praying inside a chapel: Will have much happiness.
Being outside a chapel: Will be very fortunate.

CHARITY:
Being charitable: Less fortune awaits you in business affairs.
Receiving charity: Domestic affliction.
Giving to charity: Financial gains.
Doing charity work without hesitation: You have a dangerous enemy.
Giving clothing to charity: People are laughing at you.
Giving food stuffs to charity: Will have hard work ahead.

CHARMS:
Of a charm: Beware of jealous friends.
Wearing a charm: Will have an important decision to make soon.
Buying a charm to ward off evil: Will marry soon.
Selling a charm: Unhappiness.

Receiving a charm as a gift: Will soon experience many ups and downs.

CHARTER:
Chartering a wagon: Another person is enjoying what you hoped to win.
Chartering a ship: Luck and prosperity.
Chartering an automobile: Hard work ahead.
Chartering any kind of machinery: Financial gains.

CHASTISE:
Chastising the children: Happy and prosperous life.
Being chastised: Will be unfortunate in financial matters.
Others being chastised: Are being deceived.
Chastising another: Will have ill-tempered husband or wife.
Being chastised by others: Troubles ahead with business partner.
Being chastised by the family: Triumph over enemies.

CHATTER:
Of chattering: An elopement will cause much gossip.
Other people chattering: They are gossiping against you.
Many people chattering: Will be cheated by friends.

CHEATING:
Of cheating: Take care of own self.
Having been cheated: Don't trust false friends.
Cheating in a gambling game: Are confronted with insurmountable obstacles.
Having been cheated in gambling: Use caution in business affairs.
Others cheating in gambling: An enemy is seeking your ruin.

CHECK:
Of checks: Financial gains.
Having checks: A change in life will soon come.
Giving a check: Accord among friends.

Receiving a check: Will overcome enemies.

Receiving a check returned without funds: Are being deceived.

Giving a check without funds to cover it: An enemy is seeking your ruin.

Losing a check: Warnings of trouble ahead.

CHECKBOOK:

Of a checkbook: Will escape a present peril easily.

Handling own checkbook: Dignity and distinction.

Writing checks from a checkbook: Good times are coming.

Others writing checks in own checkbook: Business disappointments.

Losing the checkbook: Secret enmity of some person.

CHECKING:

Checking numbers: Appetites will create enemies.

Checking business accounts: Will enjoy happiness in the future.

Checking on wife: You are doing wrong to an innocent person.

Checking on husband: Unfitted for position of loyal married person.

CHEEKS:

Beautiful cheeks: Joy and contentment.

Rosy cheeks: Long life.

Pale cheeks: Will be in need of provisions.

Nice cheeks: Will have good health.

A woman dreaming of her own cheeks: Will be loved very much.

A man dreaming of his own cheeks: Will have plenty of joy.

CHEERING:

Of cheering: Will have bad luck.

Others cheering: Avoid spending too much money.

Hearing the sound of cheering: Be careful of own actions.

CHEESE:

Of cheese: Worry caused through own hasty actions.

Buying cheese: Are being deceived by those nearest you.

Having cheese: Opposition in love affairs.

Eating cheese: Health and many pleasures.

Foreign cheese: Are prone to liking only the best things.

Cheese made in own country: Change for the better.

Homemade cheese: Good luck to one for whom you care.

CHEMISE:

A woman dreaming of her chemise: Will hear gossip concerning herself.

A woman taking off her chemise: Dissolution in love.

A woman putting on her chemise: Will be loved very much.

A woman washing her chemise: She will be loved.

CHEMIST:

Being a chemist: Business affairs are not good.

Of a chemist's shop: Be cautious in business dealings.

Being in a chemist's shop: Will be married soon.

CHERRIES:

Cherries hanging on a tree: Losses in business will come soon.

A cherry tree without cherries: Will have good health.

Eating cherries: Will be involved in agreeable matters.

Having cherries in the house: Good health.

Cooking cherries: Will have an illness very soon.

Rotten cherries: Will be disappointed by lover.

Having dark cherries: Will be sorry about present enterprises.

Eating cherries in alcohol: Will be cheated by best friends.

A man dreaming of picking cherries: Will be deceived by women.

CHESS:

Playing chess: Difficulties ahead in your path.

Others playing chess: Fortune will depend upon results of the game.

Winning a game of chess: Approaching money.

Losing a game of chess: Troubles ahead.

CHEST:

Having a big chest: Will make many debts.

Having a small chest: Love affairs will be good.

Having an empty chest: Be prepared for a disappointment.

Having a full chest: Family arguments.

CHESTNUTS:

Having chestnuts: Will have domestic afflictions.

Eating chestnuts: Will have some advantages if careful.

Buying chestnuts: Will be disappointed by lover.

CHEW:

Of chewing: Will have to overlook own faults.

Others chewing: Will have peace of mind and happiness.

Children chewing: Advancement in own affairs.

CHICKENS:

Of one fine chicken: Will be fortunate in love.

Several chickens: Will have many good friends.

Chickens laying eggs: Joy and contentment.

A chicken sitting on her eggs: Joy and happiness.

A chicken with her chicks: Will receive a favor.

Eating chicken: Will be afflicted.

Cooking chicken: Will make considerable money.

Killing a chicken: Profit.

CHILBLAINS:

Of chilblains: You have desires that will bring disgrace.

Having chilblains: A misunderstanding will be cleared up.

Others having chilblains: Will receive unexpected news.

Children having chilblains: Will receive unexpected money.

CHILDREN:

Of children: A woman will become pregnant soon.

Several children: Will have abundance in life.

Little children: Disappointment and sorrow.

Pretty children: Happy and successful career.

Children at play: Good deeds will bear fruit.

Children falling: Loss in business.

Having many children of your own: Success in business.

Adopting children: Own children will dislike those adopted.

Children being killed: Misery caused by parents.

Talking to own children: Losses in business.

Children being sick: Obstacles are ahead.

A child being crippled: Troubles await.

Children studying: Will have a great deal of fun.

A mother holding her child against her breast: Child will have bad health.

A child with her nurse: Mother will have another child.

Being a bastard child: Will have trouble raising all your children.

A man dreaming of being with his child: Riches.

CHIMNEY:

A tall chimney: Fortunate events to come.

Chimney of own house: Will receive good news.

A cracked chimney: Big catastrophe ahead.

Smoke coming from a chimney: Prosperity.

A chimney falling down: Joy.

CHIMNEY SWEEPER:

Of a chimney sweeper: Will be falsely accused.

Having chimney sweeper clean chimney: Family embarrassments.

A chimney sweeper with face all black: Will do mediocre business.

Hearing chimney sweeper calling for work: Will make big profits.

CHIN:
Of own chin: Good business in the future.

Having a large chin: Will receive money.

Having a beautiful chin: Poverty.

Other people having a double chin: Will be complemented for doing good.

Other people hurting their chin: Good success.

CHINA:
Of own china: Financial gains from a faraway place.

Fine china: Good luck in gambling.

Buying china: Happiness in your marriage.

CHINESE:
Several Chinese people: Will make a long trip.

Being in the company of Chinese: Will have impossible desires.

Being in a Chinese home: Will have much security.

CHIPS:
Of chips: Will have business success or win a wager.

Handling chips: Will collect money soon.

Playing with chips: Loss of business.

CHISEL:
Of a chisel: Will have peace of mind and happiness.

Owning a chisel: Will obtain desires through energetic work.

Using a chisel: Will learn lessons at own expense.

Buying a chisel: Will make a public appearance.

CHLOROFORM:
Giving chloroform: Will have emotional sorrow.

Being chloroformed: A pleasant surprise is in store.

Others being chloroformed: Expect good business.

CHOCOLATES:
Of chocolate candy: Will have a congenial occupation.

Eating chocolates: Will receive a gift soon.

Chocolate powder: Will have happiness and health.

Buying chocolate: A short period of troubles will be followed by prosperity.

Drinking chocolate: Will receive a marriage proposal.

CHOIR:
A choir singing: Happiness in love.

Singing in a choir: Will hear from an old friend.

Hearing a choir singing: You have one loyal friend.

CHOKING:
Of choking: Will live a long life.

Others choking: Will be abandoned by lover.

Children choking: Recovery from an illness.

CHOOSE:
Of choosing: Will have a sickness that may result in an operation.

Choosing too fast: Overexertion of yourself.

Choosing a beautiful woman: Will have plenty of money.

Choosing a wealthy man: Will have misery.

Choosing employees: Family disagreements.

CHRIST:
The birth of Christ: Will have peace, joy, and contentment.

Christ being in the Garden: Will have big wealth.

Christ in the Temple: Efforts will be rewarded.

Christ being crucified: Enemies will be defeated.

Resurrection of Christ: Will have good hopes in life.

Talking to Christ: Will receive a big consolation.

CHRISTEN:
Attending a christening: Will achieve hopes and desires.
Members of family being christened: A new life lies ahead.
A friend's child being christened: Contentment.
A lady dreaming of a christening: Will soon be married.

CHRISTMAS:
Attending church on Christmas day: Will receive God's blessings.
Of Christmas: Will have happy family affairs.
Being at a Christmas party: Will have new good friends.
Going Christmas caroling: Great financial gains.

CHURCH:
A church being built: Will have difficulties to surmount.
Several churches being built: Big happiness.
Building a church: You are loved by God.
Entering a church: Will receive a kindness.
Being seated in a church: Will change habits.
Talking in a church: Have plenty of envious friends.
Praying in church: Consolation and joy.
A church being fully decorated: Will receive an inheritance.
Being in a church during mass: Will receive what you are hoping for.
Hearing a dispute in a church: Will have family troubles.
Being in a church convent: Will have peace and contentment.
Singing in a church choir: Will hear from an old friend.
Being with a priest in a church: Happy marriage and success.

CHURCHYARD:
Of a churchyard: Will have a pleasant life.

Being in a churchyard: Will have a happy family.
Other people in a churchyard: Will live a long life.

CHURN:
Of churning: A difficult task is ahead.
Making butter from churning: Prosperity will attend you.
A single man dreaming of churning: Will have a happy marriage.
A young woman dreaming of churning: Will have energetic, thrifty husband.

CIDER:
Having cider: Will have fortune if you attend to business.
People drinking cider: Will have quarrels and hatred.
Buying cider: Will gossip about own private affairs.
Selling cider: Act very cautiously.

CIGAR:
Smoking a cigar: Success in everything.
Having an unlit cigar: Will have misfortune.
Having a lit cigar: May have good hopes.
Others smoking cigars: Prosperity awaits.

CIGARETTE:
Lighting a cigarette: Signifies new plans.
Holding a half-smoked cigarette in hands: Postponement of love.
Smoking a cigarette to the end: Great success.
A man and woman smoking cigarettes together: Conclusion of hopes.

CIGAR SHOP:
Of a cigar shop: Should save money for a rainy day.
Being in a cigar shop: Attempt to be economical.
Buying cigars in a cigar shop: Business will fail.

CINDERS:
Of cinders and ashes: Expect a big disappointment.

Throwing cinders away: Success in business.

Others throwing cinders away: Good times are coming.

CIRCUS:
Of a circus: Future unhappiness.

Watching a circus performance: Loss of money.

Taking children to a circus: Important and beneficial events to come.

CISTERN:
A brimful cistern: Financial matters are improving.

A half-full cistern: Unhappiness because of own careless habits.

A nearly empty cistern: Will be unfortunate in business.

CITIZEN:
Being a good citizen: Will hear good news.

Being a bad citizen: Will pay a visit to a tomb.

Becoming a citizen: Will have hard work ahead.

Being refused citizenship: Will make money.

Many citizens: Unhappiness.

CITY:
An inhabited city: Will be very rich.

A large city: Will have much ambition.

Seeing a city in the distance: Will have much success.

A city burning: Poverty.

Being in a large city: Conclusion of hopes.

Being in a small city: Must take good care of business.

A city in ruins: Will have illness in the family.

Going through a city: Will receive sad news from a friend.

A beautiful city: Slow recovery of business losses.

CITY HALL:
Of City Hall: Will attain desires slowly but surely.

Going to City Hall: Victory over persecution.

Being married at City Hall: Unpleasant events ahead.

Being employed at City Hall: Will enjoy great prosperity.

Doing business at City Hall: Will enjoy a free life.

CLARET:
Drinking red wine: Be careful in business dealings.

Buying claret wine: Disappointment in love.

Serving claret wine with dinner: Misfortune in love affairs.

CLAY:
Of clay: Own ideas are not clear.

Working with clay: Will make good profits.

Baking white clay: Good business prospects.

Baking clay made from bricks: Big fortune ahead.

CLEAN:
Of cleaning: Embarrassment and quarrels.

Cleaning yourself: Will have an everlasting friendship.

Cleaning the teeth: Happiness.

Cleaning children: Will achieve victory over enemies.

Cleaning house: Will receive news from an absent person.

CLERGYMAN:
Of a clergyman: Disappointment in love affairs.

Many clergymen: Will receive a letter from abroad.

Confiding in a clergyman: Expect unhappy news.

Being in the company of a clergyman: Will have an honorable position.

CLIFFS:
Of cliffs: Will have a big fire that will ruin everything.

Going up a cliff: Conclusion of affairs.

Being on top of a cliff: Do not undertake any business risks.

Descending from a cliff: Don't trust your friends.

Being on a cliff with others: Happy love affairs.
Pushing someone from a cliff: Will see a big riot.

CLIMBING:
Of climbing: Prosperity in business.
Being unable to climb: Present efforts are not good enough.
Climbing a mountain and reaching the summit: Will gain a fortune.
Climbing but failing to reach the summit: Cherished plans will fail.
Climbing a ladder to the top: Success in business.
A ladder breaking while climbing: Will have unexpected difficulties.
Climbing a tree: Will receive a good position.
Climbing the stairs of a house: Will overcome all obstacles.

CLOAK:
Of an old cloak: Will receive good news from a friend.
Putting on a new cloak: Sorrow and grief will come to an end.
Tearing a cloak: Separation from all that is dear to you.
Buying a cloak: You are wasting good time.
Fixing a cloak: Will be exact in own affairs.

CLOCK:
Hearing a clock strike the hours: Will be married soon.
A church or city clock: Will enjoy a comfortable life.
Having a wall clock: Will have happiness.
Buying a wall clock: Will receive important business news.
A clock being stopped: Will be spared from illness.

CLOGS:
Putting on clogs: Prepare for a wedding in the near future.
Buying clogs: Good times are coming.
Other people wearing clogs: Will make a big profit.

CLOSET:
Of a closet: Will have plenty of money which will be squandered.
Having money in a closet: Sickness of a female person.
Clothes hanging in a closet: Big fortune.
Linens being in a closet: Happiness in the home.

CLOTH:
Of cloth: Certain and secure profit.
Linen cloth: Will make big earnings.
Woolen cloth: Will make profits from own products.
Velvet cloth: Will have an amorous conversation.
Silk cloth: Big joy.
Indianhead cloth: Wrongdoings will be recognized.
Frame for making cloth: Efforts are being wasted.

CLOTHES:
Having plenty of clothes: Troubles to come.
Putting on clothes: Will receive good news from a stranger.
Having no clothes on: Will receive plenty of money.
Being partly dressed: Will have prosperity.
Buying many clothes: Success in love.

CLOUDS:
Stormy and dark clouds: Will have many sorrows.
Clouds passing away: Good fortune awaits.
The sky being without clouds: Conclusion of own hopes.
The sky being full of clouds: Arguments between business partners.
Beautiful white clouds: Will become a miser.
Very black clouds: Unhappiness.
Downpour of rain from the clouds: Will have hard days ahead.
Clouds clearing away: Will have a disagreeable attitude.

CLOVER:
Of clover: Will have a prosperous future.

Clover in blossom: Misfortune and sorrow.

Being in a field of clover: You are in love.

CLOWN:

Being dressed as a clown: Will receive news of a death.

A clown performing: Others think you are wicked.

Being in the company of a clown: Troubles ahead.

A clown being hurt: Will receive an unexpected gift.

A clown making love to a woman: You have many hypocritical friends.

CLUB:

Being in a club: Will meet acquaintances of long ago.

Meeting friends in a club: Happiness in the family.

Being at a club party: Financial losses.

Being refused admittance to a club: Will take good care of business.

CLUMSY:

Being clumsy: Will overcome troubles in business.

Employees being clumsy: Don't confide in relatives so much.

Children being clumsy: Will receive good news.

Other people being clumsy: Good results in love affairs.

COACH:

Driving in a coach alone: May find yourself in difficulties.

Driving in a coach with other people: Beware of treachery.

Others driving a coach: Will be cheated by friends.

COAL:

Being in a coalpit: You are in grave danger.

Coal burning brightly: Happiness in the family.

Coal burning slowly: Beware of enemies.

A fiery coal: Reputation is in doubt.

Coal extinguished: Unfounded jealousy.

Coal burning in a fireplace: Will be tenderly loved and enjoy pleasures.

Handling coal: Will be extremely fortunate.

Buying coal: Will receive big profits.

Swallowing coals in medicines: Secret affection.

Completely dead coals: Troubles ahead.

Coal burning in a stove: Beware of untrue friends.

Sitting in a coal bin: Will be abandoned by lover.

Selling coal: Will have enough money to live comfortably all your life.

Children playing with coal: Will enjoy a happy future.

COAL MINE:

Being in a coal mine: Will not be fully satisfied in own affairs.

The blackness of a coal mine: Will have a certain amount of contentment.

Digging coal from a coal mine: Abundant means.

Being a worker in a coal mine: Will receive unexpected money.

COAT:

Of a new coat: Are about to receive honors.

Wearing a new coat: Beware of business troubles.

Wearing an old coat: Prosperity is coming.

Wearing a torn coat: Will receive big profits.

Wearing another person's coat: Will be forced to seek a friend's help.

Losing a coat: Will soon face financial ruin through speculation.

Getting a coat dirty: Will lose a good friend.

COAT OF ARMS:

Of a coat of arms: Will have bad luck.

Having a coat of arms: Will be highly honored by women.

Own coat of arms on the door of own house: Business failure.

COAXING:
Of coaxing: A dangerous request will be made of you.
Being coaxed: Immediate marriage.
Others coaxing: Will have emotional sorrow.

COBBLER:
Of a cobbler: Misfortune will come.
Being a cobbler: Troubles ahead.
Going to a cobbler: Misfortune is very near.
Having shoes fixed by a cobbler: Will overcome enemies.

COBWEB:
Seeing and brushing away a cobweb: Triumph over an enemy.
Destroying a cobweb: Misfortune is near.
Others destroying a cobweb: Danger in own love.

COCK:
Hearing a cock crow: Great prosperity.
Hearing a cock crow while asleep: Will receive good news.
A cock being in the house: Will get married.
Cocks fighting: Will have quarrels.
A dead cock: Happiness in the family.

COCKATOO:
Of a cockatoo: Discovery of a secret.
Buying a cockatoo: Will have arguments with friends.
Keeping a cockatoo in a cage: Will realize own indiscretion.
Hearing a cockatoo talking: A false friend is nearby.

COCKLES:
Of cockles: Expect bad news from afar.
Having cockles: Improvement in own circumstances.
Gathering cockles: Will receive a sad letter.

COCOA:
Of cocoa: Will be madly in love.
Buying cocoa: Happiness in the family.

Drinking cocoa: Will have a very good future.
Making cocoa: Abundant means.

COCONUT:
A coconut tree: Will receive a fortune from parents.
Buying coconut: Will have a love affair.
Eating coconut: Will receive a large sum of money.
A large tree full of coconuts: Women are gossiping.

CODE:
Consulting a law code: Will have a big fight.
A tax code: Advantageous events in business.
A business code: Success in own affairs.
Deciphering a code: Good news of improvement in business.

COFFEE:
Making coffee: Great domestic happiness.
Drinking coffee: Friends are discussing your wedding plans.
Selling coffee: Financial losses.
Buying coffee: Will have the best reputation in business.
Roasting coffee: Will have a visitor.
Grinding coffee: Will overcome obstacles.
Burning coffee: Will be surrounded by evil.
Pouring coffee: Security is forthcoming.
Growing coffee: Great financial gains.
Of a coffee shop: Will be deceived.
Being in a coffee shop with good people: Highly considered by friends.

COFFIN:
Of a coffin: Will soon marry and own your own house.
Many coffins: Will incur large debts.
An elaborate coffin: Death of a partner.
A friend in a coffin: Serious illness of a dear friend.
Coffin of the head of the family: Must contend with unpleasant matters.

Own coffin: Someone is attempting to cheat you.

A coffin of someone else: Inheritance.

Being in a coffin: Abundance.

Stealing a coffin: Are ashamed of receiving a fortune.

COGWHEELS:

Of cogwheels: Will have a fresh outlook on own affairs.

Many cogwheels: Will achieve success in plans from now on.

A broken cogwheel: Approaching money.

COINS:

Of coins: Great financial gains.

Silver coins: Will have family troubles.

A girl dreaming of silver coins: Will be jilted by her lover.

Copper coins: Sickness.

Nickel coins: Good work will be your fortune.

Having gold coins in the hands: Misfortune.

Assembling all kinds of coins: Will receive good news.

Counting coins: Will make a considerable profit.

Stealing coins: Long sickness.

Spending coins: Will risk failure in own plans.

Finding coins: Good fortune in domestic affairs.

Seeing all kinds of coins: Promotion in own affairs.

COLD:

Feeling cold: Will have comfort and friendship.

Having a bad cold: Security is forthcoming.

Mate having a cold: Abundant means.

Children having a cold: Good times are coming.

COLLAR:

Putting on a new collar: You are loved too much.

A man's collar: Gains in speculations.

A woman's fur collar: Family love.

A woman having a white collar on her dress: Prosperity.

Having a dirty collar: Shows fickleness on the part of the loved one.

COLLECTION:

Contributing to a collection: Will take a long trip very soon.

Others contributing to own collection: Unexpected news.

Making a collection for poor people: Will have wealth.

COLLEAGUE:

Having colleagues: Will have litigations.

Dealing with colleagues: Big business gossip.

Hitting a colleague in anger: Birth of first son in the family.

Death of a colleague: Unhappiness.

COLLEGE:

A man or woman dreaming of being at college: Will receive bad news.

Children going to college: Will be deceived.

A woman dreaming of being inside a college: Will have a child.

A man dreaming of being inside a college: A change in life to come soon.

College buildings: Advancement will come to you.

COLLISION:

Of a collision: Will have a serious accident.

Being hurt in a collision: Disappointments in business.

Being unhurt in a collision: Will make a love conquest.

Dying in a collision: Will live a long life.

COLONEL:

Being a colonel: Will be surrounded by evil.

A woman dreaming of being married to a colonel: Save money for old age.

A colonel in uniform: Dissatisfaction in love.

Unmarried woman dreaming of a colonel: Will marry a banker.

COLONIES:

Of the colonies: Willl receive an unexpected visit.

Going to the colonies: Good financial affairs.

Being in the colonies: Good times are coming.

Returning from the colonies: Will have an important result.

Being deported from the colonies: Danger is ahead.

Being deported to the colonies: Will hold a religious mission.

COLORED PEOPLE:

A colored woman: Great financial gains.

A colored man: Security is forthcoming.

A colored man and woman together: Big financial gains.

Mulatto men and women: Good luck in money matters.

COLORS:

Azalea: Big joy.

Azure blue: Promotion in employment.

Navy blue: Prosperity through other people.

Black: Will have a very unfortunate time.

Brown: Big friendship.

Crimson: Pleasant news from a friend.

Gold: Will do business with people far away.

Green: Good fortune in love affairs.

Gray: Will receive a letter with good news.

Mauve: Unhappiness.

Orange: Fortune is near at hand.

Pink: Glorious success.

Purple: A joyful journey.

Red: Quarrels with friends.

Scarlet: Family quarrels.

Silver: Will be fortunate in all dealings.

White: Success in undertakings.

Yellow: Important but bad changes will occur in own affairs.

Several colors mixed together: You have false friends.

COLUMBINE:

Of a columbine: Will visit luxurious surroundings.

Having a columbine: Advancement will come soon.

Receiving a columbine as a gift: A change in life will soon come.

COLUMBUS DAY:

Celebrating Columbus Day: Will be going fishing.

Columbus discovering America: Good business transactions.

The statue of Columbus: Postponement of success.

The fleet of Columbus' ships: Rapid success of hopes and desires.

COLUMN:

Of any kind of a supporting column: Home will be robbed.

Leaning on a column: Will become disappointed in best friend.

Workers erecting a column: Abundance of money.

COMB:

Buying a comb: Misfortune.

Using a comb: Affairs are in confusion.

Losing a comb: Your love is not as strong as it once was for someone.

Borrowing another's comb: Loss of money.

Own comb being borrowed by others: Difficulties in business.

COMBAT:

Of combat: Will be humiliated.

Engaging in a combat and being successful: Love and happiness.

Engaging in combat and being unsuccessful: Difficulty and worry.

Helping others in a combat: Reconciliation with enemies.

COMBING:

Combing own hair: Loss of a lover.

Combing a young girl's hair: Loss of friendship.

Combing a boy's hair: Loss of money.

Own hair being combed by others: Loss through someone trusted.

Others combing their hair: Death of a relative.

Hair being combed by a beautician: Honor.

A beautician combing a rich woman's hair: Big fortune ahead.

COMEDIAN:

A male comedian: Will handle business automatically.

A female comedian: Good results in affairs.

Being a comedian: You harbor bad desires in your mind.

Being a poor comedian: Loss of money and disgrace.

COMEDY:

Of a comedy: Will receive a long-awaited letter.

Acting in a comedy: Be prepared for bad news.

Watching a comedy: Will succeed in undertakings.

Reading a comedy play: Security is forthcoming.

A friend playing in a comedy: Beware of untrue friends.

COMET:

Of a comet: Unusual distinction will come to you.

A comet falling: Coming troubles.

Several comets: Approaching sorrow.

Several comets falling: Loss of love.

COMFORT:

Living in comfort: Will receive bad news.

Comforting children: Approaching money.

Comforting other people: Will be fortunate in love.

Being comforted by others: Happiness in love.

COMMAND:

Being commanded by others: Anger and authority.

Commanding others: Unexpected money.

Commanding children: Will receive a valuable gift.

Receiving a government command: Death of an enemy.

COMMANDER:

Of a commander: Will receive unpleasant news.

Being a commander: Will receive pleasant news.

Being the commander of a vessel: Will make a love conquest.

Being promoted to a commander: Triumph in own affairs.

COMMERCE:

Of commerce: Death of people while on a trip.

Having own commerce: Will receive a favor in the near future.

Doing a small trade: Treason and persecution.

Being in the steel trade: Loss of friends.

Having commerce dealings in wool: Profit.

Having commerce dealings in silk: Pleasure.

Having commerce dealings in taffeta: Joy.

Having commerce dealings in linen: Approaching money.

Having commerce dealings in cotton: Affliction.

Being important Chamber of Commerce official: Will be robbed.

COMMISSION:

Collecting a commission: Inheritance and riches.

Paying a commission: Loss of friends.

Working on a commission basis: Beware of untrue friends.

Receiving a commission of authority: Hard work ahead.

Receiving a government commission: Beware of enemies.

COMMITTING:

Committing good actions: Financial gains.

Committing bad actions: Will be cheated by friends.

Committing a crime: Danger through a secret.

Committing immoral actions: Rivals will take sweetheart's affection.

COMMODORE:
Of a commodore: Will have a vigorous mind.
Being a commodore: Dignity and distinction.
Being the commodore of a yacht: Will have pleasant social activities.
A commodore giving orders: Will be greatly annoyed.

COMMUNICATE:
Communicating news: Security in business.
Communicating orders: Will receive a grave injustice.
Communicating bad news: Must rely upon own vigor.
Communicating a secret: A change in life will soon come.

COMMUNION:
Going to communion: Will receive many blessings.
Going to communion with others: Security in affairs.
Not going to communion: Will learn unpleasant news.
Taking children to communion: Will receive good news.
Relatives going to communion: Will receive a sad letter.

COMMUNITY:
Having a community business: Will soon have a law suit.
Having community property: You don't plan affairs very well.
Having a community property settlement: Will have very big projects.
Disposing of community property: Will have a long life.

COMMUTE:
A married woman commuting: Someone with evil intent is watching you.
A married man commuting: You are deceived.
A single man commuting: A false friend is nearby.
A single woman commuting: Happiness is assured.

COMPANION:
Being with a pleasant companion: Poverty.
Being with an unpleasant companion: Financial losses.
Conversing with several companions: Peril of rain.
Having dealings with companions: Will be lazy.

COMPANY:
Having company: Bad times are ahead.
Having good company: Will not make good progress.
Having undesirable company: Will be cheated by a friend.
Having a company meeting: Triumph over enemies.

COMPARE:
Comparing children with others: Stepfather is unpleasant to your child.
Comparing documents: Will enjoy security in business.
Comparing accounts: Will be surprised by sad news.
Comparing qualities: Danger through a secret.
Comparing likenesses: Will be jilted by a lover.

COMPASSION:
Of compassion: Happiness.
Others having compassion on you: Fortune.
Having compassion for children: Joy.
Having compassion for poor people: Will have bad affairs.
Having compassion for mate: Unsatisfied curiosity.

COMPETE:
Competing with rivals: Will soon experience ups and downs.
Taking part in a competition: Unsuccessful affairs.
Children taking part in a competition: Big joy.
Others competing with you: Loss of money.

COMPLAIN:
Of complaining: You become angry over unimportant things too easily.
Receiving complaints: Unhappiness.
Complaining to others: There is no foundation for your hopes.
Making a legal complaint: Important event, very beneficial.

COMPLEXION:
Of own complexion: Great success.
A beautiful complexion: Avoid rivals.
A person with a white complexion: Glory.
A person with a brown complexion: Will have good friends.
A person with a black complexion: Good times are coming.

COMPLICE:
Having a complice with you: Will be guilty of foolish actions.
Having a good complice: A change in life will soon come.
Doing wrong things with a complice: Suffering because of own foolishness.
Several complices: A false friend is nearby.

COMPLIMENT:
Receiving compliments on business: Will enjoy good profits.
Receiving compliments from a man: Vanity.
Receiving compliments from a woman: Vainglory.
A young girl receiving compliments from a man: Joy.
A young man receiving compliments from a girl: Prosperity.
Complimenting children: Will receive a dog as a gift.
Children complimenting their parents: Family happiness.
Others complimenting you to receive favors: Will soon have a fight.

COMPOSE:
Being a musical composer: Vanity.
A musical composition: Good business.
Composing printing: Extravagant in spending money.

Composing literature: Beware of coming rain.
Composing music yourself: Will receive plenty of money.

CONCEIT:
Being conceited: Will have unhappiness.
Others who are conceited: Will have abundant means.
Children being conceited: Unhappiness.
Mate being conceited: Will have everlasting love.
Friends being conceited: Will take a boat trip.

CONCERT:
Being at a concert as a participant: Unexpected news.
Singing at a concert: Will receive plenty of money.
Others at a concert: Will receive an inheritance.
A sick person dreaming of a concert: Will soon recover.

CONCUBINE:
Of a concubine: Security.
Having a concubine: Will have good enterprises.
Being member of a concubinage: Will live a long time.
A household recognizing a concubine: Will have a good financial condition.

CONDEMN:
Being condemned: Your conscience is not clear.
Having been condemned: Will make a fortune at a lottery.
Relatives being condemned: Will live a long life.
Others being condemned: Death of an acquaintance.

CONDOLENCE:
Receiving condolences: Death.
Relatives giving condolences: Unhappiness.
Receiving condolences from people far away: Fortune.

Offering condolences to the family of a dead person: Sickness.

CONDUCT:
Having good conduct: Loss of a friend.
Having bad conduct: Joy.
Conducting affairs correctly: Inheritance.
Conducting affairs wrong: Will have many changes.
Conducting business: Happiness.
Conducting military troops: Good changes ahead.
Conducting children at school: Family reunion.
Being a conductor of a train or bus: Inheritance.

CONFECTIONS:
Making dainty fancy desserts: Will have pleasure and profit.
Eating confections: Will soon be in love.
Receiving confections as a gift: Will have much success.
Giving confections as a gift: Will be cheated.
Others making confections: Wishes will not be realized.

CONFESS:
Confessing to a crime committed: Happiness.
Confessing to cheating on a mate: Loss of a friend.
Confessing sins to a priest: Must put business in order.
Children confessing to their parents: Financial gains.

CONFESSION:
Making a confession to a friend: Will have great success.
Friends confessing to you: Will have good luck.
Going to confession: Will soon be told a secret.
Receiving confession: Others will reveal their secrets to you.

CONFETTI:
Purchasing confetti: Social disappointment.

Throwing confetti: Will receive a letter with good news.
Others throwing confetti at you: Love and happiness.
People throwing confetti into a crowd: Big business profit.

CONFIDE:
Confiding news to a friend: Misfortune in love affairs.
Confiding in your mate: Must rely upon own vigor.
Confiding in children: Important and very beneficial event to come.
Others confiding in you: Good times are coming.

CONFISCATE:
Having own things confiscated: Dangerous enterprises ahead.
Confiscating other peoples' things: Own affairs are in confusion.
Being released from confiscation: Will make an unexpected gain.
Confiscation of property: Premonitions will be realized.

CONFLICT:
Having a conflict: Will participate in dangerous affairs.
Having a legal conflict: Will soon be tricked.
Losing a conflict: Will make unexpected earnings.
Winning a conflict: Will make a profit through speculations.

CONFUSION:
Of confusion: Will be defrauded of money.
Being confused: Will make an unexpected big profit.
Relatives being in a state of confusion: Family arguments.
Others being in confusion: Will be deceived.

CONGRATULATE:
Of congratulations: Must control passions.
Receiving congratulations: Financial gains.
Receiving congratulations from influ-

ential people: Will enjoy good humor.

Sending congratulations: Joy.

Congratulating children: Approaching money.

Congratulating others: Will have financial gains.

CONGREGATION:
Of a congregation: Will receive very sad news.

Being a member of a congregation: Will incur debts.

Being among a religious congregation: Will be very worried.

Attending meetings of own congregation: Recovery of money.

CONGRESS:
Of congress: Will meet a thief.

Being in congress: A false friend is nearby.

Attending a congressional session: Will soon be cheated.

Others attending congressional session: Will take a long trip abroad.

Being a congressman: Loss of all hopes in business.

CONJURER:
Being a magician: Social disappointments.

A conjurer performing tricks: Will have good clothes.

Being a conjurer and performing tricks: A mystery will be solved.

Others being a conjurer and performing tricks: Advancement in position.

CONQUEST:
Of conquest: You expect too many favors from other people.

Conquest of a woman: Must rely upon own good judgment.

Conquest of a man: Avoid rivals.

A victory: Triumph over enemies.

CONSCIENCE:
Having a clear conscience: Happiness.

Having a worried conscience: All will go well.

Being worried about relatives' conscience: Abundant means.

Other peoples' conscience: Better times are ahead.

CONSENT:
Consenting to another's request: Discovery of lost valuables.

Others consenting to your request: Will have good health.

Refusing consent: Will have a vigorous mind.

CONSOLATION:
Of consolation: Will receive good news from far away.

Receiving consolation from others: Big disgrace is ahead.

Being consoled by children: Bad days ahead.

Consoling others: Future loss of business.

CONSPIRE:
Of conspiring: Will have an automobile accident.

Conspiring with others: You bring on own personal troubles.

Others conspiring against you: Will have uneasiness.

Being a conspirator: Will be badly burned in a fire.

CONSTRUCTION:
Of construction: Will soon be molested.

Constructing own home: Adversity.

Constructing a home for others: Annoyance.

Constructing an altar at a church: Joy and consolation.

Constructing tombs: Sickness.

Constructing roads: Confusion in business affairs.

Constructing docks: Will have many things on your mind.

Constructing other things: Big profit ahead.

CONTAMINATION:
Things being contaminated: Future disgrace.

Having contaminated things: Danger.

Foodstuff being contaminated: Loss in business.

Other things being contaminated: Will have hard times.

CONTENT:
Being content: Better times to follow.
Others being content: A mystery will be solved.
Family being content: Change in your environment.
Children being content: Approaching money.

CONTRABAND:
Of making contraband: Danger through a secret.
Having partners in contraband dealings: Worry will be smoothed away.
Being apprehended while smuggling contraband: Doomed for disappointment.
Selling the smuggled contraband: A serious disaster is ahead.

CONTRACT:
Drawing up a contract: Ill health.
Making a purchase contract: Will have good health right up to death.
Signing a contract of sale: Will be informed of an accident.
Others making contracts: Will pass away very soon.

CONTRADICT:
Contradicting others: Business will be satisfactory.
Being contradicted by friends: Jealous people are nearby.
Being contradicted by relatives: Family arguments.
Being contradicted by mate: Avoid rivals.

CONVENT:
Being in a convent: A happy engagement.
Others being in a convent: Coming ill health.
Becoming a nun in a convent: Happiness, though not a wealthy marriage.

CONVERSATION:
Having a conversation with important people: Prosperity.

Having a conversation with a group of people: Danger of rain.
Having a conversation in the evening with a group: Gossip.
Having a conversation with a priest: Hard days are ahead.

CONVERT:
Of converting: Must endure tribulation.
Converting to another religion: Will have a quiet, happy life.
Converting others to own ideas: Very beneficial and important event to come.
Converting foreign money: Will fall into disgrace.

CONVICT:
Of a convict: Will live a long life.
Being a convict: Will be cheated by friends.
Convicts who are in prison: You have a loyal friend.
Convicts escaping from prison: Shame and sorrow.

CONVICTED:
Being convicted in Court: Prosperity is on the way.
Not being convicted: Good financial matters.
Others being convicted: Business will be satisfactory.

CONVULSION:
Having convulsions: Prosperous married life.
Members of family having convulsions: Good financial matters.
Others having convulsions: Will be invited to a dance.

COOK:
Being a cook: Poverty.
Being the cook at a restaurant: Will be cheated by friends.
A male cook: You expect too many favors of other people.
A female cook: Great joy is in store.
A young girl being a cook: Will soon become engaged.

COOKIES:
Making cookies: Will receive good news.
Buying cookies: Must rely on own good judgment.
Others making cookies: You enjoy sports.
Receiving cookies as a gift: Will have a prosperous married life.
Giving cookies as a gift: You should mend your ways in life.

COOKING:
Of cooking: Divorce is in sight.
A man cooking: Will be invited to a party.
A woman cooking: Beware of treachery.
Others cooking: Will benefit in the near future.
Several people cooking at the same time: Success in love.

COP:
Being with a policeman: Ambitions will be realized.
Other people with a cop: Good news is on the way.
Being a cop: Troubles caused from prying into others' affairs.

COPPER:
Of copper: Present desires are impossible to realize.
Buying copper: A false friend is nearby.
Selling copper: Will make plenty of money.
Handling copper: Will receive unexpected visit of important person.

COPULATE:
Of uniting in sexual intercourse: Happiness is assured.
Others who are copulating: Abundant means.
Yourself having sexual intercourse: Financial gains.

COPY:
Copying a letter: Happiness in the home.
Copying legal papers: Everything will work out as desired.

Others copying: Will have emotional sorrow.
Being in the copy business: Misery and troubles.

CORAL:
Of coral: An old friend will return soon.
Wearing coral: Will meet with a former sweetheart.
Buying corals: Will receive a letter with money.

CORD:
Knotting a cord: Friendships will be strengthened.
Unraveling a cord: An engagement will be broken.
Unraveling many knots in a cord: Will receive an important gift.

CORK:
Removing a cork from a bottle: Will hear good news from a friend.
Pushing a cork into a bottle: Will have an unexpected visitor.
Having several corks: Will soon receive a gift.

CORKSCREW:
Using a corkscrew: Illness.
Others using a corkscrew: A mystery will be solved.
Opening a bottle with a corkscrew: Danger through a secret.

CORN:
Corn growing: Will have plenty of money.
Eating corn: Success in all your affairs.
Harvesting corn: Will hear good news.
A field with large ears of corn: Big financial gains.
A field without ears on the stalks: Doomed for disappointment.
A rich person dreaming of eating bread made of corn: Wealth.
A poor person dreaming of eating bread made of corn: Poverty.

CORNER:
Being in a corner: Doomed for disappointment.

Others being in a corner: Loneliness and trouble.

Putting articles in a corner: A mystery will be solved.

Putting a child in the corner: You are not sincere.

CORNET:

Hearing a cornet played: Family quarrels.

Playing a cornet: Discovery of lost valuables.

Hearing children playing a cornet: Change for the better.

Buying a cornet: Joy without profit.

CORNS:

Having corns on the feet: Fortunate business venture.

Cutting corns from the feet: Business prosperity.

Cutting the corns on others' feet: You have a loyal friend.

CORONATION:

The coronation of a king or queen: Will receive unexpected fortune.

Coronation of a beauty contest queen: Are deceived by closest friend.

Daughter being crowned queen: Neighbors can be relied upon.

CORPORATION:

A strong corporation: Will have dominion over people.

Having a corporation: You enjoy amusements too much.

Having a businessmen's corporation: Don't be swayed by present events.

Having a corporation of armed people: Will have good enterprises.

CORPSE:

The corpse of a relative: Unhappy love affairs.

The corpse of other people: Loss of money.

Several corpses: Peril of death.

A corpse in the water: Arguments with lover.

A corpse with clothes on: Happiness.

A corpse being lowered into a grave: Separation from a loved one.

A corpse at a morgue: Marriage or other happy events.

The corpse of an animal: Business troubles.

CORSET:

Of own corset: Another person is enjoying what you desired.

Wife's corset: Avoid rivals.

The corset of others: Will be jilted by lover.

The corset of sweetheart: Temptation will come.

Losing a corset: Will find a new person for whom you care.

Buying a corset: Will have a vigorous mind.

COSTUME:

Having several different costumes: Will live a long life.

A man in a riding costume: A great effort will be required of you.

A woman in a riding costume: Pleasant work and good news.

The costume of a priest: Avoid rivals.

Officers in uniforms: Will realize high ambitions.

Having masquerade costumes: Important and very beneficial events to come.

Others in different costumes: Will escape an unhappy position.

COTTAGE:

Living in a cottage: Better times to follow.

Others living in a cottage: Will receive good news.

An empty cottage: Loneliness and trouble.

COUCH:

Of an empty couch: Troubles ahead.

Sitting on a couch alone: An enemy is seeking your ruin.

Sitting on a couch with husband: Triumph over enemies.

Sitting on a couch with a loved one: Danger in love matters.

Sitting on a couch with a friend: Hard work awaits.

Sitting on a couch with children: You have great will power.

Sitting on a couch with a dog: You have faithful friends.

COUGHING:
Of coughing: Indiscreet people are nearby.
That you are coughing: Good health.
Others coughing: Good friendship.
Children coughing: Good earnings.

COUNCILMAN:
Being a councilman: An enemy is seeking your ruin.
Being in the company of a councilman: Do not speculate.
Having dealings with a councilman: Will improve your estate.

COUNT:
Being a count: People are testing your character.
Being in the company of a count: Do not speculate.
Dealing with a count: Opposition in love affairs.
Being friendly with a count: Will go to prison.
Of a countess: Humiliation.

COUNTERFEIT:
Receiving counterfeit money: A mystery will be solved.
Making counterfeit money: Will receive a promotion at the job.
Handling counterfeit money: Will be asked to help someone.

COUNTERPANE:
A bedspread being torn: Will have an accident.
A bedspread being pulled from the bed: Better times will follow.
A bedspread being dirty: Will have very good fortune.
Buying a new bedspread: Big love and friendship.

COUNTING:
Of counting: Ambitions will be satisfied.
Counting money: Profit.
Counting different items: Will suffer in own affairs.
Counting and finding items missing: Results in business are unsure.

Others counting: Joy.
Counting men: Jealousy.
Counting women: Will be tormented.

COUNTRY:
Going to the country: Danger of losing an estate.
Going on a picnic in the country: Danger of death.
Living in the country: Persecution by those trying to take an estate.
Having business in the country: Joy.
Being in the country with the family: Profit.
Company visiting you in the country: Good health.
The country at night: Melancholy and weakness.
The country on a bright sunny day: Illness of the mind.
Going to the country from a small town: Will take a long trip.
Going to the country from a big city: Will receive letter with sad news.
A vegetable garden in the country: Unhappiness.
Growing corn in the country: Will enjoy great financial profits.
Growing barley in the country: Great riches and happiness ahead.
Country property being well situated: Happiness.
Family giving you a fine piece of property: Will have a beautiful wife.
Property being very fertile: Will have a good and honest wife.
Having a large piece of property: Riches proportioned to size of property.

COURT:
Being in court: Important and very beneficial events to come.
Going to court: Business losses.
Having been in court: Loss of prestige.
Being requested to go to court: High consideration of others.
Being punished by a court: Travel and prosperity.
Being acquitted by a court: Serious disaster is ahead.

COURTED:
Being courted: Doomed for disappointment.
Courting someone else: Love affairs are not good.
Being courted by a married person: Good luck.
Being courted by an unmarried person: Will have happiness.

COURT PLASTER:
Handling court plaster: Recovery from an illness.
Binding a cut with court plaster: Will improve your estate.
Having court plaster: Will receive an unexpected visit.
Buying court plaster: You expect too many favors from others.

COUSIN:
Of a cousin: Relatives will ask you for help.
Several of own cousins: Misfortune in love affairs.
Being in the company of a cousin: Unexpected bad news.
Being in the company of all your cousins: Danger in love.

COVER:
A table cover: Will receive a favor from important person.
A bed cover: Great honors and good fame.
Covering a wagon: Gossip.
Coverings for furniture: Misery.

COW:
Of a cow: Prosperity.
Several cows: Great prosperity in all ventures.
Being chased by a cow but escaping: Watch own affairs carefully.
Milking a cow: Will make good financial profits.

COWSLIPS:
Of this wild flower: Unexpected good news.
Holding cowslips in the hands: Will have a love affair.
Picking cowslips: Will receive a long-awaited letter.

CRAB:
A live crab: Will have a new lover.
A dead or boiled crab: Disappointment with lover.
Many crabs in a fish market: Danger is ahead.
Eating crab: Avoid rivals.

CRAB APPLE:
Having crab apples: Will be happy in love affairs.
Eating crab apples: Will be wounded and have unhappiness.
Buying crab apples: Profit.
A crab apple tree: Will have good earnings.

CRADLE:
An empty cradle: Misfortune will come soon.
A cradle with a baby in it: Avoid rivals.
A lovely baby in a cradle: Big prosperity.
Rocking own baby in a cradle: Illness in the family.
A young woman dreaming of a cradle: Reconsider your present conduct.

CRAMPS:
Having cramps: Will have a fit of temper.
Others having cramps: Worry.
Relatives having cramps: Family quarrels.
Children having cramps: Riches.

CRANE:
Being a crane operator: Troubles are ahead.
A crane lifting heavy weights: Will lose personal property.
Lifting something with a crane: Loneliness and trouble.

CRAWL:
Of crawling: Love affair will not prosper.
Others crawling: Doomed for a big disappointment.
Crawling over rough places: Good opportunities have been neglected.

CRAZY:

Being crazy: Will be the object of much flattery.

Relatives being crazy: Will receive many costly gifts.

Other people being crazy: A mystery will be solved.

CREEK:

Of a creek: Will have new experiences and take a short trip.

A dry creek: Will have a big disappointment.

Others in a creek: Another person is enjoying what you hoped to win.

CREMATE:

Being cremated: Business failure if advice of others is followed.

Requesting cremation at death: Abundant means.

Mate being cremated: Poverty.

Cremating a member of the family: Will receive a legacy.

Others being cremated: Will possess abounding health.

CREPE:

A person dressed in crepe material: Must endure deep sorrows.

Handling crepe: Lovers' quarrels and separation may follow.

A widow dressed in crepe: Will have a happy life.

CREW:

Of a crew at work on a vessel: Expect bad news.

Of a crew not working on a ship: Avoid your rivals.

Members of a crew on shore: Good events will come as a surprise.

CRIBBAGE:

Playing a game of cribbage: Important decisions must be made.

Watching a game of cribbage: Your advice will be sought.

Winning a game of cribbage: Will escape a present danger.

Losing a game of cribbage: Warning of troubles.

CRIES:

Hearing happy and joyous cries: Expect bad news.

Hearing cries of trouble or distress: Everything will go well.

Hearing cries of children: Change for the better.

CRIME:

Of a crime being committed: Another person is enjoying what you desired.

Being caught while committing a crime: Will be sorely tempted.

Others committing a crime: Danger through a secret.

CRIMINAL:

Of a criminal: Troubles are ahead.

Being a criminal: Family quarrels.

A criminal being arrested: Big catastrophe ahead.

A criminal being executed: Triumph over enemies.

CRIMSON:

Of the color crimson: Unexpected pleasant news from a friend.

Using things of a crimson color: Will take a long trip.

Materials of crimson color: Good times are coming.

Buying dresses of crimson color: Dignity and distinction.

CRIPPLE:

Of a crippled person: Will receive help from an unexpected source.

Being crippled: Kind people are nearby.

Relatives being crippled: Warning of trouble.

Child being crippled: Will have happiness.

Several crippled people: Triumph over enemies.

Members of family being crippled: Expect too many favors from others.

Friends being crippled: Will become a beggar.

Being badly crippled: Will have annoyances over a prolonged lawsuit.

A crippled person limping: People are talking badly about you.

A crippled rich woman: Unsuccessful business affairs.

A crippled man in prison: Business will be at a standstill.

A crippled woman in prison: Will be duly punished for wrongdoings.

CROCHET:
Of crocheting: Troubles caused by prying into affairs of others.

Sweetheart crocheting: You are very ambitious.

Others crocheting: Will have a change in environment.

CROCODILE:
Of a crocodile: You are in the grip of a deceitful people.

Killing a crocodile: Warning of troubles ahead.

Many crocodiles: Big catastrophe ahead.

CROCUS:
Of this flower: Suitable time to pursue courtship.

Having a crocus: Avoid rivals.

Receiving a bouquet of crocus: Good luck to one for whom you care.

Giving a bouquet of crocus: Will be very fortunate in everything.

CROSS:
Of a cross: Warning of trouble.

Having a cross on the feet: Will have emotional sorrow.

A cross on a grave: You need help.

Wearing a cross: Will have the protection of friends.

Others wearing a cross: Will be in misery.

A cross in the church: Big joy.

Praying on a cross: Will receive wishes.

CROSS-PURPOSE:
Being at cross-purposes with someone: Joy, pleasure, and health.

Others being at cross-purposes: Accord among friends.

Enemies being at cross-purposes: You are being deceived.

CROSSROAD:
Unmarried people dreaming of a crossroad: Will soon be engaged.

Married person dreaming of a crossroad: Loss of loved mate.

Relatives being at a crossroad: Recovery from illness.

Friends being at a crossroad: Secret enmity of some person.

CROW:
Of a crow: Disappointment in everything.

Crows flying: Grief and misfortune.

Crows flying over the head: Death in the family.

A large flock of crows: Serious disaster ahead.

Hearing the croak of crows: Illness of children.

A woman dreaming of a crow: Death of her husband.

A man dreaming of a crow: Death of his wife.

CROWD:
Of a crowd: Happiness is assured.

Being in a crowd: Advancement within position.

Friends being in a crowd: New interests and surroundings.

Enemies being in a crowd: Beware of jealous people.

CROWN:
Having a crown on the head: Will benefit through other people.

Being crowned: Will have the friendship of important people.

A royal crown: Will have plenty of happiness.

Placing a crown on another's head: You are worthy of advancement.

Having a gold crown on the head: Big protection of high officials.

Having a crown of flowers: Big success.

Having a crown of iron: Beware of business transactions.

Having a crown of tin: Loss of fortune.

Having a crown with a cross on it: Will benefit through a death.

CRUCIFIX:
Of a crucifix: Will be involved in trouble with other people.

Having a crucifix: Will have big happiness.

Praying to a crucifix: Will receive high honors.

CRUEL:
Being cruel to others: One near to you is in need of help.

Others being cruel to you: Will receive good news.

Others causing cruelty: Unhappiness in all affairs.

CRUMBS:
Cleaning crumbs from the table: Big joy.

Feeding crumbs to birds: Temptation will come.

Birds eating crumbs: Will receive valuable gifts.

Cooking with bread crumbs: Must rely on own good judgment.

CRUSH:
Crushing something: Big losses.

Crushing food: Will enjoy good humor.

Other people crushing food: Will have good days ahead.

Crushing food for children: A relative will have a terrible death.

Crushing insects: Will have plenty of money.

Crushing strawberries: Misery.

CRUST:
Being reduced to eating crusts: Business affairs will be prosperous.

Others eating crusts: Change for the better.

Making a crust pudding: Abundant means.

CRUTCHES:
Using crutches: You will be self-supporting.

Others using crutches: Will not achieve all you hoped from your labors.

Being able to walk without crutches: Will receive plenty of money.

CRYING:
Of crying: Domestic trials are on the way.

Others crying: Will have to render aid to others.

Members of the family crying: Will receive good news.

CRYSTAL:
Buying crystal: Will soon be given nice gifts.

Having crystal: Change for the better.

Being given crystal: Happiness is assured.

CUBS:
Of one cub: A friendly hint will be given.

Many cubs: Will have emotional sorrow.

Many cubs in a cage: Death of an enemy.

CUCKOO:
Of a cuckoo singing: Misfortune in love affairs.

A cuckoo shouting: Joy and good health.

Many cuckoos: Important and beneficial events to come.

CUCUMBER:
Of cucumbers: Violent love.

Buying cucumbers: Recovery from an illness.

Growing cucumbers: Good health.

Eating cucumbers: Abundant means.

Using cucumbers to make a salad: Avoid spending money for foolish things.

Being ill and dreaming of cucumbers: Recovery.

CUP:
Drinking from a cup: Good times are coming.

Having an empty cup: Will have emotional sorrow.

Breaking a cup: Death of an enemy.

Having an elegant cup: Fortune in love affairs.

Drinking from a gold cup: Advancement in own affairs.

Receiving a cup as a gift: You have faithful friends.

CUPBOARD:
An empty cupboard: Business will not prosper.
A full cupboard: Change for the better.
Putting things in a cupboard: Will recover from losses.
Taking things out of a cupboard: You have many loyal friends.

CUPID:
Of cupid: Will receive sad news.
Several cupids: Will find a hidden treasure.
Venus giving birth to cupid: Infirmity or death.

CUPPING:
Of the process of drawing blood from surface of body: Speedy recovery.
Using cupping process on the shoulders: Will practice usury.
Using cupping process on animals: Increase in profits.

CURATE:
Of a curate: Disappointment in love affairs.
Being with a curate: Will receive an honorable position.
Many curates: Will receive a letter from abroad.
Confiding in a curate: Expect unhappy news.

CURBSTONE:
The curbstone on a river bank: An outsider is interfering in affairs.
The curbstone on the bank of a lake: Will have fun with friends.
The curbstone of a street: Must complete a present job in a hurry.
The curbstone of a house: Someone is attempting to bring harm.

CURLS:
Having curls: Complete change in own affairs.
Putting up own curls: New environment and better times in view.
Others putting up your curls: Suitable time to push your suit.
Other people having curls: Will have emotional sorrow.

Rolling up curls: Loss of a friend.
Curling daughter's hair: Will have great motherly love.
A man dreaming of someone curling hair: His wife is unfaithful.

CURRANTS:
Black currants: Warning of trouble.
Brown currants: Advancement in own business.
Buying dry currants: An enemy is seeking your ruin.
Buying currant jelly: Will be deceived by friends.
Cooking currants in pudding or cake: Wealth.

CURRY COMB:
Of a curry comb: Happiness.
Using a curry comb on a horse: Will receive good advice from friends.
Others using a curry comb on a horse: Will receive help from a stranger.
Cleaning a curry comb: Will receive unexpected money.

CURSE:
Of cursing: Will have bad luck.
Being cursed: Ambitions will be realized.
Hearing curses: Difficulties have been surmounted.
Hearing others curse you: Warning of love troubles.

CURTAIN:
Of many curtains: Own curiosity will bring damages.
Pulling a curtain aside: Will be warned in time.
Others pulling curtains aside: Warning of trouble.
Putting up new curtains: Will entertain a prominent guest.

CUSHION:
Having a few cushions: Will make a good marriage.
Having plenty of cushions: Difficulties and business worries.
Cushions belonging to others: Discord among friends.
Lying on several cushions: Change for the better.

CUT:
Being cut: Will be betrayed by a friend.
A cut healing: Will have good earnings.
A cut not healing: Will be paid for your services.
Treating a cut: Big joy.
Children being cut: Approaching money.
Cutting off the head of a bird: Will have pleasures.
Cutting off the head of animals: Joy.
Cutting off the head of another person: Revenge will be sought.
Cutting stones: Profit.
Cutting grass and shrubs: Fortune in business.
Cutting with a saw or file: Unpleasant events are ahead.
Being a cutter: Infidelity.

CUTTLEFISH:
Of cuttlefish: Failure of enemies.
Many cuttlefish: An important decision must be made in a hurry.
Buying cuttlefish: Change in environment.
Eating cuttlefish: Good times are coming.

CYCLING:
Of cycling: Will make a visit at some distant place.
Others cycling: Luck and prosperity.

Relatives cycling: Misfortune in love affairs.
Children cycling: Abundant means.

CYCLONE:
Of a cyclone: Intense sorrow will come to you.
Being in the area of a cyclone: Warning of troubles.
Property being damaged by a cyclone: Social activities of a happy nature.
Ships at sea being damaged by a cyclone: Death of an enemy.

CYPRESS:
Of this heavy rich satin: Troubles caused by prying into others' affairs.
Having cypress material: Delay in the conclusion of your business.
Buying a dress made of cypress: Advancement in financial position.
A cypress tree: A friend is trying to help you secretly.

CYPRUS:
Taking a trip to Cyprus: Change for the better.
Being among the people of Cyprus: Advancement in own position.
Buying Cyprus wine: Dignity and distinction.
Drinking Cyprus wine: Abundance of money.
Selling Cyprus wine: An illegitimate son will be born.
Of the island of Cyprus: Joy.

D

DAFFODILS:
Of daffodils: Happiness in love affairs.
Daffodils growing out of doors: Will have a long happy future.
Receiving daffodils as a gift: Happiness is assured.

DAGGER:
Of a dagger: Expect news from an absent person.

Many daggers: Beware of treachery.
Others with daggers: Happiness is assured.
Carrying a dagger: Advancement in own position.
Attacking someone with a dagger: Own plans will be realized.
Being wounded by a dagger: Another person is enjoying what you hoped for.

DAHLIA:
Of a dahlia: Will be very happy with lover.
Many dahlias in a garden: Avoid rivals.
Having them in a vase in the home: Financial affairs will improve.

DAIRY:
Of a dairy: Good luck.
Buying produce from a dairy: A change for the better.
Working at a dairy: Failure of enemies.

DAISIES:
Of daisies in a garden: You are headed for success.
Picking daisies: Great happiness in love.
Having them in a vase in the home: Important and very beneficial events.

DAMASCUS:
Going to Damascus: Will receive a legacy.
Coming from Damascus: Will receive unexpected money.
Buying damask woven silk: Will have many friends.
Having damask silk with flowered pattern: Wealth.
Having damask deep pink roses: Affairs will be booming.

DAMSON:
Having this small dark purple plum at home: Anxiety.
Damson hanging on a tree: Important and very beneficial event to come.
Picking damson from the tree: Avoid rivals.
Eating damson: Will have troubles caused by false companions.

DANCE:
Of dancing: Success in love.
Others dancing: Great success in business.
Little children dancing: Much joy and a happy home.
Watching friends dance: Good news concerning a friend.

Watching others dance: Will receive good news.
Dancing fancy dances: Big prosperity.
Dancing with great grace: Success in enterprises.
Dancing before sick people: Change for the better.
Dancing on a steel rope: Joy and loving children.

DANDELIONS:
Of dandelions: Happiness in love affairs.
Picking many dandelions: Will be very fortunate in love affairs.
Buying dandelions: Will be invited to a party.
Growing dandelions: Big joy.

DANGER:
Being in danger: Success and honor.
Facing danger: You may expect success.
Avoiding danger: Troubles will come to you.
A lover being in danger: Failure.
A married person being in danger: Disaster is ahead.

DARK:
Being in the dark: Difficulties ahead.
Falling and hurting yourself in the dark: Expect changes for the worse.
Succeeding in groping way out to the light: Big success.
Others being in the dark: Loneliness and trouble.
Children being in the dark: Illness.
Walking in the dark: Recovery of money.

DARNING:
Of darning: Will be introduced to a new and kind friend.
Others darning: A mystery will be solved.
Members of the family darning: Will live a long life.

DATES:
Eating dates: You will experience want.
Buying dates: Will be admired by a member of the opposite sex.

90

Receiving a gift of dates: Troubles caused by false companions.
Giving a gift of dates: Will have to take a disagreeable journey.

DAUGHTER:
A parent dreaming of a daughter: Pleasure and harmony in the home.
Own daughter playing: Happiness is assured.
Several daughters gathered together: Advancement in own position.
Talking to a daughter: Will have emotional sorrow.
A mother dreaming of her only daughter: Will become pregnant soon.
An adopted daughter: Serious disaster ahead.

DAWN:
A very clear dawn: Will receive unexpected help.
A cloudy dawn: Death of an enemy.
A rainy dawn: Good times are coming.

DAYS:
It being your birthday: Will have a short life.
Own name day: Great joy and pleasure.
A holiday during the week: Fortune.
A holiday on Sunday: Will receive money.
Pay day: Will receive an injustice.
Election day: Do not despair, troubles will soon be over.

DEAD:
Being dead: Happiness and wealth are in store.
Dead bodies: A wedding will take place.
Kissing the dead: Will have a long life.
Speaking to a dead relative: Will receive news from a living relative.
Speaking to a dead friend: Change for the better.
A dead person speaking to you: Death of a relative.
Touching a dead person: Will receive sorrowful news.
An enemy being dead: News of a birth.

An unknown person dead: Inheritance and prosperity.
A dead person holding you: Death is near.
Fighting with a dead person: Sickness.
Talking with a dead person: Will live a long life.
Being in the company of a dead person: Loss of friends.
A dead person lying in an open coffin: Will have indigestion.
Giving a gift to a dead person: Loss of money.
Receiving a gift from a dead person: Slow recovery of money.
Helping to put a dead person in a grave: Success over enemies.
A dead person that is really alive: Loss of legal matters.
A person dying after already thought dead: Big sorrow in the family.
A person dying and does not talk: Death will come soon.

DEAF:
Being deaf: A big fortune is coming to you.
Other people who are deaf: Change for the better.
Going deaf very suddenly: Advancement in own position.

DEATH:
The death of a pregnant woman: Will receive a fortune from abroad.
The death of a young girl or boy: Will have a big happy family event.
The death of a wife: Separation from friends.
The death of a husband: Death of a relative.
Wanting death: Will have good health for a long time.
Someone coming to life after death: High honor.
The death of several people: Big happiness.

DEATH MARCH:
Hearing a death march played: Good luck for one for whom you care.
Playing the death march: Important and very beneficial event to come.

Military people playing the death march: A false friend is nearby.

DEATH WATCH:
Keeping a death watch: Immediate marriage.
Keeping death watch with a criminal before execution: Big joy.
Keeping death watch with a dying relative: Inheritance.

DEATH'S HEAD:
The skull of a dead person: May discover some hidden secret.
The skull of a relative: Luck and prosperity.
Holding the skull of a dead person in hands: Death of an enemy.

DEBTS:
Paying debts: Important and very beneficial event to come.
Owing debts to other people: You are goodhearted.
Others repaying debts owed you: Expect a loss.
Having no intention of paying debts: Catastrophe ahead.

DECEMBER:
Of the month of December during that month: Will be happy in life.
Of December during other months: Good financial revenues.
Being born in December: Will live a long life.
Being born on December 25th: Will have blessings from God.
Children being born in December: Rapid success in life.

DECK:
Being on the deck of a ship: Big joy.
Being on the deck of a ship during a storm: Troubles are ahead.
Being on the deck of a ship during calm weather: Unhappiness is awaiting.
Being on deck with a member of opposite sex: Unhappy marriage.

DECORATE:
Decorating own room: Losses in business affairs.
Decorating a house: Loss of a friend.

Decorating a window: Take advantage of opportunities.
Decorating a show window: Change for the better.
Decorating a grave: Will have very little joy.

DEDUCT:
Deducting valuable things: Good results in business.
Deducting money from bills owed: Will soon have a family argument.
Others deducting money from bills owed you: Assist one who needs money.
Deducting amounts illegally: Will have big fortune.

DEEDS:
Signing a deed: You are in danger.
Having already signed a deed: Loss of money.
Others signing a deed to you: Loss of affection.
Receiving payment of a deed: Will have good health until death.

DEER:
Of a deer: Will receive glad news.
Several deer: Will receive plenty of money.
A herd of deer: Great friendship.
A herd of deer running away: Financial distress.
Killing a deer: Will receive an inheritance.
Others killing a deer: Will have good earnings.
A deer and a rabbit on the run: Avoid rivals.
A deer jumping: Troubles ahead.
Having the horns of a deer: Will be cheated by friends.
Having the skin of a deer: Will receive inheritance from elderly person.
Shouting because of missing a deer: Will go into bankruptcy.
Eating the meat of a male deer: Difficult times ahead.

DEFEND:
Defending yourself: You have one loyal friend.

Others defending themselves: Will be offended.

Being unable to defend yourself: Will live a long life.

Defending relatives: Important and beneficial event to come.

Defending children: Luck and prosperity.

DEFORM:

Being deformed: Shame and sorrow.

Others who are deformed: Beware of false appearances of others.

Children being deformed: Small family disagreement.

Relatives being deformed: Be on guard against spiteful gossip.

A young lady dreaming of being deformed: Will break her engagement.

DELICATE:

Having delicate health: Change for the better.

Others having delicate health: Will be vigorous in business activity.

Children having delicate health: Avoid rivals.

Relatives having delicate health: Warning of troubles.

DELIGHT:

Being delighted: Excessive happiness.

Others being delighted: Expect troubles at home and business worries.

Relatives being delighted: Triumph over enemies.

Children being delighted: Financial gains.

DELIRIOUS:

Being delirious: Danger through a secret.

Others being delirious: A friend is trying to help you secretly.

Relatives being delirious: Must control your passions.

Children being delirious: Approaching money.

DELUGE:

Of a deluge of rain: Bad luck in love affairs.

Others being in a deluge: Will soon have an accident.

Home being lost in a deluge: Luck and prosperity.

Crops being lost in a deluge: Financial disaster ahead.

DEMOCRACY:

Of a democracy: Danger of fire.

Belonging to a democracy: False friends are nearby.

Forming a democracy: Will enjoy a long life.

Belonging to a democratic party: Will win a lawsuit.

DEMOLISH:

Of demolishing: People are talking against you.

A house being demolished: Will have successful ventures.

A building being demolished: Will be accused of wrongdoings.

People demolishing machinery: Will receive money soon.

DENTIST:

Being in a dentist's chair: Will have cause to question friends' sincerity.

Others in a dentist's chair: Business partners are not sincere.

Children in a dentist's chair: Will hear false reports about friends.

Friends in a dentist's chair: Misfortune in love affairs.

DEPART:

Of departing: Will barely avoid an unhappy event.

Departing for a place of pleasure: Danger of losing property.

Loved ones departing: Failure of projects.

Departing with others: Death of an enemy.

Others departing unwillingly: Unhappiness or death.

DERBY:

Watching a derby: Will receive big fortune.

Others watching a derby: Triumph over enemies.

Having a horse running in a derby: Avoid rivals.

Attending a derby with a loved one: Approaching good times.

Attending a derby with other people: Failure of enemies.

DESCENDANT:
Of descendants: Unhappy days are ahead.
Talking to a descendant: Postponement of success.
Being the first in line of descendants: Family quarrels.
The descendants of other people: Will live a long life.

DESERT:
Traveling across a desert: Shame and sorrow.
Crossing a desert in a sand storm: Difficulties with a cherished plan.
Crossing a desert in bad weather: Will be cheated by friends.
Crossing a desert with others: Accord among friends.
Others crossing a desert: Warning of trouble.

DESERTION:
Deserting the home: Will incur large losses.
Deserting your wife: Unhappiness.
Deserting your children: Will receive news from an absent friend.
Deserting your business: Will discover the truth of a secret.
Deserting from the army: Unhappiness in love.

DESIGN:
Of designing: Will receive a proposition and turn it down.
Designing a dress: Will discover a secret.
Designing a sketch: An enemy is attempting to cause harm.
Designing a plan: Will be involved in an argument.
Children designing pictures: Will win a lawsuit.

DESIRE:
Having a desire: Will receive bad news.
Desiring something unobtainable: Abundance.
Receiving something desired: Dishonor.

Desiring someone's wife: Beware of being hurt by coming events.
Desiring someone's husband: Happiness in new love.
A woman desiring to have children: Unfriendliness of other people.
Desiring money: Loss in business.

DESK:
Working at a desk: Bad luck.
Working on an open desk: Expect good news.
A closed desk: Will have emotional sorrow.
Others working at several desks: A mystery will be solved.
Working on a desk at home: Happiness is assured.
Working at a lawyer's desk: Advancement in own position.
Working at an accountant's desk: Overwork on scientific matters.

DESPAIR:
Of despair: Luck and prosperity.
Being in despair: Domestic happiness.
Not being in despair: Abundant means.
Others being in despair: Will have a change for the better.

DESSERT:
Having dessert alone: Avoid rivals.
Having dessert with others: Accord among friends.
Others eating dessert without you: Death of an enemy.
Not enjoying a dessert: Expect business losses.

DESTROY:
Of destroying something: Shame and sorrow.
Others destroying things: Big catastrophe ahead.
Having destroyed something: Warning of troubles.
Somebody having destroyed your things: Triumph over enemies.

DESTRUCTION:
Of destruction: Misfortune in business.
Causing destruction to many things: Will have fights with friends.

Army causing destruction: Small fights in the future.

Others causing destruction: You have foolish desires.

DETECTIVE:

Being questioned by a detective: You have one loyal friend.

Others being with a detective: Loneliness and trouble.

Others being taken away by a detective: Death of an enemy.

Being blamed by a detective: Financial gains.

DETEST:

Of detesting something: Abundant means.

Detesting other people: Will have emotional sorrow.

Being detested by others: Good luck to one for whom you care.

Detesting a particular person: Will quarrel with an old friend.

Detesting a relative: Family quarrels.

DEVIL:

Of the devil: Travel and prosperity.

A young girl dreaming of the devil: A happy marriage will occur soon.

An elderly sick person dreaming of the devil: Expect trouble.

Poor people dreaming of the devil: Big catastrophe ahead.

Children dreaming of Satan: Sickness.

The devil with a big horn and long tail: Misfortune in love affairs.

Hitting the devil and vanquishing him: Triumph over enemies.

Having a conversation with the devil: Will be cheated by friends.

Fighting with the devil: You are in much danger.

Being taken away by the devil: Serious disaster ahead.

Wounding the devil: Abundant means.

Being chased by the devil and running away: Legal attachments.

Seeing the devil while praying: Will resist temptation.

DEVOTION:

Praying with devotion: Will have joy and happiness.

Others praying with devotion: Change for the better.

Wife and husband having devotion for each other: Happiness is assured.

Children having devotion for parents: Important and beneficial events to come.

DEW:

Seeing the dew at dawn: You have one loyal friend.

Refreshing dew falling: Abundant means.

Dew on dead bodies: Big joy.

DIAMONDS:

Of diamonds: Failure in own personal matters.

Having diamonds: Fortunate dealings in business and speculations.

Losing diamonds: Poverty and ill health.

Finding diamonds: You have a good lover.

Owning many diamonds: Success and honor will be conferred upon you.

Others wearing diamonds: Will make a big profit.

Buying diamonds: Will have emotional sorrow.

Selling diamonds: Serious disaster ahead.

Stealing diamonds: Will have big business losses.

Of fake diamonds: Death of an enemy.

DICE:

Playing with dice: Fortune will change.

Winning while playing with dice: Will receive an inheritance.

Losing while playing with dice: Losses through speculation.

Others winning while playing with dice: Recovery from loss of money.

Others cheating while playing with dice: Abundant means.

DICTIONARY:

Consulting a dictionary: Triumph over enemies.

Others consulting a dictionary: Quarrels and loss of a friend.

Children studying with a dictionary: Luck and prosperity.

Buying a dictionary: Change in environment.

DIET:
Of dieting: Dissolution of hopes.

Being weak from dieting: Loss of wealth.

Dieting too much: Danger of sickness.

Others who are dieting: You have a kind heart.

Friends dieting: Will have a lawsuit.

DIFFICULTY:
Being in great difficulty of any kind: Change for the better.

Having personal difficulties: Good times are coming.

Having financial difficulties: Will receive money.

Having dangerous difficulties in own life: Big happiness.

Sweetheart having difficulties: Will surely be kind and agreeable.

Others having difficulty: All will be well.

Relatives having difficulty: Happiness is assured.

DIGGING:
Of digging: Life will have many ups and downs.

Digging in good soil: Will have plenty of money.

Digging in loose soil: Plans will succeed.

Others digging: Advancement in own position.

A professional digger: Change in environment.

Digging graves: Death of an enemy.

Digging holes for trees: Accord among friends.

Digging up a dead person's body: Infidelity.

Digging out someone who was buried alive: Terrible misfortune.

DILIGENT:
Being diligent: Good fortune.

Children being diligent at school: Will be offended by others.

Employees being diligent: Will have an accident in the street.

Being diligent with personal affairs: Will receive good news.

DINING HALL:
A hotel dining room: Joy.

A military dining hall: Will have a quiet old age.

A prisoner's dining hall: You should mend your ways in life.

A hospital dining hall: Important and very beneficial event to come.

Being with others in a dining hall: Unhappiness in love affairs.

DINNER:
Having dinner: Warning of trouble.

Having friends for dinner: Triumph over enemies.

Having relatives for dinner: Must control your nerves.

Having dinner with a large group: Will enjoy companionship of friends.

Others giving a dinner party: You have one loyal friend.

DIPLOMA:
Having a diploma: Will lead to success.

Others having a diploma: Temptation will come to you.

Children having a diploma: Will live a long life.

Being handed a diploma: Own talents are being neglected.

DIRECTOR:
Being a director: Will receive good news.

Being appointed as director: Will win a lawsuit.

Being director of a corporation: Joy and profit.

Resigning position as director: Humiliation.

DIRT:
Dirt being thrown at you: Will suffer abuse.

Throwing dirt at others: Serious disaster ahead.

Clothes being dirty: Will escape some contagious disease.

Stepping into dirt: Will be leaving your abode.

Falling into the dirt: Affairs will soon begin to prosper.

Being dirty yourself: Illness.

Others who are dirty: Illness in the family.

Dirt created by humans: Discovery of lost valuables.

Dirt in a church: Will be punished by God.

DISAPPEAR:
Of disappearing: Will be robbed.

Realizing things have disappeared: Will have a large profit.

Mate disappearing: Will have a happy life.

Money or jewelry disappearing: Money will come easily.

Friends disappearing: Sickness in the family.

DISAPPOINT:
Being disappointed: Success in matters dreamed about.

Disappointing others: Misfortune in love affairs.

Others being disappointed in you: Are in the grip of deceitful people.

Lovers being disappointed: Danger through a secret.

DISAPPROVE:
Of disapproving: Disagreements in the family will cause unhappiness.

Others disapproving: Will be involved in a car accident.

Disapproving of others' opinions: Honor and consideration.

Receiving disapproval of family: Will enjoy good results in business.

DISARM:
Being disarmed: Dignity.

Disarming thieves: Will soon be robbed again.

Disarming a member of the family: Success in enterprises.

Disarming friends: Will soon have an increase in the family.

Disarming enemies: Will have money difficulties for a long time.

DISASTER:
Being in a disaster: Will have good earnings.

Others being in a disaster: Avoid rivals.

A woman dreaming of a disaster: Suitable time to pursue endeavors.

A man dreaming of a disaster: Good times are coming.

DISCIPLINE:
Of discipline: Will be reprimanded.

Disciplining others: Will be frightened by coming events.

Being disciplined by others: Will be punished by the law.

Disciplining children: Must be more cautious of your actions.

People ignoring discipline: An enemy desires to become a friend again.

Disciplining prisoners: Will be hurt by gossip of others.

DISCUSSION:
Having a discussion: Warning of trouble.

Discussing subjects with other people: Danger through a secret.

Hearing others having a discussion: Shame and sorrow.

A man and wife having a discussion: Danger of fire.

DISEASE:
Having a disease: Warning of treachery.

Others having a disease: Will make money illegally.

Lovers dreaming of a disease: Good times are coming.

Having a disease in the stomach: Waste of money.

Having a disease in the brain: Will be fortunate and honored.

Having an unknown disease: Big financial gain.

DISFIGURE:
Being disfigured: Unexpected happiness.

Others who are disfigured: Will be cheated by friends.

Relatives being disfigured: Luck and prosperity.

Disfiguring a lover: You have one loyal friend.

DISGRACE:
Having been disgraced: Accord among friends.
Others in disgrace: Are surrounded by enemies.
Others disgracing you: Will be prosecuted by enemies.
Relatives being in disgrace: Hard work awaits.
Children being in disgrace: Good times are coming.

DISGUISE:
Disguising yourself: Will have troubles that are not very serious.
Having disguised yourself: Will take a long trip and change residence.
Disguising yourself with fancy costumes: Avoid rivals.
Others being disguised: Triumph over enemies.
Relatives being disguised: Important and very beneficial events to come.

DISGUST:
Being disgusted: Will have friends in foreign countries.
Being disgusted with attitude of others: Infidelity.
Being disgusted with relatives: Will not accomplish plans.
Others being disgusted with you: Will have misery.

DISH:
Breaking dishes: Domestic troubles.
Others breaking dishes: Must control your passions.
Chipping a baked enamel dish: Will receive plenty of money.
Dropping a plate belonging to a scale: Big fortune is ahead.

DISHCLOTH:
An ordinary dishcloth: Will have a small unimportant argument.
Dishcloth made of rough material: Unknown person will give good advice.
Washing with a dishcloth: Will receive important and good news.

Washing dishcloths: Be cautious in business ventures.
Throwing a dishcloth away: Be careful of heart condition.

DISHONEST:
Being dishonest: Will receive a document pertinent to own affairs.
Others being dishonest: Are within grip of deceitful people.
Family members being dishonest: Misfortune in love affairs.
Others acting dishonestly: Temptation will come to you.

DISHONOR:
Being dishonored: Sorrow and unlucky events in near future.
Having been dishonored: Great scandal ahead.
Other people being dishonored: Prompt engagement.
A relative being dishonored: Family discord.

DISINHERIT:
Being disinherited: Will sustain a serious loss.
Disinheriting a relative: Will have good earnings.
Others being disinherited: Change in your environment.

DISLIKE:
Disliking someone: Will have emotional sorrow.
Someone disliking you: Will have worries.
Being disliked by others without caring: Will have abundant means.
Others disliking you: Difficulties will be overcome.
Being disliked by member of the family: Happiness is assured.

DISMISS:
Having been dismissed from business position: Advancement in position.
Dismissing an employee: Doomed for disappointment.
Others being dismissed: A mystery will be solved.

DISOBEDIENT:

Having been disobedient: A difficult choice is before you.

Children being disobedient: Prompt engagement.

Husband and wife being disobedient: Loneliness and trouble ahead.

Others being disobedient: Will be accused and have a big quarrel.

Relatives being disobedient: Change for the better.

DISPUTE:

Having a dispute: Will have a happy life.

Having a dispute with relatives: Obstacles will be avoided.

Having a business dispute: Discovery of lost valuables.

Others having a dispute: Good times are coming.

DISTANCE:

Being at a distance from family: Big catastrophe ahead.

Being at a distance from husband: Will hear good news.

Being at a distance from wife: Another person is enjoying what you desired.

Friends being at a distance: Doomed for disappointment.

Others being in distant places: Big catastrophe ahead.

DISTRESS:

Being in distress: Will have family quarrels.

Children being in distress: Warning of trouble.

Wife or husband being in distress: Will have emotional sorrow.

Others being in distress: Will have big gains in fortune.

Putting others in distress: Warning of trouble.

DISTRICT ATTORNEY:

Of a district attorney: Unexpected worries.

Being in presence of a D.A.: Will have self-respect.

Being accused by a D.A.: Will be amorous, have happiness and delight.

Being brought before D.A. by a policeman: Satisfaction and moral content.

DISTRUST:

Distrusting others: Accord among friends.

Being distrusted by others: Will have a serious illness.

Distrust between husband and wife: Long and happy life.

Distrusting other members of family: Change for the better.

DISTURB:

Being disturbed: Will receive news from faraway.

Others who are disturbed: Happiness is assured.

Being disturbed by others: Persecution from an enemy.

DITCH:

Being in a ditch: Rapid recovery of good health.

Others in a ditch: Will have financial difficulties.

Being pushed into a ditch: Beware of unexpected difficulties.

Walking through a ditch: Will be cheated by someone.

Digging a ditch: Discovery of a secret.

Digging a very deep ditch: You are prone to being too egotistic.

DIVING:

Of diving: Loss of money through speculation.

Others diving: Warning of troubles.

Children diving: Dignity and distinction.

Members of family diving: Business undertaking will be risky.

DIVORCE:

Wanting a divorce: Domestic happiness.

Being divorced: Security.

Obtaining a divorce and receiving alimony: Prosperity.

Relatives being divorced: Bad gossip by friends.

Children being divorced: Big joy ahead.

Friends being divorced: Danger through a secret.

Enemies being divorced: Lucky and prosperous life.

DIZZY:

Being dizzy: Hard work with no results.

Others being dizzy: Unhappiness.

Members of family being dizzy: Avoid rivals.

Children being dizzy: Beneficial gains.

Being dizzy from effect of alcohol: Probable loss of money.

DOCK:

Of a dock: Danger in love affairs.

Being alone on a dock: Must endure grief.

Being on a dock with a sailor: Secret enmity of some person.

Being on a dock with workmen or stevedores: Good business prospects.

DOCKYARD:

Being in a dockyard: Will have plenty of savings.

Of a dockyard: Will have a fight with best friend.

Workmen in a dockyard: Will have good earnings.

Sailors in a dockyard: Happiness will come soon.

DOCTOR:

Going to a doctor: Will have mastery over many things.

Calling a doctor for yourself: Will live a long life.

Calling a doctor for children: New interests and surroundings.

Calling a doctor for relatives: Rapid recovery.

Calling a doctor for friends: Suitable time to pursue endeavors.

A doctor visiting patients: Big wealth.

Others calling a doctor: Troubles ahead.

Being a doctor: Joy and profit.

Becoming a doctor: Financial gains.

DOCTRINE:

Teaching Testament doctrine: Will receive high, honorable position.

Enforcing government doctrine: Will be betrayed by enemies.

Learning the principals of doctrine: Will be arrogant with friends.

Being a teacher of doctrine: Will have hard times and poverty.

DOG:

The dog spoken of in Dante's book: Unexpected journey.

Of dogs: Happiness.

Own dog: Will receive favors from a friend.

A dog belonging to others: Warning of trouble.

A white dog: Fortune is near at hand.

A brown dog: Are mistrusted by someone.

A black dog: Beware of treacherous friends.

A gray dog: A faithful friend is nearby.

A big dog: You have many friends.

A small dog: Beware of enemies.

A hunting dog: Will receive gifts from a stranger.

A racing dog: Loss of a lawsuit.

A watchdog: Arguments between husband and wife.

A bird dog: An old lover still loves you.

A police dog: Quarrels with a business partner.

A helping dog for blind people: Will have to fast.

Pretty little dog: Will be visited by an unwelcome guest.

Friendly dog: All will be well.

Unfriendly dog: Will receive help from a good friend.

An English dog: Will receive an invitation to a party.

A German dog: Will be deeply in love.

A greyhound: You will be seduced.

A bulldog: Will quarrel with girl friends.

A dog guarding a wounded person: Affairs will be useless.

Mountain dog: Will have trustworthy friends.

Sheep dog: Will encounter deceitfulness.

A bastard dog: Faithfulness between lovers.

A dog with a shaggy coat: Your lover is truthful.

A happy dog: Loss of a lover.

A sad dog: Fear of persecution.

A dog sleeping: You need have no fears.

A yelping dog: Imminent danger.

A frothing dog: Change for the better.

A courageous dog: Your help is faithful to you.

A lost dog: Will receive bad news.

A barking dog: Beware of quarrels.

A dog fighting: Beware of thieves.

Dogs causing destruction: A mystery will be solved.

A dog tearing clothes: Gossip among own family.

A dog biting others: Gossip by friends.

Being bitten by a dog: Will be double-crossed by someone you trust.

Dogs playing together: You are in danger.

A male dog playing with a female dog: Lovers are cheating on each other.

A male dog loving a female dog: Realization of all desires.

A dog and cat playing: Big love disputes.

A dog and cat fighting: Arguments with relatives.

A dog belonging to others: Avoid rivals.

Being chased by a dog: Reputation is being injured by others.

Single people dreaming of a dog: Will be seduced.

Married people dreaming of a dog: Will soon have a quarrel over love.

DOLLS:
Of dolls: Domestic happiness.

Having dolls: You are prone to flirt too much.

Girls playing with dolls: Will have very good luck.

Buying a doll: Prosperity.

Dolls belonging to others: Rapid recovery from an illness.

DOMINO:
Playing dominoes: Will have a small triumph over difficulties.

Winning while playing dominoes: Happiness is assured.

Losing while playing dominoes: Avoid rivals.

Playing dominoes with children: Big joy.

Playing dominoes with the family: Change for the better.

Playing dominoes with a loved one: Unhappiness in love.

Playing dominoes with friends: Important and beneficial events to come.

DONKEY:
(See **ASS.**)

DOOR:
Of a door: Money will soon come to you.

A doorway: Fortune is near at hand.

Own door: Will become annoyed.

Entering door of own house: Will be cheated by friends.

Door being closed: Avoid speculation.

Door being open and entering: You have a loyal friend.

A house with many doors: You will lose your money.

A burning door: Death of a person living in the house.

Breaking down a door: Will soon be arrested.

A broken door: Will receive good news from a person faraway.

Being unable to escape from a door: Happiness and long life.

Other people's door: Luck and prosperity.

The door to a city: Happiness in married life.

DOORMAN:
Of a doorman: Sickness and infirmity.

Being a doorman: Will be obedient and passionate.

Giving orders to a doorman: Will be persecuted.

A doorman being killed: Will receive an honorable position.

DORMER WINDOW:
Looking out of a dormer window: Rapid recovery.
Falling from a dormer window: Sickness is ahead.
Seeing others at a dormer window: Avoid rivals.

DOUBLE:
Of anything that is double: Don't place too many hopes in the future.
Going somewhere on the double: Will enjoy good food.
Two children riding a double bicycle: Will have honest reliable friends.
A double-yoked egg: A member of the family will have an accident.
A double marriage of family members: Are unfitted to fill your position.

DOUBT:
Being in doubt: It is safe to rely on a good friend.
Others doubting you: You distrust your friends.
Being doubted by lover: Good luck.
A wife doubting her husband: A long happy future.
A husband doubting his wife: Happiness is assured.

DOVE:
White doves: Bountiful crops and faithful friends.
Hearing a dove cooing: Probable death of the father.
A woman dreaming of doves: Fortunate affairs at home.
A dove as the representation of the Holy Spirit: Happiness.

DOWRY:
A woman giving a dowry to her husband: People will take good care of you.
A man giving property to his bride: Expect much uneasiness.
Giving a dowry to daughters: Will earn more money.

A widow's dowry: Will make a good change in your life.

DRAGON:
Of a dragon: Great riches.
Many dragons: Big disappointment in love.
A military man dreaming of a dragon: Will have plenty of money.
A navy man dreaming of a dragon: Will be visited by superior officer.
A young girl dreaming of a dragon: Big joy.

DRAPER:
Of a person who makes draperies: Must control your passion.
Being in the company of a draper: Prompt engagement.
Being a draper and dealing in cloth: A change in life will come soon.

DRAPERIES:
Draperies of one color: You are conceited.
Draperies with a flowered print: Will receive dinner invitation from prominent people.
Cloth draperies of one color: Will receive good news.
Silk draperies of one color: Joy.
Married women dreaming of draperies: Will give birth to many children.

DRAWBRIDGE:
A closed drawbridge: Will realize high ambitions.
An open drawbridge: Will pardon enemies.
A drawbridge being drawn up: Will take an unexpected journey.
A drawbridge being lowered: Financial losses.

DRAWERS:
Of an open drawer: Suitable time to pursue flirtations.
Opening a drawer: Happiness is assured.
Opening a locked drawer: Will discover a secret.
Being unable to open a closed drawer: Beware of troubles ahead.

A married woman dreaming of her drawers: Unfaithful to the man who loves her.

A married man dreaming of his drawers: Shame and sorrow.

A single girl dreaming of her drawers: Will soon be engaged.

A single man dreaming of his drawers: Will be engaged to a rich girl soon.

DREAM:

Consulting someone about your dreams: Expect news from faraway.

Dreaming nice things: You have impossible desires.

Dreaming of being rich: Will be disillusioned.

Dreaming of being poor: Change in your position.

Others dreaming: Will have emotional sorrow.

DRENCH:

Being drenched: Danger of fever for you or someone nearby.

Others being drenched: You expect too many favors of others.

Drenching by force: A mystery will be solved.

Causing someone to drink: A false friend is nearby.

DRESS:

Receiving a beautiful dress: Will be helped by an unknown man.

Buying a new dress: Health and happiness.

Changing dresses: Will suffer because of own foolishness.

Owning a daring evening gown of various colors: You have many friends.

Wearing a daring evening dress: Sickness.

A beautiful dress: Money worries will soon pass.

An embroidered dress: Will receive favors from an unknown person.

Having nice dresses: Efforts will succeed.

Simple dresses: Will have success in love.

Dresses of various colors: Will meet a nice person.

A house dress: You are very neglectful.

Dark dresses: Financial gains.

A mourning dress: Death of a relative.

Wearing a cheap dress: Will be annoyed by friends in the future.

Others wearing evening dresses: Shame and sorrow.

A tight dress: Sickness.

A dress that is too large: Will have good employment.

Wearing a torn dress: You are unaware of good fortune.

Sewing up a torn dress: You are neglecting your own children.

Desiring to tear up a dress: Success in love affairs.

Tearing a dress: Your fortune is in danger.

Others tearing your dress: Will receive the help of a friend.

Staining a dress: People are talking against you.

Washing a dress: Will be a good wife.

Partially unsewed dress: Will be disregarded by friends.

A dirty dress: Will be blamed by friends.

Being badly dressed: Warning of troubles.

A dress that is out of style: Danger of fire.

Dresses of elderly people: Will attend a baptism.

A nun's dress: Will receive great honors.

Losing a dress: You expect too many favors from other people.

A loose dress: Will be cheated by friends.

A pregnant woman wearing her loose dress: Luck and prosperity.

Stealing a dress: Success in own enterprises.

A closet full of dresses: Constant love of social pleasures.

A closet without dresses: Family quarrels.

Owning a light-blue dress: Promotion in own employment.

A navy-blue dress: Misfortune will be avoided.

Taking off a blue dress: Unreasonable contempt for danger.

Owning a black dress: Joy.

Wearing a black dress: A marriage will take place soon.

Wearing a black dress at a funeral: Inheritance.

Taking off a black dress: Misery.

Wearing a black silk dress: Will receive what you desire.

A brown dress: Will have a high social position.

A gold dress: Will be rich very soon.

Wearing a gold-trimmed dress: Honor and joy.

Wearing a gold-trimmed dress with furs: Abundance of money.

A green dress: Expect a big fortune.

A gray dress: Will receive a letter with good news.

A mauve dress: Unhappiness.

A pink dress: Glorious success.

A purple dress: Death of a friend.

A red dress: Will be respected by other people.

Taking off a red dress: Will lose your temper.

A tan dress: Financial gains.

A white dress: Happiness.

Wearing a white dress: Big fortune.

Owning a white silk dress: Joy.

Wearing a yellow dress: Fortune and honor.

Taking off a yellow dress: Jealousy.

DRINK:

Wanting a drink and cannot find water: Misfortune.

Muddy, dirty water: Will be cheated by friends.

Warm water: You have loyal friends.

Drinking clear spring water: Big joy.

Drinking very cold water: Triumph over enemies.

Drinking milk: Abundant means.

Drinking blood: Success in everything in life.

Drinking out of a clean cup: Immediate employment.

Relatives drinking: Prompt engagement.

Drinking from a spring: Complete recovery from an illness.

Drinking pure water from a glass: Will soon get married.

Drinking liquor: Beware of an accident.

Drinking water from a pitcher: Will have pleasant companions.

Drinking white wine: Happiness.

Drinking from a glass half full of wine: Sickness is ahead.

Being thirsty and drinking fresh water from a glass: Will be very rich.

Drinking until satisfied: Desires will be satisfied.

Drinking in company of friends: Change in your environment.

Other people drinking: Big sorrow.

Drinking something sweet: Will be violently loved.

Getting drunk from drinking sweet things: Someone will make you rich.

DRIVING:

Of driving: Discovery of lost valuables.

Other people driving: Expect monetary losses.

Relatives driving: Listen to suggestions of friends.

Loved one driving: Avoid rivals.

DROPS:

Measuring drops: Will soon have a small sum of money left to you.

Others measuring drops: Don't keep track of small monetary values.

Putting medicine drops in water: Advancement within position.

A nurse putting drops in water: Important and very beneficial event to come.

DROPSY:

Having dropsy: Will be imprisoned.

Others having dropsy: Are prone to squander money.

Relatives having dropsy: Will make a dishonorable fortune.

Friends having dropsy: Are being deceived.

DROUTH:

Of a drouth: Beware of business losses.

Dry, parched fields: Another person is enjoying what you hoped to win.

A lengthy dry spell: Will soon experience ups and downs.

Rain falling after a long drouth: Luck and prosperity.

DROWN:

Of drowning: Will lose all that you have.

Relatives drowning: Big ruin ahead.

Being rescued from drowning: Expect help from a friend.

A businessman drowning: Will go into bankruptcy.

Other people drowning: Joy and triumph.

Being drowned by others: Loss of money.

Drowning own children: Will have an unhappy trip.

Husband or wife drowning: Serious disaster is ahead.

Rescuing others from drowning: A friend will reach a high position.

Children being rescued from drowning: Will have prosperity and high position.

DRUGS:

Having drugs: Infirmity.

Taking drugs: Affliction.

Being ordered to take drugs: Morale will be raised.

Refusing to take drugs: Affairs will be in confusion.

Being given drugs by a doctor: Will have the protection of friends.

Giving drugs to relatives: Are surrounded by much gossip.

Giving drugs to children: Successful speculation.

Making drugs: Loss of money.

Others taking drugs: Suitable time for flirtation.

Having medicine chest full of drugs: Good business but no profit.

A drug store: Will begin a new business.

Selling drugs: A dishonest man is nearby.

DRUMS:

Hearing drums playing: Will gain great success.

Playing a drum: Big joy.

Others playing a drum: Will have emotional sorrow.

Marching in a parade and playing a drum: Luck and prosperity.

Buying a drum: Will have a loss of small importance.

Children playing a drum: Will not have sufficient money.

DRUNK:

Being drunk: Will have financial troubles.

Others who are drunk: Will lose money through another person.

Being very drunk: You will go mad.

Relatives being drunk: Riches and health.

A person being drunk without liquor: Danger through a secret.

A woman being drunk: Will commit some bad action.

Becoming drunk with good wine: Will make acquaintance of a high person.

Being drunk and feeling sad: Treachery by relatives.

Being drunk from water: Will become rich through big connections.

Several drunken people: Will be guilty of foolish actions.

Being sick from drunkenness: Squandering of household money.

Others who are sick from being drunk: Dishonor.

Children being drunk: Fortune will increase.

Being drunk and vomiting: Loss of money in gambling.

Being drunk and having heart pains: Infidelity of a lover.

Husband being drunk constantly: Bad future.

Getting drunk with cheap wine: Will have fleeting pleasures.

Enemies being drunk: You will be slandered.

DRY:

Of drying: Will be taken care of by someone.

Drying yourself: Joy.

Drying other people: Prosperity.

Drying children: Riches and profit.

Drying dishes: Hard work will bring good returns in money.

Drying pots and pans: Will receive news from faraway.

Drying clothes: Will be visited by an unwelcome person.

DUCKS:

Of ducks: Failure of enemies.

Being attacked by wild ducks: Trouble in business affairs.

Ducks flying: Marriage and a happy family life.

Hunting ducks: Big success.

Killing a duck: Will have a disaster in traveling.

Eating duck: Honor and fortune.

Catching a duck: Malicious gossip by friends.

A wild duck dead: Don't forget your friends.

Ducks swimming: Beware of great danger.

Other people eating duck: Big joy.

DUEL:

Having a duel to save your honor: Beware of your rival.

Having a duel with a swordsman: Big family embarrassment.

Having a duel with a friend: Big happiness.

Having a duel with a walking stick: You will dominate friends.

Being wounded in a duel: Will have emotional sorrow.

Being killed in a duel: Warning of trouble.

DUET:

Singing in a duet: Good fortune in love and marrage.

Hearing others singing a duet: Domestic happiness.

Hearing children singing a duet: A mystery will be solved.

Hearing friends singing a duet: Temptation will come to you.

DUKE:

Of a duke: Will receive good news.

Being a duke: You flirt too much.

Meeting a duke: Will be guilty of doing improper things.

Dating a duke: New love affairs are in sight.

DUMB:

Being dumb: Will have a family quarrel.

Being unable to speak: Avoid speculation.

Members of family being dumb: A crippled child will be born.

Other people being dumb: Do not discuss your business plans.

DUMPLINGS:

Making dumplings: Fortune will change for the better in near future.

Making dumplings from potatoes: Pleasant surprise awaits.

Eating dumplings: Aspirations will be realized.

Others eating dumplings: Success in all affairs.

DUN:

Being dunned for payment: Will have financial success.

Being a creditor: Will have unhappiness.

Others being dunned: Serious trouble.

Relatives being dunned: Good expectations in business.

Being dunned by many people: Big misery.

Dunning a partner: Beware of damages.

Being dunned by a partner: Misery for a short time.

Pursuing your creditors: Will have some unhappiness.

Being pursued by creditors for payment: Will receive unpleasant visit.

Receiving payment of money owed by others: Security in business.

DUNGEON:

Being in a dungeon: Family happiness.

Others being in a dungeon: You have many enemies.

Escaping from a dungeon: You have loyal friends.

Being unable to escape from a dungeon: Expect business losses.

DUSK:
Being in the dusk: Must struggle against adverse circumstances.
Others being in the dusk: A slight difficulty is ahead.
Relatives being in the dusk: Will receive money.

DUST:
Dusting off clothes: Good business ventures.
Dusting furniture in the house: Death of a good friend.
Dusting books and ornaments: Happy days ahead.
Using a feather duster to brush away dirt: Attempting to hide wrongdoing.

DWARF:
Of a male dwarf: Will have a vigorous mind.
A well-formed female dwarf: Will have a healthy body.
Friends being dwarfs: They will bring you many pleasures.
Ugly dwarfs: Illness and misfortune.
Unknown dwarfs: Will be attacked by friends.

DYE:
Dyeing own hair: Warning of trouble.
Dyeing another's hair: Joy without profit.
Others dyeing their hair: Will suffer through own foolishness.
Putting rouge on cheeks: Will live a long life.
Dyeing materials: Misery.

A person who dyes materials: Must endure a long infirmity.
Dyeing clothes: Business is very confused.
Dyeing with light colors: Sickness is forthcoming.
Dyeing with yellow or dark colors: Family member will have a high fever.
Making a mess while dyeing clothes: Expect a very expensive present.

DYING:
Of dying: Will receive empty promises.
Relatives dying: Will receive a big inheritance.
Children dying: Will receive fortune from abroad.
Kissing a dying person: Loss of a lawsuit.
Friends dying: Triumph over enemies.
Others are dying: Doomed for disappointment.

DYSENTERY:
Having dysentery: Will receive a very costly gift.
Taking medicine for dysentery: A good future is ahead.
Children having dysentery: Will be invited to a banquet.
Recovering from dysentery: Will receive news of a marriage.
Entire family having dysentery at the same time: Domestic troubles.

E

EAGLE:
An eagle flying: Good fortune is ahead.
Killing an eagle: Wealth and nothing to prevent achieving goal.
A dead eagle: Expect money losses.
Being attacked by an eagle: Expect many difficulties.
A wounded eagle: Loss in love affairs.

An eagle high up on a statue: Will realize high ambitions.
An eagle perched on a mountaintop: Fame and money.
Carrying an eagle: Shame and sorrow.
A woman dreaming of several eagles: Will have a famous son.
Owning an eagle: Honors and business profits.

An eagle standing up: Many soldiers will die.
An eagle falling on you: Warning of danger.
A bald eagle: Will have a prominent political position.

EARRINGS:
Of own earrings: Congenial work and good news.
Losing own earrings: A period of sorrow is about to come.
Earrings of others: Big friendship.
Wearing earrings: Will be cheated by friends.
Giving own earrings to someone: Big quarrel.
Receiving earrings as a gift: Avoid rivals.

EARS:
Feeling own ears while dreaming: Will discover a secret.
Having trouble with own ears: Trouble from unexpected source.
Having nice ears: Big success with an intimate friend.
Having a cut in the ears: Disappointment through a friend.
Having ears stopped up: Domestic troubles.
A man dreaming of one ear being stopped up: Troubles because of partner.
A woman dreaming of one ear being stopped up: Big gossip by friends.
Having only one ear: Will lose your job.
Having something heavy hanging on the ears: Will have a struggle in life.
Having small ears: Friendship with a wealthy person.
Having big ears: Will be helped by a friend that cares for you.
Having long ears: Public shame and sorrow.
Having the ears pierced: Domestic loss.
Cleaning own ears: Will have faithful friends.
The ears of a donkey: Will be an honest servant.

The ears of a dog: Honesty between husband and wife.
The ears of a deer: Will have big success.
The ears of any wild animal: Will be deceived by friends.
Having the ear drum broken: Will defend yourself well with fists.
The ears of corn, wheat, rye, or grain: Will have abundant means.

EARTH:
Of the earth: Loss of a friend.
Kissing the earth: Will be humiliated.
Eating the earth: Long sickness.
Being put under the earth: Danger of disaster.
Being buried in the earth: Will have plenty of money.
Earth being black: Sorrow.
Owning good earth or land: Will have a fine wife.
Enclosed earth being given to a man: He has a good wife.
Earth with pleasant pastures: Will have good children.
Earth full of vegetables: Are in the grip of deceitful friends.
Earth full of corn, wheat, rye, or grain: Much luck and prosperity.
Lying on the earth: Death of some person.
A farmer working the earth: Big profits coming.
Escaping an eruption of the earth: Good luck is on its way.

EARTHQUAKE:
Feeling an earthquake: Death of a relative.
Being in the area of an earthquake: Loss of a close friend.
The earth trembling from an earthquake: Loss in business matters.
A city destroyed by an earthquake: A change in life will soon come.
Earthquake occurring in the East: Difficulties must be overcome.
Earthquake occurring in the West: Warning of troubles.
Earthquake occurring in the North: Change in environment.

Earthquake occurring in the South: Will have emotional sorrow.

EARTHWORM:
Of earthworms: Secret enemies are endeavoring to cause ruin.

Earthworms coming out after a rain: Humiliation caused by friends.

Having earthworms on the body: Will be rich.

An area full of earthworms: Will have a contagious illness.

EARWIG:
Of an earwig: An enemy will cause trouble.

Earwigs being on others: Beware of enemies.

Many earwigs: Recovery from an illness.

EASEL:
Having an easel: Good times are coming.

Working at an easel: Mind is concentrating on lofty meditation.

Others working at an easel: Will have happiness.

EAST:
Of the East: Are about to be sent on a long journey.

Being in the East: Will hold a religious position.

Others being in the East: Will have important results.

Returning from the East: Financial gains.

EASTER:
Having a happy Easter: Coming happiness.

Spending Easter with others: Bad days are ahead.

Others celebrating Easter without you: Good times are coming.

Being in an Easter parade: Temptation will come.

Others in an Easter parade: Danger through a secret.

EATING:
Of eating: You are being deceived.

Eating until you are full: Good financial affairs.

Overeating: Discovery of valuables.

Eating with the hands: Danger is ahead.

Eating on the floor: Somebody will take something away from you.

Eating in company of others: Will soon receive what you desired.

Eating with the family: Big joy is ahead.

Others eating: Death of an enemy.

Eating broiled meat: Good fortune.

Eating salads: Advancement within position.

Eating cheese: Sickness.

Eating turnips: Will quarrel with friends.

Eating fruits: Happiness is assured.

Eating salted things: Gossip by friends.

Eating fat things: Warning of an illness to come.

(See listings of meats, vegetables, fruits, and so on, e.g., **BEEF.**)

EAVESDROP:
Of eavesdropping: Will be lucky with the opposite sex.

Secretly eavesdropping on a conversation: Unexpected good fortune.

Friends eavesdropping on own conversation: Approaching money.

Others eavesdropping on secret conversation: Money is coming to you.

EBONY:
Of ebony wood or tree: Will take a trip to a foreign country.

Having ebony wood: Will meet someone from abroad.

Buying ebony wood: Success in business.

Being given things made with ebony: Will have good earnings.

ECHO:
Hearing an echo close by: Will receive a visit from good friends.

Hearing an echo faraway: Will hear of some good fortune.

Hearing an echo in a cavern: Triumph over enemies.

ECLIPSE:
The eclipse of the sun: Will incur losses.
The eclipse of the moon: Will have small misfortune.
Watching the eclipse of the moon with the family: Happiness.
Watching the eclipse of the moon with a loved one: You are deceived.

EDUCATION:
Not having an education: Will suffer through own foolishness.
Seeking an education: Fortune will likely smile on your efforts.
Children having an education: Children will cause trouble.
Having a restricted education: Loss of money.

EELS:
Of one eel: Immediate recovery from an illness.
Holding an eel: Will be attended by good fortune.
A dead eel: Will vindicate yourself.
Catching a dead eel: Warning of suffering.
Catching a live eel: You are very clever.
Many eels in the water: You are overworking.
Many dead eels: Will get out of prison.

EGGS:
Fresh eggs: Good news.
Many broken eggs: Will quarrel and have lawsuits.
Eating eggs: Foretells an early marriage.
Having very fresh eggs: Will receive money.
Having old eggs: Unpleasant news.
Broken eggshells: Loss of money.
White eggs: Will receive some advantageous news.
Having brown eggs: Will receive bad news.
Having red eggs: Will be threatened by someone.
Eggs of different colors: Great disappointment.

Buying eggs: Infidelity by a loved one.
Cooking eggs: Gossip by friends.
Chickens laying eggs: Abundant means.
The eggs of a fish: Will have hard times ahead.
Making a mess with eggs: Will be persecuted.
Beating eggs with an egg beater: Death of a relative.
The empty shells of eggs: Will be eating too much.

ELASTIC:
Of elastic: Fortune will improve.
Having something made of elastic: Good times are coming.
Having an elastic corset: Big joy.
Putting elastic bands on bundles of things: Beware of jealous friends.

ELBOW:
Having nice elbows: Good times are coming.
Having a dirty elbow: Will have misery.
Having a pain in the elbow: Difficulties ahead.
Children having a pain in their elbow: Use caution in business ventures.

ELDERBERRY:
Of elderberries: Social activities of a pleasant nature.
Picking elderberries: Financial gains.
Eating elderberries: Abundant means.
Buying elderberry jam: Will have a vigorous mind.

ELECTION:
Assisting with an election: Rapid success of own hopes.
Others at an election: Important and very beneficial events to come.
Filling an office after an election: Change in environment.
Winning the election: A false friend is nearby.

ELECTRICITY:
Using electricity: Will be greatly surprised by a coming event.
Being shocked by electricity: Will be cheated by friends.

Others handling electricity: Use caution in business ventures.

Handling electrical devices: Accord among friends.

ELEPHANT:

Of an elephant: Fear and danger for rich people.

A poor person dreaming of an elephant: Will have a good, new position.

Feeding an elephant: An important person will befriend you.

Getting on the back of an elephant: Good fortune.

Many elephants: Prosperity.

Others with elephants: Will receive assistance from a friend.

Giving water to an elephant: Will be of service to an influential person.

An elephant at a circus: Danger of death for a relative.

An elephant escaping from a circus: Family quarrels.

An elephant being free: Will enjoy much independence in life.

ELEVATOR:

Coming down in an elevator: Will be overwhelmed by misfortune.

Going up in an elevator: Increase in wealth and advancement in position.

Being in an elevator with others: Avoid rivals.

Being in an elevator with the family: Financial gains.

An elevator being out of order: Warning of troubles.

Being stuck between floors in an elevator: Will have emotional sorrow.

ELF:

Of an elf: Important and very beneficial event to come.

Children dreaming of an elf: Children will be very friendly.

ELM:

Of an elm tree: Rapid success of own hopes.

Being under an elm tree: Social activities of a happy nature.

Others under an elm tree: Doomed for disappointment.

Relatives being under an elm tree: Money will come easily during life.

ELOPE:

Married person dreaming of eloping: Are unfitted to fill your position.

Single person dreaming of eloping: Unhappiness in love affairs.

A young girl dreaming of eloping: Loss of reputation will follow.

Children eloping: Must mend your ways in life.

Friends eloping: Failure of enemies.

EMBALM:

An embalmed body: Big honors.

A relative's body being embalmed: Must rely on own good judgment.

A dignitary being embalmed: Are doing work with diligence.

An animal or bird embalmed: You expect too many favors from others.

EMBARK:

Troops embarking on a ship: Failure of enemies.

Navy sailors embarking on a ship: Enemies will be defeated.

Merchant seamen embarking on a ship: Happiness is assured.

Others embarking on any craft: Prosperity in love.

EMBARRASS:

Being embarrassed: The more embarrassed the greater your success.

Others being embarrassed: Happiness.

Embarrassing friends: Immediate success of all hopes.

Being embarrassed by children: You are acting too old-fashioned.

EMBRACE:

Embracing relatives: Watch out for treachery.

Embracing children: Big joy is ahead.

Embracing a stranger: Will entertain an unwelcome guest.

Being embraced by others: Financial gains.

Being embraced by unknown person: Suitable time to pursue flirtations.

Wife or sweetheart embracing someone else: Loneliness and trouble.

Husband or boyfriend embracing others: Will have a long life.

EMBROIDERY:
Of embroidering: Will make the best of everything.
Having embroidered on a dress: Honor and riches.
Having embroidered linens: Joy and profits.
Embroidering something for loved one: Will be accepted in society.

EMERALD:
Of an emerald: Will experience difficulty over an inheritance.
Having emeralds: Will have the greatest good fortune possible.
Selling own emeralds: Separation from a loved one.
Buying an emerald: Good business with a person faraway.

EMIGRATE:
Of emigrating: Will receive a letter from a friend in a foreign country.
Others who are emigrating: Watch out for treachery.
Having trouble with emigration authorities: Big joy is ahead.
Being refused admittance by emigration authorities: Danger through a secret.

EMPEROR:
Being an emperor: Will make plans to run away.
Being presented before an emperor: Will take a long journey.
Being married to an emperor: Loss of reputation.

EMPLOYER:
Of own employer: Will have a change in own position.
Speaking to own employer: Will be advanced shortly.
Being hired by an employer: Must mend your ways in life.
Being fired by an employer: A mystery will be solved.
Own employer going out of business: Will have a vigorous mind.
Employing other people: Their interests will clash with yours.

EMPLOYMENT:
Being unable to find employment: Misfortune in love affairs.
Having good employment: Good times are coming.
Finding employment for others: Much poverty is ahead.
Being at employment office seeking a job: Change for the better.

EMPRESS:
Being an empress: Loss of your lover.
Being presented before an empress: Loss of dignity.
Being married to an empress: Happiness is assured.

EMPTY:
Home being empty: Big catastrophe is ahead.
Having an empty barrel: Big poverty.
Pouring from an empty jar: Unexpected gains.

ENCHANT:
Being enchanted: Evil influences are nearby.
Others being enchanted: Will give financial aid.
Relatives being enchanted: Loss in business matters.
Enchanting others: Will realize high ambitions.
Resisting an enchantment: Your advice will be sought by many.

ENCOURAGE:
Being encouraged: Will be offended.
Needing encouragement: You are being unjust because of jealousy.
Encouraging a sick person: Will receive monetary assistance.
Encouraging children: Will have arguments with mate.
Encouraging friends: Will have sorrow because of own actions.
Being encouraged by relatives: Unhappiness.

END:
Hearing the end of something: Good times ahead.
Watching the end of a play: Very surprising things will occur.

The end of the world: Joy without profit.

The end of others: Recovery from an illness.

ENEMA:

Of the syringe used in giving an enema: Confusion in business.

Giving an enema: Will be sick over love affairs.

Being given an enema: Unhappiness.

Taking an enema yourself: Will be short of money.

ENEMY:

Meeting an enemy: Good fortune.

Being in the company of someone disliked: Catastrophe is ahead.

Speaking with an enemy: Be cautious in dealings.

Being taken away by an enemy: Will be embarrassed by friends.

Fighting with enemies: Will be deceived by friends.

Hating an enemy: Loss of your fortune.

Killing an enemy: Great joy and pleasures in life.

Winning out over an enemy: Will succeed in a law suit.

ENGAGEMENT:

A young person dreaming of being engaged: Will not be very popular.

A broken engagement: May have to endure disappointments.

A social high-class engagement: Troubles are ahead.

Engagement of others being broken: Will have emotional sorrow.

Engaged person being strong or beautiful: Dishonesty.

Engaged person being quiet or simple: Future will be good.

ENGAGEMENT RING:

Wearing an engagement ring: Big joy.

Others wearing an engagement ring: Avoid rivals.

Relatives wearing an engagement ring: Their happiness is assured.

Returning an engagement ring: A change in life will come soon.

ENGINE:

Of an engine: Must endure trials.

An engine in motion: Expect difficulties in the near future.

Driving an engine: Change in environment.

A steam engine: Money will come easily during entire life.

A gas engine: Important and very beneficial event to come.

An engine being out of order: Watch out for treachery.

An engine stopped: Financial gains.

ENGLISH:

Of an English person: A good friend has ulterior motives in his mind.

Many English people: False friends are nearby.

Going to England: Creditors will press for payment.

Living in England: Desires will not be realized.

Having love affair with English person: Will have an unknown sickness.

ENGRAVE:

Engraving on metal: Change of work.

Engraving on hard wood: Social activities of a happy nature.

Being an engraver: Death of an enemy.

An engraver of seals: Misfortune in love affairs.

ENJOY:

Of enjoying yourself: Accord among friends.

Others enjoying themselves: Your happiness is assured.

Enjoying a wedding: Will have difficulties and disappointments.

ENLIST:

A woman dreaming of enlisting: She will find a fine husband.

A man dreaming of enlisting: Postponement of success.

Relatives enlisting: A false friend is nearby.

Children enlisting: Family quarrels.

Others enlisting: Advancement within position.

ENTERPRISE:

Beginning a new enterprise: Be prudent in order to avoid ruin.

Undertaking a good enterprise: Sad news awaits.

Being forced into a bad enterprise: Will make a great deal of money.

Others being in good enterprises: Big changes awaiting.

ENTERTAINMENT:

Enjoying good entertainment: Family quarrels.

Leaving before entertainment is over: Will miss a good opportunity.

Feeling uncomfortable at an entertainment: Big joy and money ahead.

Liking the entertainment: Sorrow caused by own carelessness.

Being with others at an entertainment: Will soon have money.

Being with relatives at an entertainment: Joy without profit.

ENTRANCE:

Going through entrance of public place: Desires will be realized.

Going through entrance of private place: Will have a glorious future.

Making a solemn entrance: You are too goodhearted.

Making a grand entrance in society: Prepared to hear of a death.

ENVELOPES:

Of an envelope: Will receive sad news.

A closed envelope: Difficulties are ahead.

Opening an envelope and removing the contents: Worry will be smoothed away.

Putting a letter in an envelope: Discovery of lost valuables.

Receiving an envelope with many letters: Big disappointment in love.

Mailing an envelope: Luck and prosperity.

Buying envelopes: Change for the better.

ENVY:

Envying others: Triumph over enemies.

Being envied by others: Financial gains.

Being envied by friends: Will have a vigorous mind.

Being envied by relatives: Will live a long life.

Being envied by enemies: Are being watched by one with evil intentions.

EPAULETS:

Wearing fringed shoulder ornaments: Honor and consideration.

Others wearing epaulets: Will have a military or naval lover.

Lover wearing epaulets: Will be guilty of foolish actions.

Enemies wearing epaulets: Will have much dignity.

EPICURE:

Being a connoisseur or fine gourmet: Will be jilted by lover.

Fine gourmet: You have one loyal friend.

Others being an epicure of fine foods: Good times are coming.

Enjoying fine food yourself: Must control passions.

EPILEPSY:

Being an epileptic: Will have large gains.

Children having epilepsy: Will be frightened.

Relative having epilepsy: Worries and cares will be taken care of.

Others having epilepsy: Will receive unexpected money.

EPITAPH:

Of an epitaph on a tomb: A wedding will occur, or a baby will be born.

Relative's epitaph on a tomb: Big success in the family.

An epitaph on a statue: Dignity and distinction.

The epitaphs on soldiers' graves: New interests and surroundings.

EQUATOR:

Of the equator: Will have new happiness in life.

Passing the equator on a ship: Will be baptized again on the ship.

Others passing the equator: Beware of enemies.

EQUIPMENT:
Of any kind of equipment: Poverty.
Buying any kind of equipment: Will receive unexpected money.
Selling business equipment: Will receive a valuable gift.
Getting equipment for the house: Are jealous of neighbor's fortune.
Getting equipment for a store: Good business is ahead.

ERMINE:
Wearing an ermine coat: A false friend is nearby.
Owning an ermine coat: Will invest in real estate.
Buying an ermine coat: Must attempt to save money.
Selling an ermine coat: Will be cheated.

ERRAND:
Going on an errand: Harmony in the home.
Completing an errand successfully: Expect business troubles.
An incompleted errand: Loss of a lover will be your fate.
An errand being unsuccessful: Important and very beneficial event to come.

ESCAPE:
Escaping from confinement: A rapid raise in the commercial world.
Escaping from accident or injury: Good things will come during life.
Escaping from difficulties: Success in personal affairs.
Escaping from fire: Triumph.
Escaping from drowning: Will have anxious moments but success will come.
Escaping from a furious animal: Treachery is near at hand.
Being unable to escape: Honor and joy.
Relatives escaping from danger: Financial gains.
Others escaping from danger: Will be cheated by friends.

ESTATE:
Having an estate: Will live a long life.
Owning an estate: Avoid rivals.
Selling an estate: A change in life will soon come.
Another person's estate: Will have a devoted marriage partner.

ETERNITY:
Of eternity: Will be very happy.
Living into eternity: Valid existence of time.
Being immortal: Happiness in the family.

EUROPE:
Of Europe: Joy without profit.
Seeing Europe on a map: Advancement within employment.
Taking a trip to Europe: Will make important acquaintances.
Taking a trip to Europe with others: A rival will take your sweetheart.
Visiting several European countries: Good financial affairs.
Returning from European countries: Quarreling with friends.
Being deported from European countries: Big job is ahead.
Being deported to European countries: Danger through a secret.
Being a citizen of European countries: Will receive false news.
Having business with European countries: Failure of enemies.

EVACUATE:
Evacuating household items from rooms: Will have unhappiness.
Evacuating a house: Will receive bad news.
Evacuating place of business: Will make money in the future.
Others evacuating property: Will lose money by gambling.
Others evacuating furniture in payment of debts: Death of distant relative.

EVAPORATE:
Of things evaporating: Will fall into poverty.
Perfume evaporating: Liking someone when meeting and receiving a kiss.

Unpleasant odors evaporating: Disappointment in love.
Ether or alcohol evaporating: Will live a long life.
Steam evaporating: Must rely on own good judgment.

EVE:
Being Eve: Prosperity.
Being Eve and being naked: Financial gains.
A young girl dreaming of being Eve: A change in life will come soon.
Speaking to Eve: Misfortune in love.

EVENING:
Having a wonderful evening: Shame and sorrow.
Having an evening of celebration: Danger through a secret.
A prosperous evening spent with others: Will realize high ambitions.
Others at an evening party: Worries will end happily.

EVERGREEN:
Having an evergreen bush: You have one loyal friend.
An evergreen tree: Will live a long life.
Several evergreen trees: Hard work ahead.

EVIDENCE:
Having evidence about some thing: Bad reputation.
Giving evidence in court against a criminal: Will be saved by a friend.
Others giving evidence against you: Watch out for treachery.

EVIL SPIRITS:
Having evil spirits: Be careful in business affairs.
Driving evil spirits away: Avoid rivals.
Evil spirits causing sorrow: Will be cheated by friends.
Evil spirits impairing happiness: Will have mastery over many matters.

EWE:
Of a ewe: A large family and prosperous times to come.
Many ewes together: Riches and abundance.

Ewes fighting among themselves: Will work hard and have suffering.
Rich people dreaming of ewes: Dishonor.
Poor people dreaming of ewes: Joy and wealth.

EWER:
Of a full widemouthed jug: Will be cheated by friends.
Having an empty ewer: A friend is trying to help you secretly.
Breaking a ewer: Social activities of a happy nature.
Receiving a ewer as a gift: Important and beneficial event to come.
Drinking from a ewer: Money will come easily during life.
Children drinking from a ewer: Joy in the family.

EXAMINATION:
Having an examination: Are unfitted to fill your position.
Passing an examination: Expect business worries.
Answering all questions correctly: Financial gains.
Not answering questions correctly: Congenial work and good news.
Children passing an examination: Will realize high ambitions.
Others passing an examination: Doomed for disappointment.

EXAMPLE:
Of example: Will be a model in your life.
Being an example to children: Will obtain a high position.
People being good example: Will make success of business.
People being bad example: Will write a death sentence.

EXCEED:
Of exceeding: Will work hard on a new enterprise that will end well.
Exceeding others in business: Disappointments in love affairs.
Children exceeding others: A false friend is nearby.
Being exceeded by others: You are envious of others' belongings.

EXCHANGE:
Exchanging articles in a store: Discovery of lost valuables.
Exchanging articles with another person: Expect business losses.
Exchanging articles with family members: Troubles and difficulty.
Exchanging wives between relatives: Rapid success of own hopes.
Exchanging a blonde for a brunette: Will be married again.

EXCITE:
Being happily excited: Postponement of success.
Being unpleasantly excited: Successful completion of plans.
Being excited by other people: Poverty.
Other people exciting you to anger: Will suffer starvation.

EXCREMENT:
Of excrement: Will have plenty of money.
Babies' excrement in diapers: Will have great advantages.
Excrement of animals: Will make a big profit.
Any other kind of excrement: Will receive a gift.

EXCURSION:
Being on an excursion: Be on guard against married associates.
Taking an excursion with friends: Beware, this friend may not be true.
Taking an excursion with family: Important and beneficial event to come.
Husband and wife taking an excursion: Postponement of success.
Others taking an excursion without you: Financial gains.

EXCUSE:
Making an excuse: Will suffer loss through own foolishness.
Others making excuses to you: Will live a long life.
A partner making excuses: Happiness is assured.
Children making excuses: Financial gains.

Friends making excuses: Avoid enemies.

EXECUTION:
Of an execution: Success of undertakings will be doubtful.
Own execution: Must control passions.
Execution of lover: Will suffer through own foolishness.
Execution of sweetheart: Avoid rivals.
Execution of a guilty person: Triumph over enemies.
Execution of an innocent person: Will be jilted by a lover.
Attending an execution: You have unfaithful friends.

EXECUTIONER:
Of an executioner: Catastrophe and ruin.
Being an executioner: Death of a small child in the family.
An executioner preparing to kill someone: Fortune.
The executioner failing in his duties: Will have a small illness.

EXECUTOR:
Appointing an executor: Important and very beneficial event to come.
Having been appointed the family executor: Will live a long life.
Having been appointed an executrix: Joy and fortune.
Someone else acting as an executor: A false friend is nearby.

EXERCISE:
Of exercising: All will be well.
Feeling tired from exercising: Beware of monetary losses.
Enjoying vigorous exercise: You are being deceived.
Exercising with members of the family: Fortune and joy.
Wife and husband exercising: Persecution and treachery.
Others exercising: Failure of enemies.

EXHAUSTED:
Being exhausted: Social activities of a happy nature.

Others being exhausted: A mystery will be solved.

Mate being exhausted: Abundant means.

Children being exhausted: Be cautious in your dealings.

EXHIBITION:
Of an exhibition: Difficulties are ahead.

Visiting an exhibition: Financial losses.

Going to an exhibition with others: Unexpected good fortune awaits.

Going to an exhibition with family: Warning of troubles.

EXILE:
Being exiled: Foretells serious losses.

Going to be exiled: Postponement of success.

A woman dreaming of being exiled: Must sacrifice pleasure to take a trip.

Returning from exile: Happiness during life.

Being exiled because of guilt: Will have a skin disease for years.

EXPEDITION:
Going on an expedition: Will carry out your purposes.

Planning an expedition but not going: Big catastrophe ahead.

Failing to reach goal on an expedition: Expect money losses.

Others failing their goal on an expedition: Business worries.

EXPERT:
Of an expert: Will be loved by someone new.

Talking with an expert: Stupid gossip is being spread about you.

Taking advice from an expert: Will be humiliated.

Being an expert yourself: Will have a good harvest.

EXPLORER:
Of an explorer: You are surrounded by false friends.

Being an explorer: Will soon have trustworthy acquaintances.

Going exploring: Sickness.

Discussing a discovery with an explorer: Will receive bad news.

EXPLOSION:
Of an explosion: Friends will disapprove of your actions.

Being injured in an explosion: Must endure vexation.

Face being scarred by an explosion: Will be unjustly accused.

Being enveloped in flames after an explosion: Friends trespass on rights.

Others being in an explosion: Danger to a relative.

Being guilty of causing an explosion: Friends will lose confidence in you.

EXPRESS:
Traveling on an express bus: An enemy is seeking your ruin.

Traveling on an express train: Be careful not to offend superiors.

Mailing an express letter: Danger through a secret.

Receiving an express letter: Will be cheated by friends.

EXQUISITE:
Having exquisite taste: Will be sorry for present actions.

A lady of exquisite beauty: Will incur many debts.

Meeting an exquisite man: Joy without profit.

Flirting with an exquisite woman: Will have a sad future.

EXTINGUISH:
Extinguishing a fire: Great danger is ahead.

Extinguishing a flame: Will not have sufficient money.

Extinguishing a light: Serious quarrels over love.

Extinguishing a law suit: Will be persecuted by a woman.

EXTRAVAGANT:
Being extravagant: Shame and sorrow.

Others being extravagant: Financial gains.

Wife being extravagant: Will realize high ambitions.

Husband being extravagant: Use caution in business ventures.

EYES:
Of many eyes: Good results in business.
Having beautiful eyes: Love and joy.
Having blue eyes: Tremendous joy.
Having black eyes: Misery.
Having brown eyes: Happiness.
Having green eyes: Unexpected big wealth.
Having red eyes: Illness.
Having hazel eyes: Gossip by friends.
Having crossed eyes: Will be short of money.
Having big eyes: Will receive a large inheritance.
Having small eyes: You are deeply loved.
Having green and blue eyes: Big financial gains.
Having grim eyes: Good business.
The eyes of a healthy person: Business success.
The eyes of a sick person: Will have a long life.
Eyes being wide-open: A change in life will soon come.
Having good eyesight: Good health.
Losing your eyesight: Children are in danger of death.
Children's eyes: Financial gains.
Admiring the eyes of your wife: You are unfaithful to your wife.
Admiring the eyes of your husband: May expect a baby.
Being worried about the eyes: Be careful of your actions.

Being worried about children's eyes: Someone is working secretly against you.

EYEBROWS:
Of own eyebrows: Financial gains.
Brown eyebrows: Big fortune.
Black eyebrows: Big joy.
Bushy eyebrows: Financial gains.
Narrow eyebrows: Big sorrow.
Long eyebrows: Happiness in love.
Eyebrows falling out: You have an unfaithful lover.
Eyebrows of a relative: Public esteem.
Eyebrows of husband: Success in love.
Eyebrows of wife: Considerable fortune.
Eyebrows of children: Financial gains.
Eyebrows of enemies: You are being deceived.

EYEGLASS:
Wearing an eyeglass: Will fall into disgrace.
Other people wearing eyeglasses: Good news will be received from a friend.
Enemies wearing eyeglasses: A change in life will soon come.

EYELIDS:
Beautiful eyelids: Happiness in life.
Unusually expressive eyelids: Success in love.
Small eyelids: Considerable fortune.
Big eyelids: Will have a long life.

F

FABLE:
Telling a fable: Important and very beneficial event to come.
Hearing others tell a fable: Must mend your ways in life.
Telling a fable to children: Big joy.

FACE:
Seeing own face in a mirror: Will not succeed in own plans.
A beautiful face: Quarrels among lovers.
A bright happy face: Good luck is ahead.
An ugly face: Unhappiness in love affairs.
A smiling face: Financial gains.
A repulsive face: Failure of enemies.
Children's faces: Postponement of success.
Faces of absolute strangers: Change of residence.

Washing own face: Repentance for sins.

FACTORY:
People entering a factory: Important and beneficial event to come.
Factories belonging to others: A false friend is nearby.
Being in a factory: Big riches in the future.
Building a factory: Death of a friend.
Buying a factory: You will be blessed.
Selling a factory: Sickness is ahead.
A paper factory: Affairs will prosper.
A silk factory: Affairs will go from bad to worse.
A velvet factory: Will entertain an unwelcome guest.
A linen factory: Use caution in business ventures.
A dish factory: Will live a long life.
A pottery factory: Will be visited by a good friend.
A clothing factory: Congenial work and good news.

FAGOT:
Many bundles of sticks or twigs: Will receive false news.
Carrying bundles of fagots: Unhappy days are ahead.
Others carrying bundles of fagots: You are being cheated by a friend.
Children carrying bundles of fagots: Change for the better.

FAILURE:
Being a failure: Will realize high ambitions.
Relatives being a failure: Use caution in business ventures.
Others being a failure: Postponement of success.
Husband being a failure: Are unfitted to fill your position.

FAINT:
Having fainted: Foretells illness.
Suffering injury from fainting: Rapid success of own hopes.
A member of the family fainting: A false friend is nearby.
Children fainting: Unhappiness in love affairs.

Other people fainting: Postponement of success.

FAIR:
Being at a fair: Social activities of a happy nature.
Others going to a fair: Change for the better.
Going to a fair with the family: Postponement of success.
Going to a fair with friends: Will have emotional sorrow.

FAIRY:
Of a fairy: Will have a contented life.
Children dreaming of fairies: You should mend your ways in life.

FAITHFUL:
Being faithful: Will become jealous.
Having a faithful mate: Happiness between children and parents.
Having faithful children: Beware of rivals.
Having faithful relatives: Happiness is assured.
Having faithful friends: Sickness.

FALCON:
Of a falcon: Own fortune will increase.
Holding a falcon in your hands: Pleasure.
Others holding a falcon: Are surrounded by enemies who are envious.
Falcons flying: Will be cheated by friends.

FALL:
Falling from a high place: Misfortune is ahead.
Falling from a medium height: Loss of honor.
Being injured in a fall: Will endure hardship and lose friends.
Falling and being frightened: Will experience some trouble.
Falling without injury: Will be victorious in your struggles.
Falling to the floor: You are menaced by danger.
Falling from a bridge: Madness.
Falling and arising again: Honor.

Falling in a grave hole: A catastrophe is ahead.

Falling in the water: Risk of death for the dreamer.

Falling in the ocean: Will have bad health.

Falling in the ocean and then awaking with a start: Honor and wealth.

Being thrown in the ocean by enemies: Will be persecuted.

Others falling: Will be promoted.

Relatives falling: Triumph over enemies.

Children falling: Joy without profit.

Enemies falling: Do not confide your secret.

Friends falling: You are being deceived.

FALSEHOOD:

Telling a falsehood: Will live a long life.

Others telling falsehoods to you: Will be cheated by friends.

Others telling falsehoods: You have many enemies.

Husband or wife telling falsehood to the other: Will suffer from own folly.

Children telling parents falsehoods: Will realize high ambitions.

FAME:

Having fame: Will have dealings with authorities.

Someone else achieving fame: Will be rich through own work.

Children achieving fame: Will live a long life.

Mate achieving fame: Failure of enemies.

FAMILY:

Of own family: Be cautious in your ventures.

Having a large family: Prosperous times are in store.

Having a small family: A friend is trying to help.

Having no family or relatives: You are being deceived.

The family of other people: Failure of enemies.

FAMINE:

Of enduring famine: Triumph over enemies.

A continued famine: Will live in great comfort.

Others suffering famine: Business will suffer.

Having plenty following a famine: Will be very rich.

FAMOUS:

Being famous: Losses and changes for the worse.

Children becoming famous: Rapid success of own hopes.

Husband becoming famous: He is in love with another woman.

Other famous people: Sorrow is about to come.

FAN:

Having a fan: News of a pleasant nature will come soon.

A young woman dreaming of being fanned: Will soon be married.

A single lady fanning herself: Will soon form profitable acquaintances.

A woman losing her fan: A close friend will drift away.

A woman buying a fan: She is interested in another man.

Others with fans: You have many rivals.

A rival with a fan: Loss of money.

FANTASY:

Of fantasy: Will enjoy good things.

Seeing things in fantasy: Will be very disillusioned.

A beautiful woman in fantasy: Will soon love someone else.

A handsome man in fantasy: Loss of money.

FAREWELL:

Bidding farewell to someone else: Be cautious in business ventures.

Bidding farewell to relatives: Will receive painful news.

Bidding farewell to children: Worry will be smoothed away.

Others bidding you farewell: Must control passions.

Husband and wife bidding farewell: A false friend is nearby.

FARM:
Owning a large farm: Will inherit money.
Owning a small farm: Will realize high ambitions.
Buying a farm: Big harvest for the farmer.
Selling a farm: Will have to struggle.
Visiting a farm: Good health.
Others visiting your farm: Rapid success in own affairs.
Working on own farm: Great success in business.
Relatives working on a farm: Will take a safe journey.
Hiring people to work on a farm: You should mend your ways in life.
Working a farm all alone: Material success.
Making paths on a farm: Hard work ahead.
A farm burning: Considerable fortune ahead.
A prosperous farm: Advantages in business, matrimony, and inheritance.
A vacant farm: Misery.
Farm belonging to others: Congenial work and good news.

FARTHING:
Being given a farthing: Loss in business.
Giving others a farthing: Worry will be smoothed away.
Changing an English farthing: Misery.

FASHIONS:
Studying a fashion magazine: Danger through a secret.
Watching a fashion show: Will have a long life.
Fashion models in a store window: Family quarrels.
Others being in a fashion show: Watch out for treachery.
Taking family to a fashion show: Postponement of success.

FASTING:
Of fasting: Big honor.
Members of family fasting with you: Big wealth.
Fasting according to own religion: Happiness is assured.

FAT:
A woman dreaming of getting fat: She will be abandoned by her lover.
A young girl dreaming of growing fat: Will be married soon.
A man dreaming of growing fat: Will soon be a free man.
A married woman dreaming of growing fat: Happy days are ahead for her.
A woman dreaming of getting really fat: Big wealth and honest love.
Children getting fat: Happy change for the dreamer.
Relatives getting fat: Wealth.
Other women being fat: Dishonest and dangerous activities.
Other people who are fat: Postponement of success.
Eating fat: Success in love affairs.
Cooking with fat: Good business ventures.

FATHER:
Of own father: Happiness.
Father being in a happy mood: Loss in business.
Father being dead: A big catastrophe is ahead.
Father being poor: All desires will be accomplished.
Own father passing away: Will not have success in business.
Talking to your father: Virtue.
The father of other people: A false friend is nearby.

FATHER-IN-LAW:
Of own father-in-law: Important and very beneficial event to come.
Father-in-law being dead: Will be threatened by people.
Father-in-law being alive: Bad luck.
Others' father-in-law: Will be difficult to escape approaching troubles.

FATIGUE:
Being fatigued: Coming success in some venture.
Others being fatigued: Friends are endeavoring to destroy you.
Mate being fatigued: Abundant means.
Children being fatigued: Be cautious in your dealings.

FAULT:
Being at fault: Will be reprimanded by friends.
Children being at fault: Shame and sorrow.
Husband being at fault: A false friend is nearby.
Wife being at fault: A mystery will be solved.
Partner being at fault: Will live a long life.
Others being at fault: Doomed for disappointment.

FAVOR:
Doing a favor for others: Loss of friendship.
Others doing you a favor: Loss of money.
Receiving a favor from relatives: Warning of arguments.
Receiving a favor from a loyal friend: Change of surroundings.
Receiving a favor from a loved one: Death of an enemy.

FAVORITE:
Of a favorite person: Joy.
Being a favorite person of other people: Will receive a thing you like.
Favorite relatives: Unhappiness.
Favorite friend: Will be asked for money.

FEAR:
Having fear of something: Someone will take care of you.
Overcoming own fears: Everything will go well.
Having persisting fears: Will meet with deceit and treachery.
Not knowing reason for fear: Do not trust one you now trust.
Having great fears: You are a person of extraordinary courage.

FEAST:
Having a feast: Expect difficulties in the near future.
Preparing a feast: Another person is enjoying what you desired.
Relatives having a feast: Will receive happy news.
Children having a feast: Happiness.
Enemies having a feast: Misery is ahead.
Others having a feast: Joy and contentment.

FEAT:
Accomplishing great feats: Failure and humiliation.
Others accomplishing great feats: Postponement of success.
Friends accomplishing great feats: Hard work is ahead.

FEATHER:
White feathers: Will be very lucky.
Black feathers: Will be very unlucky.
Red feathers: Good business ventures.
Brown feathers: Success.
Gray feathers: Wealth.
Light-blue feathers: Realization of own ambitions.
Tan feathers: Prospect of a journey.
People wearing feathers in hats: Rapid success of own hopes.
Collecting feathers: Will have joy during life.
Wearing a tuft of feathers: Great honors will come to you.

FEATURES:
Not remembering a person's strange features: Important introduction.
Features with blue-green eyes: New friendships.
Features with dark eyes: Will have a lover.
Features with hazel eyes: Important event to come.
Features with a bearded face: A traveler will return.
Smiling features: A wish will be granted.

FEBRUARY:
Of February during this month: Good month for business.

Receiving a gift during February: Treason from lover.

Giving birth to a child during February: Will have many worries.

February during another month of the year: Illness.

Being born in February: Important and very beneficial events to come.

Children being born in February: Will succeed in political life.

FEEBLE:

Being feeble: Will live a long life.

Always being feeble: Must gasp for air to breathe.

Others being feeble: You are looking for money.

Children being feeble: Financial gains.

FEED:

Feeding small children: Financial gains.

Feeding animals: Affairs will prosper.

Others feeding children: You are being deceived.

Others feeding animals: Someone is endeavoring to destroy you.

FEET:

Of own feet: Jealousy.

Feet hurting: Likely to have troubles of humiliating nature.

Others' feet next to yours: Will soon make a trip.

Burning own feet: Failure in own affairs.

Having a broken foot: Loss of a relative.

Kissing the feet of another person: Will change your conduct.

Children's feet: Big disappointment.

Bathing own feet: Will have trouble and be molested.

Bathing feet in the ocean: Shame and sorrow.

Bathing feet in a river: Illness.

Bathing feet in a basin: You are too greedy.

Having dirty feet: Will be in danger.

Having feet cut off: Will have an operation.

Own naked feet: Unexpected misfortune.

Having own feet dislocated: Illness in the family.

Feet being scratched by others: Do not pay attention to enemies.

Feet itching: Joy without profit.

Having big feet: Will live a long life.

Having small feet: Worry will be smoothed away.

The feet of animals or birds: You have faithful friends.

Measuring distances in feet: Happiness and good humor.

A ruler marked in feet: You are a smooth talker around ladies.

FENCE:

Climbing a fence: Own efforts will meet with success.

Falling from a fence: You are attempting more than you can complete.

Climbing through a fence: Will obtain money in questionable manner.

Others climbing a fence: Death of an enemy.

FENCING:

Of fencing: Good adventures are ahead.

Others fencing: Misfortune in love affairs.

Enemies fencing: Beware of jealous friends.

Teaching fencing: Will experience many ups and downs.

FENDER:

Standing on a fender: Will soon travel to a foreign country.

Others standing on a fender: Accord among friends.

Denting a fender: Someone is endeavoring to destroy you.

Others denting your fender: Good times are coming.

FERRET:

Of this small animal: Be on guard against spiteful gossip.

Using a ferret to hunt: Will have a vigorous mind.

A ferret hunting rabbits: Approaching money.

A ferret hunting rats: Will have emotional sorrow.

FERRY:
Of a ferry boat: Expect the visit of a friend.
Being on a ferry boat alone: Danger is nearby.
Being on a ferry boat with others: Success in love.
Being on a ferry boat with family: Good times are coming.
Others on a ferry: Triumph over enemies.
Friends being at a ferry: You have a loyal friend.
Enemies being at a ferry: You are being watched by one with evil intent.

FESTIVAL:
Of a festival: Expect difficulties in the near future.
Preparing a festival: Another person is enjoying what you desired.
Others at a festival: Joy and contentment.
Being at a festival with relatives: Will receive happy news.
Being at a festival with children: Happiness.
Enemies being at a festival: Misery is ahead.

FETTERS:
Being set free from chains: Will escape some difficulty.
Not being free of fetters: Bad news is ahead.
Others being bound in fetters: Burdens are about to depart.
Relatives being bound in fetters: You have several loyal friends.
Enemies being bound in fetters: You are being deceived.
Cutting your fetters: Will have worries for a short time.

FEVER:
Having a very high fever: Friends will tell you lies.
Suffering from a fever: Will be bothered by petty worries.
Children having a fever: Will get what you desired.
Relatives having a fever: Financial gains.

Friends having a fever: Will be cheated by friends.

FIANCE:
Of own fiancé: Will have sad experiences.
Daughter's fiancé: An argument will soon be overcome.
Son's fiancée: A disagreement will be settled.
Another person's fiancé: Will have a vigorous mind.

FIASCO:
Making a ridiculous failure: Will realize high ambitions.
Others making a fiasco: Postponement of success.
Children making a fiasco: Bad business ventures.
Husband making a fiasco: Are unfitted to fill your position.

FIDDLE:
Of a fiddle: Big prosperity.
Playing a fiddle: A change in life will come soon.
Others playing a fiddle: Will have emotional sorrow.
Owning a fiddle: Avoid rivals.

FIELD:
Of a field: Will make a good marriage.
Being in a field: Happiness.
Working in a field: Hard work is ahead.
Buying a field: Will have much hospitality.
A field of grain: Pleasant friends.
A field of oats: Prosperity.
A field of corn: Good earnings.

FIEND:
Of a fiend: Travel and prosperity.
A young girl dreaming of a fiend: A happy marriage will soon take place.
Married people dreaming of a fiend: Happiness and long married life.
Being taken away by a fiend: Serious disaster is ahead.
A young man dreaming of a fiend: Will soon be engaged.

FIFE:
Having a fife: Advancement within your position.
Hearing a fife played: Will take a trip to see a relative in the army.
Others playing a fife: Luck and prosperity.

FIGHT:
Of being in a fight: Misfortune in love affairs.
Others being in a fight: Recovery from an illness.
Being beaten in a fight: Will have opposition in love.
Winning a fight: Will overcome your difficulties.

FIGS:
Of figs during their season: Pleasure and honors.
Figs when out of season: Sorrow.
Eating figs: Squandering of wealth.
Having dry figs: Loss of fortune.

FIGURES:
Of figures: Dignity.
Dreaming of figures and not remembering the number: Pleasant social affairs.
Seeing many people and figuring how many: Satisfaction of ambitions.
(See also **NUMBERS.**)

FILBERTS:
Of these nuts: Will make financial gains.
Eating filberts: Abundant means.

FILE:
A nail file: A mystery will be solved.
A machinist's file: Unpleasant news will arrive soon.
Several files: Will realize high ambitions.
Using a file: Will have new work to do.
Putting papers in a file: Are confronted with insurmountable obstacles.
Taking papers out of a file: An enemy is seeking your ruin.
A filing cabinet: Discovery of lost valuables.

FILL:
Of filling: Will be involved in a secret transaction.
Filling bottles: Happiness for the woman of the house.
Filling pockets: Honor.
Filling a handbag: Will receive a gift of jewelry.
Filling a hole: You enjoy amusements too much of the time.

FILM:
Having film: Avoid rivals.
Buying film: Possible journey abroad in the near future.
Using film: Guard what you say carefully.
Others using film: Much discussion is going on concerning you.

FIND:
Finding something: Loss in business.
Finding a valuable article: Big misfortune in business.
Others finding valuable things: Shame and sorrow.
Finding someone naked: Will find new employment.
Finding someone lost in a forest: Will have an unsettled future.
Finding a child: Will have a very complicated lawsuit.
Finding a tree: Dissolution.
Finding various other things: Infidelity.
Finding gold and silver: Will have many worries.

FINGERS:
Fingers being covered with gold rings: Will be married soon.
Having pains in the fingers: Big joy.
Pale fingers: Your love will be reciprocated.
A finger bleeding: Be careful not to lose money.
Nice fingers: Will do much charitable work.
Cutting the fingers: Will quarrel with friends.
Having fingers cut off: Loss of friends.
Having finger nails cut: Dishonor.
Burning the fingers: Are envied by many people.

Having long fingers: Marriage will not last long.

Having short fingers: Inheritance.

Having more than five fingers: Will make new friends.

Having less than five fingers: Joy and love.

Breaking the fingers: Will have a good marriage.

FIRE:

Poking up a fire in a fireplace: You have no control of your temper.

A blazing fire: Great joy will come to you.

Lots of smoke but no flames: Will be disappointed.

Being unaware of a fire: You are loved very much.

Firemen putting out a fire: Will receive good news.

A burning fire without smoke: Will have plenty of money.

Someone falling into a fire: Misfortune.

Relatives burning in a fire: Will soon have a high fever.

Watching a fire being put out: Poverty.

Being in a fire: Triumph.

A dead fire: Will have bad fortune.

A small fire: Expect good news.

A large fire: Expect serious changes in your affairs.

A big fire burning: Will soon have a quarrel.

Being burned in a fire: Business damaged.

Throwing water on a fire: Will lose your temper.

Fire falling from the sky: Desolation.

Starting a fire: Will allow yourself to be seduced.

An artificial fire: Will become pregnant soon.

Taking something from a fire with hand: Will surmount obstacles.

Extinguishing a fire completely: Will be compensated.

FIREARMS:

Of firearms: Coming quarrels.

Owning firearms: Financial gains.

Carrying firearms: Will have a lawsuit.

Selling firearms: You are in the company of ruffians.

FIRE ENGINE:

Of fire engines: Danger ahead.

Fire engines going to a fire: Will have peace.

Fire engines returning from a fire: Will receive a big disappointment.

Being a fireman on a fire engine: Will realize high ambitions.

Being the head fireman: Riches and fortune.

FIRESIDE:

Sitting by a fireside alone: Will be happy in love.

Sitting by a fireside with others: Are being deceived by friends.

Sitting beside a fireside with family: Will live a long life.

Sitting beside a fireside with fiancé: Will soon get married.

FIREWORKS:

Of fireworks: A baby will be born soon.

Watching a fireworks display: Will suffer through own foolishness.

Watching fireworks with children: Joy without profit.

Watching fireworks with relatives: Family quarrels.

FIR:

The dark coloring of fir trees: Will be cheated by friends.

A fir tree with many green leaves: Prosperous but hard work ahead.

Several fir trees: Congenial work and good news.

Cutting down fir trees: Will solve present troubles easily.

FIRMAMENT:

Of the moonlit heavens: Financial gain.

Viewing firmament with a loved one: Luck and prosperity.

Viewing firmament free of clouds: Big fortune is ahead.

Viewing firmament obscured by clouds: Unhappiness.

FISH:
Fish swimming freely about: Good fortune.
Catching fish: You will be loved very much.
Dead fish in a store: Expect troubles.
Fish in shallow water: Loss of reputation.
A fish market: Will obtain a high honorable position.
A woman dreaming of fishes of many colors: Illness.
A man dreaming of fishes of many colors: Will quarrel and suffer.
Having fish: Will enjoy pleasures that will cost money.
Cooking fish: Marriage.
Eating boiled fish: Joy.
Eating fried fish: Big worries.
A dead fish in a stream: Loss of hope.
Fish hatching: Will have difficulties in bearing a child.
Catching a large fish: Joy and profit.
Catching a small fish: Ruin in proportion to size of fish.
Red-colored fish: Big contentment.
Salted fish: Will have to fight to avoid misery.
Salmon fish: Dissatisfaction.
Other people fishing: Will have children with poor health.
Children fishing: Joy and health.
Relatives fishing: Difficult business enterprises.
Eating cod fish: Will receive good news.
Buying cod fish: Will have an unexpected visitor.

FISHERMAN:
Of a fisherman: Expect very good news.
Being a fisherman: Happiness assured.
Many fishermen: A large measure of prosperity awaits.
Being in the company of a fisherman: Unexpected fortune.

FISHING:
Going fishing: Loss of a friend.
Fishing with a loved one: Will enjoy expensive pleasures.
Fishing with relatives: Be on guard against spiteful gossip.
Enemies fishing: A mystery will be solved.
Fishing with a rod: Loneliness.
Fishing with nets: Will do business with smart women.
Fishing in the sea: Be on the lookout for treachery.
Fishing in a river: Unhappiness in love affairs.
Fishing in a canal: Will realize high ambitions.
Fishing in a pond: Must rely on own good judgment.
Fishing from a rock: Important and very benefical events to come.

FIST:
Using your fists: Good news to come.
Hitting someone with your fist: Will enjoy a very long friendship.
Children hitting with their fists: Will be insulted.
Other people fighting with fists: Will have a delay in business.

FIT:
Having a fit: Family quarrels.
Others having a fit: Illness is ahead.
Children having a fit: Physical disorders.
Husband or wife having a fit: Loss of present position.
Enemies having a fit: Will be annoyed by petty quarrels.

FLAG:
Carrying a flag: Honor will come to you.
A flag floating in the breeze: Will escape from threatened misfortune.
Viewing a display of flags: Triumph over enemies.
White flags: Success in own undertakings.
Navy-blue flags: Will have prosperity through other people.

Light-blue flags: Promotion within employment.

Yellow flag: Important changes in your affairs.

Red flag: Warning of quarrels with friends.

Green flag: Good fortune in love affairs.

Black flag: Will be unfortunate.

Brown flag: Big friendship.

Gold flag: Will do business with people faraway.

FLAGON:

Of a flagon: Danger through a secret.

A flagon of liquor: Illness.

Drinking from a flagon of wine: Shame and sorrow.

Others drinking from a flagon: Avoid rivals.

FLAGPOLE:

A small flagpole: Arguments and war.

A big flagpole: Victory.

Holding a flagpole: Security.

Breaking a flagpole: Hard work.

FLAME:

Of flames: A lovers' quarrel will end in joy.

Dark flames: Danger in love matters.

Uncontrolled flames: Difficulties ahead.

Flames being under control: Will receive good news.

FLANNEL:

Of flannel: Unhappiness.

Wearing flannel underwear: Sickness.

Wearing a flannel suit: Will have unpleasant events ahead.

Wrapping something in flannel: You are guilty of wrongdoing.

FLASH:

Of a flash of light: Will be cheated by friends.

A flash from a torch or searchlight: Important news causing success.

Buying a flashlight: You are being watched by one with evil intent.

Using a flashlight: A secret will be solved.

FLASK:

Of a flask: Will ignore your friends.

Owning a flask: Enjoyment.

Drinking wine from a flask: Troubles caused by drinking too much.

A flask full of water: Will be rich.

Breaking a flask: Losses.

Others drinking from a flask: Be on guard against gossip.

FLATTERY:

Being flattered by others: Their attention is false and insincere.

Flattering other people: You will be defrauded.

Flattering your mate: Will live a long life.

Flattering a fiancé: Must control passions.

Flattering friends: Will experience many ups and downs.

FLAX:

Of flax: Will have success in all you undertake.

Having flax: A change in life will soon come.

Spinning flax: Will have a long life.

FLEAS:

Of fleas: Unhappiness.

Catching a flea: Will be worried.

Killing a flea: Will encounter obstacles.

Being bitten by a flea: Will be rich.

Many fleas: Enemies desire revenge.

Fleas being on children: Will entertain an unwelcome guest.

A woman dreaming of fleas: She has an inconsistent lover.

FLEEING:

Fleeing from someone: Disappointment and sorrow.

Fleeing from friends: You expect too many favors from other people.

Fleeing from enemies: Worry will be smoothed away.

Others fleeing: Will be cheated by friends.

FLEET:

Of a naval fleet: Will receive a letter from a loved one.

A merchant marine fleet: Will receive a letter from a friend.

A naval fleet in a parade: You are being deceived.

A naval fleet on maneuvers: Changes in business.

A foreign naval fleet: Will entertain an unwelcome guest.

FLIES:
Of flies: Will be annoyed by friends.

Many flies: Will do something very foolish.

Flies on children: Will have an honest lover.

Flies on a dog or cat: Will live a long life.

Flies being around food: Postponement of success.

Being bitten by a horsefly: Sorrow is about to come.

Being bitten by a wasp: Will be persecuted by envious friends.

FLIRT:
Of flirting: Prosperity.

Others flirting with you: Big happiness.

Flirting with a married woman: Beware of treachery.

Flirting with a married man: Suitable time to pursue a courtship.

Flirting with an unmarried girl: Avoid rivals.

Flirting with an unmarried man: You will be deceived.

Flirting with a divorced person: Will realize own ambitions.

Flirting with a widow: Financial gains.

Flirting with a widower: Will be guilty of foolish actions.

FLOAT:
Of something floating: All will go well.

Having trouble staying afloat: Expect troubles ahead.

Others floating: A false friend is nearby.

A dead person floating near a beach: Will live a long life.

A dead fish floating near the beach: Danger through a secret.

An empty boat floating: Will have a change in surroundings.

FLOOD:
Of a big flood: Will be jilted by lover.

Saving yourself from a flood: You have one loyal friend.

Relatives being in a flood: A false friend is nearby.

Others being in a flood: Will be unfortunate in love affairs.

Floods causing devastation: Worry will be smoothed away.

The ruin caused by floods: Postponement of success.

FLOOR:
Sweeping your floor: Be cautious in your ventures.

Washing the floor: Financial gains.

Sitting on the floor: Will realize high ambitions.

Sleeping on the floor: Will live a long life.

A dirty floor: Congenial work and good news.

Having the floor repaired: Loss of money.

FLOUR:
Buying flour: Will be making money.

Having flour: Abundance.

Cooking with flour: Loss of a friend.

Burning flour: Danger is ahead.

Making pastries with flour: A happy life is ahead.

Dealing in the flour market: Will make risky speculations.

FLOWER:
Of flowers: Great happiness.

Blooming flowers: Pleasures are ahead.

A young woman dreaming of receiving flowers: Will have many suitors.

Gathering flowers: Will marry soon.

Receiving flowers from faraway: Will be an heir to a fortune.

Picking flowers from a plant: Big benefit.

A florist's yard full of flowers: Will have big losses.

Painted flowers: Will be worried.

Artificial flowers: Misfortune in business.

Receiving flowers as a gift: Big joy.

Being greeted with flowers: Pleasure and contentment.

Flowers blooming in May: Will have a better future.

Own preferred flower: Will be blessed.

White flowers: Small difficulties.

Yellow flowers: Big difficulties.

Red flowers: Death.

Pink flowers: You are in love.

Bright-colored flowers: Gloom is in store.

Flowers of various other colors: Financial gains.

Having flowers out of season: Obstacles are ahead.

Flowers in the house: Pleasure and joy.

Plants of flowers: Will have plenty of money.

Picking flowers: Will have a steady friendship.

A yard full of flowers: Will have weakness in your body.

Smelling the scent of flowers coming from the yard: Loss of friends.

Throwing flowers away: Violent quarrels.

Throwing away blossoming flowers: Will suffer from own carelessness.

FLUSH:

Of flushing the bathroom: Be on guard against spiteful gossip.

Flushing water from a sink: Family unhappiness.

Flushing a boiler: Fortune will arrive a little late.

Flushing pipes: Will fall into poverty and misery.

FLUTE:

Of a flute: Money will come easily during life.

Playing the flute: Financial gains.

Others playing the flute: Expect difficulties.

Children playing the flute: Will receive news of a birth.

FLUTTER:

Birds fluttering: Infidelity.

Many birds fluttering: Avoid rivals.

Birds fluttering on branch of a tree: Beware of a family member's actions.

Ducks fluttering in the water: Your sweetheart has ulterior motives.

FLYING:

Of flying: Congenial work and good news.

Flying at a high altitude: Big fortune.

Flying at a low altitude: Ruin is ahead for you.

A plane flying in distress: Loss through investments.

Being an aviator: Ambitious plans are possibly beyond power to accomplish.

Flying in a plane: Profitable speculation.

Others flying: Be on the lookout for treachery.

Owning a plane: Success in all enterprises.

FLYING FISH:

Of a flying fish: Will be cheated by friends.

Flying fish going through the air: Will be deceived.

Several flying fishes flying one after the other: Happiness.

FLY NET:

Using a fly net: Happiness.

Catching flies and butterflies with a fly net: Have unrighteous desires.

Buying a fly net: Persecution.

Breaking a fly net: Things will go well for you.

FOAL:

Of a foal: Will receive news of the birth of a child.

Many foals: Postponement of success.

A foal running after her mother: Approaching good days.

A foal sucking milk from her mother: Triumph over enemies.

FOAM:

Foam created from brushing teeth: Will be very fortunate.

Foam created from cooking foods: Will be surrounded with cheerful friends.

The foam of a horse's mouth: You have loyal friends.
Foam coming out of a dog's mouth: Are unfitted to fill your position.

FOG:
A dense fog: Business will be bad.
Ground fog moving up into the sky: Will have a big disappointment.
Fog clearing away: Happiness in love.
Fog clearing away to sunshine: Will have a long and happy marriage.
Traveling through a fog: Financial worries.
Emerging from a fog: Will have a tiresome journey.

FOLD:
Folding something: Death of a friend.
Others folding things: Will succeed in your business.
Folding clothes: Will realize high ambitions.
Folding household linen: Big financial gains.

FOLIAGE:
Of fallen foliage: Dangerous illness.
Having a crown of foliage: Big honors.
The foliage of figs: People are envious of you.
Eating boiled foliage: Dissension within the family.
Green foliage: Pleasures are in store for you.
Dry foliage: Sickness.
Brown foliage: Joy.
Grape foliage: Will lose your temper.
Dead foliage: Undertakings will not succeed.

FONT:
Of a spring font: Important and very beneficial events to come.
A font in a public park: You have one loyal friend.
A font filled with water in a garden: A change in life will soon come.
A font inside a sacred building: Will be abandoned by lover.

FOOD:
Of food: Happiness.
Eating food: Joy.

Leftover food: Will soon have trouble.
Food that has gone bad: Loss of money.
Eating food like a glutton: Be cautious in business ventures.
Not having enough food: Death of an enemy.
Eating food and not being satisfied: A false friend is nearby.
People selling food: You will receive some money.
Others eating food: Rapid success of own hopes.
Children eating food: Fortune in love affairs.
Tasting food: Loss of friends.

FOOLISH:
Having committed foolish actions: Will have financial gains.
Others committing foolish actions: Joy without profit.
Children doing foolish actions: Will receive money soon.
Mate being foolish: Financial gains.
Lover being foolish: You should mend your ways in life.
Two engaged people being foolish: Both will suffer from their foolishness.

FOOT:
Of own foot: Jealousy.
Having a broken foot: Loss of a relative.
Foot hurting: Likely will have humiliating troubles.
Having a dirty foot: Will be in danger.
Cutting the foot: Will have an operation.
Own foot being naked: Unexpected misfortune.
Having foot dislocated: Illness within the family.
Having a big foot: Will live a long life.
Having a small foot: Worry will be smoothed away.
The foot of own children: Big disappointment.
The foot of other people: Will soon make a trip.

FOOTBALL:
Playing football: Good business ventures.
Winning a football game: Future is secured.
Not scoring in a football game: Will have a long life.
Watching a football game: You may expect worries.
Others scoring in a football game: A friend will cause worries.
Children playing football: A friend is trying to help.
Husband playing football: Triumph over enemies.

FOOTMAN:
Of a footman: Avoid rivals.
Having a footman at your service: Unexpected troubles.
Being a footman: A false friend is nearby.

FOOTPRINTS:
Footprints of a woman: Rapid success of own hopes.
Footprints of a man: Use caution in business ventures.
Own footprints: Luck and prosperity.
Footprints of children: Will surmount difficulties.
Footprints of others: A friend is trying to help you secretly.

FOOTSTEPS:
Stepping up on a footstep: Great success.
Stepping down from a footstep: Will hear good news.
The footstep of own house: Will live a long life.
The footstep of a neighbor's home: Will be deceived.

FOP:
Of a silly person: Someone is endeavoring to destroy you.
Several silly people: Accord among friends.
A married woman dreaming of a male fop: Should mend your ways in life.
A married man dreaming of a female fop: Will have a new love affair.

An unmarried woman dreaming of a male fop: Lover has inferior position.

FORCE:
Using great strength to force something: Will be dominated by others.
Using force against other people: Your hopes will be realized.
Forcing others to do your will: You allow others to dominate you.
Using force against a prisoner: Despair.
Forcing a safe open: Will buy an old-fashioned safe.

FOREHEAD:
Having a fine forehead: Will attain power.
The forehead of others: Will begin a new business venture.
A large forehead: Will enjoy high spirits.
A smooth forehead: Will have much influence.
An ugly forehead: Vexation.
A wounded forehead: Will discover an unknown treasure.

FOREIGN COUNTRY:
Of a foreign country: Will be deceived.
Going to a foreign country: Your happiness lies at home.
Being in a foreign country alone: A change in life will soon come.
Being in a foreign country with others: Will have new business ventures.
Being in a foreign country with a lady: Will be guilty of foolish actions.
Being in a foreign country with a man: Must control passions.
Being in a foreign country with loved one: Luck and prosperity.

FOREIGN CURRENCY:
Of foreign currency: Promotion in your affairs.
Possessing foreign currency: Family troubles.
Buying foreign currency: Will have a loss in business.
Selling foreign currency: Change for the better.

Making payments in foreign currency: Financial gains.
Receiving foreign currency: You are being deceived.

FOREIGNERS:
Meeting foreigners: Discovery of lost valuables.
Being in the company of foreigners: Happiness is assured.
Marrying a foreigner: Will be fortunate in love affairs.
Falling in love with a foreigner: Will live a long life.
Disliking a foreigner: Undertakings will not succeed.

FOREST:
Of a dense forest: Someone will care a lot for you.
Being alone in a forest: Social activities of a happy nature.
Being with others in a forest: Will be cheated by friends.
A forest fire: Glad news.
Wandering around in a forest: Inheritance.
Relatives being in a forest: Will be jilted by your lover.
Strolling through a forest: Pain is ahead for you.
A forest with unusually high trees: Good business affairs.

FORGE:
Of a blacksmith shop: Your love is not secured.
A blacksmith forging: Troubles over love affairs.
The fire and sparks from a forge: Serious quarrels over love.
Being a blacksmith: Will be in need of money.

FORGERY:
Being guilty of forgery: Will receive unexpected money.
Others committing forgery: Friends are not telling you the truth.
Forging a signature: Richness is ahead.
Others forging your signature: Financial gains.

FORGET:
Of forgetting: Business will not improve from present condition.
Forgetting a date: Disappointment in love.
Forgetting to mail a letter: Will receive bad news.
Forgetting to pay a bill: A mystery will be solved.
Forgetting a loved one: Fortune is near at hand.

FORGET-ME-NOT:
Of a forget-me-not: You are beloved and remembered by many.
Having forget-me-nots: Will live a long life.
Receiving forget-me-nots as a gift: Big gain in love.
Giving forget-me-nots as a remembrance: Important and beneficial event coming.
Receiving a bouquet of forget-me-nots: A faithful friend loves you.

FORK:
Of forks: Big family quarrels.
Eating with a fork: Happiness is assured.
Using a fork to cook: You have parasites near you.
Others using forks: Reconciliation with an enemy is impossible.
Guests using forks to eat: Rapid success of own hopes.
Receiving a gift of forks: Doomed for disappointment.

FORLORN:
Feeling forlorn: Will have family quarrels.
Being miserably forlorn: Will regain a cheerful state of mind.
Others being forlorn: Worry will be smoothed away.

FORSAKE:
Forsaking something dear: Failure of enemies.
Others being forsaken: Will have much affection.
Being forsaken by a loved one: Hard work awaits you.

Forsaking a loved one: Loneliness and trouble.

FORT:
Of a fort: Troubles and losses in store.
Being in a fort: Avoid rivals.
Being in a fort with others: Will forgive someone in disgrace.
Being honored when entering a fort: Will receive an unexpected gift.

FORTUNE:
Having own fortune told: Great struggle in real life.
Reading fortune on a spinning wheel: Beware of danger.
Receiving a fortune: Trouble and losses.
Receiving a fortune from relatives: Success in everything.
Being fortunate in business: Gay occasion to come.
Being fortunate in love: Will lose plenty of money through gambling.
Being fortunate in politics: Will have a steady position.

FORTUNETELLING:
Being a fortuneteller: Good times are coming.
Having own fortune told: Serious disaster is ahead.
Telling another's fortune: Special activities of a happy nature.
Hearing a fortune told to others: You have a loyal friend.

FOSSILS:
Digging fossils from the earth: Will hear of the illness of someone.
Possessing fossils: Will meet an old friend.
Digging many qualities of fossils: A mystery will be solved.

FOUNDATION:
The foundation of own house: Will give money to charity.
The foundation of other buildings: Will soon take a long trip.
A foundation being built: Death of someone you know.
Children having a good foundation for school: Will make good resolutions.

FOUNDRY:
Of a foundry: Will receive compensation.
A foundry in operation: Try to economize on expenses.
A foundry making steel: Gossip and disappointment.
A foundry making large bells: Do not be concerned with idle talk of others.

FOUNTAIN:
Of a sacred fountain: Devotion will bring success.
A full fountain: Happiness and long life.
A fountain with high sprays: An unusually good thing will happen soon.
Being at a fountain of clear water: Will be very happy in love.
A large fountain: Abundance and health.
A fountain spraying water: Profitable operation in business matters.
Being at a fountain with sweetheart: Great happiness & success in love and marriage.
A fountain with muddy water: Good luck to come later.
A fountain with littered water: Troubles and vexation.
Washing yourself at a fountain: Joy and prosperity.
Drying yourself at a fountain: Poverty or death.
A dry fountain: Big desolation.

FOWL:
Of domestic birds: Will enjoy eventful life without ups and downs.
Many birds: Considerable earnings.
Owning birds: Will receive a favor from an unknown person.
A beautiful bird: Fortune in love.

FOX:
Of a fox: An enemy or rival is among your acquaintances.
A fox being killed: Will overcome a threat of trouble.
A fox with a beautiful coat: Beware of deceitful friends.
Killing a fox: Success in all undertakings.

Surprising a fox: Beware of thieves.
Catching a fox in a trap: Will have a fight with friends.
A tame fox: Your love is misplaced.
Children playing with a baby fox: People are abusing your kindness.
Many foxes: You have many enemies.
Buying a fox: Will be cheated by friends.

FOXGLOVES:
Having foxgloves: You are unfitted to fill your position.
Buying foxgloves: Should mend your ways in life.
Receiving a gift of foxgloves: Luck and prosperity.

FRAGILE:
Breaking something fragile: Hopes will not be realized.
Mailing something fragile: Happiness.
Receiving a gift of something fragile: Will make good resolutions.
Receiving fragile things that are broken: Will go to prison.

FRAGRANCE:
A pleasant fragrance: Important and very beneficial event to come.
An unpleasant fragrance: Bad results, not too serious.
A preferred fragrance: Small success.

FRANCE:
Going to France: Own future is uncertain.
Being a Frenchman: You are undecided in business matters.
Sightseeing in France: Your resolutions are wise, be determined about them.
Marrying a Frenchwoman or Frenchman: Will go to prison.

FRANTIC:
Being frantic: Strenuous times followed by a peaceful holiday.
Others being frantic: Advancement within own position.
Relatives being frantic: Will receive a small inheritance.

FRAUD:
Being defrauded: Big treachery.

Committing fraud: Coming prosperity.
Being defrauded by relatives: Deception in love.
Being defrauded by others: Enemies will try in vain to cause loss of reputation.

FRECKLES:
Face being covered with freckles: Unpleasant discovery about a friend.
Having freckles all over the body: Will be dearly loved.
Looking at own freckles in a mirror: Loss of a lover.
Children having freckles: Discovery of an enemy.

FREEMASON:
Being a freemason: A mystery will be solved.
Becoming a freemason: Will have new friends.
Other fraternal members: Will take a journey faraway.

FREEZE:
Being freezingly cold: Will be compensated for having a kind heart.
Freezing without a coat on: Must attempt to regain stolen things.
Other people freezing: Good results in own enterprises.
Things freezing in an icebox: Will receive false information.

FRENCH:
Being of French nationality: Danger through a secret.
Speaking French: Success in love affairs.
Marrying a Frenchwoman: Will have plenty of clothes and linens.
Marrying a Frenchman: Must control passions.

FRETTING:
Of fretting work: Another person is enjoying what you desired.
Being adorned with fretting: Change in environment.
The fretting work in a leaf: Temptation will come to you.

FRIDAY:
Of Friday: Dignity and honor.

Things to happen on following Friday: Will be falsely accused.

Good Friday: Will have prosperity in the family.

Attending church on Good Friday: Must bring domestic affairs into order.

FRIENDS:

Friends being happy: Pleasant tidings.

Friends being troubled: Sickness is near at hand.

Saying good-by to a friend: Painful experiences ahead.

Arguing with a friend: Joy.

Being separated from a friend: Friends are endeavoring to destroy you.

Friends being in trouble: Will receive unexpected good news.

A friend being naked: Will have a big fight.

Embracing a friend: Treason.

Talking with a friend in a room: Joy and consolation.

Laughing with friends: Will dissolve your partnership.

Making new friends: Will be in mourning soon.

FRIGHTENED:

Being badly frightened: Great success.

Being frightened by children: Will prosper with perseverance.

Frightening other people: A change in life will come soon.

Being frightened in your sleep: Will discover a secret.

FRINGE:

Things with a fringe: Vanity.

Having clothes with fringes: Will make love to the opposite sex.

Buying fringe to put on something: Will receive false news.

Draperies with a fringe: Will have an indefinite future.

FROGS:

Being given frogs: Will receive an unexpected gift.

Buying frogs in a store: Will meet people who admire you.

Watching frogs: Success in business.

Catching frogs: A self-inflicted injury will occur soon.

Killing frogs: A false friend is nearby.

A woman seeing a bullfrog: Marriage with wealthy widower with children.

Hearing frogs croaking: Pleasure awaits.

Frogs in water: Will receive money.

Eating frogs: Will receive wealth.

FROST:

Of a frost: Will travel abroad.

Frost damaging your plants: Many troubles ahead.

A thick frost: Advancement within own position.

Frost melting under the sun: Approaching money.

FROWN:

Of frowning: Much domestic happiness.

Others frowning: You have confidence in friends.

Children frowning: Advancement within own position.

Friends frowning: Misfortune in own affairs.

FRUIT:

(The meaning of "fruit" varies according to color and kind. See by name each particular fruit dreamed about.)

FRYING:

Frying food: Will be taken care of during old age.

Frying food for a party: Will have an unfortunate quarrel.

Frying eggs: Will have financial gains.

Frying chicken: Will live a long life.

Frying potatoes: Will be loved dearly by someone new.

FRYING PAN:

Cooking in a frying pan: Unhappiness in love affairs.

Burning food in a frying pan: Accord among friends.

Others cooking with a frying pan: Difficulties in business affairs.

Buying a frying pan: Suitable time to pursue courtship.

FULL:

A house full of people: Will have good earnings.

Cupboards being full: Will have plenty of money.

A huge refrigerator full of food: Are being too stuck-up with neighbors.

Stomach being full of food: Joy and pleasure.

FUN:

Having lots of fun: Rapid success of own hopes.

Others having fun: Money will come easily during life.

Having fun with relatives: Happiness in various matters.

Having fun with children: Doomed for disappointment.

Having fun with friends: Change for the better.

Having fun with important people: Honor and happiness.

FUNERAL:

Being present at a funeral: Will be lucky in love affairs.

Going to a funeral with a loved one: You are envied by enemies.

Going to a funeral with other people: Good health.

Going to a funeral with family: Loss of friends.

Being a pallbearer at a funeral: Will do something foolish.

Attending funeral of best friend: Long life.

Attending funeral clothed in black: Loss of husband or wife.

A woman attending a funeral in mourning: Unhappy married life.

FUNERAL SERVICE:

Attending a funeral service of relatives: Death of a friend.

Attending a funeral service of a friend: Embarrassment in affairs.

Attending a funeral of a brother or sister: Prosperous days ahead.

Attending a funeral of mother or father: Small sickness is ahead.

Attending a funeral of your mate: Misfortune.

FUNNEL:

Of a funnel used for pouring liquid: You are an incorrigible person.

Pouring liquid through a funnel: Gossip by friends.

Others using a funnel: Will slowly attain your goal.

The funnel of a ship: Honor and riches.

FUR:

Possessing furs: Will receive a large inheritance.

Fine furs: Riches and honor.

An ermine fur: Big wealth and riches.

A mink fur: People are being false to you.

Being covered with fur: Health and long life.

Owning a mink coat: Your lover is faithful to you.

Owning a skunk coat: Some man will fall in love with you.

Owning a fox coat: Treachery by friends.

Owning coats of other furs: Security in business.

FURIOUS:

Being a furious person: Will be compatible.

Being exceptionally furious: People are gossiping against you.

A woman being furious: Jealousy over your lover.

A man being furious: Unhappiness in love affairs.

Others being furious: You are hated by people.

Children being furious: They are disliked by their neighbors.

Two beloved people being furious: Joy and long happiness.

A furious animal: A friend is defending your name.

Many furious animals in a cage: Good times are coming.

FURNACE:

A furnace with a dead fire: Good luck.

A furnace with a burning fire: Money will come easily during life.

Lighting a furnace: Troubles caused by own children.

Putting out a furnace: Good news to come.

Someone else lighting a furnace: Your servants are not faithful.

FURNITURE:
Beautiful furniture: Abundant means.

Common furniture: Will be a person of the working class.

A wealthy woman having nice furniture: She will do something foolish.

A common person dreaming of nice furniture: Much love.

A business girl dreaming of having furniture: Will earn own living.

FUTURE:
Of own future: Will have a chance to patch up an old quarrel.

Own future not being good: Much joy in affections.

Own children's future: Happiness is assured.

G

GABLE:
Of a gable: Good advice will be given to you.

Being at the window of a gable: Will lead to good fortune.

The gable window of own home: Discovery of lost valuables.

The gable of other peoples' homes: Warning of trouble.

GAG:
Having a gag in your mouth: Will soon be kissed by a pretty lady.

Being unable to get free from a gag: Expect serious trouble ahead.

A young girl dreaming of a gag: Will meet a man who takes her fancy.

A lady dreaming of a gag: She will fall in love with a man.

GAIETY:
Of having gaiety: Big catastrophe is ahead.

Being in a place of gaiety: Advancement within own position.

Enjoying gaiety with your mate: Good times are coming.

Enjoying gaiety with your lover: Danger in love matters.

GAIN:
Making a big gain: Misfortune in love affairs.

A successful business gain: A big catastrophe is ahead.

Making a gain by cheating: Shame and sorrow.

Making a real-estate gain: Will be fed well during life.

Gaining through gambling: Will have good friendship.

Making a gain under unfair advantages: Recovery from an illness.

GAITERS:
Of gaiters: Will be very fortunate in love affairs.

Wearing gaiters: A tiresome journey is ahead.

Others wearing gaiters: Big joy.

Wearing regular shoes with gaiters: Dignity and distinction.

GALA:
Being at a gala party: Secure profit.

Being at a gala party with friends: A false friend is nearby.

Being at a gala party with your mate: Change of residence.

Being at a gala party with sweetheart: Will have many servants.

GALE:
Of a gale: Financial gains.

Being in a gale: Rapid success of own hopes.

Being on a ship during a big gale: Will realize high ambitions.

Being in a small boat during a gale: Financial troubles and losses.

GALLANT:

Being gallant to a lady: Satisfaction and good health.

A married woman being gallant to a man: Good fortune in business.

A man being gallant to a young unmarried lady: Inconsistency in love.

A man being gallant to a widow: Good results in business affairs.

GALLERY:

Of a gallery: A false friend is attempting to bring harm to you.

Being in a gallery: Financial gains.

Falling from a gallery: Family quarrels.

A gallery of paintings: Big honors and fortune.

A commercial gallery: Fortune in business affairs.

GALLON:

Of a gallon: Happiness.

A gallon of liquor: Abundant means.

A gallon of wine: Good times are coming.

A gallon of vinegar: Avoid rivals.

A gallon of water: Health and prosperity.

A gallon of milk: Will live a long life.

A gallon of oil: Financial gains,

GALLOP:

An easy gallop: Think well before acting.

A fast gallop: Important and very beneficial events to come.

Galloping on a horse: Will have emotional sorrow.

A jockey galloping on your horse: Good times are ahead.

Several horses galloping: Rapid success of own hopes.

GALLOWS:

Of a gallows: Happiness is assured.

Having to die on the gallows: Will obtain an honorable position.

A public gallows: Will be greatly honored.

Hanging on the gallows: Dignity and money.

Others being hanged on the gallows: Ruin is ahead of you.

A relative being hanged on the gallows: Will be persecuted.

Someone you know being on the gallows: Avoid rivals.

GAMBLING:

Of gambling: Financial gains.

A gambler: Affairs will go as you desire.

Winning at gambling: Social activities of a happy nature.

Loosing at gambling: Will be relieved of pains.

Gambling with dice: Inheritance.

Gambling with checkers: Will lose money.

Gambling with chess: You are wasting your time.

Gambling with cards: Loss of prestige.

Gambling at roulette: Vain hopes.

Gambling at a spinning wheel: Discovery of lost valuables.

Gambling at a slot machine: Doomed for disappointment.

Gambling at a pinball machine: Postponement of success.

Gambling with a friend and winning: Loss of a beloved one.

Gambling with a friend and losing: Will love someone else.

Children playing childish gambling games: Fortune in own affairs.

GAME:

Taking part in a game: Financial gains.

Others playing a game: Worry will be smoothed away.

Winning while playing a game: Misfortune in business.

Your side winning a game: Loneliness and trouble.

Your side losing a game: Important and very beneficial event to come.

Children playing games: Fortune in own affairs.

Children playing blindfolded games: You are being deceived.

GANGRENE:
Having gangrene: Loss of friends.
Others in family having gangrene: Family happiness.
Own leg being cut off because of gangrene: Hard work is ahead.
Others having leg cut off because of gangrene: Friends are not loyal.

GANGWAY:
Going up the gangway of a ship: A mystery will be solved.
Coming down the gangway of a ship: Avoid rivals.
Crossing a gangway: Will receive hostility from a rival.
Other people going up a gangway: Loss of money.
Other people coming down a gangway: Loss of friends' confidence.
Sailors or officers being on a gangway: Luck and prosperity.

GAOL:
Of this place of confinement: Will have a long life.
Being put in a gaol: Success in spite of present difficulties.
Being released from a gaol: Great and good fortune.
Others being in a gaol: A big disgrace will come to you.

GARAGE:
Of a garage: Affairs will take a turn for the better in near future.
An empty garage: Either husband or wife is cheating on the other.
A garage full of cars: Will have good health and money.
Putting a car in the garage: Money will come easily during life.
A garage burning: Congenial work and good news.

GARDEN:
Of the garden of Eden: Suitable time to pursue love affairs.
A well-kept garden: Good money matters.

A neglected garden: Danger through a secret.
A neighbor's garden: Will have prosperity.
A friend's garden: Unpleasant times are ahead.
Relative's garden: Success in spite of present difficulties.
A beautiful garden: Increase in fortune.
A barren garden: Death in the near future.
Taking care of a garden: Will soon receive money.
A disorderly and dirty garden: Will go into bankruptcy.
Walking in a garden: Joy.
A garden full of trees: Big happiness.
A garden with beautiful flowers: Imminent matrimony.

GARDENER:
Of a gardener: Present activities will soon make you rich.
Being a gardener: Increase of fortune.
Being the gardener of own garden: Wealth is near at hand.
A gardener not taking care of a garden: Misfortune.
A gardener pruning trees: Joy and matrimony.
Another person's gardener: Will receive news of the death of a friend.

GARLAND:
Of a garland: Financial gains.
Having a garland of flowers: You are in love.
Receiving a gift of a garland of flowers: Luck and prosperity.
Sending a gift of a garland of flowers: Be careful of rivals.

GARLIC:
Of garlic: Discovery of a secret.
Eating garlic: Will have a big quarrel.
Buying garlic: Will be irritated by other people.
Cooking with garlic: You are disliked by those working under you.
Growing garlic in a garden: People detest you.

Giving children garlic to eat: They will realize high position.

People who don't like garlic: Are unfitted to fill your position.

GARRET:

Of this watchtower or place of refuge: Discovery of lost valuables.

Being in a public garret: Advancement in position will come soon.

Being in the garret of own house: Happiness is assured.

GARROTER:

Having on an iron collar used for execution by strangulation: Abundant means.

Others with a garroter on neck: Be firm in convictions, you are right.

A criminal with a garroter on neck: Violent opposition to opinions.

GARTER:

A woman dreaming of her garters: Postponement of success.

A woman dreaming of losing her garters: Will have a jealous lover.

Loosening garters: A false friend is nearby.

Garters falling down: Postponement of success.

Someone picking up your garters: You have a loyal friend.

Lost garters being returned: Will be helped with difficulties.

Lost garters not being returned: Troubles will increase.

Garters of other people: Will realize high ambitions.

Finding only one garter: Fortune in love.

Finding several garters: Illness.

GAS:

Lighting a gas flame: Will find way to avoid threatened misfortune.

Blowing out gas flame: Enemies are seeking to injure you.

A gaslight being poor: Your interests will suffer.

GAS LAMP:

Having a gas lamp: Business will come to a standstill.

Lighting a gas lamp: Will have plenty of money.

A gas lamp already lit: Passion in love.

Blowing out a gas lamp: Loss of hope in love.

A decorative gas lamp: People are telling you lies.

A gas lamp going out suddenly: Expect a catastrophe.

The gas lamp of others: Good love affairs and domestic happiness.

GASOLINE:

Of gasoline: Use caution in business ventures.

Buying gasoline: Financial gains.

Selling gasoline: Rapid success in business.

Others buying gasoline: Postponement of success.

GATE:

Of a gate: You are very much in love.

Passing through a gate: Will be shocked with receipt of bad news.

A broken gate: Misfortune.

A closed gate: Will be oppressed with insurmountable difficulties.

Locking a gate: Success in business.

Other people being at your gate: Friends are being untrue to you.

The gate of others: Will be cheated by friends.

GATHER:

Of gathering various things: You will have good food.

Gathering wood: Good friendship.

Gathering flowers: Good relations with relatives.

Gathering roses: Joy.

Others gathering things: Postponement of success.

Gathering money: Will lose money.

Gathering papers: Be careful of speculation.

Gathering books: Profit.

Gathering love letters: A secret weighs heavily on your conscience.

GAUZE:

Of gauze: Congenial work and good news.

Using gauze: Financial gains.

Throwing gauze away: Pleasant social activities.

Other people using gauze: Others are concealing their feelings for you.

GAVOTTE:

Dancing a gavotte: Calm and happy future.

Others dancing a gavotte: Important and very beneficial event to come.

Young girls and men dancing a gavotte: Big loss of money.

Dancing a gavotte with sweetheart: Will receive an inheritance.

GAZELLE:

Of this graceful antelope having lustrous eyes: Big joy.

Having a gazelle: Will fall in love.

A young girl dreaming of a gazelle: Will have rough suitor but true husband.

GEESE:

Of geese: Misfortune at sea.

Geese flying: Will take an extensive journey.

Eating geese: Good fortune.

Hearing geese quacking: A death within the family circle will occur.

Geese swimming: Fortune will increase.

Plucking geese: Inheritance.

Wild geese: Your friends have forgotten you.

Others eating geese: Joy.

GEMS:

Of gems: Happiness through love.

Buying gems: Fortunate business transactions.

Selling gems: Misfortune in love affairs.

Putting gems around the neck: Financial gains.

Other people wearing gems: Discovery of lost valuables.

Receiving a gift of a gem: Danger through a secret.

Relatives having gems: Sickness within the family.

GENERAL:

Being a general: Honors will come to you.

Being an artillery general: Will receive plenty of money.

Being an army general: Will receive several favors.

Generals marching in a parade: Use caution in your ventures.

A friend being promoted to general: Unhappiness in the home.

GENTRY:

Being with the gentry: A change in life will soon come.

A country girl dreaming of the gentry: Will work in a large city soon.

A lady dreaming of the gentry: Will marry a nobleman from abroad.

GEOGRAPHY:

Of a geography book: Your love will be refused by someone.

Studying geography book: Be very cautious in everyday affairs.

Children studying geography: Will soon be afflicted with minor pains.

Being a geography teacher: Danger in own affairs.

Buying a geography book: Present worries are needless.

GERANIUM:

Of geraniums: Considerable wealth.

Picking geraniums: You will always be loved.

Throwing geraniums away: Family quarrels.

Smelling the scent of geraniums: Will receive good news.

Receiving a bouquet of geraniums as a gift: Your lover is jealous.

Buying a geranium plant: Will have plenty of money.

Geraniums belonging to others: High honors.

White geraniums: Difficulties.

Yellow geraniums: Sorrow.

Pink geraniums: Will be visited by a beloved person.

Red geraniums: Sickness.

Red geraniums with black spots: Death.

GHOST:

Of a ghost appearing: Good luck.

Being frightened by a ghost: Expect troubles ahead.

Having no fear of ghosts: Will pull through difficulties.

A ghost speaking to you: Beware of enemies.

GIANT:

Meeting a giant: Will attain success.

Killing a giant: Abundant means.

A monstrous giant: Much success.

A giant being in the company of others: Triumph in love affairs.

GIDDY:

Of being dizzy: Family quarrels.

Feeling ill or giddy: Things will change for the better.

Children being giddy: Hard work will bring a change for the better.

GIFT:

Receiving a gift: Will have riches and receive a marriage proposal.

Receiving a gift from a loved one: Success and good luck.

Giving a gift: Bad luck.

Receiving several gifts: Beware of person from whom you receive them.

Giving a gift to relatives: Good hopes.

Receiving a gift from an important person: Will receive many honors.

Receiving gifts from relatives: Postponement of success.

Receiving a Christmas gift from friends: Treason

Receiving a Christmas gift from relatives: Will have many admirers.

Reciving a gift from a son: Tribulations.

Receiving a gift from a daughter: Opposition.

Receiving a gift from a woman: Big friendship.

Receiving a gift from a man: Change of fortune.

Receiving a ring as a gift: Will marry a wealthy person.

GILDING:

Of covering something with gold: A present will be offered to you.

Others gilding: Friends have ulterior motives.

Working as a gilder: A false friend is nearby.

GILT:

Having something that resembles gold: Happy life.

Having garments covered with gold lace: Great honor.

Others wearing gilt garments: Postponement of success.

Buying gilt articles: Will have plenty of money.

GIN:

Drinking gin: Will have a short life.

Drinking gin with friends: You have deceitful friends.

Drinking gin with a loved one: Fleeting pleasures.

Buying gin: Will have many changes in life.

Serving gin: You have false friends.

Receiving gin as a gift: Family quarrels.

Giving gin as a gift: False favors.

Breaking a bottle of gin: Will be visited by a friend.

GIRDLE:

Wearing a girdle: A period of sorrow is about to come.

Others wearing a girdle: Will strive for money rather than honors.

Relatives wearing a girdle: Happy life.

Enemies wearing a girdle: A mystery will be solved.

Young women wearing girdles: Avoid rivals.

GIRL:

A beautiful girl: Increase in business affairs.

An intelligent girl: Big fortune.

Talking to a girl: Happiness and tranquility.

A single man dreaming of kissing a girl: Good luck.

A married person dreaming of kissing a girl: Domestic troubles.

Kissing several girls: Big success.

A girl in a window: Big disputes.

A girl running: Will catch a thief.

A girl crying: Will be embarrassed by a friend.

An exceptionally beautiful girl: Abundant means.

Saving a girl from danger: Will be extremely loved.

A kind girl: Happiness in love affairs.

Receiving surprising news from a girl: A long-delayed reply will arrive.

A man dreaming of being a girl: Will play a female part on stage.

GLADIATOR:
A gladiator in combat: Will have plenty of money.

A gladiator being at a festival: Something will happen to cause sorrow.

Several gladiators in combat: Change in environment.

A gladiator being killed: Unhappiness.

GLASS:
Of a glass: Luck and prosperity.

Cutting glass: Postponement of a wedding.

Breaking a mirror: Death caused by an accident.

Breaking a window glass: Trouble is ahead.

Cleaning window glass: Your happiness is in danger.

Changing a window glass: May go to prison.

A glass factory: Fortune is ahead.

Being in the company of a woman dealing in glass: Happiness.

Drinking out of a glass: Danger.

Drinking a glass of water: Will be married soon.

Breaking a drinking glass without water in it: Death of a woman.

Breaking a water glass and spilling water: Children will be healthy.

Spilling water without breaking the glass: Death of a child.

Spilling a glass of wine: Good news.

Spilling water on clothes from a glass: Death of one you know.

A dirty glass: Congenial work and good news.

A businessman dreaming of breaking a glass: Fortune in business.

Receiving a gift of glasses: Birth of children.

Wearing eyeglasses: Will have an honorable position.

Buying eyeglasses: Failure of own affairs.

Children wearing eyeglasses: Congenial work.

Others wearing eyeglasses: Must rely on own good judgment.

GLEANER:
Being a gleaner: Plenty of money ahead.

Gathering grain after a reaper: Big prosperity.

Others being gleaners: Beware of false friends.

GLOBE:
Of a globe: Luck in own affairs.

Of a globe-trotter: Will have good friends.

Taking a trip around the globe: Will have a long life.

Others going around the globe: Will receive help from friends.

GLOOM:
Of the gloom: A possible change for the better.

Being in very dark gloom: Don't hesitate to grasp an opportunity.

Others being in the gloom: Much unhappiness.

GLOVES:
Wearing old gloves: Happiness.

Wearing torn gloves: Many disappointments.

Carrying gloves in the hands: Prosperity and pleasure.

Losing own gloves: Will be thrown onto own resources.

Finding a pair of gloves: Early marriage.

Others wearing gloves: Postponement of success.

Buying gloves: A false friend is nearby.

Getting gloves dirty: Loneliness and trouble.

Being a glovemaker: Will obtain a high position.

GLOW:
Of a brilliant glowing scene: Improvement in fortune.
Feeling a very hot glow: Important and very beneficial event to come.
Feeling the glow of passion: Will have a vigorous lover.
Having a glowing expression: A change in life will come soon.
Feeling a glowing sensation after exercise: Triumph over enemies.

GLOWWORM:
Of glowworms: You have a loyal friend.
Many luminous insects: Will have a chance to do a great kindness.
A firefly in the dark: You will be repaid later.

GLUE:
Using glue: You have a faithful friend that you can trust.
Others using glue: You are deceived by best friends.
Buying glue: Will realize own ambitions.

GLUTTON:
Being a glutton: You are in danger of poverty.
Relatives being gluttons: Do not expect any money.
Other people being gluttons: Expect big business losses.
Children being gluttons: Will lose all of your estate.

GNAT:
Of gnats: Losses and troubles.
Gnats being on others: Loss of money.
Killing gnats with poison: A friend is trying to help you secretly.

GOAL:
Reaching a goal in life: Financial gains.
Not reaching a goal in life: Luck and prosperity.
Others reaching their goal in life: Important and very beneficial event.
Making a goal while playing a game: Failure of enemies.
Others making a goal in a game: Will have a long life.

GOAT:
Of a goat: Will be rich.
Many goats: Abundance.
Goats fighting: Will suffer soon.
Owning many goats: Abundance and riches.
Keeping goats in a pen: A false friend is nearby.
Herding goats: Will be abandoned.
Being butted by a goat: You have many rivals.
White goats: Luck will be very erratic.
Black goats: Unreliable friends.
Black and white spotted goats: Use caution in own affairs.
Killing a goat: Happiness.
The horns of a goat: Poverty.
A baby goat: Fortune in gambling.
Being a goat: Realization of this dream.
A female goat: Will overcome enemies with care and prudence.
Rich people dreaming of leading goats: Dishonor.
Poor people dreaming of leading goats: Will have plenty of money.

GOBLET:
Breaking a goblet: Loss of business.
Drinking out of a goblet: Happy times.
Drinking out of a colored goblet: Loss of friends.
Others drinking out of a goblet: Unhappiness in life.

GOD:
Praying to God: Much prosperity.
Worshiping God: Sickness.
Hearing God speak to you: Intense enjoyment.
Talking to God: Joy and happiness.
God putting his arms around you: Will receive that prayed for.
Seeing God face to face: Will have much joy.
God granting you what was desired: Will realize high ambitions.

GOING:
Going somewhere in a big hurry: You are a very happy-go-lucky person.
Going somewhere in a carriage: Will have many pleasant memories.

Going somewhere in a car: Death.
Going places with men: Good news.
Going around the fields: Happiness in business.
Going around the forest: Will receive sad news.
Going around limping: Laziness.
Going around hiding: Persecution.
Going around very slowly: You are neglecting your fortune.
Going to your death: Happiness.
Others going places: Will receive unexpected valuable gift.
Women going places: Abundant means.

GOITER:
Having a goiter: Death.
Others who have a goiter: Will receive unexpected news.
Children having a goiter: Will have fights in the future.
Friends who have a goiter: Will be invited to a banquet.

GOLD:
Finding gold: An inheritance will soon be yours.
Seeing gold: Every enterprise will bring success.
Losing gold: Financial distress.
Digging for gold: Unexpected fortune will come through own efforts.
Working with gold: Misfortune.
Clothes being embroidered with gold: You are highly thought of by others.
Making rings from gold: Loss of time.
Imitation gold: You will be plenty rich.
Exchanging gold: Will lose your temper.
Throwing gold away: Big sorrow.
Handling gold in a business venture: You are a tempermental person.
Melting gold: Someone is doing you wrong.
Taking gold from others: Big fortune.
Stealing gold: You will get into trouble.
Counting gold: You are attempting to deceive friends.
A mixture of gold and silver: Will have a large loss.

The color of gold: Will do business with people faraway.
Materials of any kind in gold color: Abundant means.
Buying clothes of gold color: Approaching money.
Gold plating: Will receive high honors.

GOLDFISH:
A young woman dreaming of goldfish: Will marry into wealth.
A married woman dreaming of goldfish: Will soon be divorced.
Dead goldfish: Disappointments to come.
Having goldfish in a bowl in own house: Financial gains.
Children playing with goldfish: Much contentment.
Buying goldfish: Matrimony within the family.

GOLD MINE:
Of a gold mine: Will have good health.
Discovering a gold mine: A big fortune is ahead.
A poor gold mine: Misfortune.
Working a gold mine: Financial gain.
A gold mine belonging to others: You are being cheated by friends.

GOLF:
Playing golf: Wife will give birth to a son.
Spending much time playing golf: Business affairs need attention.
Winning a golf contest: Important and very beneficial event to come.
Having a bad golf score: A false friend is nearby.
Playing golf with friends: Much joy.

GOLF LINKS:
Playing on golf links: Will have a busy life at home.
Playing on a golf link with others: Are unfitted to fill your position.
Enemies playing on a golf link: Warning of troubles.

GONDOLA:
Of a gondola: Happy but unromantic life.

Being in a gondola with your mate: Good days are ahead.

Being in a gondola with a lover: Love will not last very long.

Others being in a gondola: Warning of trouble.

GONG:

Having a gong in own house: Pleasant work and good news.

Hearing the noise of a gong: An exciting event will happen in the family.

Hearing the gong of a ship: Avoid trifling with important matters.

GOOD:

Of good things: Misfortune in love.

Doing good to others: Joy and pleasure.

Others doing good to you: Profit and gains.

Children doing good things: A baby will be born late in life.

Saying good things about others: Will be embarrassed.

People saying good things about you: Will be deceived by friends.

GOOSE:

Of a goose: Misfortune at sea.

A goose flying: Will take an extensive journey.

Eating goose: Good fortune.

A goose quacking: A death in the family circle will occur.

A goose swimming: Fortune is increasing.

Plucking a goose: Inheritance.

Others eating goose: Joy.

A wild goose: Your friends have forgotten you.

GOOSEBERRY:

Making gooseberry jam: Avoid rivals.

Making gooseberry pie: Will be jilted by your lover.

Having gooseberries: Important and very beneficial event to come.

Gathering gooseberries: Brighter business prospects.

Eating gooseberries: Doomed for disappointment.

Buying gooseberries: Loneliness and trouble.

Picking gooseberries: A mystery will be solved.

GORSE:

Of this evergreen shrub: Good fortune will come your way.

Picking the yellow flowers of a gorse: Luck and prosperity.

Others having gorse flowers: Unhappiness.

GOSSIP:

Being the object of gossip: Pleasant surprises are in store.

Gossiping about others: Will realize high ambitions.

Relatives gossiping about you: Family arguments.

Friends gossiping about you: You are being deceived.

Enemies gossiping about you: Will suffer through own foolishness.

GOUT:

Having gout: Vexation.

Having gout for a long time: Must avoid overstrain because of weakness.

An old person having gout: Will have misfortune in business.

A young person having gout: You are in danger.

Having gout on the hands: Will soon have an illness.

Having gout on the feet: Will have misery.

Having gout in any other joint: Financial losses because of a relative.

GOVERNMENT:

Having a government position: Social activities of a happy nature.

Being offered a government position: Good times are coming.

Others having a government position: Troubles are ahead.

Losing a government position: Will soon experience many ups and downs.

GOWN:
Wearing a beautiful gown: Misfortune in love affairs.
Own gown being shabby: Advancement within own position.
Own gown being torn: Luck and prosperity.
Gown being pulled away and being left naked: Abundant means.

GRACE:
Asking God for grace: Will have important changes in life.
Receiving grace: Will make good earnings.
Saying grace on food: Will be returned to perfect health.
Asking grace for a prisoner: Abundant means.

GRAIN:
A large amount of grain: Financial gains.
A small amount of grain: Troubles are ahead.
Harvesting grain: Big gains.
Grain standing in the field: Will receive plenty of money.
Carrying the grain to the barn: Luck and prosperity.
Grain catching fire: A serious disaster is ahead.
Sowing grain in a field: Big joy.
A very large field of grain: Good marriage and good business.
Selling grain: Financial gains.

GRAMMAR:
Of a grammar book: Much work is ahead.
Children going to grammar school: Abundance.
Teaching grammar school: Will receive good news.
Children completing grammar school: Prosperity.

GRAMOPHONE:
Having a gramophone: Pleasant news received from faraway.
Hearing records played on a gramophone: A mystery will be solved.
Others playing records on a gramophone: Unexpected discovery will be made.
Buying a gramophone: Family happiness.

GRANDPARENT:
Being a grandparent: Will realize high ambitions.
Speaking to a grandparent: Sudden death.
Grandchildren being with grandparents: Advancement in health condition.
Talking in the dream to grandparents: Inheritance.

GRAPES:
Of a field full of grapes: Will live a long life.
Eating grapes: Will be burdened with many cares.
Children eating grapes: Will have a wide influence.
Handling grapes on the vines: Eminence will be yours.
Making wine out of grapes: Abundant means.
White grapes: Victory over enemies.
Black grapes: Be cautious in your business affairs.
Red grapes: Will have a small contradiction.
Having large grapes: Considerable fortune.
Harvesting grapes: A big fortune is ahead.
Destroying grapes: You should mend your ways in life.
Buying grapes: Be cautious in business ventures.
Selling grapes: Worry will be ended.
Having gooseberry grapes: Will receive an unexpected invitation.
Having raisins made from grapes: Postponement of success.
Having dry grapes: Loss of money.

GRASS:
Of grass: Wealth to those in business.
Very long grass: Illness.
Cutting the grass: Long life.
Green grass flourishing: Failure of enemies.

Dogs or animals eating grass: Poverty is ahead.

A woman dreaming of grass: Happiness with her lover.

A literary person dreaming of grass: Good reputation.

An artistic person dreaming of grass: Big joy.

GRASSHOPPER:

Of grasshoppers: Will enjoy a short period of fancied success.

Grasshoppers in own yard: Bad omen for sick people.

Killing grasshoppers: Arrival of an unexpected person.

Others killing grasshoppers: Expect the arrival of a thief.

GRATE:

Of a grate: Unhappiness.

Cooking meat on the grate of an oven: Will enjoy liberty again.

Cooking fish on the grate of an oven: Sickness followed by death.

Breaking a grate: Worries ahead.

A grate used for barbecue: Will have the love of a rich person.

GRATITUDE:

Being grateful to someone: Surprising events will happen.

Others expressing gratitude to you: Events will happen to a loved one.

Receiving gratitude from children: Will live a long life.

GRAVE:

A newly prepared grave: Will suffer through the sins of others.

Walking on a grave: Unhappy married life.

Of own grave: Enemies are trying to bring disaster to you.

Digging a grave: Big obstacles are ahead.

Walking on another person's grave: Death is very near at hand.

Grave space being open: Will receive news from afar.

The grave of your father: Inheritance.

Building a grave: Loss of friends.

Destroying a grave: A wedding will take place soon.

Visiting relatives' graves: Sorrow.

Visiting enemies' graves: Big matrimonial dinner.

Visiting graves in a monastery: Large and happy family event.

GRAVEL:

Walking on a rough gravel path: Big obstacles are ahead.

Repairing something with gravel: Will take a journey.

Others doing gravel work: Will have small business.

GRAVY:

Making gravy: Loss of rugged health.

Eating gravy: Will overcome every obstacle.

Others making gravy: Financial success.

GRAY:

The color gray: Will receive a letter with good news.

Material of any kind in gray color: Wealth.

Buying clothes of gray colors: Important and very beneficial event to come.

GRAY HAIR:

A man dreaming of having gray hair: Difficulties followed by success.

A woman dreaming of having gray hair: Will realize high ambitions.

Being in the company of a gray-haired person: Abundant means.

GREECE:

Going to Greece: Loss of a lover.

Being a Greek: You will be cheated.

Traveling in Greece: Will have good means coming soon.

A Greek marrying a foreigner: Gossip by women.

Other nationalities marrying a Greek: Humiliation and misery.

GREEN:

The color green: Good fortune in love affairs.

Materials of any kind in green: Abundant means.

Buying clothes of green color: Financial gains.

GREENFINCH:
Of a greenfinch: Stick to your work and undertakings.
Owning a Texas sparrow: Will avoid losses.
Killing a greenfinch: You are confronted with insurmountable obstacles.

GREENGAGE:
Of this greenish-yellow plum: You are fortunate in love.
Picking greengages from a tree: Pleasure and happiness.
Having greengages out of season: You will be insulted.
Having jam or jelly made from greengages: Will have a big friendship.

GRENADIER:
Being a grenadier: Happiness in love affairs.
A married woman dreaming of a grenadier: Will have a happily married life.
A young girl dreaming of a grenadier: Will marry a civilian soon.

GREYHOUND:
Of a greyhound: Will overcome enemies.
Owning a greyhound: Will win at the races.
A greyhound belonging to others: Will win at a lottery.
A greyhound racing: Will receive a letter with good news.

GRIEF:
Of suffering grief: You will be happy soon.
Children suffering grief: Joy and merry times ahead.
Relatives suffering grief: Something good will happen to a loved one.
Enemies suffering grief: Unhappiness.

GRIND:
Of a grinding machine: Big earnings.
Grinding coffee: Troubles at home.
Grinding pepper: Sickness and sorrow.
Grinding corn: Good fortune.
Grinding grain: Will be very rich.

Grinding colored stones: Loss of own hopes.
Grinding materials for dyeing: Discord within the family.

GRINDSTONE:
Of a grindstone: Death of a relative.
Using a grindstone: Good fortune will attend your efforts.
Others using a grindstone: Loss of the friendship of several friends.
Children using a grindstone: Life of great activity with financial success.

GROAN:
Of groaning in a dream: Avoid rivals.
Hearing children groaning: Will live a long life.
Relatives groaning: Financial gains.
Hearing enemies groaning: You have one loyal friend.

GROCERIES:
Buying groceries: Will have a life of ease.
Eating the groceries: Big joy.
Others buying groceries: Important and very beneficial event to come.
Relatives buying groceries: Luck and prosperity.

GROOM:
Of a groom: Hard work awaits.
Being a groom: Legal affairs will be made known to you.
Several grooms: Will have to contend with ruffians.
The groom of an enemy: Things will go as planned.

GROPE:
Of groping: Affairs are improving, so do not despair.
Groping your way along: An introduction will cheer you shortly.
Groping for something in the dark: Use caution in your affairs.

GROTTO:
Of a grotto: Good changes in present financial conditions.
Being taken to a grotto: Will have many friends.
Going to a grotto to eat: Will receive an inheritance.

Having a big party in a grotto: A big fortune is ahead.

Being taken by force into a cave: Perilous journey ahead.

GROUND:

Being stretched out on the ground: Humble status for some time to come.

Others stretched out on the ground: Death of a friend.

The ground in own yard: Money and profit.

The ground of others: Financial losses.

The ground floor of own home: Long illness.

The ground floor of any inn: Loss of a friend.

GROWING:

Of growing: Will become an important person.

Being grown up: Honor.

Good stuffs growing: Riches.

Children growing: Happiness.

GRUEL:

Of gruel: Good luck.

Eating gruel: Do not have friends addicted to strong liquors.

Cooking gruel: Will have a big advantage in life.

Buying gruel: Approaching money.

GUARD:

Being on guard against danger: Avoid uncouth speech.

Being a security guard: Will be saved from a big danger.

Being a night guard: A big sorrow is ahead.

Hitting a guard: Will soon have joy.

A guard taking away a prisoner: Will be insulted by friends.

Being taken away by a guard: Will have a secure fortune.

Killing a guard: Loss of money.

A presidential guard: You are waiting for useless help.

The guard of a park: You have a good heart.

GUESS:

Making a guess: Are desirous of knowing future but unable to do so.

Making correct guesses: Will have a good adventure.

Guessing about peoples' personal affairs: You have deceitful friends.

Other people guessing about you: Will be cheated.

Guessing the ages of people: Poverty.

GUEST:

Having a guest call on you: Important and very beneficial event to come.

Many guests: Great difficulties in business.

Others having guests: Beware of illness.

Unwelcome guests: Unhappiness in love affairs.

GUIDE:

Being a guide: Hard work awaits.

Being guided by others: Pay attention to suggestions of a friend.

Others being guided: Loss of money.

Guiding people around: Will receive kind assistance from a good friend.

GUILTY:

Being guilty: Must endure tribulation.

Others being guilty: Treason.

Mate or lover being guilty: Will receive inheritance from an old lady.

Enemies being guilty: Death of a member of the family.

GUITAR:

Playing a guitar: Will have small pleasures in life.

Hearing a guitar played: Will have a vigorous life until death.

Being pleased by guitar music: Love and joy.

Guitar music being interrupted: Will be cheated by friends.

A young woman dreaming of hearing a guitar: Temptation through flattery.

GULF:

Of a gulf: Change for the better.

Being in a gulf: Departure of a person for whom you care.

Others being in a gulf: Avoid rivals.
Being in a boat in a gulf: Will overcome troubles.
Landing at a gulf port: Joy without profit.

GUM:
Having gum: Financial delays are indicated.
Chewing gum: Someone will stick by you.
Others chewing gum: You may have cause to regret actions.

GUMS:
Of own gums: Discord among the family.
Gums being inflamed: Unfavorable results in affairs.
Childrens' gums being sore: Will receive an unexpected guest.
Gums being treated by a dentist: Death of a friend.

GUN:
Having a gun: Danger is ahead.
Receiving a gun as a gift: Honor.
Buying a gun: Good earnings.
Hearing a gun fired: Loss of employment.
Shooting a person with a gun: Big dishonor.
Being shot by a gun: A serious illness threatens.
Having shot someone with a gun: A loved one will pass away.
Others firing a gun: Will be an invalid for some time.
Shooting an enemy with a gun: Will have a law suit.
A rifle with a bayonet: Separation of partners.
Traveling with a gun: Will soon get married.

A gun merchant: Will dissolve a corporation.

GUNPOWDER:
Having gunpowder: You should mend your ways in life.
A man dreaming of gunpowder: Immediate change of residence.
A woman dreaming of gunpowder: Will divorce her husband.
A young girl dreaming of gunpowder: Will marry a soldier.

GUTTER:
Being in a gutter: Hard times to come.
Friends being in a gutter: Will take a trip in the near future.
Enemies being in a gutter: Triumph over enemies.
Finding something valuable in a gutter: Will receive a financial reward.

GYMNASTICS:
Doing gymnastics in a gymnasium: Worry will be smoothed away.
Relatives doing gymnastics: Troubles are ahead.
Children doing gymnastics at a gym: Financial gains.
Owning a gym for gymnastics: You should attend to business better.

GYPSY:
Of a gypsy: You are prone to change your mind very often.
A gypsy telling a fortune to a woman: Will have an unfortunate marriage.
A gypsy telling a fortune to a married woman: Is jealous of her husband.
A gypsy telling a fortune to a man: Will be jealous of wife without cause.

H

HABIT:
Having good habits: Will receive good news.
Having bad habits: Sickness.

Having a special habit: Will be welcomed wherever you go.
Relatives having bad habits: Will be humiliated.

Others having bad habits: Warning of troubles.

HADDOCK:
Of haddock: Good health.
Buying haddock: Will have mastery over many matters.
Cooking haddock: You have more friends than you thought.
Fishing for haddock: Own stupidity will cause you danger.
Eating haddock: Accord among friends.

HAG:
Of a hag: You are being watched by someone with evil intentions.
Seeing a hag: Gossip and scandal about women friends.
Talking with a hag: You should mend your ways in life.
Being scared by hag: Abuse of confidence.

HAIL:
Of hail falling: Difficulties are ahead.
Being out in a hail storm: Disappointment.
Others being in a hail storm: Big sorrow.
Crop being ruined by a hail storm: Abundant means are ahead.

HAIR:
Having red hair: You are telling something untrue.
Having brown hair: Will be a voluptuous person.
Having white hair: Dignity.
Having blond hair: Friendship.
Having black hair: Will be in a car accident.
Hair turning gray: Must endure pains.
Having a pony tail hair-do: Will have many vain desires.
Having a crew cut hair style: You are being cheated.
Being satisfied with the way own hair looks: Will have a new sweetheart.
Of own hair: Continued prosperity.
Own hair getting thin or falling out: Will have emotional sorrow.
Worrying because own hair is turning gray: Separation from family.

Other peoples' hair: Own affairs will need careful attention.
Of curly hair: You will be antagonistic.
Short black curly hair: Unhappiness.
The short hair of prisoners: You will be victorious.
A conductor's long hair: Happy days to come.
A man having long hair: Dignity.
A man having very little hair: Fortune.
Hair falling out: Loss of friendship.
Hair burning: Death of someone you know.
Short hair: Poverty.
Long hair: Will receive something important.
Having hair cut: Profit.
Cutting own hair with scissors: Wealth.
Dyeing own hair: Vanity.
Someone pulling your hair: Enemies are trying to harm you.
Having trouble taking hair down: Will work hard a long time.
Brushing the hair: Will be short of money.
Putting up own hair: Will have many things on your mind.
Washing own hair: Sorrow.
Allowing hair to be cut up to your ears: Unhappiness.
Having hair well combed: Friendship and end to bad business.
Having hair snarled: Long legal action.
Eating hair: Joy.
Hair growing from the edge of the mouth: Sudden death.
Hair growing on the back of the hands: Financial gain.
Hair growing on the face of a woman: Danger of losing fortune.
A woman going bald: Financial losses.
Mussing up own hair: Family quarrels.
Having a permanent: Danger in love matters.
Having very long white hair: High hopes.
Having beautiful long hair: Will overcome enemies.

Having hair as long as body of the person: Are being deceived by mate.

A man having short white hair: Happiness.

HAIRDRESSING:

Going to a hairdresser: Postponement of success.

Going with a friend to a hairdresser: Will be envied by friends.

Having only hair done at hairdresser: Will take a trip.

Having hair dyed blond: You will regret your actions.

Having hair dyed black: A mystery will be solved.

Having hair dyed red: Will lose a friend.

Having hair dyed auburn: Postponement of success.

Having hair dyed white: Abundant means.

Enemies being at a hairdresser: Doomed for disappointment.

Going to a hairdresser with sweetheart: Joy without profit.

Taking daughter to a hairdresser: Good news from faraway.

Having a wig made by a hairdresser: Danger is imminent.

Conversing with a hairdresser: Death of a friend.

Being a hairdresser: Will attend a large ball.

HAIRPIN:

Of hairpins: You are being deceived.

Handling hairpins: Will visit a novel place of amusement.

Finding others' hairpins on the floor: A friend is watching you.

Buying hairpins: Approaching money.

Losing hairpins: A change will come soon.

Finding hairpins of a rival woman: Will be guilty of foolish actions.

HALIBUT:

Eating halibut: Good luck to one for whom you care.

Buying halibut in a store: Will be generous to friends.

Cooking halibut: Expect pregnancy in the near future.

Catching halibut: Your desires are unsatisfied.

Receiving halibut from others: Will realize high ambitions.

HALL:

Being in a hall: A two-faced companion will injure your reputation.

Being in a hall with others: Will receive bad news.

Having a meeting in a hall with friends: Good, new relationships.

Meeting in a hall with enemies: Advancement within own position.

HALLMARK:

Of a hallmark: Reputation will be injured by a two-faced friend.

A hallmark being stamped on gold and silver: Big joy.

A hallmark being missing on your gold articles: You are being deceived.

HALO:

Of a halo: Present troubles will lead to good fortune later.

Seeing a solar halo: Rapid success of own hopes.

Seeing a lunar halo: Change in own environment.

A luminous circle of light surrounding something: Emotional sorrow.

HALTER:

Of a halter: A former playmate will become your marriage partner.

Putting a halter on a horse: Prosperity in business and success in love.

Hitching a haltered horse to a carriage: Warning of trouble.

Halter straps worn by women: Will overcome obstacles.

HAM:

Buying a ham: Will incur debts.

Having ham: Don't trust friends.

Boiling a ham: Big profit.

Slicing a ham: Financial gains.

Broiling a ham: Important and very beneficial event to come.

Eating ham: Joy and profit.

Serving ham to others: Family quarrels.

HAMLET:
Of a hamlet: Will live a long happy life.
Reading Shakespeare's *Hamlet:* New interests and surroundings.
Seeing the play *Hamlet* at a theater: A rival will steal your sweetheart.

HAMMER:
Having a hammer in own hands: Pleasant work and good news.
Hammering on wood: Avoid rivals.
Hammering on plaster: Will be jilted by a lover.
Others holding a hammer: Temptation will come to you.
Others hammering: Financial condition will be better in the future.
The sound of a hammer being used: You have one loyal friend.
Hearing many people hammering: Happiness in love affairs.

HAMMOCK:
Being in a hammock: Happiness with lover is assured.
Others being in a hammock: A serious disaster is ahead.
Relatives being in a hammock: Will have emotional sorrow.
Children being in a hammock: Misfortune in love affairs.

HAMPER:
Having an empty hamper: Will have jealous quarrel with sweetheart.
A hamper being full of linen: Shame and sorrow.
Taking linen from a hamper to wash: Triumph over enemies.

HAND:
Of own hands: Perfect accord between husband and wife.
Having a big hand: Will be a big lover.
Having a small hand: Infidelity.
Own hand being cut: Will incur debts.
Burning own hand: Loss of employees.
Hands being clean: Will overcome troubles.
Hands being dirty: Be careful with own affairs.
Shaking hands: Unexpected good event.

Having hands tied: Great difficulties.
Having swollen hands: Wealth.
Kissing hands: Friendship and good fortune.
Washing own hands: Big work is ahead.
Having a handful of hair: Will be annoyed by friends.
A woman's hand being cut off: Her husband will run away.
A child's hand being cut off: The children will elope soon.
A man's hand being cut off: Must take better care of own business.
Unmarried people dreaming of their hands: Will love and be loved.
Working with the right hand: Happiness.
Writing with right hand: Joy.
Working with the left hand: Contrariety.
Writing with left hand: You are in love.
The hands of a watch or clock: Big unhappiness.

HANDBAG:
Of a handbag: Passing riches.
Blue handbag: Happiness.
Black handbag: Unhappiness.
Red handbag: Affairs will go well.
White handbag: Success in undertakings.
Buying a handbag: Will be loved.
Finding a handbag: Bankruptcy.
Finding an empty handbag: Good results in enterprises.
Finding a full handbag: Negligence.
Finding a handbag with a coin purse in it: Good results in business.
Finding a handbag with cigarettes in it: Good luck.
Receiving a handbag as a gift: Irritation and loss of temper.
Giving a handbag as a gift: Will encounter opposition.

HANDCUFFS:
Being handcuffed: Annoyance caused by enemies.
Others being handcuffed: Will conquer all obstacles.

Relatives being handcuffed: Will get out of troubles.

Enemies being handcuffed: Good prospects for own business.

A dangerous prisoner being handcuffed: Will receive a letter with money.

HANDKERCHIEF:

Losing a handkerchief: Broken engagement.

A torn handkerchief: Serious troubles between lovers.

Giving a handkerchief as a gift: Will cry for a long time.

Using a handkerchief to blow nose: Will be loved by people.

A linen handkerchief: Will soon become ill.

A silk handkerchief: You are egotistical.

An embroidered handkerchief: You are prone to conceit.

Wiping sweat away with a handkerchief: Troubles are ahead.

Putting a handkerchief around the neck: Beware of enemies.

Buying a handkerchief: Be careful of new ventures.

Receiving a handkerchief as a gift: Will receive a gift.

HANDWRITING:

Seeing handwriting on paper: Will make excuses to people.

The handwriting of others: Will receive legal documents.

Handwriting on a wall: Will find out the truth.

Handwriting a letter: Dignity in love.

HANG:

Hang up something: Illness.

Hang up own clothes: Must control your passions.

Hang up children's clothes: Avoid rivals.

Hang up visitors' clothes: Change in own environment.

HANGING:

Of being hanged: Abundant means.

Being sentenced to hanging: Exceptional honors will be yours.

Someone who is going to be hanged: Will enjoy excellent meat at meals.

Other people hanging: Good luck to the person in the dream.

A friend hanging: Your lover will be faithless.

A relative hanging: Wealth and great honor.

A stranger being hanged: Deception and false friends.

A criminal hanging: Will make money in a shameful manner.

Someone hanging without cause: You are prone to being stingy.

Being freed just before hanging: Will realize own ambitions.

HAPPY:

Of being happy: Will realize your ambitions.

Increased happiness: Bad business ventures according to degree of happiness.

Husband and wife being happy: Joy and success.

Children being happy: Rapid success of own hopes.

Relatives being happy: Worry will be smoothed away.

Friends being happy: A false friend is nearby.

Other people being happy: Avoid rivals.

Employees being happy: Pleasant social activities.

HARBOR:

A harbor without ships: Misery.

A harbor with ships: Will be taken care of all your life.

Being alone in a harbor aboard a ship: Financial gains.

Being with loved one in a harbor aboard a ship: Falsehoods to be exposed.

Being in a harbor of a lake: Will take a trip.

Being in a harbor at sea: Will discover a secret.

A harbor far away: Good news.

HARE:

Of a hare or rabbit: Failure of enemies.

A hare running: Change of occupation.

Several hares on the run: Very good business ventures.

Eating rabbits: Will quarrel with a friend.

Shooting hares: Happiness.

Having hares in the back yard: Big friendship.

HAREBELLS:

Of gathering bluebells: Will find a true lover.

Making harebells into a bouquet: Many people are envious of you.

Picking harebells: Will be cheated by friends.

Being given harebells: Joy and honor.

HAREM:

Of a harem: You are prone to luxurious living.

Living in a harem: The truth will come out.

Other women in a harem: Secret things are the subject of gossip.

Men being in a harem: Will triumph in own affairs.

Turks being in a harem: Abundant means.

Far Eastern people in a harem: Financial gains.

Foreigners being in a harem: Change for the better.

HARMONICA:

Of a harmonica: Will receive some money.

Buying a harmonica: Abundant means.

Playing a harmonica: Will receive unexpected good news.

Hearing a harmonica played: A big fight is ahead.

Others playing a harmonica: Arguments within the family.

HARMONIUM:

Of a harmonium: Sickness is near at hand.

Hearing a harmonium played: Happiness is ahead.

Playing a harmonium: Happy but solemn occasion to come.

Others playing a harmonium: Will be invited to wedding of a friend.

HARMONY:

Being in harmony: Joy and contentment.

Others being in harmony: A friend is helping you secretly.

Hearing musical harmony: Happiness.

Having harmony within the family: Change in environment.

HARNESS:

A harness for a dog: An introduction will lead to friendship.

Buying a dog harness: You will be very much in love.

A harness for a horse: Advancement in own love affairs.

Buying a horse harness: Will be tempted by a new love.

HARP:

A harp being broken: Illness of a lover.

Playing a harp: Do not trust friends too far.

Others playing a harp: Dissolution.

A daughter playing the harp: She will not have a happy marriage.

Enemies playing the harp: Will enjoy expensive pleasures.

A harp being played at a theater: You have one loyal friend.

HARROW:

Of a harrow: Failure of enemies.

Buying a harrow: Luck and prosperity.

Using a harrow: Prompt and good business.

Others using a harrow: Change for the better.

HASH:

Eating hash: Petty vexations and sorrow.

Making hash: Will be visited by several family friends.

Others making hash: Avoid rivals.

HASSOCK:

Of stuffing a hassock: Disappointment in love.

Praying with a hassock under the knees: Beware of rivals.

Having feet on a hassock: Triumph over rivals.

HART:

Of a male deer: Quarrels and losses.

Killing a hart: Will receive an inheritance.

Eating the meat of a hart: Difficult times.

(See also **DEER.**)

HARVEST:

Having a good harvest: Misfortune in love affairs.

Workers harvesting: Money will come easily.

Having an abundant harvest: Nature favors you.

A poor harvest: Troubles in love affairs.

HARVEST FLY:

Of a harvest fly: You are prone to laziness.

Catching a harvest fly: Will suffer hunger.

Not catching harvest flies: Will have a bad harvest.

Killing harvest flies: Will receive news of someone's operation.

Hearing many harvest flies singing: Arrival of an unwelcome guest.

Hearing harvest flies singing at noon: Arrival of musicians.

A sick person hearing them singing: Will be robbed by thieves.

Harvest flies jumping: You are surrounded by boisterous people.

HAT:

A woman's hat: Recovery from an illness.

A man's hat: Will have emotional sorrow.

Losing your hat: Beware of false friends.

Finding your hat: Worry will be smoothed away.

A woman wearing an unusual hat: Big admiration.

Wearing a new hat: Wealth.

Wearing an old hat: Poverty or danger.

Wearing a straw hat: You are prone to conceit.

Wearing a big hat: Joy and prosperity.

Someone else wearing a hat: Joy and contentment.

Taking your hat off to someone: Humiliation.

The wind blowing a ladies' hat off: She will lose her freedom.

A man who makes hats: Will be doing useless work.

A woman who makes hats: Fortune and happiness.

HATBOX:

An empty hatbox: Worry will be smoothed away.

A full hatbox: Disappointment concerning a party.

Opening a hatbox: A gay occasion to come.

Closing a hatbox: Change for the better.

HATCHET:

Of a hatchet: Danger of death.

Owning a hatchet: It is impossible to reconcile with enemies.

Others with a hatchet: Warning that your life is in danger.

A friend with a hatchet: Will be in danger soon.

Enemies with a hatchet: Anxiety and trouble.

HATE:

Being hated without reason: Will possess many true friends.

Hating others: Be careful not to do them wrong unconsciously.

Hating enemies: Will win a lawsuit.

Being hated by friends: Will have new, good friends.

Hating some of own relatives: Happiness in domestic affairs.

HAWK:

Of a hawk: Your fortune will increase.

A hawk flying: Losses caused through intrigue.

Several hawks together: Be careful in business speculations.

Shooting a hawk: No obstacles will be insurmountable.

HAWKER:
Of a hawker: A new influence is about to enter your life.
Talking to a hawker: Be reserved with present associates.
Buying from a hawker: Will have dealings with a woman.

HAWTHORN:
Of this spring blossom: Accord among friends.
A white hawthorn: Will have considerable money.
A pink hawthorn: Happiness is assured.
Smelling the fragrant flowers of hawthorn: Big joy.

HAY:
A field of hay: Exceptional prosperity.
Loading hay: Will have a life of ease and freedom.
Cutting hay: Success in love affairs.
A stack of hay: Abundant means.
The smell of hay: Will have a small accident.
The smell of rotten hay: Loss of money.

HAY CART:
Of a hay cart: Change of residence.
A hay cart being full: Illness.
Being on a hay cart: Dishonor in life.
Coming down off a hay cart: Loss of honor.

HAYSTACK:
Of a haystack: You are laying the foundation for a prosperous future.
Losing something in a haystack: You are being deceived.
Finding something in a haystack: Abundant means.
Lying on a haystack with sweetheart: Must rely on own vigor.

HAZARD:
Of a hazard: A good future is ahead.
Escaping from a hazard: Will be involved in car accident but not hurt.
Being hurt by a hazard: Will incur money losses.

A building being a safety hazard: Will go into bankruptcy.

HAZELNUT:
Of hazelnuts: Will marry into wealth.
Buying hazelnuts: Arguments and discussions.
Picking hazelnuts: Father or mother are in danger of death.
The hazelnut tree before picking: Difficulty in love.

HEAD:
Of own head: Big fortune.
Having a nice head: Do not take risks.
Own head being turned sideways Will receive something good unexpectedly.
Having a headache: Difficulties are ahead.
Washing your head: Overwhelming misfortune.
A head without a body: Disappointment.
Many heads: Dishonor in love.
A three-headed person: Honor and money.
A bald head: Will be loved.
A pointed head: Long life.
A huge head: Good business transactions.
A large, rounded head: Dignity.
A small head: Beware of your enemies.
A black head: Success in own business.
A white head: Big earnings.
A very very small head: Will be loved very much.
Having a round head: Loss of your wife.
A head with long flowing hair: Big honor.
A head well combed: Headed toward danger.
A head poorly combed: Will be raped.
Having a clean-shaven head: Will be ashamed.
Having a head cut in half: Success in everything.
Having your head cut off: Pleasure and honor.

Cutting another's head off: You will surpass your friends in success.

Holding own head in hands: Will have a brain disease.

Holding another person's head in your hands: Loss of a relative.

An unmarried person dreaming of holding a head in hands: Big happiness.

Holding a dog, horse, or donkey head in hands: Will be enslaved.

A colored person's head: Will take a long journey.

A dead person's head: Will discover a secret.

A sick person dreaming of a large head: Will get well soon.

The head of a bird: Change within own position.

The head of a wild animal: Victory over enemies.

The head of a lion: Will be a very important person.

The head of a wolf: Honor.

The head of a deer: Triumph over enemies.

The head of a calf: Big consolation.

The head of a dog: Great humiliation.

HEALTH:

Being in poor health: Will be saved from a big peril.

Recovering health after an illness: Must rely upon business intelligence.

Children being in good health: Honor.

Family being in good health: Will attain fame.

Relatives being in bad health: Persecution.

Children being in bad health: Fortune.

Husband or wife being in bad health: Pleasant happenings to come.

Friends being in bad health: Death of a friend.

HEAR:

Hearing someone nearby: Will have a vigorous mind.

Hearing relatives talking: A change in life will soon come.

Hearing children: Financial gains.

Hearing others: You are being deceived.

HEARSE:

A hearse being at a church: Worry will be smoothed away.

A hearse taking a dead person to the grave: Happiness.

A military hearse conveying the dead: Will have emotional sorrow.

HEARSAY:

Of hearsay: Unhappiness in the home.

Hearsay from others: Unhappiness in your business.

Hearsay from friends: Beware of deceit, and trust few people.

Telling others hearsay: Will be making an important change shortly.

HEART:

Having a happy heart: Good business.

Having a wounded heart: Separation of husband and wife.

Having a big heart: Sickness.

Being heartless: Triumph in business.

Losing your heart: Death is near.

Having pains in your heart: Long sickness.

Blood passing to heart slowly: You have insulted your best friend.

The heart of a woman: She will leave her husband.

The heart of a man: He will love another woman.

The heart of an unmarried person: Elopement and marriage.

Eating heart meat: Happy love affairs.

Cooking heart meat: Successful future.

Being out of breath because of heart trouble: Will surpass friends.

Having a heart disease: Big illness.

HEARTH:

Of the hearth of own home: Happiness.

The floor of a hearth: Will have good fortune.

Cooking on the fire of a hearth: Will be successful in everything.

The grate of a hearth: Advancement in own affairs.

HEAT:

Having heat in your face: Friends are gossiping about you.

Suffering from heat: You have no reason to worry.

Being in a very heated place: A friend is betraying you.

Being very hot: Happiness is assured.

HEATER:

Of a heater: Important and very beneficial events to come.

Lighting a heater: Advancement within own position.

Putting out a heater: Change in own environment.

Buying a new heater: Are prone to frivolity.

HEATHENS:

Going to a savage country among heathens: Will enjoy contented home life.

Being among heathens: Profitable life.

A priest going among heathens: Dignity and distinction.

HEAVEN:

Of the heavens surrounding the earth: Big happiness.

The heavens being clear: Joy.

The heavens being dark: Recovery of money.

The heavens without the sun: Recovery from an illness.

The heavens without the stars: Will receive bad news.

Being in heaven: An immediate marriage.

Going to heaven: Prosperity.

HEAVY:

Of heavy articles: Wealth.

Carrying something heavy: Children will be born into the family.

Others carrying heavy things: Will receive unexpected money.

Laborers carrying heavy things: Will be courted.

Friends carrying heavy things: Use caution in business affairs.

Children carrying heavy bundles of books: Big honors in the family.

HEDGE:

A hedge surrounding entire home:

Will not have any obstacles to overcome.

A green hedge: Happiness.

Bare hedges: Sadness and distress.

HEDGEHOG:

Of a hedgehog: Failure of enemies.

Killing a hedgehog: Rapid recovery of losses in own affairs.

A defensive stronghold fortified with mines: Danger in love matters.

HEELS:

Of own heels: Misfortune in love affairs.

Having a wounded heel: Will have innumerable troubles.

Having pains in the heels: A false friend is nearby.

The heels of other people: Change for the better.

HEIRLOOM:

Having a personal heirloom: Do not be dominated by friends.

Putting an heirloom away: You will be humiliated.

Receiving a piece of property as an inheritance: Family quarrels.

HELL:

Of hell: Complete change of your circumstances.

Being in hell: Good times are coming.

Running away from hell: Joy.

Returning from hell: Disappointment.

Hearing the people in hell groaning: Will live a short life.

HELMET:

Of a helmet: Pleasant visitors.

Wearing a helmet: Avoid extravagances.

Buying a helmet: You will need all of your savings.

Others wearing helmets: Avoid rivals.

HELP:

Requiring help: Attempt to understand the heart of your acquaintances.

Hiring help: Will have hard work ahead.

Firing help: You expect too many favors of others.

Having reliable help: Misery.
Asking for financial help: Joy.
Receiving help from a dog: Will be double-crossed by a woman.

HEMP:
Smoking a cigarette of hemp or marijuana: Prompt engagement.
Being addicted to hemp and taking it: Postponement of success.
Buying hemp: Warning of trouble.

HEN:
Of a hen: Financial gains.
A hen laying eggs: Expect good luck.
A hen with her chicks: Will have many children.
Setting a hen: Promises fulfillment of a long-cherished wish.
A hen house: Big family joy.

HERBS:
Of herbs: Will be loved very much.
Herbs growing vigorously: Good fortune.
Herbs with their flowers: Abundant means.
Cutting herbs: Will have a long life.

HERD:
Of many herds of cattle: Joy.
Gathering a herd together: Fortune.
Having a fat herd of cattle: Good times ahead.
Having a herd of skinny cattle: Will be very short of money.
Milking a herd of cattle: Will earn money.

HERMAPHRODITE:
Having both male and female reproductive organs: Will have emotional sorrow.
Others being hermaphrodites: Will be guilty of foolish actions.
The son of Hermes and Aphrodite joined in one body: Happiness.
A hermaphrodite sailing vessel with two masts: Will take long journey.

HERMIT:
Of a hermit: If you had been more daring, you would have gained more.

Being a hermit: You are being deceived by a friend.
Becoming a hermit: Will soon become sick.

HERO:
Of a hero: One who is treating you cool will have a change of heart.
Being a hero: Happiness is assured.
A relative being a hero: Triumph over enemies.

HERRING:
Of herring: Will take a trip.
Catching herring: Desires will be satisfied.
Eating herring: Good luck to one for whom you care.
Buying herring: Will be generous to friends.
Cooking herring: Expect pregnancy in the near future.
Being given herring by others: Will realize high ambitions.

HICCOUGH:
Having a siege of hiccoughing: Will travel soon.
Relatives hiccoughing: Sorrow and loneliness.
Others hiccoughing: Will be separated from friends.

HIDE:
Of hiding: Bad news will soon reach you.
Relatives hiding: You are being deceived.
Others hiding: Avoid rivals.

HIGH SCHOOL:
Being in high school: Quarrels will end happily.
Teaching high school: Will be happy because of innocence.
Children going to high school: Modesty.
Children graduating from high school: Happiness.

HIGHWAYMAN:
Of a highwayman: Abundant means.
Being robbed by a highwayman: Big joy.

Others being robbed by a highwayman: Misfortune in love affairs.

Being frightened by a highwayman: Will be kidnaped.

Being beaten by a highwayman: Loss of relatives, children, and property.

Being wounded by a highwayman: Will be deprived of money.

Being killed by a highwayman: Loss of inheritance.

HILLS:

Climbing up hills: Good fortune.

Reaching the crest of a hill: Will have to fight against envy.

Climbing hills easily: Future will be very good.

Having difficulties in climbing a hill: Sorrow.

Others climbing a hill: You have one loyal friend.

Climbing a hill with relatives: Financial gains.

Several hills: Will have easy earnings.

HIPS:

Of own hips: Pleasant work and good news.

Hips of children: Will live a long life.

Hips of others: You are being deceived.

Hips of enemies: Triumph over enemies.

Hips of your wife: Will be rich.

Hips of your husband: Husband is cheating on you.

Having very big hips: Will have money.

Having strong hips: Good health.

Having broken hips: Loss of money.

Breaking own hips: Sickness and loss of children.

Having an operation on the hips: Misplaced confidence in mate.

Hip being injured and bleeding: Large losses to the family.

Being hit on the hips: Mate will cause family embarrassment.

HISTORY:

Of past history: Big honors.

Reading a history book: Will go into bankruptcy.

Being a history teacher: Security in business.

Consulting a book on ancient history: Your fortune is at expense of others.

Reading modern history books: Don't believe lies being told by others.

HIT:

Hitting someone: Present situation will get worse.

Being hit by someone: Death of a friend.

Being hit by a bandit: Changes in personal relations.

Being hit by a friend: Improvement of personal situation.

Being hit by a relative: Fortune in business.

Hitting a relative: Will take a long trip.

Other people hitting you: Misfortune in business.

People hitting each other: Shame will fall upon you.

Being hit by a wild person: Will gain the love of one you desire.

HIVE:

A hive without honey or bees: Dangerous undertakings.

A hive full of honey and bees at work: Good times are coming.

Taking honey from a hive: An enemy is seeking your ruin.

HOARSE:

Being hoarse because of a cold: Warning of trouble.

Others being hoarse from a cold: Danger in love matters.

Speaking with a hoarse sound: A serious disaster is ahead.

HOBBY:

Spending time at favorite hobby: Joy without profit.

Others spending time at their hobby: A change in life will come.

Children spending time at their hobby: Financial gains.

HOE:

Several shapes of hoes: Good hopes for the future.

Using a hoe: Will be a competent person.

Using a hoe to cultivate own garden: Improvements to come very soon.

HOGS:

Of hogs: Will have good earnings.

Hogs being well fed: Prosperity to come.

Hogs being thin: Children will cause petty vexations.

Many hogs: Will receive money after the death of a relative.

Buying hogs: Will have joy.

Selling hogs: Will be hated by friends.

A wild hog: A friend will try to cause harm.

Others who have hogs: Avoid rivals.

HOLD:

Holding something firmly in hands: Will be noted for bravery.

Losing hold of something: Gossip.

Holding investments: Intrigue.

Holding one you love in your arms: You are too egotistic.

Holding children in your arms: Happiness.

HOLE:

Making a hole: Will make a long trip.

Others making holes: Good times will come in the future.

Falling into a hole: Illness.

Creeping into a hole: Will come in contact with undesirable people.

HOLLY:

Of holly: Beware of vexations.

Picking holly: Will live a long life.

Being given holly: Postponement of success.

HOME:

Of a home: Financial security.

Own home: Happiness within the family.

Other peoples' homes: Will have a law suit coming up.

Building a home: Honor without joy.

Others building a home: Will have much consolation.

Changing homes: Small fortune.

Your home burning: Honor and dignity.

Staying at home: Will have an easy life.

A home trembling: Small loss of money.

Other people coming to your home: Sorrow.

Visiting an old home: Will have cause to rejoice.

Old home being dilapidated: A relative will die.

Own new home: Prosperity especially for lovers.

Having a corner home: Will be fortunate.

A home being demolished: Loss of your property.

Entering own home on a sunny day: Will buy real estate.

A big fire burning a home: Inheritance.

A home burning with dark smoke: A mystery is ahead.

A small home: Joy and contentment.

Receiving a home as a gift: Good hopes.

Going upstairs in a home: Loss of your lover.

A home of correction: Will have dealings with a judge.

HOMICIDE:

Planning to commit homicide: Will have a long life.

Other people committing homicide: Will have security.

Friends committing homicide: Will avoid a danger.

HOMOSEXUAL:

Of homosexual people: Financial gains.

Meeting a homosexual person: Recovery of lost money.

Homosexuals being arrested: Must control your passions.

HONEY:

Having honey: Business success.

Eating honey: Big success in all own dealings.

Being given honey: Financial gains.

Making honey on a farm or in back yard: Big prosperity.

HONEYDEW MELON:
Of a honeydew melon: Good success.
Having honeydew melons: Good news from a loved person.
Growing honeydew melons: Success in love affairs.
Buying a honeydew melon: High hopes.
Eating honeydew melon: Sick people will recover from an illness.

HONEYMOON:
Going on a honeymoon: Changes in your life will come.
Being on own honeymoon: You are being deceived.
Children going on their honeymoon: Joy without profit.
Relatives going on their honeymoon: Will take a small trip.
Friends going on their honeymoon: Disappointment.

HONEYSUCKLE:
Of honeysuckle: Will have a happy marriage.
Honeysuckle being in flower: Will change residence to a better one.
Gathering honeysuckles: Much prosperity.

HONOR:
Receiving an honor: Joy in life.
Being honored: Beware of false promises.
Losing your honor: Death of a friend.
Others receiving honors: Will lose money.

HOOKS:
Of hooks: A present will be given to you.
Having hooks: Will find a valuable article.
Catching things with a hook: Will have mastery over many things.
Using a hook: False friends are nearby.

HOOP:
Of a hoop: Big joy.
Handling a hoop: Assurance of happiness.

Fastening with hoops: Accord among friends.

HOPE:
Having hope: Loss of good friends.
Losing hope: Good days are ahead.
Having good hopes for family: Danger is ahead.
Hoping for success of children: Big arguments ahead with relatives.

HORN:
Hearing the sound of a horn: Unexpected and joyful news.
Blowing a horn: Social activities of a happy nature.
Others blowing a horn: You are being deceived.
Blowing a horn while hunting: Gossip will cause unhappiness.
Having horns on the head: Dignity and dominion.
A man having horns on his forehead: Danger of a disease that brings death.
Animals with large horns: Expect sorrow.
Animals with small horns: Joy and happiness.
The horns of a bull or cow: Quarrels.
The horns of wild animals: Magnificence.
Receiving a set of horns as a gift: Will receive sad news.
Buying horns: Good business transactions.
Other people having horns: Will be desperately in love.

HORNETS:
Of a hornet: Triumph over your enemies.
Many hornets: A rival will seek to injure you just for spite.
Killing a hornet: Be on guard around friends.
Others killing hornets: Joy.

HOROSCOPE:
Buying a horoscope book: Approaching money.
Being told your horoscope: Will be badly tormented.

Reading own horoscope: Will be embarrassed.

HORSE:
Being mounted on a horse: Wealthy marriage.

Riding a horse and being thrown: Use caution in business ventures.

Someone coming to visit on horseback: Expect good news.

A horse being shod: Financial gains.

Putting shoes on own horse: Financial gains.

A horse running away: Disappointment and misfortune.

A female horse: Will be married to a beautiful lady in near future.

A horse hitched to a carriage: Good business is on the way.

Wild horses: Will have many good business transactions.

White horses: Joy.

Black horses: Will be molested.

Red horses: Big prosperity.

Brown horses: Tremendous joy.

Tan horses: Will realize own ambitions.

Gray horses: Money will come easily during life.

Horses of other colors: Good business is on the way to you.

Buying a gray horse: Good fortune.

A horse being ridden by a woman: Will be reconciled with friends.

A horse being ridden by a man: Big earnings.

A racing horse: Quarrels with friends.

A castrated horse: Happiness.

A cavalry horse: Good things will happen soon.

A horse with a short tail: Friends will desert you when you are in misery.

A horse with a long tail: Friends will help select your wife.

A dead horse: Will have good yearly earnings.

A wounded horse: Bad results in enterprises.

Showing horses at a fair: Big luck.

Riding a horse: Will meet a rich foreign woman.

Riding a horse not belonging to you: **Will have big benefits.**

Losing a horse: Loss of friends.

Riding a dangerous horse: Will work hard and make money.

Hitting a horse to make him obey: Honor and dignity.

Friends riding a horse: A friend will make love to your wife.

A horse being in the water or a stream: Will be in misery.

A horse limping: Will encounter opposition.

HORSESHOE:
Finding a horseshoe: Will receive a legacy.

Losing a horseshoe: Family quarrels.

Putting a new shoe on a horse: Misfortune in love.

HOSPITAL:
Of a hospital: Misery.

Being a patient in a hospital: Hopes for good business.

Being in a religious hospital: Divine hopes.

Being in a mental hospital: Must control passions.

HOSTLER:
Of a stable groom: You are in favor with fortune.

Having a hostler take care of your horses: Abundant means.

Own hostler at work: Big financial gains.

Others working as a hostler: Change of surroundings.

HOTEL:
Of a hotel: Success of hopes in near future.

Living in a hotel: Will have a life of ease.

A very fine hotel: Will take a long journey.

Being in a hotel with your sweetheart: Wealth will come to you.

Making your home in a hotel: A mystery will be solved.

HOTHOUSE:
Of a hothouse: Doomed for disappointment.

Being in a hothouse: Important and **very beneficial event to come.**

Many plants and flowers being in a hothouse: Luck and prosperity.

HOUNDS:
Of hound dogs: Success will come after much struggling.
Hound dogs at work: Luck and prosperity.
Owning a hound dog: Change of surroundings.

HOUR:
The hour showing on a clock: Discovery of a secret.
A clock chiming the hour: Fortune.
A cuckoo giving the hours: Unexpected wealth.
Looking at the hour on a wristwatch: Will lose a friend.
Seeing the hour on a clock in the street: Will donate to charity.

HOUSE:
Of a house: Financial security.
Own house: Happiness within the family.
A house belonging to others: Will have a lawsuit coming up.
Building a new house: Honor without joy.
Changing houses: Small fortune.
A house burning: Honor and dignity.
Others building a house: Will have a big consolation.
Friends visiting your house: Sorrow.
A house being torn down: Warning of sad news.

HOWL:
Hearing dogs howling: Will receive bad news.
Hearing wild animals howling: Enemies will get the best of you.
Hearing people howling: Will have hard work in the future.
Friends howling: You are prone to arrogance.

HUMIDITY:
Of humidity: Will contract an illness shortly.
Being in a humid country: Will work the mind very hard.
It being a humid day: Will be corrupted.

Suffering from the humidity: You are prone to arrogance.

HUMMINGBIRDS:
Of hummingbirds: Rapid success in own affairs.
A great many hummingbirds: Successful business.
Owning a hummingbird: Will travel to a foreign country.

HUMOR:
Being in a good humor: Disagreements and unhappiness.
Being in a bad humor: False friends are nearby.
Husband or wife being in a bad humor: Foolish gossip is being spread.
Other people being in a bad humor: Fortune in business.
Sweethearts being in a bad humor: Will encounter someone you love.
Sweethearts being in good humor: Will make a long trip.
Boss being in a bad humor: Will receive an invitation to dinner.
Relatives being in a bad humor: Family disagreements.

HUNCHBACK:
Being a hunchback: Will be humiliated.
Talking to a hunchback: Happy love affairs.
A male hunchback: Changes to come.
A female hunchback: Will have a period of many trials.

HUNGER:
Being hungry: Malicious gossip.
Children being hungry: Important and very beneficial event to come.
Other people being hungry: Failure of enemies.
Enemies being hungry: Will be cheated by friends.

HUNTING:
Of hunting: Your endeavors are too weak.
Going hunting: Will be accused by friends.
Being on a hunting party: Big earnings.

Actually hunting: Will have a happy life.

Husband hunting: You are economical and industrious.

Children hunting: Financial gains.

Hunting small animals: Disappointment.

Hunting big animals: Coming prosperity.

Hunting a fox: Will conquer all difficulties.

Returning from a hunting trip: Certain earnings.

Missing an animal while hunting: Failure of own desires.

Changing your place of hunting: You will succeed.

Many people hunting: Will receive a big fortune.

HURDLES:
Of hurdles: Will be unjustly accused.

Fixing hurdles: Must clear yourself of false suspicions.

Others arranging hurdles: Will hear from an old acquaintance.

HURRICANE:
Of a hurricane: Loss of friends.

Being in a hurricane: Be very careful of your actions.

Losing property in a hurricane: Will live a long life.

The devastation from a hurricane: A mystery will be solved.

HURRY:
Being in a hurry: Danger of an accident.

Children being in a hurry: Important and very beneficial event to come.

Friends being in a hurry: Will live a long life.

Enemies being in a hurry: Doomed for dissappointment.

HURT:
Being hurt: Will be plenty rich.

Children being hurt: Financial gains.

Relatives being hurt: You are being watched by one with evil intent.

Enemies being hurt: Family quarrels.

HUSBAND:
Of a husband when not married: Big joy.

Having a good husband: Avoid rivals.

Liking someone else's husband: Trouble is ahead.

Wanting to divorce your husband: Must control your passions.

Losing husband by death: Important and very beneficial events to come.

Marrying a second husband: Luck and prosperity.

A husband divorcing his wife: Quarrels with one dear to you.

Others flirting with your husband: Will live together all your life.

HUSSAR:
Of a European cavalry: Unreturned affection will be your fate.

Being with a hussar: Will have a civilian lover.

Several hussars: Joy without profit.

HUT:
Being in a hut: A big catastrophe is ahead.

Being in a hut with the family: Triumph over enemies.

Enemies being in a hut: Will have a vigorous mind.

HYACINTH:
Having a hyacinth on clothes: Will have an everlasting marriage.

Having hyacinth given to you: You have one loyal friend.

Of this precious gem: Will have a faithful husband.

Friends wearing a hyacinth: Someone is endeavoring to destroy you.

Enemies wearing a hyacinth: Misfortune of others.

Relatives wearing a hyacinth: Sickness in the future.

HYDROPHOBIA:
An animal having hydrophobia: Robbery and losses.

Own dog having hydrophobia: Guard your treasures.

A dog with hydrophobia biting someone: Abundant means.

HYMNS:
Singing hymns: Plans will be successful.
Hearing others singing hymns: Recovery from an illness.
Hearing hymns being sung by friends: Fair business prospects.
Hearing foreigners singing hymns: Contentment.
Singing hymns in church: Own affairs will be completed well.

HYPOCRITICAL:
Being hypocritical: A false friend is cheating you.

Having dealings with a hypocritical person: Riches and honor.
Realizing that you are hypocritical: Security in business.
Being hypocritical in love: Will receive a gift.

HYSTERICS:
Having hysterics: Will have a vigorous mind.
Children having hysterics: Do not allow yourself to be dominated.
Relatives having hysterics: Be firm in order to achieve success.

I

ICE:
Of a lot of ice: Big business prosperity.
Sliding on the ice: Disaster threatens.
Breaking through the ice: Anxiety without cause.
Running on the ice: Warning of deception in love.
Walking with others on the ice: Do not be too daring.
The ice in own refrigerator: Happiness in love.
A farmer dreaming of ice: Good harvesting.
Working people dreaming of ice: Money-making.
Merchants dreaming of ice: Improvement in business.
Business man dreaming of ice: Obstacles in their affairs.
Military men dreaming of ice: Promotion within their ranks.
Ladies dreaming of ice: Will make a long journey.
Young people dreaming of ice: Will soon be in love.

ICEBERG:
Of an iceberg: Will have a trial in court.
A vessel used to break up icebergs: Good luck.

A vessel breaking up icebergs: Make big efforts and you will triumph.

ICE CREAM:
Eating ice cream: Success in every undertaking.
Buying ice cream: Danger through a secret.
Making ice cream: Financial gains.
Children eating ice cream: Will live a long life.
Enemies eating ice cream: They must endure starvation.

ICICLES:
Of many icicles: Poverty.
Icicles hanging from the eaves: Ill health.
Icicles melting and dropping water: Loss of a loved person.

IDIOT:
Of idiots: Some unexpected good fortune awaits.
Many idiots: Will have a vigorous mind.
Being an idiot: Are on the way to receive a cabinet post.
Children being idiots: Will have a prominent place in life.

IDLENESS:
Being idle: Will have to work hard.

Other people being idle: Success in own business ventures.

Employees being idle: Important and very beneficial event to come.

IDOL:

Of an idol: Intentions are to commit an injustice against another.

Idolizing a saint: You are loved very much.

Being idolized by others: Will be apprehensive over business.

Idolizing your children: Must conceal your feelings better.

IGNORANCE:

Being ignorant: Success will crown your efforts.

Dealing with ignorant people: Recovery from an illness.

Children being ignorant: Abundant means.

ILL-BRED:

Being an ill-bred person: Don't let other people scare you.

People who are ill-bred: Will have an accident caused by other people.

Being among ill-bred people: Success in your affairs.

Friends who are ill-bred: Must control your temper.

ILLNESS:

Having an illness: Misfortune in love affairs.

Children having an illness: Consolation and happiness.

Relatives having an illness: Unhappiness.

Enemies having an illness: Great temptation will not be favorable for you.

Visiting people with an illness: Will find a way to attain own goal.

A woman dreaming of having an illness: Despair.

Sweetheart having an illness: Must forego some anticipated pleasure.

Other people having an illness: Someone you know will go to prison.

Many people in a hospital with illness: Joy and profit.

Having a brain illness: Fortune.

Having a stomach illness: You waste money.

Having an unknown illness: Wealth.

ILLUMINATE:

Of rooms illuminated: Misery and afflictions.

Halls that are illuminated: Great and good fortune.

Sweetheart being in an illuminated place: Exceptional good fortune.

Enemy's house being illuminated: Be on the lookout for treachery.

IMAGE:

Of an image: You are very diligent in your work.

The image of a dead person: Expect the death of a relative.

The image of a saint: Failure in business and love.

The image of own children: Misfortune in love affairs.

The image of dead relatives: Postpone an important decision.

Several beautiful images: Pleasure and friendship.

IMPALE:

Being impaled on railings: Will be threatened by enemies.

Others being impaled upon railings: Trouble is ahead.

Escaping from an impaled condition: Happiness.

Being tortured or punished: Triumph is certain.

IMPATIENT:

Being impatient: Will reach own goals slowly but surely.

Being impatient with children: Will receive a letter containing money.

Being impatient with friends: Gossip.

Being impatient with business people: Happiness.

Others being impatient: Will receive punishment from God.

IMPORTER:

Being an importer: Be diligent in your own work.

Being importer of general merchandise: Will be ashamed of actions.

Being importer of different animals: Will enjoy much wealth.

Others being importers of merchandise: Security in enterprises.

IMPOTENT:

Of lacking power: Will soon have an illness.

Lacking the power of sexual intercourse: Will have unforeseen wealth.

Being impotent yourself: Will receive a legacy.

Others being impotent: Hope for good earnings.

IMPUDENT:

Being impudent: Lack of modesty.

Other impudent people: Change of surroundings.

Others being impudent to you: Will be rescued in business transactions.

Others being impudent: Will be cheated by friends.

INACTIVE:

Being inactive: Good days are ahead.

Having inactive properties: Loss of sweetheart.

A man being inactive: Unhappiness in love.

A woman being inactive: Will not have a boyfriend or husband.

Others being inactive: Will lead a worried life.

INCENSE:

Of incense: Big flattery.

Burning incense before the arrival of a loved one: Will pay respects.

Incense burning in church: Your troubles are ended.

Others burning incense: Will receive pleasing attentions.

Burning incense in own home: Flattery by lovers.

INCOME:

Having a comfortable income: You should mend your ways in life.

Having insufficient income: Warning of troubles with relatives.

Own income getting very low: Important and very beneficial events to come.

Relatives with a big income: Use caution in business ventures.

Friends with a big income: A false friend is nearby.

INCOME TAX:

Paying own income tax: You have stingy relatives.

Being unable to pay income tax: Financial losses.

Receiving a refund on income tax: Success in own enterprises.

Cheating on payment of income tax: Beware of big losses.

Having income tax raised: Will be assisted by a friend.

INCONSTANT:

Being inconstant: Will soon fall in love.

A woman dreaming of being inconstant: Will receive sad news.

A man dreaming of being inconstant: Will have worry and shame.

Others who are inconstant: Are surrounded by enemies trying to bring harm.

INCREASE:

Increasing financial standing: Be careful of expenses.

Increasing own business: Satisfaction.

Increasing bank account: Vanity.

Increasing the family: Happiness.

INDECENT:

Being indecent: Will be put in your place.

A man being indecent: You live strictly for success of business.

A woman being indecent: Will be double-crossed by several sweethearts.

Friends being indecent: Will incur debts from moneylenders.

Being put in jail for indecency: Will enjoy excellent business.

INDEX:

Consulting the index of a book: Postponement of success.

The index finger: Don't expect so many favors from others.

Pointing at people with index finger: Must rely upon own vigor.

Others pointing at you with index finger: Will have many things to learn.

INDIA:

Going to India: Will have emotional sorrow.

Being in India: A big catastrophe is ahead.

Traveling to India with sweetheart: You are in the grip of deceitful people.

Returning from India: Happiness is assured.

Relatives being in India: Will receive message from unfriendly woman.

A native of India: Will have an adventure soon.

Being an Indian: Financial gains.

INDIGENT:

Of a poor person: Good fortune.

A woman dreaming of a poor person: Will inherit wealth.

Relatives being indigent: Will earn money.

Many indigent people: Poverty.

Grown children being indigent: Big happiness.

Enemies being indigent: Family quarrels.

INDIGO:

Putting indigo in water: Will take a journey over water or seas.

Dyeing material with indigo: Will have a long stay away from own home.

Others dyeing things with indigo: Immediate success.

INDUCE:

Of inducing: Will enjoy solitude.

Inducing others to your will: Will incur damages.

Being induced by others to their will: Waste of time on preliminaries.

Taking advantage of inducement over others: Will have a clear conscience.

INDUSTRY:

Having an industry: Will be very embarrassed.

Others having an industry: Important

and very beneficial event to come.

Others working in industry: Good times are coming.

Being an industrious person: Every effort put forth will be good.

INFANT:

A newborn infant: Pleasant surprises are awaiting.

A helpless infant: Warning of coming trouble.

A beautiful infant: Peace and joy.

A newborn infant in diapers: Good events to come.

An infant nursing: Long illness.

A wetnurse nursing your infant: Beware of threats.

The infant of another person: Unhappiness in love affairs.

INFERIOR:

Being inferior: You are prone to being too apprehensive.

Having an inferiority complex: Good event to come.

Dealing with inferior people: Fidelity.

Feeling inferior in business dealings: Will be in need of money.

INFIRM:

Being infirm: Look out for many troubles.

Others who are infirm: Affection.

An elderly person being infirm: Will realize high ambitions.

Children being infirm: Worry will be smoothed away.

Relatives being infirm: Postponement of success.

Enemies being infirm: Financial gains.

INFIRMARY:

Being in a hospital infirmary: Coming misfortune.

Others being in an infirmary: Pleasant work and good news.

Enemies being in an infirmary: Misery.

Children being in an infirmary: Starvation.

Relatives being in an infirmary: Difficult times are ahead.

Leaving an infirmary completely recovered: Will overcome difficulties.

Being treated by religious person at an infirmary: Will be helped by God.

Being in a mental infirmary: Must control your passions.

INFLUENTIAL:

Being influential: Will be offended by an inferior person.

Other influential people: Will be surprised by unexpected good news.

Dealing with influential people: Will be told of termination of job.

Acquiring an influential position: Will marry a beautiful rich woman.

INFLUENZA:

Having influenza: Fortune is ahead.

Members of family having influenza: A secret will be discovered.

Children having influenza: Will lead a simple and honest life.

Dying from influenza: Faithful friends will show compassion toward you.

INGRATITUDE:

People being ungrateful: Something is preying on your conscience.

Family being ungrateful: Must rely on own good judgment.

Relatives being ungrateful: Will be visited by someone asking a favor.

Children being ungrateful: Will be in misery.

Being ungrateful to others: Will triumph over persecution.

INHERITANCE:

Receiving an inheritance: Death in the family.

Not receiving an inheritance: Death of a brother.

Receiving a small inheritance: Affliction.

Being cut off from an inheritance: Will fall into misery.

INJURY:

Being injured by someone else: You have a rival in business or love.

Injuring someone else: Danger is ahead.

Injuring yourself: Abundance in everything.

Children having an injury: Joy without profit.

Relatives having an injury: Freedom from troubles.

Enemies having an injury: Advancement within own position.

INK:

Of a bottle of ink: Happiness is assured.

Spilling ink: Your love is not reciprocated.

Buying ink: Financial gains.

Changing colors of ink: Family quarrels.

Drinking ink: Fulfillment of fondest hopes.

Children writing with ink: You have one faithful friend.

Writing love letters with ink: Treason.

Writing business letters with black ink: Loss in business affairs.

A young woman dreaming of ink: She will be slandered.

INMATE:

Being an inmate of a prison: Happiness within the family.

Of a prison inmate: Accord among friends.

An inmate being released: Small fortune.

A long-time inmate of a prison: Will receive big fortune.

An inmate escaping from prison: Plentiful means.

Inmates working in prison: Good events.

An inmate killing himself in prison: Everlasting friendship.

An inmate killing another inmate in prison: Big arguments.

An inmate being executed: Beware of illness.

INN:

Being at an inn: Will have emotional sorrow.

Resting at an inn: You possess great courage.

A beautiful inn: Will be tormented.

Being a regular customer at an inn: Loss of money.

Being at an inn with your mate: Unhappiness.

Being at an inn with your sweetheart: Insecurity is ahead.

Finding a friend at an inn: Contentment.

Being at a celebration held at an inn: Will have misery in old age.

Being at an inn with children: Advancement within own position.

Being at an inn with relatives: Change for the better.

Being at an inn with friends: Triumph over enemies.

INNKEEPER:

Being an innkeeper: Will have many worries.

Having a fight with an innkeeper: Will enjoy much good business.

Not paying the innkeeper: Gossip will injure prestige.

A female innkeeper being guilty of immoral actions: Honor and pride.

INNOCENT:

Being innocent: You are a very passionate person.

Knowing that you are not innocent: Will acquire a new and important position.

An innocent person being found guilty: Fortune is ahead.

Members of family being innocent: Will have business arguments.

INQUEST:

Being at an inquest: Prosperity.

Others at an inquest: Warning of trouble.

Enemies being at an inquest: A big catastrophe is ahead.

Conducting an inquest: Change for the better.

An inquest being ruled in your favor: Financial gains.

INQUISITIVE:

Being inquisitive: Do not have despair in your heart.

Relatives being inquisitive: Don't interfere in others' business.

Others being inquisitive about you: Poverty.

Law being inquisitive about own affairs: You cannot know the future.

INSANE:

Of being insane: Big financial gain.

Relatives being insane: Long life.

Friends being insane: Unhappiness.

Others who are insane: Your plans will prove successful.

Committing something insane: Big quarrels.

A woman dreaming of being insane: Will be a widow.

A man dreaming of being insane: Will divorce his wife.

A young girl dreaming of being insane: Will have a happy marriage.

A divorced woman dreaming of being insane: Will give birth to a child.

A young single woman dreaming of being insane: Her child will be prominent.

INSECT:

Of dirty insects: Gold and silver in abundance.

Having insects in own house: Be considerate of others.

Killing insects outside own home: Financial gains.

Killing insects inside own home: Abundant means.

Killing insects with poison: A mystery will be solved.

INSOLENCE:

Being insolent to others: Expect difficulties ahead.

Others showing insolence to you: Important and very beneficial event to come.

Children showing insolence: Will have a vigorous mind.

Employees showing insolence: Will find a new sweetheart.

Friends showing insolence: Worry will be smoothed away.

Employer being insolent to employees: Will be cheated by friends.

INSTRUCTION:

Giving instructions: A friend will seek your aid.

Receiving instructions: Will need sympathy from friends.

Giving instructions to employees: A rival will take what you desire.

Instructing children: Failure of enemies.

Man and wife instructing each other: Will live a long life.

Receiving instructions from a judge: A change in life will soon come.

Receiving instructions from an attorney: Financial gains.

Receiving religious instructions: Worry will be smoothed away.

INSTRUMENT:

Of instruments: Will make an advantageous matrimony.

Musical instruments: Will have a great deal of fun for a long time.

Surgical instruments: Must expect to endure pain.

Buying musical instruments: Great happiness.

Using surgical instruments: Dissension within the family.

Various other kinds of instruments: Big reunion of the family.

INSULT:

Insulting someone else: You have deceitful friends.

Being insulted by others: A season of sorrow is coming.

Being insulted by friends: Troubles are ahead.

Insulting friends: Will suffer through own foolishness.

Being insulted by enemies: Change of occupation.

Insulting enemies: Luck and prosperity.

Being insulted by relatives: Change of residence.

Being insulted but not resenting it: Beware of troubles ahead.

INTEGRATION:

Of integration: Triumph over enemies.

Being in the process of integration: A change in life will soon come.

Others adopting integration: Triumph in life.

INTEMPERANCE:

Of being intemperate: You should moderate your habits.

Showing intemperance by excessive drinking: Troubles are ahead.

Others showing intemperance in excessive drinking: Quarrels.

INTEREST:

Paying interest: Will receive bad news.

Receiving an interest payment: Unhappiness.

Being overcharged in interest percentage: Death.

Owing interest: Will have reason to become jealous.

Others owing interest to you: Big changes are ahead.

INTESTINES:

Having pains in own intestines: Misfortune in love.

Children having pains in the intestines: Consolation and happiness.

Relatives having pains in the intestines: Unhappiness.

Sweetheart having pains in the intestines: Must forego pleasure.

Others having pains in the intestines: Will receive a visitor.

Enemies having pains in the intestines: Unfavorable results in own affairs.

Having part of own intestines removed: Family quarrels.

Relatives having part of intestines removed: Loss of money.

Children having part of intestines removed: Doomed for disappointment.

Eating the intestines of animals: Big fortune is ahead.

INTRIGUE:

Of intrigue: Affliction and misery.

Being intrigued with gambling: Will enjoy social pleasures.

Being intrigued with a lottery: Treason.

Being intrigued with science: Will have hard times ahead.

A married man being intrigued with another woman: Good prospects.

A married man being intrigued with another man: Much gossip.

Unmarried people being intrigued with opposite sex: Despair.

Other people being intrigued: Loss of an enterprise.

Being intrigued with a conceited person: Ridiculous arrogance.

INUNDATE:

Being inundated: You will be out of danger.

Viewing much inundation: Expect losses of all kinds.

Own land being inundated: Worry will be smoothed away.

Own home being inundated: A friend is trying to help you secretly.

INVALID:

Being an invalid: Will recover from an illness.

Recovering from invalid state: Postponement of success.

Children being invalid: Expect difficulties on the way to success.

Relatives being invalid: Pleasant work and good news.

Friends being invalid: All your own affairs will go well.

Enemies being invalid: Use caution in business ventures.

Being invalid for the rest of your life: Will soon receive money.

INVENTOR:

Being an inventor: High honors.

Other inventors: Will be compensated through their work.

Children becoming inventors: Luck and prosperity.

INVENTORY:

Preparing to take an inventory: Good changes in own business.

Taking an inventory: Abundant means.

Others taking an inventory: Will realize high ambitions.

Having good results from an inventory: Joy and profit.

INVISIBLE:

Of something invisible: Important and very beneficial event to come.

Everything being invisible: Prompt engagement.

Finances being invisible on statements: Change for the better.

Loved one being invisible: A warning that something will be discovered.

Invisible things in a church: Expect success.

INVITATION:

Receiving an invitation: Good news from faraway.

Receiving a written invitation: Failure in own affairs.

Receiving a printed invitation: Shame and sorrow.

Receiving an invitation from a loved one: Financial gains.

Receiving a business invitation: Doomed for disappointment.

Sending an invitation to relatives: Quarrels within the family.

Sending invitations to friends: Avoid rivals.

Sending an invitation to business people: Financial gains.

Sending an invitation to a prominent personality: A mystery will be solved.

INVULNERABLE:

Being invulnerable: Will realize high ambitions.

Being threatened but not injured: Will live a long life.

Being slightly wounded: Important and very beneficial event to come.

Others being invulnerable: Business quarrels.

IRON:

Of iron plates: Difficulties are ahead.

Gray iron: Must control your passions.

Black iron: Will be cheated by friends.

Melted iron: Happiness is assured.

Iron bars: Discovery of lost valuables.

Angle bars made from iron: Accord among friends.

Buying iron: Will receive news from abroad.

Selling iron: Money will come easily.

Red-hot iron: Quarrels.

Cutting iron: Postponement of success.

Hammering iron: Success in love.

Using a pressing iron: Financial gains.

IRONING:
Ironing clothes: Will experience trouble because of a rival.
Ironing a man's clothes: Comfortable home and increasing love.
Ironing dresses: Quarrels with husband.
Ironing linen: Keep yourself free of any ties.
Ironing silk materials: Unexpected help will come to you.
Ironing starched clothes: Illness within the family.

IRON MOLD:
Of an iron mold: Dissolution in love.
Stamping linen with an iron mold: Serious illness within the family.
Others stamping with an iron mold: Immediate recovery.

ISLAND:
Being on an island: Your conscience is not clear.
Others being on an island: Rapid recovery from an illness.
Being on an island with family: Important and very beneficial event to come.
Being on an island with relatives: Family quarrels.
Leaving an island: Important and very beneficial event to come.
Leaving relatives on an island: Difficulties are ahead.

An island covered with green vegetation: Travel, wealth, and honor.
A heavily populated island: Must struggle for prominence in life.

ITCH:
Having an itch: Your fears and anxieties are groundless.
Having an irritating rash: Unexpected arrival of friends.
Children scratching an itch: Unhappy departure of a friend.
Having a sore caused from itching: Troubles from several women.
Friends having an itch: Will be happy with present condition.

IVORY:
Possessing ivory: Will have a literary talent.
Buying ivory: You have one true and trusted friend.
Selling ivory: Misery.
Giving ivory as a present: Money will come easily during life.

IVY:
Growing ivy: Beware of a broken engagement.
Ivy growing on trees: Will have much grief.
Ivy growing on a house: Wealth.
Ivy growing on a friend's house: Will enjoy rugged health.
Having ivy in a pot in the house: Happiness is assured.

J

JACK:
Of a jack: A false friend is nearby.
Using a jack: Be on guard against spiteful gossip.
Playing cards and holding the jack of clubs: Will have a good friend.
Playing cards and holding the jack of hearts: Will have a true lover.
Playing cards and holding the jack of spades: An enemy is nearby.
Playing cards and holding the jack of diamonds: A false friend is nearby.

JACKAL:
Of a jackal: You are being watched by someone with good intentions.
Owning a jackal with a yellow color: Financial gains.
Others owning a jackal: Postponement of success.
Children being with a jackal: You have one loyal friend.

JACKASS:
Of a jackass: Plenty of business is ahead for you.

Owning a jackass: Will have a dispute with best friend.

Chasing a jackass: Scandal is being spread about you.

Taking a jackass from the barn: Love affairs will be ended.

Hearing a jackass bray: Disgrace.

JACKDAW:

Of this bird commonly known in Europe: Happiness in love.

Catching a jackdaw: Immediate marriage.

Having a jackdaw in a cage: Poor harvest.

A young girl dreaming of having a jackdaw: Will soon become engaged.

JACKET:

Wearing a dark-colored jacket: Infirmity.

Wearing a sport jacket: Financial gain.

Wearing an evening jacket: You will be deceived.

Wearing a house jacket: Infidelity.

Wearing a waiter's jacket: Luck and prosperity.

JACOBEAN:

Of Jacobean furnishings: Will enjoy a quiet life.

Jacobean architectural work: Will gain by experience.

JACOBIN:

Of a Jacobin society member: Abundance of love.

A Jacobin fancy pigeon: Will have several lovers.

JADE:

Wearing jade: Prosperity.

Wearing green jade: Big financial gains.

Having jade ornaments in your ears: Will receive unexpected news.

A jade necklace: Marriage will last forever.

Buying jade: Financial gain.

Selling jade: Loss of money.

Others wearing jade ornaments: Death of a relative.

JAIL:

Being in jail: Public esteem.

Being in jail for a long time: Bad destiny.

Being promptly released from jail: Use caution in business activities.

Being in a dark jail: You have a secret friend.

Being in jail for life: Will receive a big favor.

Being in jail because of friend's wrongdoing: Sorrow.

Friends being in jail: Family happiness.

Enemies being in jail: Short-lived fortune.

A woman dreaming of being in jail: Must endure much suffering.

JAM:

Making jam: Will have many charming friends.

Buying jam: Will have a happy home.

Giving children jam to eat: Family happiness.

Receiving jam as a gift: Postponement of success.

JANUARY:

Of January during the month of January: Financial gains.

Of January during other months: A mystery will be solved.

Being born in the month of January: A false friend is nearby.

Children being born in January: They will like sports.

JAR:

Of an empty jar: Will receive a letter from abroad.

A full jar: Will have wealth late in life.

A jar with candy in it: Worry will be smoothed away.

Breaking a jar: Rapid success of own hopes.

JASMINE:

Jasmine in blossom: Will realize high ambitions.

Having a bouquet of jasmine: You have one loyal friend.

A young girl dreaming of jasmine: Will soon receive proposal of marriage.

A widow dreaming of jasmine: She will be married within the year.

JAUNDICE:
Having jaundice: Unhappiness in love affairs.
Children having jaundice: Financial gains.
Husband having jaundice: Quarrels with his sweetheart.
Relatives having jaundice: Your fortune is secure.
Enemies having jaundice: Sickness and poverty.

JAW:
Having the jaw injured: Disagreements with lover.
Recovering from a jaw injury: You have conquered initial difficulties.
A solid jaw: Discovery of lost valuables.
A flabby jaw: Difficulties are ahead.
A beautiful jaw and lips: Changes for the better in own affairs.
A deformed jaw: Use caution in business ventures.
The jaw of a relative: Financial gains.

JAY:
Of a jay: Happiness in love.
Catching a jay: Immediate marriage.
Having a jay in a cage: Poor harvest.
A young girl dreaming of having a jay: Will soon become engaged.

JEALOUS:
Being jealous: Prepare yourself for unpleasant news.
Being jealous of husband: Be cautious in your ventures.
Being jealous of wife: Pleasant social activities.
Being jealous of children: Family quarrels.
Being jealous of sweetheart: Important and very beneficial event to come.
Being jealous of your religion: Hope in God.

JELLY:
Making jelly: Good fortune.
Having jelly: Sure sign of long life.
Eating jelly: Happiness in family life.
Having plenty of jelly: Will enjoy a long life.

JELLYFISH:
Of a jellyfish: Warning that house will catch fire.
Having jellyfish: Don't give away your heart.
Others having jellyfish: Postponement of success.

JEOPARDY:
Being in jeopardy: Loneliness and trouble.
Children being in jeopardy: Financial gains.
Friends being in jeopardy: A serious disaster is ahead.
Enemies being in jeopardy: A big catastrophe is ahead for them.
Sweetheart being in jeopardy: Immediate success of love affairs.

JERUSALEM:
Of Jerusalem: Will have bitter experiences.
Going to Jerusalem: Will take a long journey.
Being in Jerusalem: Dignity and command.
Praying in Jerusalem: Will be respected in society.
Many people worshiping in Jerusalem: Children will have abundant means.

JESUS CHRIST:
Of Jesus Christ: Good hopes ahead.
Offering prayers to Jesus Christ: Will become a celebrity.
Talking to Jesus Christ: Will be consoled.
Offering thanks to Jesus Christ: Will give charity to needy people.

JET:
Of this well-polished black mineral: Danger is ahead.
Others handling jet: A change in life will come soon.

Having an ornament made of jet: Will suffer through own foolishness.

JETTY:
Being on a jetty extended in a harbor: Will have money coming.
Someone falling from a jetty into the sea: You are being deceived.
Others being on a jetty: A change in life will come soon.
Relatives being on a jetty: Will travel to another country.

JEW:
Of a Jew: Financial gains.
Dealing with a Jew: Domestic joy.
Having business relations with a Jew: Abundant means.
Being married to a Jew: You will entertain welcome guests.
Having several Jewish friends: Will be guilty of foolish actions.
Receiving a favor from a Jew: Unexpected fortune and success.
A Jewish temple: Financial gains.

JEWEL:
Having jewels: Unhappiness in love affairs.
Buying jewels: Will have an accident.
Wearing jewels: Will suffer because of envy.
Stealing jewels: Are in danger of committing some disgraceful act.
Receiving a gift of jewels: You are hated by someone.
Admiring jewels: Will experience extravagance.
Giving a gift of jewels: Will experience ruin.
Selling jewels: Loss of money.
Being a jeweler: Will cheat friends.

JIG:
A married woman dancing a jig: Be careful not to cause jealousy.
A woman dancing the jig with a man: A change in life will come soon.
A man dancing a jig with a woman: He is in love with her.
A young girl dancing a jig: She will soon become engaged.
Others dancing a jig: Must control your passions.

JILT:
A married man being jilted: Will have happiness in his married life.
A widower being jilted by a single woman: Financial gains.
A woman jilting a man: Frivolity.
Others being jilted: Will be guilty of foolish actions.
An unmarried man being jilted: Will have good luck with other women.
A married woman jilting a secret lover: Will have worries over love.
An unmarried woman jilting a lover: Unhappiness.

JINGLE:
Hearing the jingle of small bells: Innocent flirtation.
Hearing the jingle of a dog's bell: Imminent engagement.
Hearing the jingle of cattle bells: Amusements.
Hearing the jingle of sleigh bells: Will realize high ambitions.

JOCKEY:
Of a jockey: Be on the lookout for treachery.
A jockey winning a race: Money will come easily during life.
A jockey losing a race: Will be cheated by friends.
A woman dreaming of a jockey riding at full speed: Unexpected proposal.
A young girl being fascinated with a jockey: Proposal of marriage.

JOINT:
Of own joints hurting: Change for the better.
Own leg joints hurting: Happiness.
A young girl having pains in her joints: Will win affection of her lover.
Children having pains in the joints: Plenty of money.
Relatives having pains in the joints: Domestic joy.

JOKE:
Telling a joke: Will enjoy good humor.
Listening to good jokes: Extreme misery.

Telling dirty jokes: Will make a big profit.

Telling very funny jokes: Will endure affliction.

Hearing children telling jokes: Unhappiness will be consoled.

JOKER:
Of a joker: People will take advantage of you.

Being a joker: Light company will bring no good.

Joker being used in playing cards: Suitable time to pursue courtship.

Joker not being used in playing cards: Will lose money.

JOLLY:
Being jolly: People are endeavoring to destroy you.

Others being at a jolly gathering: Use caution in speculation.

Being too jolly: Will lose plenty of money.

JOURNEY:
Going on a journey: Profits if the journey is pleasant.

Going on a disagreeable journey: Big disappointment.

Going on a journey on horseback: Will surmount your obstacles.

Walking all the way on a journey: Hard work is ahead.

Taking a journey in a carriage: Big fortune.

Taking a journey in a car: Abundant means.

Taking a journey by steamer: Accord among friends.

Taking a journey by plane: Family quarrels.

A long journey: You will be able to avoid unpleasant things.

Going on a journey armed: Will soon get married.

Going on a journey with a sword at your side: Will be married in a month.

Taking a journey on a rough road: Everything will turn out well.

Having stormy weather during a journey: Be careful in own affairs.

Relatives taking a journey: Change for the better.

Enemies taking a journey: Failure of enemies.

Taking a journey with children: Happiness is assured.

JOY:
Of joy: Will receive bad news.

Being very joyous: Good health is ahead for you.

Children being very joyous: Good times are coming.

JUBILEE:
Of a jubilee: Will marry early in life.

Being at a jubilee: A fortune will be left to you by a rich relative.

Married people going to a jubilee: Your hopes will be realized.

A young woman dreaming of a jubilee: Will soon become engaged.

JUDGE:
Being summoned by a judge: Sorrow and trouble.

A judge taking your side: You will come out well from worries.

Being a judge and making decisions: Unhappiness.

Being an arbitration judge: You have several good friends.

A judge of the peace: Hard times.

Being found guilty by a judge: Will have high social standing.

Being acquitted by a judge: A big fortune is coming to you.

JUGGLER:
A juggler performing his tricks: Beware of enemies.

Others being entertained by a juggler: Deception by an impostor.

Being taught tricks by a juggler: Will have abundance.

JUGS:
Having a jug: Loss of money because of others.

Breaking a jug: Death.

A jug already broken: Good times are coming.

Drinking out of a jug: Illness.

Drinking water out of a jug: A mystery will be revealed.

JULY:
Of the month of July during July: Will be happy in love.
July during other months: Use caution in your affairs.
Being born in July: Rapid success of own hopes.
Children being born in July: Will have good earnings in life.

JUMP:
Making a jump: You are very inconsistent in love affairs.
Making a high jump: Will escape a present danger.
Failing to make the jump: Life will be almost intolerable.
Jumping over a ditch: An enemy is seeking your ruin.
Others jumping: Will overcome enemies with perseverance.
Jumping over a hurdle: Will receive happy news.
A kangaroo jumping: Pleasant social activities.
Killing a kangaroo while jumping: Inheritance.
Jumping in the water: Will be persecuted.
Jumping in the air: Loss of present position.
Jumping in the presence of others: Will lose a law suit.

JUNE:
Of the month of June during June: Will have good earnings.
June during other months: Avoid rivals.
Being born in June: Must rely on own good judgment.
Children being born in June: Will realize high ambitions.

JUNGLE:
Of a jungle: Financial affairs will cause anxiety.
Being in a jungle: Economize while there is still time.
Others being in a jungle: Discovery of lost valuables.
Killing a wild animal in a jungle: You have several loyal friends.

JUNIPER:
Of juniper shrubs or trees: Someone will speak evil about you.
The blue berrylike fruits of junipers: Be cautious in all dealings.
Eating the fruit of junipers: Important and very beneficial event to come.

JURY:
Being appointed to a jury: Death of an enemy.
A jury being formed: Will overcome difficulties.
A jury seated in the court: Failure of enemies.
A jury pronouncing their verdict: Change for the better.

K

KALEIDOSCOPE:
Of a kaleidoscope: Big fortune.
Losing colored glass fragments from a kaleidoscope: Inheritance.
Handling a kaleidoscope: Frivolity.
Others handling a kaleidoscope: Do not take things too lightly.

KANGAROO:
Of a kangaroo: Hostility of someone will cause great anxiety.
Being attacked by a kangaroo: Exercise great care of reputation.
A dead kangaroo: A big catastrophe is ahead.
A kangaroo being in a cage: Failure of enemies.

KEEL:
Of the keel of a ship: News from a lover at sea.
The keel of a ship being scraped: Warning of trouble.

The keel of a ship being laid: Happiness is assured.

The keel of a ship being damaged: Will have good earnings.

KEEPER:
A keeper of game: Financial gains.

A keeper of a park: Danger in love matters.

A keeper of an inn: A rival will take affection of sweetheart.

A keeper of a drinking place: Financial gains.

KEEPSAKE:
Of a keepsake: Luck and prosperity.

A friend asking for a keepsake but not giving one: Big worries.

Being given something for a keepsake: A change in life will soon come.

Receiving articles from a relative for keepsake: Good luck.

KEG:
Of a keg: Unexpected money.

An empty keg: Change of surroundings.

A keg filled with liquid: Better times.

A keg being filled with fish: Prosperity.

KENNEL:
Of a kennel: Will suffer humiliation.

An empty kennel: Will be invited to someone's house.

A kennel full of dogs: Do not go alone so as to avoid quarrels.

The shop of a kennel: Advancement within own position.

KETTLE:
Of a kettle: Hard work awaits.

A kettle of boiling water: Troubles will soon end.

An empty kettle: A change awaits.

A bright kettle that is very clean: Big losses in business.

KETTLEDRUM:
Having a kettledrum: Trouble.

Playing a kettledrum: Anxiety.

Others playing a kettledrum: Business losses.

Buying a kettledrum: Change of surroundings.

KEYHOLE:
Peeping through a keyhole: Big losses.

Others peeping through a keyhole: Quarrels.

Enemies peeping through a keyhole: Death of an enemy.

Relatives peeping through a keyhole: Frivolity.

KEYS:
Having a key: Will become very enraged.

Having lover's keys: You will come out well from a present danger.

Having a broken key: Illness.

Finding several keys: Peace and happiness in the home.

Losing own keys: Misfortune in love affairs.

Giving keys to someone: Good fortune in home life.

KHAKI:
Of cloth for khaki uniforms: You are surrounded by anxieties.

Wearing a khaki uniform: Frivolity.

Army people in khaki uniforms: A rival will take your sweetheart.

Buying a khaki uniform: Approaching good times.

KICK:
Being kicked: You will have many powerful adversaries.

Kicking someone else: Dignity and distinction.

Kicking enemies: Financial gains.

Kicking friends: A friend is trying to help you.

KID:
Of a kid: Happiness in the home.

Own kids: Abundant means.

Relatives' kids: Joy without profit.

Other people's kids: Warning of family quarrels.

KIDNAP:
Being kidnaped: Change in your environment.

A girl being kidnaped: Misfortune in love matters.

A boy being kidnaped: A catastrophe is ahead.

Kidnapers being arrested: Approaching money.

KIDNEY:
Of kidneys: Will be in mourning and have worries.
Having pains in the kidney: You trust yourself too much.
Having a kidney operation: Loss of money.
Buying kidney: Unhappiness.
Eating kidney: Will be visited by an uninvited person.
Other people refusing to eat kidney: Will receive good news.

KILLING:
Of killing someone: Death for the dreamer.
Someone wanting to kill you: Will live a long life.
Killing a serpent: Separation.
Killing a businessman: Security.
Killing a friend: Will have good health.
Killing father or mother: A big catastrophe is ahead.
Killing an enemy: Warning of trouble.
Killing a defenseless person: Sorrow and failure.
Killing a beast: Victory and high position.
Killing birds or bees: Big damage in business.
Killing and then eating an animal: Big profit in business.

KILTS:
Wearing kilts: Congenial work and good news.
A woman wearing kilts: Happiness in marriage.
A man wearing kilts: You are dealing with deceitful people.
A Highlander in a kilt costume: Will receive news from abroad.

KING:
Of a king: Will encounter deceit in love matters.
Going to see a king: Good fortune.
Sending a letter to a king: Danger.
Having an interview with a king: Rebellion in own home.

A king surrounded by his court: Will be deceived by friends.
The king of the church: You will be pardoned for your sins.

KINGFISHER:
Of a kingfisher: Will have good fortune.
Several kingfishers: Financial gains.
A kingfisher flying across the water: Recovery of lost money.

KISS:
Of a kiss: Much affliction.
Kissing sweetheart during the day: Bad luck.
Kissing sweetheart at night: Danger.
Kissing mother: Success.
Kissing father: Joy.
Kissing a brother or sister: Many pleasures.
Kissing husband or wife: Marital happiness.
Kissing someone on the face: Coming success.
Kissing the hands: Good fortune.
Kissing a married woman: Unhappiness.
Kissing a single woman: Will be deceived.
Kissing a dead person: Long life.
Kissing a friend: Failure in your affairs.
Kissing the earth: Humiliation.
Kissing the backside of a person: Will be deceived by a woman.

KITCHEN:
Of a kitchen: Will be subject to unkind gossip.
A bare kitchen: Expect money soon.
An untidy kitchen: Will receive news from faraway.
A very neat kitchen: Arrival of a friend.
A fire lighted in the kitchen: Will have changes in your help.
A gas range being in the kitchen: Misery.
A coal stove in the kitchen: Misfortune in business.
Preparing a meal in the kitchen: Will soon be divorced.

Others preparing a meal in the kitchen: Gossip.

A male chef preparing meals: Will receive an invitation to dinner.

KITE:
Making a kite: You will risk all through speculation.

A kite flying easily in the breeze: Expect success.

A kite flying low: Good times will come in the future.

A kite flying very high: Big joy.

KITTEN:
Of new born kittens: Recovery from an illness.

Kittens with their mother: Will have emotional sorrow.

A kitten being hurt: Death of an enemy.

A kitten not being hurt: Will come out well from a present danger.

KNAPSACK:
Of a knapsack: An enemy is seeking your ruin.

Soldiers carrying a knapsack: Difficulties ahead for a short time.

Carrying a knapsack on own back: Troubles are ahead.

KNAVE:
Of the knave on cards: Trouble and quarrels.

Several knaves: Big disputes with friends.

A male servant: Dignity and distinction.

Employing a male servant: Failure of enemies.

KNEE:
Of knees: Sickness.

Own knees being badly injured: Will suffer humiliation.

Own knees being slightly injured: Affairs will turn out all right.

Bent knees: Long illness.

A broken knee: Poverty.

Falling on the knees: Misfortune in business.

The knees of a woman: Good luck.

The knees of a married woman: Prosperity.

The knees of a single woman: Suitable time to pursue courtship.

The knees of a young girl: Marriage to the girl of your choice.

Knees being very tired: Recovery from an illness.

Having a dislocated knee: Will be unemployed.

Cutting own knees: Will have obstacles in business.

Recovering from a cut knee: Fortune and joy.

The knees of animals: Hard work awaits.

KNEEL:
Kneeling on knees and praying: Happiness and honors.

Children kneeling to pray: Joy and prosperity.

Relatives kneeling: Financial gains.

Enemies kneeling: A mystery will be solved.

Friends kneeling: Will be cheated by friends.

Kneeling in a church or tabernacle: Desires will be accomplished.

KNELL:
Being announced by a bell or toll: Bright times are in store for you.

Others being announced by a knell: Joyful times.

Announcing others with a knell: Joy without profit.

KNICKKNACK:
Of these small ornaments: Social activities of a happy nature.

Handling knickknacks: Unhappiness.

Others handling knickknacks: Domestic troubles.

Buying knickknacks: Triumph over enemies.

KNIFE:
Of a knife: Will be invited to a big dinner.

A sharp knife: Many worries.

A rusty knife: Discontent and vexations at home.

A broken knife: Failure in love.

A kitchen knife: Quarrels with friends.
A butcher's knife: Good times are coming.
Having many knives: Quarrels.
A table knife: Will have a big argument.
Having a pocketknife: Separation of lovers.
Finding a knife: Failure in business.
Cutting yourself with a knife: Must curb your emotions.
Being wounded with a knife in the neck: Will be insulted by friends.
Two knives in the position of a cross: Someone will be killed.

KNITTING:
Of knitting: Will have peace in the home.
Doing fancy knitting: Will have a loving husband.
A young woman knitting: Will make a hasty marriage.
Mother knitting: Will have obedient children.
Children knitting: Prosperity in the home.
Enemies knitting: Undertakings will be crowned with success.
Others knitting: You are being deceived by friends.

KNOCK:
Of knocking: Guard your tongue.
Others knocking: Good times are coming.

Relatives knocking: Approaching money.
Enemies knocking: Misfortune in love affairs.

KNOT:
Of a knot: Warning of infidelity.
Making knots: Will have a vigorous mind.
Knots made by others: A change in life will soon come.
Relatives making knots: Frivolity.
Enemies making a knot: Will have reason for anxiety.
Sailors making knots in ropes on a ship: Abundant means.
Tying a knot: Will soon meet one who will be a true friend.
Untying a knot: Will escape some danger.

KNUCKLE:
Knocking with own knuckles: Your affections are not required.
Others knocking with their knuckles: You will be betrayed.
Being wounded by knuckles: Avoid rivals.

KURSAAL:
Of a public hot springs: Will journey to a new home across the sea.
Going to a *Kursaal:* Will receive news from a distant friend.
Many people being at a *Kursaal:* Will be jilted by a lover.
Relatives being at a *Kursaal:* Good times are coming.

L

LABEL:
Of labels: Will receive important news.
Putting a label on a package: You may expect a surprise.
Putting a label on a trunk: Will soon take a long trip.

LABORATORY:
Of a laboratory: Big peril.

Being in a laboratory: Security.
People working in a laboratory: Be cautious in business ventures.

LABOR DAY:
Of Labor Day: Domestic contentment.
Being in a Labor Day parade: Big joy is ahead.
Working on Labor Day: Will receive a good deal of money.

Laborers fighting on Labor Day: Will eat more than usual in the future.

LABORER:
A laborer working: Prosperity in own business.
Many laborers working: Will have abundant means.
A laborer tilling the ground: Profit.
A laborer working with right hand only: Happiness in the family.
A laborer working with left hand only: Momentary troubles.
Laborers resting: Loss of wealth and mate.
Laborers fighting: Will undergo a public crisis.
Punishing laborers: Persecution.
Hiring laborers: Profit.
Paying laborers: Will be loved by people.
Firing laborers: Beware of actions of neighbors.

LABURNUM:
Of this poisonous shrub: Will have a vigorous mind.
Having the bright yellow flowers of Laburnum: Triumph over enemies.
Others handling Laburnum: You are being deceived.

LABYRINTH:
Of such a place: Will unravel some mystery.
Being in a labyrinth: A mystery will be solved.
Becoming confused in one: Are surrounded with unhappiness.
Finding the way out: Your perplexities will be happily solved.
Not being able to find way out: Beware of domination by untrue friends.

LACE:
Of lace: Every desire will be realized and will have many lovers.
A young girl dreaming of making lace: Will have handsome and wealthy husband.
Making lace: Financial gains.
Buying lace: Danger through a secret.

Buying a lace dress: Will have a vigorous mind.
Giving a gift of lace: Misfortune in love affairs.
Buying a lace stole: Frivolity.
Receiving lace from sweetheart: Will live a long life.

LACKEY:
Of own lackey or valet: Avoid rivals.
Own lackey waiting on you: Will have good earnings.
Own lackey waiting on others: Friends are endeavoring to destroy you.
Own lackey attending to relatives: Financial gains.

LADDER:
A tall ladder: Will be jilted by your sweetheart.
Climbing a ladder: Unusual happiness and prosperity.
Descending a ladder: Disappointments in business.
Falling from a ladder: Failure.
Climbing a circular ladder: Will attain own goal.
Descending a circular ladder: Worry will be smoothed away.
Being dizzy when on a ladder: Important and very beneficial event to come.
Climbing a rope ladder: Profit.
Carrying a ladder with you: Will rescue someone.
Raising a ladder up to a window: Will encounter a tender person.
Climbing a ship's gangway: You will be robbed.
Others climbing a ladder: You have faithful friends.
Climbing a house ladder: Success.
Climbing the ladder of a fortress: Advantageous lawsuit.
Jumping from a ladder: Will obtain a good position.
Climbing a stepladder: Unexpected good fortune.

LADIES:
Of a lady: Gossip in your house.
Several ladies: Slander.
A beautiful lady: Weakness.

Many beautiful ladies: False accusations.

A beautiful long blond-haired lady: Happy events.

A beautiful long-haired brunette lady: Sickness.

Hearing voice of a lady without seeing her: Departure of the dreamer.

A convention of ladies: Will realize high ambitions.

Ladies at a party: Will live a long life.

A lady of court: Vanity.

Being a maid of honor: Will have many friends.

A lady gambling: Will be deprived of money.

A high-class lady dealing cards: You have made mistakes in figures.

Being in the company of a lady: Gossip.

A lady being burned in a fire: Unhappiness.

Saving a lady from a fire: Sickness.

LADLE:
Of a ladle: Danger through a secret.

Using a ladle: Will receive news from an absent friend.

Others using a ladle: Unhappiness.

LADYBIRD:
Of a ladybird: Unhappiness in love affairs.

Others having a ladybird: Postponement of success in business.

Killing a ladybird: Be cautious in business ventures.

LAKE:
A muddy lake: Unhappiness in business.

A clear lake: Success will attend every venture.

A large lake: Big love affairs.

A lake with smooth water: Will be jilted by your lover.

A boat sailing on a lake: Expect conflicts within the home.

A boat rowing on a lake: Success in business.

A lake with rough water: You are faced with difficulties.

Rain falling on a lake: Will overcome worries with patience.

Fishing in a lake: Advancement within own position.

LAMB:
Lambs in a field: Much tranquillity.

Buying lambs: Will receive a big surprise.

Eating lamb: Tears.

Owning lambs: Profit and consolation.

Selling lambs: Happiness.

Finding lost lambs: You will win a lawsuit.

Killing lambs: You will be tormented.

Giving a lamb as a gift: Will live a long life.

Carrying a lamb: Prosperity, good future, and devotion.

Eating lamb on Easter: Lasting friendship.

A herd of lambs grazing in a field: Will be frightened.

LAME:
Of a person who is lame: Big disappointment.

Being lame yourself: Business troubles.

Others being lame: Will have a minor sickness.

Children being lame: Good earnings.

LAMENT:
Of lamenting: Big joy.

Weeping from sorrow: Failure of business transactions.

Others lamenting: Will hear good news.

Children lamenting: Abundant means.

LAMP:
Of a lamp: Business will come to a standstill.

Lighting a lamp: Will have to offer explanations to people.

A lighted lamp: Passion.

A bright lamp: Good luck in a small venture.

Turning out a lamp: Coolness in love.

A very dim lamplight: Will work hard and face difficulties.

Many lamps: Your path in life will be an easy one.

A lamplight going out: Failure of your plans.

A plain unlit lamp: You will fall in love.

Lamps in the homes of others: Warning of trouble.

LAND:
Fertile land: You are about to get married.

Barren land: Troubles will follow.

Land covered with trees: Poverty.

Land covered with grass: Happiness.

Possessing land: Change of occupation.

Being ordered off land by owner: Expect bitter disappointment.

Moving away from a land: Expect changes in occupation.

LANDING:
Landing from a ship: Bad luck.

Landing from a plane: Be on the lookout for treachery.

Others landing: A false friend is nearby.

Relatives landing: Use caution in business ventures.

An important personality landing: Will realize high ambitions.

LANDLADY:
Being a landlady: Rapid success of own hopes.

Discussing business with a landlady: Important and very beneficial events.

Bawling out a landlady: Will live a long life.

Paying rent to a landlady: Will realize high ambitions.

LANDLORD:
Of a landlord: Domestic troubles.

Being a landlord: You have loyal friends.

Having business transactions with a landlord: Danger through a secret.

Being insulted by a landlord: Change for the better.

Talking to a landlord: Unexpected fortune.

LANDSCAPE:
A fine open landscape: Dignity and distinction.

A landscape obscured by hills: Many troubles and obstacles.

A beautiful landscape: Luck and prosperity.

An ugly landscape: Avoid rivals.

LANDSLIDE:
Of a landslide: Loneliness and trouble.

Repairing a landslide: Discovery of lost valuables.

Causing a landslide: Triumph over enemies.

LANGUAGE:
Speaking in own language: You are not sincere.

Learning foreign languages: Should practice modesty.

Speaking in foreign languages: Honor.

Hearing others speaking foreign languages: Will be victim of circumstances.

Children learning foreign languages: Happiness in love.

LANTERN:
An extinguished lantern: Be careful of deceit by a friend.

A signal lantern: Will have important and responsible position.

A magic lantern: Will suffer dissolution.

Putting out a lantern: Poverty and sickness.

A beautiful flame inside a lantern: Joy and happiness.

A dim lantern: Domestic troubles.

A lantern going out: Expect worries and difficulties.

LAP:
Sitting in the lap of opposite sex: Will receive good news from friends.

A mother holding children on her lap: Change of surroundings.

A married man holding a woman on his lap: Great humiliation.

A stenographer sitting on lap of boss: An enemy is seeking your ruin.

LARD:
Of lard: Triumph over enemies.

Cutting lard: Loss of someone dear to you.

Eating lard: You love money too much.

Buying lard: Triumph over enemies.

LARDER:

Of a larder: Another person is enjoying what you desired.

Putting foodstuffs in a larder: Family quarrels.

Having a full larder: Luck and prosperity.

Having an empty larder: A mystery will be solved.

LARK:

Of a lark: Will have a long life.

A lark singing happily: You have one loyal friend.

A lark in a cage: Failure of own plans.

A lark being dead: Someone is endeavoring to destroy you.

LASH:

Being lashed: Avoid rivals.

Lashing someone else: Troubles caused by someone you love.

Several people being lashed: Doomed for disappointment.

Enemies being lashed: Recovery from an illness.

LATE:

Being late: Your opinions will be sought.

Being late to a meeting: Are confronted with insurmountable obstacles.

Others being late: Loss of money.

Friends being late: You are being deceived.

Employees being late: Warning of troubles.

LATHE:

Of a lathe: Will enjoy contentment.

Using a lathe: Misfortune will come to friends.

Being a lathe operator: Fortune is near at hand.

Others using a lathe: Will fall in love.

LATIN:

Learning Latin: Will find good employment.

Reading Latin: Triumph over enemies.

Speaking Latin: Beware of having a fall.

Children learning Latin: Will have strong character.

LAUGH:

Someone laughing: Be careful with love affairs.

Several people laughing: Take precautions against gossipers.

Being laughed at by a woman: She will deceive you.

Children laughing: Approaching money.

Enemies laughing: A rival is undermining your work.

Hearing someone laugh: Indicates loss.

LAUNDRY:

Of a laundry: Will be unusually happy in the company of people.

Doing own laundry: Someone will render service to you.

Of a public laundry: Will see an unknown dead person.

Washing laundry under a fountain: Joy and prosperity.

Washing laundry of sweetheart: Marriage will not take place.

LAUREL:

A beautiful laurel: Big profits.

Being given a laurel: Will receive money from relatives.

A laurel for the head: Unexpected gift from a friend.

Picking laurels: Inheritance.

A laurel plant: Pleasure.

Being surrounded by laurels: Prosperity and pleasure.

Holding laurel branch as sign of peace: Advancement in own position.

A woman dreaming of smelling perfume of laurel: Will have many children.

A young girl dreaming of smelling perfume of laurel: Marriage soon.

A man dreaming of smelling perfume of laurel: Good business ventures.

Men dreaming of a laurel tree: Fortune in enterprises.

Widows dreaming of laurel tree: Will fall to temptation.

Unmarried women dreaming of laurel tree: Will soon be married.

Married women dreaming of a laurel tree: Will have many children.

LAVENDER:

Of the lavender shrub: Take bad actions of others with a grain of salt.

A bunch of lavender flowers: Plenty of money.

Dried lavender flowers being among linen: Marriage soon.

Lavender perfume: Will be fortunate in gambling.

Lavender silk material: You are blessed by the church.

Any other lavender material: Success in own affairs.

LAW:

Being a law enforcement officer: Will have obstacles to overcome.

Beginning a law litigation: Serious business troubles ahead.

Others starting law action against you: Consider plans well before acting.

Being an attorney-at-law: Will realize high ambitions.

LAWN:

Of own lawn: Your affairs will prosper.

Cutting own lawn: Will receive an unexpected visitor.

A lawn needing to be cut: Will receive sad news.

The lawn of others: Postponement of success.

Others cutting their lawn: A false friend is nearby.

Children playing on a lawn: Will receive an unwelcome guest.

A dog sleeping on a lawn: Approaching money.

Sprinkling own lawn: Long life.

Walking on a lawn: Will have anxiety.

A smooth green lawn: Prosperity and well-being.

LAWN TENNIS:

Of a lawn tennis court: Will secure employment.

Playing lawn tennis: Will take interest in own friends.

Playing lawn tennis with a man: Success.

Playing double match with a male partner: Will be in mourning.

Playing single match with a woman: Warning of falling in love.

Playing double match with a female partner: Big fortune ahead.

Winning a game of lawn tennis: Will have a minor sickness.

LAWSUIT:

A man starting a lawsuit for divorce: People will think little of you.

A woman starting a divorce lawsuit: Happiness in the family.

Beginning a lawsuit: Use caution in business ventures.

Appealing a lawsuit: Will be cheated by friends.

Winning a lawsuit: Avoid speculation.

Losing a lawsuit: Will have a passing illness.

Starting a lawsuit for business transactions: Will suffer losses.

Others starting a lawsuit for business transactions: Involves money losses.

A lawsuit against you to get money owed: You spend money too freely.

A lawsuit to recover money owed to you: Success.

LAWYER:

Being a lawyer: You are considered to be well to do.

Dealing with a lawyer: Will have many worries.

Hiring a lawyer: You will not have good results.

Dismissing a lawyer: Reconciliation with an enemy.

Paying a lawyer: A lawsuit will fail.

Dealing with opposing lawyers: Failure of enemies.

Having a meeting with a lawyer: Will have good earnings.

Children becoming a lawyer: Happiness is assured.

Husband being a lawyer: Big joy.

Being introduced to a lawyer: Bad tidings.

Speaking to a lawyer: Loss of property.

Someone else speaking in favor of a lawyer: Misfortune.

LAZY:

Being lazy: Trouble for those near you.

A lazy couple: Legal matter will end in marriage.

Husband being lazy: An unknown person is working against you.

Wife being lazy: Dignity and distinction.

Children being lazy: Will marry wealthy people.

Employees being lazy: Worries will be smoothed away.

Others being lazy: Warning of trouble.

LEAD:

Sheets of lead: Difficulties are ahead.

Melted lead: Happiness is assured.

Bars of lead: Discovery of lost valuables.

Buying lead: Will receive news from abroad.

Selling lead: Money will come easily during life.

Cutting lead: Postponement of success.

Hammering lead: Success in love.

Pressing lead: Financial gains.

Making boxes out of lead: Accord among friends.

LEAK:

Of a leak: You are wasting your time in love.

A gas leak: Death of a relative.

Having a pan that leaks: You are loved by those around you.

A bathtub leaking: You will meet an important personality.

A pipe leaking: Should find a wider scope for your activities.

A roof leaking: Misfortune is ahead.

A car leaking: You have a faithful wife.

Own radiator leaking: Birth of a child is near.

LEAN:

Leaning against a wall: Help those near you that are in need of money.

Leaning against another person: Will receive substantial assistance.

Children leaning against you: Happiness.

People leaning against each other: Will receive a letter from abroad.

LEAP:

Of leaping: You are very inconsistent in your love affairs.

Leaping in the air: Loss of your present position.

Leaping in the water: Will be persecuted.

Leaping in the presence of others: Will have a losing lawsuit.

Making a high leap: You will come out well from a present danger.

Falling back from a leap: Life will be almost intolerable.

Leaping over a ditch: An enemy is seeking your ruin.

Others leaping: Will overcome enemies with perseverance.

LEAP YEAR:

It being leap year and your being single: Marriage within the year.

Getting married during leap year: Marriage will not last long.

Being born in leap year: Will live a long life.

A relative dying during leap year: Will inherit money from a relative.

Children getting engaged in leap year: Will never marry this person.

LEARN:

Of learning something by experience: Good luck to one for whom you care.

Learning something mentally: Unhappiness.

Children learning their lessons: Will have few difficulties in life.

Learning a lesson in life: Are undertaking more than can be completed.

Learning to write: Happiness.

Learning a foreign language: Unhappiness in love affairs.

Learning a new trade: Things will come slowly to you.
Learning that you have been deceived: Will receive a legacy.
Learning of the arrival of relatives: Unexpected earnings.

LEASE:
Signing a lease: Persecution by justice.
Asking someone to sign a lease: Prison.
Canceling a lease: Uncertain future.
Suing someone for a lease: Reconciliation with an enemy.
Taking a lease on a house: Avoid rivals.
Taking a lease on a shop: Business is secure.
Taking a lease on land: Will be fortunate in love affairs.

LEATHER:
Of a leather shop: Failure of enemies.
Buying leather: Happiness within the family.
Working with leather: Financial gains.
Selling leather products: Luck and prosperity.
Giving a gift made of leather: Family quarrels.
Receiving a leather purse as a gift: Doomed for disappointment.
Having a harness, handbag, or belt of leather: Financial gains.

LEAVES:
A tree in full leaf: Important and very beneficial event to come.
Picking green leaves: Will receive money.
Blossoms among leaves: Two people are very happy together.
Falling leaves: Will have a dangerous sickness.
Green leaves: Health and happiness.
Wilted leaves: You are very determined in decisions.
Dry leaves: People are malicious toward you.
Fig tree leaves: People are saying bad things about you.
Grape leaves: You are prone to losing your temper.
Laurel leaves: Joy.

Eating leaves: Quarrels.
A crown of leaves: Honor.
Using leaves for seasoning: You like to eat too much.
Cooking leaves: Approaching money.
Autumn leaves falling: Disappointment in love.
Wind blowing leaves from trees: Unhappiness in domestic affairs.
Leaves on the ground: Quarrels with friends.
Leaves on a stem with fruit: Happy marriage.
Leaves covering the earth in back yard: Divorce.
Leaves of paper: Diligence will make money.

LECTURE:
Giving a lecture: Will be disappointed if you do not control your tongue.
Giving a long lecture in public: Will become tangled in a litigation.
Hearing a lecture in a public square: Will be disappointed in friends.
Giving a political lecture: Avoid rivals.
Receiving a lecture from a superior: Troubles ahead.
Lecturing to children: Big joy.

LEDGER:
Of a ledger: Long life.
A ledger with figures on it: Discovery of lost money.
A cash ledger book: Financial gains.
Writing on a ledger: Will collect money.
Finding mistakes on a ledger: Warning of troubles.
Balancing a ledger: Discovery of own errors made in life.

LEECH:
Of this bloodsucking worm: Doomed for disappointment.
Killing a leech: A false friend is nearby.
Many leeches being around: Loss of money.
A square sail leech: Important and very beneficial event to come.
Handling a square sail leech: Luck and prosperity.

LEEK:
Of this cultivated biennial plant: Will realize high ambitions.
Eating the leek type of onions: Financial gains.
Eating the leaves of leek plant: Advancement in own position.
Leeks being in a coat of arms emblem: Dignity and distinction.

LEFT:
Being left by someone: Must control your passions.
Leaving someone else: Will have emotional sorrow.
Being left without any reason: News of the death of a friend.
Having left your house: Will prosper in own business.
Having left your family: Dishonor and humiliation.
Having left your children: Will be prosecuted.
Children left by others: Good business affairs.
Being left by a woman: Greater success in life.

LEFT-HANDED:
Being left-handed: Triumph for naturally left-handed people.
Developing left-handed traits: Loss of relatives.
Writing left-handed: Happiness in love.
Working left-handed: Honor and riches.
Fencing left-handed: Loss of a relative.
Boxing left-handed: Loss of friends.
Eating left-handed: Control your manners.
Driving a left-handed car: The future is clear for you.
Walking on left-hand side of street: Will marry a rich person.

LEG:
Of well-formed legs: Will win some contest.
Thin legs: Will be ridiculed.
A wooden leg: Will lower yourself in the sight of friends.

An injured leg: Financial difficulties.
Swollen legs: Loss of money.
Having beautiful legs: Joy and happiness.
Having a leg amputated: Loss of a friend.
Women marching with pretty legs: Change in your condition.
Losing a leg: Loss of a relative.
A married woman dreaming of having beautiful legs: Will take a long trip.
Bruising own leg: Financial difficulties.
A four-legged animal: Will have plenty of money.

LEGACY:
Receiving a legacy: Use caution in business ventures.
Receiving a legacy from an unknown person: Financial gains.
Receiving a legacy and arguing with relatives about it: Loss of money.
Making a legacy to relatives: Will be upset because of difficulties.

LEGISLATION:
Preparing a law for legislation: Important and very beneficial event to come.
Having enacted legislation: Avoid rivals.
A large group considering legislation: Advancement in own position.

LEGISLATOR:
Of a legislator: Shame and sorrow ahead.
Being a legislator: Doomed for disappointment.
Becoming a legislator: Will be abandoned by friends.
Many legislators together: Will be cheated by friends.

LEMON:
Of a lemon tree: You should mend your ways in life.
An unripened lemon: Frivolity.
A lemon blossom: Will take a trip abroad.
Ripe lemons: Will fall in love.
Eating lemons: Unhappiness.
Drinking lemon juice: Good health.
Eating sweet lemons: Prosperity.

Squeezing lemons: Will get rid of enemies.

Drinking a hot lemonade: Improvement in health.

Making medicine from sweet lemons: Will be good for your health.

LEND:

Lending money: Will want money yourself before long.

Lending articles: An enemy is seeking your ruin.

Lending clothes: Trouble is ahead.

Lending your car: Change in environment.

Lending household items: Doomed for disappointment.

Lending machinery: You should mend your ways in life.

Others lending you money: Failure of affairs.

LEOPARD:

Of a leopard: Victory over enemies.

Being attacked by a leopard: Success.

Killing a leopard: Will have many changes but finally victory.

A leopard being in a cage: Enemies seek to cause injury but will fail.

Many leopards: Will go abroad on business.

Hearing a leopard roar: Will suffer grief.

Leopards fighting: Sickness.

Leopards scuffling: Will have cruel suffering.

Leopards running: Serious illness.

A leopard dying: Death of a prominent person.

A leopard being tied with chains: Will receive a surprise from an enemy.

Surprising a leopard: Beware of deceitful friends.

Being afraid of a leopard: Will be persecuted by enemies.

Being triumphant over a leopard: Avoid rivals.

The skeleton of a leopard: Will soon have money.

Baby leopards: Joy and happiness.

LEPROSY:

A man dreaming of having leprosy: Will have a sickness.

A woman dreaming of having leprosy: Will be helped by a wealthy man.

Others having leprosy: It is within own power to overcome worries.

Children having leprosy: Financial gains.

Relatives having leprosy: Will have good earnings.

Enemies having leprosy: Misfortune in own home affairs.

LESSON:

Preparing for a lesson: Great joy.

Learning a lesson: Abundant means.

Taking lessons: Happiness.

Children preparing their lessons: Good luck.

Giving lessons to children: Good times are coming.

Giving lessons to adults: Change of surroundings.

Giving lessons to foreign persons: Dignity and distinction.

Giving lessons to blind people: Good luck to one for whom you care.

Receiving lessons: You will come out well in life.

Correcting people's lessons: Happiness is assured.

LETTER:

Receiving a letter: Great wealth awaits.

Receiving a letter from a wife or husband: Failure of enemies.

Receiving a letter from a lover: Prompt engagement.

Receiving a letter from a friend: Will have good earnings.

Receiving a letter from children: Abundant means.

Receiving a letter from relatives: Will come out well from a present peril.

Receiving a letter from a suitor: Will make an advantageous marriage.

Receiving a business letter: Be cautious in all your affairs.

Receiving letters with money: Hopes have been accomplished.

Having a letter of exchange: Unexpected profit.

Writing letters to an attorney: Misfortune.

Reading an interesting letter: Will take a long vacation.

Sealing a letter: Will be successful in all your affairs.

Tearing a letter: A rival will take the affection of your sweetheart.

Destroying a letter of business: Insurmountable obstacles confront you.

Mailing a letter: Will receive interesting news.

Others reading your letters: Take precautions against being deceived.

Reading romantic letters: Will forget your troubles.

Reading political letters: Will be assisted by a conceited person.

Reading a chain letter: Happy advancement.

Sending a letter: Be careful not to betray your secrets.

Sending a letter to a husband or wife: Joy.

Sending a letter to a lover: Announcement of a marriage.

Sending a letter to a friend: Will take an extensive voyage.

Sending a letter to children: Will have a good future.

Sending a letter to relatives: Family quarrels.

Sending a letter to a suitor: Will overcome your enemies.

Sending a business letter: Warning of troubles.

LETTER CARRIER:

A letter carrier bringing letters: Unpleasant news will reach you.

Hearing the whistle of a letter carrier: Will have an unexpected guest.

Being handed a special delivery by a letter carrier: Luck and prosperity.

A letter carrier putting mail in own box: Failure of enemies.

Giving a letter to a letter carrier: Will be hurt through jealousy.

A letter carrier not having letters for you: Disappointments.

LETTUCE:

Having lettuce: Poverty and illness.

Eating lettuce: Own affairs are in a mess.

Picking lettuce from a garden: Danger in love affairs.

Buying lettuce: Will have emotional sorrow.

Washing lettuce: Will be guilty of foolish actions.

LEWD:

Of a lewd person: Will be jilted by your lover.

Reprimanding a lewd person: Unhappiness in love affairs.

A lewd person being arrested: Be cautious in your dealings.

LIBEL:

Being libeled: Much success in life.

Having other people libeled: Will overcome enemies.

Others being libeled: Misfortune in business.

A wife or husband libeling each other: A divorce will take place.

LIBRARY:

Of a library: Will make rapid progress.

Owning a library: Will need to consult a judge.

Borrowing a book from a library: Poverty.

Consulting books at a library: You are prone to laziness.

LICE:

Of lice: Good luck.

Many lice: Abundant means.

Killing many lice: Dishonor.

Finding lice on own clothes: Approaching money.

Finding lice in the hair: Will be very rich.

Finding lice on other people: Misfortune in love affairs.

Having lice on own body: Will have plenty of money soon.

Killing body lice: Will be surrounded by many friends.

LICENSE:

Having obtained a license: Will have a change in occupation.

Applying for a license: Change of surroundings.

A license being granted to you: Dignity and distinction.

Having been refused a license: Important and very beneficial event.

Others receiving a license: Sorrow.

Others being refused a license: A change in life will come to you soon.

LICKING:

A dog licking you: Luck and prosperity.

A dog licking others: Good times are coming.

Being licked by a baby: You will come out well in life.

Others licking you: Happiness.

A horse licking your hand: Danger in love affairs.

Others being licked: A friend looks to you for guidance.

LIE:

Of telling a lie: Will live a long life.

Being told a lie by others: Will be cheated by friends.

Others telling lies: You have many enemies.

Husband and wife telling lies to each other: Will suffer through own folly.

Children telling lies to parents: Will realize high ambitions.

Telling lies in court: Will have trouble caused by own misconduct.

LIFEBOAT:

A lifeboat aboard a ship: Will have opposition in all your affairs.

A lifeboat being on shore: Expect difficulties.

A lifeboat floating at sea: Triumph over enemies.

Many lifeboats floating at sea: Luck will change for the better.

A lifeboat being in a river: Warning of trouble.

A lifeboat being in a lake: A mystery will be solved.

A lifeboat being smashed: Change for the better.

A lifeboat being built: Advancement in own affairs.

A lifeboat saving lives of people: Will have a peaceful life.

Buying a lifeboat: Dignity and distinction.

LIFT:

Of lifting something: Recovery from an illness.

Lifting something very heavy: Warning of troubles.

Being lifted by others: Will overcome enemies with perseverence.

Lifting a child: Dignity and distinction.

Others being lifted: Some person has secret enmity for you.

Lifting something with machinery: Approaching money.

A woman being lifted by a man: Much joy.

Ascending in a lift: Success is very probable.

Descending in a lift: You will have a doubtful life.

LIGHT:

Light being on: Inheritance.

Light being dim: Will have sickness.

Light being bright: Good health.

Light being obscured: Difficulties are ahead.

Light going out: Danger in love affairs.

A light in the distance: Safe return from extensive travel.

Turning a light on: Success in business.

Turning a light out: You are being cheated by your lover.

Others turning lights on: Will recover from an illness.

Others turning lights off: Warning of a small operation.

A light on a ship in the distance: Will take a trip with sweetheart.

A light on a ship in port: Will be introduced to important person soon.

Lighting a lamp: Happiness.

Putting out light of a lamp: Bad news from a friend faraway.

Turning light on in bedroom: Unfortunate event will happen.

LIGHTHOUSE:

Being in a lighthouse: Will have a good healthy life.

Going to a lighthouse: Success in business.

Returning from a lighthouse: Will receive a letter from a relative.

Seeing a lighthouse in a calm sea: Will have a peaceful life.

Seeing a lighthouse through a storm: Happiness will come soon.

LIGHTNING:

Of lightning: High honors.

Lightning striking a house: Death of a friend.

Lightning striking trees: Discord between partners.

Being struck by lightning: Death of a relative.

Others being struck by lightning: Will meet a lustful woman.

Lightning striking the water: Success is certain.

Lightning killing animals in a field: Your life is in danger.

Lightning striking at night: Troubles and quarrels.

LILAC:

Of lilacs: Conceit.

Having lilac perfume: Will receive a gift from a friend.

Receiving a gift of lilacs: You do not care about appearances.

Giving lilacs to others: Change of surroundings.

LILY:

Of lilies in season: Much happiness.

Lilies out of season: Loss of all hopes.

Growing lilies: An early marriage will take place.

Buying lilies: Do not expect help from others.

Selling lilies: Must depend on your own efforts.

Lilies withering: Will be guilty of own foolish actions.

Throwing lilies away: Thoughtless actions will cause your downfall.

Receiving a bouquet of lilies as a gift: Frivolity.

LIME:

Drinking the juice of a lime: Approaching money.

Of lime: A good event will happen soon.

A large heap of lime: Small property soon to be left to you.

Buying lime: Advancement within own position.

Handling lime powder: People will put your feelings to a test.

Using lime in work: Be on guard against enemies.

LIMP:

Of limping: Will be dishonored.

Having to rest because of a limp: Hard work awaits.

Being unable to take a trip because of a limp: Favorable business ventures.

Relatives limping: Restrain yourself from speculations.

Enemies limping: Be cautious in all your dealings.

LINDEN:

Of a linden tree: Good news.

A dry dead linden tree: An enemy is seeking your ruin.

Cutting down a linden tree: Danger in love affairs.

LINEN:

Of linen: Wealth and pleasure.

Being dressed in clean linen: Good luck.

Others dressed in linen: Will inherit money.

Children dressed in linen: Expect good news before long.

Linen being dirty: Serious loss in business.

Linen being stained: Misfortune in love affairs.

Changing linen clothes: Expect to overcome worse difficulties.

Handling linen: Gossip by friends.

Hanging linen up to dry: End of your troubles.

Linen of own family: Abundance.

Wearing a white linen dress: Much joy is ahead for you.

Fine linen lingerie: Great fortune.

Having much fine linen lingerie: Wealth is ahead.

LINING:

Of materials used for linings: Vanity.

Taking the lining out of a dress: Beware of rivals.

Taking the lining out of a man's suit: Will have an argument.

Buying material for linings: Will receive an unexpected visitor.

LINT:

Of a large amount of lint: Must exercise prudence.

Wrapping a wound with lint: Be forgiving or you will regret it.

Others wounds being wrapped with lint: Prosperity is ahead.

Buying lint to wrap wounds: Your life is protected.

LINTEL:

Of a horizontal beam spanning an opening: Important changes.

Being under a lintel: Will move to a larger home.

Placing a lintel on a superstructure: Luck and prosperity.

LION:

Of a lion: Future dignity.

A woman dreaming of hearing a lion roar: Unexpected promotion.

A man dreaming of hearing a lion roar: Will be admired by women.

Being chased by a lion: Disgrace.

Killing a lion: Financial independence.

An angry lion: Expect misfortune caused by jealousy.

The cub of a lion: Will have a valuable friendship.

Being attached to a lion: Success.

Killing a lion: Will have many changes but finally achieve victory.

A lion being in a cage: Enemies will fail in attempt to injure you.

Several lions: Will go abroad on business.

Hearing a lion roaring: Will suffer grief.

A lion dying: Death of a prominent person.

A lion tied with a chain: Will be surprised by an enemy.

Surprising a lion: Be on the lookout for deceitful friends.

Being afraid of a lion: Will be persecuted by enemies.

Being triumphant over a lion: Avoid rivals.

The skeleton of a lion: Will soon have money.

LIONESS:

Of a lioness: Family fortune.

A lioness with her babies: Joy and happiness.

A lioness fighting with a lion: Sickness.

A lioness scuffling: Will have suffering.

A lioness running: Serious illness.

A lioness killing a lion: Beware of jealous friends.

A lioness dying when delivering small lions: Will receive money.

A lioness eating meat: Will have much wealth.

A lioness at a circus: Will have many helpful friends.

Being attacked by a lioness: Will live a long life.

Having a small lioness as a pet: Will receive a marriage proposal.

LIPS:

Of own lips: Approaching money.

Thin lips: Vexation.

Thick lips: Unhappy marriage.

Sore lips: Poverty.

Beautiful lips: Will have mastery over many matters.

A man kissing a woman's lips: Good business affairs.

A woman kissing a man's lips: Will have many advantages.

Children's lips: Postponement of success.

Lips of strangers: Change of residence.

Repulsive lips: Failure of enemies.

LIPSTICK:

Wearing lipstick: You are surrounded by false friends.

Other people wearing lipstick: Treason and false friendships.

Buying lipstick: Frivolity.

Catching a man with lipstick on his lips: Troubles from sweetheart or wife.

LIQUOR:
Drinking liquor: You have loyal friends.
Drinking liquor with ice: Immediate employment.
Being thirsty for liquor: Misfortune.
Drinking liquor in a large glass: Much joy.
Drinking liquor in a small glass: Many worries.
Drinking clear-colored liquor: Happiness.
Drinking dark-colored liquor: Sickness is ahead.
Drinking liquor in the company of a female friend: Will be very rich.
Drinking liquor with male friends: Change of environment.
Drinking liquor with own wife: Your marriage will last forever.
Drinking liquor with relatives: Family quarrels.
Drinking liquor with enemies: Expect financial losses.

LISP:
Hearing someone speaking with a lisp: Be cautious of rivals.
Many people speaking with a lisp: Friends are insincere.
Children speaking with a lisp: Friends are attempting to cheat you.

LISTEN:
Someone listening to you: Don't let people get the best of you.
Listening to others: Sickness.
Listening to the advice of others: Poverty.
Listening to advice of important people: Take heed to advice given.
Listening to children: Joy.
Listening to mate: Family arguments.

LITTER:
Of a litter: You have a fine family.
A dog's litter: Worries will soon pass.
A pig's litter: Approaching money.
Litters of other animals: Good times are coming.

LITTLE:
Being little in size: You will have plenty of affection.
Being little in weight: Take care of own health.
Having little children: Great joy.
Others being little: You will rise high in life.

LIVER:
Having plenty of liver: Illness.
Having spoiled liver: Misery.
Eating liver: Will have good health.
Having liver of animals without horns: Inheritance to come soon.
Having liver of animals with horns: Will soon be very rich.
Eating liver to have better health: Approaching money.
Giving children liver to eat: Will have happy family.
Enemies eating liver: Will win a lawsuit against an enemy.

LIVERY:
Having a livery servant: Great success.
A master having a livery servant: Will be annoyed.
A lady having a livery servant: Advancement in her position.
Livery servants of enemies: Danger in love affairs.
Livery servants of friends: Triumph in life.

LIZARD:
Of a lizard: Enemies will cause you injury.
Killing a lizard: Will regain lost fortune.
Having a lizard in a cage: Will have a good reputation.
Having a belt made of lizard skin: Marriage will last until death.
Having a bag made of lizard skin: Will have money all during life.
Having shoes made of lizard skin: Will be very healthy.
Friends having articles made of lizard: Treachery.

LOAD:
Of carrying a load: You will be very charitable.

Children carrying a load: Happiness.
Enemies carrying a load: You will be jilted.
Relatives carrying a load: Danger through a secret.

LOBBY:
Of a lobby: Joy.
Being in a lobby: Beware of treacherous friends.
The lobby of own home: Will remain in present surroundings.
Meeting people in a lobby: Dishonor.
Friends being in a lobby: You have no loyal friends.

LOBSTER:
Of a lobster: Domestic happiness.
Eating lobster: Happiness in love affairs.
Children eating lobster: Richness in the family.
Enemies eating lobster: Enemies are endeavoring to destroy you.
Friends eating lobster: You have only one loyal friend.
Relatives eating lobster: Doomed for disappointment.

LOCK:
Of opening a lock: Happiness is assured.
Being unable to open a lock: Beware of trouble ahead.
A woman opening a lock: Will be unfaithful to the man who loves her.
A man opening a lock: He is flirting with several women.
An opened lock: Suitable time to pursue your courtship.
Being unable to find keys for a lock: Be careful in money matters.
Finding the key for a lock: You will pull through your troubles.
Having keys for locks: Avoid speculations of any kind.
Possessing many locks: You have very stingy relatives.

LOCKJAW:
Having lockjaw: A serious disaster is ahead.
Others having lockjaw: Loss of money.

Dying because of lockjaw: You are being deceived.
Recovering from lockjaw: Will marry a nagging partner.

LOCOMOTIVE:
Of a locomotive: Will travel a great deal.
A locomotive coming toward you: Arrival of friends.
A locomotive going away from you: Will be jilted by a lover.
A locomotive going full speed: Quick rise to wealth.
A wrecked locomotive: Loss of prosperity.
Two locomotives hooked together: Big worries are ahead.
Being a locomotive engineer: Difficulties will be overcome easily.

LOCUST:
Of the locust plant: Happiness will be short-lived.
Having locust honey: Will have a big dinner.
Eating locust honey: Change in environment.
Picking locust: You have one loyal friend.

LODGING:
Looking for temporary lodging: Important matters will be delayed.
Finding temporary lodging: Loneliness and trouble.
Finding permanent lodging: Happiness in home life.
Finding a beautiful lodging: Good times are coming.

LOG:
Of logs of wood: Abundant means.
Fallen trunks of trees: Happiness is assured.
Cutting logs of wood: Will not have any earnings.
Cutting trunks of trees: Misery and affliction.
Carrying logs of wood: Will be offended by a friend.

LONELY:
Of loneliness: Happiness is assured.

Being lonely: Worry and misfortune.

Being lonely and not seeking company of others: Approaching money.

Others being lonely: Some person holds secret enmity for you.

LONGING:

Of longing: Reconciliation with a former enemy.

Others longing: You will be guilty of foolish actions.

Relatives longing: Family arguments.

Friends longing: Change of surroundings.

LOOK:

Looking at a beautiful human being: Abundant means.

Looking at other things: Advancement in life.

Looking forward to something: A change in life will soon come.

Looking straight in the eyes of a man: Triumph over enemies.

Looking straight in eyes of a woman: Suitable time to pursue courtship.

Looking at a person with a side glance: Worries of all kinds are coming.

LOOKING DOWN:

Looking down from a very high place: You are very ambitious.

Looking down from a hill: You have a restless desire for love.

Looking down from a window: Do not go too far in your schemes.

Looking down from a home: Change in environment.

LOOKING GLASS:

Of a looking glass: Treason.

A woman looking at herself in a looking glass: Friends are cheating you.

A man looking at himself in a looking glass: Be careful of business.

A business executive looking into a mirror: Staff is not giving support.

A young girl looking into a mirror: Advisable to change boyfriends.

A married woman looking into a mirror: She is unfaithful to her husband.

A lover looking into a mirror: Sweetheart is not really faithful.

A widow looking into a mirror: Should find out the real underlying motive.

LOOKING UP:

Looking up at a mountain: Hard work awaits.

Looking up at a monument: Will surmount your obstacles.

Looking up at the sky: Proceed with plans with all confidence.

Looking up at a window: Must control your passions.

Looking up at a home: Good luck is coming to you.

LOOM:

Looming above the surface of the sea: Luck and prosperity.

Looming above the surface of the land: Money will come easily during life.

Making yarns into fabrics on a loom: Good times are coming.

Of a loom: Recovery from an illness.

LOOPHOLE:

Of a loophole: You have the ability to see far ahead.

Making loopholes: Ability will aid in attaining own wishes.

Others finding loopholes: Misfortune in love affairs.

Others falling into a loophole: Will have emotional sorrow.

LORD:

Speaking to a lord: Social success.

A lord speaking to other people: Will have high authority.

A woman speaking to a lord: Momentary gains.

A young girl speaking to a lord: You have many personal matters.

LORRY:

Of a truck running on rails: Suitable time to pursue courtship.

Being on a lorry: You should mend your love life.

Others being on a lorry: Rapid success of own hopes.

Children being on a lorry: Financial gains.

Enemies being on a lorry: A mystery will be solved.

Friends being on a lorry: Important and very beneficial event to come.

LOSING:

Losing an article: Difficulties ahead.

Losing a boyfriend: Shame and sorrow.

Losing a girl friend: Will suffer because of own foolishness.

Losing a wife: Avoid rivals.

Losing a husband: Temptation will come to you.

Losing a child: Domestic troubles.

A woman losing her wedding ring: Good times are coming.

Losing own shoes: A serious disaster is ahead.

Losing clothing: You are in the grip of deceitful people.

Losing other household items: Troubles caused by own efforts.

Losing own dog: Dignity and distinction.

Losing own car: Approaching money.

LOST:

Being lost in the streets: Joy without profit.

Having lost the friendship of friends: Changes in love affairs.

Having lost own home: Be more careful of financial matters.

Having lost own business: You will be humiliated.

Having lost at gambling: Your worries are over.

Having lost blood: Will be in need of financial help.

Having lost the nose: Warning of trouble.

Having lost your hearing: Beware of jealous friends.

LOTHARIO:

Of a seducer of women: Unhappiness in love affairs.

Flirting with a Lothario: Be on the lookout for treachery.

Being loved by a Lothario: Family quarrels.

Loving a Lothario: You should mend your ways in life.

LOTTERY:

Of a lottery: You do not deserve success.

Playing a lottery: Small risks are ahead.

Being interested in a lottery: Unknown enemies are around you.

Holding lottery tickets: Good luck.

Lovers holding a lottery ticket: Unhappy association.

A lottery drawing: You will make money.

Lottery numbers being upside down: Engagement to a worthless person.

LOTTO:

Playing lotto: Will be in agreeable company.

Holding a lotto ticket: You have a bad chance in life.

Playing lotto with a sweetheart: Frivolity.

Winning at lotto: Good times are coming.

LOVE:

Being in love: Will live happily during life.

Love being unwanted: Will have heart trouble.

Being loved: Prosperity.

Being in love with yourself: Vanity.

Loving your work: Prosperity is ahead.

Loving someone very much: Fortune and joy.

Trying to make love to someone: Unhappiness.

Not succeeding in love: Will marry and live happily.

Being in the company of a lover: Will not succeed in marital life.

Being in love with two people: Faith and confidence will be abused.

Sweethearts being in love: Beware of jealous friends.

Loving your children: Happiness.

Being loved by children: Quarrels over which child is loved most.

Loving your husband: Avoid rivals.

Others loving your husband: Will live happily together all your life.

Loving your wife: Luck and prosperity.

Others loving your wife: Troubles are ahead.

Loving your relatives: Loss of money.

Being loved by relatives: Financial losses.

Loving your friends: Will receive news of a friend's death.

Being loved by friends: You will hear false promises.

LOVE LETTERS:

Writing a love letter: Happiness.

Reading a love letter: Will receive good news.

Receiving many love letters: Frankness is an admirable quality.

Tearing up love letters: Unhappiness.

Saving treasured love letters: Will find out the truth.

LOVE TOKEN:

Giving a love token promise: Suitable time to pursue courtship.

Receiving a love token promise: You are being deceived.

Others knowing about a love token promise: Be cautious.

LUCKY:

Being lucky in business: Are confronted with insurmountable obstacles.

Being lucky in love affairs: Be cautious of mental abilities.

Man and wife dreaming of being lucky in love: Do not trust affections.

Sweethearts dreaming of being lucky in love: An enemy is seeking your ruin.

LUGGAGE:

Having very heavy luggage: Loss of money.

Having light luggage: Will receive some money very soon.

Having luggage that is easy to handle: Will overcome difficulties.

Losing own luggage: Family quarrels.

Lovers losing their luggage: Broken engagement.

Relatives losing their luggage: Beware of business speculation.

Finding own luggage: Will have difficulties in your path.

LUMBER:

Of lumber: Big disappointment.

Having plenty of lumber: Unhappiness.

Buying lumber: Will be in need of money.

Burning lumber: Will receive unexpected money.

Piles of lumber: Will face a troublesome task.

Curved lumber: Will be in disgrace.

Owning a lumberyard: Do not allow others to lead you.

Of a lumberyard: You will make inevitable errors.

Ebony lumber: Will accomplish intentions through diligent work.

Sandal lumber: You hesitate too much in your affairs.

Cedar lumber: You have false friends.

LUNATIC:

Of a lunatic: Will receive surprising news.

Being a lunatic: Warning of troubles.

Friends being lunatics: Death of an enemy.

Keeping company with lunatics: Will be guilty of foolish actions.

Being in an asylum: Danger in love matters.

LUNG:

Of lungs: Will have a serious illness.

Having a sickness of the lungs: Loss of health and property.

Being wounded in the lungs: Domestic loss.

Having a lung removed: Disappointment in desires.

Spitting mucus from the lungs: Will suffer big losses.

LUXURY:
Being in luxury: Misfortune in love affairs.
Having luxurious surroundings: Will be humiliated.
Showing off luxurious things: Your ego will make many enemies.
Receiving luxurious gift: Family quarrels.
Losing your luxurious life: Loss of money through bad debts.
Luxury in love: A rival will take sweetheart's affections.
A luxurious family life: Domestic and family quarrels.

LYING:
Of lying: Will live a long life.
Others lying to you: Will be cheated by friends.
Husband or wife lying to each other: Will suffer from own foolishness.
Children lying to parents: Will realize high ambitions.
Others telling lies: You have many enemies.

LYNX:
Of a lynx: Will suffer persecution.
A lynx being in a tree: Will discover the secret of an enemy.
A lynx being on a roof: Will live a long life.

M

MACARONI:
Of macaroni: You are prone to being a parasite.
Eating macaroni: Will never be hungry.
Making macaroni: Will fall in love with a maid.
Cooking macaroni: Hard work and perseverance will bring happiness.
Buying macaroni: Will be invited to a dance.

MACE-BEARER:
Of an officer who carries a mace: Dignity and distinction.
A mace-bearer using a club as a weapon: Someone holds secret enmity.
Being a mace-bearer: Danger in love affairs.

MACHINERY:
Of machinery: You live a very proper life.
Machinery run by steam: Richness and happiness.
Being afraid of machinery: Be careful in new ventures.
Being injured by machinery: Failure in your purposes.
Buying machinery: Hard work is ahead.

Being interested in machinery: Good profits.
Others handling machinery: You have false friends.
Selling machinery: Prosperity.
Repairing a piece of machinery: Dignity and distinction.

MACKEREL:
Of a dead mackerel: Expect trouble.
Mackerel in a fish market: Will obtain a high, honorable position.
Catching a mackerel: You will be loved.
Having mackerel: Expensive pleasures.
Cooking mackerel: Marriage.
Eating mackerel: Joy.
Children eating mackerel: Good health.
A woman dreaming of a mackerel: Illness.
A man dreaming of a mackerel: Will have quarrels and suffering.

MACKINTOSH:
Putting on a mackintosh: Passing anxieties.
Taking off a mackintosh: Look out for gossipers.
Buying a mackintosh: Will have plenty of money.
Losing a mackintosh: Success.

MAD:

Being insane: Happiness.

A man dreaming of being mad: You love someone very deeply.

A woman dreaming of being mad: Will have a son who becomes famous.

A young girl dreaming of being mad: Will marry soon.

Becoming mad: Long life.

A raving mad person: Unhappiness is ahead.

A mad person being dead: Will have a new love.

MAD DOG:

Of a mad dog: A falsehood will be unmasked.

Owning a mad dog: An unfair accusation will be proven so.

Killing a mad dog: Will have a contented future.

MADONNA:

Of a madonna: Abundance.

Talking with a madonna: Fortune and consolation.

A picture of a madonna: Riches.

Entering a church and finding madonna's picture missing: Must endure pain.

MAGAZINE:

Of a magazine: Will receive news from faraway.

Buying a magazine: Will be relieved of worries.

Selling a magazine: Loneliness.

Giving away a magazine: Friendship.

Losing a magazine: Poverty.

Writing articles in a magazine: Be careful to avoid a loss.

MAGGOT:

Of a maggot: Change for the better.

Many maggots: Change in environment.

Killing maggots: Failure of enemies.

MAGIC:

Of magic: A change will come in your affairs.

Reading about magic: Will receive news from an unexpected source.

Discussing magic: Loss of a friend.

Being involved with unpredicted magic events: Progress in enterprises.

MAGISTRATE:

Of a magistrate: Will progress in own affairs.

Being summoned by a magistrate: Sorrow and trouble.

A magistrate being in your favor: Will overcome worries.

Being punished by a magistrate: Hard times ahead.

Being acquitted by a magistrate: A big fortune is coming to you.

Being a magistrate: Do not trust relatives.

MAGNATE:

Of a magnate: Will fall in love.

Being in the company of a magnate: Dignity and distinction.

Marrying a magnate: Luck and prosperity.

Divorcing a magnate: Will have abundant means.

MAGNET:

Of a magnet: Success and security in business but do not be reckless.

Using a magnet: An elevated trend in your affairs to come.

A woman dreaming of using a magnet: Wealth will be hers.

A man dreaming of using a magnet: Loss of honorable life through a woman.

Professional people using magnet for work: Long lasting love.

MAGNIFYING GLASS:

Of a magnifying glass: Business will be enlarged.

Using a magnifying glass: Glorious future.

Buying a magnifying glass: Discovery of lost valuables.

Reading with a magnifying glass: Will live a short life.

MAGPIE:

Of a magpie: Someone is trying to steal something from you.

A magpie being in a cage: Will have a long life.

A magpie in the morning: Success in affairs.

A magpie in the evening: You will be badly cheated.

MAID:

A girl dreaming of being a maid: Disappointment in love.

A married woman dreaming of being a maid: A false friend is nearby.

An elderly woman dreaming of being a maid: Will have plenty of income.

Being a maid: Insurmountable obstacles are ahead.

Having several maids: Prosperity.

Marrying a maid: Your employer will fall in love with you.

MAIL:

Mailing a package: Will receive a gift.

Mailing a letter with a check: Will receive good news.

Mailing documents: A false friend is cheating you.

Mailing items of value: Will become jealous.

MAKE-UP:

A beautiful woman using make-up: Beware or you will be deceived.

A plain woman using make-up: Will have troubles in love affairs.

Being an arrogant, conceited woman and making-up: Danger of loss of estate.

A man dreaming of a woman using make-up: Loss of authority.

A woman dreaming of using make-up: Satisfaction and good income.

Putting a net over own hair: Will have a terrible headache.

MALICE:

Having malice for some person: Misfortune in love affairs.

Having malice for many people nearby: Persecution.

Having malice for own family: Unhappiness.

Having malice for own sweetheart: Danger through a secret.

Having malice between husband and wife: Changes in family life.

MALT:

Of malt: Failure of enemies.

Adding water to malt causing fermentation: Good luck to one for whom you care.

Making malt from barley: A period of wealth is coming.

Making a malted milk: Avoid rivals.

MALTA CROSS:

Being an officer decorated with a Malta Cross: You have loyal friends.

Being presented with this honor: Will have good fortune by merit alone.

A civilian being decorated with the Malta Cross: Luck and prosperity.

MAMMOTH:

Of this type of Indian elephant: Insurmountable obstacles confront you.

A mammoth being trained: Will have good earnings.

A mammoth being in a cage: Will receive an unexpected gift.

MAN:

A tall man: Good luck.

An armed man: Sorrow.

A bald-headed man: Abundance.

A fat man: Bad ventures.

A furious man: Disgrace.

A naked man: Beware of whom you meet.

A horrible-looking man: Will have no friends.

A dirty man: Family quarrels.

A man with a beard: Loss of temper.

A haughty, proud man: Someone loves you secretly.

A man in a park: You will be frightened.

A savage man in a forest: You will be cheated.

A dead man: Loss of a lawsuit.

A handsome man: Big satisfaction and joy.

A woman dreaming of a handsome man: Will have a terrible quarrel.

A young girl dreaming of a handsome man: Look out for gossip.

A prominent man: Abundance.
Hearing a speech by a prominent man: Dishonor.
Talking with a prominent man: Improvement in own business.
A political man: Happiness.
Being seen in the company of a political man: Disgrace to yourself.
A man dreaming of an unknown man: Glory and honor.
A woman dreaming of an unknown man: Boundless wealth.
A man dressed in white: Excessive good luck.
A man dressed in black: Misfortune.
A man who is a murderer: Security.
A man fighting with a wild animal: Good friendships.
Killing a man: Will have a long life.
A man being executed: Loss of business.
A man being hanged: Sickness.
A man with a crown: Big profit.
A man with a cross in the summer: Good enterprises.
A man with a cross in the winter: Bad business.

MANACLES:
Of being handcuffed: Will be annoyed by enemies.
Others wearing manacles: Will conquer all obstacles.
Relatives wearing manacles: Will get out of trouble.
Enemies wearing manacles: Good prospects for own business.

MANGLE:
Of a mangle: Good times are coming.
Using a mangle to smooth sheets: Change for the better.
Others using a mangle: Temptation will come to you.
Buying a mangle: Will triumph over enemies.

MANICURE:
Of a manicure: Happiness is assured.
Being a manicurist: Will marry a wealthy man.
A woman having a manicure: Will marry a man much older than herself.

A man having a manicure: Will have a happy marriage.

MANIKIN:
A manikin in a show window without clothes on: Financial gains.
A manikin in a show window with clothes on: Beware of being jilted.
A woman fixing a manikin in a show window: Avoid rivals.
Buying a dress from a manikin: Frivolity.

MANNA:
Of this divinely supplied food: Will have good earnings.
Having manna: Unexpected riches.
Supplying manna to others: Approaching money.
Taking manna as a mild laxative: Discovery of lost valuables.

MANSERVANT:
Of a manservant: Will be cheated by friends.
Being a manservant: Someone with evil intent is watching you.
Having a manservant: A change in life will come soon.
Firing a manservant: Unexpected troubles.

MANSION:
Seeing a distant mansion: Advancement.
Being in a mansion: Wealth.
Owning a mansion: Pleasure of short duration.
Having several mansions: Will be molested.
Having a small mansion: You are an innocent person.
Living in a mansion: Sorrow.
Demolishing a mansion: Someone will take something from you by force.
Burning a mansion: Foolishness.
Having a mansion in a city: You will spend much money.
Having a regal mansion: People are ungrateful to you.
Others being in a mansion: You are surrounded by jealous people.

209

MANSLAUGHTER:
Being the object of a manslaughter: Will avoid danger.
Committing manslaughter: Security and long life.
Being acquitted of manslaughter: Be cautious in own enterprises.
Being found guilty of manslaughter: Warning of divorce.

MANTEL:
Of a beautiful mantel: Beware of treachery.
A clock sitting on a mantel: Beware in whom you place your trust.

MANTLE:
Wearing a mantle on own shoulders: Dignity.
Putting on own mantle: Will have new employment.
Taking off own mantle: Will be disgraced.

MANUFACTURE:
Of manufacturing material: Will be active in making money.
Selling manufactured materials: Will realize high ambitions.
Working at a manufacturing plant: Services will be rendered to you.
Owning a manufacturing plant: Financial gains.
Manufacturing playing cards: Will escape a danger.
Manufacturing pots and pans: Death of someone.
Manufacturing combs: Unhappiness in marriage.
Manufacturing starches: Poverty and misery.

MANURE:
Of fertilizing soil with manure: Prosperity.
Buying manure: Wealth.
Selling manure: Abundant means.
Handling manure: Good profits.

MAP:
Of a colored map: Will have plenty of money.
Studying a map: Change of residence.
Consulting a map: Changes in business or employment.
Buying a map: Will take a long trip abroad.

MARBLE:
Of a marble quarry: Will enjoy success in business.
Having marble things in own house: Security.
Polishing marble: Will receive an inheritance.
Marble being scratched: Affection will brighten your life.
Buying marble: Will attend a funeral.

MARCH:
Of the month of March during this month: Enemies will cause damages.
Of March during other months: Unhappiness.
Being born in March: Everything will go your way in life.
Children being born in March: They will succeed to highest aspirations.

MARCHING:
Of marching: Fortune in business.
Marching in the company of women: Change of surroundings.
Marching with flags: Unexpected news.
Marching with soldiers: Wealth.
Marching at a fast pace: Advancement and success in business.

MARIGOLD:
Of this flower: You will be fortunate.
Picking marigolds: Unexpected money.
Receiving a bouquet of marigolds: Will incur debts.
Giving marigolds to others: Beware of bad influences working against you.

MARIJUANA:
Of the marijuana plant: Will be melancholy.
Smelling marijuana: Will have much protection.
Smoking marijuana alone: Will dream of unattainable things.
Smoking marijuana with one of opposite sex: Security in love.
Being arrested for smoking marijuana: You love amusements too much.

MARINER:
Of a mariner or a sailor: Will take a perilous trip.
Being a mariner: Restlessness and changes in affairs.
A woman dreaming of being with a mariner: News received from faraway.
A man dreaming of being in company of a mariner: Arrival of friends.
Several mariners: Misery.

MARKET:
Of an empty market: Expect difficulties and trouble.
Idly looking through a market: Loss of opportunities.
Being in a market: New friendships.
Making purchases at a market: Good health.
Selling something at a market: Money will come easily during life.
Being in a small market: Small infirmity.
Going to a fish market: Will have a prominent position.
Going to a meat market: Will receive honors.

MARMALADE:
Making marmalade: Troubles and worries.
Eating marmalade alone: Beware of untrue friends.
Eating marmalade in company of others: Wealth.
Giving marmalade as a gift: Good love affairs.

MARQUIS:
Of a marquis: You are becoming too proud.
Being a marquis: Will receive difficult favors.
Being in the company of a marquis: Will be fortunate in love.
Dealing with a marquis: Opposition in love affairs.
Being friendly with a marquis: Will not get married.
A married woman dreaming of a marquis: Will achieve something favorable.

Unmarried women dreaming of a marquis: Will soon be married.
Others being a marquis: Humiliation.

MARRIAGE:
Of a marriage: Warning of ill health.
Getting married: Melancholy.
Assisting at a marriage: Will have pleasing news of little importance.
A second marriage: Will make money.
Giving sister away in marriage: Big peril.
Children participating in a marriage: Good news.
A woman dreaming of marriage to an old man: Sickness and trouble ahead.
Giving a daughter away in marriage: Good times are ahead.
A widower dreaming of marriage the second time: Happiness until death.
Being a bridesmaid at a marriage: Will get married very soon.
Being a flower girl at a marriage: Will have a happy future.
The marriage of a priest: Success in life.
Being a bride or groom: Profit.
A young woman dreaming of being an unhappy bride: Enemies seek her downfall.
A bride being with her parents: Danger.
Being a beautiful bride: Joy.
Being a plain bride: Advantages in life.
Being an ugly bride: Unhappiness.
Being a blond bride: Joy without profit.
Being a brunette bride: Inheritance.
Being a virgin bride: Big honor.

MARROW:
Of marrow: Will receive good news.
Buying marrow: Loss of wealth in the family because of relatives.
Cooking marrow: Happiness and prosperity.
Eating marrow: Will make good profit.

MARSH:
Of a marsh: Constant friendship.

Having a tract of marshland: Temptations in love will come to you.
Being stuck in a marsh: Big joy.
Getting out of a marsh to firm ground: Abundant means.

MARTYR:
Being a martyr: Honor and public approval.
Making a martyr of someone: Will be oppressed by others.
Making martyrs of children: Stinginess will cause damages.
Making martyrs of innocent people: Poverty.
Others making a martyr of you: Will be saved from death.

MARY:
Of Mary the mother of Jesus: Much happiness within the family.
Ladies with the name Mary: A big fortune is ahead for you.
Wife being named Mary: Honor without profit.
Having a daughter named Mary: Must rely upon own vigor.
Mother being named Mary: Will have fortune in business.
Loved one being named Mary: Will receive a large favor from someone.

MASCOT:
Of a mascot: Unexpected news will change your future prospects.
Having a mascot: Will come out well from a present danger.
The mascot of a ship: Important and very beneficial events to come.
Having a mascot in the home: Good luck in family affairs.
Having a mascot in own car: Will live a long life.

MASK:
Of a mask: Beware of rivals.
Wearing a mask: Will make plenty of money.
Someone with a mask on: Beware of deceitful neighbors.
Others wearing a mask: Will be injured through falsehood and envy.
Enemies wearing a mask: Treachery.

MASON:
Of a mason: Distinction in work.
Being a mason: Warning of troubles.
A mason at work: Will be guilty of foolish actions.
Employing several masons: Losses due to illness.
Several masons building a house: Dignity in the family.

MASQUERADE:
Of a masquerade party: Someone will trick you.
Being at a masquerade party alone: Prosperity.
Being at a masquerade party with loved one: Successful life ahead.
Being queen of a masquerade party: Enemies seek your downfall.

MASS:
Of mass: Wealth will come soon.
Going to mass: Will have much satisfaction in the near future.
Going to mass alone: Your conscience is not clean.
Going to mass with your family: Happiness in the family.
Attending mass: Good sign for future well-being.
Attending mass every week: Will receive what you desire.
Attending a musical mass: Great joy.
A priest telling mass: You will be free from slavery.
Others being at mass: Dignity and distinction.
Attending mass several times: Abundant riches.
Of a mass of things: A close friend will visit you soon.

MASSACRE:
Of a massacre: Loss of personal belongings and wealth.
Hearing of a massacre: Will make money.
Being massacred: Will receive damages in own affairs.
Many people being killed in a massacre: Death of a friend.

MASSAGE:
Of a massage: Will have a pleasant life.

Having a massage in a public place: Your efforts will be rewarded.

Giving a massage to a woman: Will soon receive unexpected money.

Giving a massage to a man: Will have difficulties to surmount.

Giving a massage to a sick person: Will receive a kindness from someone.

MAST:

Of the mast of a ship: Will take an important journey soon.

Very high masts: Will have a long and pleasant journey.

Climbing a mast: Will have mastery over many matters.

Sailors climbing on masts: Change of surroundings.

Enemies climbing a mast: Danger will come to them.

Relatives climbing a mast: Will live to a ripe old age in happiness.

MASTER:

Of the master of a ship: Good times to come.

Being the master of a ship: Approaching money.

Being the master of own home: Prosperity.

Being the master of own business: Happiness is assured.

Being the master of a dog: You do not have faithful friends.

Being the master of own children: Abundant means will come to you.

Having a master: Good times are coming.

Being a dancing master: Frivolity.

Being a school master: Your earnings will increase.

Being a master of languages: You are being deceived.

Being a fencing master: Your friends are not loyal.

The master of a chapel: Will have troubles in love affairs.

MASTIFF:

Of this smooth-coated dog: Beware of false suspicions.

Being bitten by a mastiff: Troubles in love affairs.

Two mastiff dogs fighting: Death of a friend.

Two mastiff dogs playing: You like to eat too much.

A woman dreaming of a mastiff dog: Her lover is faithful to her.

MAT:

Of a mat: Sorrow.

A mat being at the door: Indicates trouble.

A mat being in a room: Failure of enemies.

A mat made of straw: Warning of poverty.

MATCHES:

Of matches: Own efforts will bring riches.

Having a box of matches in pocket: Financial gains are at hand.

Having matches at home: Misfortune in love affairs.

Buying matches: Expect some money.

MATRON:

Of a matron: Will live to a very ripe old age.

Arguing with a matron: Death is near.

Being a matron: Will have happy days ahead.

Becoming a matron: Dangers in the family.

Being a disliked matron: Will make money.

MATTRESS:

Of a mattress: Heavier responsibilities and duties will come to you.

Having a mattress: Worries ahead.

Buying a mattress: Will lead an easy life.

Repairing own mattress: Desires will be accomplished.

MAUSOLEUM:

Of a mausoleum: Serious troubles.

Visiting a mausoleum: Long sickness.

Being in a mausoleum: Illness.

Others being in a mausoleum: Death of a close friend.

MAUVE:

Of the color mauve: Unhappiness.

Materials of any kind in mauve color: Warning of troubles.

Buying clothes of mauve color: Financial losses.

MAY:
Of the month of May during this month: Do not be discouraged.

Of May during other months: Financial losses.

Being born in May: Undertakings will be successful.

Children being born in May: Will live a long life.

Flowers blossoming in May: Disappointment and bad news.

May 1st being international Labor Day: Will work hard in life.

MAYPOLE:
A tall maypole: Good times are coming.

A maypole wreathed in flowers: Joy without profit.

Many maypoles in an open area: Important and very beneficial events to come.

MAZE:
Of a maze: A mystery will be solved.

Being in a maze: You are surrounded by unhappiness.

Finding way out of a maze: Perplexities will be happily solved.

Not finding way out of a maze: Beware of domination by insincere friends.

MEADOW:
Of meadows: Undertakings will be successful.

Grass growing in a meadow: Will make a good marriage.

Hay growing in a meadow: Pleasant friendships.

Being in a meadow: Happiness.

Buying a meadow: Will have much hospitality.

MEAN:
Being mean: Happiness.

Being mean to others: Will have a fight in the near future.

Others being mean to you: Will be ignored by friends.

Members of family being mean: Will soon take a long trip.

MEANS:
Not having sufficient means: Beware of people who will bring damages.

Having sufficient means: Poverty.

Other people without sufficient means: Unhappiness.

Friends having sufficient means: Postponement of success.

A man having more means than necessary: Loss of personal property.

A woman having more means than necessary: Family disaster.

MEASLES:
Of having measles: Fretting and worry will interfere with own business.

Other people with measles: Will be troubled over love affairs.

Children having measles: Happiness is ahead.

Relatives having measles: Approaching money.

MEASURING:
Of measuring: Big commercial gains.

Measuring ingredients for cooking: A warning to be careful.

Measuring size of own body: Abundant means.

Measuring own clothing: Beware of enemies.

Measuring own house: Be careful, you may lose more than you save.

Measuring the temperature: Good times are coming.

Measuring anything else: Lack of attention is detrimental to own affairs.

MEAT:
Of meat: Happiness.

Boiled meat: Melancholy.

Broiled meat: Good times are ahead.

Roasted meat: Will receive God's blessings.

Fried meat: Will be paid well to kill someone.

Raw meat: Will receive news of the death of a friend.

Eating raw meat: Wealth.

Veal meat: You will cheat someone.

Pork meat: Will be very fortunate.

Beef meat: Will have an easy life.
Lamb meat: Happiness is assured.
Deer meat: Will have worries.
Fowl or bird meat: Will collect money.
Wild meat: Will have many troubles.
Buying meat: Will gain money in gambling.
Throwing meat away: Danger is very close to you.
Cutting raw meat: Inheritance.
Carving cooked meat: Financial gains.
Cooking meat for yourself: Change in surroundings.
Cooking meat for other people: Misfortune in love affairs.

MEDAL:
Of a medal: Will come out well from a present peril.
Wearing medals: Merry times are to come soon.
Someone else wearing medals: Danger in love affairs.
Army and navy personnel wearing medals: Financial gains.

MEDICINE:
Of a medicine chest: Big joy without profit.
Taking medicine: Troubles are not serious; persevere, and you will succeed.
Taking pleasant medicine: Troubles will end in ultimate good.
Taking bitter medicine: Will attempt to injure one who trusts you.
Giving medicine to friends: Accord among friends.
Giving medicine to children: Hard work awaits.
Giving medicine to relatives: Be cautious in all your dealings.

MEDITERRANEAN SEA:
A map of the Mediterranean Sea: Will have emotional sorrow.
Visiting towns on the shores of this sea: Future prosperity.
Traveling to the Mediterranean Sea: Good times are coming.
Returning from a trip to the Mediterranean Sea: Financial gains.

MEDLAR:
Of this small Eurasian tree: Big earnings and good life.
Eating fruit from a medlar tree: Enjoyment will cease and troubles begin.
Eating this fruit with others: Will enjoy favorable events.
Buying the fruit of a medlar: Pleasant circumstances.

MELANCHOLY:
Being in a melancholy state: Will realize high ambitions.
Others being melancholy: Separation of lovers.
A young girl being melancholy: Disappointment from a broken engagement.
Married people being melancholy: Pleasant work and good news.

MELODY:
Hearing a pleasant melody: Success will attend you.
Singing a melody: A false friend is nearby.
Hearing others singing a melody: Certain and happy marriage.
Playing a melody: Affairs will prosper.

MELONS:
Of melons: Big earnings and good life.
Eating melons: Consistency in love.
Raising melons: Good fortune.
Having a melon: Good success.
Buying a melon: Good sign for love affairs.
A sick person dreaming of eating melons: Will get well soon.

MEMORIAL DAY:
Of Memorial Day: Will have good health and blessings.
Visiting relatives' graves on Memorial Day: Rapid and good future success.
Decorating graves on Memorial Day: Will enjoy security for a long time.
Attending church on Memorial Day: Will receive good news very soon.

MEMORY:
Having a loss of memory: Family dishonor.

Regaining memory: Will rise in the world shortly.

Friend having a loss of memory: You should mend your ways in life.

Friend regaining memory: Will acquire something big.

Children having a loss of memory: Will live a long life.

MENAGERIE:

Of a menagerie: Expect difficulties in business.

Being in a menagerie with wild animals: Postponement of success.

Others being in a menagerie: They have a reputation for gossip.

Working in a menagerie: Good times are coming.

MENDICANT:

Of a beggar: A period of sorrow is about to come.

Being a mendicant: You have one loyal friend.

A mendicant begging in the street: Failure of enemies.

Being a mendicant and begging: Affairs are prospering.

Being accosted in the street by a mendicant: Difficulties ahead.

Assisting a mendicant: Will overcome troubles.

People you know begging: Will receive the help of a good friend.

MENDING:

Of mending: Will have an inferior and miserable position.

Others mending: Be cautious in love adventures.

Mending children's clothes: Financial gains.

Others mending your clothes: Family quarrels.

A young woman mending clothes: Will be a great assistance to her husband.

MERCURY:

Of mercury: Will have money.

Taking mercury in medicine: Will become disgusted with friends.

Handling mercury: Will be well thought of by other people.

Walking on mercury: Income will raise considerably.

MERIT:

Receiving merit: Will have a better future.

Being given merit for accomplishments: Will receive unexpected fortune.

Children receiving merits: Profit.

Someone receiving merit without deserving it: Loss of money.

MERMAID:

Of a mermaid: Misfortune in love affairs.

A mermaid being on the bow of a ship: End of love affairs.

A mermaid being on the bow of a sailing vessel: Are deceived by a lover.

MERRIMENT:

Of merriment: Expect difficulties in home life.

Having much merriment: Will suffer because of own foolishness.

Others having much merriment: Warning of troubles.

MESMERISM:

Of being hypnotized: Confidence will be betrayed.

Mesmerising others: Triumph over enemies.

Others who are mesmerised: New interest and surroundings.

MESS:

Things being in a mess: You idolize money too much.

Making a mess of things: Will be made love to by unexpected person.

Children making a mess: Will receive a legacy.

Sailors' mess hall: Will be very fortunate in business transactions.

MESSAGE:

Of a message: Will change to a better position.

Receiving a message: Security in business.

Sending a message: Unpleasant circumstances.

Sending a message to relatives: Danger through a secret.

Receiving a message from relatives: Important and very beneficial event.

Sending a message to a sweetheart: Beware of rivals.

Receiving a message from a sweetheart: A big catastrophe is ahead.

METALS:
Of metals: Riches.
Buying metals: Approaching money.
Selling metals: Abundant means.
Melting metals: You are confronted with insurmountable obstacles.

METAMORPHOSIS:
Of metamorphosis: Will take a trip.
An animal experiencing metamorphosis: Gossip.
Plants going through metamorphosis: Will change residence.
Humans changing to animals: Will improve present position.

MICE:
Of mice: Troubles through a business associate.
Only one mouse: Troubles caused by a friend.
A cat killing mice: Victory over enemies.
Mice being caught in a trap: You will be slandered.
Mice playing: Dishonor.
A dog catching mice: End of troubles.

MICROSCOPE:
Of a microscope: Increase in the family.
Using a microscope: A mystery will be solved soon.
A chemist using a microscope: Dignity and distinction.
A doctor using a microscope: Recovery from an illness.
A jeweler using a microscope: Abundant means.

MIDWIFE:
Of a midwife: Discovery of a secret.
Being a midwife: An enemy is seeking your ruin.

Helping a midwife: Good times are coming.
A doctor using a midwife: Will receive news from faraway.

MIGNONETTE:
Of this type of flower: You are being deceived.
A mignonette out of season: Loss of all hope.
A mignonette in season: Great happiness.
Raising mignonettes: An early marriage will take place.
Buying mignonettes: Do not expect help from others.
Selling mignonettes: You must depend on your own efforts.

MILDEW:
Mildew developing: Will be introduced to an attractive stranger.
Something going mildew: Be careful of own private papers.
Removing mildew from vegetables: Rapid recovery.

MILESTONE:
Of a milestone: Some person holds secret enmity for you.
Placing a milestone: Warning of troubles.
Placing several milestones: Will be cheated by friends.

MILK:
Of milk: Misfortune in love affairs.
Drinking milk: Great joy.
Selling milk: Fortune in love affairs.
Spilling milk: Loss of business.
A large container full of milk: Unexpected fortune.
Milking a cow: Good times are coming.
Getting lots of milk from a cow: Prosperity in love affairs.
Having large quantities of milk: Good health.
Giving milk to other people: Will lead a charitable life.
Selling large amounts of milk: Abundant harvest for the farmer.
A woman selling milk: Large profits for business people.

A young girl milking a cow: Safe journey for the traveler.
The milk of a donkey: Riches.
The milk of a woman: Gossip.
A married woman having plenty of milk: She will be pregnant again.
An old woman having milk: Big wealth.

MILK PAIL:
Of milk pails: Misfortune in love affairs.
Carrying full milk pails: Good news concerning a birth.
Carrying an empty milk pail: You are being deceived by a lover.
Having several full milk pails: Change in environment.

MILL:
A metal mill: Will overcome enemies with perseverance.
A timber mill: An enemy is seeking your ruin.
A cloth mill: Good times are coming.
A manufacturing mill: Danger in love matters.
A mill grinding grain: Shame and sorrow.
A sawmill: Will receive bad news.
A windmill: Will be badly deceived.
An old mill: Sickness and misfortune.
A new mill: Inheritance from a rich relative.
Lovers dreaming of being in a mill: Big happiness.

MILLER:
Of a miller: Will be cheated by friends.
A woman dreaming of a miller: Will marry a man poorer than she thought.
Being a miller: Hard work awaits.

MILLET:
Of this type of cereal: Much happiness.
Birds eating millet: Approaching money.
Planting millet: Will overcome enemies with perseverance.
Buying millet: Change of surroundings.
Selling millet: Hard work awaits.

MILLINER:
Of a milliner: You have too much vanity.
Being a milliner: Money comes easily to you.
Buying hats from a milliner: Will encounter debts.
A milliner selling hats: Will have money coming in the near future.

MILLIONAIRE:
Of a millionaire: Listen to the advice of friends.
Receiving money from a millionaire: Will be very tired from hard work.
Receiving a favor from a millionaire: Will enjoy happiness.
Returning money to a millionaire Don't let people cheat you.

MILLSTONE:
Of a millstone: Increase in the family.
Using a millstone: Take better care of of your dealings.
An old millstone: Sickness or misfortune.
A new millstone: Success.

MINCE PIES:
Of mince pies: Great joy.
Making a mince pie at Christmas time: Joy without profit.
Making a mince pie other times of the year: Will have a vigorous mind.
Eating mince pie: Good fortune is ahead.

MINE:
Of a mine: Own business will increase.
Going down into a mine: Trust only proven friends.
Coming up out of a mine: You have an unfaithful wife.
Owning a mine: Promise of future work.
Digging for a mine: Good times are coming.
Closing a mine: A big catastrophe is ahead.
Having a big coal mine: Plenty of work and little profit.
Having an iron mine: Unhappiness.
Having a gold mine: Will be guilty of foolish actions.

Being a miner: Danger in love matters.

MINISTER:
Of a minister: Happiness that will not last long.
A minister being with a judge: Expect serious disappointment.
A minister preaching: A big catastrophe is ahead.
A minister giving advice: Warning of troubles.
The black clothing of a minister: Danger of death.
A minister being outside a church: Misfortune in love affairs.
A minister being in the company of a woman: Frivolity.

MINK:
Of a mink: Abundant means.
A mink coat: Joy without profit.
Buying a mink coat: Your husband is deceiving you.
Receiving a mink coat as a gift: A change in life will come soon.
Others wearing a mink coat: You are in the grip of deceitful people.
Relatives wearing mink coats: Family quarrels.
Selling a mink coat: Will have a new husband that is better.
Wearing a mink hat: A rival will take affections of sweetheart.

MINT:
Of a mint building: Troubles caused by prying into affairs of others.
Working at the mint: Will have emotional sorrow.
Minting paper money: Change of surroundings.
Minting coins: An enemy is seeking your ruin.
Minting postage stamps: Will take a long trip abroad.
A sick person dreaming of the mint: Will soon recover.
A healthy person dreaming of the mint: Better spirits.

MINUET:
Of a minuet: Domestic happiness.

Dancing a minuet with your wife: Unhappiness.
Dancing a minuet with a friend: Good fortune.
Dancing a minuet with a handsome man: Approaching money.
Dancing a minuet with sweetheart: Danger in love matters.

MINUTE:
The minutes on a clock: Will have a happy future.
Counting the minutes: Good results in a business deal.
Minutes passing by quickly: Loss of a relative.
Waiting for minutes to pass: Riches.

MIRACLE:
Of a miracle: Unexpected events will astonish you for a while.
Believing in miracles: Recovery from an illness.
Others telling of being present at a miracle: Insurmountable obstacles.

MIRAGE:
Of a mirage: Be careful in business ventures.
A woman dreaming of a mirage: Friends are cheating you.
A man dreaming of a mirage: Bad fortune in business.
A young girl dreaming of a mirage: It is advisable to change boyfriends.
A business executive dreaming of a mirage: Your staff is not honest.
A lover dreaming of a mirage: Your sweetheart is not faithful.

MIRE:
Of a mire: Will have security.
Getting stuck in the mire: Honors and riches.
Getting out of the mire: Worries will soon pass.
Others sinking in the mire: Anxiety and advancement.

MIRROR:
Of a mirror: Discouragements.
Seeing yourself in a mirror: Illness.
Seeing husband in a mirror: Will be unfairly treated.

Seeing a loved one in a mirror: Wealth.

Seeing others in a mirror: Unhappy marriage.

A broken mirror: Unexpected death of a relative.

A woman looking at herself in a mirror: Friends are cheating you.

A man looking at himself in a mirror: Be careful in own business.

A young girl looking in a mirror: She should change boyfriends.

A business executive looking in a mirror: Staff is not loyal to you.

A widow looking in a mirror: Find out her ulterior motives.

MISCARRIAGE:

Having a miscarriage: Happiness.

A married woman having a miscarriage: Abundant means.

An unmarried woman having a miscarriage: Will have a legacy.

A divorced woman having a miscarriage: Will marry a rich man.

MISCELLANEOUS:

Of miscellaneous things: Will receive good news from faraway.

Gathering miscellaneous things: Honor and profit.

Receiving miscellaneous papers: Unsuccessful enterprises.

Miscellaneous household things: Will receive an unexpected visitor.

MISCHIEF:

Getting into mischief: Will do wrong to others.

Children getting into mischief: Arrival of a friend.

Husband getting into mischief: Will abuse the confidence of others.

Others getting into mischief: Misery and annoyance.

MISCONDUCT:

Having misconduct yourself: Will be menanced by danger.

A mate having misconduct: Postponement of a trip.

Children having misconduct: Affairs will turn out very well.

Relatives having misconduct: Infidelity in family affairs.

MISCOUNT:

Miscounting money: Happiness.

A cashier miscounting money: Will have a comfortable life.

Miscounting purchases: Good earnings in business.

Others miscounting: Will have an increase in revenue.

MISER:

A miser near his safe counting money: Inheritance will come to you.

A woman being a miser: Triumph over enemies.

Being a miser: You are unfitted to fill a good position in life.

Hoarding more money: Will be unfortunate in business.

MISERABLE:

Being miserable and in despair: Don't let temper get the best of you.

Others who are miserable and in despair: Be prepared to die.

A miserable person burning himself: Unhappiness and sickness.

Friends who are miserable: Affliction.

MISFORTUNE:

Having misfortune yourself: Fortunate stroke in business.

Others having misfortune: Danger in love affairs.

Lovers having misfortune: Great success.

Enemies having misfortune: Beware of jealous friends.

Relatives having misfortune: Will gain through gambling.

MISS:

Being a beautiful miss: Will engage in risky speculation.

Being a young miss: Honor and fortune.

Being a miss in later life: Will talk with a handsome man.

Missing money: Gossip within the home.

Missing a boat: Happiness.

Missing a train: Dishonor.

Missing other means of transportation: Property is in danger.

Missing valuable articles: A happy matrimony will take place.

MISSIONARY:

Of a missionary: Change to more interesting work.

Being a missionary: Will have many faithful friends.

Working with a missionary: Unhappiness because of desertion.

Going faraway with a missionary: Good times are coming.

MIST:

Of mist: Approaching money.

Being enveloped in a mist: Unhappiness in the home.

Mist clearing away: Troubles will be passing ones.

Being in the mist with a loved one: An enemy is seeking your ruin.

MISTAKE:

Having made a mistake: Avoid conceit.

Others making a mistake: Be sure of your information before acting.

A wife and husband making a mistake: Take counsel before taking action.

Making mistakes in accounts: What you desired will not be realized.

MISTLETOE:

Of mistletoe: You will be fortunate.

Picking mistletoe: Will receive unexpected money.

Receiving mistletoe from someone: Happiness.

Giving mistletoe to others: Good luck and prosperity.

MOAN:

Moaning because of pain or grief: Be on guard against untrue friends.

Children moaning: Abundant means.

Other people moaning: Be cautious in all your dealings.

MOCK:

Being mocked: Take care not to be swindled.

Others being mocked: Will be asked to assist others.

Children being mocked: Do not neglect own affairs.

Being mocked by friends: You are in the grip of deceitful people.

MOLD:

Of a mold: Good luck to one for whom you care.

Using a mold: Important event concerning happiness.

A cooking mold: Do not speculate in your affairs.

Others using a cooking mold: Someone nearby is in trouble.

A mold used for casting metals: Luck and prosperity.

A mold used for frames: Betrayal by a friend.

The shape of a mold: Financial gains are coming your way.

Molding bread: Inheritance coming to you from a friend.

Molding food: Save your money or you will not keep it long.

MOLE:

Of a mole: Danger in love affairs.

Having moles: Unknown enemies.

Catching this animal: Will rise to prominence.

Being on a mole alone: Must endure grief.

Being on a mole with sailors: Some person holds secret enmity for you.

MOLLUSK:

Of these shellfish: Mysterious happenings will claim your attention.

Catching mollusks: Approaching money.

Eating mollusks: Do not believe too readily all you hear.

Selling mollusks: Abundant means.

Cooking mollusks: Will be visited by several friends.

MOLT:

Of something molting: Be wise and sever doubtful associations.

Hair molting: An invitation will bring new opportunities.

Feathers molting: Will make new friends.

MONARCH:

Of a monarch: Will be deceived in love affairs.

Going to see a monarch: Good fortune.

Sending a letter to a monarch: Danger.

Having an interview with a monarch: Rebellion within the home.

A monarch surrounded by his court: Will be deceived by friends.

MONASTERY:

Of a monastery: Worldy affairs will prosper.

Being in a monastery: Warning of troubles.

Entering a monastery: Will receive many honors.

Leaving a monastery: Must suffer much affliction.

Praying in a monastery: Will have joy and happiness.

Being seated in a monastery: Will have changes in affairs.

Conversing in a monastery: Will soon commit a sin.

A monastery being fully decorated: Will undergo trials for inheritance.

MONEY:

Possessing money: Great financial gains.

Handling money: Will be deceived.

Collecting money: Will have petty vexations.

Paying money: Prosperity awaits you.

Receiving money: Impending changes.

Finding money: Danger and business loss.

Losing money: Success.

Counting money: Happiness.

Assembling money: Will receive good news.

Stealing money: Long sickness.

Spending money: Will risk failure of plans.

Changing paper money: Difficulties are your own fault.

Changing gold money: Misfortune.

Changing silver money: Will receive a visit from friends.

Changing copper: Bad luck.

Changing nickel: Obstacles are ahead.

Handling foreign paper money: Financial losses.

Handling foreign gold money: Beneficial gains.

Handling stocks: Risk of failure.

Handling checks: Danger.

Of a money changer: Will receive unpleasant news.

MONK:

Of a monk: Family quarrels.

Several monks: Travel that will prove unpleasant.

Meeting a monk: Recovery from illness.

Meeting several monks: Will have pain and grief.

Wanting to become a monk: Must control your passions.

Being a monk: Will suffer loss.

Conversing with monks: Will soon commit a sin.

A monk being in the company of a woman: Frivolity.

MONKEY:

Of monkeys: You have deceitful friends.

Monkeys chattering: You will be flattered.

Monkeys climbing: Enemies will seek your ruin.

Feeding a monkey: Betrayal by a friend.

Monkeys being in a cage: Opposition in love.

Monkeys dancing: Good business in real estate.

Poor people dreaming of monkeys: Earnings and hope in love.

Rich people dreaming of monkeys: Troubles ahead and illness.

Children dreaming of monkeys: Success in coming years.

MONOCLE:

Wearing a monocle: Pleasant and happy future.

A man wearing a monocle: Must recognize own faults.

Others wearing a monocle: Treason and gossip.

MONSTER:
Of a monster: Good times are coming.
A monster in the sea: Expect misfortune.
A monster on dry land: Good luck.
A monster being killed: Death of an enemy.
Being pursued by a monster: Sorrow and misfortune will overwhelm you.

MONUMENT:
Of a monument: Success is coming your way.
Visiting a monument with others: Will be rewarded for your efforts.
The monument of a prominent person: Honor and great fame.
A monument being made to you: Death of an enemy.
Monuments in a cemetery: Discovery of lost valuables.
Others viewing a monument: Danger in love affairs.

MOON:
A full moon: Intense enjoyment of life.
The moon shining brightly: Good luck.
The moon being free of clouds: Success in love.
The moon being clouded over: Interruption in comforts of life.
A new moon: Will be very fortunate in business.
A blood-red moon: Indicates strife.
The reflection of the moon in water: Will fall in love with handsome man.
The eclipse of the moon: Expect reverses in affairs.
The moon falling from the sky: Loss of money.
The moon moving toward the sun: Happiness.
The moon at sunset: Death of a prominent person.
Being illuminated by the moon: Will receive big favors from a woman.
Going to the moon: Your desires are impossible.
A woman dreaming of the moon getting bright: Big profit.

A man dreaming of the moon getting bright: Honor and joy.
A woman dreaming of the moon becoming dark: Loss of money.
A man dreaming of the moon becoming dark: Unhappiness.
A woman dreaming of a dark moon: Illness of the mother, sister, or daughter.
A man dreaming of a dark moon: Illness of the brain or eyes.
A young woman dreaming of a dark moon: Will make a long trip.

MOONSHINE:
Of the moon shining: Happiness in wedded life.
Seeing the moonshine with a sweetheart: Insurmountable obstacles ahead.
Married people seeing moonshine together: Devoted family life.
Young unmarried people seeing the moonshine: Will soon be married.

MOOR:
Of moorlands: Prosperity.
Walking over moorlands alone: Joy and contentment.
Walking uphill in moorlands in company of others: Abundant means.
A very large moorland: Constant friendship.
A vessel moored: Misfortune in love affairs.
Mooring a vessel yourself: Happiness is assured.
Other people mooring a vessel: Good times are coming.

MOP:
Of a mop: Must be careful to avoid coming troubles.
Using a mop: Advancement within own position.
Buying a mop: Good luck to one for whom you care.
Throwing a mop away: Approaching money.
Others using a mop: Misfortune in love affairs.
Mopping own room: Will succeed in everything.

Mopping own apartment: You are trusted by people.

Mopping a cellar: Will undertake bad business.

Mopping the front of own house: Will have friends visit you.

Mopping up dirty things: You will leave your home.

MORNING:

Of a beautiful morning: Your fate is protected.

A cloudy morning: Big profit.

A rainy morning: Will have many advantages in life.

A foggy morning: Be confident in yourself.

Getting up early in the morning: Big success.

Seeing children in the morning: Good times are coming.

Seeing relatives in the morning: Death of an enemy.

Seeing friends in the morning: Dignity and distinction.

MORTGAGE:

Holding a mortgage: Will have plenty of money to pay all debts.

Others holding a mortgage: Misfortune in your business.

Giving a mortgage: Financial crisis in your affairs.

Paying a mortgage: Financial gains.

Others paying you a mortgage: Good times are coming.

MOSAIC:

Of mosaic work: Will have ups and downs.

Doing mosaic work: Will hear of the death of a relative.

Buying mosaic works: Will have small profit.

Having a mosaic floor in the home: Happiness.

MOSQUE:

Of a mosque: Ignorance keeps you from being a firm believer of your faith.

An Islamic mosque: Joy and profit.

The mosque of Omar at Jerusalem: Will come out well from present danger.

A Turkish mosque: Will have emotional sorrow.

A hidden mosque: Beware of ignorant people.

Worshiping in a mosque alone: Good luck is coming your way.

Worshiping in a mosque with others: Will have many faithful friends.

Worshiping in a mosque with family: Abundant means.

MOSS:

Of a moss plant: Someone is attracted to you.

Having moss: Will have a free life.

Seeing moss flowers: Take care of your correspondence.

Receiving moss flowers: Write guardedly, seal and post carefully.

MOTH:

Of moths: Rivals will attempt to harm you.

Moths being in the home: Be careful with your speech and actions.

Killing moths: Expect quarrels with your sweetheart.

Moths destroying things: Quarrels between wife and husband.

Moths eating clothes: Someone nearby is in trouble.

Throwing away moth-eaten clothes: Your help is not faithful.

Having moths in the house: Will have some slight trouble.

MOTHER:

Of own mother: Good luck.

Living with own mother: Security.

Talking with own mother: Good news.

Mother being dead: Danger to property and you personally.

Mother being in danger: High dignity in life.

Mother being healthy: A family gathering will take place.

Seeing own mother while you are faraway: Will return home soon.

Embracing own mother: Expect good fortune.

Hitting own mother: A catastrophe is ahead.

Mother being crazy: Your business holdings are in danger.

Killing your mother: Inevitable death in the family.

MOTHER-OF-PEARL:

Of mother-of-pearl: Happiest time lies in the future.

Buying mother-of-pearl: Will live a long life.

Receiving a gift of mother-of-pearl: Increase in the family.

Giving a gift of mother-of-pearl: You are surrounded by deceitful friends.

MOTORCAR:

Of a motorcar: Will receive important news.

Owning a motorcar: Will receive an important gift.

Driving a motorcar: Will have success in your business.

Escaping from the path of an oncoming motorcar: Avoid rivals.

Riding in a motorcar alone: Will have new surroundings.

Riding in a motorcar with a woman: Scandal will be connected with name.

A woman driving a car alone: Will have average success.

Driving a car at night: You are keeping secrets from friends.

Driving a car in the rain: Will hear from friends living abroad.

Driving a car with sweetheart: Weaknesses will be known.

Driving a car with wife: Will have a long life.

Driving a car with children: Happiness in the family.

Driving a car with relatives: Gossip is ahead of you.

Driving a car with friends: Will soon discover a secret.

Driving a car with your lover: Must control your passions.

Having a car accident: Approaching money.

MOUNTAIN:

Of a mountain: Delivery of a baby will be very painful.

A mountain being covered with snow: Will receive a big favor.

A mountain falling: Ruin of a prominent person.

Climbing to the top of a mountain: All will go well in own affairs.

Descending a mountain: Will have success of small importance.

A mountain climber: Will receive a visit from an unwelcome person.

A high mountain: Will struggle in your affairs.

A very high mountain: Big happiness.

A small mountain: Will undertake a short trip.

Seeing a fire on top of a mountain: A big catastrophe is ahead.

MOURN:

Being in mourning over parents: Family quarrels.

Being in mourning over relatives: Invitation to a dance.

Wife or husband being in mourning for each other: Emotional sorrow.

Wearing black mourning clothes: Misfortune will follow.

Lovers wearing black mourning clothes: Beware of misunderstandings.

MOUTH:

Of a mouth: Will become drunk.

Own mouth: You should guard your tongue.

A big mouth: A friend is worth more than money.

A very large mouth: Friendship and plenty of money.

A small mouth: Money to come.

A very small mouth: Great love.

An open mouth: Generosity.

A tightly closed mouth: Sickness.

Being unable to open the mouth: Peril of death.

A dirty mouth: Desperation.

An infected mouth: Public shame.

A mouth full of food: Treason by friends.

A mouth full of wine: Big pleasures to come.

Mouth of children: High honors.

Mouth of relatives: Unhappiness.

Mouth of friends: Misfortune will follow.

Mouth of enemies: Will live a long life.

Mouth of other people: Poverty.

Mouth of animals: Starvation.

MOVIE:

Of movies: Frivolous invitations.

Going to a movie alone: Be cautious in love affairs.

Going to a movie with wife: Loneliness and trouble.

Going to a movie with husband: A mystery will be solved.

Going to a movie with children: Will live in wealth.

Going to a movie with sweetheart: Great joy.

Going to a movie with friends: An enemy is seeking your ruin.

A beautiful movie: Change of surroundings.

An unpleasant movie: Will be guilty of foolish actions.

Performing in a movie: A change in life will come soon.

Someone you know performing: warning of troubles.

MOVING:

Of moving: Social activities of a happy nature.

Moving from one house to another: Discovery of lost valuables.

Moving from one apartment to another: Loneliness and trouble.

Moving from one store to another: Obstacles in business.

Moving furniture from one house to another: Change for the better.

Moving from one city to another: Happiness is assured.

Others moving: You are being deceived by best friends.

MOWING:

Of mowing: A false friend is nearby.

A man mowing his own lawn: success in business.

A woman mowing her own lawn: Happy life.

Others mowing their lawn: Postponement of success.

MUCUS:

Mucus from own nose: Will have unfriendly people nearby.

Mucus from children's nose: Good health.

Being unable to stop nose from running: Big earnings.

Mucus from other people's noses: Blessings in your affairs.

MUD:

Of mud: Will live a long life.

Mud being in the street: Advancement within own position.

Walking in the mud: Family disturbances.

Having mud on own clothes: Your reputation is being attacked.

Scraping mud off own clothes: Will escape the slander of enemies.

Others having mud on clothes: Good fortune awaits you.

MUDDLE:

Of things being in a muddle: Take no risks at all in business.

Making a muddle of things: Pleasure from a re-established friendship.

Own affairs being in a muddle: Watch your footing especially in high places.

Business being in a muddle: Business will take a turn for the worse.

Others being in a muddle: Triumph over enemies.

MUFF:

Owning a beautiful muff: Will have no money.

Wearing a muff: Promises a life free from continual changes.

Buying a muff: Unfaithfulness on the part of someone trusted.

Others wearing a muff: Be on guard against spiteful gossip.

MULBERRIES:

Of mulberries: Avoid rivals.

Eating mulberries: Will marry when very old.

Buying mulberries: Luck and prosperity.

Picking mulberries: Will live a long life.

Making mulberry jelly: Happiness is assured.

An unmarried woman eating mulberries: Will make a prosperous marriage.

An unmarried man eating mulberries: Will have a fortunate journey.

MULE:

Of a mule: Beware of sickness.

Being kicked by a mule: Dissappointment in love.

Owning a mule: Disappointment in your marriage.

Using a mule to pull a cart: Changes for the better.

A female mule: Business will increase.

MULTIPLY:

Multiplying figures: Don't trust acquaintances.

Others multiplying figures: You are being deceived.

Various things multiplying: Watch enemies closely.

Plants multiplying: Someone is endeavoring to destroy you.

MUMMY:

Of a mummy: A change in life will come soon.

Mummies well preserved: Be confident in yourself.

Seeing mummies in company of your sweetheart: Will soon get married.

People embalming mummies: Danger in love maiters.

MURDER:

Of a murderer: Triumph over enemies.

Murdering someone: Sorrow and failure.

Others committing a murder: Will live a long life.

Committing a murder: Disgrace through some dishonorable act.

A murderer being arrested: A change in life will come soon.

Being murdered: An enemy is attempting to injure you.

Seeing a murder committed: Sorrow because of the actions of others.

MUSCAT:

Of these European grapes: Suitable time to pursue courtship.

Buying muscat sweet wine: Are in the grip of deceitful friends.

Drinking muscat wine: Prompt engagement.

Having muscat wine: Riches and honors.

Offering muscat wine to others: Good times are coming.

MUSCLE:

Own muscle hurting: Important and very beneficial event to come.

Being unable to move arm muscles: Will have emotional sorrow.

Being unable to move leg muscles: Will suffer because of own foolishness.

Having a pain in the neck muscle: Misfortune in love affairs.

Children having sore muscles: Good times are coming.

MUSEUM:

Of a museum: Discovery of lost valuables.

Visiting a museum alone: Postponement of success.

Visiting a museum with a loved one: Worry will be smoothed away.

Visiting a museum with family: Will realize high ambitions.

MUSH:

Of this cooked cereal: Good times are ahead.

Cooking mush: Varying fortune.

Eating mush: Will enjoy your money.

Giving mush to children to eat: Abundant money.

MUSHROOMS:

Of mushrooms: Big advancement in all your affairs.

Many mushrooms: Luck and prosperity.

Eating mushrooms: Big distinction in life.

Business partners eating mushrooms: Be cautious in dealings with them.

Gathering mushrooms: Your ventures will be fortunate.

Digging only one mushroom: A corporation will be dissolved.

Digging many mushrooms from the earth: Long life.

MUSIC:

Hearing melodious music: Big pleasures in life.

Hearing pleasant music at a concert: Will receive some money.

Enjoying good music at a theater: Consolation of misfortune.

Hearing harsh and unpleasant music: Will be greatly disappointed.

Hearing jazz music: Will become very uncomfortable.

Hearing opera music and singing: Will hear very welcome news.

MUSIC BOX:

Of a music box: Avoid rivals.

Hearing a music box playing with a loved one: Frivolity.

Putting money in a music box: Danger in love matters.

A music box playing favorite song: Change of surroundings.

MUSIC HALL:

Of a music hall: All own affairs will prosper.

Attending a music hall alone: Pleasant news from an absent friend.

Going to a music hall with a loved one: Renewal of old friendships.

Going to a music hall with family: Will do a cunning and underhanded thing.

MUSICIAN:

Of musicians: Will become drunk.

Being a musician: Sudden changes in life.

Not being a musician: Will have a showdown with your lover.

Being a professional musician: Will move to another district.

Being a beginner musician: Will soon become engaged.

An unmarried person being a musician: Will fall in love and be engaged.

A young girl being a musician: Will have a proposal from a rich man.

MUSKET:

Of a musket: Will receive a passionate love letter.

Many soldiers carrying muskets: Honor and joy.

An empty musket: You have enemies within the family.

A loaded musket: Financial gains.

Firing a musket: Loss of profits.

Relatives firing a musket: Will be annoyed by relatives.

Others firing a musket: Big quarrels.

MUSSEL:

Of this type of shellfish: Luck and prosperity.

Gathering mussels: Will make big money.

Eating mussels: Hard work is ahead.

Cooking mussels: Failure of enemies.

Buying mussels at a fish market: Someone will make a proposal to you.

Buying mussels in cans: Will change to a better position.

Giving mussels to others: Will come out well from a present peril.

Receiving mussels as a gift: Joy without profit.

MUSTACHE:

Of a mustache: Will have disputes with a superior.

A big mustache: Increase in own fortune.

An ugly mustache: Will be publicly disgraced.

Short mustaches: Small disagreements.

A very small and thin mustache: Small money earnings.

A woman admiring a mustache: She should guard her virtue.

Having a mustache: Will be a betrayer of women.

MUSTARD:

Of mustard: Do not make hasty decisions.

Eating mustard: Will deeply repent for actions.

Relatives eating mustard: Danger through speaking too freely.

Friends eating mustard: Avoid repeating confidences.

Cooking with mustard: Warning of troubles.

Mustard in powder form: Bad luck will come soon.

Mustard being on the table: Will have arguments and disputes.

Buying mustard: Beware of friends.

MUTILATE:
Of mutilating something: Triumph over enemies.

Mutilating a part of own body: Good financial gains.

Having a leg mutilated: Avoid rivals.

Having an arm mutilated: You are being cheated by friends.

Having a hand mutilated: Recovery of money.

Having a foot mutilated: Recovery from an illness.

MUTINY:
Of a mutiny: Beware of untrue friends.

Watching a mutiny: Be cautious with business matters.

Taking part in a mutiny: You are unhappy with present position.

Being wounded in a mutiny: Infidelity.

Overcoming a mutiny: Advancement within own position.

Others taking part in a mutiny: Friends will cease to annoy you.

MUZZLE:
Putting a muzzle on a dog: Happiness in love affairs.

Putting a muzzle on other animals: Enemies are under control.

Putting on a respiratory muzzle: Will have a vigorous mind.

Others putting a respiratory mask on you: Recovery from an illness.

MYOPIA:
Of being nearsighted: You are being watched by one with evil intent.

Children being nearsighted: Good times are coming.

Other people having myopia: Friends will cheat you.

Getting glasses to cure myopia: Failure of enemies.

MYRTLE:
Of this European species of shrub: Gratification of desires.

Blossoms of the myrtle shrub: Will have pleasures that you desired.

Picking branches of myrtle: Luck and prosperity.

MYSTERY:
Of a mystery: Something will happen that will puzzle you.

A mystery being explained: Avoid rivals.

Hearing of a mystery: You have loyal friends.

Having mysterious friends: Will suffer because of own foolishness.

N

NAG:
Of nagging someone: Will receive pleasant news.

Being nagged by others: Circumstances will improve.

Being nagged by relatives: Loneliness and trouble.

Being nagged by children: Advancement within own position.

NAILS:
Of own fingernails: Will have a dispute.

Cutting own fingernails: Quarrels.

Others cutting your fingernails: Dishonor in the family.

A man dreaming of nails growing long: Prosperity in business.

A woman dreaming of nails growing long: Success in love.

Extra long fingernails of a woman: Big profit.

Having very short nails: Loss of money.

Breaking own fingernails: Misery and affliction.

People chewing fingernails: Will be shunned by higher class of people.

Fingernails of other people: Success in life.

Children's nails growing: You or someone dear to you will have an accident.

Of carpenter nails: Big losses.

Steel nails: Illness.

Copper nails: Sorrow.

Horseshoe nails: Will be worried by bad news.

Hammering nails: Divorce.

Selling nails: You will make money.

Buying nails: Your reputation is in dispute.

NAIVE:
Acting so: Good health and interesting friends.

NAKED:
A woman dreaming of being naked: Unhappiness.

A man dreaming of being naked: Public disgrace.

A beautiful naked woman: Good earnings.

A plain naked woman: High ambitions.

An ugly naked woman: Desires will not be granted.

A young beautiful girl being naked: Arrogance.

Wife being naked: Relatives are talking about you.

Many naked women: People have a high opinion of you.

Counting naked people: Will receive good news.

Men and women together who are naked: Dignity.

Naked people running: Loss of ambitions.

Sleeping with a naked person: Big commotion.

Sleeping with a naked woman away from home: Someone is doing you wrong.

Walking around the streets naked: Disappointment through friends and relatives.

Married people being naked: Plenty of wealth.

NAME:
Hearing own name called: Will receive good news.

Other people calling your full name: Will receive a visitor.

Being called by wrong name: Will be unfortunate in love affairs.

Calling sweetheart's name: Will be visited by one who cares for you.

Calling children's name: They will become prominent people.

NAPKIN:
Of napkins: Will be visited by socially prominent person.

Using a napkin to clean mouth: Will be respected by people.

Having embroidered napkins: Marriage will take place soon.

Receiving a gift of napkins: Family quarrels.

A child's napkin or bib: Healthy life.

NAPPING:
Dreaming one is: Good luck will follow.

NARCISSUS:
Of this flower: Will be fortunate if the flower is not kept at home.

Picking narcissus: Unexpected money.

Keeping narcissus indoors: Happiness is not certain.

Receiving a bouquet of narcissus: Will fall in love with a wealthy man.

Giving narcissus to others: Beware of bad influences.

NARCOTIC:
Of narcotics: Will keep your promises.

Being a narcotic addict: Will make good financial gains.

Others who are narcotic addicts: Will make good business speculations.

NARGHILE:
Smoking this Oriental water pipe: Abundance.

Others smoking a narghile: Realization of desired love affairs.

Of seeing the tobacco through the water: Many women will pursue you.

NARROW:

Of a narrow path: An insignificant event will happen.

Struggling along a narrow path: With extreme effort will achieve success.

Others struggling along a narrow path: Will obtain what you dared not hope for.

Enemies on a narrow path: Will receive an honorable position.

NATURE:

Of nature: Coming fortune.

Being good-natured: Will be relieved of pain.

Being bad-natured: Gossip.

Others who are good-natured: Important events will soon transpire.

Relatives who are bad-natured: Will take a trip.

Mate being good-natured: Will have a long life.

Mate being bad-natured: People nearby are trying to destroy happiness.

NAVAL BATTLE:

Of a naval battle: Will receive a promotion.

Being in a naval battle: Will be double-crossed in love.

Winning a naval battle: Will soon be married.

Losing a naval battle: A great service will be rendered by a relative.

People being killed in a naval battle: Happy family life.

Falling in the water during a naval battle: Long life.

NAVEL:

Painful or swollen: Will receive unpleasant news regarding father or mother. If neither parent is living, sadness due to waste of an inheritance.

NAVIGATE:

Navigating a small vessel: You have changeable humor.

Navigating a large vessel: Will be shunned by women.

Being a navigator: Abundant means.

A man dreaming of a vessel run by steam: Good news coming unexpectedly.

A woman dreaming of a vessel run by steam: Unfavorable news.

Being aboard a navigated vessel: Joy and security.

NEATNESS:

Putting everything in order: You must discipline your temper in order to rise in work or society.

NAVY:

Of navy personnel: Loss of business.

Being in the navy: Sickness.

Being released from the navy: Honor.

A married man dreaming of being in the navy: His wife is cheating on him.

A wife dreaming of husband being in the navy: He commits adultery.

Boys being in the navy: Financial gains.

High-ranking navy officers: Troubles in love.

Noncommissioned navy personnel: Will obtain your goal.

Enlisted navy personnel: Business ruin.

Friends being in the navy: Sickness.

Enemies being in the navy: Loss of fortune.

NECK:

Of own neck: False friends surround you.

The neck of others: You are too deeply in love.

Neck of children: Will be proud of their intelligence.

An unusually large neck: Honor.

An unusually long neck: Riches.

A small neck: Will meet with opposition.

A fat neck: Will receive plenty of money.

A very flabby neck: Will be in an accident.

Neck having a double chin: Good position in society.

Seeing three heads on one neck: Abundant money.

Being strangled at the neck: You are a "yes" person.
Being tied up by the neck: Will be the slave of a woman.
Having a tumor on the neck: Illness to come.
Neck being bandaged: Will make new friends.
Neck being infected: Will receive news of the death of a friend.
Neck aching: Money coming to you soon.
Injuring own neck: Will have good love affairs.

NECKLACE:
Of a beautiful necklace: Realization of desired love.
Wearing a necklace around the neck: Abundant means.
Someone putting a necklace on you: Long married life.
Losing a necklace: Will receive a visitor.
Receiving a gift of a necklace: Will possess the one you love.
Husband giving a necklace to his wife: Will have a luxurious home.
Giving a necklace to sweetheart: Will make her a slave.
A necklace for children: You are a virtuous person.

NECKTIE:
Difficulty putting it on: An argument with a lover or a relationship that should be broken off.
Numerous: Some freedom will soon be lost.

NECTAR:
Drinking: You will accumulate honor and wealth, possibly through marriage.

NECTARINES:
Of nectarines growing: Good health.
Eating nectarines: A hypocritical woman will cause a calamity for you.
Picking nectarines: Coming prosperity in love.
Others eating nectarines: Hard work awaits.

NEED:
Being in need of money: Poverty.
Being in need of a doctor: Riches.
Being in need of a nurse. Good business.
Being in need of a maid: Will encounter opposition.
Being in need of love: A corporation will be dissolved.
Being in need of a friend: Happiness.
Others needing you: Good business.

NEEDLE:
Of needles: Persecution in love.
Having needles: Intrigue.
A sewing needle: You love too deeply.
A darning needle: You will fall in love.
Knitting needles: You are too egotistic.
Threading a needle: Family burdens.
Searching for a needle: You worry without cause.
Finding a needle: You have appreciative friends.
Losing a needle: Disappointment in love.
Needles made of steel: Long life.
Pricking yourself with a needle: You are overly affectionate.

NEEDLEWORK:
Of needlework: Treachery.
Doing needlework: Should distrust one that you now trust.
Others doing needlework for you: Inheritance.
Young girls doing needlework: Loss of friends or relatives.
Receiving a gift of needlework: Will take a long trip.
Giving a gift of needlework: High hopes.

NEGATIVE:
Of something negative: Big dissolution.
Photographic negatives. You have the ability to see and avert danger.
Developing negatives: Disappointment in married life.
Printing from a negative: Are surrounded by people who adore you.
Buying negatives: Loss of money.
Burning negatives: Beware of drinking too much.

NEIGH:
Hearing a horse neigh: Good luck to one for whom you care.
Hearing several horses neighing at once: Big joy.
Hearing a donkey neigh: Disgrace for you.

NEIGHBOR:
Of a neighbor: Misfortune in business.
Own neighbors: Misfortune in love.
Meeting a neighbor: Will have unwelcome guests.
Visiting with neighbors: Family quarrels.
Socializing with neighbors: Will be embarrassed.
Being very friendly with neighbors: Loss of money.

NEPHEW:
Of own nephew: Long life.
Many nephews: Will have good health.
Having disputes with nephews: Business will come to an end.
Liking your nephews: Profit.
Disliking a nephew: Good results in own affairs.
A nephew being killed: Embarrassment in business.
A nephew being naked: Will have good luck in love.

NERVOUS:
Being nervous: Good luck.
Others being nervous: You have a faithful friend.
Having a serious nervous condition: Will discover a treasure.
Relatives being in a nervous condition: Warning of troubles.

NEST:
Of a nest: Wealth will increase.
A full nest: Fortune.
An empty nest: Termination of business.
Finding a nest: Approaching wedding.
Finding a nest with broken eggs: Prosperity.
Finding a nest with dead babies: Honor.
The nest of a bird: Domestic happiness.

A nest with only one bird in it: Profit.
A snake's nest: Dishonor.
A cricket's nest: Fortune.
A pigeon's nest: You have bad humor.
Only one pigeon in a nest: Pleasant surprise.
A scorpion's nest: Big dissatisfaction.
A crocodile's nest: Gossip by other people.

NET:
Of a net: Love affair will go on the rocks.
Someone using a net: Will fall in love soon.
Using a net: Success in business.
A woman dreaming of using a hair net: Marriage will last forever.
Catching something in a net: Will receive a surprise.
Catching a woman in a net: Plenty of money.
Catching fish in a net: Change of temperature and much rain.
Catching birds in a net: Big worries ahead.

NET BALL:
Of the game being played: You will become upset.
A man dreaming of playing net ball: Inconsistency in love.
A woman dreaming of playing net ball: Divorce.
Others playing net ball: Fortune will be delayed.
A net ball getting lost: Don't expect letters from those you love.
Children playing net ball: Will receive good news.

NETTLES:
Walking among nettles without being stung: Happiness.
Being stung by nettles: Will be discontented.
Others being stung: Unhappiness.

NEW:
Having new things: Joy.
Having new clothes, hats, or shoes: Big profit.
Other people with new clothes: Changes in your condition.

Receiving something new: Good events in near future.

Giving new things to others: Will be angry over bad news received.

NEWS:

Hearing good news: Good fortune and many friends.

Hearing bad news: Satisfaction.

Giving good news: Great curiosity.

Giving bad news: Will learn of the loss of a relative.

Hearing good news from children: Honor in life.

Hearing bad news from children: Must refrain from anger.

NEWSPAPER:

Reading a newspaper: Death is nearby.

Others reading a newspaper to you: They are telling you untruths.

A daily newspaper: Common gossip.

A weekly newspaper: Advancement in business.

A Sunday newspaper: Will have a short life.

Buying a newspaper: Will receive a very great love.

Selling a newspaper: Friends are deceiving you.

Tearing a newspaper: Poverty.

Throwing a newspaper away: Dishonor.

NEW YEAR:

Of the new year: An improvement in circumstances is at hand.

Beginning a new year with friends: Be careful of an unscrupulous rival.

Beginning an even-numbered year: Will have very little money.

Beginning an odd-numbered year: Will inherit plenty of money.

Being drunk at a New Year's party: Love affairs will improve.

Proposing on New Year's Eve: Marriage will last forever.

Getting married on New Year's Eve: Marriage will not last long.

A boy being born on New Year's Eve: Will become a prominent person.

A girl being born on New Year's Eve: Will marry a wealthy person.

Committing adultery on New Year's Eve: Imminent separation.

NIB:

Breaking the point of a pen: An enemy is seeking your ruin.

Repairing a nib: Change in surroundings.

Buying a new nib: Advancement in children's condition.

NIBBLE:

Of nibbling: Be careful of what you write and sign.

Nibbling in a public place: Be careful in whom you confide.

Nibbling in a friend's home: Are surrounded by deceitful people.

Others nibbling: Beware of enemies.

NICE:

Of something nice: Sure profit.

Being nice: Momentary pleasure.

People being nice to you: Happiness.

Having nice things given to you: Unhappiness.

Having nice children: Joy.

Many nice children: You will become pregnant.

People being too nice and using flattery: Beware of deceitful people.

NICKNAME:

Having a nickname: Will make money from your work.

Giving a nickname: Will receive a present.

Giving others a nickname: Contentment.

Nicknaming your children: Family will be increased.

NIECE:

Of a niece: Will have a long life.

Several nieces: Good health.

Having a beautiful niece: Will have difficulties and worries.

A man flirting with a niece: Danger of death.

Dating a niece: You are wasting your time.

Marrying a niece: Joy.

A niece being killed: Unhappiness.

A niece getting married: You are cheating in love affairs.

NIGHT:
Of the nighttime: Misfortune.
Being in the dark: Will hear of engagement of a friend.
Friends on a dark night: Will attend a funeral.
Children on a dark night: Big family satisfaction.
Enemies on a dark night: Embarrassment.
Entering a dark place at night: Will win at gambling.
House being in the dark at night: Fortune is ahead.

NIGHT BIRDS:
Of night birds: Prosperity.
Hearing night birds singing: Good love relationship.
Being scared by a night bird: Will receive money.
Killing a night bird: Joy.
Many night birds: Disgrace.

NIGHTCAP:
Serving a nightcap to a loved one: You will expect a good night kiss.
Lingering over a nightcap: You are madly in love.
Caught having nightcap at someone else's home: Beware of jealousy.
Having a nightcap with many people: Good fortune is ahead.

NIGHTINGALE:
Of a nightingale: Will be jilted by your lover.
Listening to nightingales singing at night: Good times are coming.
Many nightingales singing together: Restored health to an invalid.

NIGHTMARE:
Having a nightmare: Treachery from one you trust.
Having a nightmare including other people: Abundant means.
Having a nightmare including children: Wealth.

NIGHTSHADE:
Of this narcotic herb: Will have emotional sorrow.
Eating the fruit of this deadly plant: New interests and surroundings.
This narcotic herb being made into belladonna ointment: Approaching money.

NIGHT WALK:
Of walking at night: Trouble.
Relatives walking at night: Loss of money.
Children walking at night: Misfortune.
Husband or wife walking at night: Mates distrust each other.
Friends walking at night: Will receive news from faraway.
Enemies walking at night: Disaster is ahead.

NINEPINS:
Of this bowling game: A rival will take sweetheart's affection.
Playing ninepins: Your affairs are unsettled.
Others playing ninepins: Will soon experience many ups and downs.
Sweetheart playing ninepins: Will have disappointments in love.

NOBILITY:
Belonging to a family of nobility: Obstacles in business.
Being a nobleman or woman: Sickness.
Ancestors being among nobility: Fortune and honor.
Being appointed duke or earl: Poverty.
Having titles conferred on family members: Good news.
A young girl dreaming of lord in love with her: Will marry a poor person.
Having a title through inheritance: Possibility of losing fortune.
Other people of nobility: Few financial gains from work.

NODDING:
Of nodding: Internal disturbances.
A young girl dreaming of nodding in church: Will marry a young husband.
A man dreaming of nodding in

church: Will marry the minister's daughter.

A widow dreaming of nodding in church: Will marry a rich man.

A widower dreaming of nodding in church: Will marry a religious girl.

NOISE:

Hearing noises: People are gossiping about you.

Hearing a loud noise: Quarrels among friends.

Hearing a loud noise in the street: Defeat in your plans.

Hearing children making noise: Will receive letter with good news.

Visitors making a noise: Success in your affairs.

NOODLES:

Of noodles: Will be visited by imposing people.

Making noodles: Infidelity.

Buying noodles: Will enjoy pleasures.

Eating noodles: Will cause damages to enemies.

Cooking noodles: Will receive unexpected news.

NOON:

Of noontime: Control yourself in greediness for food.

Dreaming of noon at any other time: Beware of catching pneumonia.

Having a noon meeting with others: Success in own affairs.

Eating a noon meal: Will be sure of taking a trip.

NOOSE:

Of a noose: Obstacles and competition.

Having a noose: Use moderation.

Being hanged in a noose: Persecution.

Others being hanged in a noose: Commendation for your actions.

NORTH:

Of the northern part of the world: A journey is ahead of you.

Traveling northward: Inheritance.

Birds or planes flying north: Discovery of a treasure.

House facing north: Will receive plenty of money.

Being in northern places: Struggles will end with success.

NORTH AMERICA:

Being in North America: Will be involved in a scandal.

Going to North America from abroad: Poor success in business.

Going abroad from North America: Social events.

Being deported from North America: Will meet new friends.

Being deported to North America: Advancement within own position.

NOSE:

Of own nose: Poverty.

Having a beautiful nose: Good character and self-confidence.

Having a small nose: Your life will be a failure.

Having a big nose: Be careful with investments and speculation.

Having nose cut off: Gossip by friends.

Having nose frozen: Adultery.

Not having a nose at all: Big friendships.

Having stuffed-up nose: Beware of wrong being done to you.

Having a nose bleed: Sure sign of disaster.

Hurting your nose: Beware of treachery.

Other people with big nose: Avoid lending money.

The nose of a beautiful woman: Increase in the family.

The nose of a beautiful young girl: Will have many friends.

A curved nose: Infidelity of a woman.

An ugly nose: Will become rich.

A long nose: People will hate you.

An unusually large nose: Plenty of money.

Nose of children: Friendships.

Nose of friends: Adultery.

Nose of enemies: Beware of danger caused by enemies.

Noses of many people: Discord within the family.

NOSEBLEED:

Of having a nosebleed: Will be disillusioned.

Children having a nosebleed: Take good care of yourself.

Relatives having a nosebleed: Will require financial assistance.

Friend's nose bleeding: Will receive a gift from someone.

Enemy's nose bleeding: Will go to jail.

NOSEGAY:

Of a nosegay of flowers: Happiness is assured.

Picking flowers for a nosegay: Hopes will be short-lived as the blossoms.

Being given a nosegay of flowers: Will incur debts.

NOTARY:

Of a notary: Wedding of a friend.

Going to a notary to get papers notarized: You have curious friends.

Taking others with you to a notary: Changes in your life.

Being a notary: Good earnings.

Receiving the advice of a notary: Embarrassment in your business.

Son becoming a notary: Family satisfaction.

NOTION DEPARTMENT:

A woman going to a notion department: Will soon be married.

Buying items at a notion department: Loss of friends.

Working at a notion counter: Will have a hard life ahead.

Others buying items at a notion department: Loss of money.

NOVEL:

Reading a novel: Will hear of the wedding of a relative.

Writing a novel: Unhappiness.

Printing a novel: Be careful of business affairs.

Buying a novel: Refrain from speculation in the stock market.

NOVEMBER:

Of the month of November during that month: Will have happiness.

Of November during other months: Money will come easily in life.

Being born in November: Will have financial gains.

Children being born in November: Will have high position in science world.

NUGGET:

Of a nugget of precious metals: Riches and honor.

Having several nuggets of different metals: Will receive money very soon.

Having nuggets of gold: Abundant means and good luck.

NUISANCE:

Being a nuisance to others: Will receive considerable fortune.

A friend being a nuisance: Will receive unbelievable news.

Relatives being a nuisance: Unhappiness in love.

Creditors being a nuisance: Exercise moderation in desires.

Enemies being a nuisance: Complete ruin in business.

Children being a nuisance: You will be deceived.

NUMB:

Feeling numb: Good results in your affairs.

Legs being numb: Big happiness.

Arms being numb: Big success.

Right hand being numb: Will receive the visit of a friend.

Left hand being numb: Will receive the visit of an undesirable person.

Children's body being numb: Plenty of money.

NUMBERS:

Of numbers in general: Dignity.

Counting numbers: Will receive good news.

Counting number of people: Will be in command of your affairs.

Counting number of people present: Satisfaction of your ambitions.

Counting without finding the correct number: Will be deceived.

Others counting the number of people: Big love satisfaction.

Remembering the number dreamed: Will win if you gamble just a little.

Not remembering the number dreamed: Social events.

Number 1: Ambition and passion.

Number 2: Final end to a romance.

Number 3: Will be fascinated with religion.

Number 4: Will have great power and strength.

Number 5: Happiness in married life.

Number 6: Perfection in work.

Number 7: Will be efficient and active during life.

Number 8: Complete conservation of property.

Number 9: Affliction and uneasiness.

Number 10: Happiness in the near future.

Number 11: Will struggle with a litigation.

Number 12: Will have the best of everything.

Number 13: Will treat things with contempt.

Number 14: Will incur loss because of other people.

Number 15: Will have a merciful disposition.

Number 16: Happiness and love.

Number 17: Dishonor and shame.

Number 18: Will become accustomed to fatigue.

Number 19: Unhappiness.

Number 20: Will be severe and strict.

Number 21: Everything will work out as planned.

Number 22: Will discover the secret of a scientific mystery.

Number 23: Revenge.

Number 24: Will receive rudimentary doctrine.

Number 25: Birth of an intelligent child.

Number 26: Business will be very beneficial.

Number 27: Will be firm and have a good mind.

Number 28: Will receive love and affection.

Number 29: Will attend a wedding.

Number 30: Will become a celebrity.

Number 31: You have active qualities of power.

Number 32: Pure in design and expression.

Number 33: If a man, will be honest; if a woman, will have a miscarriage.

Number 34: Love for glory.

Number 35: Harmony in the family and good health.

Number 36: A genius will be born.

Number 37: Affection between loved people.

Number 38: Will have an excessive desire for gain.

Number 39: You are envious of other people.

Number 40: Marriage reception.

Number 41: Deprivation of good name.

Number 42: Short unfortunate trip.

Number 43: Will attend a church service.

Number 44: Will become an influential person.

Number 45: Loss of virginity.

Number 46: Will have big productive powers.

Number 47: Long and happy life.

Number 48: Will go to court to receive a judgment.

Number 49: Will receive affection from a person of the opposite sex.

Number 50: Will forgive each other.

Number 60: Will become a widow.

Number 70: Will be introduced to a prominent person.

Number 71: Worship of nature.

Number 75: Change in the temperature of the world.

Number 77: Will receive a favor from a friend.

Number 80: Will recover from an illness.

Number 81: Will soon become a dope addict.

Number 90: Will become blind in the near future.

Number 100: Will receive a Divine favor.

Number 120: Will get a government position.

Number 121: Will be praised by the community.

Number 200: Danger will come through hesitation.

Number 215: Calamity is near.

Number 300: Will become a philosopher.

Number 313: Blessings will soon come.

Number 350: What you hoped for will come soon.

Number 360: Change of residence.

Number 365: The stars are in your favor.

Number 400: Will undertake a long trip.

Number 490: Will hear a sermon by a priest.

Number 500: Will win an election.

Number 600: Will do everything perfect.

Number 666: Enemies are laying a plot for you.

Number 700: Will have strength and power.

Number 800: Will be the head of a state.

Number 900: Hunger is very near.

Number 1000: Will receive clemency.

Number 1095: Will be depressed because of loneliness.

Number 1360: Will be vexed.

Number 1390: Will soon be persecuted.

NUN:

Of a nun: Infidelity in love.

Many nuns: You are a helpful person.

Nuns singing: You have high intelligence.

A nun with an abbott: Will be very smart.

Being helped by nuns: Will receive money.

A nun helping sick people: Contentment.

A school nun: Great tranquillity.

A nun tending children: Jealous people are around you.

A nun leaving your home: You have many enemies.

A nun living in your home: Good fortune.

Several nuns with your friends: Will attend a funeral.

Nuns with your enemies: Peril of death.

A woman praying with a nun: Loss of husband.

Nuns caring for children: Disagreement between lovers.

NURSE:

Of a nurse: Will have a big fight.

Being a wet nurse and feeding a child: Will receive unpleasant news.

Nurses in a hospital: Joy and contentment.

Nurses in a home: Financial damages.

Needing the help of a nurse: Will be pregnant.

A nurse with a doctor: Misery.

Hiring a nurse: Good future.

A woman dreaming of being a nurse: Will gain high position by sacrifice.

NURSERY:

Of a nursery: Will have many children.

Being in a nursery: Things will not run smoothly.

Babies being in a nursery: Disturbed love.

Bringing a baby home from a nursery: Will live a long life.

NURSING:

Of nursing: High honor.

Nursing husband or wife: Constant love.

Nursing children: Will receive good news.

Nursing parents: Peril of death.

Nursing relatives: Will receive an inheritance.

Nursing someone back to health: Will be surprised by a friend.

Others nursing you: Big fortune.

NUT:

Of nuts: Difficulties.

Gathering nuts: Success in love affairs.

Eating nuts: Big obstacles are ahead.

Eating nuts with bread: Success in life.

Eating nuts without skin: Beginning of a new love affair.
Eating nuts as a dessert: Important wish will be granted.
Cracking nuts: Success in business.
A nut tree: Will have good health.
Walnuts: Will receive a gift.
Pecans and other similar nuts: Riches.
Several kinds of nut trees without fruit: Satisfaction in life.
Hiding nuts: Discovery of a treasure.

NUTCRACKER:
Of nutcrackers: Family arguments.
Using a nutcracker: Will have unhappy days.
Holding nutcrackers in your hands: Reflect well on own actions.
Pinching hands with a nutcracker: Happiness in love affairs.

NUTMEG:
Of several cans of different nutmeg: Changes in own affairs.
Buying nutmeg: Changes in business will lead to overland travel.
Using nutmeg: Will receive an unexpected visitor.
Others using nutmeg: Danger in love affairs.

NUTRITION:
Receiving nutrition: Unhappiness.
Giving children nutrition: Dignity and ambition.
Giving nutrition to others: Small worries.

Giving nutrition to animals: Fortune and riches.

NUTSHELL:
Of nutshells: Will have plenty of money.
Cracking nutshells: Happy marriage.
Stepping on nutshells: Will receive a large inheritance.
Throwing away nutshells: Good luck and prosperity.

NUT TREE:
Of a nut tree: Riches.
Being up in a nut tree: Dignity and good news.
Being in the shade of a nut tree: Worries caused by an important friend.
Being asleep under a nut tree: Happiness.
Having a picnic with family under a nut tree: Much satisfaction in life.
Friends being under a nut tree: Sickness.
Being with a sweetheart under a nut tree: Failure in love affairs.

NYMPH:
Of a naked nymph: Will fall in love very soon.
A beautiful nymph in a veil: Will live a very long life.
A nymph in the clouds: Peril of death.
Several people admiring a nymph: Termination of business.

O

OAK TREE:
Of an oak tree: Money and long life.
Climbing an oak tree: Misfortune for a relative.
Resting under a wide-spreading oak tree: Long happy life and much wealth.
A dead oak tree: Death of a close friend.
Many beautiful oak trees: Immediate prospects.

Healthy young oak trees: Will have financial gains in future years.
A withered oak tree: Business loss.
Leaves having fallen from an oak tree: Loss of love.
An oak tree being cut down: You are deceived.
An oak tree lying in your path: Death of an enemy.

OAR:
Of an oar: Frivolity.

Handling oars: Disappointment in love.

Losing an oar: Failure of own plans.

A broken oar: Interrupted pleasure.

Rowing in a small boat: Good business transactions.

Rowing in a big boat: Financial gains.

Rowing alone: Will have a vigorous mind.

Rowing with others: Expect to face difficulties.

Children rowing: Success in life.

Others rowing: An enemy is seeking your ruin.

Sailors rowing: Danger in love matters.

Enemies rowing: Warning of troubles.

OASIS:

Of an oasis: Will come out well from a present danger.

Finding an oasis when wandering in a desert: You can rely on a friend.

Being with others in an oasis: Misfortune in love affairs.

OAT:

Of oats: Poverty.

Growing oats: Success in business.

Green unripened oats: Be careful in business.

Harvesting oats: Financial gains.

Selling oats: Be cautious in all dealings.

OATH:

Of taking an oath: A good position will be yours.

Others taking an oath: Will receive bad news from a friend.

Relatives taking an oath: Death of a relative.

Business people taking an oath: Change of surroundings.

Enemies taking an oath: Will suffer humiliation.

Husband or wife taking a marriage oath: Prosperity.

Husband and wife taking an oath after their marriage: Foretells divorce.

OATMEAL:

Of oatmeal: Good times are coming.

Cooking oatmeal: Varying fortune.

Eating oatmeal: Will enjoy a well earned fortune.

Children eating oatmeal: Abundant means.

OBEDIENT:

Being obedient: Will have a good future.

Being obedient to others: Will have a commonplace career.

Others being obedient to you: Will command riches and exert wide influence.

Children being obedient: Family happiness.

Own help being obedient: Will make big gains in business.

A woman being obedient: Brighter days are in store.

A young woman being obedient: An admirer is seriously attracted to you.

OBELISK:

Of this four-sided pillar: Will move to better surroundings.

Several obelisks: Wealth.

Being on top of an obelisk: Will make good purchases.

Viewing an obelisk with a loved one: Joy without profit.

OBITUARY:

Receiving obituary notice of a relative's death: Approaching money.

Receiving obituary notice of a friend's death: Good news from faraway.

Reading obituary notice of someone you know: News of a marriage.

Reading obituary notice of an enemy: Danger in love affairs.

OBJECT:

A visible object: Will have mastery over many matters.

A tangible object: Will soon experience many ups and downs.

An object arousing pleasure: Change to better surroundings.

An object arousing pity: Hard work awaits.

OBLIGATION:

Of being under obligation: Warning of troubles.

Being under obligation to a friend: Hard work awaits.

A friend being under obligation to you: Riches.

Others being under obligation to you: You are being deceived.

Relatives being under obligation to you: Financial losses.

Being under obligation to relatives: Dignity and distinction.

OBLIQUE:

Of an oblique: Warning of troubles.

Being under an oblique: A rival will take affection of sweetheart.

OBSCURE:

Of something not clearly expressed: Danger in love matters.

Of something obscured: Difficulties are in store for you.

Of something undefined: Warning about incurring debts.

OBSERVATORY:

Of an observatory: Beware of unreliable friends.

Being in an observatory: A solitary life will be your fate.

Being with friends in an observatory: Advisable to reject these friends.

OBSTINATE:

Being obstinate: Will be degraded.

Others being obstinate: Will have a quiet conscience.

Children being obstinate: Unexpected fortune.

Friends being obstinate: Will do bad business.

OCCUPATION:

Having an occupation: Good times are coming.

Not having an occupation: Frivolity.

Liking your occupation: Will live a long life.

Detesting your occupation: Good fortune in every way.

Making good earnings at occupation: Family quarrels.

Making small earnings at occupation: Beware of jealous friends.

OCEAN:

Of the ocean: Prosperity.

A calm ocean: Stormy wedded life.

A rough ocean: Will have few difficulties.

Having ocean waves lashing a boat: Business disaster.

Being in a vessel on the open, smooth ocean: Fortunate business.

Being in a vessel on the open rough ocean: Will have big troubles.

Being in a vessel that sinks in the ocean: Termination of love affairs.

OCTOBER:

Of the month of October during this month: Profit and success.

Of October during other months: Will have unhappiness.

Having a dream during October: Will enjoy the fruits of hard work.

Being born in October: Prosperity and abundance.

Children being born in October: Will have a high position at a university.

OCULIST:

Of an oculist: Will discover a secret.

Being an oculist: A mystery will be solved.

Going to an oculist for an examination: Fortune is ahead.

Buying glasses from an oculist: Dignity and distinction.

Going with others to an oculist: Distrust your friends.

Taking children to an oculist: Prosperity.

Meeting friends at an oculist: You are being watched.

ODOR:

Of fragrant odors: Contentment.

Unpleasant odors: Vexation.

Pleasing odors: You will excel in everything.

Offensive odors: Unreliable servants are in your employ.

Very strong odors: Prostitution.

Smelling odor on hands: Will suffer because of own foolishness.

Smelling odor of the body: Will be guilty of foolish actions.

Smelling the odor of feet: Beware of going to prison.

Smelling bad odors in a house: Hard work awaits.

Smelling bad odors in a public room: A change for the better is needed.

OFFENSE:

Receiving an offense: Good times are coming.

Committing a public offense: An enemy is seeking your ruin.

Someone offending a woman: Family quarrels.

A woman being offended by a man: Troubles are ahead.

A man being offended by another man: A mystery will be solved.

Giving cause for an offense: Triumph over enemies.

Offending a public person: Will suffer humiliation.

Being offended by relatives: Are confronted with insurmountable obstacles.

OFFER:

Receiving an offer: Expect an improvement in your position.

Someone making a good offer to you: You will be cheated.

Making an offer for services: You must work hard.

Making an offer to the church: Will meet with prominent personalities.

Making an offer to a woman: Big friendships will develop.

Making an offer to a man: Will have emotional sorrow.

Making an offer to a public institution: Approaching money.

OFFICE:

Having an office: Honesty will bring you prosperity.

Losing your office: Joy without profit.

A landlord putting you out of your office: Troubles in love affairs.

Getting a new office appointment: Unhappiness in married life.

Working in an office: Guard your health.

Opening an office: You will be insulted.

Having a job in the office of the press: Unfavorable news.

Having a collecting agency office: Financial disaster.

Holding a government office: Will suffer humiliation.

OFFICER:

Of an officer: Good business transactions.

Being an officer: Triumph over all affairs.

Being among other officers: Will obtain success in your affairs.

Being appointed an officer: Dignity and distinction.

Being dismissed as an officer: Warning of troubles.

OGRE:

Of this giant monster: Beware of difficulties and obstacles.

Killing an ogre: You have jealous friends.

An ogre eating human beings: Obstacles between you and your sweetheart.

OIL:

Of oil: Will have an abundant harvest.

Having dealings in oil: Fortune.

Digging for an oil well: Profit.

Refining oil: Control your business affairs.

Selling oil: Death of an enemy.

Buying oil: You are being deceived.

Using olive oil: Big joy.

Using linseed oil: Will make money.

Taking castor oil: Happiness.

Taking cod liver oil: Unexpected good business.

Spilling oil: Loss of business.

Frying food in oil: Big advantages.

Storing olive oil: Pleasant events to happen soon.

Artists and painters using oils: Large earnings.

Contractors using oil for business: Quarrels with partners.

OILCLOTH:

Of oilcloth: Treachery will cause suffering.

Using oilcloth: Good fortune.

Covering furniture with oilcloth: Will receive bad news.

Using an oilcloth tablecloth: Will receive very sad news.

Buying oilcloth: Sickness.

OINTMENT:
Of ointment: Will be offended.

Using ointment: Slight illness to come.

Using ointment on a sore: Will have good health.

Using ointment on other people: Will be abandoned by friends.

Buying ointment: Good health.

OLD:
Being old: You are being foolish.

Becoming old: Will achieve fame.

Being very old: Will have bad relationship with a young woman.

Having dealings with old people: Be prudent.

OLD-FASHIONED:
Of being old-fashioned: Death of a friend.

Having old-fashioned ideas: Short-lived happiness.

Wearing old-fashioned clothes: Dissension in home life.

Dealing with old-fashioned people: Business will prosper.

OLD MAID:
Of an old maid: You are prone to having a bad temper.

Many old maids together: Will enjoy happy events.

Being an old maid: Big sorrow.

Remaining an old maid: Will be offended by a proposition.

OLD MAN:
Of an old man: Will have troubles.

Being an old man: Honor and distinction.

Being a rich old man: Good health.

An old man dreaming of courting an old woman: Good business enterprises.

OLD SWEETHEART:
Thinking of an old sweetheart: Happily wedded life.

Embracing an old sweetheart: Will receive an unexpected gift.

Making up with an old sweetheart: Will have a prominent position.

Marrying an old sweetheart: Family quarrels.

OLD WOMAN:
Of old women: Big sorrow.

A very old woman: Unhappiness in the distant future.

Being an old woman: Freedom from troubles.

Old women being at a party: Good family reputation.

Belonging to an old woman's club: Jealousy of friends.

An old woman dreaming of being courted by old man: Her love is faithful.

OLIVES:
Of an olive tree: Great happiness.

Planting an olive tree: Imminent marriage.

A young man dreaming of planting an olive tree: Will have many children.

A married woman dreaming of planting an olive tree: Joy and prosperity.

A man dreaming of planting an olive tree: Abundance.

Picking a branch from an olive tree: Happiness and prosperity.

Smelling the scent of an olive branch: Success in enterprises.

A woman smelling the branch of an olive tree: Will have many children.

A young girl smelling an olive branch: Will soon get married.

A woman dreaming of olives: Will have many daughters.

A young girl dreaming of olives: Immediate engagement and marriage.

A man dreaming of olives: Good results in business affairs.

Eating olives: Happiness in domestic life.

Picking olives from the tree: Will make money.

Picking olives from the ground: Hard work ahead of you.

Putting olives in a bottle: Will have a long life.

Taking olives out of a bottle: Social pleasures.

OMNIBUS:

Of an omnibus: Will be helped by friends.

Riding alone in an omnibus: Will make fantastic gains.

Many people riding the same omnibus: Obstacles in your path to fortune.

Riding an omnibus with wife or relative: Sickness in the family.

Riding an omnibus with children: Will have a virtuous family.

Enemies taking an omnibus: An accident will occur.

ONION:

Of onions: Disputes.

Pulling onions out of the ground: Revelation of a secret.

Eating onions: Quarrels with employees.

Cooking onions: Will be visited by a friend.

Planting onions: Unexpected good fortune.

Buying onions: Your feelings will be hurt.

Seeing onions growing: Rivals will press you hard.

OPAL:

Of this gem: You will come out well from a present peril.

Having an opal: Fortunate business transactions.

Wearing an opal: Misfortune in love affairs.

Buying an opal: Happiness through love.

Selling an opal: Disputes with sweetheart.

Other people wearing an opal: Discovery of lost valuables.

OPERA:

Going to the opera: Family disorder.

Being at the opera: Confusion in your business.

Seeing comical opera: Good results in business affairs.

Enjoying comical opera: A child will be born.

Seeing a foolish opera: Too little work and too much fussing.

Seeing a dramatic opera: Fortunate events ahead of you.

Seeing a melodramatic opera: You are too superstitious.

Theatrical people being at the opera: Happiness in love affairs.

Hearing grand opera: A long absent friend will return soon.

Seeing a complete season of operas: Confronted with domestic chores.

OPERATION:

Going to have an operation: Will have much pain.

Undergoing an operation: Success will come to you.

Having an operation: Beware of untrue friends.

Watching an operation: Will be very lucky.

Operation not being a success: Corruption.

Operation being a success: You have plenty of friends.

Performing an operation yourself: Wealth.

Another doctor helping with an operation: You will be deceived.

A nurse assisting with an operation: Success in life.

OPIUM:

Of opium: You are negligent in your affairs.

Prescribing opium as medicine: Will suffer humiliation.

Taking opium: Social disgrace.

Taking opium with others: Bad changes in life will soon occur.

Encouraging friends to take opium: Worries are ahead for you.

OPPONENT:

Of an opponent: Will win against rivals.

Fighting with an opponent: Doomed for disappointment.

Having disputes with several opponents: Opposition and quarrels to come.

OPTICIAN:
Going to an optician: Will make much money.
Buying glasses from an optician: Attempting to hide age because of shame.
Wearing glasses from an optician: You are living an extravagant life.
Being an optician: Money comes easily to you.
Selling glasses: Will have good earnings.
Taking children to an optician: Family security.

ORANGE:
Eating oranges: You will injure yourself.
Selling oranges: True love.
Buying oranges: Disappointment in love.
Making orange marmalade: Death of soldiers.
Of an orange tree: Will shed tears.
Planting an orange tree: Will make an unsuccessful trip.
Peeling oranges: Death of a relative.
The color of orange: Fortune is near at hand.
Orange-colored materials: Good times are coming.
Buying orange-colored clothes: Small financial gains.

ORANGE BLOSSOM:
Picking orange blossoms: Marriage.
Making a crown of orange blossoms: Will be happily married.
Wearing a crown of orange blossoms: Your virginity is safe.

ORATORY:
Giving an oration: You are a very affable person.
Listening to an oration: Will receive an inheritance.
Delivering an oration: Loss of a friend.
Being an orator: Beware of minor troubles.

ORCHARD:
Being in an orchard: You have good friends.

Being in an orchard with children: Family happiness.
Walking in an orchard: Every wish will be realized.
Gathering fruit in an orchard: Will never realize desires.
An orchard being stripped of fruit: Will lose advancement opportunities.
Plentiful fruit in an orchard: Good fortune.
Scarce fruit in an orchard: Your fortune will improve with patience.
Ripe fruit in an orchard: Expect great success.
Green fruit in an orchard: You have bad friends.

ORCHESTRA:
Of an orchestra: Fortune will come soon.
Hearing an orchestra: Expect great success.
An orchestra performing: Unhappiness.
Hearing an orchestra playing in the distance: Loss of relatives.
Attending an orchestra concert with family: Small wealth ahead.
An orchestra conductor: Happiness in the family.
Someone you know being an orchestra conductor: Completion of business.

ORCHID:
Of orchids: Happiness is assured.
Having orchids: Luck and prosperity.
Buying an orchid: Abundant means.
Giving an orchid to an unmarried woman: Short engagement.
Giving an orchid to a married woman: Beware of jealous friends.
An unmarried girl receiving orchid as a gift: Prompt engagement.

ORDERS:
Giving orders: Will be grateful for a service rendered to you.
Obeying orders: Will have a large family.
Taking orders: Sadness.
Wearing military orders or medals: Will have setbacks in hopes.

Giving orders to children: Advancement in love affairs.

Putting things in order: Will be obedient to superiors.

Ordering things through the mail: You are too gullible.

ORGAN:

Of a church organ: Friends are endeavoring to assist you.

Selling an organ: Painful experiences.

Hearing organ music: Arrival of relatives.

Playing an organ: Loss of relatives.

Playing an organ in church: Inheritance.

Playing an organ at home: Anxiety.

Hearing loud unpleasant organ music: Family discord.

Hearing a funeral march played on an organ: Favorable love affairs.

Buying an organ: Will be in mourning soon.

Organs of the body: Birth of a girl.

Organs of sick people: Despair.

Smelling organs: Prosperity.

Hearing organs: Personal honors.

Organs of sick old people: People are saying bad things.

Having solid organs: Will have a big family.

Having flabby organs: Will discover one who is double-crossing you.

Having healthy organs: Riches.

Having oversized organs: Birth of a boy who is deformed.

Having organs removed: Loss of one whom you love dearly.

Having unhealthy organs: Death of father or mother.

ORIENT:

Of the Orient: Will soon take a long trip.

Oriental people: Romantic happiness that will not last.

Oriental countries: Small measure of happiness.

Traveling to the Orient: Take little stock in people's promises.

Being among Oriental people: Good chance of getting married.

Returning from the Orient: Will have comfortable living.

Returning from the Orient with someone else: Unhappiness.

Bringing things back from the Orient: Waste of time.

Being an Oriental yourself: You have the world's blessings.

ORPHAN:

Of an orphan: Will receive profits from a stranger.

Several orphans in an orphanage: Change of surroundings.

Adopting an orphan: Happiness is assured.

A child becoming an orphan: Will receive a legacy.

ORNAMENT:

Of ornaments: Frivolity.

Wearing ornaments: High honors.

Giving ornaments to others: Extravagance.

Others wearing ornaments: Coming trouble.

Church ornaments: Will have good spirit.

Flower ornaments: Will have pleasure and fortune.

Having various other kinds of ornaments: Family happiness.

OSTLER:

Of a stableman: You are in favor with fortune.

Having an ostler taking care of own horses: Abundant means.

A stableman at work: Big financial gains.

Other people's ostler: Change of surroundings.

OSTRICH:

Of an ostrich: Miserly habits.

Wearing a hat with ostrich feathers: A slight ailment will cause worry.

Others wearing hats with ostrich feathers: Watch your diet.

Buying ostrich feathers: Friends know that you are guilty.

OTTER:
Of an otter: Untrue friends will hurt your feelings.
Many otters: Will be harrassed by many debts.
Catching an otter: Good fortune.
An otter eating fish: An absent friend will soon return.

OTTOMAN:
Of an empty ottoman: Warning of troubles.
Sitting on an ottoman alone: An enemy is seeking your ruin.
Sitting on an ottoman with husband: Triumph over enemies.
Sitting on an ottoman with a loved one: Danger in love matters.
Sitting on an ottoman with a friend: Hard work awaits you.
Sitting on an ottoman with children: You have a great deal of will power.
Sitting on an ottoman with a dog: You have faithful friends.

OUNCE:
Counting ounces of liquid: Will be hurt through secret affairs.
Counting ounces of medicine: Danger.
A chemist measuring ounces: Security and long life.
A nurse measuring ounces: A baby may be born.

OVEN:
Of an oven: Riches.
An oven being lighted: Abundance.
Turning off an oven: Will be of service to someone.
Baking in an oven: Affairs will come to a standstill.
Cooking good food in an oven: Business will improve slightly.
An oven being very hot on the outside: Happiness.
Burning food in the oven: You are drifting into bad paths.
Cooking food too long in an oven: Take no risks.
A woman dreaming of a hot oven: Will be widely loved.
An oven in which bricks are baked: Big profit in business.

OVER-ALLS:
Of over-alls: Bad luck.
Working in over-alls: Will be repaid for your kindness.
Having dirty over-alls: Be careful of your diet.
Tearing over-alls: Beware of illness.
A woman dreaming of a man in over-alls: Doesn't know loved one's character.

OVERBOARD:
Falling overboard: Misfortune.
Others falling overboard: Speculation will cause loss of money.
Throwing people overboard: Fortune.
A sailor falling overboard: Big prosperity.
Committing suicide by jumping overboard: Will take a long trip abroad.

OVERCOAT:
Of an overcoat: Dignity.
Wearing an overcoat: Will soon receive a high position.
Taking off an overcoat: Disgrace.
Others putting on an overcoat: Your help will be sought.
Others taking off an overcoat: They will fall into disgrace.
Overcoat of a woman: Joy without profit.
Overcoat of children: Substantial means.
Throwing an overcoat away: Will be annoyed.
Cleaning an overcoat: Will lose sustenance money.
Buying an overcoat: Will be a person of honor.
Selling overcoats: Will receive some money.

OVERFLOW:
Water overflowing: Will receive an unexpected proposal.
A river overflowing: Change of surroundings.
The bathtub overflowing: You have unattainable desires.
A barrel overflowing: Happiness.
A tank overflowing: Death of a friend.

OVERHANG:
Of something overhanging: Will have small disappointments.
Something overhanging your body: Loss of money.
Pictures overhanging height of body: Misfortune in love affairs.
Pictures of saints overhanging: Will have a happy life.

OVERTAKE:
Overtaking someone else: Personal happiness.
Being overtaken by others: You like to eat too much.
Being overtaken by enemies: Advancement in position and good influence.
Overtaking other things: Must moderate your desires.

OVERTURN:
Overturning in an automobile or truck: Small loss of money.
Objects being overturned: Big joy.
Children being overturned while playing: Abundance of money.
A woman being overturned riding a horse: Marriage will not last long.
A man dreaming of being overturned riding a horse: Death of an animal.
Overthrowing an enemy: Honor and distinction.

OVERWORK:
Being overworked: Unhappiness.
Overworking help: Will have dealings with Justice Department.
Overworking children: Changes in present condition.
Overworking animals: Good friendships.
Overworking a machine: You will get into trouble.

OWL:
Of an owl: Unhappiness.
Catching an owl: Happiness.
Killing an owl: Great happiness.
Hearing the hoot of an owl: Warning of the approach of a deceitful person.
Hearing owls screaming: Someone will die.

OXEN:
Of one ox: Profitable business undertakings.
A herd of oxen: Prosperity in affairs.
An ox in the pasture: Will rise rapidly in present position.
Oxen grazing peacefully: Should watch speculations.
Oxen plowing: Good earnings.
Oxen pulling a cart: Fortune in love.
Oxen eating grass: Big joy in life.
Oxen running: Will have troubles caused by enemies.
Oxen pulling up a hill: Unhappiness in love.
A fat ox: Your fortune will increase.
Lean oxen: Fortune will decrease.
Oxen fighting: You have enemies.
Killing oxen: Riches.
Oxen sleeping: Loss of friends.
Buying oxen: Will have wealth.
Selling oxen: Be careful in buying and selling shares.
Oxen without horns: Favorable developments in own affairs.

OYSTERS:
Of oysters: Luck and prosperity.
Gathering oysters: Will make lots of money.
Eating oysters: Hard work is ahead.
Eating friend's oysters: Will have riches.
Oysters at a market place: Promise of many children.
Opening a can of oysters: Happiness in love affairs.
Buying oysters: Someone new will fall in love with you.
Giving a gift of oysters: You need courage to succeed in life.
Receiving a gift of oysters: Joy without profit.

P

PACK:
Packing for a journey: Business worries will keep you at home.
Relatives packing for a trip: Happiness in the family.
A woman packing clothes for a trip: She may leave her husband.
A man packing clothes for a trip: He is guilty of foolish actions.
Packing something to mail: Abuse of confidence.

PACKAGE:
Preparing a package: Will make a short trip.
Mailing a package: Unhappiness because of children's actions.
Carrying a package: Worries caused by children's health.
Carrying a big package: Big disappointment.
Carrying a small package: Will have to face trouble.
Receiving a package: There is someone that loves you dearly.
Opening a package: Marriage will last forever.
Receiving a package from children: Love affairs are not very good.

PADDOCK:
Of a paddock: Happiness is assured.
Being in the paddock of a racecourse: Do not speculate.
Being inside the paddock of a pasture: Surprising news of an engagement.
Others being inside a paddock: An engagement will be called off.

PADLOCK:
Of a padlock: Good luck.
Opening a padlock: Happiness is assured.
Being unable to open a padlock: Beware of trouble ahead.
A man opening a padlock: He is flirting with several women.
A woman opening a padlock: Will be unfaithful to the man who loves her.

An open padlock: Suitable time to pursue courtship.
Having the key of a padlock: Avoid speculation of any kind.
Losing the key of a padlock: Be careful in money matters.
Finding the key of a padlock: You will pull through your troubles.

PAGE:
Pages of books: Will be abused.
Pages of letters: Will enjoy the confidence of other people.
Many pages of other things: Riches.
Assembling pages together: Fortune.
Being paged: Misfortune in business.
Paging others: Fortune in love affairs.

PAGEANT:
Of a pageant: You should not judge appearances.
Watching a pageant on a float: Do not pay attention to other things.
Children being in a pageant: Happiness.
Friends being in a pageant: You are being deceived.
Enemies being in a pageant: Misfortune in business.

PAGODA:
Of a pagoda: Unexpected news will cancel a journey.
Being inside a pagoda: Happiness is ahead for you.
Being with others inside a pagoda: Change of surroundings.
Others being inside a pagoda: Beware of jealous friends.
Lovers dreaming of a pagoda: Immediate separation.
Unmarried person dreaming of a pagoda: Engagement will be canceled.
Married person dreaming of a pagoda: Make the most of opportunities.

PAIL:
Of a pail: Good harvest.
An empty pail: Poverty.

A full pail: You have many close friends.

Buying a pail: Be careful of new business ventures.

Selling pails: People will confide in you.

A clean pail: Will have plenty of money.

A dirty pail: Will be cheated by friends.

PAIN:

Having pain in the heart: Sickness.

Having pain in the teeth: Unhappiness.

Having pain in the ears: Malicious gossip against you.

Having pain in the stomach: Pleasant social activities.

Having pain in the shoulders: Use caution in business activities.

Having pains in the chest: Financial gains.

Having pains in the throat: Discovery of lost valuables.

Having delivery pains: Death.

Having pains in the legs: Will receive good news.

Having pains in the feet: Will get out of trouble.

Having pains all over the body: Success.

Lovers dreaming of having pains all over: Their love is secured.

Others being in pain: Your life is full of mistakes.

Children being in pain: Persecution by an enemy.

PAINT:

Painting the face: Joy without profit.

Covering cheeks with paint: You are deceitful.

Painting the face of a woman: She deceives you.

An overly painted lady: Do not trust her.

A paint job on a house being completed: Domestic affliction.

PAINTER:

A painter at work: Pleasant life.

Being a painter: Happiness in your employment.

Having a paint shop: Abundant means.

A painter going up a ladder: Important and very beneficial events ahead.

A painter coming down a ladder: Unhappiness in love affairs.

Many painters at work: Worry will be smoothed away.

A painter using enamel: Long-lasting marriage.

Others who are painters: Money is getting low.

PAINTING:

Painting own portrait: Will live a long life.

Painting another's portrait: Friends will be false to you.

Painting portrait of ancestors: Will be gratified.

Painting portrait of children: Difficulties will be overcome.

Painting a landscape: Will make good purchases.

Painting various pictures: Satisfaction in home life.

PAIR:

Having a pair of anything: You are undecided about marriage plans.

A pair of twins: A remarkable event is about to happen.

A pair of earrings: Poverty.

Husband and wife as a pair: Must do work that you do not like.

A pair of shoes: Disagreements in family affairs.

Having a pair of scissors: Gossip concerning private life.

PALACE:

Of a palace: Pleasures of short duration.

Many palaces: Big real estate dealings.

Living in a palace: People esteem you highly.

Entering a palace: Beware of enemies who desire to harm you.

PALE:

Being pale: Untruthful gossip.

Going pale from fright: Riches.

Children being pale: Honor.

A loved one being pale: Family quarrels.
A friend being pale: Happiness.
Relatives being pale: Family quarrels.
Others who are pale: Danger and perhaps death.

PALISADE:
Of a palisade: Happiness.
Being inside a palisade: Will hear news of an engagement.
Others being inside a palisade: An engagement will be called off.

PALL:
Of a black velvet covering: Will have a short life.
Putting a pall over a coffin: Will receive a legacy.
Putting a pall on an altar: Great sadness because of a death.
Concealing things with a pall: Beware of sickness.

PALLBEARER:
Being a pallbearer: Great affection.
Four pallbearers carrying a coffin: Honor.
Many pallbearers: You are a distinguished person.
Military officers being pallbearers: Will be deceived by a woman.
Poor people being pallbearers: Will suffer constant harrassment by enemy.

PALM:
Of the palm of the hand: Inheritance from a distant relative.
A hand with a beautiful palm: Happiness and joy.
Smelling perfume on a palm: Prosperity and abundance.
Holding the palm of a married woman: She will have children.
Holding the palm of an unmarried woman: She will soon be married.
Kissing the palm of a woman's hand: Friendship and good fortune.
Putting engagement ring in palm of a woman's hand: Dignity and honor.
Having own palm read: Abundance and success.

The palm of a child's hand: Domestic peace.

PALM TREE:
Of a palm tree: Great success.
Several palm trees: Will receive a high and honorable position.
Friends being under a palm tree: Difficulties will be overcome.
Young girls dreaming of a palm tree: Will soon be married.
A woman dreaming of palm trees: Will have children.
A man dreaming of palm trees: Will enjoy fame and success.
Businessmen dreaming of palm trees: Successful speculation.
Professional people dreaming of palm trees: Will flourish in profession.

PALPITATE:
The heart palpitating: A death will come soon.
Suffering from heart palpitation: True and constant friendships.
Feeling children's heart palpitating: Success in enterprises.
Feeling palpitations of a sick person: Big disputes.

PAN:
Of one pan: Short-lived unhappiness.
Several pans: Loss of money.
Cooking in a pan: Will enjoy devotion of others and virtue.
Buying pans: Will receive plenty of money.
Others having pans: Receipt of money will be delayed.

PANCAKE:
Making pancakes: Will be successful.
Eating pancakes: Persevere in present undertakings.
Others making pancakes: Will find a way out of difficulties.
Others eating pancakes: Business associate will cause difficulties.
Cooking pancakes: Will have unexpected guests.
Burning pancakes: Failure in business ventures.

PANSY:
Pansies in own garden: Contentment.

Pansies in another's garden: Big changes for you.

Having a bouquet of pansies: Happiness.

Having a corsage of pansies: Will assist at a wedding.

Receiving a gift of pansies from a man: Your love is secured.

Growing pansies: You will have a big family.

PANTALOONS:

Women wearing pantaloons: Will be lucky in love affairs.

A woman dreaming of someone else in pantaloons: Security in her love.

Young girls wearing pantaloons: Confidence in the future.

A woman dreaming of wearing pantaloons and a mask: You are very gullible.

PANTHER:

Of a panther: Victory over enemies.

Many panthers: Will go abroad on business.

Being attacked by a panther: Success.

Killing a panther: Many changes but finally victory.

A panther being in a cage: Enemies will fail in attempts to injure you.

Hearing a panther roar: Will suffer grief.

Panthers fighting: Sickness.

Panthers scuffling: Will have cruel suffering.

Panthers running: Serious illness.

Panthers dying: Death of a prominent person.

Panthers tied with chains: Will receive a surprise from an enemy.

Surprising a panther: Watch out for deceitful friends.

Being triumphant over a panther: Avoid rivals.

The skeleton of a panther: Will soon have money.

Being afraid of a panther: Will be persecuted by enemies.

Baby panthers: Joy and happiness.

PANTRY:

Being in a pantry: Success in all your affairs.

Preparing something in a pantry: Will succeed in present endeavors.

Being with others in a pantry: Will always have obstacles to overcome.

Fixing drinks in a pantry: News from one you haven't heard from in a long time.

Spilling something in a pantry: A lover is thinking of you.

PAPER:

White paper: Innocence.

Colored paper: People are watching you secretly.

Painted paper: Joy of short duration.

Printed paper: Good faith.

Poor quality paper: Will receive news from a friend.

Paper that is written on: You like to argue.

Paper used to print newspapers: Loss of temper.

Paper being manufactured: Will have a good job in own line of work.

Handling paper: Losses are threatening.

Unmarried people handling papers: Love quarrels.

Married people handling papers: Marital disagreements.

Children handling paper: They will have a brilliant future.

Enemies handling papers: Will be served with legal papers.

Dirty paper: Your actions will be questionable.

Clean paper: Will escape with only slight money losses.

Folded paper: Small disappointment.

PAPERING:

Of papering a room: Illness of a friend.

Being a paper hanger: You are deceitful.

Others papering rooms: Imminent peril.

Seeing wallpaper: Will encounter trouble.

PAPRIKA:

Of paprika: Will become very irritated.

Buying paprika: Profit.

Using paprika on food: Will have many pleasures in life.

Spilling paprika on the floor: Misfortune in love affairs.

PARACHUTE:

Of a parachute floating downward: Be careful not to go to extremes.

Coming down in a parachute yourself: Sorrow within the family.

Many people coming down in parachutes: Increase in the family.

People being killed upon landing in a parachute: Dishonor for enemies.

PARADE:

A parade of marching soldiers: Faithful love of a woman.

A parade of drilling soldiers: A change in life will soon come.

A parade of young girls: Increase in the family.

A parade of young boys: Happiness.

A parade of boy scouts: You will forgive your enemies.

A religious parade: Treachery.

A national parade: Work without happiness.

A union parade: Improvement in family conditions.

A parade of protest: Great satisfaction will come to you.

A parade of happy people: Will receive a gift.

PARADISE:

Going to paradise: Happy marriage.

Being in paradise: Forgive those who have wronged you.

A farmer dreaming of paradise: Abundant harvest.

Young girls dreaming of paradise: Will have sorrow.

Not being wanted in paradise: Will have an accident.

Men being thrown out of paradise: Breakup of the family.

Women being thrown out of paradise: Misery.

Enemies being in paradise: Abundant means.

PARALYSIS:

Having paralysis: Dishonor.

Becoming paralyzed: Arguments within the family.

Others that are paralyzed: Misfortune in love affairs.

Relatives being paralyzed: Death of an enemy.

Children being paralyzed: A change in life will soon come.

Husband or wife being paralyzed: Will lose affection for each other.

Enemies being paralyzed: Financial losses.

PARAPET:

Kneeling on a parapet: Danger and worries.

Falling on a parapet: Difficulties will be overcome by own efforts.

Others being on a parapet: Contentment.

Others falling from a parapet: Misfortune in love affairs.

PARASOL:

Carrying a parasol over the head: Someone will come to your aid.

Having an open parasol: Will have prosperity.

Having parasol open to protect you from the sun: Wealth.

Opening a parasol in the house: Love affairs are on the rocks.

Others with an open parasol: Birth of a child.

Others with a closed parasol: Sickness.

Borrowing a parasol: Misunderstandings with a friend.

Lending a parasol: Will be hurt by false friends.

A beautifully colored parasol: Your lover will displease you.

PARCEL:

Of a parcel: Troubles.

Having a parcel: Unhappiness caused by children.

Receiving a parcel: Will receive money.

Sending a parcel: Prosperity.

Opening a parcel: This parcel may have an affect on your luck.

Carrying a parcel: Expect a change of circumstances.

PARCHED:
Of something being parched: Will take a trip to a hot country.
Many things being parched: Someone will confide in you.
Receiving parched things: Will have sorrow.
An old parched document: Happiness is secured.

PARCHMENT:
Of parchment documents: Fortune and riches.
Receiving documents written on parchment: Troubles with legal affairs.
Sending documents written on parchment: Appointment to a new position.

PARDON:
Pardoning someone else: You have a secret that hurts deeply.
Being pardoned by others: Discomfort.
Pardoning children: Will despair after giving pardon.
Husband and wife pardoning each other: Humiliation and disgrace.
Asking pardon for an offense: Warning of troubles.
Criminal asking for pardon: It will not be granted.
Children asking for your pardon: Unhappiness.
Lover asking for pardon: Remorse.
Asking pardon from God: Great joy.
Being pardoned by a priest: Will have a vigorous mind.

PARENTS:
Of own parents: Will have dealings with the law.
Visiting own parents: Will receive bad news.
Accompanying parents: Difficult times ahead.
Of parents after they are dead: Prosperity.
Parents of other people: Death of a friend.
A parent being naked: Big family disagreement.

Being a grouchy parent: Will receive bad news.
Embracing a parent: Treachery.

PARIS:
Going to Paris: You are being watched by someone.
Visiting Paris: You are prone to enjoying amusements too much.
Being in Paris alone: Contentment.
Being in Paris with a woman: Good results in own affairs.
Others going to Paris: Annoyance will cause arguments.

PARISH:
Of a parish: There are no clouds ahead in your future.
Being inside a parish: Prosperity.
Being a member of a particular parish: You are headed in dangerous ways.
Being the pastor of a parish: Your own affairs are very confused.

PARK:
Of a park: Pleasure and happiness.
Walking in a beautiful park: Increase in the family.
Strolling through an untidy park: Reverses in business.
Children playing in a park: Happiness in love.
Sitting in a park alone: Increase in your fortune.
Sitting in a park with sweetheart: Enemies will be punished.

PARLIAMENT:
Of a parliament in session: Will be cheated.
Visiting a parliament: Quarrels.
Being a member of parliament: Advancement in present position.
Being with parliament officials: Death of a friend.

PARRICIDE:
Of a person who kills his parents: Will live a quiet life.
Being a parricide: Business affairs will go bad.
Other people being parricides: Treason by friends.

A member of family being a parricide: Ideas and actions will create enemies.

PARROT:
Of a parrot: Riches.
Enjoying the chatter of a parrot: Flattery from a deceitful person.
Children talking to a parrot: You have confidence of friends.
A parrot chattering too much: Will be flattered by someone.
A parrot that talks very little: Difficult work ahead.
A parrot laying an egg: Increase in the family.
A young engaged girl dreaming of a parrot: Inquire about fiancé's family.

PARSLEY:
Of parsley: You will be approached by a rich man.
Eating parsley: Affliction.
Cooking parsley: People are talking against you.
A woman dreaming of eating parsley: Will be deceived.
A man dreaming of eating parsley: Will desert his home.
Growing parsley: Success will be achieved through hard work.
Family eating parsley: Good health and large family.
Buying parsley: Security.

PARSNIP:
Of parsnips: Failure in love.
Eating parsnips: Success in business.
Cooking parsnips: You are indebted to someone.
Buying parsnips: Sickness that will not last long.
Growing parsnips: Will have a long life.

PARTING:
Parting with a friend: Will have a life of vexation.
Parting with enemies: Success in every undertaking.
Parting with relatives: Bad financial business.
Parting with wife: Riches.

Parting with husband: Dangers.
Parting with children: Death in the family.

PARTNER:
Finding a partner: Have no fears.
Having a partner: You are prone to arguing.
Losing a partner: Your success is sure.
Having a prominent partner: Good business.

PARTRIDGE:
Of a partridge: Many small troubles.
A partridge flying away: Will succeed in your business.
A partridge landing: Will meet with great success.
Many partridges: Will achieve goals by hard work.
Killing a partridge: Abundant means.

PARTY:
Being at a party: Joy without profit.
Being with others at a party: Unexpected fortune.
Giving a party: Quarrels.
Others giving a party for you: Disappointment in love.
Being at a party without a partner: Life holds good things for you.
Taking children to a party: Hopes are vanishing.
Being at a wild party: Will be a victim of gossip.
Someone getting hurt at a party: Will have a long life.

PASSAGE:
Of a narrow passage: Work ahead for you.
Being with others in a passage: Happiness in the family.
Finding something in a long passage: Will overcome great difficulties.
Reading a passage in the Bible: Will be captivated by a fine person.
Reading a passage in a book: Will have a constant friendship.
Reading a passage in a dictionary: Honor.
Taking passage on a boat: Will avoid unhappiness.

Taking passage on a plane: Will have obstacles in your path.

PASSENGER:
Being a passenger: Watch out for your family.
A man dreaming of being a passenger on a boat: Big unhappiness.
A woman dreaming of being a passenger on a boat: Days without troubles.
A man dreaming of being a passenger on a plane: Treachery.
A woman dreaming of being a passenger on a plane: She is very jolly.
Oncoming passengers: Better circumstances.
Outgoing passengers: Will have an opportunity to acquire property.
Children being passengers: Family discord.
Friends being passengers: Realization of own ambitions.

PASSION:
Being passionate: Prosperity.
A woman being passionate: She will be justified.
A man being passionate: Passing love.
A wife being passionate: A better future awaiting her.
A husband being passionate: Changeable in love.
Other passionate people: Honor of short duration.

PASSION FLOWER:
Of a passion flower: Must control your passions.
Picking a passion flower: Inherited wealth.
Having a bouquet of passion flowers: Many faithful friends.
Smelling a passion flower: Sacrifice and sorrow.

PASTE:
Making paste: Will have a big argument.
Pasting papers together: Will receive sad news.
Pasting various items together: You have very smart enemies.

Pasting household things: You have greedy people around you.
Pasting material together: Happiness in love in days to come.
Others using paste: Loss of a friend.
Enemies using paste: Success in your plans.

PASTOR:
Of a pastor: Must pay more attention to property holdings.
Talking with a pastor: Must take better care of personal affairs.
Taking advice from a pastor: Increase in possessions.
Being a pastor: Profit.

PASTRY:
Of a pastry shop: You love good things.
A candy and pastry shop: Joy and profit.
People making pastry: Beware of spending money foolishly.
Making pastry yourself: Riches.
Eating pastries: You will love a businessman.
A man dreaming of eating pastries: Will fall in love with a teen-ager
Cooking fancy pastries: Will face contradiction.
Making a cake: Suffering.
Making a pie: Troubles.
Making cookies: Will discover a secret.
Children eating pastries: Good results in own enterprises.
Eating pastries with almonds: Will be justified in your actions.
Using plenty of butter in pastries: Great satisfaction.
Buying pastry: Will find out something startling.
Selling pastry: Will be relieved of pains.

PASTURE:
Of a pasture: Success.
Cattle grazing in a green pasture: Long life.
Having a large pasture: Much happiness.

A pasture belonging to others: You are being deceived.

Being in a pasture: Happiness and wealth.

Owning a pasture: Embarrassment in affairs.

Being in a wooded pasture: Profit.

Running around in a pasture: Disappointment in marriage.

Being with others in a pasture: Good earnings.

PATCH:

A patch being on own clothes: Inherited wealth.

Putting a patch on children's clothes: Will avoid sickness.

Patching relative's garments: Will receive news of a marriage.

Patching own underclothes: Joy and profit.

PATCHWORK:

Doing patchwork: Money will come to you in an unexpected way.

Others doing patchwork: Other people's love for you is sincere.

Doing patchwork for others: Will hold the affection of your lover.

PATENT:

Applying for a patent: Will be bothered by people.

Obtaining a patent: Will have good earnings.

Being refused a patent: Will be talking with the devil.

Making money from a patent: Will enjoy a happy love life.

PATH:

Walking in a broad straight path: Unhappiness.

Walking in a narrow path: Adversity.

Walking on a rough path: Embarrassment.

Walking with someone down a path: Will better your position in life.

Walking leisurely down a path: Your affairs will flourish.

Meeting obstacles along a path: Difficulties to be faced in the future.

A young girl walking along a path with boyfriend: Will marry very rich man.

A married woman walking along a path with husband: Divorce.

Two people in love walking along a path: Will meet a prominent person.

PATIENCE:

Having patience: Long healthy life.

Losing patience: Success in love.

Others losing patience with you: Will hear of the birth of a boy.

Mates losing patience with each other: Will incur loss of small importance.

Other people being impatient: Fortune in affairs.

PATRIARCH:

Of a patriarch: Will enjoy a contented life.

Talking to a patriarch: Will receive much publicity.

The appointment of a patriarch: Will live a long life.

Being a patriarch: Will have joy and prosperity.

PATRIOTIC:

Being patriotic: Abundance.

Not being patriotic: Danger ahead.

Others who are patriotic: Must endure much suffering.

Relatives being patriotic: Waste of family wealth.

PATROL:

Of a patrol: Will have a loss of small importance.

Watching a patrol: Will be repaid for money loaned.

Being taken to prison by a patrol: Good name in society and publicity.

PATRONESS:

Of a female patron: Peril of war.

Being a patroness: Will live a contented life.

Arguing with a patroness: Much commotion with no good results.

Being insulted by a patroness: People are saying bad things about you.

PATTERN:

Of a pattern: Quarrels in the family.

Making a pattern: Small vexation.

Buying a pattern: Worries will be overcome.

Ordering a pattern: You will collect money.

PAVEMENT:

The pavement in front of own house: Bad news ahead.

Falling on the pavement: Danger ahead.

The pavement of the street: Will fall into a trap.

The pavement in a warehouse: Will secure a good job.

PAW:

Of paws: Will be offended by a person with bad manners.

The paws of a dog or cat: Friends far away are thinking of you.

The paws of wild animals: Will have joy of short duration.

PAWN:

Going to a pawnshop: Unexpected help will come to you.

Receiving money from a pawnshop: Future and troubles are taken care of.

Taking articles to be pawned: You do not make plans well.

Redeeming articles pawned: Good fortune ahead.

PAWNBROKER:

Going to a pawnbroker: Affairs will take a turn for the better.

Being a pawnbroker: Troubles at home.

Pawnbroker not returning own articles to you: Unfaithful sweetheart.

Renewing pledges at a pawnbroker: Indiscretion of mate causes troubles.

PAY:

Paying a bill that is due: Misery and poverty.

Paying a debt: Financial gains.

Others paying a debt to you: Recovery from an illness.

Paying a debt for someone else: You are not in your right mind.

Paying a bill that you shouldn't: Will be guilty of foolishness.

Having to make payments: Superiors do not favor you.

PEACE:

Having peace: Will have a quarrel.

Making peace: Will have a fight.

Remaining peaceful: Loss of money.

Mates making peace between each other: Increase of affection for children.

Lovers making peace between each other: Good results in affairs.

Making peace with friends: Important and very beneficial events to come.

PEACH:

Of peaches on a tree: Promised attainment of fondest hopes.

Picking peaches from a tree: Sickness in the home.

Many trees loaded with peaches: Earnings will be good.

Eating peaches in season: Contentment.

Eating peaches out of season: Will receive a favor.

Eating peaches with other people: Love worries.

Children eating peaches: Their future is secured.

Friends eating peaches: You are financially secure.

Relatives eating peaches: Good times are coming.

Other people eating peaches: Will have emotional sorrow.

PEACOCK:

Of a peacock: Will be disappointed.

Catching a peacock: You are too ambitious.

A dead peacock: Own good plans will fail.

Hearing the chirping of a peacock: A big rain will come and cause damage.

The beautiful feathers of a peacock: Joy without profit.

A farmer dreaming of a peacock: Will have a good harvest.

A woman dreaming of a peacock circling: Riches.

A man dreaming of a peacock circling: Will have troubles.

A beautiful woman dreaming of a peacock: Elevation to a high position.

PEARLS:
Of pearls: Misery.
Many pearls: Unhappiness and tears.
Threading pearls: Loneliness.
Gathering pearls from the sea: You are penniless.
Finding pearls: Will earn success through hard work.
Buying pearls: Will succeed to your goal.
Receiving a gift of pearls: Very happy and successful marriage.
A string of pearls breaking: Grief and sorrow.
Restringing a broken strand of pearls: Success.
Losing a set of pearls: Will make new friends.
Giving a gift of pearls: Are trying to gain favors by giving a gift.

PEARS:
Of pears: Will have a wonderful time.
Picking pears: Amusements.
Eating pears: Dignity.
Eating green pears: Damages.
Eating ripe pears: Great joy.
Other people eating pears: Momentary troubles.
Children eating pears: Husband will always be faithful to you.
Friends eating pears: You are financially secure.
Relatives eating pears: Husband and wife will always be faithful.
Many trees loaded with pears: Prospects are good.
Shaking pears from a tree: Success is assured.

PEAS:
Of peas: Good health and long life.
Cooking peas: Will encounter contagious disease.
Boiling peas: Big sickness.
Shelling peas: Recovery of an illness.

Eating peas: Rugged health and increasing riches.
Peas on the vines: Fortunate undertakings.
Planting peas: Fulfillment of ambitions.
Children eating peas: They will succeed in everyday activities.
Peas growing in the garden: Financial gains.
Dried peas: Large earnings acquired in a shady manner.
Peas not completely cooked: Exercise patience in your affairs.

PEASANT:
Of a peasant: Good future ahead of you.
A businessman dreaming of a peasant: Successful enterprises.
Many peasants at work: Will succeed in family life.
Hiring peasants to work: Will have good health.
Dismissing peasants: Misery.
Making peasants work hard: Business plans will prosper.

PEBBLES:
Of pebbles: Jealousy.
Finding pebbles: Competition will cause trouble.
Handling pebbles: Sickness.
Making a walk with pebbles: Unhappiness.
Various colored pebbles: You are too proud.
Cutting pebbles: Joy and pleasure.
Sorting pebbles: Will avoid trouble.
Sitting on pebbles: Will be delivered from a difficult situation.
Picking up pebbles: Melancholy.

PEDDLER:
Of a peddler: Business is booming.
Meeting a peddler: Good business undertakings.
Talking to a peddler: Sickness.
Being a peddler: Will receive sad news.
Ignoring a peddler: You are too haughty.
Sending a peddler away: Infirmity of friends.

Many peddlers: You have deceitful companions.

PEDESTRIAN:
Of a pedestrian: Will overcome enemies with perseverance.
Many pedestrians: Will be successful in business undertakings.
Bumping into pedestrians: Are confronted with insurmountable obstacles.
Being a pedestrian: Honor and fame.
A pedestrian coming toward you: Will attend a funeral.
A pedestrian falling down: One of married partners is cheating.
A pedestrian being hurt: Fortune in business dealings.

PEEL:
Peeling fruits: Death of a relative.
Peeling vegetables: Will invite friends for dinner.
Peeling eggs: Will be visited by a loved one.
Skin peeling: Unhappiness.

PEN:
Of a pen: Big unhappiness.
Writing with a pen: Will receive news from absent friends.
Buying a pen: Will live a long life.
Writing with an old-fashioned pen: Honor.
Writing with a fountain pen: You have false friends.
Writing with a quill pen: People are gossiping about you.
Writing love letters with a fountain pen: You are being deceived.
Writing letters in bed with a pen: Annoyance.
Children using a pen: Fortune in family affairs.

PENANCE:
Offering penance: Be reserved with strangers.
Asking for penance: Will live to an advanced age.
Others asking for penance: A dangerous influence is near when traveling.

Giving penance to someone: Will have wonderful health.

PENCIL:
Of pencils: You are influenced by good things.
Receiving pencils: Beware of the person who gave you the pencils.
Giving pencils: Will separate from the one to whom you are giving them.
Buying pencils: Business success.
Sharpening pencils: Your accounts are in order.
Children using pencils: They will enjoy good health.

PENDULUM:
Of a pendulum: Will receive unexpected message.
A pendulum that has stopped: Long and healthy life.
Starting a pendulum: Will take a long journey.
A pendulum sitting on a mantel: Beware of treacherous friends.

PENINSULA:
Of a peninsula: Will receive damages.
Being on a peninsula: Will be tortured by friends.
Living on a peninsula: Will enjoy good nutrition.
Others going to a peninsula: Big unhappiness.

PENITENCE:
Making penitence: Will live a long healthy life.
Sorrow for having to pay penitence: Gossip by neighbors.
Relatives making penitence: Family disagreement.
Being ordered to give penitence: Infidelity.

PENSION:
Receiving a pension: Will be called upon to make a decision.
Being refused a pension: You have a loyal friend.
Others receiving a pension: Be careful of your decisions.
Relatives receiving a pension: Will make a stock investment.

PEONY:
Of a peony: Loss of temper.
Having peonies: Anxiety.
Receiving peonies: Annoyance.
Giving peonies: Deceitful companions.

PEOPLE:
Happy people: Will be respected in society.
A large group of people: Dignity and respect.
Counting people: Will receive orders from a superior.
People coming to your house: Will have sorrow and tears.
People coming uninvited: Unhappiness.
People who are armed: Will be visited by army officers.
Blind people: Misfortune.
People dressed in white: Loss of friendship.
People dressed in black: Unhappy events in near future.
Elderly male people: Will have fortune.
Elderly female people: Will suffer disgrace.
Influential male people: Will be persecuted.
People in high office: Honor and dignity.
Being courted by women of high class: Misery and wrongdoings.
Being with noble people: High honors.
The lowest class of people: Don't let your boss mistreat you.
Having dealing with low-class people: Hold firm to principles.
Having protection of low-class people: You expect too many favors of others.

PEPPER:
Of pepper: You are satisfied with enough food.
Buying pepper: Will receive good news.
Grinding pepper: Will receive bad news.
Eating pepper: People are saying bad things about you.

Burning the tongue with pepper: Idle gossip will cause injury.
Sprinkling pepper on food: Lasting affection in love.
Smelling pepper and sneezing: Talents within the family.

PEPPERMINT:
Of peppermint: You are proud of children.
Eating peppermint: Will attain your goal.
Receiving peppermint from others: You have deceitful companions.
Giving peppermint to others: Friends will come to rescue if needed.
Giving peppermint to children: Make sure of your plans.

PERAMBULATOR:
Of a perambulator: Unpleasant events are ahead.
Being a perambulator: Responsibilities will hamper you.
A perambulator being with others: Jealousy.

PERCH:
Of a perch: A high position is in store for you.
Climbing to a perch: Will succeed in business ventures.
Climbing to a perch on top of a tree: Do not alter friendships.
Others climbing to a perch: Disaster for fondest hopes.
Enemies climbing to a perch: Danger in love matters.

PERFORM:
Of performing: You attach too much importance to appearances.
Others performing: Will overcome enemies.
Performing in something with others: Happiness.
Enemies performing: Uncertain future.
Children performing: Happy events.

PERFUME:
Smelling perfume: Happiness.
Spilling perfume: Loss of something that brings pleasure.

Buying perfume: Will find a new lover.

Buying cheap perfume: Corruption.

Buying expensive perfume: Jealousy of friends.

Not having perfume: Friends will abuse your confidence.

Breaking a bottle of perfume: Disaster to fondest hopes.

Losing a bottle of perfume: Loss of your lover.

A man preferring a special perfume: A friend will seduce his wife.

A woman preferring a special perfume: Cheating in love affairs.

Receiving bottle of perfume as gift: Will be embraced by unknown person.

Stealing a bottle of perfume: A rival will take away your sweetheart.

Using perfume of other people: Strong attachment for this person.

Giving a gift of perfume: Big profit.

Smelling a man's perfume: Beware of people searching for love.

Smelling perfume on children: They are doing something wrong.

Smelling odor of perfume in a church: God's blessings on you.

Smelling odor of perfume in a house: Frivolity.

Making perfume: Will receive good news from friends.

Making perfume and giving to friends: Good news regarding money.

Mixing perfumes: Pleasant news.

Having a lot of perfume: Frivolity.

A woman putting perfume on a man: You are too proud.

A man putting perfume on a woman: Adultery.

PERIL:

Of peril: Will live in disgrace.

Being in peril: Many obstacles are ahead of you.

Getting out of peril: Affairs will end successfully.

Children being in peril: Unhappiness.

Friends being in peril: You will be penniless.

Enemies being in peril: Bankruptcy.

PERJURY:

Committing perjury: Misfortune will befall you.

Having committed perjury: Postponement of business affairs.

Others committing perjury: Loss of friendship.

Others committing perjury against you: Business will prosper.

Husband or wife committing perjury against each other: Divorce.

PERMIT:

Asking for a permit: Will soon receive relief from pains.

Being refused a permit: Delay in affairs.

Obtaining a permit: Prosperity.

Receiving a marriage permit: Will have many children.

Receiving a building permit: Will do business with an ungrateful woman.

PERSECUTE:

Being persecuted: You enjoy a clear conscience.

Being persecuted falsely: Loss of a friend.

Being persecuted by family: Unhappiness within the family.

Being persecuted by the law: Beware of treachery by friends.

Persecuting others: Contentment.

PERSIAN:

Of a Persian: Laziness.

Being a Persian: Be careful of your business dealings.

Many Persian people: Plans will not materialize.

Being in company of Persian people: A marriage will soon take place.

PERSIAN MELON:

Of Persian melons: Success in love affairs.

Eating Persian melons: Will receive news from a loved one.

Buying Persian melons: Joy without profit.

Growing Persian melons: Good fortune.

Having Persian melons at home: Good success.

PERSPIRE:
Of perspiring: Great efforts will be required for own success.
Perspiring from taking medicine: Health will improve.
Perspiration odors: You have deceitful friends.
Wiping away perspiration from forehead: Small fortune ahead for you.
Wiping perspiration from body: Proposal of marriage.
Children perspiring: Will succeed in undertakings in life.
Enemies perspiring: Loss of money.
Relatives perspiring: Will be rewarded for own good efforts.
Men perspiring: Will be badly treated by creditors.

PEST:
Of pests: Honor and dignity.
Having pests in own house: Will have plenty of money.
Having pests in the garden: Small prosperity.
Having pests in the bedding: Prosperity beyond fondest hopes.
Pests being in others' houses: Loss of friendship.

PESTILENCE:
Of pestilence: Beware of revealing personal affairs.
Causing pestilence: Will undertake a very tiring business.
Friends causing pestilence: Will squander fortune.
Others causing pestilence: Must rely on own good judgment.

PETROLEUM:
Of petroleum: Warning of trouble.
Having petroleum: Danger of dispute with business associates.
Using petroleum: Guard against double cross by enemies.
Buying petroleum: Danger of family disputes.

PETTICOAT:
Of petticoats: Will have many amusements.

Wearing petticoats: Warning of conceit and wasteful expenditures.
Having petticoats: Will soon have a love affair.
Buying petticoats: Exercise moderate mode of living.
Changing a petticoat: Fondest desires will meet with disaster.
Mending a petticoat: Changes in love affairs.
Losing a petticoat: Difficulties in married life.
A young woman losing her petticoat: Loss of affection by her lover.
An unmarried woman losing her petticoat: Will have a marriage proposal.
Petticoats for small girls: Good family undertakings.
A white petticoat: Will receive a beautiful gift.
Colored petticoats: A marriage will soon take place.
A torn petticoat: Unhappiness for a long time.
Embroidered petticoats: Will contract a contagious disease.

PEWTER:
Of things made of various alloys: Contentment and joy.
Having utensils made of pewter: Will have money but not wealth.
Buying utensils made of pewter: Good times are coming.
Using pewter dishes and pots: Will overcome your difficulties.

PHANTOM:
Of a phantom: Disappointment is in store for you.
A phantom dressed in white: Joy and consolation.
A phantom dressed in black: Avoid bad temptations.
Many phantoms: Will be in a state of desperation.
Lovers dreaming of a phantom: The one you love cannot make up her mind.
Unmarried people dreaming of a phantom: Avoid quarrels with friends.

Married people dreaming of a phantom: Do not travel; fate is against you.

Business people dreaming of a phantom: Avoid lending money or giving credit.

PHEASANT:

Of a pheasant: Prosperity beyond own hopes.

Eating pheasant: Everything will come successfully to you.

Cooking pheasant: Big happiness.

Holding a pheasant on a finger: Profit and joy.

Having a pheasant sitting on shoulders: Will have very good health.

Killing a pheasant: Abundant means.

PHILOSOPHY:

Of philosophy: Loss of time.

Studying philosophy: Will undertake a foolish venture.

Working hard at philosophy: Must fight very hard to make money.

Being a philosopher: Will be very hard up for money.

PHOTOGRAPH:

Of own photograph: Misfortune in love affairs.

Photographs of others: Dignity and distinction.

Others taking your photograph: Will suffer loss in speculations.

Taking photographs of others: A rival with take sweetheart's affection.

Taking photographs of children: Approaching money.

Taking photograph of relatives: Joy without profit.

Taking friend's photograph: You are deceived by friends.

Taking a photograph of a dead person: Happiness is assured.

Having a photograph of someone dear hanging around neck: Prosperity.

Receiving or giving own photograph: Treason.

PHYSICIAN:

Of a physician: Will have mastery over many matters.

Being a physician: Joy and profit.

Calling a physician for children: New interests and surroundings.

Calling a physician for yourself: Suitable time to pursue courtship.

Calling a physician for relatives: Rapid recovery.

Others calling a physician: Troubles ahead.

Others calling a physician for you: Will live a long life.

A physician visiting patients: Big wealth.

PIANO:

Of a piano: All of own affairs will prosper.

Having a piano: Successful business undertakings.

Playing the piano: Disputes.

Children playing the piano: Disputes with relatives.

Relatives playing the piano: Disagreements in family affairs.

Others playing the piano: Gossip among friends.

Hearing a piano played: Affairs will prosper.

Hearing sweetheart playing the piano: Certain and happy marriage.

Owning a piano: Beware of jealous friends.

Selling a piano: Loneliness and disappointment.

PICK:

Picking different things: Will have good food.

Picking up someone: Will receive good news.

Picking up children: Inheritance.

Picking flowers: Good relations with relatives.

Owning a pickup truck: Failure of enemies.

Using a pickup truck: Important and very beneficial events to come.

Others using a pickup truck: Be on guard against spiteful gossip.

PICKLE:

Of pickles: A mystery will be solved.

Making pickles: Temptation in love will come to you.

Buying pickles: Financial gains.

Eating pickles: Your life will be marked by lack of ambition.

Giving pickles to others: Important and very beneficial event to come.

Receiving pickles from others: False friends are nearby.

Throwing pickles away: Your troubles are ended.

PICNIC:

Of a picnic: Danger through a secret.

A happy picnic: False friends are gossiping about you.

Others having a picnic: Failure of enemies.

Attending a picnic: Deep enjoyment of life and success.

Having a picnic with children: Luck and prosperity.

Having a picnic with relatives: Will realize high ambitions.

Having a picnic with friends: Doubtful results in love affairs.

PICTURE:

Of pictures: Will be happy in love affairs.

Pictures on a wall: Honor.

Painting pictures: Big joy.

Buying pictures: Will suffer loss through speculation.

Selling pictures: Work without profit.

Receiving a gift of a picture: Immediate success of own hopes.

Having a relative's picture hanging on the wall: Vanity.

Pictures of naked women: Public disgrace.

Pictures of naked men: Unhappiness in love affairs.

Pleasing pictures: Double cross by one you trust.

Taking pictures off the wall: Are envied by your enemies.

Other people having pictures: Enemies are endeavoring to destroy you.

Owning a collection of pictures: Will suffer through ingratitude.

A collection of ancient pictures: Danger in love affairs.

A collection of modern pictures: Take care of your dealings.

PIE:

Of pies in a pastry shop: Dissension within the family.

Cooking a pie: Joy in the home.

Eating a pie: Good fortune is ahead.

Making a pie to give to others: Will come out well from your perils.

Receiving a pie as a gift: A friend is seeking your ruin.

Giving children pie to eat: Hard work awaits you.

Giving relatives pie to eat: New interests and surroundings.

PIER:

Of a pier: Will bring happiness to someone else.

Being on a pier alone: Warning of trouble.

Being on a pier with others: Danger is ahead.

Others being on a pier: Be cautious in all your affairs.

Workmen being on a pier: Will have good earnings.

Sailors being on a pier: Happiness will come in the near future.

PIG:

Of pigs: Will have good earnings.

Pigs being well fed: Prosperity to come.

Pigs being thin: Children will cause petty vexations.

Many pigs: Will receive money after the death of a relative.

Buying pigs: Will have joy.

Selling pigs: Will be hated by friends.

Wild pigs: A friend will attempt to harm you.

PIGEON:

Of pigeons: Big success.

White pigeons: Consolation.

Gray pigeons: Devotion.

Brown and white pigeons: Good business enterprises.

Many pigeons: You are engaged in charitable work.

A pigeon's roost: Imminent marriage.

Pigeons flying: Good news will soon be received.

Pigeons walking on the ground: Important news from faraway.

Pigeons lighting on ledges: Favorable love affairs.

Two pigeons fighting: Changes in own affairs.

PILGRIM:

Of a pilgrim: Welcome to all who come to your door.

A female pilgrim: Affairs will change for the better.

Being with a pilgrim woman: Happiness.

Being a pilgrim yourself: You are too independent.

A gathering of pilgrims: Desires will be satisfied.

Pilgrims migrating to new places: Poverty.

Giving money to pilgrims: Fulfillment of fondest wish.

PILL:

Of many pills: Will take a journey abroad.

Taking pills yourself: Important responsibilities entrusted to you.

Giving pills to others: Will suffer severe criticism.

Giving pills to children: Happiness within the family.

Giving pills to relatives: Sweet satisfaction.

Taking many pills each day: Will be healthy.

Buying pills: Use caution in business ventures.

PILLOW:

Of a pillow: A life of ease and plenty awaits.

Many pillows: Hard work.

Not having pillows: Persecution.

Having head on many pillows: Will have a good marriage.

Being surrounded by pillows: You are too feminine.

A soiled or untidy pillow: Expect troubles of your own making.

Clean pillows: Attainment of own goals.

Children lying on pillows: Expect an increase in the family.

PILOT:

Being a pilot: You are the master in your love affairs.

A pilot directing a ship: Success in business.

A pilot flying an airplane: Will accomplish own desires.

A pilot causing damage to a ship: Joyous times ahead.

A pilot crashing but no one being hurt: Defeat by rivals.

A pilot crashing and everyone being killed: Trouble will come from faraway.

PIMPLE:

Of pimples: Riches.

Having pimples on the body: Will have good earnings.

Squeezing pimples: Will have a large amount of silver.

PIN:

Of pins: Small contradiction.

Having many pins: Serious trouble with a friend.

Buying pins: Will have good earnings.

Using pins while sewing: Good health.

Pricking yourself with a pin: Disagreements in love affairs.

Others using pins: Will be contradicted.

Throwing pins away: Long life ahead of you.

PINAFORE:

Of a pinafore: Happiness.

Wearing a pinafore: Be circumspect in your actions.

A young woman dreaming of wearing a pinafore: Will have ups and downs.

Tearing a pinafore: Small benefits.

Tying a pinafore: Will receive big honors.

A blue apron: Gossiping of other women.

Pinafore being lost: Loss of sweetheart.

PIN CUSHION:

Of a pin cushion: Undertakings will be accomplished.

A pin cushion without pins: A life of ease awaits.

A pin cushion with many pins: Dissatisfaction.

Giving a pin cushion as a gift: Be on guard with your friends.

PINEAPPLE:

Of pineapples: Will be fortunate in all affairs.

A pineapple tree: Good news.

Peeling skin from a pineapple: Good relationships with neighbors.

Eating pineapple: Short-lived love affairs.

Slicing pineapple: Be cautious in relationships.

Cooking pineapple: Love affairs will last forever.

Giving pineapple to children to eat: Will learn of new schemes.

Receiving pineapples as a gift: Comfortable domestic surroundings.

Giving a gift of pineapple: Will receive a social invitation.

PINE:

Of things made of pine: Danger concerning your income.

Using pine wood: Happiness.

Buying pine furniture: Happiness in love affairs.

Working with pine wood: Devotion to affairs.

PINE TREE:

Of a pine tree: Tremendous happiness.

Many pine trees: Family reunion.

Cutting branches from a pine tree: Will enjoy a good life.

Cutting down a pine tree: Congenial work and good news.

PINK:

Of the color pink: Glorious success.

Pink material of any kind: Will have a happy family life.

Buying pink clothes: Recovery of lost money.

PINKING:

Of pinking material: Will receive consideration from others.

Others' pinking material: Failure of enemies.

Material that has been pinked: Joyous times and new clothes.

PIPE:

Of pipes: Unusual good events.

Smoking a pipe: Sweet satisfaction.

Filling a pipe: Disagreeable position.

Putting a pipe away: Pride without advantage.

Breaking a pipe: Security.

Having several pipes: Great peace of mind.

Dirty pipes: Misery.

Other peoples' pipes: Affliction.

Receiving a pipe as a gift: Advancement in own business.

Giving a pipe as a gift: Important and very beneficial event to come.

Putting out a pipe: Loss of a friend.

Buying a pipe: Will be visited by an old friend.

PIRATE:

Of a pirate: Beware of your friends.

Many pirates: Love affair has reached a very low point.

Being a pirate: Journey and financial gains.

Being a victim of a pirate: Deceitful associate will cause pain.

Being harmed by pirates: Exciting times ahead.

PIROUETTE:

Doing a pirouette: Much gratitude.

Others doing a pirouette: Will receive money.

Young girls dancing a pirouette: Health and prosperity.

Many dancers doing a pirouette: An employee is cheating you.

Daughter dancing a pirouette: She will marry a band leader.

PISTOL:

Of a pistol: Recovery of health.

Hearing the sound of a pistol being fired: Misfortune.

Firing a pistol: Hard work with little results.

Carrying a pistol: Will be disliked by people.

Other people firing a pistol: Will learn of schemes to ruin you.

Owning many pistols: Profit.
Being an officer and carrying a pistol: Treachery.
Friends carrying a pistol: Will be annoyed.
Enemies carrying a pistol: Loss of temper.

PIT:
Of a pit: Will have a nice complexion.
Going down into a deep pit: Business affairs will decline.
Going down into a shallow pit: Decline in love affairs.
Falling into a pit: Indifference and coolness to love.
Hurting yourself in a pit: Will have troubles confronting you.
Being forced to go down into a pit: Will risk fortune and health.
Falling into a pit and being hurt: Great sorrow and misfortune.
Walking along and falling into a pit: Will escape danger.
Others being in a pit: Failure in business.
Many people being killed in a pit: Enemies will endeavor to destroy you.

PITCH:
Pitch used to repair cracks: Will make money.
Pitch used on the bottom of ships: Honor and dignity.
Pitching in a ball game: Honor.
Others pitching a ball game: Will obtain money easily.
Children pitching: Undertakings will be accomplished.
A pitcher who has lost a game: Reputation is in danger.

PITCHER:
Of a pitcher: Many joys and good luck.
A colored pitcher: Unlucky events to come.
A pottery pitcher: Will lose money.
A pitcher being full: Fidelity.
A pitcher being empty: Infidelity.
Breaking a pitcher: Love affairs will come to an end.

Throwing a pitcher away: Will have a new lover.

PITY:
Being pitied: Humiliation.
Having pity for someone else: Small vexation.
Having pity on relatives: Expect disappointment.
Being pitied by friends: Will receive a gift.
Having pity on friends: Health and joy.
Having pity on poor people: Affairs are in confusion.
Having pity on sick people: Luck and prosperity.

PLACE:
Of a meeting place: Will have many faithful friends.
Arranging things in place: Good love relations.
Placing things in correct order: Many people are interested in your future.
Placing things in wrong order: Will discover a false friend.

PLAGUE:
Having the plague: Wealthy marriage.
Other people having the plague: Lucky discovery of money.
People dying of the plague: Joy and pleasure.
Friends dying of the plague: Delivery from suffering and pain.
People recovering from the plague: Good earnings in business.
Someone who can cure the plague: Realization of desires.
Rats being killed that caused the plague: Will be an influential person.

PLAID:
Of plaid material: Good health.
Many plaid materials: Kind companions.
Wearing plaid garments: Will have fortune.
Children wearing plaid garments: Abundant means.
Relatives wearing plaid garments: Family quarrels.

Enemies wearing plaid garments:
Happy events.
Others wearing plaid garments: Good
hopes.

PLAIN:
Of a vast open plain: Success.
An open plain covered with grass:
Matrimony.
Being on a beautiful plain: Joy and
prosperity.
Children being on a large open plain:
Will make a pleasure trip.
Relatives being on a large open plain:
Material gains.
An arid plain: Unhappiness and dis-
tress.
A fruitful plain: Will have a life of
ease and pleasure.

PLANE:
Of a plane: Indifference.
Using a carpenter's plane: Life will
be shortened.
Others using a plane: Success in un-
dertakings.
A carpenter using a plane: Squander-
ing of money.
Owning a plane: Satisfaction.
Sharpening the blade of a plane: Rec-
ognition of rights.

PLANET:
Of a planet: Avoid being so superstitious.
A planet falling: You are working in
vain to achieve a desire.
Own horoscope planet: Long life and
fortune in old age.
Children's horoscope planet: Loss of
a mate.

PLANK:
Of a plank: Happiness.
Many planks: Will be disturbed during
a love affair.
Cutting planks: Disappointment.
Planks falling down: Enjoyment in
life.
Planks piled up: Public disgrace.
Others handling planks: Unfortunate
business affairs.
Buying planks: Will be in a restless
state of mind.

Selling planks: Will have a satisfactory
trip.

PLANT:
Of a plant: Obstacles in business.
Many plants: Joy without profit.
Small plants: Children will grow up to
to be very intelligent.
Watering plants: Good health.
Planting plants: Satisfaction in busi-
ness.
Plants in a garden: Good earnings.
Plants in the home: Dignity and dis-
tinction.
Plants used to make medicines: Un-
happiness will disappear.

PLASTER:
Of plaster: Unhappiness.
Handling plaster: Will soon experience
many ups and downs.
Plaster coming off the wall of own
house: Family troubles.
Plaster being on the floor of own
home: Will suffer humiliation.
Plaster falling on you: False accusa-
tions are being made against you.

PLATFORM:
Of a platform: Will marry one you
least expected.
Being on a platform: Beware of hasty
judgments.
Performing on a platform: Death of
an enemy.
Making a political speech on a plat-
form: Approaching money.
Watching a parade from a platform:
Triumph in love affairs.

PLAY:
Of a play: Beware of jealous friends.
Attending a play: Fulfillment of own
dearest desire.
Others attending a play: Will live a
long life.
Friends attending a play: Recovery
from an illness.
Taking part in a play: Will overcome
enemies.
Someone you know taking part in a
play: You are being deceived.
Attending a play with family: Avoid
rivals.

PLEAD:
Of pleading: Take confidence in your own powers.
Others pleading for you: Confidence will soon be proven to you.
An attorney pleading for you: Important and beneficial events to come.
An attorney pleading for others: Postponement of success.
Pleading in defense of children: Shame and sorrow.
Pleading in own defense: You have loyal friends.
Pleading in others' defense: Luck and prosperity.

PLEASURE:
Having pleasure: Another person is enjoying what you hoped to win.
Others having pleasure: A mystery will be solved.
Children having pleasure: Congenial work and good news.
Friends having pleasure: Will be cheated by friends.
Sweetheart having pleasure: Frivolity.

PLEURISY:
Of pleurisy: Will soon have an illness.
Having pleurisy: Must rely on own vigor.
Relatives having pleurisy: Take better care of own health.
Friends have pleurisy: Will have very good business.

PLOT:
Of a plot of land: Important correspondence will come.
Buying a plot of land: Changes and surprises.
Selling a plot of land: Surprising changes in own affairs.
Having a cemetery plot: Possible engagement.

PLOUGH:
Ploughing a field: Will not achieve success at first, it will come later.
Others ploughing a field: Hard work is ahead.
Being unable to plough: Will overcome troubles with perseverance.

A farmer ploughing a field: Happiness in married life.
Young people ploughing: Happy life for the patient lover.

PLUG:
Of plugs: Will have a big dispute soon.
Plugging a hole with cement: Will make the acquaintance of a new lady.
Plugging a hole in a vase: Will have many love affairs.
Plugging a pipe: Will marry a rich woman the second time.

PLUM:
Of plums: Happiness.
Eating plums: Will experience a disappointment.
Buying plums: Will have a quiet old age.
Selling plums: Good financial standing.
Plums out of season: You are forcing affection upon the opposite sex.
Dried plums: Obstacles.
Green plums: Never-ending friendship.
Black plums: Bad business.
Gathering ripe plums: Innocence.
Gathering green plums: Efforts will fail.
Receiving a gift of plums: Make plans carefully.
A plum tree: Your position is not satisfactory.
Picking plums from a tree: Change of position in employment.
Picking plums from the ground: Difficulties.

PLUME:
Wearing a plume in own hat: Honor.
Others wearing a plume: Unhappiness.
Daughters wearing a plume in hat: Public honor especially if white feather.
Relatives wearing a plume: Unexpected gains.
Friends wearing a plume: You will be tortured.
White plume: Riches.

Black plume: Postponement of business affairs.

Being covered with feather plumes: Satisfaction.

PLUNDER:
Of plundering: Unhappiness and delay in own affairs.

Others plundering: Troubles in love affairs.

Relatives plundering: Will have worry and suffering.

Plundering yourself: Bad results in own affairs.

Being plundered by others: Misfortune.

PLIERS:
Of pliers: Joy and profit.

Using pliers: Will make a cake in the near future.

Buying pliers: Will receive unpleasant news.

Mechanics working with pliers: People are making jokes about you.

PNEUMONIA:
Of pneumonia: Will have a long illness.

Having pneumonia: Loss of your estate.

Children having pneumonia: Dissolution of own hopes.

Relatives having pneumonia: Domestic quarrels.

Others having pneumonia: Health is in danger.

Dying from pneumonia: Will suffer big losses.

POACH:
Of poaching eggs: Guard your speech.

Making poached eggs: Everything you undertake will be accomplished.

Eating poached eggs: Much happiness.

Poaching in soft ground: Will have a vigorous mind.

Escaping from poaching into soft ground: Will live a long life.

POCKET:
Of pockets: Will meet stingy people.

Own pockets: Will have covetous relatives.

Mate's pockets: Will win at gambling.

Relative's pockets: Misery.

Friend's pockets: Beware of scandal.

Enemy's pockets: Will make up with enemies.

POCKETBOOK:
Of a pocketbook: Will have emotional sorrow.

Own pocketbook: Big joy.

Losing a pocketbook: Quarrels with closest friends.

Finding a pocketbook: Luck and prosperity.

Relative's pocketbook: Discovery of a secret.

A lady's pocketbook: Attainment of almost every desire.

POETRY:
Of poetry: Tranquillity.

Reading poetry: Happiness in love affairs.

Reading poetry out loud: Death of a relative.

Writing poetry: Changes in love affairs.

Being a poet: Will have a hard life ahead.

POISON:
Of poison: Will be disregarded by others.

Taking poison yourself: Will contract the plague.

Others taking poison: Will encounter opposition.

Giving poison to someone: Separation from a loved one.

Throwing poison away: Success regardless of all obstacles.

Dying from taking poison: Be careful of giving credit and lending money.

Friends taking poison: Do not speculate in stock market.

Recovering from the effects of poison: Difficulties will be overcome.

Poisoning someone's drink: Dishonesty of a person you now trust.

Buying arsenic poison: Will meet with contrariety.

Taking arsenic poison: Will have a contagious disease.

POKER:
Playing poker: You have good tastes.
Playing poker with friends: Total loss in your affairs.
Playing poker with unknown people: Doomed to be disappointed.
Playing poker with people who are cheating: Financial gains.
A man dreaming of playing poker: Attainment of almost every desire.
A married woman dreaming of playing poker: She is cheating on husband.
An unmarried woman dreaming of playing poker: Should guard virtue carefully.

POLICE:
Of a police station: You are very tired.
Being arrested by police unjustly: Will win over every rival.
Being arrested by police with cause: Misfortune will attend you.
Police handcuffing an arrested person: Will live a long life.
Being at a police station for questioning: Happiness.
Being with friends at a police station: Loss of money.

POLICEMAN:
Of a policeman: Friends are not being true to you.
Being arrested by a policeman: Security with good work.
Killing a policeman: Will have pleasure ending with unhappiness.
A policeman arresting other people: Misfortune is near.
A policeman arresting your friends: Will have delayed joy.

POLITE:
Being polite: Will be in need of bread.
Others being polite to you: Will receive an invitation to a party.
Children being polite: Will increase property possessions.
Friends being polite: Beware of being double-crossed.

POMEGRANATE:
Of a pomegranate: Will fall heir to riches.

A pomegranate tree: Will receive good news.
A blossoming pomegranate tree: Prosperity.
A pomegranate tree with fruit on it: Joy and pleasure.
Breaking a pomegranate into two pieces: Persecution from tax collector.
Eating pomegranates: Happiness and good health.
Taking the juice from a pomegranate: Hard work ahead of you.
Having a basket full of pomegranates: Will be guilty of foolish actions.
Pomegranates being spoiled: Troubles ahead of you.

POND:
Of a pond: Will quarrel with a loved one.
A clear pond: Wealth and lasting friendship.
A muddy pond: Quarrels within the home.
A quiet pond: Great affection between sweethearts.
A pond full of dead fish: Will soon go into bankruptcy.
A pond full of live fish: Abundance and riches.
A dry pond: Poverty.
A very small pond: You are surrounded by much gossip.
A very big pond: Good times are coming.

PONY:
Of a pony: Will marry a beautiful girl.
A beautiful pony: Will acquire a beautiful house.
An ugly pony: Will marry an ugly wife.
A newly born pony: Will have a woman who loves you very much.
Pony running: Hard work ahead.
Several ponies: Investments will bring profits.
Buying a pony: Embarrassment.
Selling a pony: Unpleasant news.
Feeding a pony in your hand: Will be kissed by a woman.

Children playing with a pony: Will be seduced by a woman.

Children riding ponies: Will be freed of bad accusations.

POOL:

Of a pool: Fortune is ahead of you.

A pool full of water: Will have good business.

A pool with very little water: Refrain from stock market speculation.

A dirty pool: Prosperous business.

A dry pool: Will forgive your enemies.

POPE:

Of the Pope: You expect too many favors of others.

Visiting the Pope: Must rely upon own vigor.

The death of a Pope: Postponement of success.

Talking with the Pope: Will have good humor and fortune.

Receiving the Pope's blessings: Will be helped by one for whom you care.

POPPY:

Of poppies: Will have intelligent children.

Picking poppies: Will have a dispute with your sweetheart.

Having poppies in the house: Change for the better in own affairs.

Giving poppies away: Successful pleasure trip.

Red poppies: You are too superstitious.

Poppies of various other colors: Will acquire riches in near future.

PORCH:

Of a porch: Honor.

Walking under a porch: Riches.

Sitting on a porch: Will be visited by a delightful person.

Eating on a porch: Will have to be satisfied with present conditions.

PORCUPINE:

Of a porcupine: You are a stingy person.

Several porcupines: Enemies are attempting to bring harm to you.

Eating porcupine meat: Will have a touchy business affair.

A pregnant woman dreaming of a porcupine: Will have ugly children.

PORT:

Of a port: Annoyance.

Landing in a port: Happiness.

Being with others in a port: Will receive news from faraway.

A vessel arriving in port: Death of a guest in the home.

Sailors coming ashore at port: Troubles in marriage.

Arriving at a foreign port: Happiness in love.

A beautiful port: Will be defrauded.

A sea port: Discovery of a secret.

A port on a lake or river: Will take a long voyage.

PORTER:

Of a porter: Good health.

Having a porter helping you: You are a faithful mate.

Having a porter take baggage: Confidence in self.

A porter loaded with luggage: Your demands have been refused.

A porter carrying others' luggage: Will lose confidence in yourself.

Being a porter: Misfortune.

PORTRAIT:

Of a portrait: Will be happy in love affairs.

Own portrait: Will live a long life.

Receiving a gift of a portrait: Immediate success of own hopes.

Having a portrait of relatives: Vanity.

The portrait of your sweetheart: Long-lasting love.

Having a portrait of children: Children will attain a high position.

A portrait of a friend: You are being deceived.

PORTUGAL:

Going to Portugal: Delay in affairs.

Being in Portugal: Will enjoy good music.

Portuguese people: Will receive good news from faraway.

Being with Portuguese people: Will receive a surprise.

POSITION:
Of own present position: Will be teased by small children.
Having an honorable position: Joy.
Being in an embarrassing position: Will receive happy news soon.
Losing your position: Will receive sad news in the near future.

POSSESS:
Possessing wealth: You are much too arrogant and stubborn.
Possessing something gorgeous: Pleasure, joy, and riches.
Possessing a good piece of property: Wife as beautiful as property good.
Possessing something well situated: Will have a beautiful wife.

POST:
Of a post: Beware of misfortune.
Several posts standing: Joy and contentment.
People setting posts: Victory.
A signpost in the street: Big honors.
A post that has been knocked down: Sickness in near future.
Playing around a post: Family disaster.

POSTER:
Of a poster: Security.
Hanging a poster: Infirmity.
Making a poster: Reconciliation.
Sending posters: Unhappiness in love.
Receiving posters: Will have good friends.
Drawing posters: Will argue about a bill for food.

POSTERITY:
Of posterity: Will have blessings.
Immediate posterity: Family arguments.
Oldest generation of own posterity: Will have a big fortune coming.
Own posterity: Don't trust those who say they are in love with you.

POSTILLION:
Riding as a guard: Will receive good news.

A postillion falling from a horse: Will receive annoying news.
Several postillions riding as escorts: Fortune.
A postillion being killed: Domestic arguments.

POSTMAN:
Of a postman: Good news.
Being a postman: Loss of real estate.
Giving a letter to a postman: Listen to the advice of friends.
Receiving mail from a postman: Happiness.
Receiving special delivery letter from a postman: Great love.

POSTMASTER:
Of a postmaster: Someone is trying to cheat you.
Being a postmaster: You enjoy eating too much.
Arguing with a postmaster: You will make money.
A postmaster being fired: Family quarrels.

POST OFFICE:
Of a post office: Will be offended by someone.
Being in a post office: Will be victorious through honesty.
Mailing a letter at the post office: Will have obstacles in your path.
Receiving a letter from the post office: Change of residence.
Registering a letter at the post office: Change of companions.
Buying stamps at a post office: Unpleasant things awaiting.
Finding post office closed: Dissension in love affairs.

POT:
Of a pot: Disagreeable news.
A pot being on a stove: Will make good commercial profits.
Filling a pot with food: Will move about often.
Buying new pots: Devotion.
Throwing away old pots: People respect you.
Buying a complete set of pots: Disappointment to come.

Cooking food in a huge pot: Be careful of plans and keep them to yourself.

Burning yourself on a pot: Loss of a dearly loved one.

POTATO:

Of potatoes: Will have a very quiet future.

Planting potatoes: Dearest plans will materialize.

Digging potatoes: Big success in own efforts.

Peeling potatoes: Will have many troubles.

Boiling potatoes: Will entertain an unwelcome guest.

Frying potatoes: Will marry a husky girl.

Baking potatoes: Will have arguments with sweetheart.

Eating mashed potatoes: Your dreams will come true.

Eating potato salad: Investments will bring profits.

Feeding potatoes to pigs: Will be enticed by a woman.

POTENT:

Being potent: Hard work awaits you.

Being potent in own work: Warning to be prudent.

Being potent in own love affairs: Happiness in love.

Having sexual potency: Financial gains.

Having control of potency: Discovery of own errors in life.

POUCH:

Of a pouch: Prosperous business.

Owning a pouch: Things will come to you slowly.

Filling a pouch: Beware of foreign people.

Having an empty pouch: Poverty.

Losing a pouch: Loss of business.

POULTRY:

Of poultry: Considerable trouble is ahead.

Buying fresh poultry: Consolation.

Cleaning poultry: Someone will give you money.

Buying young poultry: Will have a change in own position.

Buying fryers: Considerable earnings.

Buying stewing poultry: Profit without glory.

Buying fat poultry: Family quarrels.

Buying an uncleaned chicken: Great courage.

Giving a gift of poultry: Loss of a friend.

POUND:

Of pounding: Unhappiness in love.

Pounding food: Contentment.

Pounding on a door: Unhappiness.

Hearing others pounding: Death of a woman while delivering a child.

A pound of weight: Very important and beneficial event to come.

POVERTY:

Being in poverty: Will soon incur a loss.

Other people in poverty: Will give beneficial service to others.

Many people in poverty: Unpleasant family affairs.

Crippled people in poverty: Love argument.

Falling into poverty: Will have many children.

Being in poverty and very sick: Will have many debts to pay.

Family falling into poverty: Future riches.

Friends being in poverty: Health and joy.

POWDER:

Of powder: Paternal joy.

Using face powder: Lasting love.

Using body powder: Will have many boyfriends.

Using perfumed powder: Something is troubling you.

Using white powder: Joy.

Using flesh-colored powder: Love.

Using a dark powder: Happiness.

Sprinkling powder on sweetheart's body: Sweetheart will get sick.

Buying powder: Opposition in your marriage.

Receiving a gift of powder: Treacherous friends.

Giving a gift of powder: Jealousy of friends.

Handling gunpowder: Death of your enemies.

Filling cartridges with gunpowder: Misery.

POWER:

Being powerful: Will have a big loss.

Having power in your position: Good future.

Taking advantage of your power: Will receive good news.

Using your powers to hurt others: Will fall into disgrace.

Own power going to your head: You will go crazy.

POWER OF ATTORNEY:

Preparing a power of attorney: Joy in the family.

Giving power of attorney to someone: Don't trust help of strangers.

Receiving power of attorney: Will place trust in someone under you.

Giving power of attorney to lawyer: Will have illness but recover soon.

Canceling a power of attorney: Will have trouble with finances soon.

PRAISE:

Receiving praise: Are surrounded by scandal.

Giving praise: People are gossiping about you.

Hearing others praise you: You have faithful friends.

Praising God: Abundant means.

Praising your children: Jealousy by other members of family.

PRAY:

Of praying: Honors and riches.

Praying in church: Desires will be accomplished.

Praying to God: Much happiness.

Praying to Jesus Christ: Riches.

Praying to the cross of Jesus Christ: Infidelity.

Praying for someone else: Poverty.

Other people praying for you: Happiness.

Praying for someone who has died: Will attain your desires.

Praying and having prayer heard: Fortune.

Praying and it not being heard: Misfortune.

Praying to possess a lady: Good reputation.

Praying for someone to do something for you: Bad consequences.

PREACHER:

Of a preacher: Satisfactory results in own plans.

A preacher preaching at a pulpit: Many worries at present.

Being a preacher: Will have many ups and downs.

Hearing a preacher from out of town: Misfortune is coming.

An important preacher: Inheritance from a relative faraway.

Of a precipice: People are making fun of you.

Falling into a precipice and being killed: Will be dishonored.

Falling into a precipice and living: Will be honored by others.

Walking away from a precipice: Will overcome all troubles.

Others falling into a precipice: Avoid travel and change of plans.

A woman dreaming of falling into a precipice: Will give birth to a child.

PREGNANT:

Being pregnant: Health will soon improve.

A married woman dreaming of being pregnant: Marital unhappiness.

Unmarried woman dreaming of being pregnant: Trouble and injury through scandal.

A man dreaming that his wife is pregnant: She will give birth to a boy.

A widow dreaming of being pregnant: She will marry very soon.

A widower dreaming of a pregnant woman: Will have plenty of money.

A young girl dreaming of being pregnant: Won't get married for long time.

A young man dreaming of getting girl friend pregnant: Remorse of conscience.
(See also **TABLE OF DREAMS ON PREGNANCY** in Preface.)

PREMATURE:
Making premature plans: You are prone to being too impatient.
Making premature plans for a trip: Will be persecuted.
Making premature plans for marriage: Quarrels.
Making a premature start in business: Poverty.
Premature delivery of a child: Change in plans.

PRESCRIPTION:
Having a prescription: Will overcome present unhealthy condition.
Asking doctor for a prescription: Will enjoy much happiness.
Refilling a prescription: Will recover completely from an illness.
Filling prescription for the family: Will buy new clothes.
A doctor writing a prescription: Good hopes ahead.

PRESENT:
Receiving a present: Will have pleasant reunion with a friend.
Receiving a present from a loved one: Success and good luck.
Receiving a present from others: Bad luck.
Receiving several presents: Beware of person from whom you received them.
Giving a present to a relative: Good hopes.
Receiving a present from an important person: Will receive many honors.
Receiving a present from relatives: Postponement of success.
Receiving a Christmas gift from relatives: Will have many admirers.
Receiving a Christmas present from friends: Treason.

PRESIDENT:
Being a president: Honors.
Being elected president: Will receive

blessing from God.
Being re-elected president: You are committing adultery.
Being impeached while president: Treason by friends.
Losing presidential position: Good news.

PRESS:
Of a press: Beware of untrue friends.
Working at a press: Inheritance.
Owning a press: Quarrels over inheritance.
Printing on a press: Public disorder.
A money-printing press: Will eat bitter bread.
A wax press: Will receive an invitation to a wedding.
An olive press: Don't rely on friends.
A wine press: Riches and fortune.
Pressing dresses: Frivolity.
Pressing underclothes: Unhappiness.
Pressing men's clothes: Fortune.
Pressing children's dresses: Riches.

PRICE:
Asking the price of an item: Perfect tranquillity.
Paying the price asked for an item: Beware of external appearances.
Arguing about price of an item: Good news.
Refusing to pay the price asked: Health will not be good.
The price being too low: Death of a person you know.
Being cheated on a price: Must moderate your passions.

PRICK:
Of pricking yourself: A gift will be made in a loving spirit.
Others getting pricked: Public disgrace.
Being pricked with a needle: Misfortune in love affairs.
Being pricked with a thorn: Loss of present position.

PRIDE:
Having pride in yourself: You ignore other people.
Pride being harmful to you: People are gossiping about you.

Pride not letting you humble yourself: Will hear sad news.

Other people having pride: Persecution.

PRIEST:

Of a priest: Inheritance is near at hand.

Talking to a priest: Will have a position of importance.

Confessing sins to a priest: You are dealing in dangerous affairs.

A woman dreaming of confessing to a priest: Won't marry one she loves.

A young girl dreaming of confessing to a priest: Will break engagement.

A priest being in the street: Loss of money in business transaction.

A priest being aboard a ship: Bad weather and shipwreck.

Family going to see a priest: Quarrels within the family.

PRIME MINISTER:

Of a prime minister: Happiness of short duration.

Talking with a prime minister: People are trying to deceive you.

Asking for audience with prime minister: Much work with little profit.

Others visiting a prime minister: You take things too seriously.

Being a prime minister: You have enough money to buy without care.

PRIMER:

Of a school primer: Good news.

Carrying a school primer with you: Will find something that was hidden.

A prayer book: Consolation for misfortunes.

Carrying a prayer book with you: Prosperity.

PRINCE:

Of a prince: A present will be given to you.

Meeting a prince: Honors and riches to come.

Going with a prince: Will have a large fortune.

Asking permission for audience with a prince: Success in business.

Killing a prince: Will receive news of the death of a loved one.

Talking with a princess: Will have self-conceit.

Seeing a princess: Will be very arrogant with friends.

Residing with a princess: Peril of death.

PRINT:

Of printing: Beware of enemies.

Having something printed: Inheritance.

Watching printing being done: Success.

Printing letterhead: Legal troubles over inheritance.

Printing calling cards: Patience will not be an advantage to you.

Printing official documents: Will be discredited by the public.

Printing newspapers: Will enjoy much success.

Printing books: Rely upon own vigor.

Reprinting books: Your future is secure.

Of a printing office: Long life.

Operating a printing office: Will experience bad luck.

Looking at a printing proof: Beware of gossip.

Watching the printing process: Guard against dangerous friends.

PRINTER:

Of a printer: Hidden family secrets.

Being a printer: Must exercise extreme economy.

Others who are printers: Will experience poverty.

A relative who is a printer: Family fortune.

Printers in the printing business: Decline in business.

PRISON:

Of a prison: Happiness in the family.

Being put in prison: Good luck.

Being in prison: Joy.

Remaining in prison: Will receive a large favor.

Getting out of prison: Short-lived fortune.

PRIVATE:
Being a private in the army: Will have happiness in the near future.
Being in a private place: Joy and good results in love.
A man being in private room with a beautiful woman: Separation from wife.
A man being in private room with an ugly woman: Big quarrels.
A woman being in private room with a man: Public dishonor and arrest.

PRIZE:
Receiving a prize: You fear an enemy.
Giving a prize: Good friendship.
Others receiving a prize: Infirmity.
Friends receiving a prize: Will have an illness in the family.
Enemy receiving a prize: Beware of gossip.

PRIZE FIGHT:
Of a prize fight: You do not have control of yourself.
Being in a prize fight: Good food.
Winning a prize fight: Bad business ahead.
Losing a prize fight: Will lose at gambling.
Being a prize fighter: Humiliation and misery.

PROCESS:
Beginning a legal process: Will have an everlasting friendship.
People in good health losing a legal process: Sickness.
Sick people losing a legal process: Recovery of health.
Winning a legal process: Will enjoy gladness.

PROCESSION:
Of a procession: Honor and joy.
Watching a procession: Advancement within own position.
A religious procession: Treachery by a friend.
A procession of priests: Beware of untrustworthy friends.
A procession of happy people: Will receive a gift.

A married person dreaming of a procession: Long-lasting marriage.
Lovers watching a procession: Happiness.
Unmarried person being in a procession: Good luck for many years.

PRODUCER:
Being a producer of farm products: Profit.
Being a music producer: Passing fortune.
Being a theatrical producer: Honor and joy.
Producing many children: Will win money at a lottery.

PROFANATION:
Violating sacred things: Will suffer terrible pains.
Relatives violating sacred things: Misery.
Friends doing profanation: Will receive a legacy.
Other people doing profanation: Will incur large debts.

PROFANE:
Profaning the name of God in vain: Will have financial losses.
Others being profane: Will have a fight and lose a friendship.
Teaching children not to be profane: Will have a happy family.

PROFESSOR:
Of a professor: Will be invited to a solemn occasion.
A male professor teaching: Must control your passions.
A female professor teaching: Important and very beneficial events ahead.
Being a professor: Will have sorrow.
A professor teaching only women: Friends will cheat you.
A professor teaching only men: Danger through a secret.
A woman being a university professor: Sickness.
A man being a university professor: Unhappiness in love affairs.

PROJECT:
Of a project: Will receive a gift.
Making business projects: You are wasting time.
Making pleasure projects: You find amusements in unfavorable places.
Making financial projects: Desires will be accomplished.

PROMISE:
Making a promise: Will be disillusioned.
Not keeping a promise: Unceasing embarrassment.
Accepting a promise: Will receive good news.
Receiving a promise: Fortune.
Receiving a promise of matrimony: Will accomplish own desires.
Refusing a promise of matrimony: Good fortune.

PROMONTORY:
Of a promontory: Outstanding events are just around the corner.
Viewing a promontory in the distance: Will be disillusioned.
Being on top of a promontory: Financial gains.
Others being on a promontory: Change in environment.
Enemies being on a promotory: You are in the grip of deceitful people.

PROPERTY:
Of property: Marriage to a wealthy person.
Looking at property: Riches.
Receiving property as a gift: Will have agreeable conditions.
Giving a gift of property: Will have a big family.
Buying property: Will have plenty of wealth.
Selling property: Will marry a young person.
A prospective buyer of property: You are a dreamer.
Having a business on own property: Will receive wonderful news.
Selling property in the country: Disgrace.

Possessing property in the country: Fortune.
Having a large estate of property: Unhappiness.
Inheriting property: Will be in mourning.

PROPHET:
Of a prophet: Don't rely on unfaithful promises of others.
Being a prophet: Will receive a financial loss.
Making prophesies: Will be involved in dangerous and mysterious things.
Others prophesying to you: Rely on own good judgment.

PROPOSAL:
Making a proposal: Will be invited for dinner.
Receiving a proposal: Good fortune and joy.
Refusing a proposal: Unsatisfied curiosity.
Accepting a proposal: Will be tormented by doubts.
Others making proposals: Family quarrels.
Relatives making proposals: Will have a quiet old age.

PROPOSITION:
Receiving a proposition: Will receive good news.
Making a proposition: Dignity and distinction.
Accepting a proposition: Great joy.
Refusing a proposition: Change of surroundings.
Others refusing a proposition: Warning of trouble.
Relatives accepting a proposition: Promise of matrimony.
Enemies accepting a proposition: Approaching money.

PROSECUTOR:
Of a prosecutor: You are being deceived.
Being a prosecutor: You have plenty of friends.
Arguing with a prosecutor: Innocence will be proven.

A prosecutor going against your enemies: Honor and distinction.

Others being prosecuted: Business will decline.

PROSPECTIVE:

Making prospective plans for purchases: Curiosity.

A man dreaming of a prospective wife: Unhappiness with wife.

A woman dreaming of a prospective husband: Will receive very happy news.

A prospective job or position: Desires will be accomplished.

PROSTATE:

Having pains in prostate gland: Loss of friends.

Having an operation on prostate gland: Damages in business.

Relatives having a prostate operation: Will discover a secret.

Others suffering with prostate troubles: Dissension between partners.

PROSTITUTE:

Of a prostitute: Good times are coming.

Being a prostitute: An enemy is seeking your ruin.

Visiting a prostitute: Troubles in home life.

Many prostitutes: Honor and blessings.

White prostitute: Liberation from troubles.

Mulatto prostitute: Recovery from a long illness.

Negro prostitute: Changes in luck.

A well-built naked prostitute: Good hopes.

Pregnant prostitute: Pleasant family news.

A dead prostitute: An important person will fall in love with you.

Unknown prostitutes: Glory, honor, and success.

Embracing a prostitute: Will take a long trip.

Receiving a prostitute into own house: Good business ventures.

A prostitute dancing: Will go back to your sweetheart.

A very kind prostitute: Will receive a bad business report.

Hearing a prostitute speak without seeing her: Will change residence.

Lying with a prostitute: Security.

A prostitute who thinks she is a man: Will give birth to a boy.

PROTECTION:

Needing protection: Will realize high ambitions.

Asking for protection: You expect too many favors from friends.

Protecting a mate: Worries will be smoothed over.

Protecting children: Curiosity will be satisfied.

PROTEST:

Making a legal protest: Will receive an invitation to dinner.

Protesting own innocence: Are looking for a fortune but unable to find it.

Others protesting to you: Will have a large family.

Protesting actions of enemies: Will enjoy long-lasting health.

PROTOCOL:

Of protocol: A good future is assured.

Doing things according to protocol: Family joy.

Doing things against rules of protocol: People are gossiping about you.

Handling protocol documents: Make plans for a rainy day.

Handling a protocol book: Will receive a promise of matrimony.

PROUD:

Of being proud: Doomed for disappointment.

Being proud of family: A false friend is nearby.

Being proud of work: You are prone to being a know-it-all.

Being proud of having a good business: Failure of enemies.

PROVIDE:

Providing for the family: Will be compensated with salary for work done.

Providing for a mate: Beware of being cheated.

Providing for children: Will receive riches at a later date.

Providing means for charity: Good earnings and profit.

Providing things for business: Will be disillusioned.

PROVISION:

Of provisions: Wealth.

Buying provisions: Will take a trip and not return.

Others buying provisions: Many years of happiness.

Giving provisions to others: Exciting times are ahead.

Many provisions being stored in a cellar: Disappointment in hopes.

Being hungry and can't buy provisions: Business troubles.

Being hungry and having plenty of provisions: Loss of money.

PROVOKE:

Being provoked by others: Luck and prosperity.

Provoking a friend: Will be tormented by doubts.

Provoking a lover: Curiosity will not be satisfied.

Provoking employees: A mystery will be solved.

PROVOST:

Of a provost: You are making plans for a love affair.

Being the provost of a prison: Will receive blessings.

Being the provost of a university: High honors ahead.

Being the provost of military police: Will have fights with friends.

PUBLIC:

Of the public: Curiosity will be satisfied.

Being among the public: Make plans for your old age.

Relatives being among the public: Warning of trouble.

Friends being among the public: Friendless.

A public riot or revolt: Happiness in the family.

PUBLIC HOUSE:

Of a public house: Will be invited to a friend's home.

Drinking in a public house: Carelessness in business affairs.

Lovers dreaming of being in a public house: Deceit by one loved and trusted.

Married people dreaming of being in a public house: Much unhappiness.

Businessman dreaming of being in a public house: Danger around corner.

Farmer dreaming of being in a public house: Bad crops.

Owning a public house: Will work hard to recover from losses.

Being with friends in a public house: Worries.

Relatives being at a public house: Exciting times are ahead.

PUDDING:

Of a pudding: Treachery.

Eating pudding: Will make money.

Cooking a pudding: Will have pains in your heart.

Buying a pudding: Terrible gossip is being spread about you.

Receiving a pudding as a gift: Sickness.

Giving a pudding as a gift: Will discover a secret.

Eating pudding at a banquet: Big troubles ahead.

Children eating pudding: Financial improvement in the family.

PULPIT:

Of a pulpit: Will achieve a good standing among people.

Being at a pulpit: Honor and blessings.

Giving a sermon from a pulpit: Hard work ahead.

Friends giving a sermon from a pulpit: Will have many tears.

A priest giving sermon from beautiful pulpit: Slow business affairs.

PUMP:

Of a pump: Will have money.

Pumping clear water: Business will prosper.

Pumping dirty water: Worries.

Pumping muddy water: Will talk to people who annoy you.

Using a pump run by a motor: Will receive disgusting news.

Operating a pump by hand: Will receive sad news.

Using a fire pump: Will receive surprising and bad news.

PUMPKIN:
Growing pumpkins: Will be dishonored.

Picking pumpkins: Death of a relative.

Buying a pumpkin: Will receive bad news.

Making a pumpkin pie: A treacherous friend is seeking revenge.

Eating pumpkin pie: Will contract a serious disease.

Buying a pumpkin pie: Misfortune in love affairs.

PUNCH:
Drinking punch: Unpleasant news to come.

Making punch: Loss of money.

Offering a drink of punch to someone: Bad reputation.

Punching someone with your fist: Will be annoyed.

Being punched by someone else: Good times to come.

Punching a friend: Misfortune in love affairs.

Punching an enemy: New interests and surroundings.

PUNISH:
Being punished: Unexpected pleasure at hand.

Punishing someone else: Will receive news from absent people.

Punishing children: Lasting friendship.

Being punished by a court: Humiliation.

Executing punishment to offenders: Unjustifiable jealousy.

PUPIL:
The pupils of eyes: Treachery in love.

Pupils of loved one's eyes: Big disappointment.

Pupils in school: Unhappiness.

Being a pupil of night school: Will have adversity in affairs.

PUPPET:
Of puppets: Employees are not efficient enough.

Being a puppet: Will be loved by ladies.

Handling puppets: Will have a family argument.

An important person dreaming of puppets: You have faithful help.

PUPPY:
Of a puppy: Will be invited to a joyous party.

Many puppies: You are not prone to becoming intimate with people.

Owning puppies: Will give money to charity.

Buying a puppy: Will have much happiness.

PURGATORY:
Of purgatory: Sickness.

Being sent to purgatory: Will travel a long distance.

Others being in purgatory: Abundant means.

Ancestors being in purgatory: Approaching money.

Relatives being in purgatory: Good luck to one for whom you care.

PURIFY:
Purifying something: You are dedicated to unusual hobbies.

Purifying eatable things: Will suffer a delay in affairs.

Purifying own soul: Will have sorrow because of sins.

Doctors purifying instruments: Will be hit by someone.

PURPLE:
Of the color purple: Will take a joyful journey.

Having a purple dress: Happy marriage.

Having a purple coat and hat: Honor.

Having purple flowers: Loss of own estate.

Having purple materials: Loss of friends.

PURSE:
Of a purse: Happiness.
Finding a purse without money: Misunderstanding between relatives.
Finding a purse with money in it: Increase in the family.
Lovers dreaming of finding a purse: Happy life.
Lovers dreaming of losing a purse: Expect difficulties or illness.
Buying a purse: Will attend a wedding.
Receiving a purse as a gift: Carelessness.
Giving a purse as a gift: Will accomplish your goals.

PURSUE:
Being pursued: Will enjoy a clear conscience.
Being pursued by women: Contentment.
Being pursued by a man: People are talking badly about you.
Being pursued by the law: Will make gains in the future.
Others being pursued: Will receive high honors.

PUSH:
Of pushing: Change of marital status.
Pushing against a door: Obstacles will be removed from your path.
Pushing other heavy objects: Obstacles will be surmounted.
Others pushing: Will be depressed by sad news.

Being pushed by others: Prosperity.
Pushing children to do correct things: Abundance.

PUTTY:
Of putty: Hard work is ahead.
Using putty: Good results from material work.
Buying putty: Fortune in love.
Using putty in own house: Will soon have a fight at home.
Others using putty: Don't listen to foolish gossip.

PUZZLE:
A puzzle you can solve: Good luck ahead.
A puzzle you can't solve: Expect heavy losses in business.
Others working on puzzles: Will be guilty of foolish actions.
Relatives working on puzzles: Expect trouble with relatives.
Solving a puzzle: Pleasant surroundings.

PYRAMIDS:
Of pyramids: Successful future.
Viewing pyramids with relatives: Abundance and prosperity.
Married people dreaming of pyramids: Will attain a high position.
A young woman dreaming of pyramids: She is unhappy in choice of husband.
A widow dreaming of pyramids: Another marriage is assured.

Q

QUACK:
Of a quack: Changes of surroundings.
Being under the care of a quack: Nuisance to society.
Being a quack: Will overcome enemies.
Others going to a quack: You are very stubborn in undertakings.

QUADRILLE:
Of a quadrille dance: Big joy.

Dancing a quadrille: Misfortune in love affairs.
Dancing a quadrille with sweetheart: You are a very lovable person.
Dancing a quadrille with your wife: Honor and joy.

QUADRUPEDS:
Of animals having four feet: Good friends.

Small quadrupeds: Will receive pleasant news.

Quadrupeds the size of a dog: Happiness.

Quadrupeds the size of a horse: Contrariety in love.

Quadrupeds being killed: Will suffer misery.

QUAIL:

Of quails: Will receive unpleasant news.

Flying quails: Good times ahead of you.

Dead quail: Contrariety.

Rotten quails: Arguments.

Quails coming from a pond or sea: Someone will steal something from you.

Many quails: Will have bad business ventures.

QUAKER:

Of a quaker: Are confronted with insurmountable obstacles.

Dealing with a quaker: Public disgrace.

A quaker doctor: Carelessness will cause serious loss.

Being a quaker doctor: Riches and good business.

A quaker community: Are surrounded with jealous people.

QUANTITY:

A quantity of articles: Will suffer misery.

Buying in quantity: You are blessed with good friends.

Selling things in quantity: Avoid squandering money.

Storing quantity of things: Happiness and enjoyment.

Sending or giving quantities of things: Will be persecuted.

QUARANTINE:

Being put in quarantine: Will avoid a danger.

A house being quarantined: Will forgive friends.

A vessel being quarantined: Will make good earnings.

QUARREL:

Starting a quarrel: Prosperity in business affairs.

Quarreling with wife or husband: Will be guilty of foolish actions.

Quarreling with a sweetheart: Will make up very soon.

Quarreling with a friend: Loss of money.

Having a family quarrel: Opposition to face at home.

Having a quarrel with a partner: Will have mastery over many matters.

Having business quarrels: Warning of trouble.

QUARRY:

Falling into a quarry: You have untrustworthy friends.

Falling into a quarry and getting out: Discovery of a secret.

Falling into a quarry and unable to get out: Expect serious troubles.

Others falling into a quarry: Fortune and happiness.

Of a stone quarry: Difficult days are ahead.

Digging in a stone quarry: Unhappiness in love.

Selling stone from a quarry: Will be slave to prejudice.

Enemies owning a stone quarry: Will enjoy success in business.

QUARTER:

Having a quarter: Will be unfortunate in business affairs.

Receiving a quarterly payment: Will have a great deal of happiness.

Paying a bill quarterly: Will begin gambling.

Receiving a quarter of something: Will have a delay in business affairs.

QUAY:

Of an artificial landing by navigable water: Danger in love affairs.

Being alone on a quay: You will suffer grief.

Being on a quay with sailors: Secret enmity of a person.

Being on a quay with workmen or stevedores: Good business prospects.

QUEEN:
Of a queen: Deceit in love affairs.
Sending a letter to a queen: Danger.
Going to see a queen: Good fortune.
Having an interview with a queen: Rebellion within the home.
A queen surrounded by her court: Will be deceived by friends.
A madonna queen of the church: Will be pardoned of your sins.

QUESTION:
Answering questions correctly: All will go well in life.
Answering questions incorrectly: You should mend your ways in life.
Refusing to answer a question: Change of surroundings.
Refusing to accept an answer to question: Warning of troubles.
Someone asking questions to you: Unhappiness in own love affairs.
Asking questions of children: Will receive good news.
Asking questions of relatives: Great joy.
Asking questions of wife: Congenial work and good news.
Asking questions of husband: Avoid rivals.
Asking questions of friends: Sorrow is about to come.

QUEUE:
Of a queue: Re-established friendship.
Waiting in a queue: Will lead to marriage.
Being in a queue with your family: Be on guard against spiteful gossip.
Others in a queue: Important event very beneficial.

QUICK:
Acting quickly: Unhappiness.
Children acting quickly: Realization of hopes.
Relatives acting quickly: Family arguments.
Doing wrong because of quick actions: Embarrassments will cause harm.

QUICKSAND:
Of quicksand: You are surrounded with many temptations.
Handling quicksand: Do not be indiscreet.
Something sinking into quicksand: Will be cheated by friends.

QUICKSILVER:
Of quicksilver: Will be invited to a big festivity.
Handling quicksilver: Loss of friends through false reports.
Others handling quicksilver: Gossip is being spread about you.
Buying quicksilver: An expected pleasure at hand.

QUIET:
Being quiet: Unhappiness.
Asking people to be quiet: Will have a fit of temper.
Quieting fighting people: Will make peace with friends.
Quieting children: Happiness.
Quieting neighbors: Will have a happy future.

QUILT:
Of a quilt: Financial gains.
A soiled quilt: A mystery will be solved.
A beautiful quilt: Will realize own ambitions.
A quilt being straight on a bed: Will live a long life.
A quilt falling from the bed: Social activities of a happy nature.

QUINCE:
Of this applelike fruit: Will fall heir to plenty of money.
This Central Asiatic tree: Will receive good news.
A quince tree blossoming: Prosperity.
A quince tree with fruit on it: Joy and pleasure.
Eating quinces: Good health and happiness.
Picking quinces: Will be annoyed by your enemies.
Cooking quinces: Will be persecuted by a woman of ill fame.
Making jelly from quinces: Will be persecuted by your creditors.
Spoiled quinces: Trouble is ahead for you.

QUININE:

Of quinine: Will have a healthy life.
Taking quinine: Greater happiness will brighten your life.
Buying quinine: Great joy without profit.
Giving quinine to children: Riches all their life.
Giving quinine to relatives: Be cautious in all your dealings.

QUIVER:

Of quivering: Happiness brought through joy at home.

Others quivering: A marriage will take place.
Quivering and trembling badly: Will realize high ambitions.
Relatives quivering: Doomed for disappointment.

QUOITS:

Of a flattened ring-shaped piece of iron: Loneliness and trouble.
A woman dreaming of quoits: Disagreeable and difficult work to face.
A man dreaming of quoits: Will have quarrels.

R

RABBI:

Of a rabbi: Fortune.
Being a rabbi: Will be in financial misery.
Talking to a rabbi: Joy.
Arguing with a rabbi: Will make peace with enemies.

RABBIT:

Of a rabbit: Failure of enemies.
A rabbit running: Change of occupation.
Several rabbits on the run: Very good business ventures.
Eating rabbit: Will quarrel with a friend.
Shooting rabbits: Happiness.
Having rabbits in own back yard: Great friendship.

RACE:

Of a race: Big fortune is ahead.
Running a race: Must persevere if you desire success.
Running a race and winning: Distinction and honor.
Running a race and losing: Will have many competitors in your affairs.
Others running a race: You are being deceived.
Friends running a race: Misfortune in love affairs.
A jockey running in a race: A change in life will soon come.

Member of family running a race: Will suffer humiliation.
A dog race: Will have mastery over enemies.

RACECOURSE:

Of a racecourse: New interest and surroundings.
Many people at a racecourse: Pleasant company but danger of losses.
Relatives being at a racecourse: Abundant means.
Friends being at a racecourse: Death of a loved one.
Enemies at a racecourse: Discovery of a secret.
Important personalities at a racecourse: Hard work awaits you.

RACE HORSE:

Of race horses: Attempt to economize while there is still time.
Owning a race horse: Luck is with you.
Riding a race horse: Do not speculate in business.
Betting on a race horse: Misfortune in love affairs.
Your race horse winning: You have many enemies.
Your jockey winning: A rival will take sweetheart's affection.
Your race horse losing: Will have many competitors.

Your jockey losing the race: Financial losses.

RACE TRACK:
Being at a race track: Will have happy days ahead of you.
Training horses at a race track: Big fortune.
Exercising horses in a race track: Happy events to come.
Being hurt at a race track: Will visit someone staying at an inn.

RACKET:
Hearing a racket: Loss of leisure.
Making a racket: New friendship.
Creating a very loud racket: Frivolity.
Others making a racket: Warning of troubles.
A tennis racket: Good luck to one for whom you care.
Own tennis racket: Will hear news from abroad.
Playing with a tennis racket: Will have mastery over many matters.
Others with a tennis racket: Beware of jealous friends.

RADISH:
Of radishes: You have a great number of enemies.
Raising radishes to sell: Prosperity.
Raising radishes for own use: Many pleasures.
Eating radishes: Will have passing troubles.
Others eating radishes: Change of surroundings.
Buying radishes: Discovery of domestic secrets.

RAFFLE:
Of a raffle: You do not deserve success.
Being interested in a raffle: Unknown enemies are around you.
Taking part in a raffle: Small risks ahead of you.
Holding a raffle ticket: Good luck.
Lovers holding a raffle ticket: Unhappy association.
Losing a raffle: Engagement will be called off.

RAFT:
Of a raft: Will soon make a journey.
A very big and long raft: Will travel for a very long time.
Sailing on a raft: Others will travel instead of you.
Buying a raft: Will change residence to distant countries.
Selling a raft: Good success.
Saving own life on a raft: Will have mastery over own affairs.
Others on a raft: Will hear false promises.
Family being on a raft: Luck and prosperity.

RAGE:
Going into a rage: Good times are coming.
Others being in a rage: Unfortunate business dealings.
Relatives going into a rage: Family unhappiness.
Going into a rage with friends: Quarrels.
Going into a rage with sweetheart: Frivolity.
A woman being in a rage: She will be justified.
A man going into a rage: Passing love.
A wife being in a rage: A better future awaits her.
A husband being in a rage: Changeable in love.
A sweetheart being in a rage: Quarrels of short duration.
Other people being in a rage: Honor of short duration.

RAGS:
Of rags: Good earnings.
A woman dreaming of herself in rags: Unhappiness.
A man dreaming of himself in rags: Public disgrace.
A girl dreaming of herself in rags: Will meet an arrogant man.
Children being in rags: Own desires will be granted.
Many people in rags: Big profit.
Friends being in rags: Will quarrel with friends.

Enemies being in rags: Recovery of lost money.

Rich people being in rags: Abundant means.

Washing rags: Unhappiness.

Gathering rags: Big arguments.

A rag man selling rags: Will be introduced to high-class people.

Being a rag dealer: Must economize for the future.

Buying rags: Will be in the company of happy people.

RAID:

Of a raid: Pleasant times to come.

A police raid: Change in environment.

An armed forces raid: Will live a long time.

An air raid: A change in life will come soon.

Own home being raided: Will have emotional sorrow.

Other people being raided: Happiness is assured.

RAILROAD:

Of a railroad: Good times are coming.

Being at a railroad alone: Rapid rise in your business.

Being at a railroad with relatives: Abundant means.

Being at a railroad with friends: Hard times are ahead.

Walking on the railroad ties: Distress and worry.

Being forced to walk the rails: Affairs will bring unmeasured happiness.

RAILROAD CAR:

Of a railroad car: Good events are ahead.

Being in a railroad car alone: Good business enterprises.

Being in a railroad car with relatives: Good business transactions.

Being in a railroad car with friends: Hard work awaits.

Being in a railroad car with children: Happy family affairs.

Others being in a railroad car: Use caution in business activities.

Enemies being in a railroad car: A catastrophe is ahead.

RAIN:

Of rain: Abundant means.

Hearing patter of rain on the roof: Great marital happiness.

Getting wet in a downpour of rain: Suffering caused by suspicion of friends.

Rain dripping into a room: Beware of false friends.

A farmer dreaming of rain without wind or storm: Good earnings and profits.

A businessman dreaming of rain: Misfortune in business.

A big downpour of rain and bad wind: Look out for rivals.

A very bad rain- and windstorm: Great joy.

Rich people dreaming of a downpour with hail: Affliction in love.

Poor people dreaming of rain with hail: Good opportunities and happy life.

Women being out in the rain: Disappointment in love.

Others being out in the rain: Great sorrow.

A rain- and hailstorm ruining crops: Abundant means ahead.

RAINBOW:

Of a rainbow: Good health and prosperity.

Being near a rainbow: Changes for the better in present position.

A married woman dreaming of a rainbow: Change in love affairs before long.

Unmarried woman dreaming of a rainbow: Will receive a beautiful present.

A young girl dreaming of a rainbow: Will have an agreeable sweetheart.

Lovers seeing a rainbow together: Happy marriage and riches.

Children seeing a rainbow: Will be healthy and intelligent.

A rainbow being over your head: Family inheritance.

A rainbow at sunrise: Big riches.

A rainbow at noon: Change for the better in your fortune.

A rainbow at sunset: Happy and joyful times are ahead.

RAISIN:
Of raisins: General prosperity.
Eating raisins: Will spend money faster than you earn it.
Raising raisins: Will receive an unexpected invitation.
Cooking raisins: Will receive several small presents.
Buying raisins: Be cautious in business ventures.
Selling raisins: You should mend your ways in life.
Having dry raisins: Loss of money.

RAKE:
Of a rake: Beware of thieves.
Using a rake: Good friends.
Farmers using a rake: Good friends will take care of your necessities.
Buying a rake: Will have plenty of money.
Raking leaves: Happy home.
Raking hay: A wedding to occur soon.

RAM:
Of a ram: You are falling into a trap.
Having many rams: Riches.
Raising a ram: Will receive an unexpected visitor.
Killing a ram: Will win a lawsuit.
Buying rams: Abundance.
Selling rams: Big gains.

RAMBLE:
Of rambling: A wish will be granted after a long delay.
Rambling alone: Honor of short duration.
Sweethearts rambling together: Small honor.
Rambling with relatives: Will have money.
Rambling with friends: Business will be good.

RANCH:
Of a ranch: Must endure unhappiness for a short time.
Working on a ranch: A wedding will soon take place.
Owning a ranch: Joy and prosperity.

Selling a ranch: Unhappiness.
Buying a ranch: Will receive good news.

RANCID:
Of rancid food: Will disregard a proposal of love.
Throwing rancid food away: Will have misfortune for a short time.
Animals eating rancid food: Will endure persecution.
Buying rancid food unknowingly: An unknown enemy will cause much damage.
Eating rancid food: Will have good health.

RANCOR:
Of rancor: Will harbor hate for other people.
Having secret rancor for someone: Will have good friendships.
Rancor existing between mates: A separation will soon take place.
Others having rancor against you: Will make good earnings in business.
Rancor existing between relatives: Will have peace and contentment.

RANGE:
Of an open expanse of range: Will be visited by sweet-talking people.
Working on the open range: Will have unhappiness.
A shooting range: Will keep busy and enjoy happiness.
Being with others at a shooting range: Persecutions.
Having a coal range: You are prone to incurring too many debts.
Cooking on a wood range: Will be falsely accused by enemies.

RANK:
Of a rank: Will overcome unhappiness.
Own rank: Own industriousness will bring money and happiness.
Rank of other people: Will receive a marriage announcement.
Being advanced in rank: Will have worries.
Being demoted in rank: Will soon make more money.

RAPE:
Being raped: Will receive a proposal of marriage.
Raping someone underage: Misfortune.
Raping someone over twenty-one: Joy and prosperity.
Being raped by a woman: Will receive an unexpected inheritance.
Friends being raped: Will be highly embarrassed.

RARE:
Of rare items: You have a highly egotistic nature.
Rare gems: Will have affliction and uneasiness.
Buying rare items: Will have big disputes with friends.
Eating rare meat: Joy and prosperity.
Eating rare vegetables: Will argue with the one you love.
Children eating rare food: Will collect money.

RASCAL:
Of a rascal: Good fortune.
A businessman dreaming of a rascal: Increase of trade and comfortable income.
A woman dreaming of a rascal: Long and happy married life.
A young girl dreaming of a rascal: Will receive a proposal of marriage.
Being a rascal yourself: Public esteem.
Many rascals: You are recognized as a perfect gentleman.

RASH:
Having a rash on the body: Beware of speaking too hastily.
Having a rash on the face: One you haven't seen for a long time will visit.
Children having a rash: You have an honest conscience.
Having a rash on the legs: Will be deeply in debt.
A friend having a rash on the face: Victory over enemies.

RASPBERRY:
Of raspberries: You are in love.
Eating raspberries: Joy and fortune.

Picking raspberries: Friends are concealing something from you.
Buying raspberries: Will suffer disillusionment.
Making jam from raspberries: Change in present position.
Giving raspberry jam as a gift: Big friendship.

RATS:
Of rats: Injury caused through deceit.
Many rats: Serious trouble to come.
Killing a rat: Success will attend all undertakings.
Catching rats in a trap: You are disliked by other people.
A cat catching a rat in the house: Unfinished business will be successful.
White rats: Will overcome troubles successfully.
Sweethearts dreaming of rats: A fortunate rival.

RATCATCHER:
Of a ratcatcher: A nice lover will find you.
A ratcatcher catching rats in a field: You are committing treason.
A ratcatcher catching white rats: Ruin of very bad enemies.
A ratcatcher catching many rats: Vindication from people who did wrong.

RAVEN:
Of a raven: Will receive bad news.
A raven flying: Your life is in danger.
A raven flapping wings: Death of a friend.
A flock of ravens flying together: Disaster.
Hearing the noise of ravens: Unhappiness.
A husband dreaming of a raven: He is making plans to be free of his wife.
A wife dreaming of a raven: Will warn husband against checking on her.

RAVINE:
Of a ravine: Will have plenty of money.
A small ravine: Peace and prosperity.

Falling into a ravine: Will work out troubles successfully.

A nearly dry ravine: A friend will render you a service.

Much water running through a ravine: People have faith in you.

RAW:

Raw eggs: Will receive a substantial amount of money.

Raw meat: Unpleasantness.

Raw vegetables: Will receive good news.

Raw poultry: Abundance.

Raw fish: Happiness.

Eating raw meat: Unhappiness in love.

Eating raw vegetables: Change in love affairs.

Eating raw eggs: Will have a new lover.

A young girl dreaming of eating raw meat: Will receive a proposal of marriage.

Raw meat in a butcher shop: A friend would like to become a lover.

RAY:

A ray of sunlight: Sickness.

Rays of sunlight shining on your bed: Life will be in danger by illness.

A ray falling from the sky: Victory over enemies.

RAZOR:

Of a razor: Danger will be encountered.

Using a razor: Warning of a coming quarrel.

Using a dull razor: Will take a trip.

Cutting yourself with a razor: Must control your emotions.

Buying a razor: Persecution.

Killing someone with a razor: Disagreeable events.

Killing yourself with a razor: Joy and prosperity.

READ:

Of reading: You are engaged in difficult work.

Reading but not understanding: Will probably lose money.

Reading a newspaper: Success will attend any undertakings.

Reading a book: Pleasures.

Reading a comic book: Joy and consolation.

Reading poetry: Will overcome obstacles.

Reading scientific books: Will meet an intelligent person.

Reading out loud: Changes ahead in your future.

Making children read out loud: Good new events.

Children reading: Will enjoy the friendship of many people.

Other people reading: Good fortune.

READY:

Getting ready: Will receive money.

Getting ready to go out: Will be told of someone's love for you.

Getting ready to eat: You should mend your ways in life.

Getting ready to take a trip: Will soon become rich.

Getting ready for bed: Will have pains in the heart.

Getting ready for work: Ambitions will increase daily.

REAPER:

Of a reaper: Will have a picnic.

Many reapers: Prosperity in business.

Many reapers at work: Abundance.

Reapers idling: Misery.

Being a reaper yourself: Abundance.

Friends being reapers: Don't listen to advice of friends.

Reaping wheat: Will receive a blessing.

Reaping wild hay: Abundance.

REAR:

The rear of own body: Unhappiness.

Having pains in the rear of own body: Imminent quarrels with family.

The rear of animals: Prosperity.

The rear of children: Increase in the family.

Family having backs turned to you: Advantages in business.

The rear of a house: Will have plenty of money.

The rear of a car: Will be assisted by friends.

The rear of a horse: Will be abandoned by friends.

The rear of a sheep: Immediate prosperity.

The rear of an engine: Will have a big fight.

A horse rearing: Success in difficult plans.

REAR ADMIRAL:

Of a rear admiral: People have a high opinion of you.

A rear admiral on a battleship: Will make money through speculation.

A rear admiral on a dock: Will receive a visit from friends.

Being a rear admiral: Domestic troubles.

Being a young rear admiral: You are a great lover of women.

Being the wife of a rear admiral: You are surrounded by lovers.

A friend who is a rear admiral: A secret will soon be explained.

Being a rear admiral at the Pentagon: Abuse of confidence.

REBELLION:

Of a rebellion: Someone inferior to you is causing much trouble for you.

Being in a rebellion: People will cease to annoy you.

Being a rebel: Are unhappy with present position.

Watching a rebellion: Be cautious with business affairs.

Taking part in a rebellion: Big satisfaction.

Being wounded in a rebellion: Infidelity.

People being killed in a rebellion: Will win at gambling.

Friends being in a rebellion: You have secret enemies.

A foreign rebellion: You are too ambitious.

Having put a stop to a rebellion: Advancement within own position.

RECALL:

Being recalled to duty: A trap is being laid for you.

Recalling people to work: Will have arguments with business partner.

Being recalled by others: Will lead a quiet life.

Being recalled to military service: Will reconcile with enemies.

RECAPTURE:

Recapturing lost money: Prosperity.

Recapturing wife: Public disgrace.

Recapturing a business loss: Will be protected by people with money.

Recapturing a love: Infidelity.

RECEIPT:

Giving a receipt: Will have modest employment.

Receiving a receipt: Good hopes for prosperity.

Signing a receipt: A thrilling time is ahead of you.

Writing a receipt: Be on guard with your most trusted friends.

Acknowledging receipt of money: Beware of being insulted.

Acknowledging receipt of a letter: Will be forgiven by friends.

The receipt of a document: Don't put too much trust in your future.

The receipt of a family letter: Peril is ahead of you.

RECEIVE:

Receiving a love letter: Unhappiness and persecution.

Receiving a gift at own house: Will have good hopes.

Receiving a ring as a gift secretly: Will have a promise of matrimony.

Receiving important personalities at own house: Riches.

Being received by other people: You lead a very carefree life.

RECEPTION:

Of a reception: Family quarrels.

Attending a reception: Will receive compensation for work done.

Attending a public dinner reception alone: Postponement of success.

Giving a reception: Will be highly thought of in society.

Giving a wedding reception for children: Will realize high ambitions.

RECIPROCATE:
Reciprocating for a favor: Will reconcile with enemies.
Reciprocating an invitation received: Will have an illness in near future.
Reciprocating the love of a friend: Will have big arguments.
Being reciprocated for a favor done: Will receive a declaration of love.

RECOGNIZE:
Of recognizing people: Will lead a quiet life.
Recognizing an old friend: Will become very upset.
Recognizing a dead person: Will be afflicted with heart trouble.
Being recognized by others after many years: Will fall in love.
Recognizing a soiled legal document: Good hopes for the future.

RECONCILE:
Being reconciled with husband: Disgrace.
Becoming reconciled with a friend: Quarrels.
Becoming reconciled with an enemy: Scandal.
Becoming reconciled with a lover: Happiness.
Becoming reconciled with own family: Deceit.
Reconciling a business transaction: Good hopes.
Reconciling an argument: Illness.
Reconciling with a creditor: Will fall into a trap.

RECORD:
Of records: You are unfitted to fill the family position.
Recording legal matters: Will enjoy much security.
Being a court recorder: Prosperity.
Buying musical records: Death in the family.
Selling musical records: Financial gains.
Playing musical records: A false friend is nearby.
Making musical records: Will enjoy social activities.

RECOVER:
Of recovering: Will live a long life.
Not recovering: Beware of treacherous people.
Children recovering: Will be protected by God.
Member of family recovering from serious illness: A mystery will be solved.
Recovering furniture: You are prone to being imprudent.

RECUPERATE:
Of recuperating from an illness: You enjoy amusements too much.
Children recuperating from an illness: Unhappiness within 48 hours.
Mate recuperating: Will receive a present.
Recuperating from a business loss: Will have happiness in near future.

RED:
Of the color red: Warning of quarrels with friends.
Materials of any kind that are red: Misfortune.
Buying red-colored clothes: Will receive a sad letter.

REDEEM:
Redeeming articles that have been pawned: Great joy.
Redeeming jewels from a pawnshop: Ingratitude for goodheartedness.
Asking others to redeem things for you: Loss of money and friendship.
Redeeming stocks from collateral: Will have the love of unknown person.

RED HAIR:
Dying hair red: Will give a party for friends.
A beautiful red-haired woman: Will receive unexpected good news.
A red-haired woman dying hair blond: Will enjoy a long happy life.
Children having red hair: Will win at a lottery.

RED-HANDED:
Being caught red-handed: Will receive unexpected joy.
Being caught red-handed while stealing: Will get rich through economy

Being caught by mate while kissing someone else: Divorce.

Catching children red-handed: Will receive an invitation to a party.

REDRESS:
Of redressing: A false friend is nearby.

Redressing church ornaments: Loss of friends.

Redressing grievances: Will soon receive good news.

Fixing clothes that are made wrong: Quietness and contentment.

REDUCE:
Of reducing: Will have splendor and joy.

Taking medicine to reduce: Will receive a gift.

Reducing expenses: Will have an unknown pain.

Reducing employee force: Misery.

Reducing drinking: Business will turn for the better.

REEDS:
Of reeds: Friends are not all true.

Handling reeds: You are deceived by business people.

Others handling reeds: Prove people before trusting them.

A bamboo reed: Will have a lawsuit.

Playing a reed instrument: Reconciliation with enemies.

Others playing a reed instrument: Will have a long and good life.

REEL:
Of a reel: Will achieve an honorable position.

Winding cotton on a reel: Your friends are not all true to you.

Winding silk on a reel: Success will be achieved by patience.

Buying reels: Affection in love.

Having a fishing reel: Loss of employment.

Seeing a fishing reel: Loss of a member of the family.

Buying a fishing reel: Loss of your subsistence.

Losing a fishing reel: Will have an irregularity in the skin.

Receiving a fishing reel as a gift: Loss of sweetheart.

Giving a fishing reel as a gift: Dignity.

REFEREE:
Of a referee: Will receive an injustice.

Being a referee: Will change position in life.

Being a referee of sports: Will enjoy a pleasant quiet life.

A court referee: Will be done wrong to by others.

A business referee arbitrating: Will lose all the money involved.

REFINE:
Of refining: You have many enemies.

Purifying while refining: You waste too much time with pleasures.

Making thinner by refining: Will enjoy good food.

People working at a refinery: Big joy.

REFLECTION:
Of own reflection in water: Lonely life.

The reflection of family in water: Visit from a strange person.

Reflection of loved one in water: Will meet and marry important person.

Reflection of children: Will achieve success.

A strange face being reflected: Separation of loved ones.

REFORM:
Of a reforming institution: Prove friends before trusting them.

Obstinate children needing reforming: Success in life.

Own children needing reforming: Will receive a high, important position.

Others' children needing reforming: Failure of enemies.

Stubborn animals needing reforming: Will receive a present from a stranger.

REFRESHMENT:
Of refreshments: Will have a happy marriage.

Serving refreshments: Will receive a small vexation.

Being offered refreshments: Unexpected joy.

Giving family refreshments: Business will go well.

Giving refreshments to children: They will achieve prominence in community.

Giving refreshments to friends: Will receive a present from a rich man.

Buying refreshments: Joy for the woman in the family.

REFUGE:

Of a refuge: You expect too many favors from other people.

Being in a refuge: Will receive help from friends.

Going into refuge with family: Will have good health.

Others taking refuge: Will be unhappy with present condition.

Taking refuge from a hurricane: Beware of bad judgments.

Taking refuge from a bad storm: Financial gains.

Taking refuge against enemies: Will soon have plenty of money.

REFUSE:

Receiving a refusal: Were too certain of receiving an acceptance.

Being refused: Prosperity.

Other people refusing: Misery and desperation.

Being refused by relatives: Prospects of better times.

Being refused by friends: Jealousy and dissension.

Children being refused: Happiness in the near future.

Refusing a gift: Will receive another gift.

Others refusing your gift: Will be embraced by sweetheart.

Refusing to accept a letter: Secret pains.

Others refusing to accept your letter: Business will turn for the better.

REGATTA:

Of a regatta: Good hopes.

Watching a regatta: Will receive favorable news.

Taking part in a regatta: Will soon be decorated.

Winning a regatta: Will inherit money from an old woman.

Losing a regatta: Will find a new lover.

Being the master of a regatta: Will be courted by many women.

Watching a sailing regatta: Joy and festivity.

Watching a rowing regatta: Will take long trip abroad with sweetheart.

REGIMENT:

Of a regiment: Security.

Being in a regiment: Confidence.

A regiment marching: Changes in own position.

A regiment taking part in a parade: Will have a large family.

A regiment winning a battle: Will make plenty of money.

A regiment losing a battle: You are surrounded by creditors.

A regiment being annihilated: Will be surrounded by beautiful women.

REGISTRAR:

Of a registrar: Will receive a proposal of marriage.

Being a registrar: Will be married for a long time.

Being a court registrar: Will receive news of many deaths.

Being registrar of an election: Happiness and contentment.

REGISTRAR'S OFFICE:

Of a registrar's office: You are at the crossroads of life.

Going to a registrar's office: Make decisions and don't look back.

Going to a registrar's office with others: Will win a large lottery.

Going to a registrar's office with loved one: Announcement of marriage.

REGRET:

Having regret: Your changeable mood will be harmful to you.

Regretting actions: Will have a bad sign of the moon.

Expressing regrets to mate: Will enjoy prosperity.

Others expressing regrets: Unhappiness will soon come to an end.

Children regretting actions: Don't be so particular.

REHEARSAL:
Of a rehearsal: Difficulties are ahead.
Being at a rehearsal: Will receive honors in the future.
Loved one being at a rehearsal: Will receive good news.
Friends being at a rehearsal: Will live to a very old age.
Children being at a rehearsal: Family contentment.

REINS:
Of the reins of a horse: Will have a high social position.
Putting bridle and reins on a horse: Conditions will soon improve.
Holding the reins of a horse: Will have a party with friends.
Pulling reins to stop a horse: Will become rich.

RELATIVE:
Of relatives: Will receive bad news.
Discussing matters with relatives: Bad luck to come.
Embracing a relative: Treachery.
Relatives being naked: Will have a very bad quarrel.
Talking with relatives: Big disappointment in family affairs.
Receiving invitation from relative: Beware of why they are inviting you.
Entertaining relatives: Danger is ahead.
Eating with relatives: Death in the family.

RELEASE:
Being released from business venture: Will have a family quarrel.
Being released from a contract: Infidelity.
Being released from prison: Will be well accepted in society.
Being released from matrimony: Unexpected joy.
Releasing someone else from a contract: Troubles will soon end.

RELIGION:
Of own religion: Quiet and contentment.

Believing in own religion: Big family argument.
Attending own religion: Will be hit by someone.
Belonging to a religious institution: Loss of enemies.
Other religious people: Death in the family.
Children being religious: Will sell your house.
Relatives being religious: Very great unhappiness.
Friends being religious: Domestic contentment.
Being a very religious person: Great happiness.
Going to church every day: Squandering of money.

REMEDY:
Taking a remedy: Will recover from an illness very soon.
Advising others of a remedy: Will collect money.
Giving children a remedy: Will be highly considered by others.
Finding remedy for business affairs: Will economize and save money.

REMOVAL:
Removing clothes to another place: Will receive a gift.
Removing yourself to another place: Poverty.
Removing your house: Will enjoy working hard.
Removing your false teeth: Expect a visitor to your home.
Other people removing things: Are in need of financial help.

RENOUNCE:
Of renouncing: Must avoid contradictions.
Renouncing a good position: Your actions are foolish.
Mates renouncing each other: You should mend your ways in life.
Renouncing a political career: Affairs will take a turn for the better.
Others renouncing their position: Will have many enemies.

RENT:
Owing rent: Will be persecuted.
Paying the rent: Beware of treacherous enemies.
Collecting rent: Good earnings and profits.
Being unable to pay the rent: Loss of a friend.
Paying rent for someone else: Unhappiness.
Paying rent for relatives: Poverty.
Paying rent on a car: Misfortune.
Having the rent frozen: Good news from faraway.
Renting an apartment: Long-lasting joy.

RENTED CLOTHES:
Renting a man's tuxedo: Will have an inheritance.
Renting full-dress evening suit: Will be threatened by sweetheart.
Renting everyday clothes for men: Loss of money through bankruptcy.
Renting sport clothes for a man: Will win at gambling.
Renting evening gowns for women: Will find a new lover.
Renting everyday clothes for women: Will receive a very expensive gift.
Renting two-piece suit for a woman: Opposition in love.
Renting fur coats: Increase in the family.
Renting a winter coat: Business will be prosperous.
Renting little girls' clothes: Will make a trip.
Renting little boys' clothes: Someone will steal from you.
Renting shoes for a woman: Sickness.
Renting boots for a man: Will have legal proceedings.

REPEL:
Of repelling others: Will be persecuted.
Repelling someone who loves you: Will have bad destiny.
Repelling a request: Will lose a friendship.
Being repelled by a woman: Will find another better than she.

REPLY:
Waiting for a reply: Beware of treachery.
Receiving a good reply: Will receive an unexpected gift.
Receiving an unfavorable reply: Affairs will improve immediately.
Sending a reply to a woman's letter: A mystery will be solved.
Sending a reply to a man's letter: Conditions will become worse.
Receiving an unfavorable reply from a woman: Will find new person to love.
Receiving a favorable reply from a man: Will enjoy pleasant social life.
Replying in a business affair: Worries will be ended.

REPRIMAND:
Being reprimanded: Will make money in business.
Reprimanding others: Will receive unpleasant news.
Reprimanding children: Consolation.
Partners reprimanding each other: Tranquillity and fortune.
Reprimanding servants: Domestic arguments.
Reprimanding your help: Joy.
Reprimanding employees: Will be sincerely loved.
Reprimanding relatives: Will receive an important offer from a superior.
Reprimanding friends: Delightful surprise is ahead.
Being reprimanded by an officer: Will discover secret enemies.
Being reprimanded by a superior: Fortune.

REPTILE:
Of reptiles: You have hidden enemies.
Killing reptiles: You are dealing with treacherous people.
Catching a live reptile: People are gossiping against you.
Many reptiles in the woods: You are too egotistic.
Having a reptile in a cage: Will win at gambling.
Others having reptiles in a cage: Be cautious in business affairs.

Being bitten by a reptile: Business is going fine.

Dying from the bite of a reptile: You are surrounded by enemies.

Relatives being bitten by reptiles: People are slandering your name.

REQUEST:

Receiving a request: Will be put under interrogation.

Receiving a request for money: Jealousy.

Receiving a request from several women: Will suffer humiliation.

Requesting things from others: You expect too many favors from others.

Mates requesting things of each other: Joy and happiness.

RESCUE:

Of a rescue: Will suffer some misfortune.

Being rescued without injury: Slight business loss.

Rescuing others: Will have a good reputation.

Being rescued from drowning: Avoid travel on the sea.

Rescuing others from drowning: Will make big financial gains.

Rescuing one who wants to die: Beware of insincere friends.

Rescuing children: Big inheritance from an unknown person.

Rescuing relatives: Family quarrels.

Rescuing a seaman: Humiliation and shame.

Rescuing enemies from killing themselves: Dangers have disappeared.

RESERVOIR:

A reservoir filled with clean water: Plenty of money in the future.

A half-filled reservoir: Declining business.

An empty reservoir: Destruction of business.

A reservoir being filled up with water: New business affairs.

RESIDENCE:

Of own residence: Beware of being seduced.

Leaving a residence: Will be persecuted.

Residence being in a prison: Will have a bad future.

Being confined to a residence: Laziness.

The residence of other people: A secret will be confided to you.

Staying at someone else's residence: Beware of damages.

RESIGN:

Of resigning: You talk too much.

Others resigning: An enemy is trying to make up with you.

Husband or wife resigning: Will gain public esteem.

Friends resigning: Will win a lawsuit.

Enemies resigning: You are an accomplice to wrongdoing.

RESIGNATION:

Handing in own resignation: Public esteem.

Others handing in resignation: Advancement in near future.

Husband giving resignation: Money gained through legal matters.

Friends giving resignation: Will have disagreeable arguments.

Being informed of enemy's resignation: Discussions about resignation.

RESIST:

Resisting the love of someone: Will be persecuted.

Not resisting advances: Discovery of lost valuables.

Other people resisting love: Will gain confidence in yourself.

Resisting wrongdoing: Luck and prosperity.

RESPECT:

Of respect: Will receive an unexpected fortune.

Being respected: Will receive money and achieve riches.

Being highly respected by children: Increase in wealth.

Being respected by others: Joy and friendship.

Showing respect to others: Tremendous catastrophe is ahead.

RESPECTABLE:
Of respectable people: Will enjoy all the pleasures and desires of life.
Being a respectable person: Will lead an easy life.
Being considered a respectable person: Big rain and change of temperature.
Having business dealings with respectable people: Work will be compensated.

RESPONSIBLE:
Being responsible for wrongdoings: Beware of escaping creditors.
Being responsible for good actions: Beware of a double cross.
Dealing with responsible people: Forthcoming happiness.
Being given a responsible job: Worries will be smoothed away.
Having responsible children: Relatives will come asking for help.

REST:
Of resting: Good luck in sporting matters.
Others resting: Will acquire a new home.
Relatives resting: Affairs are going backwards.
Children resting: Happiness in family affairs.
Friends resting: Will be informed of sad news.

RESTAURANT:
Of a restaurant: Bad health.
Entering a restaurant: Friendship.
Eating at a restaurant: Health is not very good.
Eating with children at a restaurant: Wealth.
Others eating at a restaurant: Will receive money soon.
Eating with relatives in a restaurant: Will overcome enemies with patience.
Eating at a restaurant with sweetheart: Bad financial condition.
Enemies eating in a restaurant: Will become rich by economy.
Husband and wife eating in a restaurant alone: Long happy marriage.

RESTLESS:
Being restless: You are prone to being bad-tempered.
Children being restless: Will fight in vain to achieve desires.
Mate being restless: Beware of a rival.
Dog being restless: Beware of prowlers.

RESTRICT:
Actions being restricted: Will have wealth and tranquillity.
Restricting actions of business people: Good times are ahead.
Being restricted by others: Illness.
Restricting children from wrongdoing: Family arguments.
Restricting impositions of family members: Family will ask for money.
Being restricted by government and complying: You should diet a little more.

RESURRECTION:
Of the resurrection: Long journey to religious places is ahead.
Being at resurrection site: Religious interest will bring happiness.
Attending Easter sunrise services with family: Long happy life.

RETURN:
Of returning: Unexpected joy.
Returning from a trip: Great prosperity.
Others returning after a long time: Losses soon to be made good.
Relatives returning from a trip: Jealousy within the family.
Friends returning to their home: Treachery.
Sweetheart returning home: He has been untrue to you.

REVELRY:
Watching merrymaking: Misfortune for you and others.
Participating in revelry: Good married life.
Others participating in revelry: Jealousy.
Relatives participating in revelry: Family arguments.

REVENGE:
Seeking revenge: Anxious times ahead.
Seeking revenge against a man: Humiliation.
Seeking revenge against a woman: You are considered to be very vulgar.
Seeking revenge against family: Small arguments solved.
Seeking revenge against relatives: Quarrels.
Seeking revenge against friends: Approaching money.
Seeking revenge against enemies: A rival will take sweetheart's affection.

REVIEWING STAND:
Of a reviewing stand: A death will occur.
People being on a reviewing stand: A sick friend will recover.
Being on a reviewing stand: Joy of short duration.
High officials on a reviewing stand: You have a bad temper.
Military officers being on a reviewing stand: Treason.
Politicians on a reviewing stand: Happiness in life.

REVOLVER:
Handling a revolver: Danger from water.
Using a revolver: Profit.
Firing a revolver: You will be cheated.
Children holding a revolver: Parents are unworthy.
Killing with a revolver: Will have a long life.
Enemies using a revolver: Return of good health.
Officers with a revolver: Good harvest.
Policemen using a revolver: Will receive good news from abroad.

REWARD:
Receiving a reward: Failure of plans because of overconfidence.
Giving a reward: Will enjoy things that money cannot buy.
Accepting a reward: Will have a big accident.

Declining an unjustified reward: Conceit.
Others receiving rewards: Beware of the danger of fire in your home.
Enemies receiving a reward: Approaching money.

RHEUMATISM:
Of rheumatism: Indiscretion of friends.
Having rheumatism: Will have a new lease on life and happiness.
Suffering with rheumatism: Will overcome enemies.
Relative having rheumatism: Enemies will win over you.
Friends having rheumatism: Fulfillment of plans will be delayed.
Enemies having rheumatism: Disappointment.

RHINOCEROS:
Of a rhinoceros: Success in business affairs.
Rhinoceros in a cage at a zoo: Disillusionment for those in love.
Rhinoceri fighting: Someone is seeking revenge upon you.
Killing a rhinoceros: Unsuccessful business affairs.

RHUBARB:
Of rhubarb: New and strong friendship.
Eating rhubarb: You are dissatisfied with occupation.
Cooking rhubarb: Will lose a friend through quarrels.
Buying rhubarb: Warning of trouble.
Growing rhubarb: Change for the better in affairs.
Making rhubarb pie: Will have an unexpected visitor.

RHYME:
Writing rhymes: Worry over business accounts.
Others writing rhymes for you: You are being cheated.
Writing rhymes with the help of a rhyme dictionary: Loss of money.
Reading rhymes others have written: Danger in love matters.

RIB:

Own ribs being injured: Unexpected money.

Breaking ribs: Unexpected joy.

Husband or wife breaking upper ribs: Happy events.

Relatives breaking their upper ribs: Beware of treachery among those trusted.

Husband or wife breaking lower ribs: Good fortune.

Relatives breaking lower ribs: A false friend is nearby.

Having a misplaced rib: People are gossiping about you.

Relatives having a misplaced rib: Unhappiness caused by relatives.

Having larger ribs than ordinary: Happy marriage.

Husband breaking his ribs: Good financial business.

Wife breaking her ribs: Will divorce her husband.

Friends having broken ribs: Important and very beneficial event to come.

Relatives having broken ribs: Unfitted to hold their position.

Family having broken ribs: Money will come easily during life.

Children having broken ribs: Marital discord.

Having strong ribs: Will be fortunate in marriage.

RIB OF UMBRELLA:

Umbrella having a broken rib: Financial troubles.

Several ribs of umbrella being broken: Someone will come to rescue.

Fixing broken ribs of an umbrella: Prosperity.

Ribs of lover's umbrella broken: Will have affection of a true lover.

Ribs of family umbrella being broken: Disputes.

Ribs of relative's umbrella being broken: Very bad quarrel.

RIBBON:

Of ribbons: Sincerity in love matters.

Handling many ribbons: Big satisfaction.

Tying ribbons: Will make a good trade of something.

Untying ribbons: Will make good business transactions.

Wearing ribbons yourself: Unexpected pleasant news concerning love.

A young woman dreaming of wearing ribbons: Will receive a proposal.

A young girl dreaming of other girls wearing ribbons: Rival in love.

Buying many ribbons: Carelessness in spending money.

Measuring ribbons: Entanglement in lawsuits.

Relative wearing a ribbon: Unexpected prosperity.

RICE:

Of rice: Be careful in making plans.

Eating rice: Happiness and comfort.

Cooking rice: Wealth and abundance.

Others cooking rice: Will have all the good things in life.

Eating rice with many people: Will make a good marriage.

Giving rice to children to eat: Troubles will cease.

Eating rice with family: You have many enemies.

Friends eating rice: Will entertain an unwelcome guest.

Eating so much rice that you are full: Disappointment is ahead.

Eating rice pudding: Money will come easily to you.

Growing rice: Abundance.

Selling rice: Financial gains.

Buying rice: Will realize high ambitions.

RICH:

Being rich: High honors and success.

Becoming rich: Will receive a big reward.

Not becoming rich: Will obtain small employment under wealthy person.

Others who are rich: Turmoil in business affairs.

Other people becoming rich: Affairs are flourishing.

Talking with rich people: Will have beneficial compensation.

Relatives being rich: They will have trouble in their life.

Children becoming rich: Change in environment.

RICKSHAW:
Of a rickshaw: You aren't living a good life.

Riding in a rickshaw: Discovery of a secret.

People who pull rickshaws: You work too hard.

Riding with a beautiful girl in a rickshaw: Will take a long river trip.

Others riding in a rickshaw: Death of someone living nearby.

RIDE:
Taking a ride: Illness.

Riding in a carriage: You are surrounded by jealous people.

Riding in a car: Peril of death.

Riding with others: Plans will turn out unsatisfactorily.

Riding fast in a car: Prosperity may develop.

Riding a horse: Business will go out of control.

Riding a horse and being thrown off: Satisfactory business.

Children riding a horse: Prosperity.

Children falling off a horse: Will have a happy life.

RIDDLE:
Hearing others talking in riddles: Unexpected offer from a relative.

Talking in riddles yourself: Beware of danger near at hand.

Relatives talking in riddles: Triumph over enemies.

Sweetheart talking in riddles: Must control passions.

Children talking in riddles: You will receive unexpected money soon.

RIFLE:
(See **GUN.**)

RIFLER:
Of a rifler: Death of very dear friends.

A rifler stealing household items: Will win at gambling.

Others who have been rifled: Will be disregarded by friends.

Friends being a rifler: Dissolution of hopes.

RING:
Of several rings: Large quarrel.

Wearing a ring: Troubles caused by a friend.

Receiving a ring as a gift: Matrimony in the near future.

Having a diamond ring: Great riches.

Having a ring of precious stones: Wealth.

An unmarried person dreaming of a ring with precious stones: Matrimony.

Married person dreaming of ring of precious stones: Birth of a child.

Having a large ring covered with diamonds: Will receive high honors.

Having a gold ring: Dignity.

Having a gold ring put on your finger: Honor and riches.

Having an iron ring: Hard work ahead.

Losing your ring: Big fortune.

A single girl dreaming of losing her ring: She'll be left by boyfriend.

A man dreaming of losing his ring: Fiancée will marry another man.

Receiving several rings: Security in love.

Buying a ring: Will be an important person.

Giving a gift of rings: Loss of money.

Ring being broken: Domestic unrest.

Fiancée's ring being broken: Separation of lovers.

Receiving a wedding ring: Will have a devoted lover.

Breaking a wedding ring: Divorce.

Having a ring on a chain: Good health.

Making a ring from your own hair: Declaration of love.

Giving or receiving a ring made from hair: Marriage.

RINSE:
Rinsing washed linen: Change of residence.

Rinsing children's clothes: Family security.

A young woman dreaming of rinsing children's clothes: Proposal of marriage.

A married woman dreaming of rinsing children's clothes: Will be pregnant.

Rinsing other people's washing: Will hear gossip against you.

Others rinsing your washing: Will be deceived by friends.

Men rinsing washing: Change for the better.

RIOT:
Of a riot: Financial failure.
Taking part in a riot: Misfortune in business.
Friends taking part in a riot: Persecution by an enemy.
Enemies taking part in a riot: Will receive money.
Relatives taking part in a riot: Death of a friend.
A riot ending: Will receive high honors.

RIVAL:
Of a rival: Will undertake an unpleasant enterprise.
Defeating a rival: Will prove successful in business.
Being defeated by a rival: Shame and sorrow.
A lover dreaming of having a rival: Will be lacking in love affairs.
A young woman dreaming of having a rival: Will accept her present lover.
Married people dreaming of having rivals: Big happiness.

RIVER:
Of a river: Happiness in family affairs.
Swimming in a river: Imminent danger.
Having a river flowing through the house: Big earnings.
A huge river: Danger of sickness.
Being unable to escape from a flooding river: Disillusionment.
Escaping from a flooding river: Long-lasting lawsuits.

A river of clear water: Good business.
A river of dirty water: Disgrace for disputing people.
A small river: Squandering money.
Crossing a river: Security.
A storm-tossed river: Be cautious in business affairs.
Falling into a river: Domestic quarrels.
Throwing someone into a river: Will be befriended by someone.
Children falling into a river: Carelessness in business.
Enemies committing suicide in a river: Will receive much money.
Sweetheart falling into a river: Financial gains.
Fishing in a river: Change of environment.
Drifting on the river in a boat: Imminent danger.

RIVET:
Of rivets: Will receive good news.
Handling rivets of all sizes: Will travel by road or rail.
Relatives handling rivets: Will travel by air.
Buying rivets: Beware of speculating on the stock market.
Selling rivets: Will receive good news.
Others handling rivets: Fortune in business affairs.
Doing riveting work yourself: Advancement within own position.

ROAD:
Of a road: Will have good health.
Traveling on a road: Security.
Traveling on a straight road: Lasting happiness.
Traveling on a crooked road: Discovery of a secret.
Traveling on a bad road: New undertakings will bring sorrow and losses.
Being lost on a road: Error in decisions will cause losses.
Traveling on a well-paved road: Financial gains.
Traveling on a wide road: Big fortune.
Traveling on a narrow, winding road: Will have many obstacles.
Traveling down a road with others: Will live a long life.

Traveling down a road with sweetheart: Will be cheated by friends.

ROAR:
Hearing the roar of water: A traveler will return.
Hearing the roar of animals: An enemy is watching you.
Hearing the roar of animals in the distance: Hard work is ahead.
Hearing animals roaring in a barn: Advancement within own position.

ROAST BEEF:
Of roast beef: Will receive affectionate greetings.
Buying roast beef: Big joy.
Cooking roast beef: Comfortable living.
Eating roast beef: Big earnings.
Cutting roast beef: Will win at gambling.
Putting roast beef in the oven: Imminent danger.
Serving roast beef: Will have fortunate events.

ROAST MEAT:
Of roast meat: Happiness.
A butcher cutting a roast of beef: Difficult times are ahead.
A butcher cutting a roast of pork: Will receive good news.
Cooking roast beef: Melancholy.
Cooking roast pork: Losses from gambling.
Cooking roast lamb: Blessings.
A cooked roast: Someone will cause you to worry.
Wife roasting meat: Will be taken good care of.
Others roasting meat: High hopes.
Roasting veal: Desires will be accomplished.

ROB:
Robbing someone else: Warning of trouble.
People robbing others: Approaching money.
Being robbed: Will receive plenty of money.
Being robbed of money: Will sustain a big loss.

Being robbed of your clothes: Will have good friends supporting you.
Being robbed of jewels: Will receive an inheritance.
Being robbed of securities: Will emerge well from present troubles.

ROBBER:
Of a robber: Big fortune ahead.
Being molested by a robber: A change in life will soon come.
Not being molested by a robber: Change for the better.
Escaping injury by a robber: Good times are coming.
Catching a robber: Triumph over enemies.
Killing a robber: Will have a long life.
A robber being arrested: Success in business.
A robber running away: Disappointment in love affairs.

ROBIN:
Of a robin: Will be very fortunate.
Several robins flying: Will receive something for which you wished.
Robins in a tree: Will have an important position.
Robins on a lawn: Malicious gossip is being spread about you.
A nest of robins: Domestic unhappiness.
Catching a robin: Wealth.
Killing a robin: Unhappiness.
Robins resting: Will receive false news.
Feeding robins: Big success in life.

ROBUST:
Being robust: Big worries ahead.
Entire family being robust: Will have many disillusionments.
Having robust children: Financial gains.
Having robust friends: Sickness.
Fighting with a robust person: Sorrow is about to come.

ROCK:
Of rocks: Difficulties and hard work.
Handling rocks: Will be contradicted.
Others handling rocks: Will have many enemies.

Climbing down rocks: Loss of relatives.

Having trouble climbing down rocks: Death of friends.

Climbing down rocks easily: Don't confide in friends.

Climbing up rocks the hard way: Realization of desires will be slow.

Climbing a rock with sweetheart: Will be married soon.

Kissing sweetheart on top of a rock: Marriage will last forever.

Children climbing up rocks: Abundance of money.

Children climbing down rocks: They will receive a good education.

A large rock in the sea: Will overcome enemies with perseverance.

ROCKET:

Of a rocket: Short-lived success.

Building a rocket: Must have firmer foundations for business.

Throwing a rocket: Abundant means.

Enemies being killed by a rocket: Will hear false news.

Exploding a rocket: Fortune in the family.

Many rockets: Triumph over enemies.

ROCKING CHAIR:

Of a rocking chair: Will obtain good employment.

Buying a rocking chair: Unhappiness.

Selling a rocking chair: Change for the better.

Sitting in a rocking chair: You are confronted with insurmountable obstacles.

Others sitting in a rocking chair: Enemies are watching.

Member of family sitting in a rocking chair: Will escape injury.

Relatives sitting in a rocking chair: Death of someone in the family.

Children playing in a rocking chair: Approaching money.

ROD:

Of steel rods: Unhappiness.

Brass rods: Infidelity of loved ones.

Rusty rods: Happiness

Silver rods: Wealth.

Handling rods: Big fortune in business.

ROLLS:

Of rolls: Promotion in employment.

Eating fresh rolls: Good earnings.

Eating stale rolls: Will encounter bad business.

Making rolls yourself: Good financial earnings.

Baking rolls: Change for the better.

Buying rolls: Avoid rivals.

Serving rolls to others: Abundance of money.

ROOF:

The roof of own house: Prosperity.

The roof of others' houses: Will receive many garments as a gift.

Putting a roof on a building: An enemy is watching.

Others putting a roof on a building: Will have a vigorous mind.

Painting a roof: Will live a long life.

Others painting a roof: Will be cheated by friends.

A roof leaking: Loss of money.

Fixing a leak in a roof: Will soon take a journey faraway.

Putting a new roof on a house: Good times are coming.

ROOK:

Of this European bird: Will entertain an unwelcome guest.

Many rooks: Postponement of success.

Two rooks fighting: You should mend your ways in life.

Killing a rook: A mystery will be solved.

ROOM:

Of a room: Will discover family secrets.

An apartment room: Be on the lookout for treachery.

A room in a home: Poverty.

A room that you live in: Financial worries.

An office room: Will have bad dealings with creditors.

A room at a mortuary: Danger of immediate death.

A hotel room: Death of a friend.
A boarding house room: Bad business ventures.
A room at a friend's house: Doomed for disappointment.
A prison room: Will live a long life.
The room of someone you love: Will be cheated by friends.
A newly painted room: Will be deceived.
Entering a room: Certainty of good earnings.
Being in own room: Good humor will bring happiness.
Of own bedroom: Disgrace.
A dark room: Loss of money.
A bathroom: Sickness.
Children's room: Will take a long trip.

ROOSTER:
Of a rooster: Joy and happiness.
A rooster laying an egg: Big profit.
Two roosters fighting: Family quarrels and disappointment.
A girl hearing a cock crow: She will soon have a new lover.
A lover hearing a rooster crow: He has a formidable rival.
A married woman hearing a rooster crow: Is in love with a handsome man.
A married man hearing a rooster crow: Someone else is in love with wife.

ROOT:
Of roots: Will have a difficult task to accomplish.
Roots of trees: Misfortune.
Roots of plants: Sickness will soon come.
Pulling roots of plant from ground: Others are credited with your ideas.
The roots of own teeth: Do not give any money on credit.
The roots of children's teeth: Do not weaken to friends' desires.

ROPES:
Of a rope: Will be embarrassed by friends.
Being bound with ropes: Difficult times in business affairs.

Climbing up a rope: Good luck.
Coming down a rope: Will overcome all who may seek your downfall.
The ropes of a ship: Will have news from people to whom you owe money.
Sailors using ropes on a ship: Will have a vigorous mind.
A ship tied up with ropes: Financial gains.
Ropes hanging people: Danger in own affairs.
Places being fenced with ropes: You are being deceived.
Ropes being manufactured: Prosperity is very small.

ROSARY:
Of a rosary: Will suffer because of sins.
Telling the beads of own rosary: Reconciliation with a friend.
Relatives telling the rosary: Will have sorrow.
Others telling the rosary: Good times are coming.
Someone wearing a rosary: Will suffer bereavement.

ROSE:
Of roses: Happiness.
Holding roses in hands during season: Joy.
Smelling roses during season: Happy news.
Sick people holding or smelling roses in season: Danger of death.
Holding roses out of season: Misfortune.
Picking roses: Will have a proposal of marriage.
Rose blossoms being withered and falling away: You are deceived.
Slightly faded roses: Success will come after some difficulties.
White roses: Innocence.
Red roses: Will be a bachelor or old maid.
Giving roses as a gift: Modesty.
Receiving roses as a gift: Pleasant memories of old friends.
Picking roses: You are a good lover or sweetheart.

Deep-red roses: Joyous times and fun.
Rose buds: Riches.
Picking rose buds: Increase in the family.

ROSEMARY:
Of rosemary: Desire for food will be satisfied.
Growing rosemary: Big joy.
Picking rosemary: Will have security.
Buying rosemary: Domestic contentment.
Cooking with rosemary: A birth will take place in own home.
Smelling rosemary: Will have melancholy and annoyance.

ROTTEN:
Of something rotten: Will have obstacles in love affairs.
Throwing away rotten things: Will receive money.
Others throwing away rotten things: Financial gains.
Throwing away rotten food: Will receive an abundance of money.

ROTUNDA:
The rotunda of a beautiful house: Big earnings.
The rotunda of a capital: Will have a very steady business.
Meeting people on a rotunda: Will enjoy amusements and pleasures.
Admiring a rotunda with a loved one: Big fortune.

ROUGE:
Of rouge sitting on a dresser: Someone will cheat you.
Using rouge on cheeks: Are guilty of carelessness.
Other people using rouge: Conceit.
Receiving rouge as a gift: Beware of ruffians.
Buying rouge: Will give children a high education.

ROULETTE:
Of a roulette table: Will have arguments with a friend.
People gambling at a roulette table: Will fight with an enemy.

Winning at roulette table: Will prove innocence to others.
Losing at roulette table: Will receive money from an elderly person.

ROUSE:
Having to wake up: You are threatened by danger.
Being roused by someone: Good business affairs.
Being roused by an alarm clock: You are always late.
Others waking up: A trap is being laid for you.

ROW:
People rowing: Headed toward misfortune.
Doing the rowing yourself: Change of surroundings.
People rowing in a race: Advancement within own position.
Others rowing: Don't confide secrets to friends.
A rowing club: Will have a strong rival.

ROWBOAT:
Of a rowboat: Decline in business affairs.
A rowboat on the sea: Fortune ahead.
A rowboat on a river: Will be contradicted.
A rowboat on a clear lake: Security.
A rowboat in dirty water: Unsuccessful business.
Slowly rowing a boat: You are very impatient.

ROWEL:
Having spurs: Will enjoy social activities of a happy nature.
Raking a horse with rowels: Will receive money.
Fastening the strap of rowels: Anxiety over results in business dealings.
Having many rowels: Vanity.
Having silver rowels: Riches.

RUB:
Of rubbing things: Will soon change residence.
Being rubbed: Will go to a dance party.

Rubbing someone else: Big neighborhood scandal.

Being rubbed to reduce weight: Make plans for old age.

Being rubbed with perfume: You trust relatives too much.

RUBBER:

Of rubber: Prosperity.

Using rubber for various things: Will take a long trip.

Articles made from rubber: Rebellion among relatives.

Erasing writing with a rubber: Uncertainty in actions.

Erasing love letters with a rubber: You are giving a lover the brush-off.

RUBBISH:

Of rubbish: Will meet a stingy person.

Handling rubbish: You are about to make a valuable discovery.

Throwing rubbish away: Recovery from an illness.

Others handling rubbish: You have a secret enemy.

RUBY:

Of rubies: Happiness.

Wearing jewelry with rubies: Will triumph over enemies.

Wearing a ruby ring: Will have a very faithful love.

Buying jewelry with rubies in it: Consolation.

Selling ruby jewelry: Loss of money.

RUDDER:

Of a rudder: You have an undecided mind.

A broken rudder: Business is in distress.

A ship without a rudder: Avoid taking a voyage.

A new rudder: Expect the visit of a dear friend.

A ship losing a rudder at sea: Big profit.

RUE:

Being sorry: A good future is ahead.

Rueing present condition. Will live a long life.

Regretting wrongdoings: Will be fortunate in love.

Regretting first love: Will meet a wealthy, honorable person.

Regretting wrongdoings in business: Domestic difficulties.

RUFFIAN:

Of ruffians: Someone will steal from you.

Being a ruffian: Infidelity.

Having dealings with ruffians: Will have bad conduct.

A ruffian blackmailing you: Will have riches.

RUIN:

Something being ruined: Fortune and success.

House being ruined: Triumph in business.

Marriage being ruined: You are well known for being so stingy.

A ruined city: Will receive unexpected fortune.

A financially ruined family: Will receive money unexpectedly.

Ruining yourself because of wrongdoing: Will be gravely embarrassed.

Causing ruin of other people: Will have luck and prosperity.

Other people being ruined: Will live a long life.

RULER:

Of a ruler: A mystery will soon be solved.

Being the ruler of a nation: Will receive unhappy news concerning love.

Ruling nation with a strong hand: Will be asked for money by relatives.

Measuring with a ruler: Will become financially destitute.

A professional person using a ruler: Will overcome unhappiness.

RUM:

Of bottles of rum: Will be doing a lot of drinking.

Drinking rum: Will have a very changeable mind.

Buying rum: Will have many friends.

Offering rum to friends: Infidelity.

RUMBLE:
Of strange rumbles: Death of an enemy.
Hearing rumbles from below surface of earth: Recovery from illness.
Hearing rumbles followed by an earthquake: Troubles will cause destitution.
Hearing the rolling sound of a rumble: Avoid rivals.

RUN:
Of running: Good fortune.
A woman dreaming of running: Will lose her virginity.
Running too fast: Unexpected fortune.
Running because of being scared: Security.
Running because of being afraid: Will go into exile.
Running in circles: Friends do not think very much of you.
Running naked: Will be robbed by relatives.
A woman dreaming of running naked: Will go crazy.
A sick man dreaming of running: Bad business.
A sick woman dreaming of running: Will get new clothes.
Running to catch someone: Good fortune.
A sick person running to catch someone: Happiness.
Other people running: Contentment.
Many people running in confusion: Will receive dreadful news.
Running like a madman: Riches.
Civilians running after each other: Big quarrels.
People running with clubs: Dissension in business.
Children running with clubs: Big joy.
Poor people running: Good fortune.
Wanting to run but can't: Will have a big sickness.

Running after an enemy: Victory and profit.
Running while hunting: Loss of money.
Running after a deer or a rabbit: You are a very stingy person.

RUPTURE:
Of a rupture: Will be very envious.
Having a rupture in the body: Luck and prosperity.
Having an operation on a rupture: Good luck is coming to you.
Others having a rupture operation: Death of an enemy.

RUST:
Of rust: Enemies will celebrate your misfortune.
Rusty articles: Beware of loss.
Handling rusty articles: You neglect your business.
Others handling rusty articles: Warning of trouble.

RUSTIC:
A rustic house: Will become pregnant in the near future.
Buying a rustic house: Family quarrels.
A rustic farm: You are gullible.
Several rustic buildings: Bankruptcy is near at hand.

RYE:
Of rye bread: Joy and money.
Eating rye bread: Popularity with opposite sex.
Buying a loaf of rye bread: Dignity and distinction.
Baking rye bread: Good days to come.
Serving rye bread at a meal: Fortune is secured.
Rye flour: You dress to perfection.
Cooking with rye flour: Displeasure caused by children.
Grinding rye flour: Will receive plenty of money.

S

SABLE:
Of a sable: Will take a long trip.
Possessing a sable fur: Will receive a large inheritance.
Others having a sable fur: A false friend is nearby.
Relatives having a sable fur: Will be cheated by friends.

SACK:
Of a sack: Discovery of lost valuables.
Sacks that are full: Luck and prosperity.
Sacks that are empty: Loneliness and trouble.
Filling a sack: Financial gains.
Emptying a sack: A season of sorrow is about to come.

SACRIFICE:
Making a sacrifice: Changes in environment.
Others making a sacrifice for you: Big joy.
Friends making a sacrifice for you: Approaching money.
Relatives making a sacrifice for you: Recovery of money.

SACRILEGE:
Committing a sacrilege: Will suffer much misery.
Others committing a sacrilege: Misfortune.
Relatives committing a sacrilege: Prosperity.
Enemies committing a sacrilege: Domestic joy.

SAD:
Being sad yourself: Lasting joy.
Children being sad: Good fortune in the future.
Wife or husband being sad: Good times are coming.
Relatives being sad: Family quarrels.

SADDLE:
Of a saddle: You are confronted with insurmountable obstacles.

Riding a horse with a new saddle: Joy without profit.
Riding a horse without a saddle: Bad health.
Others riding horses without saddle: A catastrophe is ahead.
Family riding a horse with a saddle: Small prosperity.
Children riding a horse without a saddle: Revise your plans.
Being a saddle maker: Will enjoy big profits.

SAFE:
Of a safe: Approaching money.
A safe filled with money: Advancement within own position.
An empty safe: Troubles are ahead.
Unlocking a safe: Anxiety caused by own failure.
Locking a safe: Plans will all go well.
Emptying a safe: Serious disaster is ahead of you.

SAFFRON:
Of saffron powder: Will fall into disgrace.
Buying saffron powder: Will receive money.
Cooking with saffron powder: False joy.

SAGE:
Of an emminent person of wisdom: Happiness is assured.
Consulting a sage person: Will have a vigorous mind.
Of the sage plant: Recovery from an illness.
Buying sage: Good luck.
Using fresh sage in food: Abundant means.
Using dried sage in food: Changes in environment.

SAIL:
Of a sail for a vessel or boat: An enemy is seeking your ruin.
Putting a sail on a boat: Dignity and distinction.
Handling several sails: Big joy.

Others raising up a sail: Misfortune in love affairs.

Others handling the sail in your boat: You are being deceived.

A square sail: Important and very beneficial event to come.

Handling a square sail: Luck and prosperity.

SAILBOAT:

Owning a sailboat: Will come out well from a present danger.

Sailing in a sailboat: Death of an enemy.

Being in a sailboat with children: Approaching money.

Being in a sailboat with sweetheart: Danger in love matters.

Others in a sailboat: Be cautious in love affairs.

SAILING:

Of sailing a boat: Happiness.

A sailor sailing a boat: Financial gains.

Sweetheart sailing alone: Will have emotional sorrow.

Sailing a very small boat yourself: Big success in everything.

A sailboat sailing in a calm sea: Death of a friend.

Sailing a boat in a stormy sea: Lasting joy.

Children sailing a small boat: Will have mastery over many matters.

SAILOR:

Of a sailor: Will take a dangerous trip.

Several sailors: Misery.

Being a sailor: Restlessness and changes in affairs.

A woman being in the company of a sailor: News from faraway.

A man being in the company of a sailor: Arrival of friends.

SAINT:

Of a saint: Will overcome enemies with perseverance.

Praying to a saint: Will overcome difficulties.

Saints being very close: Will enjoy peace and well-being.

A sinful person dreaming of a saint: Must repent.

An ill person dreaming of a saint: Foretells death.

SALAD:

Of salads: Own qualities will insure advancement in life.

Eating salads: Good luck.

Preparing a mixed salad: Approaching money.

Others preparing a salad: You are being deceived.

Eating salad in company of others: Will be guilty of foolish actions.

SALAMI:

Of many kinds of salami: Your love is very changeable and unsteady.

Slicing salami: Beware of a trap being laid for you.

Eating salami: Family arguments.

Making a salami sandwich: Will receive good news from close friends.

SALARY:

Receiving a salary: Big joy ahead for you.

Paying salary: Hard work awaits you.

Others collecting their salary: Triumph over enemies.

Others paying salary: Beware of jealous friends.

Paying a salary to your help: Financial gains.

SALE:

Of a public sale: You are in the grip of deceitful people.

A private sale: Will do good business.

Buying things at a public sale: Changes for the better.

Selling own property: Change of surroundings.

Selling merchandise: Dignity and distinction.

Others selling things: Secret enmity of some person is directed at you.

SALESMAN:

Being a salesman: Will come out well in business.

A salesman selling to you: Good times are coming.

Others buying from a salesman: Postponement of success.

A friend being a salesman: Will be cheated by friends.

SALIVA:
Of your own saliva: Happiness is assured.

The saliva of your children: Important and very beneficial event to come.

The saliva of a sick person: Avoid rivals.

Others spitting saliva: Someone is endeavoring to destroy you.

The saliva of an animal: Will overcome your enemies.

Saliva coming out of the mouth of a dog: You have many loyal friends.

Saliva coming out of the mouth of a horse: Abundant means.

SALMON:
Of salmon: Family troubles.

Catching a salmon: Accord among friends.

Eating fresh salmon: You have a loyal friend.

Eating cooked salmon: Advancement within own position.

Eating canned salmon: Approaching money.

Eating a salad with salmon in it: Will have sorrow.

Eating a salmon sandwich: Hard work awaits.

Others eating salmon: Beware of a rival.

SALON:
Of a salon: People are gossiping about you.

Going to a salon: Beware of untrue friends.

Being at a salon to have hair fixed: Humiliation.

Going to a salon with a member of the family: Watch your spending of money.

Friends being at a salon: Insurmountable obstacles confront you.

SALT:
Of salt: Abundance.

Buying salt: Good earnings will last a long time.

Using salt on food: Will have religious arguments.

Cooking food with salt: Good days are ahead.

Putting too much salt in food: Will squander money.

Spilling salt: On the right path to money if you throw salt over shoulder.

Others spilling salt: Quarrels and dissatisfaction.

Using a salt shaker: Will be a person of science.

Being a salt merchant: Will make plenty of money.

SALUTARY:
Of promoting good health by exercise: Will have a good position in life.

Taking exercises for health: You are too active in affairs.

Teaching children to live a salutary life: Happiness.

Advocating a salutary life: Beware, you are eating too much.

SALUTATION:
Sending salutations to friends: Poverty.

Sending salutations to businessmen: Will come out well from present peril.

Receiving salutations from friends: Will win at gambling.

Receiving salutations from people abroad: Loss of present position.

SALUTE:
Of someone saluting: Beware of sickness.

Saluting someone else: Reconciliation.

Being sick when you salute someone: Blessings in business.

Being saluted by friends: Will be very brave in business.

SALVAGE:
Salvaging something: Big happiness ahead.

Salvaging something from a fire: Big success in business.

Salvaging something from ruin: You are very humanitarian.

Salvaging family affairs: Advancement in financial standing.

SALVATION:
Of salvation: Happiness.
A salvation institution: Embarrassment in family life.
Being member of a salvation institution: Dignity and contentment.
Being helped by a salvation institution: Good days are coming.

SALVO:
Hearing a gun salute: Recovery of illness.
An army giving a salvo salute: Contentment.
The navy giving a salvo salute: Progress in business enterprises.
Receiving a salvo salute: Unhappy days are ahead.
Ordering a salvo salute: An enemy is seeking your ruin.

SAMBO:
Of a child born of Negro and Indian parents: Persecution.
A sambo being persecuted: Booming business.
A sambo being imprisoned: Warning of trouble.
Protecting a sambo: Recovery from an illness.

SAMPLE:
Taking samples: You are testing the ones you love.
Taking a sample of food: Happiness.
Taking samples of minerals: Prosperity.
Taking samples of various seeds: Security in business.
Taking samples of gold, silver, or brass: Will be invited to a concert.
Samples of materials: Sickness.

SANATORIUM:
Of a sanatorium: Will have good health.
Being put in a sanatorium: Treachery by relatives.
Being released from a sanatorium: Big fortune gained in gambling.

Relatives going to a sanatorium: Poverty.
Relatives being released from a sanatorium: Postponement of success.
Friends being in a sanatorium: Persecution.
Friends being released from a sanatorium: Loss of present position.
Enemies being in a sanatorium: Good financial improvements.

SANCTION:
Being sanctioned: Infidelity.
Others being sanctioned: Public disgrace.
Members of family being sanctioned: Beware of enemies.
Enemies receiving sanction: Joy and prosperity.

SAND:
Of sand: Embarrassment and uneasiness.
Handling sand: Will have many small vexations.
Working with sand: Years of hard work are ahead.
Mixing sand with cement: Success.
Others using sand: Will receive unexpected money.
A sand dune: Will be justified by friends.
Colored sand: Will receive a favor.

SANDAL:
Of sandals: Will have good health.
Wearing sandals: Will have healthy feet.
Taking off sandals: Will receive small unexpected inheritance from stranger.
Changing sandals: Will have a headache.
Throwing away sandals: Will receive an unexpected gift.

SANDPAPER:
Of sandpaper: Joy without profit.
Using sandpaper: Joy within domestic life.
A laborer using sandpaper: You are disgusted with living.
Sanding an article with sandpaper: Your imagination is too big.

SANDSTORM:
Of a sandstorm: Financial gains.

Being in a sandstorm: Will live a long life.

Being injured in a sandstorm: Important and very beneficial event to come.

Property being damaged by a sandstorm: Will build a new house.

SANDWICH:
Of sandwiches: Honor.

Buying sandwiches: Big fortune.

Making sandwiches for others: Will receive a gift.

Eating sandwiches with white bread: Enormous profit.

Eating sandwiches with dark bread: Big inheritance.

Eating sandwiches with various meats: Small profit.

Eating sandwiches made with fish: Long healthy life.

SANITARY:
Doing sanitary chores: Will live a long life.

Family helping with sanitary chores: Important events, very beneficial.

Condemning something for being unsanitary: Doomed for disappointment.

Working in a sanitary department: Improvement of career.

SAPIENT:
Of a wise person: You are prone to talk too much.

Being sapient: Confusion in business affairs.

A sapient person giving advice: You are being deceived.

Following advice of a sapient person: Avoid rivals.

SAPPHIRE:
Of sapphires: Will be happy.

A woman dreaming of wearing sapphire rings: She will be molested.

A woman dreaming of dark blue sapphires: Husband will bring great happiness.

Other people wearing sapphire rings: Disputes with best friends.

Wearing jewelry with sapphire stones: Will be seduced by force.

Wearing sapphire bracelets: You have many secret enemies.

Friends wearing sapphire rings: Will receive very pleasant news.

SARDINE:
Of sardines: You have a black mark of dishonor on you.

Eating sardines: Constant fortune.

Frying sardines: Will quarrel with friends.

Eating canned sardines: Discontent within the home.

Marinating sardines: Big profit.

Catching sardines in a net: Big inheritance.

Making sardine pie: Disagreement among relatives.

Buying sardines in a can: Troubles are ahead for you.

SASH:
Of many sashes: You are belligerent.

Handling a sash: You enjoy comical plays.

Putting a sash on: Will receive plenty of money.

Putting a sash on children: Will have a large family.

Taking a sash off children: Desires will meet with success.

SATAN:
Of seeing Satan while saying a prayer: Will resist temptations.

A sick person dreaming of Satan: Unhappy events.

Of Satan: Good business ahead.

Talking to Satan: Will never be short of money.

Being possessed by Satan: Will have a long happy life.

Having a fight with Satan: Danger.

SATIN:
Of satin: Profit and honor.

White satin: Abundant means.

Blue satin: Will have damages in own affairs.

Red satin: Will be wounded by a bullet.

A businessman dreaming of satin: Business is secured.

A lover dreaming of satin: Beware of false and flattering talk.

A beautiful single girl dreaming of satin: Will have an ardent love.

A married woman dreaming of satin: Will deceive her husband.

SATISFACTION:

Being satisfied: Will receive momentary wealth.

Receiving satisfaction from others: Will have a bad lawsuit.

Giving satisfaction to others: Loss of present position.

Giving satisfaction to friends: Will be persecuted.

SATURATE:

Of something being saturated: Abundance in proportion to saturation.

Others saturating articles: You are looking for a new business.

Relatives saturating something: Unable to find employment.

Being given something saturated: Will receive sad news.

SATURDAY:

Of Saturday: Will enjoy peace and quiet.

Working on Saturday: Uneasiness.

Not working on Saturday: Embarrassment in love affairs.

Having lots of fun on Saturday: Will be granted a favor.

SATYR:

Being a lewd person: Will be criticized by the community.

Doing indecent satyr actions: Will have immoral pleasures.

Others who are satyr: Will contract an incurable disease.

Having satyr friends: Hopes will not be realized.

SAUCE:

Of a ready-made sauce: You like good food.

White sauce: You eat too much.

Brown sauce: Will have friends for dinner.

Green sauce: Will have indigestion.

Preparing a mushroom sauce: Will receive favors from important person.

Putting sauce on food: Joy and small profit.

SAUCEPAN:

Of a saucepan: Will take care of debts.

Using a saucepan: Future is secured.

Using several saucepans: Will never be in poverty.

Others using saucepans: Beware of double cross.

Having a saucepan full: Will have good health.

SAUSAGE:

Of sausage: Domestic trouble.

Making sausage: You are a very passionate person.

Buying sausages: Contentment in life.

Cooking sausages: Contentment in home affairs.

Eating pork sausages: Will win in gambling.

Eating liver sausages: Poverty.

Young people eating sausage: They will fall in love.

Mature people eating sausages: Will have good health.

SAVAGE:

Of a savage person: Contentment in love.

Dealing with a savage person: Will receive good news.

Being hurt by a savage person: Leading a wild life.

Being savage yourself: Will have friends' protection.

Many savages: Rescue by a friend.

Fighting with a savage person: Small worries through dishonesty of others.

SAVANT:

Of a man of learning: Will have good business affairs.

Taking the advice of a savant: A woman is cheating on you.

Being a savant: Good fortune in love affairs.

Enemies going to a savant: Business will be abandoned.

SAVE:
Saving money: You have a very changeable mind.
Saving life of children: Happy events.
Saving someone from drowning: Will have dealings with honest people.
Saving someone from committing suicide: Public disgrace.
Saving someone from wrongdoings: Reconciliation with enemies.

SAVINGS:
Of financial savings: Will have good friendships.
Putting money in a savings account: You eat good foods.
Having plenty of money in a savings account: Will surprise your enemies.
Others accumulating savings: Poverty.
Children saving money: Family secret will be revealed.

SAVIOUR:
Of the Saviour: Will have good health.
Talking with the Saviour: Will have great blessings.
The Saviour granting wishes: Big joy and contentment.
Praying to the Saviour: Desires will be achieved in the future.

SAW:
Of a saw: Progression in business.
Sawing wood: Success.
Others sawing wood: Satisfaction in business.
Enemies sawing wood: Will have a long happiness.
Using a saw: Increased wealth.
A rusty saw with broken teeth: Failure.

SCABBY:
Having scabs all over the body: Will achieve great riches.
Having scab treatments: Will enjoy great fortune for rest of life.
Contracting scabs: Will win a lawsuit.
Children having scabs: Family arguments.
Dog having scabs: Will be hurt by actions of enemies.

SCAFFOLD:
Of a scaffold: Will be disillusioned.
An erected scaffold: Sickness.
Someone climbing a scaffold: Will receive a very valuable gift.
Someone being executed on a scaffold: Will live a long life.
Being on top of a scaffold: Sick people will get well.
Falling from a scaffold: Will have much pleasure.
Taking down a scaffold: Will receive an inheritance.
Several scaffolds lined up: A rival competitor will press you hard.
Many people falling from a scaffold: Will cause injury to others.

SCALD:
Being scalded: High ambitions.
Scalding own hand while cooking: Misery or sickness.
Other people being scalded: Riches.
Children being scalded: Family quarrels.
Relatives being scalded: Prosperity.

SCALE:
Of a scale: Will have good business.
Being on a scale: Will have dealings with the Justice Department.
An old-fashioned scale: Good results in a lawsuit.
Weighing children on a scale: Will be badly deceived.
Weighing various things on a scale: Arguments with friends.
Several scales: Arrest and appearance before a court.
Others being on a scale: Denotes arrest.
Relatives on a scale: Will be summoned before a court.

SCANDAL:
Of a scandal: Honor and triumph.
Being involved in a scandal: Will be offended.
Hearing of scandals: Will receive a marriage proposal.
Friends being involved in a scandal: Financial gains.

Enemies being involved in a scandal: Prosperity.

Farmers being involved in a scandal: Will have a good harvest.

SCAR:

Of a vaccination scar: Will have plenty of money.

Having a scar: Dishonor will come to you.

Having a scar from an operation: Riches.

Having a scar because of a fight: Will escape approaching danger.

SCARLET:

Of the color scarlet: Family quarrels.

Scarlet-colored materials of any kind: Danger in love matters.

Buying a scarlet evening gown: Dignity and distinction.

Buying scarlet-colored clothes: Will have sorrow.

SCARLET FEVER:

Having scarlet fever: Riches.

Children having scarlet fever: Will have determination in life.

Relatives having scarlet fever: Things will turn out for the best.

Others having scarlet fever: Have faith in yourself.

SCENT:

Smelling a bad scent: Loss of friendship with neighbors.

Smelling a bad scent in the air: Will be deceived by best friend.

Smelling scent of bad breath: Someone will trick you.

Smelling a perfume scent: Prostitution.

Having a bottle of perfume: Corruption.

Smelling perfume on others: Loss of friendship.

Smelling perfume on friends: Revelation of a secret.

Buying perfume: Will have a good harvest.

Going into a store selling perfume: Unexpected business transaction.

SCEPTRE:

Of a sceptre: Think well before making a decision.

Receiving a sceptre when being crowned: Poverty.

A queen receiving a sceptre at a coronation: Extreme misery.

Handing a sceptre to a queen: Will be in need of many things.

SCHOOL:

Of a school: Will suffer humiliation.

Going to school: Business will be in good standing.

Taking children to school: Will set a good example for children.

Children going to school alone: Family disagreement.

Children getting good grades at school: Family happiness.

Going to high school: Modesty.

Spending money for schooling: You are surrounded by boisterous people.

Being in school yourself: Increase of knowledge.

Children becoming teachers: You have promising business affairs.

Going to elementary school: Will do crazy things.

Going to grammar school: Anxiety.

Going to a swimming school: Will soon be robbed.

Going to a dancing school: Your morals make you unfit to fill position.

SCHOOLTEACHER:

Being a schoolteacher: Will have a a position of honor.

Becoming a schoolteacher: Business is secure.

Teaching school: Prohibited love.

A woman dreaming of being a schoolteacher: Will earn money by activity.

Being a high school teacher: You have many false friends.

Talking to a schoolteacher: Will receive sad news.

Being a teacher of foreign languages: Someone is cheating you.

Hiring a schoolteacher: Avoid too much amusement.

SCISSORS:
Of scissors: Will be appointed editor of a well-known newspaper.
Buying scissors: You are a very precise and proper person.
Using manicure scissors: Will live a long life.
Cutting materials with scissors: Will have an unexpected visitor.
Cutting paper with scissors: Big success.
Others using scissors: Future is not secure.
Enemies using scissors: Will suffer a business loss.
Married couple using scissors: Will have a big love quarrel.
Lovers handling scissors: Will have a big argument about love matters.

SCORPION:
Of a scorpion: Will receive damages caused by enemies.
Several scorpions: Enemies are talking behind your back.
A nest of scorpions: Will overcome enemies.
Scorpions eating lizards: You are an idealist.
A scorpion in a cage: You are surrounded by boisterous people.
Being bitten by a scorpion: Business will succeed.
Killing a scorpion: Will suffer loss through pretended friends.

SCRAPE:
Of scraping: A wedding will take place soon.
Working hard at scraping: Unhappiness.
Members of family scraping: Misfortune.
Friends scraping: Poverty.

SCRATCH:
Scratching own back: Approaching money.
Scratching yourself: Arrival of guests.
Other people scratching: Worries will be smoothed away.
Drawing blood from a scratch: Will receive bad news.

Being scratched by a woman's nails: Your love is secured.
Being scratched by children: Will receive unexpected money.
Being scratched by a cat: Sickness.
Being scratched by a dog: Will be cheated by friends.
Being scratched by rosebushes: You are being deceived.
Sweethearts scratching each other: Will be guilty of foolish actions.

SCREAM:
Of screaming: Beware of enemies.
Screaming for help: Danger in love matters.
Children screaming: Happiness.
Relatives screaming: Quarrels and arguments.
Others screaming: An enemy is seeking your ruin.

SCREEN:
Of a screen: You are attempting to hide mistakes.
Beautiful screens: Double cross by friends.
Screens dividing a room: Will attend a comedy.
Undressing behind a screen: Will enjoy beautiful things.
Buying a screen: Increase in the family.

SCULPTOR:
Of a sculptor: Change in present position.
Visiting a sculptor: Will receive honors.
Being friendly with a sculptor: Will bring about love but less money.
Posing for a sculptor: Social activities of a happy nature.
A model posing naked for a sculptor: Will realize high ambitions.
A married woman posing for a sculptor: Will be left by her husband.
A virgin posing for a sculptor: Will marry a rich man.
A widow posing for a sculptor: Suitable time to pursue her desires.

SCYTHE:
Of a scythe: Riches.

Sharpening a scythe: Shame for wrongdoings.

A small scythe: Weakness of character.

Cutting grass with a scythe: Will have a long life.

Cutting very tall grass with a scythe: Will receive much attention.

Cutting dried grass with a scythe: Sickness.

Using a scythe: Abundance of money.

SEA:

Of the open sea with small waves: Big joy.

A blue sea: Business affairs are running smoothly.

A dirty-colored sea: Small profit.

Large waves on the sea: Will receive unexpected help.

Small waves on a clear sea: Joy in administration of business.

A dead calm sea: Will make money from a business transaction.

Being on a calm sea with a loved one: Business is slow.

Falling into the sea: Beware of jealous friends.

Waking upon falling into sea: A woman's love will cause ruin and dishonor.

Falling into sea and clutching a piece of wood: Will attain goal with hard work.

Taking a bath in the sea: Honor.

Men and women taking a bath in the sea: Great honor without profit.

Being thrown by force into the sea: Sickness.

Traveling across a very smooth sea: Devoted love within the family.

Traveling on a very rough sea: Loss in business affairs.

Man and wife traveling on a rough sea: Great and lasting love.

Being at sea during a typhoon: Loss and adversity.

A high tide of the sea: Fortune in business.

A low tide of the sea: Losses.

Children being with you at the sea: Beware of jealous friends.

A lonely person dreaming of the sea: Foretells a life without love.

A girl dreaming of a stormy sea: Deep anguish because of a double cross.

SEALS:

Of seals: You are pushed on by ambitions but will never attain your goal.

A seal coming onto the beach: Will soon become pregnant.

A seal diving: Abundant means.

A sealskin coat: Approaching money.

Catching a seal: Secret enemies are working against you.

Taking oil from a seal: You have many faithful friends.

A small seal in an aquarium: Security in love.

Of the seal of the government: Will receive good advice.

Putting own seal on legal papers: Happiness.

Putting own seal on a letter: Will escape danger.

Sealing a letter: Security.

Breaking the seal on a letter: Loss of present position.

Opening a sealed letter: Warning of trouble.

SEARCH:

Searching for something: Infidelity.

Others searching: Gossip.

Searching through personal effects: Beware of thieves.

Searching through the house: Warning of trouble.

Own house being searched by the law: Tranquillity of conscience.

Others searching their personal effects: You are hated.

Searching husband's pockets: Abundant means.

Searching for a lost object: Family dishonor.

SEARCH WARRANT:

Of a search warrant: Important and very beneficial event to come.

Being handed a search warrant: A false friend is nearby.

Being found innocent: Happiness.

A search warrant being given to others: Financial gains.

SEAT:
Of a seat: Satisfaction.
A seat at a theater: Personal affairs are in confusion.
The seat of a bus or streetcar: Contentment.
The seat of a plane: Joy.
A seat in a park: You are too boisterous.
The county seat: Good things will happen.
Being seated in a comfortable chair: You are an amorous person.
Being seated alone on a divan: Disappointment.
Being seated with loved one on a divan: Happiness.

SECRET:
Having a secret: Will have a big fortune.
Being told a secret: Must control passions.
Telling a secret: Misfortune in love affairs.
Betraying a secret: Divine punishment.
A secret being whispered in ear: Public dignity to be bestowed on you.
Couples keeping secrets from each other: Diligence and hard work.
Children keeping secrets from parents: Prompt engagement.
Relatives having secrets among themselves: Insurmountable obstacles.
Friends telling you a secret: Approaching money.

SECRETARY:
Being a male secretary: Will enjoy riches.
Being a female secretary: Will enjoy a comfortable life.
A female secretary at work: Will have a good fortune ahead.
Hiring a female secretary: Will be well situated for rest of life.
Hiring a male secretary: Business disputes.
Firing a female secretary: Family discord.
Firing a male secretary: He will fall in love with a member of the family.

SECURITY:
Of security: Will do duty as a good citizen.
Having financial security: Will invest money in bonds.
Having security for old age: Will enjoy a happy future.
Mates feeling secure about each other: Family happiness.
Putting money in security for children: Joy and contentment.
Receiving security from others: Good financial speculation.

SEDUCE:
Being seduced: Will have plenty of money during life.
Seducing a very young girl: Business will run as you desire.
Seducing a woman by force: Good events will happen to you.
Being seduced but escaping: Will go roller skating.
Marrying the man who seduced you: You are dealing with frivolous people.
Own daughter being seduced: Financial gains.
A married person dreaming of being seduced: Will live comfortable life.
A widow dreaming of being seduced: Will be robbed.
A man being arrested for seducing a woman: Will have many perplexities.
A teen-ager seducing girl of same age: Death in the family very soon.

SEEDS:
Of seeds: A matrimony is being planned.
Planting seeds of grain: Riches.
Planting vegetable seeds: Discomfort in your work.
Planting flower seeds: Will suffer much pain.
Buying grain seeds: Prosperity.
Buying vegetable seeds: Misery.
Making your own seeds: Will have plenty of money.
Bird seeds: Dishonor.
A seed shop: An unknown person is talking about you.
Selecting good seeds: Misery.

SEESAW:
Of a seesaw: Big happiness.

Children playing on a seesaw: Joy in the family.

Children being hurt when playing on a seesaw: Will have a long life.

A seesaw breaking: Will have an unexpected visitor.

Handling a seesaw: Unexpected love affairs which will not last long.

SELL:
Of selling: Will make money.

Selling things of steel: Will fall into disgrace.

Selling small quantities of merchandise: Abundance and riches.

Selling milk and cheese: Unexpected big fortune.

Selling tobacco: Will have many worries.

Selling mechanical things: Unhappiness.

Selling property: Illness.

Selling jewelry: Will be loved.

Selling a business: Will have family arguments.

SEMAPHORE:
Of a semaphore station: Immediate success of own hopes.

Semaphore alphabet flags: Will receive important and good news.

A semaphore signal: Warning of troubles.

Several semaphore flags: Important and very beneficial event to come.

Officer directing traffic at a semaphore: A mystery will be solved.

SEMINARY:
Of a seminary: Treason.

Visiting a seminary: Will have a son who will become a priest.

Being a student of seminary: A false friend is attempting to cause harm.

Being the dean of a seminary: Will suffer misery.

Not being accepted into a seminary: New life will bring good profits.

SENATE:
Of the senate: Will have disputes over ridiculous things.

Visiting the senate: Will be misled by friends.

Being a member of the senate: Avoid telling lies.

Listening to arguments of senators: Will have ability to fool people.

SEND:
Sending a gift to a loved one: Good harvest.

Sending clothes in a package: Will learn of the death of a friend.

Sending business merchandise: Security in business.

Sending foodstuffs to poor people: Will receive a sad announcement.

Sending a letter or package: Many worries ahead.

SENTENCE:
Receiving a sentence: Do not confide in other people.

Being sentenced to death: Very bad events to happen.

Being sentenced unjustly in a lawsuit: People are telling lies about you.

Reading a sentence from a book: You waste time with too many pleasures.

Writing incorrect sentences in a letter: You have not a clear conscience.

SENTINEL:
Of a sentinel: Be cautious in your affairs.

Many sentinels: Beware of those in whom you have placed trust.

Being a sentinel: Change of surroundings.

A lonely sentinel: New business will take you on a journey south.

Being warned by a sentinel: Death is near.

A sentinel shooting to sound an alarm: Pleasant happenings.

Being killed by a sentinel: Desires and hopes will be accomplished.

SEPARATION:
Of a separation: Frivolity.

Husband and wife separating: Gossip by friends.

Separation of sweethearts: Idle talk by people around you.

Planning on separating from someone: Misfortune awaits.

Having a final separation: Will be guilty of foolish actions.

Others desiring your separation: Beware of shady people.

Separation of children's marriage: Inheritance.

Friends being separated: Sickness of children.

Sweetheart wanting a separation: Be cautious in business transactions.

Separating from a business partner: Success in business.

Separating from those you love: Failure of some cherished plan.

SEPTEMBER:

Of September during the month of September: Good luck.

Of September during other months: Changes for the better.

Being born in September: Abundant means.

Children being born in September: Your future is secured.

SEPULCHRE:

Of a sepulchre: Will go into ruin.

Going into a sepulchre: Misery.

Building a sepulchre: Matrimony.

Building a sepulchre for family: Birth of a boy.

Visiting a sepulchre alone: Sad news.

Visiting a sepulchre with others: Unpleasant family news.

Being in a sepulchre with partner: Good news concerning a birth.

Being in a sepulchre with sweetheart: A letter will bring happiness.

SERENADE:

Hearing a serenade: Be cautious in affairs.

Singing a serenade: Will suffer financial embarrassments.

Enjoying a serenade: Will have a lasting love.

Lovers listening to a serenade: Will have disputes and break up.

SERMON:

Of a sermon: Approaching temporary illness.

Hearing a sermon: Good fortune.

Delivering a sermon: Will have many amiable friends.

Being a preacher and giving a sermon: Wealth.

Following the advice of a sermon: You are very superstitious.

SERPENT:

Of a serpent: Ungrateful people surround you.

Many serpents: You are planning to seduce someone.

A serpent with several heads: Will seduce a beautiful girl.

Catching a serpent with several heads: Will go fishing.

Killing a serpent with several heads: Victory over enemies.

A coiled serpent: You are hated by people.

A serpent unwinding: Sickness.

A serpent moving away: Imprisonment.

Killing a serpent: Danger ahead.

A water serpent: Recovery from an illness.

Serpents in a cage at a zoo: You are too boisterous.

Being bitten by a serpent: Enemies are accusing you.

Seeing serpents in the evening: Good fortune.

Seeing serpents in the morning: Something bad will happen.

SERVANT:

Of a servant: Someone will steal from you.

A female servant: Gossip by other people.

A male servant: You are disliked by people.

Employing several servants: Persevere and stick close to your affairs.

Servants at work: Infidelity.

Being a servant: Luxury and ease.

Hiring a servant: Will have money coming.

Firing a servant: Will sustain heavy losses.

Paying a servant: Big joy.

SERVE:
Of serving: Beware of thieves.
Being served: Infidelity.
Serving a meal: Gossip by friends.
Being served a meal: Business will not go well.
Serving children: Tranquillity of conscience.

SERVICE:
Attending a church service: Contentment in own heart.
A silverware service: A servant is stealing from you.
A china service: Gossip by neighbors.
Asking for service from others: Disgrace in the family.
Giving service to others: Will incur debts.
Being of service to friends: Will receive good news from faraway.
Being of service to relatives: Will be accused by enemies.

SEX:
A man of the male sex: Will be cheated by friends.
A boy of the male sex: Luck and prosperity.
A woman of the female sex: Will live a long life.
A daughter of the female sex: Discovery of lost valuables.
A man having sexual desire: Public disgrace.
A woman having sexual desire: Immediate success of hopes.

SEXUAL ORGANS:
Sexual organs being in good condition: Will have abundance of money.
A man having a disease of the sexual organs: Poverty.
A woman having a disease of the sexual organs: Warning of troubles.
A man having deformed sexual organs: Will be punished for a crime done.
A woman having deformed sexual organs: Will have a virtuous son.
A man having unusual sexual organs: Death of a son.
A woman having unusual sexual organs: Children will have good reputation.
A woman having ovaries removed: Death of a member of the family.
Exposing the sexual organs: Danger.

SEW:
Of sewing: Big happiness.
Sewing for children: Joy.
Sewing for husband: Abundant means.
Sewing for the house: Good results in business.
Sewing clothes for yourself: Dishonor.
Fashioning new garments: Will have peace in the home.
Other people sewing: Pleasure and good health.
Enemies sewing: Poverty.
Daughter sewing: Engagement will soon be announced.
A tailor sewing: Will receive news from abroad.
A seamstress sewing: Death of a child.

SHABBY:
Of a shabby person: Future is good.
A shabby man: You are wasting your efforts.
A shabby woman: She will be a wonderful lover.
Shabby children: Good future.
Talking to shabby people: Good earnings.
Giving something to shabby people: Big profit.
Being shabby yourself: Something will hinder progress of business.
Going about in shabby clothes: New clothes will soon be yours.

SHADOW:
Of a shadow: Will be threatened by a big enemy.
Many shadows: Death of someone.
Being afraid of shadows: A child will be born.
Own shadow: Financial gains through legal affairs.
The shadow of evil spirits: Death.
The shadow of a tree: You have a faithful friend.
Being in the shadow of a tree: Will receive a proposal of love.
The shadow of friends: Beware of being tricked.

The shadow of enemies: Death will come soon.

SHAMROCK:
Of a shamrock: Arrival of an old friend.
Having a shamrock: Prosperity in love affairs.
Receiving a shamrock: News of old matters will change your affairs.
Giving a shamrock to others: Suitable time to pursue courtship.
Wearing a shamrock: A false friend is nearby.
Picking shamrocks: Big fortune.
Others picking shamrocks: Happiness in the near future.

SHAPE:
Of the shape of own body: Happiness.
The shape of a woman's body: People are flirting with this woman.
The shape of a man's body: Good business ventures.
The shape of children: Will undertake a journey.
The shape of an abnormal person: You have a good future ahead.
Shapes of things made of wax: Will go into bankruptcy.

SHARK:
Of a shark: Troubles in the near future.
Escaping from a shark: Serious illness.
Catching a shark: Affairs are running smoothly.
Being killed by a shark: Will overcome obstacles.
Being bitten by a shark but not killed: Bad results in business.
Others being bitten by a shark: Will escape from serious trouble.

SHARPEN:
Of a person who sharpens knives: Good fortune in adventures.
Sharpening knives: Beware, a traitor is nearby.
Sharpening scissors: Someone is attempting to break up a marriage.
Sharpening tools: Loss of occupation.
Sharpening a blade: Congenial partnership.

Sharpening a pencil: Dissension within the family.

SHAVE:
Of shaving: Losses in gambling.
Shaving yourself: Difficulties ahead.
Someone else is shaving you: Be careful whom you trust.
Being shaved by a barber: Don't buy shares and stocks.
Shaving on a ship or train: Do not lend any money.
Having completed a shave: You are guilty of molesting women.
A young girl dreaming of a man shaving: Matrimony.
A married woman dreaming of a man shaving: Infidelity.
A pregnant woman dreaming of a man shaving: Abortion.
A widow dreaming of a man shaving: Will fall into disgrace.
A female servant dreaming of a man shaving: Will lose her job.
Having a thin beard: Happiness.
Having a thick beard: Will make plenty of money.
Having a red beard: Will be annoyed by creditors.
Beard growing long and thick: Big increase in revenue.
A woman shaving a man: Women give you the brush off.
A woman dreaming of shaving under her arms: Liked by men because of passion.
A woman dreaming of shaving her neckline: Will refuse a proposition.
A woman dreaming of shaving her legs: Will refuse a proposal.
The shaved head of a nun: Unprofitable ambitions.

SHAWL:
Of a shawl: Someone will be cruel to you.
Wearing a shawl: Will have success in love.
Buying a shawl: Will receive a visit from a doctor.
Wearing embroidered shawl given as a gift: Unjustified gossip about you.

Relatives wearing a shawl: Will go to a funeral parlor.

Friends wearing a shawl: Must pay more attention to business.

Poor people wearing shawls: Enemies are plotting against you.

Young girls wearing shawls: You are surrounded by fast-talking people.

A large white shawl: Purity and virtue.

A black shawl: Grief.

A red shawl: You are too loose with your affections.

Various other colored shawls: Affairs will run smoothly.

Giving a shawl as a gift: Will have deep affection from one you love.

SHEARS:

Of shears to cut other peoples' hair: Joy and happiness.

Using shears: Prosperity in everything.

Using shears on animals: Advancement in own position.

Using shears to cut own hair: Will receive unexpected gift.

Buying shears: Long life.

Using shears to cut a prisoner's hair: Embarrassment in business.

SHED:

Of a shed: Riches and money.

A shed in the forest: Hard work ahead.

A shed made of wood: Economize and plan for old age.

A shed at the beach: Dignity.

Several sheds in a row: Unhappiness.

Entering a shed: Have patience with pain and it will disappear.

Others going into a shed: Treason.

SHEEP:

Of sheep: Coming success through well-conceived plans.

A flock of sheep: Abundance.

Sheep fighting: Will suffer business loss.

Wealthy people herding sheep: Dishonor and damages.

Poor people herding sheep: Joy and good earnings.

A shepherd leading sheep: Will make much money.

Having a herd of fine quality sheep: Abundance.

A shepherd leading sheep to pasture: Profit and honor.

A shepherd leading sheep through a forest: Will find valuable things.

Losing sheep: Will be abandoned.

Milking a ewe: Abundant means.

Drinking milk of sheep: Will be molested.

Squirting milk of sheep into own mouth: Engagement.

Buying sheep: Good earnings in stock speculation.

Selling sheep: Death of an enemy.

SHEIK:

A woman dreaming of a sheik: Will receive a proposal of marriage.

A man dreaming of a sheik: Will have to consult a doctor.

A sheik ruling his tribe: Hard times are in store.

Visiting a sheik with someone you love: Save while you can.

SHELF:

Of a shelf: You are an experienced lover.

Several shelves: Your desires will be opposed.

Putting things on a shelf: Will conduct business well.

Putting books on a shelf: Will soon have an accident.

Putting groceries on shelves: Family disputes.

Putting linen on a shelf: Your conscience is not clear.

Putting pans on a shelf: Unavoidable loss of money.

Putting shoes on a shelf: Death of a member of the family.

Putting hats on a shelf: Business affairs are all confused.

Putting other things on shelves: Will attain goal with hard work.

Putting pillows and blankets on a shelf: Will be deceived by one you love.

SHELL:

Of shells: Extravagance.

A clean shell: Will go into bankruptcy.

A smooth shell: Will have changes in your life.

A rough shell: Change of residence.

Gathering shells: Fleeting pleasures.

Many shellfish: Joy.

A live shellfish: Prosperity.

A dead shellfish: Will receive news of death of a friend.

SHEPHERD:

Of a shepherd: Big earnings.

A farmer dreaming of a shepherd: Unusually bountiful harvest.

Shepherds watching flocks: Good earnings ahead of you.

A shepherd being faraway from his flock: Good, long, and healthy life.

A shepherd whose flock is scattered: Big satisfaction.

Several shepherds gathering flocks: Honor of short duration.

A shepherd living in a forest: Profit.

A very young shepherd: Prosperity and good reputation.

A shepherd losing some of his flock: Will achieve success in desires.

SHILLING:

Of a shilling: Small disappointment and grief.

Counting shillings: Will fall in love with someone.

Changing shillings to pounds: Will evade going to prison.

Changing silver shillings to paper shillings: Winnings at gambling.

Changing shillings into foreign currency: Insecurity in business.

Changing shillings into gold: Danger of infirmity.

SHIN:

Of own shins: Will have many things on your mind.

Shins of small animals: Misfortune in love affairs.

Shins of cattle: You are prone to being too stuck-up.

Shins of dead animals: Sickness.

SHINE:

Rays of light shining: Success in love matters.

The sun shining: Financial gains.

Jewelry shining: Avoid extravagance.

Gold, silver, and other metals shining: Luck and prosperity.

Shining shoes: Your life will be bright.

SHINGLE:

Of shingles: You have false friends.

Buying shingles: Will fall into much money.

Buying many shingles: Will fall into disgrace.

Putting shingles on a house: Will achieve goal through hard work.

Selling shingles: Will make inevitable errors.

Nailing shingles: Loss of a friend.

Painting shingles: Will get out of debt.

Burning shingles: Will be cheated by friends.

SHIP:

Of a ship: Prosperity.

A prisoner dreaming of a ship: Will be released.

A man dreaming of a ship docking: Unexpected good news.

A woman dreaming of a ship docking: Unexpected bad news.

Lovers dreaming of a ship docking: Marriage will not be realized.

A ship sinking: Abundance of money.

A ship sinking after a collision: Good ventures in the future.

Two ships going in opposite directions: Promotion and honor.

Being on the bridge of a ship: Will take a short trip.

Being safely aboard a ship: Joy in love and security.

Being aboard a ship at sea: Abundant means.

Being aboard a ship on a rough sea: Loss of much money.

Being aboard a ship on a river: Joy if the water is smooth.

Being aboard a ship on a lake: Security in business.

Being aboard a ship during a bad storm: Infirmity.

Being aboard a ship with a loved one in bad weather: Prosperity.

Being aboard a ship with a loved one in calm sea: Security in business.
Being aboard a ship with children: Big joy.
Going aboard a ship with all of immediate family: Abundant means.
Traveling on a ship with business people: Very good fortune.
A small ship: Must rely upon your own vigor.
A small ship with sails: Will receive unexpected good news.
A small ship with all sails up: Sickness.

SHIPWRECK:
Of a shipwreck: Affairs will soon take a turn for the worse.
Losing your life in a shipwreck: Arrival of an unexpected friend.
Being saved after a shipwreck: Will have emotional sorrow.
Being shipwrecked with one you love: A big catastrophe is ahead.
Others in a shipwreck: Beware of rivals.
Being shipwrecked with family and saved: Happiness is assured.
Being shipwrecked and sinking into the sea: Loss by carelessness.

SHIPYARD:
Of a shipyard: Loss of money.
Working in a shipyard: Will have money during old age.
A shipyard building vessels: Will soon receive sad news.
A shipyard demolishing vessels: Financial gains.
Taking vessels to be repaired in a shipyard: Will be in financial distress.

SHIRT:
Of a shirt: Fortune and good things coming in the future.
An everyday shirt: Prosperous future.
An evening shirt: Abundant means.
A nightshirt: Victory over enemies.
Putting on a shirt: Will be neglected.
Taking off a shirt: Will be disillusioned in love.
Washing a shirt: You will be loved.
Ironing a shirt: You love someone who doesn't love you.

A torn shirt: Good fortune.
Buying shirts: Will be told many falsehoods.
Wearing a fancy sport shirt: Sweethearts will break up.
Wearing a knitted sport shirt: Frivolity.
A dirty shirt: Will contract a contagious disease.
Losing a shirt: Failure in love.

SHIVER:
Of shivering: Loss of a member of the family.
Dressing warmly to keep from shivering: Loss of an inheritance.
Children shivering: Children will be kidnaped.
Others shivering: Will lose money in stock market transactions.
Relatives shivering: They will soon receive new clothes.
Wife and husband shivering: Will buy something they both like.

SHOCK:
Of a shock: Will overcome enemies with perseverance.
Being shocked by bad news: Will have mastery over own affairs.
Shocking members of own family: Will overcome difficulties.
Being shocked by a loved person: Good luck.
Shocking a loved one: Your love is very changeable.
Shocking other people: Beware of a trap being laid for you.

SHOE POLISH:
Having shoes polished by professional: Will have legal deals with attorney.
Being a person who shines shoes: Pride has gone beyond reason.
A shoeshine boy shining others' shoes: Joy and contentment.
A boy polishing shoes of husband: Will receive invitation to a dance.
A shoeblack polishing shoes: Beware of rivals.

SHOES:
Of shoes: Will have no obstacles in path to achieving your goal.
Shoelaces or buckles coming undone: Quarrels with relatives.
Wooden shoes: Earnings will be very large.
Dancing with wooden shoes: Family embarrassment.
Shoes for women: Big fortune in love.
Shoes for men: Postponement of success in business affairs.
Shoes for children: Change of residence.
Going into the mud with wornout shoes: Poverty.
Having shoes with holes in the soles: Loss of money.
Losing shoes: Poverty.
Having black shoes: Bad times are ahead.
Having white shoes: Future is completely secure.
Having blue shoes: Sickness.
Having suede shoes: Will have easy and happy days.
Having high boots: Happiness.
Buying new shoes: Will have a large profit.
Having other qualities of leather shoes: Will fall into ruin.
Wealthy people having other qualities of leather shoes: Comfortable life.
Poor people having other qualities of leather shoes: Happiness.
Patched shoes: Will have big financial difficulties.
Being without shoes: Expect success in business.
Buying new shoes for children: Unexpected good results in business.

SHOE TREE:
Of a shoe tree: Heavy work ahead.
Putting shoe trees in shoes: Unfavorable news.
Putting shoe trees in boots: Will be worn out from overwork.
Buying shoe trees: Will be persecuted.

SHOOT:
Hearing shooting: Misunderstandings between married people.

Being shot: Will have an opportunity to better yourself.
Shooting with a rifle: Sickness.
Shooting with a revolver: Will be robbed.
Shooting with a shotgun: You are being deceived.
Shooting artillery: Profit.
Shooting birds: False gossip by friends.
Shooting at a target: Will take a long trip.
Shooting in a contest: Melancholy.
Other people shooting at you: Will fall into disgrace.
Shooting at other people: Honor and joy.
Shooting only one shot: Big profit.
Shooting enemies: Domestic troubles.
Shooting something but missing: Will overcome difficulties.
Shooting and killing someone: Disappointment and grief.
Lovers hearing shooting: Will have a big quarrel.

SHOP:
Of a shop: Good fortune follows efforts.
Operating a shop: Success.
Going into a shop with others: Prosperity through hard work.
Going into a shop that does small business: Love affairs are insecure.
A beautiful shop: Will have something nice happen.
A dress shop: Everything will be wonderful.
A shop for men: Will be in despair.
A linen shop: Ruin of other peoples' business.
A lingerie shop: Big success.
A barber shop: Gossip.
A food shop: Ruin of other people.
A shop burning: Loss of possessions.
A shop for children: Will receive good news.
A department store: Increase in the family.

SHORE:
Being on shore: Riches.
Going to a seaside shore: Will see one you have been thinking about.

Being on a shore with children: God will provide for you.

Being on a shore with relatives: Will avoid perils.

Being on a shore with a loved one: Will not be disappointed.

Friends being on a shore: Beware of gossip.

A boat coming into shore: Will receive a rich gift unexpectedly.

A shore used to prop something up: Will receive help from someone.

Using a shore inside the house: Don't fail to help needy people.

People putting a shore up against something: Happy life.

SHORT:

Of being short of everything: Will have happiness in old age.

Being short of money: Postponement of success.

Being short of food: Good improvements financially.

Being short in weight: An enemy is seeking your ruin.

Being short of belongings: Good days are coming.

Being short in conversation: Progress in business enterprises.

Having short clothes or trousers: Warning of trouble.

SHOTGUN:

(See GUN.)

SHOULDER:

Of own shoulders: Fortune.

Children's shoulders: Will receive a letter containing good news.

Others' shoulders: Must rely upon your own vigor.

Large muscular shoulders: Will enjoy excellent health for rest of life.

Very small shoulders: Unhappiness.

Boney shoulders: Sickness.

Beautiful naked shoulders: Will avoid danger.

A prisoner dreaming of having large shoulders: Will remain in prison.

SHOVEL:

Of a shovel: Friends will come to the rescue financially.

Using a shovel: Must rely upon own good judgment.

Children using a shovel: Big pleasures in life.

Others using a shovel: Good health.

Laborers using a shovel: Death of an animal.

Owning a shovel: You have foolish desires.

Buying a shovel: You will be robbed.

SHOW:

Showing yourself: You have too much vanity.

Showing teeth: Will have a dispute.

Showing personal belongings: Will have sexual pleasures.

Showing your figure: People feel that you are ignorant.

Showing zealous actions: All desires will be realized.

Showing childish qualities: Will enjoy a long life.

SHOWER:

Taking a shower: Abundance.

Children taking a shower: Will receive a gift.

Guests going to take a shower: Loss of money.

Others taking a shower: Riches.

SHRIMP:

Of shrimp: Will take a nice trip.

Buying shrimp: Loss of a relative by death.

Fishing for shrimp: Will have a big honor bestowed on you.

Raw shrimp: Will have a bad business transaction.

Cooking shrimp: Death of a friend.

Eating shrimp: Disgrace.

SHUFFLE:

Of shuffling: Will have good health.

Shuffling letters out of sight: Treachery from relatives.

Shuffling a deck of cards yourself: Will test the one you love.

Others shuffling a deck of cards: Warning of trouble.

Making tricks in shuffling cards: Postponement of success.

Playing a shuffleboard: Good financial improvements.

SHUT:
Of shutting: Will receive a gift.
Shutting a door: Will be highly considered.
Shutting a door in someone's face: Sickness.
Shutting a box: Happiness will soon come.
Shutting a safe: Jealousy in the family.
Shutting drawers: Joy will come in the near future.
Shutting a jewelry box: Will enjoy health.

SHUTDOWN:
Of shutting down: Big neighborhood scandal.
Shutting down your home: Fortune ahead.
Shutting down your store: You are always tardy.
Shutting down your office or business: Should make plans for old age.

SHY:
Being shy: Fortune ahead.
Mate being shy: You trust relatives too much.
Children being shy: You are surrounded by jealous people.
Others being shy: Plans will turn out unsatisfactory.

SIAMESE:
Of Siam: Prosperity.
Going to Siam: Discovery of a secret.
Returning from Siam: Will realize high ambitions.
Siamese citizens: Beware of treachery.
Having a Siamese cat: Will obtain modest employment.
Seeing a Siamese cat: Death of someone living nearby.

SICK:
Being sick: You are inclined to being melancholy.
Children being sick: Happiness.
Visiting sick people: Will find a way to reach your goal.

Loved ones who are sick: Unhappiness.
Many sick people: Joy and profit.
Being mentally sick: Fortune will be lost.
Being sick to the stomach: Squandering of possessions.
Visiting sick people at a hospital: Life will offer many pleasures.

SIDE:
Taking a side: Treachery from relatives.
Not having people on your side: Persecution.
Having people on your side: Good financial improvements.
The right or left side of own body: Beware of flirting.
The side of any other thing: Will be invited to a musical concert.
Having people walking at your side: Beware of gossip.
Sitting side by side with someone: Happiness in love matters.

SIDEWALK:
Of a sidewalk: You are prone to having a bad temper.
A sidewalk on the right: Good times are ahead.
A sidewalk on the left: Bad times are ahead.
Walking with mate on a sidewalk: Will be invited to a wedding.
Being with a loved one on a sidewalk: Will have an argument over love.
Children walking on a sidewalk: Prosperity.
Standing on a sidewalk: Will become rich by economy.
Falling on a sidewalk: Will live a long life.

SIEGE:
Of a siege: Will become an actor or actress.
A continuous state of siege: Limit your expenses.
Being inside a sieged area: You have false friends.
Being inside a sieged house: Loss of all friends.

Relatives being in a state of siege: Unhappiness.

SIEVE:
Of a sieve: You are too extravagant.
Using a sieve: You are leading a bad life.
Others using a sieve: Sickness for those using it.
Sifting flour through a sieve: You are neglecting business affairs.
Straining a cooked sauce: Will make acquaintance of a stage personality.

SIGH:
Of sighing: Big joy.
Making a very deep sigh: Good times are coming.
Hearing children sighing from fatigue: Good luck.
Hearing others sighing: Secret enmity of some person.

SIGN:
Of signing: Big success.
Signing a legal document: Will abandon the family home.
Signing a contract: Someone will confide a secret to you.
Other people signing papers: Will have a good position.
Signing an agreement: You are an idealist.
Signing a letter: Will make new friends.
Signing an unpleasant letter: Will attain aim in life.
Signing a check: Avoid squandering money.
Signing a love letter: Beware of untruthful people.
Signing a note to borrow money: Will make new acquaintances.
Making signs with hands: Beware of being seduced.
Making signs with fingers: Vanity.

SIGNAL:
Of a signal: Will be informed of unpleasant happenings.
A street signal: Happy events to come.

Overlooking a signal: Danger ahead of you.
Seeing a signal but not heeding it: Fortune.
A danger signal: Improvement in affairs.
Hearing a fire signal: Will receive interesting news.
Hearing a police signal: Will be cheated by a woman.
A woman dreaming of hearing a police siren: Will marry a rich man.
A red light signal: You are placing your life in dangerous hands.
A semaphore signal: Warning of trouble.

SIGNATURE:
Of own signature: Father and mother make you very happy.
Putting signature on wedding license: Good health.
Putting signature on a diploma: Joy.
Putting signature on a birth certificate: Riches.
Putting signature on a death certificate: Be careful of eyesight.
High official's signature on documents: Children's life is in peril.
A judge's signature on a law decision: Will uncover deceitful friends.

SIGNPOST:
Of a signpost: You have domestic enemies.
Seeing a signpost but not heeding it: A corporation will be dissolved.
Hitting a signpost: Embarrassment in affairs.
Painting a signpost: You have a faithful friend.
Destroying a signpost: Will embarrass other people.
Putting up a new signpost: Will overcome those trying to harm you.
Pasting something on a signpost: Dishonor.
Reading a signpost: Will do much work without profit.

SILENCE:
Having silence: Will soon receive news of going to war.

Being asked for silence: Good results in a business deal.

Silencing children: Fortune ahead.

Silencing a large group of people: Will receive unexpected good news.

SILHOUETTE:

Of a silhouette: Happiness.

The silhouette of own figure: Contentment in life.

The silhouette of others: Beware of strong rivals.

A man admiring silhouette of a woman: Flirtation with the admired woman.

Admiring the silhouette of a loved one: Long-lasting love.

SILK:

Of silk: Profit and honor.

White silk: Everything will go well.

Blue silk: Will receive damages in own affairs.

Red silk: Will be wounded by a bullet.

Black silk: Will receive news of a death.

Other colors of silk: Tranquillity of conscience.

Buying silk: You are in love.

Selling silk: You are incurring too many debts.

Buying silk garments: You have a maid that is cheating you.

Buying silk nightgowns: Unhappiness.

Wearing a silk negligee without a nightgown: Will receive a proposition.

Silk garments for children: Prosperous affairs.

Buying a silk dress: Honor.

Making a silk dress: Riches.

Tearing a silk dress: Simulation of joy.

A young girl wearing a silk dress: Success will crown your efforts.

Buying a silk wedding dress: Abundant means.

Wearing a silk dress: Don't believe everything you hear.

Getting dressed up in a silk dress: Someone is undermining your happiness.

Throwing away a silk dress: Will contract a contagious illness.

Receiving a silk dress as a gift: Modesty.

Getting a silk dress dirty: You are being deceived.

Cleaning a silk dress: Your desires will be realized.

SILVER:

Of the color silver: Will be fortunate in all dealings.

Buying silver-colored clothes: Happiness is assured.

Various silver-colored materials: Will have many friends.

Of silver money: Good fortune in business and love.

Having one-dollar and fifty-cent pieces: Advancement within own position.

Having twenty-five- and ten-cent silver pieces: Loss of present position.

Counting silver: Big gains.

Finding silver money: Prosperity.

Gathering silver: Loss and damages in business.

Changing silver money: Will be visited by a friend.

Handling silver: Will receive damages in business matters.

Buying silver things: Beware of enemies.

Selling silver things: Will receive money losses.

Receiving silver gifts: Good times are coming.

Giving silver gifts: New interests and surroundings.

Having a large amount of valuable silver: Will escape danger if careful.

SILVERWARE:

Of silverware: Ungratified ambitions.

Inheriting silverware: Will have friends for dinner.

Buying silverware: Will have small gains.

Selling silverware: Improvement in business matters.

Of silver plating: Must have more courage.

SIN:
Committing a sin: Be careful because of menacing dangers nearby.
Repenting of a sin: Long life and good health.
Family members committing sins: Will make a long trip.
Children committing a sin: Days of melancholy ahead.
Friends committing a sin: Your many desires will be harmful to you.

SING:
Of singing: Beware that jealousy does not ruin your happiness.
Others singing: Your life will be gladdened by many friends.
Hearing a soprano singing: Good news.
Singing operatic songs: Will be afflicted with tears.
Being a singer: Death of a member of the family.
Hearing a singer: Disappointment.
Watching a singer perform: Small sickness in the family.
Hearing melancholy songs sung: Illness.
Listening to a bad singer: Will be disappointed in life.
Hearing a singer with a raspy voice: Disputes.
Hearing birds singing: Love and joy.
Hearing singing in church: Family discord.
Hearing soft sweet singing: Good news.
Hearing a man singing: Will have convulsions.
A male operatic singer: Will receive the help of a friend.
A group of men singing: Will have a large family.
Hearing a love song: A happy event to come.
Hearing others singing: Difficulties through dealings with others.
Hearing a bass singer: Will have a big fight.
Hearing a tenor singer: Unhappiness.

SINGLE:
Being single: Loss of money.

A single person dreaming of loving someone: Will receive good news.
A single person dreaming of getting married: Indecision in choice of husband.
A single man dreaming of getting married: Will be humiliated.
A single man dreaming of taking advantage of a girl: Fighting against nature.
A single woman accepting the advances of a man: Triumph in life.
A man or woman dreaming of being single again: Gossip will cause worry.

SINK:
Of something sinking: Will fall into disgrace.
Sinking yourself: Big business losses.
Others sinking: Bad news from a friend.
Something sinking because of negligence of other people: Ruin is ahead.
Sinking a ship: Abundance of money.
People being saved from sinking: Good business ventures.
A ship sinking after a collision: Good ventures in the future.
Sinking into the mud: Ruin is coming.
Sinking and drowning in the sea: Big profit.
Sinking into a haystack: Prosperity.
A vessel sinking at sea: Loss by carelessness.

SIPHON:
Of a siphon: Loss of own job.
Using a siphon: Gossip within own home.
Others using a siphon: Something new will happen that is good.
Breaking a siphon: Property is in danger.
A man dreaming of a siphon: Will be invited to a bachelor party.
A woman dreaming of a siphon: Will be complimented on choice of fiancé.

SISTER:
Of own sister: Fortune.

Several sisters: Dissension within the family.

Arguing with a sister: Family disgrace.

Sisters insulting each other: Beware of an illness to come.

A sister arguing with a sister-in-law: Expect small fortune.

Two sisters-in-law arguing with a sister: Family shame and sorrow.

A sister arguing with a brother-in-law: Good fortune ahead.

SISTER-IN-LAW:

Of a sister-in-law: Family quarrels.

Having a sister-in-law: Advantages for the family.

A sister-in-law being dead: Pleasant desires will be yours.

Marrying your sister-in-law: Gossip by people of society.

Having many sisters-in-law: Your husband is cheating on you.

SIT:

Of sitting down: Will live a comfortable life.

Inviting people to sit down: Honors will be conferred upon you.

Sitting on a chair: Will have good gains.

Sitting on a divan: Wealth.

Being asked to sit in a chair: Honors.

Sitting on chairs in a waiting room: Good relations with other people.

Sitting on a bench in a park: Will be treated well by loved one.

Sitting on a bench at night and being seduced: Relations with insecure people.

Sitting with someone you love: Your good fortune is secured.

Sitting with friends: Unhappiness.

SITUATION:

Being in a serious situation: Will have sorrow.

Being in a complex situation: Hard work awaits.

Objects being placed in a bad situation: Use caution in business affairs.

Own job situation not being good: Good changes will come.

Friends being in a bad situation: Avoid rivals.

Own situation in life improving: Good times are ahead.

SKATE:

Of skating: Will encounter opposition.

Breaking through the ice while skating: False friends will offer bad advice.

Children skating: Luck and prosperity.

Relatives skating: Danger to come.

Others skating: You may be connected with a scandal.

SKELETON:

Of a skeleton: Will have spells of nausea.

Being a skeleton: Domestic troubles.

A skeleton of ancestors: Death in the family.

A skeleton of an animal: Will have fear because of wrongdoing.

A skeleton of someone you know: Danger or illness.

SKETCH:

Of sketches: Business affairs are in great confusion.

Making a sketch: Unhappiness.

Others making a sketch: You are surrounded by people who talk too much.

Buying sketches: Disaster in married life.

Sketches of people you know: Beware of rivals.

SKIFF:

Of a skiff: Be careful in business.

A skiff moving down a smooth river: Will be helped by a prominent person.

Rowing a skiff: Achievements and gain.

An overturned skiff: Business failure.

SKIN:

Of skin: Good fortune.

Own skin: Will have good health.

Sunburned skin: Will be cheated by friends.

Peeling own skin off: Big fortune.

Skin being disfigured: Kindness from those least expected.

Skin of a mulatto: Dispute with business partners.

Skin of a Negro: Will have benefactors.

Skin of a woman: Happiness.

Skin of a man: Good fortune.

Washing own skin: Death of someone you know.

Buying animal skins: Will take a trip.

Having animal skins dyed: Unhappiness.

Skinning an animal: Disgrace.

The skin of a cat: Will recover lost fortune.

The skin of a lion or tiger: Will find out who enemies are.

Having skins made into a coat: Will soon be rich.

Having things made from skin of a bird: Will enjoy good food.

Using skins for drums or tambourines: Will receive good news.

SKIRT:

Of skirts: Will be lazy.

A white skirt: Your tastes are high-class.

A black skirt: Adversity.

Skirts of other colors: Unhappiness in love.

Buying a skirt: Prosperity.

SKITTLE:

Of this game of ninepins: A rival will take affection of sweetheart.

Playing skittles: Affairs are unsettled.

Others playing skittles: Will soon experience many ups and downs.

Sweetheart playing skittles: Will suffer disappointment in love.

SKULL:

Of a skull: Engagement will soon be announced.

A skull being in a museum: Will receive money.

The skull of an ancestor: Will do good business.

The skull of animals: Domestic troubles to come.

SKUNK:

Of a skunk: Will be cheated by someone.

A woman dreaming of many skunks: Will be defrauded.

A man dreaming of many skunks: Will love a maiden who will cheat you.

An unmarried person dreaming of skunks: You are a cunning person.

SKY:

Of the sky: Happiness.

A clear sky: Marriage.

A red sky: Increase of wealth.

A cloudy sky: Misfortune.

A bright sky: Joy.

A golden sky: Will be threatened by a well-known personality.

A pure blue sky: You conduct yourself very properly.

An azure blue sky: Contentment in love affairs.

Ascending into the sky: Can expect honors to be bestowed.

Descending from the sky: Beware of falling.

A great expanse of flaming red sky: Desolation.

A rainbow in the sky: Peril is near at hand.

Stars looking like diamonds in the sky: Certain good earnings in everything.

Stars falling from the sky: Will be unable to have children.

The sky falling on your head: Expect to be killed in an accident.

Things falling out of the sky: Expect war.

SLAP:

Being slapped: Will find yourself in bad company.

Being slapped by a good friend: Happiness in the family.

A man slapping a woman: Success in love.

A woman slapping a man: Unfaithfulness of a loved one.

Mates slapping each other: Big success in married life.

Children slapping each other: Business is not very steady.

Slapping children: Will be treated unjustly by friends.

Friends slapping each other: Will enjoy good results in enterprises.

SLATE:
Of a slate: Luck and prosperity.
Having a clean slate: Will live a long life.
Writing on a slate: Will make new plans.
Breaking a slate: Failure of own plans.
Rubbing off a slate: Someone with evil intentions is watching you.

SLAUGHTER:
Being slaughtered: You have false friends.
Slaughtering an animal: A catastrophe is ahead.
Slaughtering a pig: Unhappy news.
Slaughtering a veal: Ruin.
Slaughtering a horse: Small earnings.
Slaughtering a lamb: Will enjoy peace for a long time.
Working at a slaughtering house: Will attain a high position in the world.
A farmer slaughtering: Will have a family reunion.

SLAUGHTERHOUSE:
Of a slaughterhouse: Caution.
Being in a slaughterhouse: Will be melancholy.
Others at a slaughterhouse: Should attempt to avoid danger.
Slaughtering being done: Unpleasant surprises.

SLAVE:
Of a slave: Will be free of troubles.
Being a slave: Happiness.
Letting a slave go free: An injustice will be done to you.
Making a slave of someone: Big enjoyment.
Many slaves: Security in love.

SLEDGE:
Of a sledge used to transport over ice: Happiness in love.
Riding on the runners of a sledge: Will have plenty of money.
Riding in a sledge: Will have good earnings and pleasure.
A sledge being pulled by several dogs: Exciting times ahead.
Many sledges being pulled by dogs: Be careful of friends you choose.
Others riding in a sledge: Do not venture too far in your business.
Of a sledge hammer: Cruelty.
Someone using a sledge hammer: Oppression.
A huge iron sledge hammer: Hard work is ahead.

SLEEP:
Of sleep: False security.
Being asleep: Be cautious in your actions.
Going to sleep: Good news.
A daughter sleeping with her mother: Adoption of an orphan boy.
A man sleeping with a woman: Enjoyment in life.
Sleeping with a very ugly man: Great unhappiness.
Sleeping with a little child: Return of love and domestic joy.
Sleeping with person of opposite sex: Affairs will go well.
Sleeping with person of own sex: Perplexing events.
Sleeping with a handsome young man: Pleasures followed by disgust.
Sleeping with a beautiful young girl: Annoyance and worry.
Sleeping with a boyfriend: Pleasures ahead.
Sleeping with a girl friend: Big enjoyment.
Sweethearts sleeping together: Delightful events to come.
A woman sleeping with a man during husband's absence: Imminent death.
Sleeping with both a mother and a daughter: Must accept things as they occur.
Sleeping with a prostitute: Will be in pain the next day.
Sleeping alone: Beware of temptation.
Sleeping with own wife: Joy and profit.
A man sleeping with one he doesn't love: Death of wife or mother.
A woman sleeping with one she doesn't love: Sickness.
A man sleeping naked with a beautiful woman: Happiness.
A woman sleeping naked with a handsome man: Treachery.

Sleeping with a Negro: Will have a very bad sickness.

SLEET:
Of sleet: Enjoyment.
A very bad sleet storm: You are surrounded by enemies.
Being in a sleet storm: Be more patient with people around you.
Others being in a sleet storm: Will receive interesting information.

SLEEVE:
Of sleeves: Will do a lot of traveling.
Short sleeves: Disgrace.
Long sleeves: Honor.
Big sleeves: Temper.
Fitted sleeves: Pleasure.
Men's sleeves: Will receive good news from a loved one.
Cutting sleeves: Will be cheated in love.
Tearing sleeves: Loss of present employment.
Embroidered sleeves: Dignity and distinction.
Others' sleeves: Will have new employment.

SLIDE:
Of sliding: Will have ridiculous disputes.
Others sliding: Comfort.
Others sliding downhill: Do not trust those you now trust.
Friends sliding: Will receive news of a wedding.
Children sliding: They will grow up normally and healthily.

SLIPPERS:
Of slippers: Contentment in own heart.
Wearing slippers: Security
An unmarried person dreaming of wearing slippers: Be careful in choice of mate.
Slippers for women: Will have to pardon enemies.
A woman wearing slippers: Good financial position.
Buying slippers: Will receive a small kindness.
Having many slippers: Will receive a large reward.

Slippers for men: Will live a long life.
A man wearing his slippers: Will lead a relaxed life.

SMALLPOX:
Having smallpox: Profit and wealth.
Being vaccinated for smallpox: Will live a long life.
Many people having smallpox: Dishonor.
Children having smallpox: Fortune.
The mark from a smallpox vaccination: Sign of beauty.
Being immune to smallpox: Will have plenty of money.
Relatives having smallpox: All will go well for the dreamer.
Family having smallpox: Will acquire unexpected wealth.

SMART:
Being smart: You have many good friends.
Having a smart mate: Happy events to come.
Having smart children: Small family arguments.
Having smart friends: Triumph and honor.

SMILE:
Of smiling: Will be relieved of pains.
Family smiling: Will suffer opposition for forty-eight to seventy days.
Friends smiling: Beware; they may not be true friends.
Children smiling: Riches.
Husband smiling: He has made good money.
Wife smiling at her husband: Will tell him of pregnancy.
Smiling girls: They have found the man they want to marry.
Smiling secretly to yourself: Other people talking will cause concern.
A woman smiling at you on the street: She has bad morals.
Walking with a smile on your face: Will have a happy life.

SMOKE:
Of smoke: Tears and doubts.
Smoking yourself: Present success.

Others who are smoking: Will be highly respected.

Smoke coming from a building: A friend is deceiving you.

Black smoke coming from a building: Glory that is short-lived.

Smoke coming from a chimney: A marriage will take place soon.

Very thick smoke: A very big disappointment will come.

Being overcome by smoke: Beware of flattery.

Children smoking: Fortune will smile upon the dreamer.

Friends smoking: Will enjoy fortune.

SMUGGLE:

Of smuggling: Not all of your plans will succeed.

Others who are smuggling: Everything will turn out for the best.

Being a smuggler: Unexpected relief from something.

Friends smuggling: Their plans will not succeed.

Enemies smuggling: Will soon be imprisoned.

SNAIL:

Of snails: Inconsistency.

Snails being in a garden: Work without financial return.

Eating snails: Will have a good financial standing.

Picking up snails from the ground: Family reunion.

Cooking snails: Happiness in the family.

Eating snails at a special party: You are highly respected.

Very huge snails: Will receive a high and honorable position.

A snail's horns showing out of the shell: Infidelity.

Buying pastry snails: Happiness.

Making pastry snails at home: Good news.

Eating pastry snails: Security in affairs.

Children eating snails: They will have a brilliant career.

SNAKE:

Of snakes: Your plans will be wrecked.

A coiled snake: Will escape from danger.

A snake ready to strike: Treachery from one you least expect.

Killing a snake: Will have victory over enemies.

Several snakes: Jealous people would like to cause your ruin.

Being unable to kill a snake: Unfortunate events that were not anticipated.

A snake with two heads: Seduction.

A water snake: Will recover from an illness.

Snakes being in a cage at a zoo: Your friends are not grateful.

SNARE:

Of snares: A change for the better.

Preparing a snare: You are surrounded by enemies.

Catching birds with a snare: Will collect a small amount of money.

Catching animals with a snare: Family reunion.

SNATCH:

Snatching something away: Unhappiness.

Other people snatching things: Unhappiness in love affairs.

Snatching a lady's handbag: Will suffer losses in the future.

Being a purse snatcher: Postponement of success.

SNEEZE:

Of sneezing: Will live a long life.

Sneezing many times: Will fall in love.

Babies sneezing: Will have minor stomach trouble.

Children sneezing: Beware of injury to children.

Others sneezing: Disaster.

SNOW:

Of snow: Good harvest.

Snow falling in a warm climate: Will be favored with good luck.

Snow falling during the winter: Abundance.

Snow falling during other seasons: You are an industrious farm laborer.

A farmer dreaming of snowing out of season: Abundant harvest.

A businessman dreaming of snowing out of season: Business difficulties.

A merchant dreaming of snowing out of season: Poor business.

A military person dreaming of snowing out of season: Battle plans will fail.

Washing yourself with snow: Relief from pain.

Eating snow: You have left your place of birth.

Driving through snow: Grief.

Very deep snow on the street: People are talking falsely.

A businessman dreaming of snow falling: Satisfactory progress in business.

Snow in the mountains: Good profits in the future.

Drifts of snow in a city: Will receive good news.

Driving through snow at night or dawn: Satisfactory reply to request.

Children playing in the snow: Will not need a doctor for a long time.

Going skiing with a sweetheart: Will have everything turn out wonderful.

SNUFF:

Of snuff: Loss of money.

Putting snuff in the mouth: Squandering of money.

Putting snuff in the nose: Will lose your temper.

Offering snuff to someone: Will meet interesting people.

A woman dreaming of putting snuff in her nose: Pleasant surroundings.

Offering a pinch of snuff to a friend: Good business dealings.

Spilling snuff on clothes: Will have trouble.

SOAP:

Of soap: Bad business.

Buying soap: Business affairs are all confused.

Selling soap: Loss of business.

Washing own body with soap: Will ask for help from friends.

Washing clothes with soap: Will receive money from rich relatives.

Using soap to take out a stain: Dishonor.

A woman dreaming of making soap: Will never experience want.

A young woman dreaming of washing with soap: Happy times ahead.

A man dreaming of washing himself with soap: Unexpected and good transactions.

Powdered soap dissolving: Will settle puzzling matters.

SODA:

Of soda: Contentment in life.

Drinking sparkling soda: You are surrounded by undesirable friends.

Drinking soda with alcohol: Will receive many gifts.

Using caustic soda: Unfortunate in love.

Buying caustic soda: Beware of enemies.

Buying sparkling soda: You have some impossible desires.

Making soda water: Hard labor is ahead for you.

SOIL:

Of soil during the winter: Will receive bad news.

Of soil during the summer: Will receive good news.

Digging in the soil: Increase in fortune.

Planting seeds in the soil: Great love within the family.

Selling soil: Must rely upon own vigor.

Kissing the soil of own property: Happiness within immediate family.

SOLD:

Having sold something: You have been cheated.

Having sold own belongings: Unhappiness and uneasiness.

Having sold something too cheap: Will have many regrets.

A poor man having sold to a rich man too cheaply: Will have more money.

SOLDIER:

Of soldiers: You are being overworked.

Soldiers drilling: Realization of hopes and desires.

Wounded soldiers: Loss of sleep.

Soldiers that you know: Loss of employment.

Soldiers turning against you: Annoyance.

Many soldiers marching: Complete change in life.

Soldiers participating in sports: Children will be very intelligent.

A young girl dreaming of soldiers: Will have many changes before settling.

Soldiers fighting: The dreamer will be victorious.

Soldiers shifting loyalty to other side: Double cross by friends.

Own son being a soldier: Plenty of money coming.

Infantry soldiers: Will receive good news.

Artillery soldiers: Unexpected good news.

Counting soldiers: You are prone to being stingy.

Hearing soldiers singing: Happy events with the family.

SOLES:

Of leather soles: Don't listen to the flattery of others.

Soles of a woman's shoes: Beware of whom you flirt with.

A young girl dreaming of soles of shoes: Misfortune and vexation.

A man dreaming of soles of shoes: Arguments in business.

Changing the soles of children's shoes: Someone will help you.

SOMNAMBULIST:

Being a sleepwalker: Take precautions in life.

A man dreaming of being a somnambulist: Will overcome sickness with care.

A woman dreaming of being a somnambulist: Domestic discussions.

Talking to a somnambulist: Will enjoy a good rest.

A man walking in his sleep: Will receive perplexing news.

SON:

Having one son: Will soon become pregnant.

Having several sons: Success in business.

Giving birth to a son when not pregnant: Happiness.

Adopting a son: Own children will dislike the adopted son.

A son being killed: Misery caused by parents.

Talking to own son: Losses in business.

Rescuing your son from danger: He will rise to eminence.

Own son being sick: Obstacles are ahead for you.

Own son being crippled: Trouble awaits.

SOP:

Of sopping up something: Will live a long life.

Dipping food in water: Congenial work and good news.

Dipping pastries in coffee: You have a loyal friend.

Soaking laundry in water: Family quarrels.

Giving money to pacify a creditor: Will suffer because of own foolishness.

SORCERY:

Being one who practices sorcery: Will have a happy life.

Talking to a sorcerer: You are too boisterous.

Taking the advice of a sorcerer: Good faith is being taken advantage of.

A very old sorcerer: Beware of deception.

A young girl consulting a sorcerer: Disillusionment over boyfriend.

SORES:

Of sores: Approaching money.

Having sores on own body: Great wealth will come to you.

Dressing sores: Will sacrifice much for others.

Others with sores on their body: You have many faithful friends.

Children with sores on their body: Abundance of money.

SORROW:

Of sorrow: Will receive sad news.

Having sorrow because of loss: Good times are coming.

Being sorrowful over the loss of a relative: Approaching money.

Being sorrowful over the loss of a loved one: Change for the better.

Being sorrowful over the loss of a sweetheart: Immediate success.

Being sorrowful over the loss of husband: Be careful with investments.

Being sorrowful over the loss of wife: Financial gains.

SOUND:

Hearing a sound: Happiness and amusements.

Hearing the sound of a trumpet: Sickness.

A loud sound made by people: Death.

Hearing the sound of pleasant music: Will have a big argument.

Hearing various other sounds: Will be visited by someone.

SOUP:

Of soup in cans: Speculations will turn out well.

Eating lots of soup: Big fortune is ahead for you.

Poor people eating a vegetable soup: Increase in earnings.

Rich people eating a vegetable soup: Will suffer much grief.

Eating bean soup: Poverty.

Eating rice soup: Prosperity.

Eating barley soup: Will have good health.

Eating onion soup: Will be cheated by friends.

Eating chicken soup: Will have sorrow.

Eating a fish soup: Happiness is assured.

Eating clam chowder: Misfortune.

Eating a bread and wine soup: Joy without profit.

SOUR:

Eating sour vegetables or fruits: Will have minor love dispute.

Buying sour vegetables or fruits: Will go into bankruptcy.

Buying sour milk: Will have a vigorous mind.

Buying sour cream: Must control your passion.

Buying sauerkraut: A change in life will soon come.

Eating sour hors d'oeuvres: Avoid rivals.

SOUTH:

Of the South: Happiness.

Taking a trip to the South: Success in love.

Going South with your family: Good times are coming.

Moving residence to the South: Advancement within own position.

Being in Southern places: Good luck in love matters.

Moving business to Southern cities: Loss of money.

SOUTH AMERICA:

Seeing South America on a map: Loss of present position.

Taking a trip alone to South America: Affairs will prosper.

Taking a trip to South America with others: Change for the better.

Going to several South American countries: Unhappiness in love affairs.

Returning from South American countries: Devoted marriage partner.

Being deported from South American countries: False friends are nearby.

Being deported to South American countries: Dissension in the family.

Touring South American countries: Financial worries.

Being a citizen of a South American country: Pleasant tidings.

Having business with South America: Will dissolve your partnership.

SOWING SEED:

Of sowing seeds: Big joy.

Having sowing seeds: Will come out well from a present peril.

Buying sowing seeds: Financial gains.

Others handling sowing seeds: Will be cheated by friends.

SPADE:

Of a spade: A new vista of contentment is ahead for you.

Having a spade: Will receive some money.

Buying a spade: Abundant means.

Using a spade: Stay on beaten track when out alone.

Laborers using a spade: Good times are coming.

Having a spade hanging at your side: Will be fortunate in love.

Killing an enemy with a spade: Will live a long life.

Wounding an enemy with a spade: Will be guilty of foolish actions.

SPANGLES:

Of a spangled plate: New interests and surroundings.

Having a spangled ornamentation: Frivolity.

Sprinkling something with spangles: An enemy is seeking your ruin.

Buying spangles: Good health.

Others handling spangles: Will be invited to a place of amusement.

SPARK:

Of a spark: Will collect much money.

A spark starting a fire: Beware of rivals.

An electric spark: Beware of enemies.

A spark causing much damage: Will receive a legacy.

SPARROW:

Of a sparrow: Hard work is ahead for you.

Many sparrows: Death of an enemy.

Catching a sparrow: Big success in business.

Feeding sparrows: Danger in love affairs.

Killing a sparrow: Secret enmity of some person for you.

SPARROW HAWK:

Of a sparrow hawk: Big danger ahead.

Several sparrow hawks: Beware of enemies.

Killing a sparrow hawk: Warning of troubles.

Others killing a sparrow hawk: Enemies are conspiring against you.

SPATS:

Of men's spats: Recovery from an illness.

Wearing spats: Will have mastery over love matters.

Others wearing spats: Someone with evil intentions is watching you.

Catching a young oyster: Beware of jealous friends.

Eating a spat: Will overcome enemies with perseverance.

A young girl eating spats: An influential man will declare his love.

A woman eating spats: A rich man is attracted to you.

A widow eating spats: Be on guard against handsome men.

SPATULA:

Of a wooden spatula: Will earn a living through hard work.

Laborers using a spatula: Obstacles in the path of children.

Painter using a spatula: Divorce.

Using a spatula in cooking: Avoid neighbors.

SPEAK:

Of speaking: You enjoy many kinds of entertainment.

Speaking with own mother: Will have good news.

Husband and wife speaking to each other: Beware of gossip by neighbors.

A man dreaming of speaking to a woman: Good ventures in business affairs.

A woman dreaming of speaking to a man: Submit yourself to the man's will.

Speaking to a friend: Suffering to come.

Speaking to an enemy: Family quarrels.

Speaking to a dog or parrot: Death.

SPEAR:
Of a spear: Happiness.
Using a spear to catch fish: Abundant means.
A spearman stabbing fish: Rapid success of own hopes.
Of a spearfish: Will receive much money from an inheritance.
Catching a spearfish: Will enjoy worldly success.
Stabbing several spearfish: A big reward will come to you.

SPECIFICATION:
Writing up specifications: Will enjoy good success.
Mailing out specifications: Efforts will bring good earnings.
Receiving specifications: Someone is attempting to cause harm.
Printing specifications: Will become drunk.

SPECTACLES:
Of spectacles: Will live to a ripe old age.
Wearing spectacles: Will come out well from a present peril.
Buying spectacles: Financial conditions will rise.
Broken spectacles: Beware of passions leading you astray.
Enjoying a theatrical spectacle: Beware of double dealings by strangers.
An appealing dramatic spectacle: Small changes in your life.
Seeing a good play with a loved one: Matrimony.

SPECTRE:
Of an apparition: Will receive very important and good news.
A spectre dressed in white: Big consolation.
A spectre dressed in black: Great sorrow is ahead for you.
A spectre disappearing: Fortune and joy.

SPELL:
Of a spell; rest from work: Success in all your plans.
Taking turns with others at work: Avoid rivals.
A spell of cold weather: Failure of enemies.
A spell of hot weather: Triumph over enemies.
Spelling words: Illness to come soon.
Misspelling words: Beware of untrue friends.

SPEND:
Spending money: Enjoyable entertainment.
Spending money in traveling: Frivolity.
Spending money on the family: Loss of good friends.
Spending money for food: Will have happy days.
Spending money on children: Will give service to an ungrateful person.
Spending money to travel: Short-lived love affair.
Spending money for amusements: Will quarrel with friends.
A man spending money on his wife: Family consolation.
A man spending money on other women: Will desert his home.
A woman spending money on a man: Will have a guilty conscience.
A woman spending money on her family: Blessings from God.
Spending money foolishly: Be careful and economize for a short time.
Spending money for charity: Affairs will improve after a long while.

SPIDER:
Of a spider: Much happiness.
Killing a spider: Pleasure.
Seeing a spider at night: Plenty of money.
Seeing a spider in the morning: Will have a lawsuit.
Eating spiders: You are a very voluptuous person.
Businessman dreaming of a spider: Good fortune is ahead.
An unmarried woman dreaming of a spider: Will receive proposal of marriage.
A spider spinning a web: Domestic happiness.

Being bitten by a spider: Marital unfaithfulness.

Several spiders: Domestic quarrels.

SPILL:

Of spilling something: You are prone to being too egotistic.

Spilling water: Happiness.

Spilling wine: Family arguments.

Spilling other liquids: Small dissension within the family.

Spilling blood: Loss in business affairs.

Spilling food: Will receive a refusal from a friend.

SPINACH:

Of spinach: Good health.

Buying spinach: Will have good earnings.

Growing spinach: Will enjoy a long life.

Eating spinach: Will be bothered by unpleasant neighbors.

Cooking spinach: Will receive gratitude from family.

Grinding spinach: Will have success in business.

SPINE:

Of the spine: Will have many unpleasant tasks to do.

Breaking the spine: Loss of money.

Not working because of broken spine: Good fortune ahead.

Others breaking their spine: Loss of wealth.

Animal's spine being broken: Death within the family.

Children having trouble with spine: Will receive good news from faraway.

SPINNING:

Of spinning cotton: Wealth.

Spinning wool: Don't neglect children if they are to become prominent.

A spinner at work: Will have good earnings.

Operating a spinning wheel: Will not be recompensed for own diligence.

Owning a spinning wheel: New acquaintances may prove untrustworthy.

An old woman dreaming of spinning: Annoyance and anxiety.

SPIRIT:

Being in good spirits: Will receive news of a death.

Being in poor spirits: Will see ghosts.

Children being in good spirits: Something is preying on your conscience.

Family being in good spirits: Beware of people who are teasing.

Friends being in good spirits: Will soon be cheated.

The Holy Spirit: Must endure fatalities.

SPIT:

Of spitting: Will be deceived.

Spitting blood: Gossip by other people.

Spitting in another's face: Will win lots of money at a lottery.

Others spitting at you: Will enjoy family love.

Children spitting at each other: Will grow up with good manners.

SPITE:

Having spite: Disagreements among friends.

Having spite against relatives: Only trust yourself.

Having spite against friends: Will lose in a game of cards.

Others having spite against you: Will run short of provisions.

SPLEEN:

Of an enlarged spleen: Will attend a big dance.

Seeing spleen at a butcher shop: Will attend a big party.

Eating spleen: Will take a very long walk.

Having illness because of the spleen: Unhappiness.

Cooking spleen: Will attend amusements very often.

SPLENDOR:

Of splendor: Will have a bright and happy life.

Being in splendor: Joy and happiness.

Others being in splendor: Family worries.

Children being in splendor: You are attempting to hide sad news.

SPLIT:
Splitting wood: Will become a pawnbroker.
Splitting cloth: Loss of entire fortune.
Splitting velvet: Will offer little resistance to advances.
Splitting property: Death of a relative.
Partners splitting up: Will be rid of an enemy.

SPONGE:
Of sponges: You are prone to being stingy.
A woman dreaming of sponges: Will have a prominent admirer.
A woman dreaming of squeezing a sponge: Lover will be in army or navy.
A young single girl dreaming of sponges: Is in a hurry to get married.
A young single girl squeezing a sponge: Will marry a man with money.
Using a sponge to wash: Waiting anxiously for something to come through.
A sponge diver: Will soon receive money.
A sponge diver dreaming of gathering sponges: Misery.

SPOON:
Of spoons: Apprehension.
Using a spoon: Happiness within the home.
Losing a spoon: Will receive sad news.
Others using a spoon: Will have an unknown illness.
Breaking a spoon: Infidelity.
A baby using a spoon: Joy in the family.
Buying spoons: Will receive some money.
Losing and retrieving a spoon from a large kettle: Good days ahead.
Using a spoon to stir: Will have company for dinner.
Eating with a spoon: Poor relationships between husband and wife.

SPOT:
Of a dirty spot: You are a good housewife.
Cleaning a spot: You are well fed.
Having a spot on own face: Someone wants to make love to you.
Having a spot on own body: Sickness.
Having spots on clothes: Melancholy.
Spots on men's clothes: Your time is well regulated.
A spot on a woman's breast: Illness to come.
A spot on the sun: Someone will scare you.
Several spots on garments of ladies: Laziness.
Spots on children's clothes: Children will grow up healthy.
Spots on a tablecloth: Disappointment of hopes.
A spot on a man's tie: Be sure to accept forthcoming promotion.

SPRAY:
Of spraying something: Honor and dignity.
Spraying perfume: Will be strong and healthy all during life.
Spraying insecticides: Will enjoy fine surroundings.
Spraying inside of house with insecticides: Agreeable life.
Spraying incense in the house: Will improve present condition.
A woman dreaming of spraying perfume on her face: Frivolity.
A woman dreaming of spraying perfume on her body: Awaiting a visitor.

SPRING:
Spring season: Will receive very good news.
The spring season during winter: A wedding will soon take place.
A fine spring day: Will be insulted by a foolish person.
Of spring water: Large wealth coming later.
Drinking a glass of spring water: Small disputes.
A dry spring: Poverty and sickness.

A spring of gushing water: Wealth and honor.

A bed spring: Will have a delightful life.

A spring used on furniture: Beware of jealous people who are nearby.

A spring used on a machine: Infidelity in love.

SPY:

Of a spy: You desired to render a service, but offer was refused.

Being a spy: Adventures will come your way.

Recognizing a spy: Protect yourself from bad influences.

Dealing with a spy: Business will run smoothly.

SQUANDER:

Of squandering: Will suffer misery.

Squandering your fortune: Will have a better future.

Other people squandering: Will suffer with pain.

Others squandering your money: Unhappy future.

SQUARES:

Of squares on various materials: Squandering of money.

Various colored squares on materials: Will encounter debts.

A woman dreaming of squares in the floor: Success.

A woman dreaming of wearing a skirt with squares in it: Happiness in love.

The squares of a checkerboard: Will be happy in all ventures.

A public square: Will have a love affair.

SQUINT:

Of squinting the eyes: You have the affection of one who loves you.

A man dreaming of squinting: Very good business.

A woman dreaming of squinting: Will have many lovers.

A young girl dreaming of squinting: Will be married within the year.

SQUIRREL:

Of squirrels: Cheating.

A man dreaming of squirrels: Will make love to his maid.

A woman dreaming of a squirrel: Will be surprised while doing wrong.

A young girl dreaming of a squirrel: Will be untrue to her boyfriend.

Children dreaming of a squirrel: They will surprise a thief.

Killing a squirrel: Will acquire a few new friends.

Petting a squirrel: Happiness in the home.

Being bitten by a squirrel: Will marry for money.

STABLE:

Of a stable for horses: Wealth.

A stable illuminated by the moonlight: Happiness in love.

A stable for pigs: You have a very weak character.

A stable for sheep: Patience will be advantageous to you.

Race track stables: Will make much money.

STAG:

Of a stag: Will receive good news.

Seeing a male deer: Will have many friends.

Avoiding a stag: Plans will be ruined.

Several stags: Big friendship.

Killing a stag: Will receive an inheritance.

Others killing a stag: Will have good earnings.

Of a stag party: You are disillusioned.

Attending a stag party: Danger is ahead.

Taking a prominent part in a stag party: Separation from friends.

STAGE:

Of a stage: Remarkable events to come.

The floor of a stage: You love pleasures too much.

Being on a stage: Disappointment in projects begun.

Building a stage: Will mourn over the loss of relatives.

Sitting in a box near the stage: Will endure terrible pains.

Being thrown out of a stage door: Will have pains in the heart.

STAIN:

A dirty stain: You are a good housewife.

Cleaning a stain: You are very well fed.

Having a stain on the body: Sickness.

Having a stain on clothes: Melancholy.

Stains on men's clothes: Your time is well regulated.

Several stains on garments of ladies: Laziness.

Stains on children's clothes: Children will grow up healthy.

Stains on a tablecloth: Disappointment of own hopes.

Stains on a man's tie: Be sure to accept coming promotion.

A stain on a woman's breast: Illness to come.

STAIRS:

Of a broad staircase: Wealth and honor.

Very high stairs: Will be jilted by your lover.

Becoming dizzy on the stairs: Important and very beneficial event to come.

Falling from the stairs: Own envy will cause suffering.

Climbing stairs: Unusual happiness and prosperity.

Climbing stairs with others: You have loyal friends.

Descending stairs: Disappointments in business.

Descending stairs with others: Danger through a secret.

STAMMER:

Of stammering: You have a very determined mind.

Other people who stammer: Fresh interests will lead to happiness.

Children stammering: They will have a good position in the future.

Friends stammering: Beware of them; they will suggest wrongdoing.

STAMP:

Of stamps: Bankruptcy.

Buying stamps: Misery.

Selling stamps: Will be making good money.

Collecting stamps: Big joy.

Receiving stamps: You have a faithful friend.

Giving stamps away: Reconciliation with an enemy.

Putting stamps on letters: Will be criticized by the press.

Putting stamps in an album: Will associate with a high official.

STAR:

Of stars: Happiness.

Dim stars: Everything will go wrong so don't place confidence in others.

Shooting stars: Great and good fortune.

Seeing stars at night: Important and very beneficial event to come.

An unusually bright star: Losses in business.

A star shining into a room: Danger of death for the head of the family.

Several stars close together: Danger of war.

Seeing brilliant stars: Prosperity and gratification of every wish.

Seeing brilliant stars with wife: Will take a trip.

Seeing brilliant stars with children: Good news.

Seeing brilliant stars with sweetheart: Realization of own desires.

A rich person dreaming of stars disappearing: Loss of money.

A poor person dreaming of stars disappearing: Death.

Stars falling from the sky: Disaster.

Stars with a tail falling from the sky: Will abandon house because of fire.

A star falling on your house: Loss of love.

A star falling on a roof: Sickness.

STARCH:

Of starching something: Success in all enterprises.

Starching ladies' blouses: You are prone to being stingy.

Starching men's shirts: Will receive unexpected fortune.

Starching collars: Must make plans for your old age.

Starching collar of a lady's dress: Some worry but much gain.

A woman dreaming of starching linen: Will marry an industrious person.

STARVE:
Of starving: Will acquire riches through courage.

Eating while dreaming of starving: Will become very rich.

Suffering from starvation: Much wealth is coming to you.

Starving for several days: Success in business and worldly affairs.

Others starving: Abundant means.

STATE:
Of the state of the country: Will soon take a trip.

Own state: Will have an easy and happy old age.

Going out of state: Will receive good news.

Moving to another state: Honor and joy.

Being a citizen of a state: Will have money in old age.

STATUE:
Of statues: Unhappiness.

Adoring a statue: Big sorrow.

A statue moving: Riches.

A statue of a saint: Wealth.

A statue of a naked woman: Honor and distinction.

A statue of a naked man: Good results in own enterprises.

Several statues: Your love is not wanted.

STEAL:
Of stealing: A gift of jewelry will be offered to you.

Being robbed: Disappointment.

Stealing valuable things: Great misery.

Stealing clothes: Will have bad results in business.

Stealing furs: Good success in all your affairs.

Others stealing: Big pleasures.

STEAM:
Of steam: Will have many disputes.

Using steam: Doubts and differences between you and the one you love.

Using steam for cleaning: Good times will come soon.

Taking a steam bath: Worries will soon clear away.

STEEL:
Of steel: Will receive good news.

Using steel: Will have good business.

Being hurt by steel: Big satisfaction.

Being hit by steel: Good results in business.

Red steel coming from the fire: Loss of blood.

Buying steel: Will be in mourning.

Cutting steel: Will receive a long-awaited letter.

STEEPLE:
Of steeples: Warning of serious troubles.

Climbing a steeple: Will have difficulties which will be overcome.

Falling from a steeple: Losses in business.

Being hurt on a steeple: Achievement of own greatest wish.

STEP:
Of steps: Will have a big fortune.

Marble steps: Will be forced to do something against own will.

Going up the steps: Fortune.

Coming down steps: Will be condemned for carelessness.

STEPFATHER:
Being a stepfather: Riches and fortune.

Arguing with a stepfather: Persecution.

Being a good stepfather: Family arguments.

Disliking a stepfather: You are abusing the confidence of someone.

STEPMOTHER:
Being a stepmother: Death is near.

Arguing with a stepmother: Persecution.

Being a good stepmother: Will live to an old age.

Disliking a stepmother: Family quarrels.

STEPPINGSTONE:

Of a steppingstone: Good fortune in love matters.

Walking on a steppingstone: Prompt love affairs.

A steppingstone being above water: Advancement in own affairs.

Walking with bare feet on a steppingstone: Will progress in everything.

STEREOSCOPE:

Of a stereoscope: Someone is attempting to catch you in a lie.

Children looking through a stereoscope: Will get rid of an enemy.

Others looking through a stereoscope: Beware of enemies surrounding you.

Viewing pleasant sites through a stereoscope: Will live a long life.

STERILE:

Being sterile: Will receive sad news.

Mates discussing inability to have children: Will adopt a child.

Members of family being sterile: Domestic happiness.

Friends who are sterile: You are too generous with loved ones.

STERN:

The stern of a ship: Will have a long life.

The stern post of a ship: Be cautious in business ventures.

The stern or back of someone: Will be double-crossed by a loved one.

The stern of animals: Disaster will come to friends.

STEVEDORE:

Of stevedores: Will be doing good things for other people.

Hiring stevedores: Important and very beneficial events to come.

Arguing with stevedores: Luck and prosperity.

Paying stevedores: Unfortunate love affairs.

Stevedores being idle: Trouble is ahead.

STEW:

Of a stew: Big money gains.

Buying meat for a stew: Will receive many presents.

Cooking a stew: Will receive a large amount of money.

Eating stew: Will receive a gift from your sweetheart.

Serving stew to others to eat: Will suffer much grief.

STEWARDESS:

Of a stewardess: People are saying bad things about you.

Being a stewardess: Unhappiness.

Falling in love with a stewardess: Will have large damages.

Marrying a stewardess: Will receive unhappy news.

Divorcing a stewardess: A guarded secret will be discovered.

A stewardess being wounded: Family unhappiness.

A stewardess being killed: Misery.

STICK:

Having a stick in your hand: Unhappiness.

Leaning on a stick: Sickness.

Hitting someone with a strong stick: Will be dominated by a woman.

Hitting strangers with a stick: Profit and good news.

Hitting relatives with a stick: Good hopes.

Pressing gunpowder into a gun with a stick: Will enjoy better days.

STIFF:

Own body being stiff: Will be molested.

Stiffness causing pain: Will have misery.

Children being stiff: Family arguments.

Mate's body being stiff: Arrival of a friend.

Having a stiff neck: Will have good business ventures.

STILE:
Of a stile: Will be in mourning over the death of a relative.
Walking warily on a stile: An enemy is trying to entrap you.
Falling from a stile: Will receive a letter with good news.
Others walking on a stile: Beware of enemies.

STILETTO:
Of a sharp-pointed dagger: Family disagreements.
Plunging a stiletto into someone: Will have feelings hurt.
Being struck by a stiletto: Discovery of lost valuables.
Wearing a stiletto on a uniform: A mystery will be solved.

STILTS:
Being mounted on stilts: You are puffed up with vain pride.
Seeing stilts: Pleasant news concerning own children.
Buying stilts: Don't offend associates by your conceit.
Others on stilts: You will have a good future.

STING:
Of a sting: Illness.
Being stung: Will have much grief.
Being wounded with a poisonous sting: Will have remorse.
Others being stung: Change of own residence.
Being stung by an insect: Unhappiness will assail you.

STINGY:
Of a stingy person: Unexpected earnings.
Being stingy with other people: Will make martyrs of people.
Being stingy with own family: Will soon receive an inheritance.
Being stingy with one you love: Will receive a considerable fortune.
Being stingy with children: Poverty.
Being a miser: Beware of enemies nearby.
Others being stingy with you: Blessings on the family.

STIR:
Stirring food: Will have an argument.
Stirring dirt: Will receive money.
Stirring soup: Financial conditions will improve.
Stirring a stew: Beware of receiving violence from someone.
Stirring various other things: Will receive bad news.

STIRRUP:
Of stirrups: Will have success in own hopes.
Fastening stirrups: Will be forced to make a trip.
Unfastening stirrups: Will receive unexpected news.
Having difficulty fastening stirrups: Violent arguments with a friend.

STOCKINGS:
Of stockings: Luck and prosperity.
Cotton stockings: Big pleasure.
Silk stockings: Will have much temptation.
Many silk stockings: Hardship.
Light-colored stockings: Sorrow.
Dark-colored stockings: Pleasure.
Wearing stockings: Happiness.
Torn stockings: Financial losses.
Stockings with a hole in them: Loss of something.
Woolen stockings: Affluence.
Cutting your stockings: Fortune.
Taking off stockings: Good days will return.
Putting on stockings: Honor and profit.
Knitting stockings: Will meet with opposition.
People selling stockings: Will receive a bad service.

STOCKMAN:
Of a stockman: Will be favorably accepted into society.
Being a stockman: Will reach your goal slowly but surely.
A stockman at work: Business affairs will go well.
Having dealings with a stockman: Will be molested.

STOCK MARKET:

Of a stock market: Poverty.

Being at the stock market: Death of a friend.

Dealing in stocks: Patience will be advantageous.

Making gains at the stock market: Will enjoy peace of mind.

Losing at the stock market: Abundance and riches.

Being a member of the stock market: Will have dealings with debtors.

STOCKPILE:

Of a stockpile: You are headed toward a lawsuit.

Moving stockpiled things: Will be involved in a public disorder.

Buying a stockpile of merchandise: Beware of enemies.

Selling stockpiled merchandise: Will receive a legacy.

STOCKROOM:

Of a stockroom: Will hear of the violent death of an enemy.

Being the clerk of a stockroom: Beware of enemies.

Receiving items from a stockroom: Will be double-crossed by friends.

Giving out items from a stockroom: Will have small arguments.

A full stockroom: Business disaster ahead.

An empty stockroom: Will put plenty of money in the bank.

STOCKYARD:

Of a stockyard: Sickness.

Working at a stockyard: Will have good fortune in the future.

Being at a stockyard: Ingratitude for good deeds done.

A busy stockyard: Will have a passing love affair.

STOLE:

A stole for women: Will have remorse of conscience.

A stole for a priest: Will be frightened by a ghost.

A woman having a beautiful stole: Will enjoy an easy life.

A woman buying a stole: Joy in the household.

Wearing a stole: You are attempting to hide wrongdoings.

Selling a stole: Someone is attempting to cause damages for you.

Losing a stole: Sickness.

STOMACH:

Stomach being full and satisfied: Riches according to the amount eaten.

Not having a full stomach: Will be invited to a dinner party.

Children having a full stomach: They will make progress in their studies.

Relatives having a full stomach: Disappointment in own hopes.

Having a large stomach: Misery and misfortune.

Having a small stomach: No one will know your secrets.

STONES:

Of stones: Angry discussions and new surroundings.

Walking on stones: Will have to suffer for a while.

Of precious stones: Good business.

Buying precious stones: Good earnings.

Admiring precious stones: Sickness.

Wearing precious stones: Abundance.

Losing precious stones: Misfortune.

Selling precious stones: Loss of money.

STOOL:

Of a stool: Honor and achievement.

Sitting on a stool: Will receive many merits.

Having your own stool at home: Will have an honorable position.

People sitting on stools: Family quarrels.

Empty stools: Will meet some friends.

STOOP:

Of stooping: Will have a quiet future.

Stooping to speak to someone: Thrilling times ahead.

Stooping to pick up something: Will be honored by everybody.

Others stooping: Will receive good news from a friend.

STORE:
Of a store: Increased wealth.
Having a store: Don't squander your money.
Being in a store: Avoid rivals.
Buying things in a department store: Joy without profit.
Buying food at a grocery store: A mystery will be solved.

STORK:
Of a stork: Foretells that you will be robbed.
Two storks together: Will marry and have good children.
A group of storks: Will marry and enjoy much prosperity.
Seeing a stork in the winter: Big disaster ahead.
A stork flying in the air: Robbers are close by.
A stork being very quiet: Arrival of enemies and holdup people.
A stork sleeping: Change of residence.

STORM:
Of a storm: Unfortunate business undertakings will cause distress.
Watching a storm: Unhappiness in love.
Being in a storm: Separation of loved ones.
Others being in a storm: Change for the better.
A storm hitting own house: Discovery of a secret.
A storm demolishing your house: People with evil intentions are nearby.
A storm damaging your house: Will have good morals.
A storm demolishing the homes of others: Big dangers ahead.

STORY:
Hearing a story: Will have much hard work ahead.
Reading a story: Wishes will be realized.
Writing a story: Unhappiness and weakness of mind.
Others writing a story: Arguments within the family.
Selling a story to a magazine: Beware of being seduced.

STOVE:
Of a stove: Will receive a long-awaited gift.
A stove with a burned-out grate: Hard times to come.
A stove filled with burning coal: Prosperity.
A gas stove: Good days are coming.
A kerosene stove: Changes for the better.
Having a stove that heats very well: Big joy and contentment.

STRANGE PLACE:
Of a strange place: Inherited money.
Being in a strange place alone: Money will come to you immediately.
Being in a strange place with others: Abundance.
Others being in a strange place: Prosperity.

STRANGERS:
Of a stranger: Will receive assistance from a friend.
Many strangers: Good and kind friends.
Being a stranger: Good fortune.
Receiving a stranger: Arrival of a friend.

STRANGLE:
Of strangling: Troubles.
Being strangled: A false friend is nearby.
Strangling someone yourself: Your wish will come true.
Others being strangled: Rapid success of own hopes.

STRAW:
Of straw: Difficulties and poverty.
Having straw: Joy.
Cutting straw: Will have much pain.
Straw in a bundle: Security in your business.
Several bundles of straw: Joy and honor.
Straw in a stable: Happiness in domestic matters.
Burning straw: Will attend a big festivity.
Selling straw: Prosperity.

Buying straw: Must work hard to overcome troubles.

A bed made of straw: Misery.

STRAWBERRY:

Of strawberries: Unexpected success.

Picking strawberries from the vines: Will make many new friends.

Eating strawberries: Big joy.

Making strawberry jam: Wealth.

Making a strawberry pie: Will succeed in business.

STREAM:

Of a stream: Meaningless joy.

Walking in a stream alone: Beware of enemies.

Walking in a stream with others: Will fall into disgrace.

Going into a stream: Ingratitude of others.

STREAMLINE:

Becoming streamlined: Will soon have a proposal of marriage.

Being unable to become streamlined: Doomed for disappointment.

Having difficulty becoming streamlined: Consolation and joy.

Others being streamlined: Will receive an unwelcome visitor.

STREET:

Of a street: Will be welcomed by everyone.

A wide and open street: Business will go well.

A long street with nice homes: Will receive a happy surprise.

A straight street full of people: Prosperity.

A street with many curves: Unhappiness.

A street with many people on it: Afflictions.

A deserted street: Great joy.

A street in bad condition: Success of own hopes in the future.

Several muddy and dirty streets: Will be molested.

Being on a street you've never been on before: Will do a lot of traveling.

STRETCH:

Of stretching: Will play a solo on an instrument.

Stretching something after washing it: Someone is attempting to destroy you.

Being unable to stretch something: Postponement of success.

Others stretching ropes: Another person received what you desired.

STRETCHER:

Of a stretcher: Will have argument over important matters.

Being carried on a stretcher: Disillusionment in own ambitions.

Family being carried on a stretcher: Will soon be free of an enemy.

The people who carry a stretcher: Avoid rivals.

A loved one being carried on a stretcher: Shame and sorrow.

STRICT:

Being strict: Immediate death of a relative.

Being strict with children: Will incur too many debts.

Being strict with employees: Will receive a legacy.

Others being strict with you: People are gossiping behind your back.

Officers being strict with rules: Worries and vexation.

STRIKE:

Of a strike: Will have a very delicate taste.

Organizing a strike: Help people in need of money.

Being damaged financially by a strike: Dignity.

Being a strike leader: Will be robbed.

Ending a strike: Will be falsely accused for something you didn't do.

Being a strikebreaker: An unknown person is in love with you.

STRING:

Of string: You have a strong power of attraction.

Having string: Will have quarrels and danger.

Using string: Must be careful in all your affairs.

Buying string: Will take a voyage in the near future.

Putting string around a package: Prosperity.

STRIP:

Being stripped: You have a great desire to do good for others.

Stripping yourself: Will have quarrels.

Others who are stripped: Arrival of a friend.

A woman of ill fame stripping herself: Unhappiness.

Being stripped by force: Will receive good advice.

STRIP TEASE:

Of a strip tease girl: Misery.

Being a strip tease girl: Will have money troubles all during life.

Being a strip tease actress: An unhappy surprise is ahead.

Many strip tease dancers on a stage: Prosperity and success in business.

Sweetheart being a strip tease girl: Will not be accepted in society.

STROKE:

Of a stroke: Wealth.

Having a stroke: Will make progress in personal affairs.

Being paralyzed by a stroke: Will have a weak mind.

Not being affected by a stroke: Beware of false friends.

Others having a stroke: Someone is trying to steal your sweetheart.

Relatives having a stroke: Will receive plenty of money in the future.

A mate having a stroke: Must rely upon own good judgment.

STRONG:

Being strong: Death of a relative.

Other strong people: Will attend a funeral.

Children being strong: Will recover from an illness.

Mate being strong: Beware of cheating on the part of your mate.

Having a strong mind: Will receive a valuable gift.

Having a strong will power: Disappointment in own ambitions.

Strong animals: Will have guilt for wrongdoing.

STRUCTURE:

Of a big structure: Good fortune in married life.

A small structure: Beware of relatives.

A structure being built: Will be badly treated by creditors.

Being inside a structure: Your future is secured.

Being outside a structure: Will work hard all during life.

STRUGGLE:

Trying to avoid a struggle: Improvement in own health.

Struggling to save yourself: Will suffer abuse.

Struggling with someone stronger than you: Will have great strength.

Struggling with a wild animal: Good fortune.

Struggling with a boy and winning: Gossip and shame.

Struggling with a woman: Will suffer through own foolish actions.

Struggling with a dead person: Sickness.

STUB:

Of checkbook stubs: Will achieve all your desires.

Own checkbook stubs: Will have the respect of others for a short time.

Adding figures from stubs: Will come to a realization of the truth.

Finding a mistake in figures on stubs: Death of a very dear friend.

STUBBORN:

Of stubborn people: Will be menaced by danger.

Being stubborn: You have ulterior motives.

Others being stubborn: Will have many loving people around.

Children being stubborn: Hopes will not be realized.

Having a stubborn mate: Will lead a pleasant life in old age.

Having stubborn relatives: A new love is growing within your heart.
Having stubborn friends: Unhappiness in love.
Dealing with stubborn animals: Infidelity.

STUDENT:
Being a student: Will be molested.
Many students: Will lead a life of crime.
Foreign students: Prosperity.
A teacher having many good students: Will achieve your goal.
A teacher having bad students: Will fall in love with one of them.

STUDIO:
Of a studio: Will receive much consolation in love.
A photographer's studio: Will receive a big disappointment.
A painter's studio: Disappointment in own ambitions.
Owning a studio: Will receive unpleasant guests.
Having a private studio: Will be free of an enemy.

STUDY:
Of studying: Will have a clear conscience.
Children studying: All desires will be realized.
Children not studying: Will abuse the confidence of others.
A mate studying: Will have an unhappy married life.
A professor studying: Will receive a proposal of marriage.

STUFFY:
Smelling a stuffy place: Will recover from an illness.
Being in a stuffy place: Unhappiness in love.
Entering a stuffy place: Have been satisfied with a very pleasant time.
Friends home being stuffy: Will make a new acquaintance.

STUMBLE:
Of stumbling: Will make a wrong move.

Stumbling and falling: Expect trouble.
Stumbling and being hurt: Financial losses.
Others stumbling: Many obstacles are ahead for you.
Children stumbling: Dignity and distinction.

STUMP:
Of stumps: Will make new friendships.
Knocking down stumps: Will have a vigorous mind.
Digging stumps out of the earth: Will receive a letter containing money.
Knocking down cricket stumps: Will meet prominent people.

SUGAR:
Of sugar: Will receive many sweet words from friends.
Buying sugar: An unfaithful friend is seeking your ruin.
Cooking with sugar: Will be cheated by friends.
Putting sugar in coffee or tea: A false friend is nearby.
Putting sugar on fruit to sweeten it: Will have a happy future.

SUICIDE:
Of a suicide: You have overstrained your mind.
Planning to commit suicide: Troubles were brought on by yourself.
Having committed suicide: Unhappiness.
Thinking of committing suicide: Must conform yourself to real life.
A woman committing suicide: Opposition in love and despair.
Others committing suicide: Will live a long life.
A husband or wife committing suicide: Permanent change in surroundings.

SUIT:
Having many suits of clothing: Loss of money.
Buying suits: Very big family quarrel.
Selling suits of clothing: Will be double-crossed.
Throwing away suits: Triumph over enemies.

SUITE:
Of a suite: Will be hampered by old-fashioned ideas.
Being with a sweetheart in a suite: Will receive unpleasant news.
Giving a party in a suite: Will be highly considered by others.
Being alone in a suite: Family disagreements.

SULPHUR:
Of sulphur: Misfortune.
Buying sulphur: Actions of others will cause sorrow for you.
Selling sulphur: Will enjoy joyful events.
Others using sulphur: Will undergo an operation.
Spraying sulphur on crops: Will enjoy a very great love.

SUM:
Of figuring sums: You are much too stingy.
Making mistakes in figuring sums: A broken relationship.
Not getting sums correct: Will have a dangerous friendship.
Correcting sums: Will soon experience ups and downs.

SUMMER:
Of summer during summer: Will have a very good harvest.
Of summer during spring: Must try to think things out very well.
Of summer during autumn: Try to avoid bad friends.
Of summer during winter: Happiness within the family.

SUMMER HOUSE:
Of a summer house: Pleasant prospects for the future.
Buying a summer house: Good hopes are ahead for you.
Building a summer house: Honor without profit.
Living in a summer house: Small fortune.
Selling a summer house: Changes in your business.
People coming to your summer house: Great sorrow.

SUMMIT:
Of a very high summit: Will be robbed.
Climbing a very high summit: Profit.
Planting a flag on a summit: Prosperity.
Celebrating with others upon reaching the summit: Unsuccessful affairs.
Descending unharmed from a very high summit: Will contract an illness.

SUMMONS:
Being served with a summons: Adverse criticism and scandal will vex you.
Issuing a summons: Unhappiness.
Accepting a summons: Postponement of success.
Refusing a summons: Will suffer humiliation.

SUN:
Of the sun: Success in love matters.
A red sun: Sickness of children.
Being in the sun: Good news and joy.
A beautiful sunrise: Success in money matters.
A beautiful sunset: Will be told false news.
A woman dreaming of a beautiful sunset: A child will be born.
A dark sun: Fortune is decreasing.
A blind person dreaming of a dark sun: Will have his sight again.
A prisoner dreaming of a dark sun: Will be let out of prison.
The sun shining on the top of a house: Danger of fire.
The sun shining where you are: Will soon have a sickness.
The sun shining on your bed: Apprehension.
An honest person dreaming of sun shining on top of his head: Glory and honor.
A dishonest person dreaming of sun shining on his head: Sins are pardoned.
People that have enemies dreaming of the sun: Will have good luck.
The sun peeping through the clouds: Troubles will soon vanish.

The sun shining brightly in a room: Big gains and prosperity.

Entering a house and seeing the sunshine: Will purchase real estate.

A married woman dreaming of sunshine in a room: Will have a virtuous child.

The sun going toward the moon: Will have some fighting.

SUN BATH:

Taking a sun bath: Unhappiness ahead.

Taking a sun bath with members of family: Will receive unexpected advances.

Taking a sun bath with a sweetheart: Will receive much affection.

Being criticized for taking a sun bath: Will win an argument.

SUNDAY:

Of Sunday: Coming change of interests.

Going to church on Sunday: Will realize high ambitions.

Having a restful Sunday: Luck and prosperity.

Working on Sunday: Will have mastery over many matters.

SUNDIAL:

Of a sundial: Coming events.

Watching a sundial: Death.

Checking a sundial: Marriage within own immediate circle.

Handling a sundial: Happiness in love.

SUNFLOWER:

Of a sunflower: Your love is not reciprocated.

A sunflower turning toward the sun: Worries ahead.

Picking a sunflower: Don't rush your affairs.

Eating sunflower seeds: Will conquer someone.

SUNK:

Being sunk into financial debts: Will have a happy life.

Being sunk into the sea: Great sadness.

A sunken ship: Will receive a large amount of money unexpectedly.

A seaman being sunk: A good future is ahead.

Various objects being sunk: Will enjoy happiness within the family.

SUN LAMP:

Of a sun lamp: Joy.

Using a sun lamp: Will have unhappiness in love.

Using a sun lamp for treatments: Will be scared by someone.

Others taking treatments under a sun lamp: Will enjoy an active life.

SUNSHINE:

Of the sunshine: Will have a long and happy life.

Sunshine being very hot: Will have ups and downs in life.

Sunshine being obscured by a cloud: Will fall in love.

The sunshine first thing in the morning: Will receive good news from faraway.

SUNSTROKE:

Of a sunstroke: Avoid rivals.

Having a sunstroke: Others will have reason to envy you very much.

Relatives having a sunstroke: Family quarrels.

Others having a sunstroke: Worry will be smoothed away.

SUPERB:

Being superb: Disappointment in own ambitions.

Dealing with a superb man: Afflictions.

Dealing with a superb woman: Will have an affair.

Having superb friends: Prosperity and good success in business.

SUPERFICIAL:

Being superficial: Give to others what rightfully belongs to them.

Acting superficial: Shame and sorrow.

Dealing with superficial people: Will desire that which others have.

Members of family being superficial: Will have insignificant worries.

SUPERINTENDENT:

Of a superintendent: Accept your destiny with resignation.

Being a superintendent: Will have arguments and suffer abuse.

Being appointed superintendent: Will enjoy a long life.

Losing job as superintendent: Death of a relative.

Being the superintendent of manufacturing plant: Big joy ahead.

SUPERIOR:

Feeling superior to others: Important and very beneficial event to come.

Being superior of a school: Will receive bad advice from others.

Being a mother superior: Will need financial help.

Children being superior to others: Family dissension.

A mate being superior to the other: Beware of rivals.

Having superiority in business affairs: Will have friends who will help.

Having political superiority: Will be harmed by talking too much.

SUPERVISE:

Supervising personal business: Misery.

Supervising military activities: Will be working in good faith.

Supervising children: Prosperity and good success.

Being supervised: Will receive good news.

SUPPER:

Of the Last Supper: Will receive blessings.

Having supper: Riches and fortune.

Having supper alone: Loneliness and unhappiness.

Having supper with others: Will spend much money in the future.

Having supper with good company: Will be harmed by actions of a friend.

Having supper with own family: Contentment.

Having a guest for supper: Misery.

Having a delicious supper: Birth of a child.

Having a business supper: Public disgrace.

Giving supper to animals: Riches.

SUPPLANT:

Of supplanting: Business activities of a good nature.

Supplanting by force: Important and very beneficial event to come.

Supplanting another person: Will be cheated by friends.

Being supplanted: You are unfitted to fill your position in life.

Supplanting roots: Trouble ahead for you.

SUPPLE:

Being supple: Reconciliation in love.

Yielding to your mate: Will find a hidden treasure.

Being supple with children: Will have joy and good results.

Others being supple to you: Will divulge a secret confided to you.

SUPPLEMENT:

Of a supplement: A friend is trying to help you secretly.

Receiving supplements to circulars: Financial losses.

Receiving supplements to a book: Business quarrels.

Sending a supplement to others: Doomed for disappointment.

SUPPLICATE:

Supplicating for grace: Another person is enjoying what you hoped for.

Children supplicating to you: Will have uneasiness.

Others supplicating to you: Beware of people taking advantage of good faith.

Supplicating a governor for grace: Will soon be molested.

SUPPLY:

Of supplies: Infidelity.

Having supplies: Arrival of a friend.

Receiving supplies: Beware of being cheated.

Buying supplies: Family arguments.

Storing supplies: Will acquire freedom from an enemy.

Selling supplies: Will have good fortune in married life.

SUPPORT:
Receiving support: Prosperity.
Supporting others: Will be acting in bad faith.
Supporting the family: You are headed toward important business dealings.
Supporting a public organization: Danger in own affairs.

SUPPRESS:
Being suppressed: Ego will bring harm to you.
Suppressing someone else: Will have a short-lived love.
Suppressing an animal: You have neighbors that you don't care for.
Others suppressing you: You are unfitted to fill position in life.

SUPREMACY:
Of supremacy: Will have unhappy days.
Having supremacy over others: Will win at gambling.
Others having supremacy: Will receive sad news.
Having supremacy in own affairs: Will find out others are telling lies.
Having supremacy over mate: Divorce.
Having supremacy over relatives: Family arguments.

SUPREME COURT:
Of the Supreme Court: Will attain goals slowly.
Having a case before the Supreme Court: Will receive unhappy news.
Losing a case before the Supreme Court: Infidelity.
Being a member of the Supreme Court: Will be married again.

SURF:
Of the surf: Will need very good tact to come out well in own matters.
The surf coming into the shore: Big joy.
Being hit by the surf: Will be guilty of foolish actions.
The surf moving out to sea again: Will have a vigorous mind.

SURF FISH:
Of surf fish: Important and very beneficial events to come.
Catching surf fish: Financial gains.
Buying surf fish: Must rely on your own good judgment.
Eating surf fish: You have a loyal friend.

SURGEON:
Of a surgeon: Will be oppressed by business enemies.
Calling a surgeon for a home visit: Illness of a friend.
Going to a surgeon's office for consultation: A long life is ahead of you.
A surgeon receiving visits of many clients: Big profits to come.
Being a surgeon: Joy and profit.

SURGERY:
Surgery being performed: Your bad doings are known by everyone.
Performing surgery yourself: Misery.
Surgery being successful: Will have long-lasting joy.
Surgery being performed on you: A mystery will be solved.

SURNAME:
Having a surname: Will be confronted with danger.
Receiving a surname: Will have fortune in the future.
Giving a surname to others: Will fall into poverty.
Giving children a surname: Fidelity.

SURPASS:
Surpassing others: You have bad advisers.
Others surpassing you in the same business: Vexation in love affairs.
Being surpassed in sports: Will have many discouragements.
Children surpassing others: Will be refused a requested favor.

SURPLICE:
Of a vest of white linen: One with evil intentions is watching you.
Wearing a surplice: Will live a long life.

Married people dreaming of a surplice: Contentment.
Single people dreaming of a surplice: Marriage will soon take place.

SURPLUS:
Having a surplus of merchandise: Will be cheating others.
Having a surplus in the home: A letter will bring bad news.
A farmer having a surplus: Will enjoy a happy life in the future.
A farmer selling surplus: Big fortune.
A store selling surplus: Will have a delicate taste.
Buying surplus: Divorce.

SURPRISE:
Of a surprise: Will receive a letter with unexpected news.
Receiving a surprise: You are surrounded by unfaithful people.
Surprising others: Will have good fortune in love.
Surprising a mate in wrongdoings: Will receive the help of a friend.
Surprising children in wrongdoings: A marriage is being planned.
Being told of a surprise: Will have a big family argument.

SURRENDER:
Surrendering to a lover: Will become even more stingy in the future.
Surrendering to the police: Will receive good news.
Surrendering to the will of your mate: Will have big earnings.
Surrendering stolen items: Must endure several sleepless nights.
An army surrendering: Unhappiness.

SURVEY:
A survey being made: You are prone to being stingy.
Making a survey: Will have good business ahead.
Writing a survey: Big problems ahead.
Reading a survey: Will receive many disillusionments.

SURVIVAL:
Of survival: Sickness of children.
The survival of a loved one: People are aware of your wrongdoings.
The survival of a business: Will be caught in a trap.
The survival of someone that was lost: Will receive good news.

SUSPECT:
Being suspected: You are accustomed to doing wrong to other people.
A mate suspecting the other: Beware of tender friendship with someone else.
Being suspected with cause: Needs will be granted.
Suspecting a relative: A woman will play a dirty trick on you.

SUSPEND:
Being suspended from your job: Success in new enterprises.
Suspending others from their job: Will incur many debts.
Being suspended in the air: Will enjoy honor and consideration by others.
Others being suspended in the air: Sickness.

SUSPENDERS:
Of suspenders: Must have faith in yourself.
Buying suspenders: Your careless words will cause anxiety.
Having old suspenders: Look out for gossiping behind your back.
Of a broken suspender: Will have to make an apology.

SWALLOW:
Of a swallow in a tree: Misfortune in love.
A swallow on a lawn: Happiness is assured.
Married couples seeing a swallow when together: Domestic happiness.
Lovers seeing a swallow: Will have faithful friends.
Of swallowing: Good news.
Having pains when swallowing: Will live to be over ninety years old.
Swallowing pills: Financial gains.
Swallowing a story that you don't believe: Frivolity.

SWAMP:
Walking through a swamp: Disappointment in love.
Sinking into a swamp: Will have big disputes.
A swamp full of dead fish: Will soon go hungry.
Being swamped with letters: Big friendship.

SWAN:
Of a swan: Joy and prosperity.
Many swans together: Good health and revelation of a mystery.
A white swan: Riches and good standing in life.
A black swan: Domestic troubles and sorrow.
Hearing the noise of a swan: Death.
Killing a swan: Business affairs need care.

SWARM:
Of a swarm of bees: Fire will be near you.
Watching a swarm of bees: Prosperity in the family.
The queen of a swarm of bees: You have many enemies that want to hurt you.
Being stung by a swarm of bees: Beware of enemies.

SWEAR:
Of swearing: Watch your actions.
Having sworn: Will receive bad news.
Others swearing: Will be blamed for your actions.
Relatives swearing: Will receive unpleasant news.

SWEEP:
Of sweeping: Happy domestic life.
Having to do the sweeping: Will receive a nice gift.
Doing the sweeping: Will live a long life.
Others sweeping: Will receive a letter with good news.
Your daughter sweeping: Your plans will not fail.

SWEETHEART:
Of a sweetheart: Will have a difficult experience.
Having a pleasing and beautiful sweetheart: Watch rivals.
Having a handsome sweetheart: Watch him very closely.
Having a changeable sweetheart: Loss of love.

SWEETS:
Of sweets: Will be cheated by friends.
Receiving sweets: Be on the lookout for a deceiving message.
Sending sweets: Be cautious in love ventures.
Making sweets: Financial gains.
Tasting sweets: Prosperity.

SWIM:
Of swimming: Will have love and pleasure.
Swimming on your back: Will have a big quarrel.
Swimming in the open sea: Prosperity.
Swimming in a river: Will encounter danger in the near future.
Swimming in muddy water: Your path is beset with many obstacles.
Swimming in a pool: Success.
Swimming to a shore: Hard work is ahead for you.
Swimming and reaching your objective: Will be successful in everything.

SWINDLER:
Of a swindler: You are a very courteous person.
Being a swindler: You are rendering services too easily.
Being swindled: Will enjoy good fortune.
Swindling other people: Be cautious with friends.
Having a swindler for a partner: You are too much of an idealist.

SWING:
Of a swing: Postponement of success.
Swinging yourself: Be cautious in your love affairs.
Swinging around in circles: A change of plans will prove very successful.
Others swinging: Will receive an important gift.

SWOON:

Of yourself swooning: Will receive valuable things from unknown person.

Another person swooning: Beginning of love.

Relatives swooning: Big quarrels.

Married people swooning: Will become rich and prosperous.

SWORD:

Of a sword: Big honors.

Wearing a sword: Will have a position of public trust.

Being wounded by a sword: Great danger is ahead.

A broken sword: Deep discouragement.

Wounding others with a sword: Good results in your business.

Being wounded with a sword by an acquaintance: Will receive a service.

Blood coming from a sword wound: Will receive a great favor.

Life being endangered by a sword: Big benefits.

Being wounded in the hand by a sword: High honors.

A woman dreaming of wounding someone: Will receive many presents.

A pregnant woman dreaming of wounding someone: Will give birth to a boy.

Hitting an unknown person with a sword: Success in your enterprises.

Being a swordsman: Will be menaced by danger.

Sharpening a sword: Security.

SYRUP:

Of syrup: Will suffer humiliation and shame.

Buying syrup: Beware of thieves.

Making syrup: Beware of enemies.

Putting syrup on food: Business affairs will become very confused.

Putting syrup on children's food: Will make good collections of money.

T

TABLE:

Of a table: Joy.

A mahogany table: Recovery from an illness.

A banquet table: Enjoyment in life.

A table with a marble top: Will have a comfortable life.

A broken table: Misery and poverty.

Breaking a table: Loss of fortune.

An empty table: Will fall into poverty.

Being seated at a table: Happiness.

Sitting at a table with own family: Happy married life.

Friends seated at a table: Accord among friends.

Children seated at a table: Luck and prosperity.

Relatives seated at a table: Change in environment.

Convention people seated at a table: Change for the better.

Marriage guests seated at a table: Happiness is assured.

Sitting at a table with sweetheart: Triumph over enemies.

TABLEAU:

Of a tableau: Approaching money.

A tableau of a naked woman: Will be happy in love.

A tableau hanging on your walls: Joy.

A married man dreaming of a tableau: You are too fond of amusements.

A married woman dreaming of a tableau: She is a frivolous wife.

A widow dreaming of a tableau: Make plans well before getting married.

A young girl dreaming of a tableau: Will marry a rich man.

TABLECLOTH:

Of a tablecloth: Financial gains.

Putting a tablecloth on a table: Abundance.

A white tablecloth: Dignity and distinction.

A colored tablecloth: Advancement within own position.

An embroidered lace tablecloth: Important and very beneficial events to come.

A clean tablecloth on a table: Will live a long life.

A soiled tablecloth on a table: Expect troubles of your own making.

A torn tablecloth: Misfortune in business.

TACKLE:
Of tackles: Financial gains.

A fishing tackle: Discovery of lost valuables.

Buying a fishing tackle: Happiness is assured.

A ship tackle: Will have good earnings.

Others lifting tackles: Important and very beneficial event to come.

A football tackle: Troubles caused by prying into affairs of others.

Securing something with a tackle: Advancement within own position.

TACKS:
Of tacks: Take care of your reputation.

Pounding tacks: Unhappiness.

A carpenter pounding tacks: Business quarrels.

A husband pounding tacks: Your quick speech and sharp wit make you feared.

A wife pounding tacks: She will outrank her rivals.

Buying tacks: Will have a lonely future.

TACTFUL:
Being tactful: Must moderate your passions.

Being tactful with children: Will receive an inheritance.

Other people being tactful: Will incur big losses.

Others being tactful to you: Joy and happiness.

TAFFETA:
Of taffeta: Profit and earnings.

Blue taffeta: Will receive damaged goods in your affairs.

White taffeta: Abundant means.

Red taffeta: Will be wounded in an accident.

A married woman buying taffeta: Will soon be pregnant.

TAIL:
Of a tail: Will be guilty of foolish actions.

A very long tail: Long-lasting comforts in life.

A short tail: Honor and success.

A red tail: Will have good business dealings.

A burned tail: Will suffer adversities.

The tail of a tame animal: Will marry an unsteady person.

The tail of wild animals: Will meet intelligent people.

The tail of a dog: Imminent success.

The long tail of a horse: Will receive assistance from friends.

A horse's tail separated from the horse: Will be abandoned by friends.

The tail of a lady's dress: Will soon have plenty of money.

TAILOR:
Of a tailor: Congenial work and good news.

A male tailor: Exercise caution in business ventures.

A female tailor: Avoid rivals.

A girl dreaming of a tailor: She will marry a man beneath her standing.

Being a tailor: Change of surroundings.

Becoming a tailor: Good times are coming.

Ordering clothes from a tailor: Joy without profit.

TALISMAN:
Of a talisman: A mystery will be solved.

A woman dreaming of a talisman: Beware of danger.

A man dreaming of a talisman: Will be cheated by friends.

A widow dreaming of a talisman: Will marry again.

A woman wearing a talisman: Beware of danger in life.

A young girl wearing a talisman: Walk carefully when crossing streets.

TALK:

Of talking: You are confronted with insurmountable obstacles.

Talking too much: Will be exposed to some malicious plans.

Hearing much talking around you: Be careful of neighbors.

Husband and wife talking very loud: Family difficulties.

Hearing relatives talking to you: Warning of troubles.

Talking to a business partner: An enemy is seeking your ruin.

Talking with friends: Will come out well from a present peril.

Talking to an enemy: Embarrassment.

Talking to mother and father: Will be granted what you asked for.

Talking to a sweetheart: Beware of jealous friends.

Talking to a woman: Good success in your business.

Talking to your superior: Will become a victim and suffer humiliation.

Talking to a dog: Unhappiness.

Talking to a parrot and other animals: Death of a friend.

TALLOW:

Of tallow: Unhappiness.

Making tallow: Will buy new furniture.

Buying tallow: Squandering of money.

Using tallow: Will have an easy life.

TALONS:

Of talons: You are being watched by one with evil intentions.

Being scratched by talons: An enemy will triumph over you.

Being scratched by animal's talons and its running away: Victory over enemies.

Being scratched by bird's talons and its flying away: Enemies will suffer loss.

Others being scratched by talons: A friend is helping you secretly.

TAMBOURINE:

Of a tambourine: Will live a long life.

Playing a tambourine: Should control your spending of money.

A husband playing the tambourine: Inconsistency.

A wife playing the tambourine: She is much in love with her husband.

A sweetheart playing a tambourine: A rival will take your place.

A young girl playing a tambourine: An old man will propose marriage.

Musicians playing a tambourine: Will be cheated by friends.

TANDEM:

Of horses harnessed one in front of another: Beware of rivals.

A man driving horses in tandem fashion: Difficulties in your affairs.

A woman driving horses in tandem manner: Difficulty through jealousy.

Driving a tandem carriage with sweetheart: Frivolity.

Driving two dogs in tandem manner: Will overcome your enemies.

Children driving a tandem bicycle: Will have new interest and surroundings.

Two lovers driving a tandem bicycle: Will quarrel because of jealousy.

TANGERINE:

Of a tangerine tree: Financial gains.

Eating tangerines: Will be saved from an injury.

Buying tangerines: Disappointment in love.

Growing tangerines: Misfortune in love affairs.

Selling tangerines: Will have a true love.

Picking tangerines: Will receive a marriage proposal.

Peeling tangerines: A death will occur in the family.

TANGLE:
Of a tangled skein of wool: Will have to contend with difficult persons.
Becoming tangled up: Patience will be well rewarded.
Being tangled in a business deal: Hard work awaits you.
Others being tangled up: Avoid rivals.

TANK:
A tank filled with wine: Good profits.
A tank filled with oil: Your sins will disappear.

TAP:
Of a tap: Trouble.
Tapping very lightly: Must control your passions.
Of a tap dance: A change in life will soon come.
Of a tap room: Good times are coming.
Drawing beer through a tap: Exercise caution in your business.
Drawing wine from a tap: Danger through a secret.
Tapping telephone wires: Some evil enemy is watching over you.
Of a water tap: Will have a good income.
Tapping a hole to start a screw into wood: Things will run smoothly.

TAPER:
Of a small wax candle: Wisdom and good fortune.
Having a small taper: Approaching money.
Carrying an unlighted taper: It is the only burden you will ever carry.
Carrying a lighted taper: Good fortune will protect your course in life.

TAPESTRY:
Of a tapestry: Big joy.
Making tapestry pictures: Joy without profit.
Painting on tapestry material: Will be deceived by friends.
Admiring tapestry: Abuse of confidence.
Buying tapestry: Enjoyment will come to you.

Decorating with tapestry: Big satisfactions in life.
Burning tapestry: Death of the head of the family.
Being a tapestry decorator: Will receive a visitor.

TAPIOCA:
Of tapioca: Good luck.
Buying tapioca: Happiness is assured.
Cooking tapioca: Good luck in some speculations.
Children eating tapioca: Family distinction.

TAR:
Of tar: Gossip will cause much vexation.
Using tar: Exercise great care in the choice of companions.
Buying tar: Beware of a double cross.
Workers putting a covering of tar on: Will be cheated by friends.

TARGET:
Of a target: Will fully succeed in getting what you desired.
Shooting at a target: Architectural plans need your attention.
Making a bull's-eye on a target: Happiness is assured.
Missing a target completely: Death of an enemy.

TARTAR:
Of tartar: Will receive unpleasant news.
Making tartar sauce: You are prone to being a malicious person.
Using wine to make tartar sauce: Will receive bad news.
Eating tartar sauce: Secret enemies are nearby.

TARTS:
Of a jelly tart: Joy and delight.
Buying a small tart pie: Fortune ahead of you.
Cooking a tart: Approaching money.
Serving tarts to friends: Danger in love matters.
Eating tarts: Sign of mastery over many matters.

Serving tarts to own family: Good times are coming.

Of a woman of loose morals: A false friend is nearby.

Being a woman of loose morals: Will live a long life.

TASSELS:

Of tassels: Cheerful company will visit you.

Fastening tassels on a mantle: Will receive a long-awaited letter.

Others handling tassels: Will receive a gift which will please you.

Tassels on corn: Advancement within own position.

TATTOO:

Hearing a call on drums or fife before taps: A change in life to come.

A tattoo telling military people to go to quarters: Financial gains.

Having your arms tattooed: Will suffer because of jealousy.

Having tattoos on your body: An enemy is seeking your ruin.

Watching someone doing the tattooing: Will be deceived by friends.

TAX:

Of taxes: Will have to endure a great sacrifice.

Filling out a tax return: Will have good earnings.

Paying taxes: Will render a service to a friend.

Being unable to pay taxes: Hard work awaits you.

Receiving a tax refund: Change for the better.

Being a tax collector: Will be proud of yourself.

TAXI:

Of a taxi: Hasty news will be sent to you.

Having a taxi: Beware of jealous friends.

Riding in a taxi: Will have success in your business.

Calling a taxi: New interests and surroundings.

Being in a taxi with another person: Be on guard against false news.

Escaping from the path of an oncoming taxi: Avoid rivals.

TEA:

Of tea: Dignity and distinction.

Buying tea: Will experience many ups and downs soon.

Making tea: Be cautious in your dealings because of an indiscreet act.

Drinking tea: Domestic unhappiness.

Drinking tea with others: Will live a long life.

Drinking tea at a teashop: Financial gains.

Drinking tea at a large party: You are being deceived.

Tea grounds: Will have many social duties.

Tea bags: Will be disappointed in a love affair.

TEACHER:

Of a teacher: Will be invited to a solemn occasion.

Being a teacher: Will have sorrow.

Teaching classes: Must control your passions.

Teaching small children: You have a loyal friend.

Teaching night school: A change in life will soon come.

Being taught: Anger over a small trifling will vex you.

Teaching only men: Danger through a secret.

Teaching only women: Will be cheated by friends.

TEAM:

Of a team of horses: Victory over enemies.

A woman dreaming of driving a team of horses: Domestic happiness.

A businessman dreaming of driving a team of horses: Success for his plans.

A farmer dreaming of driving a team of horses: Good harvest.

Of a team of players: Will change residence.

A team of players winning: High honors.

A team of players losing: Troubles in love.

Being a member of a team: Will have success.

Children being members of a team: Unexpected family reunion.

TEAR:

Of tearing: Will act in bad faith.

Tearing a dress: Gossip by friends.

Tearing cloth: Good results in business.

Tearing papers: Misfortune in love.

Tearing money: Will attain your goals slowly but surely.

Tearing love letters: Will fall in love with someone new.

Tearing valuable documents: Will have a change of mind.

TEARS:

Of tears: Opposition will end with happiness.

Crying: Will receive a gift.

Children shedding tears: Recovery of money due you.

Husband shedding tears: Happiness in marriage.

Sweetheart shedding tears: Will have consolation.

Relatives shedding tears: Will soon experience many ups and downs in affairs.

TEASE:

Of teasing: Secret desires will be discovered.

Teasing others: Will see a naked woman.

Others teasing you: Will be deserted by your wife.

Being teased by a dog: Will have quarrels with enemies.

Teasing a dog: Will have good earnings.

Being teased by friends: Will be offended by enemies.

Being teased by relatives: Will come out ahead of them in the end.

Being teased by sweetheart: You are deeply in love.

Being teased by children: Joy.

TEETH:

Of teeth: Be careful of your health.

White teeth: A wish will be realized.

A gold tooth: Corruption and sorrow.

A tooth of any other metal: Humiliation.

Infected teeth: Must give much explanation to other people.

Having black teeth: Sickness of a relative.

Having dirty teeth: Prosperity.

Not brushing teeth: Faithful friends.

Brushing teeth of children: Will borrow money from relatives.

Teeth moving: Affliction caused by friends.

Having teeth pulled: Financial losses.

Having a wisdom tooth pulled: Death of your father.

Pulling children's teeth: Joy without profit.

Being a dentist who pulls teeth: Will be making money.

Teeth falling out: Death.

Losing teeth in a fight: Loss of a relative.

Losing baby teeth: Death of your mother.

Losing your front teeth: Sickness of children.

Having teeth knocked out: Sudden misfortune.

A tooth growing in: Will receive news of a death.

One tooth being longer than the rest: Affliction from relatives.

Perfectly straight white teeth: Happiness for the rest of your life.

Brushing teeth: Misery.

Having teeth cleaned by a dentist: Will lend money to neighbors.

Having big teeth: You will be very short of money.

Teeth of children: Family quarrels.

Teeth of a loved one: Court action over an inheritance.

Teeth of a friend: Will receive good news from relatives faraway.

TELEGRAM:

Sending a telegram: Will receive news of the loss of a friend.

Receiving a telegram: Will receive unpleasant news.

A friend sending you a telegram: Loss of a friend.

Sending a business telegram: Decline in business.

Receiving a business telegram: Will collect money past due to you.

TELEPHONE:

Of a telephone: Your curiosity will be satisfied.

Making a telephone call: Advantages in business.

Receiving a telephone call: Postponement of a date.

Talking long distance on the telephone: Happiness.

Being without a telephone: Desires will be realized.

TELESCOPE:

Of a telescope: You exaggerate your troubles.

Looking through a telescope: Will have your fortune told.

Others looking through a telescope: Will be embarrassed.

Handling a telescope: Difficulties will be lessened with care.

TEMPER:

Having a temper: You are surrounded by false people.

Losing temper at family: Family happiness.

Losing temper with sweetheart: Trust will be deceived.

Losing temper at children: You have something on your conscience.

Others losing their temper against you: Success in business.

TEMPEST:

Of a tempest: Will suffer humiliation.

A tempest approaching: Affliction.

Being blown about by a tempest: People trick you because of good faith.

Being in a bad rain tempest: All desires will be realized.

A tempest blowing something down on you: Must leave present city.

Being hit on head by falling object during a tempest: Loss of property.

Something falling on own house during a tempest: Will be wounded by accident.

A tempest damaging property of relatives: Will be exiled because of love affair.

Children being in a tempest: Improvement in position.

TEMPLE:

A temple in your own country: Death of a very close friend.

A temple in a foreign country: Unusual experience is coming to you soon.

Going into a temple: Discretion will bring rewards.

Idols in a temple: Will do something unjustified.

TEMPT:

Being tempted: Will encounter obstacles in your path.

Being tempted to wrongdoing: Guard your tongue and use common sense.

Being tempted to commit sin: Difficulties will be surmounted.

Being tempted to leave husband: Will have excellent health.

Being tempted to leave sweetheart: Will meet a charming person.

Being tempted to leave wife: Big advantages in business.

TENDON:

Of tendons: Will have big arguments soon.

Own tendons: Will enjoy very vigorous health.

Tendons of relatives: Family quarrels.

Tendons of animals: Infirmity.

TENOR:

Of a tenor: Will make a new acquaintance.

Hearing tenors singing: Will have advantages in business.

Being a tenor: Will be molested by ruffians.

Hearing a tenor and soprano singing a duet: Big happiness.

Applauding a tenor: Will read good books.

TENT:
Of a tent: Will take pleasure in helping others in love affairs.
Living in a tent with family: Will undergo great changes in life.
Living in a tent with sweetheart: Arguments over love.
Living in a tent with friends on camping trip: Visitor from faraway.
Children camping in a tent: You have very good and youthful friends.
A military camp of tents: Will take a very tiresome trip.

TERM:
Of a term of office: Misfortune and worries ahead.
Getting a new term of office: Advantages in affairs.
Legal terms: Worries ahead.
Medical terms: Will receive news of illness of distant relative.

TERN:
Of this gull-like bird: Will receive unexpected good news.
Terns flying over the ocean: Visit from someone from faraway.
The quacking of a tern: Fortune.
Terns flying over land: Newly marrieds will be intelligent and faithful.
A nest of terns: Fortune and blessings on house where nest is made.
Killing a tern: Misfortune.
A tern coming into a house or a ship: Will receive news from friends.

TERRACE:
Being on a terrace alone: Will rise to a worldly position.
Being on a terrace with others: Will live a long life.
Being on a terrace with relatives: Will receive an inheritance.
Being on a terrace with prominent officials: Will be master of affairs.
Being on a terrace with children: Will have many ups and downs.
Being on a terrace with friends: Will suffer humiliation.

TERRIER:
Of a terrier: Social activities of a happy nature.

A terrier barking: Beware of quarrels.
A terrier sleeping: Avoid rivals.
A terrier biting a friend of yours: Double cross from someone you trust.
A terrier playing with children: Will have good earnings in the future.

TERRITORY:
Of a large territory: Will receive a letter from a loved one.
Being in a territory: Beware of enemies.
A state becoming a territory: Will have good business.
Going to a foreign territory: Sickness.

TERROR:
Being in terror: Secret enmity of some person for you.
A terrorist using violence against you: Death of an enemy.
A political party causing terror: Joy without profit.
Children causing terror: Good times are coming.

TEST:
A doctor making a test on you: A mystery will be solved.
Testing your ability: Discovery of lost valuables.
Testing faithfulness of mate: Avoid rivals.
Others testing you: Will have sorrow.

TESTAMENT:
Reading a testament: Changes in your environment.
Reading chapters of the Bible: Accord among friends.
Consulting the New Testament: Financial gains.
The disposition of property after a death: Abundant means.

TESTICLE:
Testicles being injured: Triumph over enemies.
Being deprived of masculine vigor: Society will get along much better.
A person being castrated: Will give a large dinner party.

Castrating an animal: Will have mastery over many matters.

TESTIFY:
Testifying under oath: Important and very beneficial events to come.
Testifying on own behalf: Good times are coming.
Testifying in favor of others: Will come out well from a present peril.
Testifying against others: Be cautious in all your dealings.

TESTIMONY:
Giving a testimony: People will honor you.
Receiving a testimony: Triumph over your enemies.
Others' testimony establishing some facts: Dignity and distinction.
Giving a testimony for a friend: Approaching money.

TETE-A-TETE:
Of a tête-à-tête: A false friend is nearby.
Having an important tête-à-tête with high-class person: Good luck.
Having a tête-à-tête dinner: Suitable time to pursue courtship.
Having a tête-à-tête with a loved one: Change of surroundings.

THANKFUL:
Of expressing thankfulness: Will lead a quiet and happy life.
Being thankful: Will be persecuted.
Others being thankful to you: Awaiting good news.
Children being thankful: Prosperity.

THANKSGIVING:
Of Thanksgiving Day: Will have good health.
Entire family being together on Thanksgiving: Big joy ahead.
Being alone on Thanksgiving: Will have blessings from God.
Spending Thanksgiving with others not of family: Contentment of heart.

THAW:
Of something thawing: Will suffer unforeseen trouble.
Being with others during a thaw:

Former adversary will become a friend.
Frozen food melting: Danger through a secret.
Ice thawing: Will be cheated by friends.

THEATER:
Of a theater: Good results in personal affairs.
Attending a theater alone: Will have pleasant new friends.
Watching a theater performance with family: Double cross of those trusted.
Taking children to a theater: Be cautious in discussing plans.
Going to a theater with sweetheart: Prosperity in everything.
Going to a theater with a large group: Will lose money.

THEFT:
Of a theft: Will incur big damages.
Being robbed: An early marriage.
Committing a theft: Loss of money on business ventures.
Stealing clothing: Loss of friends.
Stealing food: Will suffer a financial loss.
Stealing money: Hard days ahead.

THERMOMETER:
Of a thermometer: Gossip is damaging your reputation.
Taking a temperature with a thermometer: Will have a changeable life.
Buying a thermometer: Will make many trips.
Taking children's temperature with thermometer: Will be humiliated.
A thermometer registering fair weather: Good change in position.
A thermometer registering stormy weather: Financial losses.

THIEF:
Of thieves: Security in financial affairs.
A thief entering your house: Unusually good business ahead.
Catching a thief: Will be reimbursed for damages sustained in business.

Being robbed by thieves: Loss of money.

Thieves robbing others: You are too skeptical.

Killing a thief: Will have misfortune.

Arresting a thief: Death of a friend.

THIMBLE:

Of a thimble: Much happiness ahead.

Buying a thimble: Will be unable to secure employment.

A woman dreaming of a thimble: Will earn her own living.

Having a thimble on when sewing: Fortune coming soon.

Losing a thimble: Will have many troubles.

Borrowing a thimble: Many friends will make your life happy.

THIN:

Being thin: Will enjoy big earnings.

A woman dreaming of getting thin: Happy love affairs.

A girl dreaming of becoming thin: Will cry over a lost lover.

Reducing to become thin: Unexpected riches.

Suffering in order to become thin: Will receive a marriage proposal.

A man dreaming of becoming thin: Good business transactions.

THIRST:

Being thirsty: Unhappiness.

Having a very great thirst: Big catastrophe ahead.

Drinking until thirst is satisfied: Riches and contentment.

Satisfying your thirst: Will overcome troubles.

Being unable to satisfy thirst: Will not realize desires.

Children being thirsty: Children's high ambitions will be realized.

Drinking cloudy water to satisfy thirst: Will be afflicted.

Drinking hot water to satisfy thirst: Will be corrupted.

THISTLE:

Of thistles: Good news.

Pulling thistles: Will be visited by a friend.

Family pulling thistles: Small earnings.

Relatives pulling thistles out: Quarrels can be avoided with tact.

THORN:

Of thorns: Will enjoy much contentment.

Being pricked by a thorn: Warning of trouble.

Children being pricked by a thorn: Change of surroundings.

Being irritated by a thorn: Change for the better.

Having thorns on your body: Sickness.

THRASH:

Of thrashing: Will have many enemies.

Being thrashed: Good times are ahead.

Thrashing someone else: A mystery will be solved.

Being thrashed by friends: Things will go wrong in love affairs.

Beating out a fire: Will have hard times ahead.

Beating copper or lead: Will have good days ahead.

Thrashing corn: You confide in other people too much.

THREAD:

Of thread: Advancement within own position.

Gold thread: Happiness is assured.

Silver thread: Will avoid a danger.

Brass thread: Will be introduced to artists.

Steel thread: Will have to fight with opposition.

Silk thread: Big joy.

Cotton thread: Good times are coming.

Wool thread: Will come out well from a present peril.

Broken threads: Faithless friends will cause losses for you.

Winding thread: Wealth gained by thrifty ways.

Unraveling knotted thread: A mystery will be solved.

Wasting thread: Discovery of a secret.

THROAT:

Of own throat: Your hopes will be realized.

Having trouble with your throat: Financial gains.
Cutting your throat: Will have trouble caused by others.
Cutting the throat of someone else: Approaching danger.
Children's throat: Danger in love matters.

THRONE:
Of a throne: Loss of valued friends.
Being on a throne: Abundant means.
An empty throne: Warning of trouble.
A King or Pope on a throne: Big catastrophe ahead for you.
Sitting on a throne: Rapid rise to prominence.
Descending from a throne: Disappointment will be yours.

THUMB:
Of own thumb: Good times are coming.
Injuring your thumb: Expect business losses.
Burning your thumb: Envious friends surround you.
Cutting your thumb: Prevent so much spending of money.

THUNDER:
Of a thunderstorm: Will have financial troubles.
Rich people dreaming of thunder: Affliction.
Poor people dreaming of thunder: Repose.
Hearing crashes of thunder: Imminent perils.
Lightning following thunder: Death of a friend.
Being hit by lightning following thunder: A woman who is overly sexual.

THYME:
Of thyme: Approaching money.
Using thyme in seasoning: Happiness in love affairs.
Buying thyme: Abundant means.
Thyme growing: Family happiness.

TIARA:
Of a tiara: Social activities of a happy nature.

Wearing a tiara: Happiness is assured.
A girl wearing a tiara: Her ambition is beyond her reach.
A queen wearing a tiara at her coronation: Abundant means.

TICKET:
Of tickets: Good times are ahead.
Having a lottery ticket: Good results ahead.
Tickets with numbers on them: Will be a very successful person.
Having a ticket that did not win: Will receive long-expected good news.

TICKLE:
Of tickling: A misunderstanding will be cleared up.
Own nose tickling: Will be asked to lend money.
Own throat tickling: Good times are coming.
Being tickled by someone: Financial gains.
Tickling others: Will have a long illness.

TIDE:
The tide flowing in: Favorable events will soon happen.
The tide going out: Death of an enemy.
A very high tide: Change in environment.
A very low tide: Misfortune in love affairs.

TIE:
Having ties: Will have a sore throat.
Selling ties: Someone will have to take care of your business.
Wearing a tie: Luxury and grandeur.
Tying a tie: Will recover from rheumatism.
Taking off a tie: Loss of employment.
Having many ties: Unexpected fortune will come to you.

TIGER:
Of a tiger: Enemies will beset your path.
Watching a tiger: Family fortune.
A tiger running: Serious illness.

Killing a tiger: Beware of jealous friends.

A tiger dying when delivering babies: Will receive money.

A tiger performing at a circus: Will have helpful friends.

Being surprised by a tiger: Will suffer great embarrassment.

Having a small tiger as a pet: Will receive a marriage proposal.

A tiger in a cage at the zoo: Death of a prominent person.

Hearing a tiger roaring: Will suffer grief.

A tiger being tied with a chain: Will be surprised by an enemy.

A tiger eating: Will have much wealth.

TILE:
Of tiles: Attempt to increase your earnings.

Handling tiles: Be careful to avoid an accident.

Many tiles: Good business profits.

Tiles breaking: Troubles ahead for you.

Tiles falling from a roof: Death of an enemy.

TILL:
Of a till: Approaching money.

A shop till filled with money: Will have dealings with wealthy businessman.

An empty till: You have disobedient help.

A woman dreaming of taking money from a till: Will marry a rich man.

A man dreaming of taking money from a till: Will fall in love with beautiful woman.

TIMBER:
Of timber: Unhappiness.

Huge piles of timber: Will be a servant under someone.

Piles of timber falling: Will have a long engagement.

Cutting down timber: Will hear unpleasant news.

A young girl dreaming of timber: Short engagement ending in happy marriage.

Unmarried woman dreaming of old timber: Will not be engaged or married.

TIN:
Of tin: People are talking behind your back.

Shining tin objects: Will accept untrue friends as good friends.

Buying tin: Will raise your own financial position.

Selling tin: Test friends before trusting them.

Working with tin: Don't lend money too freely.

Owning a lot of tin: You have a very high character.

TINKER:
Of a tinker: Do not meddle in affairs of friends.

A tinker mending kettles and pans: Big joy.

Working as a tinker: Misfortune in love affairs.

A tinker being unable to mend something: Will have a vigorous mind.

TIPS:
Giving tips: Someone is attempting to bribe you.

Receiving a tip: Someone is attempting to bring harm to you.

Giving a tip secretly: Will soon receive announcement of a marriage.

Making a living on tips: Will not be able to have children.

Dividing tips among people: Will have a fortune achieved dishonestly.

TIPTOE:
Of tiptoeing: Contentment and happiness.

Children tiptoeing: Unexpected happenings for separated lovers.

Others tiptoeing: Be sure to mend your quarrels before nightfall.

Many people tiptoeing: Will meet people who do not have high morals.

TIRED:
Being tired: Will receive a big favor from someone.

Husband being tired: Poverty.

Wife being tired: Inheritance.

Children being tired: A mystery will soon be solved.

Employees being tired: You care more for amusements than work.

Friends being tired: Quarrels in the family.

TITLE:

Of titles: Don't let people disturb your thoughts.

Receiving a title: Gossip by neighbors.

Renouncing a title: Loss of prestige.

Carrying on a family title: Important and happy events within family.

TOAD:

Of toads: Loss and difficulties.

Catching toads: A self-inflicted injury will come.

Killing toads: A false friend is nearby.

Toads hopping away: Hard work may solve your situation.

Stepping on a toad: Friends will desert you when needed most.

Hearing croaking of toads: Pleasure awaits.

TOAST:

Making a toast during a meal: Good humor.

Hearing others making a toast: Will be free of embarrassment.

Answering a toast made at a banquet: You are near to losing a loved one.

Toasting white bread: Work and happiness.

Toasting dark bread: Riches.

Eating toast: Will make a big profit.

Serving toast to others: Losses and unhappiness.

TOBACCO:

Of tobacco: Plan and save for your old age.

A tobacco shop: Big gossip behind your back.

Smoking a cigarette: You are squandering money.

Women dreaming of smoking cigarettes: Troubles will soon vanish.

Smoking cigars: Will attend a big party.

Leaves of tobacco: Failure in love but success in business.

Rolling cigarettes: Will never have to worry about money.

Putting tobacco in the nose: You are very irritable.

Buying tobacco: Will suffer grief.

Selling tobacco: Will meet someone very interesting.

A tobacco pouch: You are squandering your money.

TOBOGGAN:

Of a toboggan: Be careful of your every step.

Having a toboggan: An enemy is seeking your ruin.

Coasting downhill on a toboggan: Will come out well from a present peril.

Others riding on a toboggan: Death of an enemy.

TOILET:

Of a toilet: Timidness will cause hurt.

Going to the toilet: Will enjoy a happy retirement.

Fixing hair or face in a toilet: Big peril ahead.

Sitting in a toilet: You are desirous of making advances to someone.

TOLERANT:

Being tolerant: Will lead an easy life.

Being tolerant with children: Pleasant events coming.

Being tolerant with employees: Will receive disfavors.

Others being tolerant of you: Will be loved by a wonderful person.

TOMATO:

Of tomatoes: Your love will last forever.

Eating tomatoes: Will have comfortable circumstances through own efforts.

Picking tomatoes: Peace and happiness in the home.

Children eating tomatoes: Return of good health.

Relatives eating tomatoes: Joy.

A married woman dreaming of eating tomatoes: Uncertainty of pregnancy.

Unmarried woman dreaming of eating tomatoes: Will achieve all desires.

Growing tomatoes: Big fortune.

Rotten tomatoes: Beware of approaching danger.

Splitting open a tomato: Persecution by a woman of ill fame.

Half-mature tomatoes on the vines: Persecution.

Making a tomato salad: Good news and contentment.

Picking a bunch of green tomatoes: Prosperity and happiness.

Making a tomato sauce: Poverty.

TOMB:

Of a tomb: Will have a long life.

Walking among tombs: Marriage.

Ordering own casket: Will be married soon.

Tombs falling into ruins: Sickness and trouble for the family.

Viewing tombs with another person: Will find suitable business partner.

Viewing tombs of prominent people: Advancement to honor and wealth.

Being put into a tomb: Inheritance.

Building a tomb: Loss of friends.

The tombs at a church or convent: Pleasant family events.

TONGS:

Of tongs: Will have a big quarrel.

Using tongs: An enemy is seeking your ruin.

Buying tongs: Misfortune in own affairs.

Enemies using tongs: Warning of troubles.

TONGUE:

Of a tongue: Will become a victim of indiscreet actions.

A woman dreaming of a large tongue: Honor and modesty.

A man dreaming of a large tongue: Will be able to discipline oneself with reason.

A dirty tongue: Will avoid a sickness.

An extra-long tongue: You must cure your nervous condition.

Burning the tongue: Troubles ahead of you.

Biting the tongue: You are a romantic person.

Children showing their tongue: They will be very intelligent.

Wagging tongues: You cannot tell when people are speaking truthfully.

TOOL:

Having many tools: Wealth.

Carrying tools: Will serve under others.

Receiving tools as a gift: Pleasant things will be done for you.

Buying tools: Many good changes to come.

Selling tools at a good price: Will collect money.

Selling farm tools: Will have a love affair.

Having machinist's tools: Will receive a gift.

Having carpenter's tools: Will receive a proposition from a woman.

Having fishing tools: Will incur loss in business.

Having silver tools: Will live a long and comfortable life.

TOOTHACHE:

Having a toothache: Will receive good news from faraway.

Children having a toothache: Happiness over letter from an old friend.

Having a persisting toothache: Fortune in the future.

Going to a dentist to cure toothache: You have no idea what love means.

Receiving relief from a toothache: Love quarrels.

TOOTHPICK:

Of toothpicks: Careless actions will cause damages.

Picking teeth with a toothpick: Will receive financial damages.

Buying toothpicks: An enemy is watching your actions.

Throwing toothpicks away: Will lead a sanitary life.

Others using toothpicks: Will have indecent people nearby.

TORCH:

Of a torch: Will be blessed with reasoning.
A lighted torch: Troubles will vanish quickly.
Lighting a torch: Will find a way out of your troubles.
An obscure torch: Love affairs will be realized.
Women holding torches: Will fall in love.
Enemies holding torches: Honor and distinction.
Holding a love torch for someone: Will fall back into sin again.
Holding a torch for a married woman: Sickness.
Holding a torch for an unmarried person: Hopes will be realized.
Holding a torch for a beautiful woman: Good and significant events to come.
An obscure torch: Love affairs will be realized.
Holding a torch at a public place: Joy and honor.
Holding a torch that has gone out: Delays in business affairs.
Holding a flaming torch: A secret will be revealed to you.
Others holding several lighted torches in hands: Discovery of wrongdoings.

TORNADO:

Of a tornado: Warning of disaster in home and business.
A furious tornado: Loss of friends.
A mild tornado: Will have disaster in own affairs.
Damages caused by a tornado: Honesty will bring victory for you.
Others' property being damaged by a tornado: Beware of actions of friends.

TORPEDO:

Of a torpedo: Riches and joy.
Handling a torpedo: Love at first sight.
Firing a torpedo: Changes in your life.
A torpedo exploding: You are surrounded by envious people.
A torpedo hitting a target: Will have joy with children.

TORRENT:

Of a torrent: Adversity.
Watching a torrent with others: Do not rush things too much.
Walking beside a torrent: Desires will be realized after a short delay.
Crossing a torrent: Will accomplish your aims.
Falling into a torrent: Achieving power is not the most important thing.
Swimming to save yourself from a torrent: Dangers ahead for you.
Others saving themselves from a torrent: Double cross by a friend.

TORTOISE:

Of a tortoise: Success and long life.
Watching a tortoise: Luck and prosperity.
Buying a tortoise: Some new person will fall in love with you.
Killing a tortoise: Good times are coming.

TORTURE:

Torturing yourself: You kill your love with your own mind.
Being tortured: Domestic hardships.
Torturing other people: Unhappiness in love.
Torturing animals: Big money losses.
Lovers torturing each other: You are unreasonable.

TOURNAMENT:

Of a tournament: Excellent news.
Being in a tournament: Joy and happiness.
Winning a tournament: Will receive mysterious news.
Losing a tournament: Will take a long trip very soon.
Others being in a tournament: Diligence will be recompensed.

TOWEL:

Of a towel: Will undergo a brief illness.
Using towels to wipe hands: Approaching money.
Using towels to dry face: Happiness in love.

Others using a towel: Recovery from an illness very soon.

Children using a towel: Will accomplish your aims.

Having guest towels in the bathroom: Beware of double cross by friends.

TOWER:

Of a tower: Long-lasting happiness.

A very high tower: Will have a long life and a pleasant old age.

Going up into a tower: Freedom from embarrassment but loss of money.

Coming down from a tower: Your wishes will not all be realized.

Others being on a tower: Much affliction.

The tower of a fortress: Will resist your enemies.

A gun salute being fired from a tower: Will be cheated.

Soldiers putting gunpowder in a gun when in a tower: Financial gains.

TOWN:

Of a town: You have a very honest heart.

Being in a town: Danger of loss of money.

A farmer dreaming of being in a big town: Warning against bad ambitions.

A townsman going to a big city: Increase in business and gains.

A woman going from a town to a big city: Employer is dissatisfied with you.

Coming from a big city to a small town: Riches and fortune.

TOYS:

Of toys: Will have a happy family.

Giving toys to children: Good times are coming.

Buying toys: Children will be clever and successful.

Receiving toys for your children: You have loyal friends.

Broken toys: Approaching illness.

TRAFFIC:

Of traffic: Public dignity and many friends are in store for you.

Being in traffic: Good days ahead.

Being held up by stopped traffic: Infidelity.

An accident in traffic: Loss of money.

Others being hurt in a traffic accident: Will undergo persecution.

Being stopped by a traffic officer: You enjoy an active life.

TRAIL:

Trailing behind someone: You are prone to being too arrogant.

Being trailed: Will have a guilty conscience.

Being trailed by a mate: Arrival of a friend.

Being trailed by a sweetheart: Success in love.

Being trailed by an investigator: Your good faith is in doubt.

TRAIN:

Of a train: Will take care of business with speed.

A mail train: Will enjoy very good business.

A cargo train: Will meet a pleasant person.

Traveling on a train alone: A lawsuit will be ruled in your favor.

Traveling on a train with the family: Advantages in life.

Traveling on a train with friends: Financial gains.

Having a long train on a dress: Unhappiness.

Someone stepping on the train of your dress: Will have a new love affair.

TRAMP:

Of a tramp: Good times are coming.

Being a tramp: An absent friend is thinking of you.

A tramp begging: A letter from a friend is on the way to you.

Tramping your feet on the floor: Change for the better.

Owning a tramp vessel: Abundant means.

TRANSFUSION:

Of a transfusion: Will expedite business very well.

Giving blood for a transfusion: Will have a dangerous sickness.

A sick man receiving a transfusion: Shame for actions.

Giving a transfusion to an animal: Family arguments.

Having a transfusion from a blood bank: Accomplishment of desires.

Spilling blood during a transfusion: Will have many headaches.

TRAP DOOR:
Of a trap door: Will receive a surprising and unpleasant letter.

A closed trap door: Reconciliation in love.

Going through a trap door: Beware of enemies.

Others going through a trap door: Joy and good results in business.

TRAVEL:
Of traveling: Difficulties in business ventures.

Traveling alone: Will avoid unpleasant events.

Traveling with your family: Will avoid unhappiness.

Traveling with loved one: Delays in personal matters.

Traveling with friends: Someone is cheating you.

Traveling with business associates: Disappointments in all affairs.

Traveling with others: Quarrels among friends.

Traveling on a train: Think before you act.

Traveling in a carriage: Will enjoy large fortune.

Traveling in a car: Happiness and family love.

Traveling on a horse: Will have dealings with obstinate people.

Traveling on foot: Hard work is ahead for you.

Traveling to foreign countries: Consider results before acting.

Traveling from your own town to another: Small success.

Traveling from another town to your own: Success depends upon hard work.

Traveling with firearms: Will soon find a wife.

Traveling with a sword at your side: Will soon get married.

TREACLE:
Of a cure for poisoning: Will hear pleasant words that you will remember.

Taking treacle: Will live a long life.

Making treacle from molasses: Joy.

Buying treacle: Recovery from an illness.

TREASURE:
Finding a treasure: You are unsettled in your affairs.

Finding a hidden treasure: Danger.

Digging for a treasure: Disgrace.

Finding a treasure chest: Inheritance.

Of a treasurer: Will receive money from relatives.

Going to the treasury: Big headaches ahead for you.

Stealing a treasure: Beware of double cross from those you now trust.

Having treasured children: You have good friends.

Having a treasured sweetheart: Will leave home of father and mother.

TREAT:
Treating someone: Wealth.

Treating guests nicely: Will be dealing with gangsters.

Treating family to a meal: Big joy.

Treating unfriendly people to a dinner: Will have fortune in business.

Treating relatives to refreshments: Someone will be unfaithful to you.

Being treated to a dinner by others: Security in business.

Being treated to a dinner by friends: Financial affairs will prosper.

Being treated to a dinner by influential people: Attain a high position.

TREES:
Of trees: Will receive favors from friends with good intentions.

Unhealthy trees: Family quarrels.

Leaves turning yellow on trees: Illness to come soon.

Tiny sapling trees: Poverty.

Cutting down trees: Will incur losses.

Trees burning: Nuisance and unhappiness.

Climbing a tree: Will have new employment.

Climbing a fruit tree: Dignity and good news.

Children climbing a tree: Sickness.

Climbing a tree with a ladder: Will attain important high position.

Resting under a tree: Will be assisted by influential friends.

Sleeping under a tree: Will be abandoned.

Falling out of a tree: Loss of employment.

A green tree: Unbounding joy will make you forget all sadness.

A barren tree: Someone is cheating you.

Cutting down a dead tree: Misfortune.

A tree without blossoms: Business will be increased.

A crooked tree: You have many enemies.

Cutting up a tree in a building: Prosperity.

Cutting down trees in someone else's garden: Will overcome enemies.

Finding a fallen tree in the road: Misfortune.

Heavily ladened fruit trees: Riches and fortune in business.

Blossoming trees: Joy and sweet satisfaction.

Fruit trees without fruit: Happy life.

Small fruit trees: Big satisfaction.

Big trees without fruit: Honors.

Fertilizing fruit trees: Will maintain good strength.

Picking fruit from a tree: Inheritance received from elderly people.

Tall straight pine trees: Will receive good news.

A Christmas tree: Joy and happiness.

The mast of a ship made from a tree: Will get assistance in time of need.

Escaping from a forest fire: Will have an unusual accident.

Apple trees: Will hear unpleasant news.

Lemon trees: Will receive great things.

Fig tree: Will take a trip.

Nut trees: Riches.

Olive tree: Peace and happiness in all desires.

Peach trees: Will have fights because of opposition in ideas.

Orange trees: Passing discontent.

Prune trees: Will be happily surprised by a visitor.

Cherry trees: Sickness.

Pomegranate trees: Will enjoy a quiet future.

Pear trees: Opposition in love affairs.

Poplar trees: Will enjoy a large harvest and good fortune.

TRELLIS:

Of a trellis: You will come out well from a present peril.

Having a trellis: A firm friendship will be the foundation of success.

Being on a trellis: Good times are coming.

Having a trellis at your summer house: Abundant means.

TRENCH:

Of a trench filled with soldiers: Will be astonished and surprised.

Being in a trench: Hopes for new employment.

Fighting in a trench: An evil influence is near you.

Others fighting in a trench: Infidelity.

Soldiers being killed in a trench: Beware of being trapped.

Own sons fighting in a trench: Will receive a fortune in time.

Of a trenchcoat: You are squandering money.

Wearing a trenchcoat: Will fight with a tempermental person.

Others wearing trenchcoats: Will be jilted by friends.

TRESPASS:

Of a No Trespassing sign: Prosperity is coming soon.

Being forbidden to trespass a premise: Attraction for a married person.

Being caught trespassing: Infidelity.

Others trespassing on your property: Will have an unpleasant future.

Friends trespassing on your property: Pleasant business dealings.

Enemies trespassing on your property: Inevitable damages to come.

Animals trespassing on property: Serious illness.

TRIAL:

Of a trial: Will witness an injustice done to someone.

Being at a trial: You have an admirer who merits your attention.

Being on trial: Will enjoy lifelong security.

Being unjustly accused at a trial: You are enjoying much passion.

Being accused by an officer at a trial: Honor and profit.

Being tried on a business matter: Success and good results.

Being on trial for wrongdoings against a woman: Will receive bad news.

Being on trial for wrongdoings against a man: Hard days ahead.

Friends being on trial: Will receive good news.

Enemies being on trial: Avoid rivals.

Relatives being on trial: Family quarrels.

TRIANGLE:

Of a triangle: Will receive a fortune in the near future.

Drawing a triangle: Will discover a secret.

A loved one drawing a triangle: You have false friends.

Other people drawing a triangle: Will have to choose between two lovers.

A laborer cutting out a triangle: Happiness will follow suffering.

Children figuring geometry triangles: Triumph over enemies.

TRIDENT:

Of a three-pronged spear: Good results in business.

A statue holding a trident: You are loved by several people.

Spearing fish with a trident: Respect and honor.

Gathering hay with a trident: Will have ups and downs in business.

An unmarried girl dreaming of a trident: Sincerely loved by a sailor.

TRIGGER:

Pulling the trigger of a firearm: Great unhappiness in the family.

A married woman dreaming of pulling a trigger: Dishonor in love affairs.

An unmarried person dreaming of pulling a trigger: Will soon be married.

Teen-agers pulling a trigger: Will receive compliments on their abilities.

Pulling a trigger against an enemy: Will be greatly criticized.

Others pulling a trigger on you: Will soon receive an advancement.

TRINKET:

Of trinkets: Your loved one is vain and fickle.

Having trinkets: Will be guilty of foolish actions.

Buying a trinket: Don't wear your heart upon your sleeve.

Others wearing a trinket: Will be cheated by friends.

TRIPE:

Of uncooked tripe: Modesty.

Cooked tripe: Will lead a simple life.

Buying tripe: Will enjoy good health.

Eating tripe: Will be complimented by sincere friends.

A dog eating tripe: Inheritance.

Serving tripe at a dinner: A business rival wants your position.

Tripe going bad: Be careful of business.

TRIPLETS:

Having triplets: Pleasures will follow pain.

Having triplets of same sex: Enemies are conspiring against you.

Having triplets of different sex: Dignity and happiness.

A woman dreaming of having triplets: Will be invited to a party.

A man dreaming of wife having triplets: Beware of unjustified gossip.

An unmarried woman dreaming of having triplets: Will soon be engaged.

TROUBLE:

Of trouble: Change of residence.

Being in trouble: Success and honor.
A married person being in trouble: Disaster ahead for you.
A single person being in trouble: Shame and sorrow.
A girl being in trouble: Will have many sweethearts.
A lover being in trouble: Failure in love.
A widow being in trouble: She will be pregnant.
Facing trouble: Will have success.
Avoiding trouble: Troubles will come to you.

TROUSERS:

Of trousers: You are prone to talking too much without meaning it.
Wearing trousers: Important honors and riches.
Taking off trousers: A woman will be faithful to you.
Putting on trousers: Increase within the family.
Having a hole in your trousers: Flirtation with a married woman.
A single girl dreaming of a man's trousers: Will have quarrels.
Trousers being dirty with mud: Hard times ahead.
A laborer's dirty trousers: Better days will come in the future.
Wearing tight trousers to a masquerade: Do not lend any money.

TROUT:

Of trout: Your troubles will be over.
Eating trout: Constant fortune.
Cooking trout: Will quarrel with relatives.
Catching trout: Will receive plenty of money.
Buying trout: Change for the better.
Trout at a fish market: Advancement within own position.
Others catching trout: Misfortune in love affairs.

TRUMPET:

Of a trumpet: Passion.
Hearing a trumpet: Will receive a surprise.

Playing a trumpet: People are curious about your affairs.
Others playing a trumpet: Imminent danger.
A musician playing a trumpet: Will receive bad news.
Children playing a trumpet: Will be very fortunate in the future.
Soldiers playing a trumpet: Bad news ahead.
A large trumpet: Pleasant activities in the near future.

TRUNCHEON:

Of a stick with branches broken off: Will discover a thief.
Using a truncheon: Will collect money.
A truncheon bracing something: Sadness.
Others handling a truncheon: Warning of thieves.

TRUNK:

Of an empty trunk: Will soon take a trip.
A full trunk: Plans for a trip have been canceled.
Many full trunks: Beware of gossip.
Taking a trunk on a trip: A wish will be realized.
A relative's trunk: A traveler will return from abroad.

TRUTH:

Telling the truth: Listen to the advice of friends.
People not telling you the truth: Your conscience is not clear.
Mates not telling each other the truth: A friend will go to prison.
Telling the truth to your children: Good fortune.
Teaching children to tell the truth: Joy.

TRYST:

Of a tryst: A reconciliation will end romantically.
Waiting at an appointed place: Misfortune in love affairs.
Waiting in a hunting ambush: Change of surroundings.
Others waiting at an appointed place: Will have sorrow.

TUB:
Of a tub: Prosperity.
A tub full of water: Happiness in married life if moderation is used.
A young girl dreaming of a tub full of water: Will soon receive a proposal.
An empty tub: Hard times are ahead.
Being in a tub: Prosperity and unhappiness.
Others being in a tub: Illness to come soon.
A tub full of wine: Prosperity.
Bringing a tub into the house: Will receive mysterious news.
Children being in a tub: You are doing extravagant things.
Husband being in a tub: Will have permanent happiness.

TUBE:
Of tubes: Prosperity.
A pile of many big tubes: Prosperity according to the amount of tubes.
Buying tubes: Will be cheated in love affairs.
Selling tubes: Grab your fortune before it passes.
A tube filled with water: Will meet someone and have an argument.
Fixing and putting tubes in place: Will have a good reputation.

TUG:
Of a tug: Business prosperity.
Riding in a tug: A mystery will be explained.
A tug pulling a barge: Dignity in society.
A tug pulling a ship: Will receive unexpected money.
A tug helping a ship in distress: Prosperity.
The crew of a tug: Satisfaction.
Hearing the whistle of a tug: You are doing something wrong.

TULIP:
Of tulips: Big joy.
Growing tulips: Happiness.
Holding tulips: Good luck.
Picking tulips: You are a good lover or sweetheart.
Gathering tulips: Will have a proposal of marriage.

Having tulips in your home: Happy news.
Receiving tulips as a gift: You have the friendship of many persons.
Giving tulips as a gift: Good times are coming.
A young girl dreaming of tulips: A short engagement will come up.
A widow dreaming of tulips: Will make a secret marriage.

TUMBLER:
Of a tumbler: Accord among friends.
Having a tumbler: Change for the better.
Drinking from a tumbler: Will have a vigorous mind.
Buying a set of tumblers: Good luck ahead of you.

TUMOR:
Of a tumor: Will be bothered by annoyances.
Having a tumor on the waist: Unhappiness caused by an inheritance.
Having a tumor on the neck: Take advantage of good luck when it comes.
Having a tumor in the throat: Victories in business transactions.
Others having tumors: Will meet the beautiful wife of a friend.
Children having tumors on the neck: Family unhappiness.

TUNNEL:
Of a tunnel: Happiness.
Going through a tunnel: A secret will be revealed.
Escaping injury in a tunnel: Business satisfaction.
Driving a car through a tunnel: Unsatisfactory business undertakings.
Going through a tunnel on a train: You have many false friends.
A tunnel being built: Many business transactions.

TURKEY:
Visiting the country of Turkey: Loss of all possessions.
Being a Turk: Beautiful women will seek after you.
The people of Turkey: Will be subjected to the will of others.

Of a turkey: Abundant harvest for the farmer.
Killing a turkey: Infidelity.
Buying turkeys: Can expect something good to come to you.
Eating turkey: Great joy.
Plucking a turkey: Will have a nervous breakdown.
Roasting a turkey: Troubles with friends.
Carving a turkey: Quarrels with business partners.
Making turkey sandwiches: Will be visited by hungry people.

TURNIPS:
Of turnips: Disappointment and vexation.
Growing turnips: Poor health.
Eating turnips: Your prospects will be very successful.
Buying turnips: You have no foundation for your hopes.
Cooking turnips: Improvement of own health.

TURTLE:
Of turtles: Opportunity for advancement will come to you.
Buying turtles: Joy without profit.
Cooking turtles: Wealth and influence.
Catching a sea turtle: A mystery will be solved.
Eating a sea turtle: You have secret enemies.
Drinking bouillon made from sea turtle: Long life and success.

TWINE:
Of twine: Avoid flirtations.
Buying twine: Suitable time to pursue your courtship.
Wrapping something with twine: You will be guilty of foolish actions.
Saving old twine: Will have an argument with a friend over small matters.
Having very thick twine: Will suffer tears because of a love affair.

TWINS:
Having twins: Happiness in the family.
A woman dreaming of having twins: Avoid rivals.
A man dreaming of wife having twins: Change of surroundings.
Having twins of the same sex: Will live a long life.
Having twins of a different sex: Dignity and distinction.
An unmarried woman dreaming of having twins: Will soon be engaged.
Having twin horses: Will come out well from a present peril.

TYRANT:
Being a tyrant: Will receive unpleasant news.
A tyrant being killed: Accomplishment of desires.
A tyrant being dismissed from office: Happiness.
Committing tyranny to others: Will win a contest.

U

UGLY:
Being ugly: Will live a long life.
Others who are ugly: Will be cheated by friends.
Children being ugly: Love quarrels with your mate.
Help being ugly: You are being watched by one with evil intentions.
A young lady dreaming of being ugly: Will break her engagement.

ULCER:
Having ulcers: Must do lots of work without profit.
Having ulcers on the legs: Will suffer affliction.
Having ulcers on the arms: Will be annoyed.
Having ulcers on ears or lips: Unhappiness.

Back being covered with ulcers: Triumph over enemies.

Having ulcers in the mouth: Loss of property.

Having ulcers in the throat: Will be ignored by everyone.

UMBRELLA:

Having an umbrella: Will have prosperity.

Carrying an umbrella: Will be annoyed by trouble and many vexations.

Carrying an open umbrella over the head: Someone will come to your aid.

Having an umbrella open inside the house: Big misfortune.

Others with an umbrella: Birth of a child.

Others with a closed umbrella: Sickness.

Borrowing an umbrella: Will have misunderstandings with a friend.

Lending an umbrella: Will be hurt by untrue friends.

An umbrella leaking: Will be displeased with your lover.

UNBECOMING:

Doing unbecoming things: You will be called to order.

Children acting unbecomingly: You live only for the success of business.

Mates acting unbecomingly: Family unhappiness.

Other people acting unbecomingly: Will suffer humiliation.

UNCLE:

Of an uncle: Success in money matters.

Being an uncle: Will make a successful matrimony.

Uncles of husband: Good times are coming.

Uncles of wife: Beware of jealous friends.

Uncles of other people: Shame and sorrow.

UNCOVER:

Being uncovered: Riches and abundance.

Children being uncovered: Misfortune in family love.

Friends uncovering themselves: Will abandon own home.

Mates seeing each other uncovered: Prosperity in business.

Uncovering food: Will collect money.

Uncovering clothes: Unhappiness.

UNDERGROUND:

Someone being underground: You desire what others have.

An underground passage: You will abuse the confidence of others.

Going through an underground passage: Worry in the future.

Having an accident underground: Will be free of enemies.

UNDERMINE:

Undermining yourself: Will be frightened.

Undermining relatives: Will take a trip.

Undermining other people: Will receive damages.

Being undermined by others: Will receive news of a marriage.

UNDERSTAND:

Understanding many things: Will receive unhappy news.

Understanding foreign languages: Will be cheated.

Understanding children: Will receive a valuable gift.

Understanding others: Honor and dignity.

UNDERTAKER:

The parlor of an undertaker: Will receive announcement of a wedding.

An undertaker removing a body from the house: Happiness.

An undertaker preparing the body for a funeral: Will sustain a loss.

Going to an undertaker's parlor: Will live a long life.

Being an undertaker: Death of a relative.

UNDRESS:

Being undressed: Gossip and malice will cause sorrow.

Undressing yourself: Will have happiness in the near future.

Undressing in privacy: A guarded secret will be discovered.

Undressing before others: People are talking badly behind your back.

Others undressing: Will be visited by a loved one.

Undressing in another's house: Will receive plenty of money.

Undressing in a hotel room: Satisfaction in love.

Undressing children: Pleasant events will occur in your life.

Husband and wife undressing in same room: Business affairs will go bad.

Undressing in public: Distress will come to you.

UNFAITHFUL:

Being unfaithful: Someone is taking advantage of your trust in them.

A man dreaming of being unfaithful to wife: Domestic unpleasantness.

A woman dreaming of being unfaithful to husband: Uncertain of pregnancy.

A man being unfaithful to his girl friend: Big fortune ahead.

A girl being unfaithful to her boyfriend: Will receive unpleasant news.

An unmarried man being unfaithful to his lover: Peril of death.

An unmarried girl being unfaithful to her lover: You are being deceived.

Other people being unfaithful to each other: Will receive money from a dishonest man.

UNFORTUNATE:

Being unfortunate: Wealth.

Being unfortunate in gambling: Will earn much money in winnings.

Being unfortunate in love with one particular person: Fortunate with others.

Engaged people being unfortunate: Dignity.

Children being unfortunate: Care will bring success.

Relatives being unfortunate: Sudden death of a relative.

Friends being unfortunate: Will be cheated by friends.

UNHAPPY:

Being unhappy: Will be visited by a judge.

A woman being unhappy with her husband: Receive invitation by prominent person.

Sweethearts being unhappy with each other: Doubt and distrust without reason.

A man being unhappy with his wife: Joy and innocence.

Children being unhappy: Will enjoy much happiness.

Relatives being unhappy: Misery in old age.

Friends being unhappy: Someone is cheating you.

Children of other people being unhappy: Good news received by letter.

UNICORN:

Of an animal with one horn: Will have anxiety caused by falsehoods.

Many unicorns together: Will receive a large sum of money.

Killing a unicorn: Losses in real estate.

Unicorns in a cage: Will be avoided by acquaintances.

UNIFORM:

Of someone in uniform: Good fortune.

Officers in uniform: Will receive a promotion.

Enlisted personnel in uniform: Will have big difficulty and afflictions.

A member of own family in uniform: Glory and dignity.

Wearing a uniform: Valor and prominence.

Selling uniforms: Friends will exert influence to help you.

Men wearing uniforms for their business: Abundance in money.

Women wearing uniforms for their business: You are too arrogant.

Women wearing military uniforms: Unfitted to fill position in life.

Servant's uniforms: Failure of enemies.

UNITE:
Being united: Loss of money through gambling.

Family being united: Happiness.

Business partners being united: Will have disagreements and sorrow.

A united country: Victory over enemies.

UNITED STATES:
(See AMERICA.)

UNIVERSITY:
Of a university: It is essential to be perfect in your studies.

Attending a university: You are fortunate in your talents.

Children attending a university: You have many faithful friends.

Other people going to a university: Triumph over enemies.

Being a professor at a university: Sickness.

UNKIND:
Being unkind: Your affections are returned with deep sincerity.

Others being unkind to you: Will make new acquaintances.

Friends being unkind to you: You have false friends.

Children being unkind to parents: You are too good to children.

Husband and wife being unkind to each other: Will have much wealth.

Relatives being unkind to you: Will discover a thief.

UNKNOWN:
Of an unknown person: Glory in the family.

A man dreaming of an unknown person: Success in affairs.

A man dreaming of unknown dark complexioned person: High honors.

A woman dreaming of an unknown person: Will make new acquaintances.

A woman dreaming of an unknown person with long hair: Great love.

Embracing an unknown person: Will take a long trip.

A man hitting unknown person with a stick: New business ventures are good.

A woman hitting unknown person with a stick: Domination over men.

UNLOCK:
Of unlocking something: A discovery will be made in your home.

Being unable to unlock a door: Beware of trouble ahead.

Being unable to unlock a drawer: Don't keep secrets from those who love you.

Not finding the key to unlock something: Be careful in money matters.

UNMARRIED:
Married people dreaming of being single: Dangerous jealousy.

Single man dreaming of remaining single: Will secure a good business venture.

A single person desiring to get married: Will receive good news.

A young girl desiring to get married: She is truthful and trustworthy.

An old bachelor wanting to get married: Will marry a healthy woman.

An old maid wanting to get married: She will marry a young man.

UNMASK:
Of unmasking yourself: Will have triumph over enemies.

Unmasking someone else: Will blush with shame.

Unmasking a prowler: Sickness and death.

Unmasking an enemy on the street: Will waste time without compensation.

UNTIE:
Of untying things: Big work is ahead.

Untying a prisoner: Unexpected events will transpire.

Untying knots in a rope: A secret will be revealed.

Untying a dog: A matrimony will take place.

Untying a horse: Faithful friends are nearby.

UPROAR:
Of an uproar: Will have to make a prompt decision.
Viewing a scene of uproar and confusion: A delayed decision must be made.
Being at the scene of an uproar: Everything will go as you desire.
Friends being in an uproar: Joy and consolation.
Enemies being in an uproar: Will live a long life.

URINE:
Of urinating: Will have to sweep the floor.
Urinating in bed: Good results in business affairs.
Urinating on a wall: Completion of a business transaction.
Others urinating on a wall: Business satisfaction.
Children urinating: Will have good health.
A urinal pot: Will have a very easy future.

URN:
Of an urn: Will receive news from a new acquaintance.
Putting hands in an urn: Good business.
Handling an urn: Death of a friend.
An urn full of ashes: Inheritance.
Others moving an urn: Will achieve distinction.
An empty urn: Death among neighbors.
A broken urn: Unhappiness.
Ashes of a relative being put in an urn: Financial gains.

USURER:
Of a person who lends money: Persecution by false friends.
Being a usurer: Business will cause much worry.
Having a usurer for a partner: Will be disliked in the community.
Others who are usurers: A friend will betray you.
Going to a usurer to borrow money: Are ashamed of your profits.

UTENSILS:
Kitchen utensils: Will have misery.
Fishing utensils: Will have fortune in business.
Writing utensils: Will avoid the danger of a double cross.
Steel utensils: Death.
Wooden utensils: Avoid squandering of money.
Lead utensils: Will receive an inheritance.
Porcelain utensils: Sickness.
Making utensils: Sorrow and unhappiness.
Being a utensil merchant: Will have to endure grief.

UTERUS:
Of own uterus: Will receive a big favor.
Having pains in the uterus: Gossip by friends.
Having the uterus removed: Will make good monetary earnings.
Relatives having the uterus removed: Loss of friends.

V

VACATION:
Making plans for a vacation: Will have many happy days.
Going on a vacation: Will have a wonderful time.
Going on a vacation with a loved one: Will be persecuted.

Returning from a vacation: Will enjoy prosperity.
Others going on a vacation: Will enjoy a considerable fortune.

VACCINATION:
Being vaccinated: You are showering affections on an unworthy person.

Needing to be vaccinated: Let your head rule your heart.

Family being vaccinated: Prosperity proportioned to number vaccinated.

Children being vaccinated: Beware of squandering money.

Being vaccinated by a nurse: Will have opposition in life.

Others being vaccinated: Enemies will occupy your time.

VAGABOND:

Of a vagabond: Attempt to avoid bad company.

Being a vagabond: Dishonor.

A vagabond wandering around: Will have a good time on a picnic.

Friends being vagabonds: Will become acquainted with dignified people.

VALENTINE:

Of Valentine Day: Excitement and joy.

Sending valentines: Will lose an opportunity to make money.

Receiving a valentine: Will take advantage of available opportunities.

A sweetheart receiving a valentine: Victory over enemies.

A sweetheart sending a valentine: Contradiction.

Married people exchanging valentines: Will receive unexpected invitation.

Children sending valentine to parents: Inheritance within a year.

VALIDATE:

Validating a ticket: Will have an abundance of property.

Validating a document: Don't rely too much on your fortune.

Validating a check: Will fall into the grip of moneylenders.

Having a valid fortune: Will hear stupid gossip.

VALLEY:

Of a valley: Be careful of your health.

Being in a valley: Warning of very bad health.

Relatives being in a valley: Do not overexert yourself.

Being in a valley with children: Will unexpectedly receive money due you.

Animals being in a valley: Honor and riches.

A beautiful valley: Be cautious in all your affairs.

Crossing a green valley: Contentment and ease.

A barren valley: Dissatisfaction and want.

VAMPIRE:

Of a vampire: Will marry for money.

A married person dreaming of a vampire: You made a bad bargain in marriage.

Fighting with a vampire: Will receive good news.

A dead person come back to life: Increase in riches.

VAN:

Of a van: Honor.

An open van: Do not act impulsively.

A covered van: Plans for a trip will not be realized.

Getting out of a van: Loss of employment.

Other people riding in a van: Good things come to one with patience.

VANISH:

Of vanishing: Consolation and joy.

Own possessions vanishing: Will have a hard life ahead.

A mate vanishing: Unhappiness.

Members of family vanishing: Will have good business.

Friends vanishing: Will live a long life.

VARNISH:

Of varnishing: Outward appearances will not fool others.

Varnishing the floor of a house: Hypocrisy.

Varnishing the doors of a house: Bigotry will bring harm to business.

Varnishing furniture: Difficult times ahead.

VASE:

An unmarried person dreaming of a vase: Immediate marriage and birth of a son.

A vase being near a fountain: Hard work ahead.

A vase full of flowers: Increase of riches.

A shop selling vases: Prosperity in the family.

A broken vase: Overwhelming sorrow to come.

Breaking many vases: Loss of friends.

A silver vase: Happiness.

Silver vase full of flowers: Good fortune.

A metal vase: Pleasant comforts in life.

Receiving a gift of a vase: Will be loved.

Breaking a vase and spilling the water: You are too concerned with appearances.

A vase made of fine pottery: Value highly loved one's attributes.

VAT:

Of a vat: You are too extravagant.

A full vat: Will be blessed with wisdom.

An empty vat: Wealth.

Many empty vats: Plan ahead for your future.

VAULT:

Of a vault: Be careful when undertaking new ventures.

Opening a vault: Difficulties will be in your path.

A full vault: Will escape danger.

An empty vault: Will receive an unexpected estate.

VEAL:

Of a veal: Joy.

Buying veal: Good fortune ahead is certain.

Cooking veal: Happiness.

Eating veal: Will always have plenty of money.

VEGETABLES:

Of vegetables: Hard work with small rewards.

Picking vegetables: Money worries will be greatly lessened by economy.

Others picking vegetables: Quarrels.

Vegetables that are still in the ground: Will suffer many afflictions.

Eating vegetables: Losses in business.

Green vegetables: Continue to persevere and retain high hopes.

Smelling odors of vegetables cooking: Will discover unpleasant secrets.

VEIL:

Of a veil: Mystery and modesty.

Having a veil: You are disguising something.

Opening a veil or folding it: Favorable circumstances.

Wearing a veil: You are secretive in your actions.

Losing a veil: Will lose your lover.

A bridal veil: Good prospects for great happiness.

A woman wearing a veil: Beware of false advice.

Arranging a veil on your head: Will be deceived.

The veil over a dead person: Will assist at a wedding.

VEIN:

Of own veins: Will have many worries.

Having swollen veins: Will have joy.

Cutting veins: Riches.

Children's veins being cut: Be cautious in all your actions.

Extracting blood from veins: You enjoy a very great love.

Blood being taken from a relative's veins: Don't believe all you hear.

VELVET:

Of velvet: Honor and riches.

Being a velvet merchant: Will be fortunate in business.

Buying velvet: You will be industrious.

Sewing with velvet: Will receive assistance from a friend.

A velvet dress: Opposition.

VENISON:

Of venison: You have furious enemies.

Eating venison: Misfortune.

Buying vension: Complete victory.

Killing a deer: Riches.

VENUS:

Of Venus: Will enjoy much security in love.

Marrying Venus: Will be respected and loved by everyone.

Having a statue of Venus: Riches in proportion to size of statue.

A naked picture of Venus: Will receive a large legacy.

VERDICT:

Hearing a juror give a verdict: Will win a case.

Hearing a verdict against you: Will prepare for a journey in a hurry.

The jury who decides the verdict: Will be hungry.

Being a juror and deciding a verdict: Will get money from a friend.

VERMIN:

Of vermin: Will receive an abundance of gold and silver.

Many vermin: Good luck.

Having vermin on your body: Don't be too severe with wrongdoers.

Vermin on other people: Someone is trying to cause you injury.

VERMOUTH:

Drinking vermouth: Must economize with earnings.

Of vermouth: Will soon have much pain in the body.

Buying vermouth: Will suffer humiliation.

Selling vermouth: Will suffer embarrassment and humiliation.

Giving a gift of vermouth: A foolish person will cause annoyance.

VERSE:

Of verses: A stupid person is causing annoyance.

Reading verses: Will succeed in your plans.

Writing verses: Will not succeed if you work alone.

Reading Bible verses: Happiness with your mate.

Verses being read aloud by others: Happiness in the family.

VEST:

A vest for a man: Hostility surrounds you.

A vest for a woman: Guard your actions.

Taking off a vest: You are too easygoing.

Buying a colored vest: Conceal your suspicions.

Not wearing a vest: Success in enterprises.

Being vested with authority: High honors.

Vesting authority in another: Will live a long life.

VEXATION:

Causing vexation: Will be deceived by one in whom you confided.

Being vexed: Prosperity.

Vexing other people: Everything will turn out for the best.

Children causing vexation: Improve conditions with correct activities.

VIBRATO:

Of singing with vibrato: Satisfaction of desires.

A tenor or soprano singing vibrato: Disagreements.

Giving lessons in vibrato: Congenial work and good news.

VICAR:

Of a vicar: Honor and dignity.

Talking to the vicar of a church: People will cause annoyance.

Receiving blessings from a vicar: Will live a long life.

Being a vicar: Will have ups and downs.

VICE:

Having a mechanical vice: You will have hard work.

Working with a vice: Will have fortune in your affairs.

Having immoral conduct: Friends will cheat you.

Others having immoral conduct: Will suffer humiliation.

Having a physical defect: Will live a long life.

Of a vice-president or governor: Will have mastery over many matters.

VICTORIA CROSS:

Receiving this honor: Will win your fortune on your own merit.

Others wearing the Cross: Secret enmity of some person.
Officers wearing the Victoria Cross: Approaching good news.
Wearing the Cross yourself: Advancement within your own position.

VICTORY:
Of victory: Unhappiness.
Gaining victory over someone: Riches and honor.
A military victory: People are laughing at you.
A political victory: Increase in taxes.
Being a member of a victorious team: Don't take sides in others' quarrels.

VICTUALS:
Serving food to others: Social pleasure.
Food being supplied to you: Good luck.
Supplying food to hotels and restaurants: Riches.
Eating many victuals: Loss of business.

VIEW:
Of a beautiful view: All desires will be realized.
A nice view in the distance: Good results in enterprises.
A misty view: Will not be successful in affairs and suffer misery.
Losing something from view: Death of a relative.
Viewing houses and trees: Loss of faith.

VIGIL:
Being on vigil: You have many things on your mind.
Keeping a long vigil: Deferred hopes.
Others keeping vigil for you: Riches and fortune.
Keeping vigil over a sick person: Will fulfill all desires.
Keeping vigil over a dead person: Happiness will be yours.

VIGOROUS:
Being vigorous: Will not have to worry about danger.
Having a vigorous love affair: Riches and earning of money.

A vigorous woman: Pleasures which may end in matrimony.
A vigorous man: Changeable love with young girls.

VILLA:
A beautiful villa: Will be very happy in the near future.
A villa being wrecked by an earthquake: Starvation.
Rebuilding a villa: Will overcome enemies.
A rustic villa: Will succeed in own hopes and desires.
A villa burning: Will serve in a war.

VILLAGE:
Of a village: Hard work ahead.
Several villages in the distance: Changes in own position.
Villages far away illuminated by the moon: Change for the better.
A village burning: Will make a pilgrimage.
The village where you live: Improved conditions in the future.

VILLAIN:
A male villain: Fortune.
A female villain: Love.
A bad villain: Will receive a gift from a loved one.
Many villains doing wrong: Will receive a letter from a loved one.
Being a villain: Will have good neighbors.

VINE:
Healthy vines: Good friendship.
Withered vines: Someone is trying to bring injury to you.
Picking from a vine: Misunderstandings will not end in your favor.
A vine of green leaves: Success will be attained soon.
Grape vines: Abundance.
Different vegetable vines: Prosperity.
Strolling among vines: Will have many children.
Cutting down vines: Must have faith to achieve fortune.
Harvesting fruit from vines: Will have good earnings.

VINEGAR:
Of vinegar: Labors will bring results at a later date.
Drinking vinegar: Family discord.
Bad vinegar: Sickness.
Fresh vinegar: Will retain good health with care.
Spilling vinegar: Loss of a friend.
White vinegar: Ruin is near at hand.
Red vinegar: Will be insulted by others.
Making vinegar from good wine: Will have a legal fight with someone.
Cooking with vinegar: Disaster in your industry.
Making vinegar sauce for a salad: Will participate in an orgy.
Making pickles with vinegar: Business will be at a standstill.
Eating foods made with vinegar: Poverty.
Buying vinegar: Abundance.

VINEYARD:
Of a vineyard: Gains through speculation.
Having a large vineyard: Abundance.
Walking through a vineyard: Prosperity.
Checking the condition of a vineyard: Beware of gossip.

VINTAGE:
Having a very successful vintage: Riches.
Helping to gather grapes for wine: Pleasure and joy.
Sick people dreaming of a vintage: Peril can be averted.
Picking grapes: Affection will be rewarded.
Carrying grapes after the harvest: Considerable wealth.
Selling grapes from a vintage: Successful operation of business.

VIOLENCE:
Violence being done to others: Will have parties with friends.
Showing violence yourself: Better days ahead.
Being attacked with violence: Joy.
Mate showing violence: Infidelity.

VIOLETS:
Wearing violets: Modesty.
Picking violets: Will have a happy marriage.
Making a bouquet of violets: Chastity.
Having double violets: High honors.
Violets out of season: Loss of friends.
Having violets in season: Success and happiness in everything.
Buying violets: Will have a lawsuit.
Receiving violets from a loved one: Will be very fortunate in love.

VIOLIN:
Of a violin: Will soon have sorrow that causes tears.
Playing a violin: Bliss between husband and wife.
Playing a violin at a concert: Consolation.
Playing a violin in solitude: Will attend a funeral.
Hearing the sweet music of a violin: Domestic happiness.
Others playing a violin: Joy.
Breaking a string of a violin: Quarrels.
Playing a cello: Happiness between husband and wife.
A base violin: Will be visited by an old friend.
A broken violin: Misfortune.

VIRGIN:
Embracing a virgin: Great happiness.
Being introduced to a virgin: Pleasures without secrecy.
Holding a virgin: Joy.
Kidnaping a virgin: Imprisonment.
A picture of a virgin: Troubles threaten.
Realizing a person is not a virgin: Much personal grief.
Knowing a virgin with many boyfriends: Be on guard and don't trust friends.
Talking to the Virgin Saint: Consolation.
A sick person dreaming of the Virgin Saint: Will recover completely.

VIRTUE:
Of virtue: You are keeping bad company.

Being a virtuous person: Many enemies are nearby.

Children being virtuous: Don't listen to the lies of others.

Having virtuous friends: Will fall into a trap.

Mates being virtuous: Will be in a precarious situation.

VISION:

Of vision: Horror and fright.

Seeing a visual image: Danger to the person who appears to you.

A lovely and charming vision: Very fortunate for a lover.

An imaginative vision: Success is certain to come.

VISIT:

Paying a visit: Obstacles are in your plans.

Visiting with relatives: Will be subject to suspicions.

A friend visiting you: Will have business losses.

A doctor visiting you: Will have advantages over others.

Visiting your friends: Your situation is not good.

Several friends visiting you: Will receive good news soon.

Returning a visit: Will have a lawsuit.

Receiving business visits: Will have sorrow that will cause tears.

VISITORS:

Of visitors: Will receive assistance from a friend.

Receiving visitors: Arrival of a friend.

Many visitors: Will be helped by friends.

Being a visitor: Will have good fortune.

Having deals with a visitor: Sickness.

VOICE:

Hearing a well-known voice: Accept the good advice of your friends.

Hearing a voice speaking to you: Will have business opposition.

Hearing several people's voices at the same time: Reverses in business.

Hearing happy voices: Will have many worries.

VOLCANO:

Of a volcano: Will receive very good news.

A volcano erupting: Events will occur soon over which you have no control.

A man dreaming of a volcano: He has dishonest servants.

A woman dreaming of a volcano: Family upsets and lovers' quarrels.

Lovers dreaming of a volcano: Deceit and intrigue by one of them.

VOLLEY:

Of a volley of arrows together: Opposition from several sources.

A burst of many things at the same time: Happiness.

Of a volley ball: Will have to make an effort to control yourself.

Playing volley ball: Attend to your needs at home.

VOLUNTEER:

Of a volunteer: You will soon be in the armed forces.

Being a volunteer: Will lose your life in a battle.

Children being a volunteer: Approaching money.

Foreign volunteers: Family happiness.

VOMIT:

Of vomiting: Big events.

Poor people dreaming of vomiting blood: Profit.

Rich people dreaming of vomiting blood: Will suffer injury.

Vomiting wine: Will lose in real-estate dealings.

Vomiting after drinking liquor: Will easily spend money won in gambling.

Vomiting food: Reputation will suffer.

Others vomiting: Will ask the service of someone else.

VOTE:

Of voting: You must be at peace with yourself to attain desires.

Casting a ballot: Will be favored by good luck.

Voting for someone you know: Hopes will be fulfilled.

Voting for political offices: Will receive good news.

Voting for people to hold position in church: Virtue and blessings of God.

VOW:

Making a vow: You must take great care in your affairs.

Breaking a vow: Bad luck for the family.

Making a religious vow: Will suffer a big disaster.

Family making a vow: Death within the family.

VOYAGE:

Being on a voyage: Will receive an inheritance.

Taking a voyage: Will receive a message soon from faraway.

Taking a voyage alone: Good times are in view in the future.

Taking a voyage to foreign countries with family: Fortune.

Taking a voyage and being in a foreign country: Reflect well upon actions.

Taking a voyage with sweetheart: Gossip.

VULGAR:

Being vulgar: Will be ridiculed by other people.

Other people who are vulgar: Will make unpleasant acquaintances.

Hearing vulgar talk: Will make the friendship of a well-known person.

Talking vulgar to others: Will be able to rely on success of good hopes.

Friends being vulgar: Will enjoy happiness in the future.

VULTURE:

Of a vulture: Will be unable to reconcile misunderstandings with a friend.

Many vultures: Will have a long illness that may bring death and misery.

A vulture devouring its prey: Troubles will cease.

Killing a vulture: Will gain victory over dangerous enemies.

A dead vulture: Conquest and misfortune.

W

WADDING:

Of wadding things together: Bad health.

Relatives wadding things together: Approaching money.

Large quantities of wadding: Troubles will cause you to lose weight.

Employees wadding cotton: Business will prosper.

WADDLE:

Of a waddle: Persecution by an enemy.

Birds waddling: Will conclude affairs satisfactorily.

Birds waddling on land: Uncertain affairs will turn out well.

An injured bird waddling: Will receive sad news.

WADE:

Of wading: Will commit a sin.

Lovers wading in clear water: Their love is not secure.

Lovers wading in muddy water: Disillusionment.

Lovers wading in rough water: Their love will fade completely.

Others wading: Will find the real truth concerning a secret.

WAFER:

Of a wafer seal: Will receive something you desire.

Using a wafer to seal a letter: Legal matters will be to your benefit.

Eating a wafer: Will have dealings in civil matters.

Receiving a wafer from a priest: Will have contentment in your heart.

Eating crackers: Profit and success.

Making wafers for family to eat: Unexpected fortune.

WAFT:
Being wafted in the air without wings: Small vexation.
Others being wafted about in the air: Someone will express gratitude.
Relatives being wafted about in the air: Long life.
Enemies being wafted about in the air: Loss of friends.

WAGER:
Making a wager: You are uncertain of what you are doing.
Accepting a wager: You are very confused in your thinking.
Winning a wager: Act cautiously and fortune will smile upon you.
Losing a wager: Will acquire wealth dishonorably.

WAGES:
Receiving wages: Danger of small thefts.
Preparing the payroll: Bad temper and disappointment.
Paying wages: Will lose money received from a legacy.
Paying weekly wages: A better future awaits.
Paying wages to laborers: Will have to work hard all during life.
Paying wages to white-collar workers: A beautiful woman will be married.
Receiving own wages: Loss.
Being refused payment of wages: Will have a lawsuit.
Not receiving wages for work performed: Bankruptcy.

WAGON:
Of a wagon: Riches will come rapidly.
Driving a wagon: Loss of money.
A loaded wagon or cart: Unexpected good fortune.
A wagon coming to your door: Riches.
Being in a wagon with a loved one: Will have tremendous good fortune.
Riding in a wagon with family: Inheritance from a distant relative.

WAIL:
Of wailing: Joy.
Weeping and wailing: Loss of someone dear to you.

Children wailing: Congenial feeling among family.
Relatives wailing: You must limit your expenditures.
Animals wailing: Will receive an inheritance.

WAINSCOT:
Of sheets of wainscot oak: Exercise caution in your business.
Wainscot lining on a wall: Will be cheated by friends.
Putting wainscot paneling on a wall: Business failure.

WAIST:
Of a blouse: Fortune that will soon pass away.
A small waist: Dishonor.
A large waist: Unhappiness.
A naked waist: Unfortunate things will happen.
Putting a belt around the waist: Unexpected money.
Fastening clothes around the waist: Happy romance.
Fastening things around another's waist: Will assist this person soon.
Having pains in the waist: Will have plenty of money.

WAIT:
Of waiting for someone to arrive: A false friend is nearby.
Waiting in readiness for action: A friend is trying to help you secretly.
Waiting on people: Advancement within own position.
Waiting for arrival of someone delayed: Insurmountable obstacles ahead.
Waiting for a loved one to arrive: Good times are coming.

WAITER:
Of a waiter: Will have money.
A waiter at a saloon: You are too confident.
A waitress: Will receive false news.
A waitress at a saloon: Gossip.
Being served by a waiter: Will become an invalid requiring a nurse.
Many waiters serving other people: You have dishonest help.

Waiters serving a banquet: Victory over enemies.

WALK:
Walking forward: Will have a change in fortune that will bring profit.
Walking backward: Loss of money.
Walking lightly: Advice from someone will bring profit.
Walking heavily: Will be acquainted with a scientist.
Walking with a wooden leg: Change in your position.
Walking very fast: Attend to pressing matters more carefully.
Walking at night: Annoyance.
Walking slowly: Disgrace and loss of money.
Walking along muddy streets: Will be molested.
Walking in the mud: Illness.
Walking on gravel: Will suffer.
Walking with a limp: Bad fortune.
Walking with crutches: Losses in gambling.
Walking over burning things: Loss of money.
Walking down a dry canal: People are working against you.
Walking down a dry river: Joy and prosperity.
Walking in water: Triumph and success.
Walking with other people: Good success.
Walking in a zigzag manner: Opposition.

WALKING STICK:
Of a walking stick: Will be slapped by someone.
Using a walking stick: Will be given assistance.
Others using a walking stick: Will have a dispute.
Putting weight on a walking stick: Prosperity.
Buying a walking stick: Will enjoy a comfortable life.

WALL:
Of a wall: Happiness.
Climbing a wall: Will overcome obstacles.

Jumping over a wall: Will realize own ambitions.
A woman dreaming of walking on top of a wall: Will have a happy marriage.
A wall being constructed: Will enjoy an industrial gain.
Falling from a wall: Must face hard work.
A wall falling down: Personal and business losses.
Many walls: Prosperity.
Many walls being torn down: Complete conclusion of affairs.
Walls being built higher: Fortune without profit.
Climbing a wall with a ladder: Joy.
Having a wall in front of own house: Troubles.
A moat surrounding a wall: Disgrace.
Building a wall: You are prone to being very stingy.

WALLET:
Of a wallet: Unexpected important news.
An empty wallet: Fortune.
A full wallet: Discovery of a secret.
Finding a woman's wallet: Will receive a small amount of money.

WALLFLOWERS:
Of wallflowers: Will see a pregnant woman.
Smelling wallflowers: Will have to contend with enemies.
Wallflowers growing: Pleasure and contentment.
Picking wallflowers: Will enjoy a good future.

WALNUT:
Of walnuts: Riches and satisfaction.
Eating walnuts: Will gain against enemies.
Cracking walnuts: You have an unsettled mind.
Making a pie with walnuts: Satisfaction.
Making cookies with walnuts: Will discover a treasure.
Growing walnuts: Embarrassment in business.

Buying walnuts: Satisfaction in business.

Selling walnuts: Will have a long life.

WALTZ:
Hearing waltz music: Abundance.

Dancing a waltz: Good humor and happiness.

Waltzing with husband or wife: Sickness.

Waltzing with lover or sweetheart: An admirer is concealing his affections.

Waltzing with children: Will win the friendship of an influential person.

Waltzing with friends: Success in enterprises.

Waltzing with people of ill fame: Prosperity.

WANDER:
Of wandering: Advancement toward achieving desires.

Wandering in the streets: Affairs will go better.

Other people wandering: Beware of being cheated by people.

Enemies wandering: Will make an unpleasant trip.

Children wandering: Advancement in business.

WANT:
Of wanting something: Will make friends with a new acquaintance.

Being in want: You are a visionary person.

Children wanting various things: Family happiness.

Relatives being in want: Will receive big news.

Mate wanting something: Arguments.

Sweetheart wanting something: Will receive an important letter with money.

WAR:
Of war: Troubles and danger.

Making war with someone: Persecution.

Watching a war: Misfortune.

Being in a war: Danger of illness.

Documents of war: Joy.

Winning a war: Happiness.

Losing a war: Loss of unimportant papers.

WARBLE:
Hearing the warble of a bird: Happiness in love.

Hearing many birds warbling: Discord between married people.

Hearing children warbling: Don't allow people to threaten you.

Hearing famous singers warble: Will receive bad news.

WARDEN:
Of a warden: Will have much happiness for a long time.

Talking to a warden: Happy holiday soon to come.

Being a warden: Will be robbed.

Receiving a favor from a warden: You are squandering money.

Removing a warden from his position: Will live a long life.

A warden having trouble with prisoners: Death of a relative.

WARDROBE:
Of a wardrobe: Honor.

Going through own wardrobe: You are pretending to be rich.

Having a large wardrobe: You are very sure of what you want.

Having a small wardrobe: Will meet a very influential person.

Adding clothes to wardrobe: Disillusionment.

Having a sloppy wardrobe: Other people are suspicious of you.

Buying dresses for a wardrobe: Many changes awaiting you.

Seeing old clothes from wardrobe: Will have fortune at another's expense.

Giving away clothes from wardrobe: A surprise awaits.

WAREHOUSE:
Of a warehouse: Money will come easily all during life.

Being in a warehouse: Success in business and married life.

Storing things in a warehouse: Curiosity.

Taking things out of a warehouse:

Change of residence.
A warehouse van: Infidelity.

WARM:
Of warm weather: Will be reprimanded.
Enjoying warm weather: Small sickness ahead.
Living in a warm climate: Jealousy.
Disliking a warm climate: Desires will cause damages.
Warming water: Will have bad thoughts in mind.
Warming food: Own timidity will cause hurt.
Keeping warm: Unhappiness.
Keeping children warm: Arrival of a friend.

WARTS:
Of warts: You are surrounded by enemies.
Having warts: Gossip.
Having warts on the body: Reputation will suffer because of actions.
Having many warts on the hands: Much money will come to you.
Others having warts on the hands: Rich friends.

WASH:
Of washing: A service will be rendered by an unknown person.
Washing in clear water: Will enjoy many pleasures in life.
Washing hands in cold water: Contentment.
Washing hands in hot water: Success.
Washing feet: Anxiety.
Washing hair or beard: Sorrow.
Washing body: Beware of immoral conduct.
Washing food: Happy life.
Washing linen: Difficulties ahead.
Washing dishes: Friends will visit at your home.

WASP:
Of a wasp: Opposition.
A hive of wasps: Will have many sorrows.
Being stung by a wasp: Losses and opposition.

The queen wasp of a hive: Gossip by jealous people.
Relatives being stung by a wasp: You have enemies among those you trust.
Children being stung by a wasp: An injustice will be done to you.

WATCH:
Of watching: You must be very cautious.
Keeping watch: Loss of money.
Watching someone you don't care for: The moon will bring rain.
Watching people's hair floating: Will be hired by an enemy.
Watching from a high window: People are spying on you.
Watching other people: Will receive good news.
Watching someone's hand: Infidelity.
Guarding something: Good health.
Guarding a secret: Guard it well from enemies.
Of a wristwatch: Good health.
Wearing a wristwatch: Loss in business.
A woman dreaming of wearing a wristwatch: Will become lazy.
A woman dreaming of receiving a gift of a wristwatch: Happiness.
A young girl receiving a gift of a wristwatch: Will receive marriage proposal.
Buying a wristwatch: Joy and tranquillity.
Selling a wristwatch: Poverty.
Having a pocket watch: Will make good money.
Buying a pocket watch: Will take a journey overland.
Being a watchmaker: Will have to do some hard work.
Fixing watches: Avoid rivals.

WATCHMAN:
Of a watchman: You are protected by silent love.
A patrol watchman: You expect too many favors from other people.
A bank watchman: You have a very kind heart.
A park watchman: Unhappiness.

An animal watchman: Honor.
Several watchmen: Friendship is near.
Being a watchman: Will be saved from danger.
Being a night watchman: Unhappiness.
Being a day watchman: Will be persecuted.
A watchman catching a prowler: Will be misled.
Being taken away by a watchman: Security.
Hitting a watchman: Happy life.

WATER:

Of water: Abundance.
Drawing water from a fountain: A beautiful young wife will bring fortune.
Drawing water from a well: Will be tormented by your wife.
Taking dirty water from a stream: Illness.
Bathing in clear water: Good health.
Bathing in dirty water: Sickness.
Drinking water blessed by a priest: Will have purity of soul.
Drinking from a glass of water: Prompt matrimony.
Being offered a glass of water: Birth of a child.
Drinking hot water: Will be molested and persecuted by enemies.
Drinking a fresh glass of water: You have a clear conscience.
Drinking ice water: Prosperity and triumph over enemies.
Breaking a glass full of water: Death of a mother and health for children.
Spilling a glass of water: Death of a child and health for the mother.
Falling into water and waking immediately: Entire life ruined by woman you marry.
Falling into very cold water: Reconciliation and happiness.
Carrying water into bedroom: Will be visited by a man with loose morals.
Water flooding house and ruining furniture: Will quarrel with enemies.
Water flooding out of own house: Your life is in danger.

Walking through water on the floor: Triumph and success.
Water flowing in a small canal: Unhappiness.
Water flowing in a river: Will receive happy news from a traveler.
A river flooding: Will receive good news concerning pending lawsuits.
Rich people dreaming of muddy water: Will fall into disgrace.
Poor people dreaming of muddy water: Will lose respect of employers.
Being bloated with water: Good fortune in the future.
Bathing in cold water with others: Good work is ahead for you.
Hiding water: Big affliction.
Serving water to people: Work and security.
Being in a boat on calm water: Prosperity in own enterprises.
Falling into rough water from a boat: Loss of fortune.
Carrying water in a jug without spilling it: Avoid trusting others with valuables.
Carrying water in a jug and spilling it: Difficulties in retaining wealth.
Carrying water in a leaky container: Abuse of confidence and theft.
Drinking clear well water: Increase of fortune.
Drinking murky well water: Will suffer ruin.
Smelly water: Sickness.
Gathering water: Will enjoy good business.
Putting roses in water: You have too great an imagination.
Pouring water on a fire: Will lose a lawsuit.
Unsalted water: Will have a very painful illness.
Salted water: Happiness.
Jumping into the water: Persecution.
Throwing dirty water away: Troubles are created by other people.
Stagnant water: Peril of death.
Water coming from a hole in the ground: Affliction.
Water in a swimming pool: Fortune.
Water falling on your head: Profit.

Being thrown into the water: Will have many things on your mind.

Putting sugar into water: Will enjoy a comfortable life.

Water disappearing: Good times are ahead.

An aquarium: Will have an argument.

Mineral water: Will recover from an illness.

Of a water spout: You worry too much for no reason.

Watering your lawn: Must rely on own good judgment.

Watering flowers in a garden: You expect too many favors from others.

WATER CARRIER:
Of a water carrier: Increase of money.

Being a water carrier: Good news will reach you.

Carrying river water: Will be annoyed by other people.

Carrying spring water: A long-expected letter will arrive.

WATERCRESS:
Of watercress: Happiness.

Growing watercress: Danger in love affairs.

Buying watercress: Will be insulted by neighbors.

Eating watercress: Increase of money.

Using watercress in a salad: Will have arguments with friends.

Picking watercress from water: Misunderstandings in love affairs.

WATERFALL:
Of a waterfall: Will be invited to a place of amusement.

A clear waterfall: Happiness.

Viewing a waterfall with others: You are being watched and gossiped about.

Taking water from a waterfall: Troubles will be very few.

WATER LILY:
Of water lilies: Your desires are out of reach.

Picking water lilies: An acquaintance will cause you trouble.

Putting water lilies in a vase: Try to gain confidence of other people.

Receiving water lilies as a gift: You are surrounded by enemies.

WATERMELON:
Of a watermelon: Good success.

Eating watermelon: Vain hopes.

Buying watermelon: Fortune.

Growing watermelon: Will receive a gift from an unknown person.

Giving children watermelon to eat: Happiness.

Sick people dreaming of eating watermelon: Will soon recover.

WATER MILL:
Of a water mill: Happiness.

Being at a water mill: Will unexpectedly receive money due you.

Business people dreaming of a water mill: Increase in business.

Farmers dreaming of a water mill: Abundant crops.

Lovers dreaming of a water mill: Will have a happy marriage.

Sweethearts dreaming of a water mill: Will soon be married.

Married people dreaming of a water mill: Happy married life.

Rich people dreaming of a water mill: Will increase their fortune.

WATER WHEEL:
Of a water wheel: Will come into a good deal of money.

A water wheel working: Hard work awaits.

Watching a water wheel working with others: Will have new friends.

Watching a water wheel with own family: Increase in money.

WAVE:
Of waves: Your life is in danger.

Waves capsizing a boat: Will be cheated by friends.

Waves breaking against rocks: Unhappiness.

Waves breaking on the bow of a ship: Abundance of money.

Waves coming onto a beach: Birth of a child.

WAX:
Of wax: Avoid lending money.

Using wax: Refuse to help friends with financial problems.

Buying wax: You are squandering money.

Waxing the floor of own house: Will need to borrow money.

Other people waxing floors: Will not be successful in enterprises.

WAYFARER:

Of a wayfarer: Congenial work and good news.

Meeting a lonely wayfarer on a path: Will make a new friend.

Being in the company of a wayfarer: Failure of enemies.

Others in the company of a wayfarer: A mystery will be solved.

WEAK:

Being weak: Rapid success of own hopes.

Mate being weak: Realization of high ambitions.

Children being weak: Financial gains.

Friends being weak: Will have good earnings.

WEALTH:

Unmarried people dreaming of wealth: Will marry poor people.

Rich people dreaming of wealth: Illness.

Poor people dreaming of wealth: Will have good earnings.

Being wealthy: Unhappiness in love affairs.

Receiving a wealthy inheritance: Family quarrels.

Having wealthy relatives: Important and very beneficial events to come.

Having a wealthy mate: Luck and prosperity.

Having wealthy friends: They will endeavor to destroy you.

WEAR:

Wearing clothing: Social activities of a happy nature.

Wearing new personal adornments: Be cautious in love affairs.

Wearing a new evening dress: Avoid rivals.

Wearing everything gracefully: Someone with evil intent is watching you.

Wearing yourself by fatigue: Family happiness.

WEASEL:

Of a weasel: Beware of those who appear to be your friends.

Having a fur coat made of weasel: Luck and prosperity.

Buying a weasel fur coat: Try to save your money.

Selling a weasel fur coat: You will be cheated.

WEATHER:

Of beautiful weather: Security in everything.

Terrible weather: Will have unpleasant news.

Windy weather: Big friendship.

Stormy weather: Enemies are seeking your ruin.

Rainy weather: You will receive a letter that will cause sadness.

WEATHER VANE:

Of a weather vane: Success in business.

Viewing a weather vane: You are overly complimented.

A weather vane changing direction from north to south: Loss of money.

A weather vane changing direction from south to north: Gain of money.

WEAVE:

Of weaving: Will be very embarrassed.

Weaving a wedding dress: Will soon purchase a wedding dress.

Ordering something from a weaver: Good news will come in a letter.

Weaving a suit: Important and very beneficial events to come.

Weaving a dress: Money will come easily during life.

WEB:

Of a web: Will take a trip in the near future.

Being caught in a web: Realization of own desires.

A large web: Big wealth.
Children finding a web: They will become prominent in life.

WEDDING:
Of a wedding: Happy days are ahead.
Being at a wedding: Big advantages will come to you.
A relative's wedding: Expect trouble in the family circle.
Husband or wife attending a wedding: Profit.
Attending a sister's wedding: Big danger.
Attending a brother's wedding: Will make money.
Attending the wedding of a virgin: Honor.
Attending the wedding of a son: Approaching money.
Attending the wedding of a daughter: Wealth.
Attending the wedding of a widow: Will make abundant money.

WEDDING RING:
Of a wedding ring: Dignity and fortune.
Losing a wedding ring: Vexation.
Receiving a wedding ring: Domestic happiness.
A wedding ring being covered with diamonds: Good health.

WEED:
Of weeds: Will face hindrances in an undertaking that promises great honor.
Pulling weeds: Happiness.
Destroying weeds: Embarrassment in business.
Burning dry weeds: All your troubles will be ended.

WEEK:
The first week of the month: Pleasure.
The second week of the month: Joy.
The third week of the month: Unhappiness.
The fourth week of the month: Happiness.

WEEP:
Of weeping: Great pleasures.

Weeping with the family: Joy and mirth.
Weeping along with grief: Will enjoy pleasures.
Children weeping: Happiness and good fortune.
Friends weeping: Will receive an unexpected gift.
Others weeping: Will receive bad news that is unimportant.

WEIGH:
Of weighing: Will overcome difficulties.
Weighing food: Will have good financial business.
Weighing packages: You are prone to have too many prejudices.
Weighing large things: Will overcome a great danger.
Weighing animals: Contentment.

WEIGHT:
Of own weight: You worry too much.
Gaining weight: Money will come easily during life.
Losing weight: Loss of money.
The weight of your mate: Financial worries.
The weight of children: Immediate success of own hopes.
The weight of relatives: Realization of your ambitions.

WEIGHTS:
Of weights: Will overcome troubles.
Using small weights: Unhappiness in love.
Making weights: Will have a large business.
Selling weights: Dignity and distinction.
Lifting weights yourself: Will have good earnings.
Mate lifting weights: Financial gains.
Children lifting weights: Family reunion.
Others lifting weights: Unhappiness in private affairs.

WEIRD:
Being weird: Will have misfortune.
Other people who are acting weird: Beware of being double-crossed.

Relatives who are acting weird: Will soon have big disputes.

Friends who are acting weird: Will show favors to a beautiful woman.

WELD:

Of welding: Worry will be smoothed away.

Being a welder: Be cautious in your business affairs.

Having something welded: Doomed for disappointment.

Others doing welding: Avoid enemies.

WELL:

Of a well: Abundance in everything.

A well full of clear water: Luck and prosperity.

Drawing water from a well: Success and profit.

An overflowing well: Death of children and losses in business.

Digging a well: Poverty.

Having a well in your back yard: Fortune.

Falling into a well: Troubles ahead for you.

A dry well: Will have some damages in own affairs.

A big well in a field, if you are married: Birth of a virtuous child.

An unmarried person dreaming of a big well full of water: Will marry soon.

A very deep well: Riches.

Dirty water in a well: Loss of your estate.

Cleaning out a well: Will suffer humiliation.

Giving well water to others to drink: Big fortune.

Giving well water to animals to drink: Loss of a child or wife.

Throwing someone in a well of water: Death for the dreamer.

WEST:

Of the Western part of the world: Will take a long trip.

Traveling westward: Riches.

Going West alone: Danger in love matters.

Going West with your family: Approaching money.

WHALE:

Of a whale: Good times are coming.

Watching a whale: Secret enmity of some person.

Engaging in whale fishing: Recovery of lost money.

Catching a whale: An enemy is seeking your ruin.

Killing a whale: Good luck.

WHARF:

Of a wharf: Will enjoy modesty and chastity.

Walking on a wharf: Will have a happily married life.

Sailors and workmen on a wharf: Loss of friends.

Bidding good-by to someone at a wharf: Will have future success.

A wharf being in poor condition: Will become drunk.

WHEAT:

Of ripe wheat: Will have a big fortune.

Harvesting wheat: Failure of enemies.

Selling wheat: Increasing money and happiness.

Buying wheat: Good times are coming.

WHEAT FIELD:

Of a wheat field: Prosperous trade.

Viewing a wheat field: Be cautious in business affairs.

Working in a wheat field: Will have a happy family.

Others working in a wheat field: Beware of jealous friends.

WHEEL:

Of a wheel: Hard work awaits.

Several wheels: Troubles are ahead for you.

A broken wheel: New interest and surroundings.

Many wheels in operation: Will have sorrow followed by joy.

Having several wheels: Recovery of money.

The wheel of a mill: You are faced with great danger.

The wheel of a car: Unhappiness in married life.

A gambling wheel: Will suffer much embarrassment.

A grinding wheel: Will have a disagreement and a fight.

WHIP:
Of a whip: Avoid rivals.
Having a whip: Will receive an affectionate message.
Using a whip: Good tidings will come shortly.
Whipping a horse: Misfortune in love affairs.
Being whipped: Will take a long trip abroad.

WHIRLPOOL:
Of a whirlpool: Will receive an inheritance in the future.
The movement of a whirlpool: A big catastrophe is ahead.
Objects floating in a whirlpool: Will receive good advice.

WHIRLWIND:
Of a whirlwind: Beware of dangerous reports.
Watching a whirlwind: Loss of money.
Losing property in a whirlwind: Will have a happy life.
The devastation caused by a whirlwind: Discovery of an enemy.

WHISKY:
Drinking whisky: Warning of bad events to come.
Buying whisky: Will have debts and difficulties.
Offering whisky to relatives: Be on the lookout for a double cross.
Offering whisky to mate: Realization of high ambitions.
Offering whisky to a lover: Temptation will come to you.
Offering whisky to friends: Warning of troubles.
Being offered a drink of whisky: A mystery will be solved.

WHISPER:
Of whispering: A rumor will be confirmed.
Whispering to your mate: Financial gains are at hand.
Whispering to children: Change for the better.

Hearing others whispering: They are endeavoring to destroy you.
Hearing friends whispering: You are being deceived.
Hearing your help whispering: Family quarrels.
Hearing relatives whispering: Advancement of financial condition.

WHIST:
Playing a game of whist: You will receive a better position.
Winning a game of whist: Will receive a large valuable gift.
Losing a game of whist: Will have arguments with friends.
Watching others winning a game: Change in environment.

WHISTLE:
Of a whistle: Scandal is being spread about you.
Handling a whistle: You are a very intelligent person.
Fixing a whistle: Will receive good advice from someone.
A broken whistle: Will have a short illness.

WHISTLING:
Of whistling: Will participate in a joyous event.
Hearing others whistling: Bad talk will injure your reputation.
Calling attention by whistling: Sudden death may occur.
A whistle being blown during a game: Happiness.
Children whistling: Big joy.

WHITE:
Of the color white: Success in undertakings.
Buying white linen: Money will come easily during life.
Various white-colored materials: Big joy.
Buying white clothes: Happiness in love.

WHITEWASH:
Of whitewash: Introduction into gay company.
Whitewashing walls: Be on the lookout for a double cross.

Whitewashing an investigation: Doomed for disappointment.

Covering up vice and crime: Use caution in business ventures.

WIDOW:

Of a widow: Will soon receive happy news.

A woman dreaming of being a widow: Joy and health.

A widow marrying: You have reached the last resort.

A widow marrying a rich old man: Happiness is assured.

A widow marrying a young man: Misfortune in love affairs.

A rich widow marrying a poor man: Insurmountable obstacles are ahead.

A widow marrying a distant relative: Change of surroundings.

WIDOWER:

Of a widower: Accord among friends.

A widower marrying a woman his own age: Realization of high ambitions.

An aged widower marrying a young girl: Will be guilty of foolish actions.

A widower marrying a sister-in-law: An enemy seeks your ruin.

A widower marrying a rich women: Will have emotional sorrow.

A widower marrying a young widow: Will have mastery over many things.

Remaining a widower: New interests and pleasures.

WIFE:

Of your own wife: Must control your passions.

Taking a wife: Accomplishment of desires.

Being called by your wife: Will be tormented.

Arguing with your wife: Will have a quarrel lasting several days.

Wife being beautifully dressed: Warning of trouble.

Own wife undressing: You must mend your ways in life.

Own wife being naked: She is cheating on you.

Wife being in a bathtub: Misfortune in love affairs.

Wife lying in the sun at the beach: Will avoid a present peril.

Wife swimming at a pool: A rival will steal her affections.

Wife being married to another: Change of affairs or separation.

A wife dreaming of being married to another man: Sudden separation or death of husband.

WIG:

A man wearing a light-colored wig: Will be refused by several women.

A man wearing a dark-colored wig: Will be loved best by women.

A woman wearing a blond wig: Will have many admirers.

A woman wearing a white wig: Will marry a rich man.

A woman wearing a dark wig: She should mend her ways in life.

A woman wearing a brunette wig: She will marry a poor man.

WILD BEAST:

Of a wild beast: Will have protection and favor of people of distinction.

Hearing the roar of a wild beast: Unexpected promotion.

Being pursued by a wild beast: Disgrace.

A wild beast in a cage: Enemies will fail in attempts to injure you.

Being attacked by a wild beast: Will live a long life.

A wild beast running: Serious illness.

Killing a wild beast: Many changes will occur but finally victory.

A dead wild beast: Death of a prominent person.

WILDERNESS:

Of the wilderness: Will have a festive occasion in your home.

An uncultivated wilderness: You expect too many favors from others.

An uninhabited wilderness: Retain your old friends.

A wilderness inhabited only by wild beasts: Hard work awaits you.

WILD FRUITS:
Of wild fruits: Postponement of success.
Picking wild fruits: Rapid success of own hopes.
Eating wild fruits: Important and very beneficial events to come.
Buying wild fruits: Family quarrels.

WILL:
Making out a will: Ill health is foretold.
Making will to a relative: Will live a long time.
Making will to wife: Wife will pass away first.
Making will to children: Long time in happiness and joy.
Making will to a friend: You will pass away very soon.
Making will to charity: Will have a very long illness.

WILLOW:
Of willow trees: A rival will take affections of sweetheart.
Making baskets out of willow branches: Approaching money.
Using a machine to cut down a willow tree: You are being deceived.
Others working with willow wood: Warning of troubles.

WINCH:
Of a winch: Your fortune is secured.
A winch lifting a heavy load: Will be protected by business people.
A winch lifting machinery from a window: Envious people surround you.
A winch loading a ship: Will make plenty of money.
The winch of a ship being broken: Postponement of success.
A farmer using a winch: You are in the grip of a deceitful person.
Using a winch yourself: Change of surroundings.

WIND:
Of a strong wind: Happiness is assured.
Battling with the wind: Untiring energy and attending success.

A mild wind: Suitable time for business transactions.
Walking with the wind: Abundant means.
Walking against the wind: Will be cheated by friends.
The wind not blowing at all: Change for the better.
The wind blowing own hat away: Future conditions will improve.
The wind turning umbrella inside out: Joy.
A ship battling against the wind: Will discover a secret.
A wind blowing away a boat's sail: Approaching troubles.
The wind sinking or destroying a vessel: Money will come easily.

WINDMILL:
Of a windmill: Will make some gains of small monetary value.
A very tall windmill: Will be content and receive a large fortune.
A windmill changing directions: Untrustworthy people surround you.
A windmill stopped: Will receive inheritance from a rich relative.
Operating a windmill: Will receive unhappy news.
A windmill moving a grinding machine: Will have to take care of many things.
A windmill moving a saw: Money will be coming soon.
Married people dreaming of a windmill: Untruthfulness between mates.
Unmarried people dreaming of a windmill: They will soon get married.
Sweethearts dreaming of a windmill: Will enjoy much happiness.

WINDOW:
An open window: Success will attend you.
A closed window: Will suffer desertion by your friends.
A broken window: Be suspicious of robbery by friends.
Jumping from a window: Will have a lawsuit.
Climbing from a window on a ladder:

Will become bankrupt.
Going out a window to descend a fire escape: Good earnings in the future.
A very big window: Very good success in business.
A window opposite your home: Disputes between brothers.
A window at the back of your home: Disputes between sisters.
Seeing people kissing in front of a window: Death of a pet bird.
Viewing something from a window: Victory over enemies.
Fire coming from a window: Will live a long life.
Throwing things from a window: Advancement within own position.

WINE:
Of a wine shop: Will give financial help to others.
Drinking wine: Will receive many good things.
Drinking white wine: Happiness.
Drinking red wine: Will become inebriated.
Drinking wine nearly black in color: Fortune and satisfaction.
Drinking misty wine: Profit.
Drinking muscatel wine: High honors.
Drinking Cyprus wine: Wealth.
Drinking Marsala wine: Business conditions will improve.
Drinking wine made from cherries: Failure of enemies.
Spilling wine: Someone will be injured and lose much blood.
Spilling red wine on a tablecloth: Disaster.
Buying wine: Will have new employment.
Selling wine: Beware of double cross.
Receiving wine as a gift: Doomed for disappointment.
Making wine: Good results in all affairs.
Getting drunk on wine: Big success.

WING:
Of wings: Will lose money.
An angel with wings: Happiness.

The wings of birds: Honor and dignity.
An angel putting wings on you: Joy and consolation.
The wings of an airplane: Will receive unexpected good news.
Wings of pet birds: Happiness in love.
Having wings yourself: Sick people will recover.
Children having wings: Will receive a legacy.
Broken wings: Loss of money.

WINTER:
Of winter: Invalidism threatens you.
A very severe winter: Happiness.
A farmer dreaming of a severe winter: Good harvest.
Navigators dreaming of a severe winter: Financial gains.
Winter weather causing damages: Death of an enemy.
Being sick during the winter: Relatives are envious of you.
Living through a severe winter: Will receive a gift.
Living through a mild winter: You are prying into affairs of others.
Living through a hot winter: Good luck and prosperity.

WIRELESS:
Of wireless: Will receive unexpected good news concerning money.
Using a wireless machine: Will have many friends.
Operating a wireless machine: Prompt engagement.
Sending messages by wireless: Family afflictions.
Receiving messages by wireless: You are very cruel.
A wireless machine being broken: You have many enemies.
Being at an office of wireless machines: Money will come easily in life.
A wireless machine being aboard a ship: Beware of danger.

WISHING WELL:
Of a wishing well: Two admirers are seeking your company.

Dropping money into a wishing well: Choose friends carefully.
Making a wish over a wishing well: Fortune for farmers.
Stealing money from a wishing well: Death in the near future.

WITCH:
Of a witch: You are being watched by someone with evil intentions.
Being scared by a witch: Abuse of confidence.
Becoming nervous because of a witch: Damages to your health.
Ignoring a witch: Beware of double cross.
Being a witch: Change for the better.
Talking with a witch: You should mend your ways in life.

WITNESS:
Of a witness: Be on guard against untrue friends.
Being a witness in court: False accusations are made against you.
Someone witnessing a document: Your actions are always proper.
Witnesses testifying on your behalf: Good results in business affairs.
Being a witness for someone else: A big catastrophe is ahead.
Having a witness for an alibi: Approaching money.
Being a witness at a divorce case: Prosperity.
Being a witness at a murder case: Small profits.
Being a witness at any civil action: Good earnings in business.
Someone witnessing unfaithfulness of mate: Family legal problems.
Being a false witness: Will go to prison in the near future.
Being a contempt witness: Insecurity in your affairs.

WIZARD:
Of a wizard: Family prosperity.
Watching a wizard: A false friend is nearby.
Being a wizard: Postponement of success.
A wizard being with the family: Im-

portant and very beneficial events to come.

WOLF:
Of a wolf: Luck and prosperity.
Being frightened by a wolf: Will be robbed by thieves.
Several wolves: Employees are abusing your trust.
A wolf running: Will have dealings with smart and treacherous enemies.
A tame wolf: Will be kissed often.
A trained wolf: Your love is badly placed.
Two wolves playing together: You have false friends.
A wolf with small babies: Disappointment and end to love.
Killing a wolf: Failure of business.
A dead wolf: You are confronted with insurmountable obstacles.
Catching a wolf: Abundance of money.

WOMAN:
Of a woman: Security in love.
A white woman: Will be free of entanglements.
A brown-skinned woman: Will have a dangerous illness.
A black-skinned woman: Will have a short illness.
A man dreaming of a dead woman: Will soon be loved by a wealthy lady.
A woman dreaming of a dead woman: Will be abandoned.
A woman dancing: Sickness.
A woman lying on a bed: Security.
A beautiful naked woman: Big unhappiness.
A woman visiting your house: Good hopes.
An unknown woman: Will entertain an unwelcome guest.
Receiving services from a woman: Will have a bad reputation.
Hearing the voice of a woman: Permanent change of residence.
Being frightened by a woman: Infirmity.

Several women: Will be humiliated.
A man dreaming of a beautiful woman talking to him: Big gossip.
A woman making advances to a man: Jealousy.
A man dreaming of a woman of ill repute: Serious disaster ahead.
Being a woman of ill repute: Will suffer humiliation.
A woman dreaming of divorcing husband: Will marry a very wealthy man.
A woman dreaming of being a man: Birth of son who brings honor to family.
A woman with white hair: Dignity and distinction.
A woman with long beautiful blond hair: Will enjoy a happy life.
A brunette with long beautiful hair: Honor and profit.
A man dreaming of woman with hair as long as she is: Adulterous wife.
Several women being at a maternity ward: Much happiness.
A man dreaming of a woman delivering a baby: Prosperity.
An unmarried woman dreaming of being pregnant: Deaf and dumb son.
A married woman dreaming of being pregnant: Will receive happy news.
A married woman dreaming of delivering a fish: Very smart children.

WONDER:
Of wondering: Poverty and broken spirit.
Wondering what will happen: You are wasting efforts.
Wondering what others are doing: You have good friends that defend you.
Wondering about health of the family: Success.
Wondering about loyalty of mate: Will have inheritance from unknown person.

WOOD:
Of wood: Scandal.
Buying wood: Will be in need of things.
Selling wood: Abundant means.

Straight piece of wood: Approaching money.
Crooked piece of wood: Disgrace.
Green wood: A change for the better to come.
Dry wood: Success will be yours through hard work.

WOODCUTTER:
Being a woodcutter: Will have many pleasures.
Working as a woodcutter: Efforts will not result in much profit.
Hiring a woodcutter: Triumph over enemies.
Being an inefficient woodcutter: Troubles ahead.

WOODS:
Many trees in the woods: Will enjoy very satisfactory business.
Walking in the woods: Will have hard work ahead.
Rich people dreaming of being in the woods: Loss of money.
Poor people dreaming of being in the woods: Profit and honor.
Many people being in the woods: Caution in business ventures.
Broken trees in the woods: Pleasant social activities.
A woods burning: Affliction.

WOOL:
Of wool: Success at home and in business.
The wool of a sheep: You are prone to using flattery too much.
The wool of a lamb: You are a very kind and easygoing person.
Selling wool: Will enjoy a comfortable life.
Buying wool: Prosperity and success.
Making material from raw wool: Will live a long life.
Selling clothes made of wool: Great unhappiness.
Buying wool clothes: Loss of a friend.

WORK:
Of work: Important and very beneficial event to come.
Being at work: Success will be yours.

Your help being at work: Realization of high ambitions.
Your family being at work: Financial gains.
Children at work: Happiness.
Others working: Will be pleasantly situated in life.
Friends working busily: Be cautious in business ventures.

WORKHOUSE:
Of a workhouse: A big legacy will come to you soon.
Being in a workhouse: Luck and prosperity.
Family being in a workhouse: Money will come easily.
Others being at a workhouse: Discovery of lost valuables.

WORKMAN:
Of a workman: Personal happiness.
A lumber workman: You handle your affairs in good order.
A steel workman: Affairs will be accomplished as desired.
A sheet metal workman: Will receive a visitor.
Plumbing workmen: Enterprises will bring great profit.
Hiring workmen: Abundance.
Being a workman: Curiosity will be satisfied.

WORKSHOP:
Of a workshop: Honor and dignity.
Being in a workshop: Will take a trip out of the state.
Others being in a workshop: Must contend with enemies.
Buying a workshop: Danger of damages.
Owning a workshop: Embarrassment.

WORLD:
Of the world: Everything will go well.
The map of the world: Contentment and tranquillity.
The world turning upside down: Everything will turn in your favor.
The world situation going bad: Double cross by someone nearby.
Discussing the world situation: Will be molested by enemies.

WORM:
Of worms: Will be the victim of intrigue.
Destroying worms: Will have money.
Others killing worms: Will go to prison.
Worms being on plants: Will receive unexpected money.
Worms being on own body: Big riches.
Worms being on body of children: Danger of an infectious disease.

WORSHIP:
Of worshiping: Great honors and riches.
Worshiping in church: Desires will be accomplished.
Worshiping the Lord: Great joy.
Worshiping at home: Unhappiness.
Family worshiping: Joy.
Teaching children to worship: Persecution.

WORSTED:
Of worsted wool: Good luck is ahead for you.
Winding worsted wool: Will receive a comfortable and good income.
Knitting with worsted yarn: Will inherit more than you earn.
Relatives knitting with worsted yarn: Postponement of success.

WOUND:
Of a wound: A false friend is nearby.
Having a wound yourself: Avoid rivals.
Lovers being wounded: Will have serious quarrels.
Children being wounded: Good times are coming.
Mate being wounded: Warning of troubles.
Others being wounded: Will be untrue to marriage vows.

WREATH:
Of a wreath: Happiness.
A wreath of beautiful flowers: High hopes and success.
A wreath of steel: Will be tormented.
A wreath of tin: Loss of an estate.
A crepe paper wreath: Will have a bad illness.

A wreath of gold: Will be protected by influential people.

Placing a wreath on someone's head: Will have the respect of people.

Being crowned with a wreath: Good friendships.

Placing a wreath on a tomb: Dignity.

WRECK:

Of a wreck on land: Sickness.

A wreck at sea: Great suffering.

Broken pieces of a ship after a wreck: Peril of death.

People in a raft after a wreck: Must endure trouble before realizing desires.

People being saved from a wreck: Danger in business affairs.

An automobile wreck: Dishonor.

Being killed in an automobile wreck: Unhappiness in the family.

Being injured in an automobile wreck: Joy and profit.

Family being killed in an automobile wreck: Will require welfare aid.

Friends being in an automobile wreck: Will suffer humiliation.

Enemies being killed in a wreck: Happiness.

WREN:

Of a wren: Rapid success of own hopes.

Watching the little birds: Will realize your ambitions.

Hearing a wren singing: Important and very beneficial events to come.

Having a wren in a cage and hearing it singing: Love quarrels.

WRESTLE:

Of wrestling: Disputes.

Wrestling with debtors: Will receive assistance.

Wrestling with very strong people: Infirmity and sickness.

Wrestling with professionals: Enemies will be punished.

Wrestling with crazy people: Death.

Wrestling with prisoners: Liberation.

Wrestling with friends: Will be elevated to a better position.

Wrestling with children: Unexpected fortune.

Wrestling with snakes: Severe punishment of enemies.

Wrestling with wild beasts: Will escape some danger.

Wrestling with sheep: Hard work ahead.

Others wrestling with crazy people: Loss of a lawsuit.

WRINKLE:

Having wrinkles in own face: Long life after a sickness.

Having no wrinkles in own face: Will have good looks rest of life.

An elderly person without wrinkles: Compliments and social pleasures.

Being wrinkled at middle age: You are very gullible.

Middle-aged men with wrinkles: Loss in business.

Elderly men with wrinkles: Loss of friendship.

Friends having wrinkles at an early age: Prosperity.

Having wrinkles in clothes: Will have small disagreements.

WRIST:

Own wrists being broken: Happiness.

Unmarried people having wrists broken: Will marry present lover.

Having a strong pulse in your wrist: Happiness.

Grabbing someone by the wrist: Sickness.

Wrist being out of place: Many good friendships.

A woman with a beautiful wrist: Will achieve all desires in life.

A woman wearing bracelets on her wrist: Imminent joy.

Having a very large wrist: Will have ulcers and very bad skin disease.

WRITE:

Writing on paper: Will be falsely accused of something.

Writing letters: Someone is stealing from you.

Of writing: Foretells a serious error which will threaten your peace.

Writing in capital letters: Joy.
Writing a report: Will be accused of slander.
Writing memoirs: Dishonor.
Writing an agenda: Infirmity.
Writing love letter to mate: Happiness and unity.

Writing a letter to relatives: Profit.
Writing a letter to children: Must put out money.
Writing a business letter: Will collect money.
Writing a reminder letter of payment due: Bad success.

X

XANTHIC:
Of flowers with a tint of yellow: Long illness.
Having several xanthics: Obstacles are ahead of you.
Picking the flowers from the plant: Big benefit.
A single person gathering the flowers: Will marry soon.

XENOGAMY:
Of cross-fertilization: Will have unexpected friends for dinner.
A woman being married to a foreign man: Congenial work and good news.
A man being married to a foreign woman: Luck and prosperity.

XENOPHOBIA:
Having hatred for foreigners: Happiness.
Disliking foreigners: Family quarrels.
Insulting a foreigner: A mystery will be solved.
Deporting a foreigner: Loss of a faithful friend.

X RAY:
Of an X-ray machine: Worry will be smoothed away.
Having own X ray taken: Doomed for disappointment.
Having a favorable X-ray report: Important and very beneficial event to come.
X-ray reports of others: Family quarrels.
Operating an X-ray machine: Will have good earnings.

XYLOPHONE:
Of a xylophone: Will receive good and important news.
Playing a xylophone: Avoid rivals.
Friends playing the xylophone: Will be cheated by friends.
Hearing a musician playing the xylophone: Financial gains.

Y

YACHT:
Of a yacht: Good luck.
A yacht under full sail: Pleasant visit in a nice place.
A yacht under full engine speed: Big joy.
A yacht sailing on a smooth sea: Prosperity.
Being on a yacht: Realization of your own ambitions.

A yacht sailing on rough sea: Disappointments.
A stranded yacht: Business ventures will cause you distress.

YANKEE:
Of a Yankee: You will fulfill your duty with honor.
Fighting with people of same nationality: Joy.

Fighting between two states: Honor.
The North fighting the South: Will receive good news.

YARD:
Of a yard: News of engagement of friends will reach you.
Being in a yard: An unwelcome friend will visit you.
Working in a yard: An admirer will soon be married.
Having an untidy yard: Will have sorrow that causes tears.
Having a well-kept yard: Family arguments.
A scrapyard: Glory and fortune.
A shipyard: Fortune.
A lumberyard: Riches.
Neighbor's yard: Must rely on own efforts.
A friend's yard: Persecution.
Planting things in a yard: Joy.
Picking flowers from a yard: Death.

YARDSTICK:
Of a yardstick: Will be cared for by others.
Using a yardstick: Will hear pleasant music.
Buying a yardstick: You are sure of not being cheated on purchases.
Mate using a yardstick: Fortune in love and business.
Salespeople using a yardstick: Will be cheated in business.

YARN:
Of yarn: Success in love affairs.
A man dreaming of yarn: Will attain business success.
A woman dreaming of yarn: Will have plenty of money.
A husband dreaming of yarn: Will have abundant means.
A wife dreaming of yarn: Will encourage husband by thrift and peace.
Unmarried people dreaming of yarn: Will soon be married.
Buying yarn: Will receive a present from an unexpected person.

YAWN:
Of yawning: Small troubles that are not serious.
Yawning at social events: You are unfitted to fill your position.
Yawning in the morning: Will be jilted by your lover.
Yawning in church: You will be humiliated.

YEAR:
Of a year: Will be feeble from age.
Leap year: Will make small profits.
A year ending in even numbers: Will have very little money.
A year ending in odd numbers: Will inherit plenty of money.

YEARN:
Of yearning: You should mend your ways in life.
Having a strong feeling of yearning: Indifference where you should be kind.
Yearning over grief and vexation: Worry will be smoothed away.
Relatives yearning: Family disputes.

YEAST:
Of yeast: Money accumulated by thrift will be left to you.
Making bread with yeast: Abundance.
Cooking with yeast: Will receive money under strange circumstances.
Buying yeast: Unusual wealth.

YELL:
Of yelling: Be cautious in business ventures.
Hearing hideous yells: Worry will be smoothed away.
Hearing noisy yells: Will have peace and money.
Yelling yourself: Family quarrels.
Mates yelling at each other: An introduction will alter your plans.
Hearing children yelling: Luck and prosperity.
Hearing relatives yelling: Unhappiness in love affairs.
Hearing others yelling: Will have strife followed by peace.

YELLOW:
Of the color yellow: Important changes in your affairs.

Yellow materials of any kind: Will have sorrow.

Buying yellow clothes: Warning of troubles.

Buying yellow silk: Will be deceived by a loved one.

YEW TREE:
Of a yew tree: Death of an aged relative.

Cutting branches from a yew tree: Will receive a big legacy.

Sitting under a yew tree: Will have a short life.

Admiring a yew tree: Will live a very long life.

YIELD:
Of yielding: Don't believe flattering talk.

Yielding to persuasive words: A false friend is nearby.

Lovers yielding to persuasive stories: Danger in love affairs.

Others yielding to your persuasive words: You have too much pride.

YOKE:
Of a yoke: You are influenced too much by an older person.

Having a yoke on shoulders carrying two pails: Abundance.

A yoke hanging garments: Try to develop your own personality.

Two animals yoked together: Luck and prosperity.

YOLK:
Of an egg yolk: Financial gains.

A double-yolked egg: Discovery of lost valuables.

Beating egg yolks: Money will be gained in speculation.

Eating a hard-boiled egg yolk: Money will come easily during life.

Eating a raw yolk of an egg: Abundance of money.

Using egg yolks to make pastries: Big fortune.

YOUNG:
An aged person dreaming of being young: Will receive happy news.

An aged woman dreaming of being young: Will have a devoted husband.

Of becoming young again: Important and very beneficial events to come.

Being young: A change for the better will not last long.

YULETIDE:
Of the yuletide: Short courtship with new admirer will end happily.

It being Christmas: Change for the better in financial position.

Family reunion during the yuletide: Business matters will improve.

Z

ZAFFER:
Of this impure oxide of cobalt: Ingratitude.

Handling zaffer: Will be molested.

Buying zaffer: Will make large profits.

Working with zaffer: Unfortunate events will transpire.

ZEAL:
Being a zealous person: Peril and misfortune.

Not being zealous: A faithful friend is thinking of you.

Others who are not zealous: Ruin in business.

Being unable to work with zeal: Discovery of a treasure.

ZEBRA:
Of a zebra: Will do extensive travel abroad.

A zebra at a zoo: Friendship is badly placed.

A mother zebra with her young: Disagreements with friends.

A zebra being attacked by wild animals: Your honor is in danger.

A zebra being fed at a zoo: Ingratitude.

ZENITH:
Of that point of the heavens vertically above you: Happiness.

An unmarried person dreaming of zenith: Good choice of husband or wife.

A married person dreaming of zenith: Unusual wealth.

Divorced people dreaming of zenith: Will marry a rich man or rich woman.

A widower dreaming of zenith: Will never get married again.

A widow dreaming of zenith: Will marry a younger man.

ZEPHYR:
Having lightweight materials: Will be molested.

Buying zephyr materials: Will have a serious accident.

Feeling a light gentle breeze: Will be insulted by a man with poor manners.

Being in the woods and feeling a west wind: Modesty.

ZEPPELIN:
Of an airship: You have ambitions far beyond your reach.

Being in a zeppelin: Will be molested.

Going up in a zeppelin: Will be insulted by a poor-mannered man.

Coming down in a zeppelin: Will receive good news.

Watching a zeppelin moving slowly: People are meddling in your affairs.

ZERO:
Of a zero: Will have a small unhappiness.

Double zeros: Will be double-crossed by a friend.

Three zeros: Will have great wealth.

It being the zero hour: Success in all ventures.

ZIBELINE:
Owning a zibeline fur coat: Will take a trip.

Buying a zibeline fur coat: Your friends are inconsistent.

Selling a zibeline fur coat: Loss of money.

Having a zibeline coat altered: Will have honor and distinction.

Other women wearing a zibeline coat: Double cross by best friend.

ZIGZAG:
Of zigzag: Will go out of your mind.

Walking zigzag: Business will endure bad consequences.

Zigzagging with a horse: Will have changes in business.

Zigzagging with a car: You will have many changeable moods.

Children going zigzag: Good days ahead.

Friends going zigzag: Avoid hesitation in making decisions.

ZINC:
Of zinc: Will achieve success through untiring efforts.

Handling zinc: You participate in too many amusements.

Buying zinc: Your future will be built on a firm foundation.

Buying articles made of zinc: Avoid speculations in gold.

Others using things made of zinc: Will have a long-lasting romance.

ZIPPER:
Zipping up own clothes: Will receive a proposition of love.

Unzipping own clothes: Will enjoy good health.

Others zipping up their clothes: Will be lucky at gambling.

Others unzipping their clothes: Will receive news of coming birth of a child.

A man unzipping a woman's dress: Will receive riches.

Buying zippers: Will be offended.

Children zipping up a zipper: Family happiness.

ZIRCON:
Having a ring made of zircon: Your friendship is badly placed.

Buying jewelry made of zircon: Will be cheated.

Selling a zircon stone: Will not receive good compensation.

Others wearing zircon jewelry: Ingratitude of friends.

ZODIAC:
Of any sign of the zodiac: Will have big fortune in the future.
Own sign of the zodiac: Will win a lottery.
Relative's sign in the zodiac: Will have arguments with relatives.
Family's sign of the zodiac: Riches.
Children's sign of the zodiac: Will be greatly loved by the children.

ZOMBI:
Drinking a zombi: Dishonor is ahead.
Making a zombi: Unhappiness.
Serving a zombi to friends: Will have a big misfortune awaiting.
Being offered a zombi by others: Will have misery in the future.

ZONE:
Of a zone: Will have good hopes for the future.
Own zone: Must endure a small unhappiness.
The zone of other people: Will have an accident.
A reserved zone: Joy without pleasure.
A military or naval zone: Will receive important news.

ZOO:
Of a zoo: Select friends carefully.
Going to the zoo alone: Will be molested.
Going to the zoo with family and children: Good hopes for the future.
Husband and wife going to the zoo: Hopes will not be realized.

Going to the zoo with sweetheart: Danger and misfortune.
Friends going to the zoo: Do not confide your secrets.

ZOOLOGICAL GARDENS:
Of a zoological garden: Will travel much in the future.
Rich people visiting a zoological garden: Poverty.
Poor people visiting a zoological garden: Will soon have money.
Visiting a zoological garden with children: Joy and contentment.

ZUCCHINI:
Of zucchini: Will receive bad news.
Growing zucchini: Will receive unexpected visit that makes you happy.
Buying zucchini: Will enjoy a very great love.
Cooking zucchini: Will have happy events.
Eating zucchini: You have the good habit of attending church regularly.
Children eating zucchini: Happiness in the family.

ZULU:
Of natives of Zululand: Will enjoy good health.
Meeting natives of Zululand: Will have long happiness.
Being surrounded by natives of Zululand: Will escape from danger to health.
Natives of Zululand being in own country: Improvement of own health.